ENCYCLOPAEDIA OF PALM AND PALM READING

A Treatise on Palmistry

ENCYCLOPAEDIA OF PALM AND PALM READING

A Treatise on Palmistry

Samudrik Tilak
M. KATAKKAR

UBS Publishers' Distributors Ltd.

New Delhi Bombay Bangalore Madras
Calcutta Patna Kanpur London

UBS Publishers' Distributors Ltd.
5 Ansari Road, New Delhi-110 002
Bombay Bangalore Madras
Calcutta Patna Kanpur London

© M. Katakkar
   79-B/1 Prabhat Road
   Between Lanes 14-15
   PUNE-411 004

1992 Edition
First Reprint   1993

Printed at Ram Printograph (India), C-114 Okhla Industrial Area, Phase I, New Delhi-110 020

ABOUT THE AUTHOR

Dr. M. Katakkar has held responsible posts in different industries, and finally retired as Chief Executive Officer in 1980. The study of Palmistry and Numerology has been his hobby since 1942. His first article 'Biological Significance of Palmistry' appeared in 1946, which heralded the beginning of his glorious career. Followed by this was his prize winning paper on Medical Palmistry. In 1972 at the 24th Annual Conference of Indian Psychiatric Society he carried his article in the Souvenir 'Palmistry in Relation to Psychiatry'. His research work and contribution of several articles on Palmistry gave him the unique position of a Medical Palmist.

He also had his brush in the form of a counter challenge, in 1985, with Dr. Abraham Kovoor, the famous Rationlist of Sri Lanka on the subject of numerology and influence of planets on human life. On his tours to Europe, Canada and USA he has also been interviewed on television, on the nature and importance of palmistry on daily life.

Dr. Katakkar has also been awarded several honours, amongst which, are Samudrik Tilak, Jyotish Mahamahopadhyaya, Daivagna Ratna, Jyotish Alankar and above all Doctor of Palmistry. Dr. Katakkar had the opportunity of reading hands of great personalities such as Mahatma Gandhi, Rajgopalachari, Vallabhbhai Patel and Morarjibhai Desai, amongst others. He is acting as an Honourary Lecturer in Palmistry and Numerology in Bhalchandra Jyotir Vidhayalaya, Pune and recently he was also nominated as President of Numerology for the 'World Peace Conference' held at Delhi in January 1989 by the World Development Parliament. This encyclopaedic work is the outcome of his rich experience.

Other books by the same author

1. Dial Your Birth Number
2. Numerology, Palmistry and Prosperity
3. Palmistry, Marriage and Family Welfare
4. Palmistry in Pictures
5. Ready Reckoner of Palmistry, Vocational Guidance and Medical Palmistry
6. Encyclopaedic Dictionary of Palmistry
7. Miracles of Numerology
8. Hasat-Khelat Hasta Samudrik (Marathi)
9. Hasta Samudrik and Sukhi Vaivahik Jeevan (Marathi)
10. Anka Jyotish and Hasta Samudrik (Marathi)

PLATE 1:
THE HAND OF MURDERER.

Plate 1 : Important observations to be noted :

1) One straight line across the palm which is a combination of Head and Heart lines. It means confusion between reason and logic on the one side and sentiments and affections on the other side.

2) The line of Life is rising high on the mount of Jupiter which indicates cruelty.

3) The line of Fate is ending on the Head line which means loss of career due to foolhardiness.

4) Cross on the mount of Saturn shows death on the scaffold.

Plate 2 : Important observations to be noted

1) The presence of the line of Via Lasciva shows lascivious tendencies and self abuse.

2) The presence of the double or triple Girdle of Venus shows uneasy constitution, bad habits developed in early younghood and a love for alcohol.

3) The double line of Head shows double role in life.

4) The broken island in the Heart line under the finger of Saturn and touching the upper line of Head is an indication of frustration in love and vengence.

5) The line of Marriage is cutting the line of Heart which is an indication of disturbed married life.

6) The life line is forked after a cross bar in the Life line which shows danger to life.

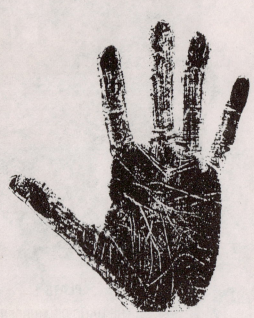

PLATE 2 :
MURDEROUS TENDENCIES.

PLATE 3 :
MURDEROUS TENDENCIES

Plate 3 : Important observations to be noted

1) The line across the hand which is a combination of the Head and Heart lines shows mysterious behaviour.

2) There is an island in the above line and the Head line is separated from the same point. It means lack of control over the mind.

3) There is a cross line cutting the (a) rising branch from the Life line, (b) the Life line itself, (c) the line of Head and (d) the line of Mercury. It means ill health, unhealthy thinking and bilious weakness.

4) There is a circle between the above cross line and the upper cross line explained in item 3 above. This circle shows a dangerous disposition.

5) The absence of Fate line on the hand shows aimless life.
6) Island in the Sun line shows loss of reputation.
7) Cross bars on the mounts show ill-luck and frustration.

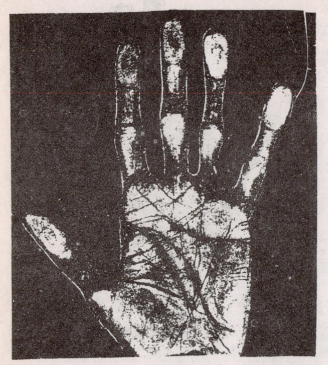

PLATE 4 :
SUICIDAL TENDENCIES.

Plate 4 : Important observations to be noted

    1) The Head line drooping down towards the mount of Moon shows suicidal tendencies.
    2) Cross on the mount of Saturn shows fatality.
    3) Abrupt ending of the Life line shows danger to life.
    4) A star on the positive mount of Mars and inside the Life line shows hot temper and irritability.

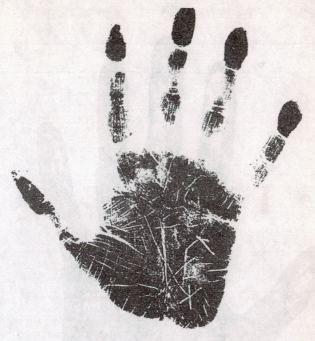

PLATE 5:

CROSS AT THE END OF VOYAGE LINE

Plate 5 : Important observations to be noted

   1) Cross at the end of the Voyage line falling out of the Life line shows danger from water.

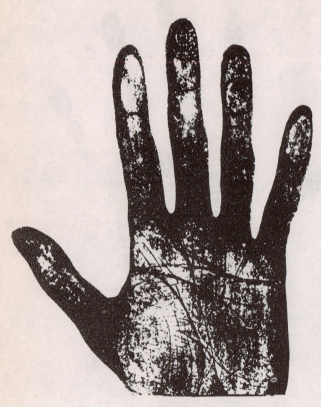

PLATE 6 :

Plate 6 : Important observations to be noted

    1) Cross at the end of the Voyage line falling out of the Life line shows danger from water (Same as Plate 5)

    2) One branch of the Heart line meets the Head line which indicates frustration in love.

    3) An island in the above branch and the Fate line runs through that island, is an indication of the person leading astray an innocent girl.

    4) An island in the Sun line just above the Heart line shows loss of reputation.

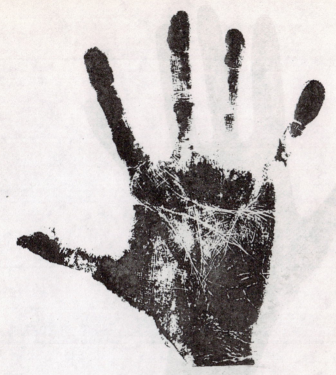

PLATE 7 :

SQUARE AT THE END OF VOYAGE LINE

Plate 7 : Important observations to be noted

    1) The Voyage line ending on a square shows escape from drowning.

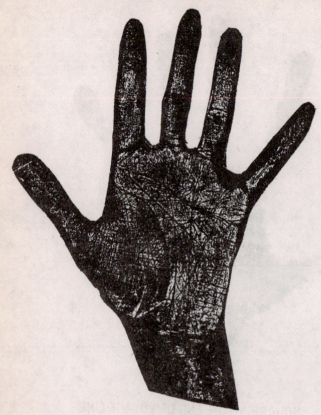

PLATE 8
THE HAND OF SUCCESSFUL ACTRESS.

Plate 8 : Important observations to be noted

1) A circle on the mount of Jupiter shows remembrance of previous birth.

2) Cross on the mount of Jupiter shows realisation of ambition.

3) The Head line is straight and starts on the mount of Jupiter which shows intelligence and brilliance.

4) The Head line is separate from the Life line which means independent nature and domination.

5) Straight lines of Fate and Sun indicate a successful career.

6) A star on the Sun line shows reputation.

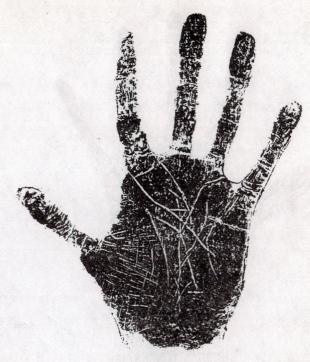

PLATE 9 :
DOUBLE LINE OF HEAD.

Plate 9 : Important observations to be noted

1) The line of Intuition indicating intuitive faculties.
2) Double lines of Head which show double role in life.
3) The above Head line starts high on the mount of Jupiter which shows extreme individuality.
4) The ring of solomon on the mount of Jupiter shows honour, reputation and deep interest in occultism.
5) Mystic Cross under the finger of Saturn and between the lines of Head and Heart shows occultism.
6) The Fate line going to the Sun mount shows fame.

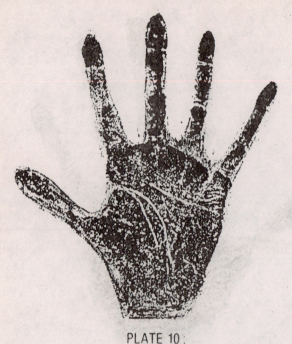

PLATE 10 :
SUICIDAL TENDENCIES.

Plate 10 : Important observations to be noted

1) The line of Head drooping down on the mount of Moon which shows suicidal tendencies.

2) The line of Life is short which shows danger to life.

3) Three lines of Marriage turning down show failure in married life.

4) The type of the hand is Psychic which indicates emotional nature.

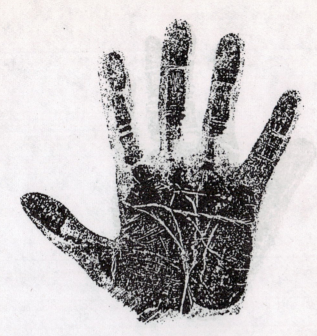

PLATE 11:

SUICIDAL TENDENCIES

Plate 11 : Important observations to be noted

1) One cross line showing the combination of the Head and Heart lines, an indication of eccentricity.

2) The line of Head separated from the Heart line and drooping down which is an indication of suicidal tendencies.

3) The fate line is wavy at the start which means family troubles.

4) The Fate line goes through the angle created by the lines of Head and Heart which shows danger to the head.

5) This Fate line is protected by a sqaure which means the accident to the head will not be fatal.

PLATE 12 :

MURDEROUS TENDENCIES.

Plate 12 : Important observations to be noted

1) The ring of Saturn found on the mount of Saturn is an inauspicious sign and shows difficulties and obstacles in life.

2) The line of Heart is present but the line of Head is absent. The line of Heart is also broken and islanded. This shows an extremely jealous nature which may commit a crime.

3) A semi circular line starts from the mount of Mars and shows its inclination towards the mount of Saturn and cuts the line of Life. It shows danger to life.

6) The fingures are short and show an impetuous nature.

7) The thumb is big and strong which shows murderous tendencies.

Preface

The study of palmistry is as old as history and various systems of palm-reading have been evolved in different countries from time immemorial. Eventhough the study has a long history, it is still a matter of prolonged and bitter controversy whether palmistry is a science. I request my readers and the students of this study to go through carefully the explanation given below so that they can have a rational outlook towards this subject.

1) Causes of discredit

It is necessary for every student of palmistry to know why this subject has never been accepted as a worthwhile study. Many causes have contributed to the degeneration of palmistry. There is intrusion of a prejudice of the majority of the educated public who regard palmistry as mere superstition and condemn it on the ground that modern scientists reject it. But they should note that in this atomic age, what they considered trivial has been discovered to contain immense power, the atom having gained immeasurable importance. If, therefore, palmistry be considered by them too trivial for their attention, I would remind them that many of the greatest truths the world has known, though once considered trivialities, have become sources of tremendous force. Another reason for the degeneration of this science is that though numerous treatises have been written on it, unfortunately the tradition and dicta of old writers, whose modus operandi in building up the science was anything but scientific, have been retained by modern authors. This together with ignorant persons practising the cheiromantic art, has brought palmistry into discredit. Thirdly, science has vigorously ignored the study of the hand regardless of the fact that occultism formed the basis of scientific discovery, that astronomy was developed from astrology, that chemistry was developed from alchemy and that it was through occultism that the path of thought was first opened leading to the development of philosophy and psycholgy. The taboo which impelled scientists to exclude cheirology from their researches, has caused the study to fall almost entirely into the hands of charlatans.

Wise men are ignorant of many things, which later every common student will come to know. Every day sciences such as the science of the hand are establishing themselves more and more firmly as concrete and exact. Once upon a time the study of the hand was regarded as esoteric and mystical. 'Mystery' says Bain is correlated to explanation; it means something intelligible enough as a fact, but not accounted for, not reduced to any law, principle or reason'. The ebb and flow of the tides, the motions of planets, satellites and comets were understood as facts at all times, but they were regarded as mysteries until Newton brought them under the laws of motion and gravity. Such is the case with the science of palm-reading. Though it was regarded as an occult study uptil now, scientific research has proved that it does not have the occult symbol it carried with it but it can be studied and practised as any other science. Voltaire has said 'There is no such thing as chance, we have coined this word to express the known effect of every unknown cause.'

Some of the standard objections and arguments raised against this science

1) Is Palmistry a Science?

Modern science has not yet found the approach by which it can bring the study of palmistry in the rigid frame work of the word 'Science'. Science has its own limitations. There are several experiences which prove the sound basis of palmistry and it is always the experience in a particular field that paves the way to further research and make that experience an exact science. However, in spite of the great development of modern science in various fields, it has failed to produce appliances and means which can prove palmistry as a science. This science has its foundation and experience and so we can call it as an emperical science.

2) Do the stars or the planets influence individual life?

I have heard that some 196 scientists all over the world, after studying the effects of the planets on the human life have come to a conclusion that the planets have no influence on the individual life. But my answer is firm and positive. Yes, the stars and the planets do have an influence on the individual being. What is the proof? I give below my own experience.

A) It was in 1942 that two street goers visited my house and asked me to show my palms to them. They were fortune tellers from the southern part of India. After stretching my palms before them they started uttering some verses (slokas) and then spotting some signs and the lines on the hand. Gradually they started sketching out my horoscope, an exact one as per one in my possession. Was it only a chance? Can we prepare, only bye chance, correct horoscope from the palm? I think, even if one could cast 10 correct horoscopes out of the 100, we cannot say it is only bye chance that these ten were correct. Science will have to investigate as to why even these ten were correct. Several other prominent dignitories have informed me that similar such horoscopes were prepared from their palms by persons from the North-East side of India and also from Nepal and Sikkim. If a horoscope can be prepared from the hand, what more proof is required to show the influence of the planets on the human being?

B) It was in 1949 that on one occassion I stayed in a hotel in Bombay. The next day morning while I was busy taking my morning breakfast, a gentleman sitting next to me started talking on the subject of astrology and in a few minutes described my horoscope to a marked degree of accuracy. I just enquired how could he do it, he said that he prepared the horoscope from my face only. How very surprising and thrilling! A horoscope could be cast from the face alone. If that is so, how can we deny that the planets have an influence on the individual being?

C) Round about 1945, the late Mr. K. M. Munshi, the Congress leader and dignitary, was the President of 'Bhavan's Journal', a monthly published in Bombay. He has contributed very valuable and informative articles on astrology and philosocphy. In one of his articles, he referred to 'The Brighu Sanhita' in the different parts of India. When he was in the city of Hoshiarpur he came across a Pandit who claimed to have an original Brighu Sanhita. The pandit referred to a particular page and started reading it. The first sentence on the page was 'You would open this page on such and such a date' (The date of Mr. K. M. Munshi's visit was mentioned).' When you will start reading, you would be surrounded by such and such persons.' The narration was absolutely true. The Panditjee went on reading. After sometime he read 'When you come to this sentence, your secretary will remind you of an important appoinment'. The moment this reading was over, the secretary came out from a neighbouring room and reminded Mr. Munshi of his appoinment with the

Maharaja of kashmir.

The above three illustrations are sufficient to prove the influence of planets on the human being.

C) Do the lines on the hand change?

Yes, the lines on the hand do change. But the change takes place in the off-shoots or the rising and falling lines from the main lines. The formation and the course of main lines do not change. Therefore the main lines indicate the path of life whereas the small lines, either appearing or vanishing, indicate the events that have to take place shortly. The lines have a psycholgical significance and the mind produces, controls or alters the lines on the palm. The main lines indicate what the natural course of the life is, new lines just beginning to form show emotions and ideas just developing within the person. Experiments are going on to catch the thought waves of man in order to understand his mind and scientists are spending years in the search for a key with which they can unlock the secrets of the human mind. One key is the hand, a perfect mirror giving insight into the working of the human mind. People can easily change their faces but not so easily their minds. The hand reveals the man as he is, not as he may pretend to be. Sometimes even small shades of the mind are seen on the hand. Hereditary and natural tendencies and those which have created profound impressions upon his mind can all be seen on the hand.

D) If everything is predetermined, what is the use of knowing one's Fate in advance?

According to Indian philosophy, there is always a struggle going on between Free Will and Predestination. The role of Predestination is to induce a thought in a particular direction. Whether to act upon the thought or not is the field of Free Will. A thought to commit a murder or a crime is according to the principle of Predestination, but to act according to the thought or not is the operation of Free Will. The palm shows what is likely to happen in the future, but we can avoid the danger by exercising our Free Will. The lines on the hand also indicate the opportunities and also the losses and scandals we have to go through. We can take advantage of the opportunities and avoid losses by taking care, well in time.

E) What is the role of Intuition in predicting events?

Events are already shown on the palm. However sometimes one sign can have several interpretations and it becomes a matter of combinations of other signs and lines on the palm so as to arrive at a definite conclusion regarding the meaning of that particular sign or line. Intuition helps to combine different possible interpretations and arrive at a conclusion. This type of intuition is required in each and every profession. For instance, even a doctor needs the help of his intuition to come to a decision based on his observation and experience to locate the exact disease of the patient. Therefore we can say that intuition is an additional aid to a palmist but not a necessity.

The purpose and the Aim of this book

There are several books written by eminent writens on palm-reading but there is not a single book which has covered all information on this subject. Moreover, there are western authors as well as eastern authors and there is a vast difference between them towards the approach to this subject.

It was therefore my strong desire to produce such a work on palmistry which would be complete in all respects and there would arise no necessity of referring to any other book on this subject. No doubt my task was huge. There were periods of big gaps when I had to discontinue my study but even then I never lost patience and persevered in the subject.

After studying several thousand cases since about 1942, I think that the approach to the whole subject of palmistry needs a radical change and a student of palmistry should be able to explain the intrinsic values of an individual, his inherent virutes, abilities and drawbacks, so that he can improve upon them and make his life more successful. It is no use knowing only how many children one would beget and whether one would have foreign travels. What is more important is to know one's abilities and also limitations. A good palmist can be a good guide in this respect.

My research in hospitals and clinics has convinced me of the utility of this subject and the possibility for further research and developement on biological and psychological significance of the hand. Chapters II and III throw more light on the subject from this point of view.

A good palmist must necessarily be a good psychotherapist. Those who go to him are already in difficulties and the important function of a palmist is to show them the path to success and guide them on proper lines.

I therefore gathered all the available knowledge on this subject and codified it in suitable chapters so as to make it a scientific subject. Every person is curious to know about the lines on his hand and this volume will help him to know the significance of the lines on his hands in a simple way. The chart and the exhaustive index at the end will be of great help to him. Thus my patience and perseverance have finally borne fruit and this volume is the outcome.

The hand reveals various developments in life and a palmist can specialise himself in any one or more of these developments. As we have a general medical practioner as well as a specialist, such as a T. B. specialist, a Heart specialist, an E.N.T. specialist etc., we can also have a general palmist who can read the hand and life in a general way or even a specialist who may study this subject from the specific angles of marriage, vocations, health, finance, psychological attitude etc. If one wants to master any of these developments one has to be conversant with the art of interpreting various combinations on the hand. This volume will assist him in his endearour.

I have tried my best to explain the study of the hand by taking into consideration all possible details of the subject according to the Indian as well as the Western systems. I do not think I have omitted any aspect of this study. The chapters have been arranged in such a manner that the student will grasp the subject without much difficulty.

I have no doubt that my readers will appreciate my efforts to handle this subject in a most scientific way and also imparting the knowledge in a systematic way. Regular study of methods and systems is the keynote to success.

There are numerous authors and scholars who have written on this subejct and I am indebted to them for the knowledge I have gained through their valuable books. (Bibliography at the end of this book)

Lastly, I may state that this work would not have been completed but for the active support and ever willing co-operation of my wife who always encouraged me in my pursuit.

79-B/1, Prabhat Road   **Dr. M.Katakkar**
Between Lanes 14 and 15,
Pune 411004. (India)

The Time Factor on the Hand

In fact this chapter should be read in continuation of chapter XVI (Lines on the hand) wherein I have explained " The Time Factor on the hand " by the division of seven.

According to the Hindu system, when a client approaches us for consultation, we have first to find out the longevity of the person. There are four methods prescribed for the purpose. (See Map of the hand on page 337 to know the lines on the hand.)

First Method
1) The Heart line which starts from the bottom of the little finger and from the mount of Mercury, if it runs upto the exterior portion of the finger of Jupiter or covers all the portion of the mount of Jupiter, the longevity is of hundred years.
2) If the Heart line goes upto the root of the Jupiter finger or upto the middle of the Jupiter mount, the longevity is upto eighty years.
3) If the Heart line runs between the fingers of Jupiter and Saturn or covers all the portion of Saturn mount, the longevity is upto seventy years.
4) If the Heart line runs upto the middle mount of Saturn, the longevity is upto sixty years.
5) If the Heart line goes upto the middle of Saturn and Sun fingers, the longevity is upto forty years.
6) If the Heart line is upto the middle mount of Sun (Apollo), the longevity is upto thirty years.
7) If the Heart line is short and goes only upto the middle of Sun and Mercury fingers, the longevity is upto twenty years only.

Second Method
According to ' Hasta-sanjivani', a method of determining the longevity is evolved from the finger of Mercury (little finger). In this

method the first upper joint of the Apollo (Sun) finger is the demarcation line.
1) If the Mercury finger is as long as this first joint of the Apollo finger, the life is of sixty years.
2) If the Mercury finger is longer than this first joint of the Apollo finger and upto one or two yavas (islands), the life is upto seventy years.
3) If the Mercury finger is as long as three yavas above the first joint of the Apollo finger, the life is upto eighty years.
4) If the Mercury finger is as long as four yavas above the first joint of the Apollo finger, the life is upto ninty years.
5) If the Mercury finger is as long as five yavas above the first joint of the Apollo finger, the life is upto one hundred years.

Third Method
1) If there are three Bracelets, well marked and faultless, the longevity is upto ninty years.
2) Two clear-cut Bracelets show a life upto seventy years.
3) Only one clear-cut Bracelet indicates life of fifty years only.

Fourth Method
Longevity is calculated on the life line at the period where the line of Mercury touches the line of life.

Note :
Before arriving at a conclusion, we should consider all the above methods, plus the one shown in chapter XVI. However as an ethics of the profession, it is necessary to keep this secret of longevity with us only and should not be conveyed to the client.

Year-wise Prospects
In order to find out good years or difficult years in one's life, we have to calculate the period from the fingers of the palm. This method is explained in the volume 'Hasta-sanjivani'.
1) We have to start counting years from the little finger of the right hand. Each finger (including the thumb) has three phalanges. The years from 1 to 15 are counted on the fingers of the right hand as shown in the chart.

2) The years from 16 to 30 are counted on the fingers of the left hand and start from the first phalange of the little finger also known as the finger of Mercury.
3) The years from 31 to 45 are counted again on the right hand and the years from 46 to 60 are counted on the left hand.
4) Thus a period of 15 years is alternately counted starting from the right hand and thereafter on the left hand.
5) Vertical lines, yavas (islands) and chakras on the phalanges are auspicious signs and indicate wealth, birth of a child, success and prosperity. On the contrary, if we notice horizontal lines, bars, broken squares, spots and stars on the phalanges, these signs indicate loss, accidents, fears, sorrow, worry, enemies etc.

With the above basic data, I will explain the significance of a particular year.

If a person wants to know about his 52nd year of age, we have to find out his 52nd year on the phalange by the method described above. We have to start counting his first year from the little finger of his right hand. Thus, the first fifteen years of his life will be shown on his right hand. The next fifteen years from 16 to 30 will be calculated on the left hand. The third phase of his life from 31 to 45 will again be calculated on his right hand. The 46th year will be calculated on the top phalange of the little finger of the left hand. This finger will cover his period of 46, 47 and 48 years. We go ahead to the ring finger, also known as the Sun or Apollo finger, which covers further three years from 49 to 51. Thereafter his 52nd year of age appears on the first or the top phalange of the middle finger, also known as the Saturn finger. We have now to see the signs on this phalange. If there are auspicious signs like a vertical line, yava or chakra, we can judge that the 52nd year will be a good year. On the contrary, if the phalange contains inauspicious signs, such as a bar, a cross line, a broken square etc., we can conclude that the year 52 is not a happy year and the person will have to face difficulties.

Before we take our final decision about the auspicious or inauspicious year by the above method of calculation, we have also to take into consideration the lines of Life, Fate and Apollo and see the markings on these lines at similar period. If the phalange of a particular finger shows a good year and the lines of Life, Fate and Apollo also indicate a good period, the intensity of auspicious year is assured. However, the phalange shows a good year but the lines do not indicate a good period or vice-versa, the year has a mixed result. If both, the phalange and also the lines show a bad period, then the person will have a period of difficulties, obstacles and sorrows.

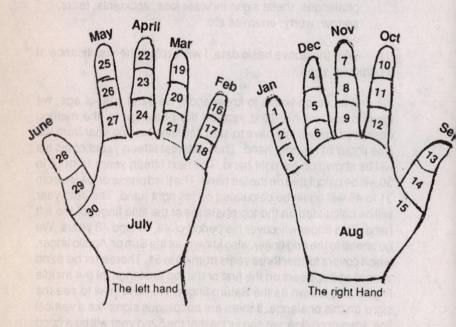

Month-wise Prospects

In order to find out month-wise prospects, following is the method. (Refer to the chart.)

The division of twelve months on both the palms is shown in the chart. On the right palm, we notice the months as follows:-
1) August - Hollow of the palm. 2) September - The thumb.
3) October - First finger. 4) November - Middle finger
5) December - Ring finger. 6) January - Little finger
Thereafter we go to the left hand.
7) February - Little finger. 8) March - Ring finger
9) April - Middle finger. 10) May - First finger
11) June - The thumb. 12) July - Hollow of the left palm.

We have now to take into consideration the time of the day at which the palm is shown to us and also the month. The whole day of 24 hours is divided into 12 equal parts of 2 hours each. The period is calculated from sun-rise. The first two hours after the sunrise are covered by the month in which the person has approached us. The next two hours are alloted to the next month, the two hours thereafter cover still next month and so on till we come to the hour of the day when the person has visited us and decide the month at that hour.

Supposing a person approaches us in the month of November at 17 hours (5 p.m.). The month of November is shown on the middle finger of the right hand. We have to allot the month of November if the person comes to us during the first two hours from sunrise. Let us suppose that the sunrise is at 6 a.m. That means the first period of two hours upto 8 a.m. is covered by the month of November. The period from 8 to 10 automatically goes to December. The period from 10 to 12 goes to January, from 12 to 14 to February, from 14 to 16 to March and from 16 to 18 to April. We have now to fix this month of April to the middle finger instead of its original month of November. Further explanation will clarify what I mean.

Now, the period falling on the first finger, the little finger and in the hollow are considered as inauspicious months. The months falling on the thumb, the middle finger and the ring finger are auspicious months. However, problems concerned with quarrels, law suits will be favourable if the period is shown on the first finger and will be unfavourable if the period falls on the thumb. We now go back to our example.

The person has visited us in the month of November and at 17 hours. This period falls on the middle finger of the right hand. As per our above calculations of every two hours, we arrive at the month of April which we have alloted to the middle finger instead of its original November month. we have to start counting the months fron April and from the middle finger. Thus May is on the ring finger, June is on the little finger of the right hand (instead of January as its original month as shown in the chart.)

We go further to the left hand and start counting July from the little finger of the left hand. August is on the ring finger, September is on the middle finger, October is on the first finger, November is on the thumb and December on the hollow of the left hand. We continue and come to the hollow of the right hand which will now be alloted to January, the thumb to February, first finger to March and April to the middle finger from where we started.

We have studied that the months falling on the little finger, the first finger and on the hollow of the palm are inauspicious. We see from the above that the months January, March and June fall in the hollow, the first finger and the little finger of the right hand respectively, and therefore, are inauspicious. Similarly, the month July falls on the little finger of the left hand , October and December on the first finger and in the hollow of the left hand. These months are also inauspicious. The other months viz., February, April, May, August, September and November are auspicious.

If the person visits us in the same month of November but between 14 to 16 hours, the month on the middle finger will be March instead of April as per our above example. In that case the auspicious and inauspicious months would be different.

Contents

Chapter		Pages
	Preface	xix
	Time Factor on the Hand	xxv
I	**Introduction**	1
	General remarks—Origin of the science—Utility of the study.	
II	**The Biological Significance of the Hand**	5
	Hand Test similar to Blood Test—Hand Print as the X-Ray.	
III	**The Psychological Significance of the Hand**	10
	The lines and their psychological interpretation.	
IV	**Importance of Hand Prints**	14
	Importance of Hand Prints—How to take Hand Prints.	
V	**The Shape of the Hand**	17
	Introduction Biological Significance of the shape of the Hand—Large and Small Hands—Bread and Short; Long and Narrow Hands—Seven types of the Hands. 1) The Elementary Hand Characteristics Nature and Temperament. 2) The Square Hand Characteristics and Temperament. The defects of the Type The Square Hand with different Types of Fingers. 3) The Spatulate Hand Characteristics and Nature. 4) The Conic Hand Three Varieties of Conic Hand. 5) The Psychic Hand Characteristics and Nature. 6) The Philosophic and Two types of Philosophers Characteristic and Nature. 7) The Mixed Hand Characteristics and Nature—Combinations of the Seven Types into three groups. 1) The Willing type. 2) The Feeling type and 3) The Thinking type—The Palm in General.	
VI	**The Division of the Hand**	47
	The Three Systems of Division—The First System. 1) The Mental World. 2) The Material World. 3) The Basal World. 4) Combination of the three Worlds—The Second System. 1) The Conscious Zone. 2) The Sub-Conscious Zone. 2) The Social Zone—The Third System. 1) The Zone of Thought. 2) The Zone of Action. 3) The Zone of Impulse. 4) The Zone of Imagination. 5) The Zone of the Thumb.	

| VII | Skin—Colour—Consistency—Flexibility | 61 |
| VIII | The Fingers | 69 |

Introduction—Smooth fingers with different tips—Knotty fingers with different tips—Short fingers with different tips—Long fingers with different tips—Fingers and their lengths. The fingers of Jupiter, Saturn. Apollo, Mercury—Space between the fingers—Leaning of fingers towards each other—Flexibility of the fingers—Phalanges—Hair on the fingers—Fingers and diseases—Skin ridges on the tips of the fingers—Signs on fingers—Zodical signs on fingers.

| IX | The Thumb | 123 |

Introduction—Evolution—Psychological significance—Biological significance—Anatomy—Small and Large Thumbs—Three positions of the Thumb. 1) High set. 2) Low set. 3) Medium set—Length of the Thumb—Shape of the Thumb—Phalanges of the Thumb—Tips of the Thumb—Knots of the Thumb—Flexibility of the Thumb—Carriage of the Thumb—Thumb in combination with other things on hand—Signs on the Thumb.

| X | The Nails | 155 |

Evolution—Anatomy—Fluted Nails—Narrow Nails—Broad Nails—Short Nails—Nails showing throat troubles—Nails showing tuberculosis—Nails showing paralysis—Almond shaped Nails—Nails showing syphilis—Cross rides on Nails—Spots on Nails.

| XI | The Hollow of the Palm | 165 |

The position of the Hollow on the Hand—The Division of the Hollow—The Quadrangle. 1) The position of the Quadrangle. The Development of the Quadrangle. 3) The Signs in the Quadrangle—The Triangle. 1) The position of the Triangle. 2) Angles of the Triangle. 3) The Signs in the Triangle.

| XII | The Right Hand and the Left Hand | 178 |
| XIII | The Mounts on the Hand | 182 |

Introduction—Mounts in General—Mount and Character—Mount and Health—Mount and Finance—Mount and Marriage Mount and Vocation—Mount in combination with other Mounts—Signs on the Mount.

| XIV | Epilogue | 311 |

Preparation of the Chart

| XV | The Hand of The President Nixon | 316 |
| XVI | The lines on the Hand | 325 |

Introduction—Theory behind the lines—Biological significance of the lines—Psychological significance of the lines—Prophetic significance of the lines—Predestination and Free-will—Study of lines : basic facts about lines—Defects in the line—Good signs on the hand—Formation of the lines on the hand—Lines

	on different types of hand—Rising and falling lines—Colour of the lines—General observation of the lines—Map of the hand—The time factor on the hand.	
XVII	**The line of Life**	342
	Introduction—Position on the hand—Normal development—Starting position—Course of the Life line—Ending position—Character of the line of Life—Defects of the line—Life line in relation to other lines—Signs on the Life line—Line of Influence—Cross lines starting from different signs—Cross lines ending on different lines.	
XVIII	**The line of Head**	400
	Introduction—Position on the hand—Normal development—Starting Position—Course of line—Ending position—Character of the line of Head—Defects of the line—Double line of Head—Head line in relation to other lines—Head line in relation to the type of hands—Head line in relation to fingers—Signs on the line of Head.	
XIX	**The line of Fate**	454
	Introduction—Position on the hand—Normal development—Starting position—Course of the line of Fate—Ending position—Character of the line—Defects of the line of Fate—Double line Fate—Fate line in relation to other lines—Line of Influence—Signs on the line of Fate.	
XX	**The line of Heart**	493
	Introduction—Position of Heart line on the hand—Normal development—Starting position of the line—Course of the line of Heart—Ending position of the line of Heart—Character of the line of Heart—Defects on the line of Heart—Double line of Heart—Heart line in relation to other aspects—Signs on the line of Heart—The Heart line and the mounts.	
XXI	**The line of Apollo (Sun)**	543
	Introduction—Position of the Sun line—Normal development—Starting position of the Sun line—Ending position of the line of Sun—Character of the Sun line—Defects in the line of Sun—Sun line in relation to other lines—Double line of Sun—Lines of Influence—Signs on the line of Sun.	
XXII	**The line of Mercury**	567
	Introduction—Position on the hand—Starting position of the line of Mercury—Course of the line of Mercury—Ending position of the line of Mercury—Character of the line of Mercury—Defects of the line of Mercury—Mercury line in relation to other lines—Double line of Mercury—Signs on the line of Mercury.	
XXIII	**Double line of Life or the line of Mars**	589
	Introduction—Position on the hand—Starting position of the	

Double line of Life—Course of the Double line of Life—Ending position of the Double line of Life—Character of the line of Mars or the Double line of Life—Defects in the Double line of Life—Double line of Life in relation to the types of hand.

XXIV	**Line of Via Lasciva**	597

Introduction—Position on the hand—Starting position—Course of the line of Via Lasciva—Ending position of the line of Via Lasciva—Character of the line of Via Lasciva—Line of Via Lasciva in relation to other lines—Signs on the line of Via Lasciva.

XXV	**Girdle of Venus**	601

Introduction—Position of the Girdle of Venus—Course of the Girdle of Venus—Ending position of the Girdle of Venus—Character of the Girdle of Venus—Defects of the Girdle of Venus—Double Girdle of Venus—Girdle of Venus in relation to other lines—Signs on the Girdle of Venus.

XXVI	**The line of Intuition**	606

Introduction—Position of the line of Intuition—Starting position of the line of Intuition—Course of the line of Intuition—Ending position of the line—Character of the line of Intuition—Defects of the line of Intuition—Signs on the line of Intuition.

XXVII	**The Bracelets**	610

Introduction—Position of the Bracelet—First Bracelet—Course of the First Bracelet—Character of the Bracelet—Defects of the Bracelet—Bracelets in relation to other lines—Signs on the Bracelets.

XXVIII	**Line of Travel and the lines on the mount of Moon**	615

Lines on the mount of Moon and the lines of Travel—Lines on the mount of showing diseases—Lines of Influence on the mount of Moon. 1) Defects in the line of Influence. 2) Signs on the line of Influence.

XXIX	**Rings of Solomon and Saturn**	621

Ring of Solomon—Ring of Saturn.

XXX	**The line of Marriage**	623

Introduction—Position on the hand—Starting position of the line of Marriage—Course of the line of marriage—Ending position of the line of Marriage—Character of the line of Marriage—Defects on the line of Marriage—Marriage line in relation to other lines—Signs on the line of Marriage.

XXXI	**The lines of Children**	636
XXXII	**Case Studies**	639
	Appendix I Signs on the Hand	657
	Appendix II	676
	Bibliography	757

CHAPTER I

Introduction

It is a matter of prolonged and bitter controversy whether palmistry is a science or not. I propose to give some facts and explanations which prove that palmistry is a natural science based on observation and medical facts. I am not endeavouring to make my readers believe in something incredible or superstitious. But I want them to pursue the study of a subject which has been made more scientific and illuminating in recent times.

The study of palmistry is receiving attention in the medical world and the science known as dermatoglyphics is advancing. However, this science has discovered only certain physical and mental illnesses from the study of the hand. There are some doctors like Dr. Charlotte Wolff who are establishing themselves as medical palmists. But the prophetic aspect of hand reading has still not been explored by modern science and it has still remained a matter of experience. Thus, today we can approach the study of palmistry from a scientific point of view as well as an empirical one and peep into the future events of man. Experience has been and will continue to be a great teacher in the technique of hand reading. Palmistry has long felt the inadequacy of mere experience and is now reaching out for all the help from growing sciences.

There is no doubt that prophecies are often to be found falsified by subsequent events. The reason for this must be sought not in the unscientific nature of this study but in our ignorance of the causes at work. The laws of Biology are not always borne out by subsequent events, but no one would, on that ground, deny that biology is not a science. The year of change in life can often be predicted much longer time in advance than the coming of a cyclone. Hence, the claim of palmistry to be regarded as a science cannot be denied on the ground that palmists lack precision and prophetic power. Palmistry is a grammar and it is to be studied just like any other grammar. Once the nouns, pronouns, verbs, etc. are digested, then the language of the hand is clear and lucid.

Origin and the History of the Science

In the Indian tradition, eight methods have been suggested for foreknowledge of good and evil. They are 1) Anga (limbs), 2) Swapna (dreams), 3) Swara (sound), 4) Bhoomi (attitude), 5) Vyanjana (marks on the body), 6) Lakshana (omens), 7) Utpatha (phenomena like earthquake), 8) Anthariksha (sky). Of all these, Anga gets the place of honour by being mentioned first. Among Anga (limbs), the hand is considered more important than even the head.

The ancient Indian sages gave out the knowledge of the hand which they gathered through three means viz. 1) Seeing (darshana), 2) Touching (sparshana) and 3) Analysing (Vimarshana). The knowledge thus gained threw light on all the aspects of life. The Indian tradition holds that the Anga Vidya was first invented by the Sea God 'Samudra'. It was thereafter developed and handed down to humanity by the sages like Narada and Gargya. Lord Skanda is held to be the patron deity of this science. Since the God Samudra is the originator of the science, the study is called the Samudrika Shastra (the science by Samudra). It is also held that all the Gods and Goddesses and all the sacred rivers have their counterparts on the palm. Hence the Hindus consider the human palm very sacred and attribute divine qualities to it.

We find further that this study of the hand spread in different countries and grew, flourished and found favour in the firmament of knowledge. We find it sanctioned by such men as Aristotle, the Emperor Augustus and many others of note.

Introduction

It is said that the Roman Emperor Caesar was so well versed in the study of the hand that on one occasion when a foreign prince presented his credentials, Caesar asked him to show his hands. After examinining them he denounced the prince as an imposter as he could not find any sign of royalty or royal descent on his hands. Several such illustrations can be quoted from India and other countries. One such example from Indian stories can be cited. When King Dushyanta denounced his wife Shakuntala and forgot her as his wife, Shakuntala approached him on a later occasion when she was carrying. But King Dushyanta, due to a curse from the Sage Durwasa, could not remember her and his memory completely failed him to recognise her as his wife. At that time the Prime Minister of the King told Shakuntala that if she gave birth to a male child and if the hand of that child showed the signs of a royal birth, the King would accept her as his Queen.

Dr. John Dee was a favourite palmist and an astrologer of the Queen Elizabeth, the daughter of the King Henry VIII. All this goes to prove that the study of palmistry is not only one of the most ancient in the world, but also one that has occupied the serious attention of the most exalted minds in history.

Utility of the study

After the above discussion, it will convince any rational person that the study of the hand has its basis and foundation. Religion explains that the lines on the hand foretell the future, civilisation proves that palmistry played an important part on many occasions, medicine gives its cognisance showing that the hand is related to the brain which rules the character of man and so his future too. Napoleon said 'perhaps the face can deceive but never the hand.' Hitler had a band of occultists. All these facts establish the authenticity of the science and its utility in everyday life. Though it is not a perfect science, as no branch of human knowledge can be, its investigations are none the less important. It does he' humanity to a great extent. A palmist is a guide and his function is to show others the periods of uplift and also the depressed periods in their lives. They have to take hints and go forward. "Forewarned is forearmed." If we can guide our children as to what study courses they should undertake, we can avoid their failures in their education to a great extent. Equally the study is useful in finding out suitable matches for young men and women so that they can lead harmonious married lives.

In brief, the study of the hand is useful to doctors in locating the diseases, to the educationists in choosing proper career for the student, to the psychiatrists in locating mental deficiencies, to the criminologists in detecting the criminal, to the law courts in finding out doubtful parentage and to the general man in building up his future. I am not over-estimating this science by giving undue praise to it, but I am putting up the exact value of the study which is entirely based on my own experience and what it can do for the humanity.

Palmistry is a treasure island. Valuable and tremendous information can be gathered from the hand. The only thing we must possess is the knowledge that the hand is a cave like that of forty thieves and we must know the keyword 'Open Sesame'. If we have the art to unfold the hand, if we have an insight into the working of the Mounts and lines on the hand, it is very easy to delineate the life of persons as vividly as anything.

CHAPTER II

The Biological Significance of the Hand

The science of Cheirosophy is divided into two parts. The first part is known as Cheirognomy which deals with the shape of the hand, the shape of the fingers, the development of the hand and the fingers and with the shape and development of the nails. This part has a biological significance. The second part is known as Cheiromancy and is concerned with the lines on the hand and their interpretation. This second part has a psychological significance with which I shall deal with in the next chapter.

In order to consider the biological significance of the hand I would point out that if we look at a person whose colour is pale, we can judge that his is not a strong constitution. If the doctor finds yellowishness in the eyes of his patient, he can conclude that the patient is suffering from jaundice. A mere glance at the tongue will convey the message of stomach trouble. All these judgments or conclusions are scientific because bodily developments and constitutions are reflected on different parts of the body and with experience in this direction, it has been discovered that colour, eyes, tongue and such other parts reflect certain diseases. Similarly, the hand is an important part of the body and it reflects many of the health defects. The colour of the hand will give an idea about the vitality of the person, while the shape of the hand tells about the shape of the brain centre and its developments. Fingers are good indicators of certain health defects. In addition to this, the nails are useful and they show the health and vitality of the person. I shall view some of these considerations and shall discuss how scientific explanation is possible for the discoveries made by the ancient scholars on this subject.

If the Mount of Venus is well developed on the hand, it is said that it indicates a passionate disposition. Uptil now the interpretation of the Mount of Venus was regarded as a superstitious matter but now scientific explanation is possible for that interpretation.

During my research in a hospital, I have found that the thumb is more affected in cases of venereal disease. The probable cause seems to be that as the Mount of Venus which is known as the third phalange of the thumb is connected with the vitality of the person and his passions, the thumb gets directly connected with the sex glands and it is natural that diseases of the sex glands should be reflected on the thumb. It is a common experience of the medical world that during the mating season the thumb of a frog gets swollen—a fact which is reflective of sexual activity.

The fingers also reveal certain peculiarities. For instance, even a casual student of palmistry knows that short fingers denote a hasty nature and an impetuous disposition. In medicine the shortness of the fingers is associated with abnormal endocrine balance which can be seen in cases of hypothyroidism, infantilism of the sex glands and in underfunctioning of the pituitary glands. Now, it is quite possible that an abnormal endocrine balance will affect the mind and the brain of the person in such a way that he will be hasty in all his action. Thus, in this case the biological condition has affected the fingers as well as the temperament. Hyppocrates discovered that the first finger shows the defects of the lungs. Any abnormal development of this finger shows diseases such as laryngitis, asthma, pneumonia and other defects of the lungs.

The middle finger or the finger of Saturn (*fig. 1*) shows a melancholy and gloomy outlook on life. In medical palmistry, this finger indicates liver and stomach condition. It is likely that a person with liver trouble has a gloomy outlook on life.

The Biological Significance of the Hand

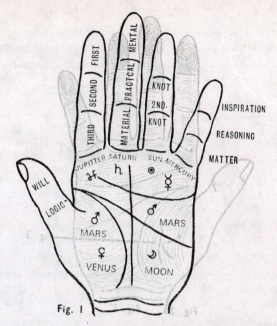

Fig. 1

General Hand (Map of the hand) Mounts and their signs

The third finger has connection with the kidneys and defects in the function of the kidney are many times noticeable on this finger.

Lastly, the fourth finger reveals the gonadic and sex troubles. I have noticed that this finger is more affected on the hands of women suffering from the troubles of the ovaries and the womb.

It will thus be clear that the significance of the signs on the hand, as explained many centuries before, can be interpreted in terms of modern science. It is now the work of medicine to take into consideration these interpretations and make discoveries as to their causes. Thus, the observations which were once regarded as superstition can have a scientific basis.

Another aspect to be noted on the hand for detecting the health defect is the pattern of the papillary ridges (*fig. 2*) found all over the hand and especially on the finger tips. It

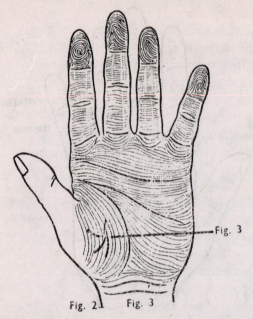

Fig. 2. Papillary Ridges   Fig. 3. Centres of tactile senses

is interesting to note that these papillary ridges are formed during the fourth month of pregnancy and they do not change throughout life. It has been a matter of observation and experience that these patterns exhibit physical and mental defects, such as kidney trouble, rheumatism, ulcer, asthma etc., which the person has acquired prior to his birth.

An interesting account of my own work in this direction will be useful to my readers and they will know how the 'Hand Test' can reveal the health defect.

During my work in a Homeopathic Clinic, I was shown a case of a lady patient and the doctor told me that she was suffering from asthma (*case 1*). After studying the hand print, I found that two other diseases affected the lady, the one was gonadic trouble and the other kidney trouble. I explained these observations to the doctor who asked me to wait. He brought her case paper and to our great surprise all the gonadic troubles were found in her history. But regarding the kidney no reference was made. After a few days when the lady patient visited for the treatment, we asked her if she ever suffered from the kidneys. To this the lady replied that she had been suffering from the disease for over twelve years and finally she got herself operated. During my discussions with the doctor later on, I was told that kidney trouble could be the cause of asthma. Thus, my examination of the hand revealed the root cause of the disease and it was a great help to the doctor who started giving her medicine on kidney.

Thus, it will be seen that there is a vast field for research in this direction and the observations of practitioners in hand-reading may be viewed scientifically by the medical science. It is clear to any one that the hand has a biological significance and the fingers, the papillary ridges and the nails give some indication about the health of the person. I call this as a 'Hand Test' and I am sure that elaborate research in the matter will enable the medical practitioners to diagonise the disease and to find out the root cause of any disease from an examination of the hand. It will also help them when the blood test will fail. It is my suggestion therefore, that the science of cheirosophy should be made an additional subject for the medical students, that arrangements for laboratory work should be made and that students for research should receive their lessons in such laboratories under the guidance of experts.

CHAPTER III
The Psychological Significance of the Hand

In the previous chapter, I discussed the hand from the biological point of view and in this chapter I shall deal with the psychological aspect of the hand. This is mainly concerned with the second division of the science of Cheirosophy which is known as Cheiromancy.

To remind my readers of the papillary ridges on the hand, I would like to mention that the papillary ridges on a Chimpanzee's finger tips bear some resemblance to those of a human being as has been shown by Dr. Cummins. All the five fingers of a monkey show the same pattern, a condition called monomorphic. Generally this condition is found in a very small percentage of people and only in subnormal people. This simian pattern of papillary ridges is very common among the feeble minded persons and imbeciles.

After the papillary ridges, we shall discuss the lines on the hand. Usually, palmistry is considered as the science of lines and has a prophetic significance. But if we take into consideration the psychological interpretation of the lines on the hand, we have grounds to say that it is a science and a further study of it on a scientific basis is possible. It has been found during the study of the hand that there is a natural course through life that every person would follow and the lines form a map of his natural life's course. If no change takes place in his mental or physical attitude and no accidents occur, this course will be followed. This explains why the lines on the hand change. It is true that the life of an individual may not undergo a revolutionary change. Nevertheless, his attitude and ideas do change from time to time and they are reflected through lines on the hand. Thus, the mind produces, controls or alters the lines on the hand. The main lines (fig. 97) indicate what the natural course of the life is, new lines just beginning to form show emotions and ideas just developing within the person. Experiments are going on to catch the thought waves of man in order to understand his mind, and scientists are spending years in the search for a key with which they can unlock the secrets of the human mind. One key is the hand, a perfect mirror giving insight in the working of human mind. People can easily change their faces but not so easily their minds. The hand reveals the man as he is, not as he may pretend to be. So it will not be wrong to connect the lines on the hand with the mind. Sometimes, even small shades of the mind are seen on the hand. Hereditary and natural tendencies and those which have created profound impressions upon his mind can all be seen on the hand.

The main lines are the direct result of the muscular activity of the hand and arm and are found where the skin folds.

The accessory crease lines are not in proportion to the manual activity of the hand owner. On the contrary lazy hands are the richest in these creases. The more sensitive a person is, the greater is his desire for self-expression and the richer is his vocabulary of gesture. These gestures involve a high degree of mobility of the hand and cause many accessory creases. The meaning of gesture is wholly psychological. It is profoundly allied with nervous and emotional reactions. We find on the Mounts of Moon and Venus small accessory lines running towards whorls or loops found on thess Mounts. These whorls or loops mark the centres of the tactile sense and the crease lines running towards them would therefore seem to have a direct connection with sensitivity (fig. 3).

From the point of view of hand psychology, the hand is divided into three zones (fig. 4). The first zone, which includes the thumb and the Index finger and the portion below them, gives knowledge of environment and conscious

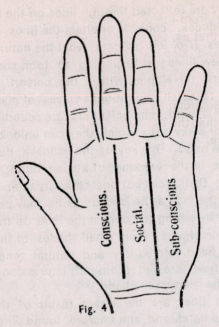

Fig. 4
Three Zones on the hand

behaviour and the will power. The second zone includes the Ring finger and the little finger and the portion below them. This zone is a good indicator of the working of the subconscious mind and the hidden characteristics of the person. The middle zone is the social zone and it indicates the social adaptability of the person.

In addition to the above, there are many other points to be taken into consideration for the study of the hand psychology. Texture of the hand will show refinement of the mind, the elasticity of the hand will reveal the adaptability and quickness of the mind, the colour of the hand will be a good indicator of the nature and temperament of the person, and the fingers and shape of the hand will mean the culture of the person, his ideas, his ambitions and many angularities of his mind.

The subject of palmistry has generally been a matter of ridicule and it has always been linked with the aspect of prophecy. But from the above proof and observations it can truly be said that as far as health defects and conditions of a person and also the psychology of the person are concerned the subject of Cheirosophy is as perfect a science as any other. Health and temperament can be judged and character-reading can be done to a marked degree, for the simple reason that the hand has a biological and psychological significance.

CHAPTER IV
Importance of Hand Prints

Before we start hand-reading, it is very necessary that we take the handprint of the person whose hands we are going to examine. Many students of palmistry do not realise the importance of hand-prints and they are under the impression that naked hands are more clear than the hand impression. But if they start taking hand-prints and make it a rule to do so, in a very short period of time, they will find from a large collection of hand-prints they shall have in their collection ; that the hand-prints are not only of great use to them, but that they notice a number of lines on the hand-prints which are not readily visible to the naked eye, even with the use of a magnifying glass. There are quite a number of advantages in taking hand impressions which can be summarised as under.

As has been stated above, the map of the hand is more clear. Especially for an advanced student of palmistry, papillary ridges on the hand are important if he want to study the hand from the health point of view. Several inherent and hereditary diseases are located on the papillary ridges and it would not be possible to study the different patterns of ridges unless we take a very clear hand-impression.

Secondly, the study of the Mounts, which forms the core of the subject of palmistry, is difficult without a hand impression. The development of any mount is easier to judge by the quantity of ink spread over that portion of the hand. Similarly, we can know without much trouble whether the particular Mount has been situated at the proper place or whether there is a displacement of the Mount. Displaced

Mounts are quite visible and their inclination on one side or the other makes a different interpretation.

Thirdly, calculations can be made to a marked degree of accuracy on a hand print, which is otherwise very difficult.

In the study of palmistry, calculating the period is more important than the mentioning of an event. For instance, a line of marriage will show that the person will be married. But the importance is to be given to the period at which he will be married. Again, a change of profession may be shown in the Fate line, but the period of change is more important. Calculations on such delicate points is quicker and smoother on a hand print than otherwise.

Fourthly, we can jot down points of observation and make our own marking on the hand print for our study of the palm. For this purpose, we can have the hand-impression before us for any number of hours. We can go on studying the print, marking various combinations, doing different calculations and finally arriving at conclusions by taking our own time. This would not be possible if we take our client's hand in ours, which may cause great inconvenience to him.

Lastly, the hand-print taken remains with us as a permanent record. It may happen that the same person may come to us after a long time and then if we have in our record his previous hand print, it will be possible for us to compare his new hand print with the old one. Some changes in the lines on the hand may be noticed.

How to take hand prints

The stamp pad ink method is more effective. In this method a thin coating of stamp pad ink is spread over both the hands by the use of a rubber roller. Both the hands are then kept on an art paper firmly. Each hand is then slowly pressed against the paper taking care that the fingers are first pressed from top to bottom. Then we have to press the portion below the fingers and gradually come down to the wrist. After this, the person may exert a little more pressure on the paper by just lifting his forearm to make a ninety degrees angle to the palm (*fig. 5*).

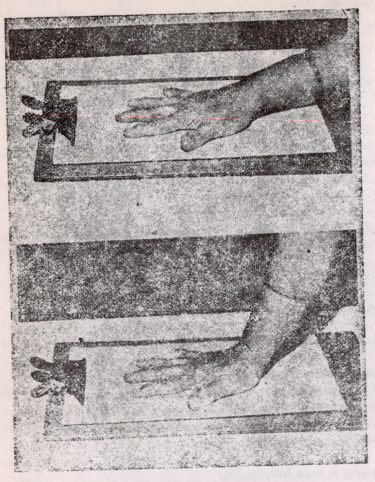

Fig. 5. How to take Hand Print

Thereafter, we should press hard from above the upper portion of the palm. This is useful to take a clear print of the hollow of the palm. In normal course, with this procedure, palms with greater hollow can also give a clear impression. Only in rare cases where the hollow is too much, we have to take a curve block of wood on which the art paper is kept and then the palm on it.

After this is done, the person removes both the hands from the art paper and we get a clear and sharp hand-impression.

CHAPTER V

The Shape of the Hand

1 Introduction

The science of the hand is based on the shape of the hand. This science is called as Cheirognomy. In this chapter, I shall give a very systematic account of the shape of the hand, and a careful study of this chapter will enable the readers to start the practice of hand-reading. There is an age old theory, that in the beginning all humanity was divided into seven types. And each type was made up of individuals disclosing certain traits. The habits and attributes, and even the physical appearance of each person in a typical group were alike.

It can be pointed out here that the shape of the hand is so important that by its study we can know the type of mind is directing the subject's activities in life. By the formation of a dog's foot we can tell for what particular kind of chase he is most suited; by the shape of a horse's hoof we can tell what is his breed and what qualities particularly distinguish him. In the same way, the shape of the hand sums up the whole of your mind and intelligence. As an acorn is symbolic of an oak tree, the shape of the hand represents the person in different shades.

There are people who fancy that they are serious, because they are of a lugubrious and miserable state of mind. The reason for their feelings is to be sought in the shape of their hands. Thus, the readers should carefully observe the hands from this point of view, which would reveal to them half of the inner life of the person.

The various shapes of hands and their suitability to various kinds of occupations is also worthy of note, and although by the exercise of will power we can alter and make up for almost any constitutional defect, yet it is true that certain types are more suited for one work than another.

2 Biological and Psychological Significance of the Shape of the Hand

The endocrine glands and the biochemistry of the cells, play an important part in developing the shape of the hand. Mongolism is very well known to the physicians. In this disease there is mental as well as endocrine deficiency and the two are probably interdependent. The palm of a Mongolian imbecile is short, broad and square. The fingers are abnormally short, in proportion to it. The thumb and the fifth finger are often minute. It is interesting to note that the fifth finger or the finger of Mercury in about ten per cent of cases, has only two phalanges instead of three. In the case of a patient suffering from acromegaly, which is a disease due to a tumour causing hyperfunctiong of the pituitary glands, every physician examines the hands, since this produces abnormally enlarged hands with huge and stout fingers. Similarly in its opposite, the under-developed pituitary glands, the hands are too small and the fingers very slender.

In the case of under-developed thyroid glands, the hand is small, fat and broad. Such hands are white and flabby with sausage-shaped fingers, the tips of which are short and usually conical, with a strikingly pointed fifth finger. Such people have a definite type of personality. They appeal to their fellows by their love for the good things of life, their desire for comfort and luxury and the atmosphere of glamour with which they surround themselves. They have very little self discipline and cannot resist the temptation to have a good time. They are good company, kind hearted and open minded, but unstable and erratic. They lack concentration and their intelligence runs on practical rather than theoretical lines.

On the contrary, a person suffering from over-developed thyroid glands, has a long bony hand with thin and bony fingers. He is active and vivacious. He cannot be pigeonholed for he is variable and capable of doing so many things.

Thus, we notice that the psychological significance of the hand is dependent on the biological composition of the individual. A good artist first studies the face of the person whose portrait he is going to paint. The square face, the oval face, the round face or the Roman face, these and all the various facial models require a careful study in posing. Each type must be posed to artistic advantage. At the same time the artist must also be a good judge of character, so as to enable him to give the proper expression to the portrait. In the same way a hand-reading expert must first fix up the type of the hand under examination. It will enable him to know the basic character of the person whose life he is going to portray.

3 Large and Small Hands

The first thing to be noted about the shape of the hand is whether the hand is large or small. There is no exact measurement which could give us a correct idea about the largeness or smallness of the hand. But the hand, on observing it, conveys a message that it is a large hand in proportion to the normal development of the hand. This is purely a matter of observation, experience and judgement. However, there should not be any difficulty in finding out a large hand or a small hand from a normal one.

Large Hands

It is very surprising to note that persons with large hands have a love for small and detailed things. Normally, we think that large hands should go in for large things and small hands for small things. But it is just the opposite. It has been observed that jewellers, watchmakers, engravers and persons who are engaged in trades, where every minute detail is to be observed, have invariably large hands. Their love for details is remarkable. Even in matters of studies and discussions, these persons never leave the subject haphazard and they have hair-splitting arguments. Such persons are therefore fit for research work, where patience is required. They always like to go to the root of a thing, and from the root to the fruit, they will examine each part carefully and gain perfect knowledge of the subject.

Large hands therefore are endowed with a spirit of minute and detail. We are told that Frederick of Prussia had large hands.

Large hands, particularly if they are hard, is a sign of physical strength and as the Greeks could not conceive beauty without strength, a large hand was to them a great beauty. Balzac, with his large conic hands liked to count the fruit on the espalier, the leaves on the hedge, the separate hair in his beard. He took delight in physiological details and might have invented the microscope, had it not been invented before he was born. Balzac was very proud of his hands.

Small Hands

Small hands display the characteristics which are incompatible with those of the large hands. Thus, they prefer to carry out big ideas, and as a rule, make plans, far too large, for their power of execution. They love to manage large concerns and govern communities. Generally, even the writing of small hands is large and bold.

There has always been an admiration for small hands which display a warm heart and delicacy of the mind.

Small-handed persons not only go in for large attempts but for too large a thing. It is towards the dwarf that a giant is irresistibly attracted and in like manner it is by the giant that the dwarf is invariably fascinated. The Pyramids, the temples of upper Egypt and of India, seem to have been built up by people whose hands were small and narrow, spatulate and smooth.

Small hands show a faculty of synthesis. Small hands which are soft, supple and rosy and with developed joints, love brilliant phrases, which like lightning, cast a sudden bright flash of wit around them. They live with their minds alone.

4 Broad and Short and Long and Narrow Hands (*Fig. 6*)

The proper hand (see the division of the hand) is either broad and short or long and narrow. A broad hand always indicates a more balanced type of mind. These people generally possess breadth of vision and have more understanding than any other type. The broad hand indicates common sense,

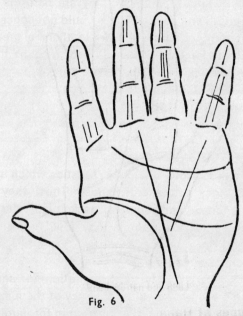

Fig. 6

Broad and short hand (common sense and undetstanding)

activity and versatility as the dominant qualities. A peculiarity to be noted of this type of the hand is that, in a majority of cases the lines on the hand are also broad. I call it a misleading type of hand, because these broad lines often convey a wrong period of any event shown by the signs on the hand. For instance, if an event is marked at the age of 30, it will often take place either 4-5 years earlier or later. Accuracy regarding the time factor is difficult with such hands. However, it does not fail to produce the characteristics shown by the shape of the hand.

The long narrow hands (*fig.* 7) belong more to a dreamer. These persons have a one track mind and lack in concentration. They are also apt to dabble in many things, but succeed in a few. This thin narrow hand indicates a strong selfish trait.

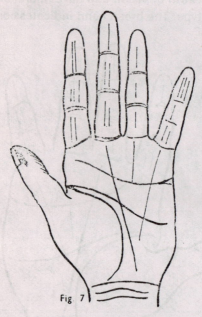

Long and narrow hand

5 Seven Types of Hand

There are seven types of the hand. They are as follows i) the elementary, ii) the square, iii) the spatulate, iv) the conic, v) the psychic, vi) the philosophic and vii) the mixed.

These seven types are sufficiently distinct from one another. Their peculiarities are clearly and distinctly described. These types cannot alter or modify themselves beyond a certain point. From these types result the various civilizations and each type asserts itself by the invincible persistence of the tendencies which it exhibits.

i) The Elementary Hand (fig. 8)

Characteristics : In appearance the elementary hand is coarse and clumsy with a large, thick, heavy palm, short fingers and short nails. There are very few lines to be seen on the palm.

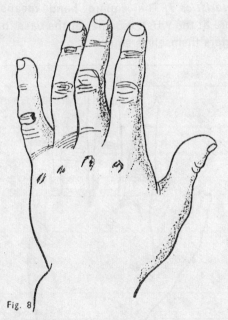

Fig. 8

The elementary hand (animal instincs, lethargy)

Nature and Temperament : 1) People of this type have very little mental capacity and lean more to the order of the brute.

2) They have little or no control over their passions.

3) The thumb being short and the first phalange of the same being more pronounced, they are violent in temper, passionate but not courageous.

4) They are without aspirations. They just eat, drink, sleep and die.

5) They are dull and sluggish.

6) They are more troubled by phantoms, spectres and oppositions in proportion to their finger tips which may be more or less conical.

7) Whatever be the form of the terminal phalange, the type is always much influenced by superstition.

ii) The Square Hand (*fig. 9*)

Characteristics: The square hand means the palm ; proper square at the wrist, square at the base of the fingers. and the fingers themselves square.

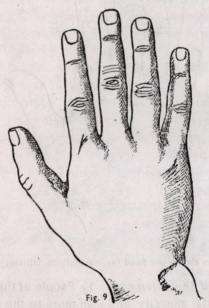

Fig. 9
The square hand (foresight, judgement)

Nature and Temperament: The square hand is called the useful hand because it is found in so many walks of life. However, it should also be noted that the square hand may have any type of fingers which will naturally reduce or

The Shape of the Hand

precipitate the characteristics of the square type. We shall deal with them later on.

1) Perseverance, foresight, and the spirit of order and conventionality are the main characteristics of the square type.

2) They are orderly, punctual and precise in manner, not however from any innate grace of nature but more from confirmity with custom and habit.

3) They do not recognise the artistic and the more beautiful aspect in a thing but they appreciate the thing from a point of view of usefulness and tradition.

4) They have the capacity to find out the difference in two things which apparently look alike and they also have the judgment to trace the likeness in two things which apparently look different.

5) They always love one law and that is tradition. They pride themselves in showing continuity in the tradition which shows that they are more bound by customs and conventions.

6) They come forward in life not because they are intelligent but because they have perseverance and patience.

7) Persons of this type are too materialistic and naturally they do not believe in anything which they do not see and they suspect the unknown.

8) Since they do not have high aspirations, they go by their good sense rather than by their genius, by their spirit and cultivated talents, rather than by the faculties of imagination.

9) This type will always look for a man who has well-cultivated thoughts, disciplined, moulded and trimmed upon a certain pattern.

If the square type is found in military occupation, it also has its own idiosyncracies and it revels in them. It will scrupulously observe its dress and be neat and clean. It feels that it should not be hungry or thirsty excepting at the regimental and prescribed hours. It will be obedient and submissive to discipline though it is bold and brave. It will have clear judgment but its wit will be neither brilliant nor refined.

Defect of the type

1) Their greatest fault is that they are inclined to reason by a twelve-inch rule and disbelieve all they cannot understand.

2) Hypocrisy and conceit, coldness, stiffness of manner and bearing, harshness of punctuality are the principal defects of persons belonging to the useful type.

I reproduce here a hand-impression representing the square type (*case 2*). The Heart line is very straight. The Head line is also straight with the end portion curving upwards, which shows a person who counts everything in rupees, annas and pies. He is sometimes punctual to a fault. Once he did not allow his wife to enter the house after her return from a trip, and kept her outside the house all the night because she returned home a day earlier than the scheduled.

The Square Hand with Small Square Fingers (*fig. 10*)

1) A person of this type has a quick grasp of things but is scrupulous.

2) He is materialistic in every sense of the term.

3) He is very hard to convince and he believes only in what he sees or hears. Sometimes he may not believe his own senses.

4) He makes money but by plodding. He may not be miserly but is business-like and practical.

5) He likes to accumulate wealth.

The Square Hand with Long Square Fingers (*fig. 11*)

This type exhibits such characteristics which are incompatible with those described above. It shows

1) high ideals and elevated views on life.

2) better logic and reasoning than the one of the previous type.

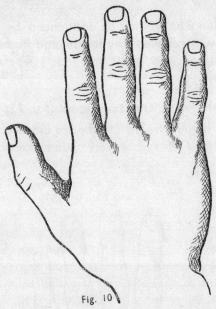

Fig. 10
The square hand with short-square fingers (quick grasp but scrupulous)

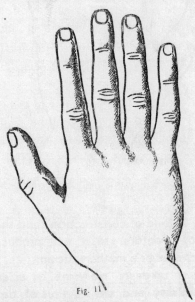

Fig. 11
The square hand with long square fingers (good logic and reasoning)

3) a person who will not be influenced by prejudice, but one who will proceed cautiously and thoroughly to logical conclusions and will find one's vocation in a scientific career.

The Square Hand with Knotty Fingers (*fig. 12*)

1) Knotty fingers by their virtue are didactic, caluclating and analytical. This is a very good combination to possess.

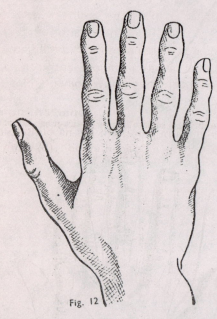

Fig. 12

The square hand with knotty fingers (analytic mind)

2) This type is fond of construction, and though it may not be the hand of inventors still it will produce a person who is a good architect or a mathematician.

3) If this type takes to medicine or science, it will choose some speciality and use its love of details in the perfection of its studies.

The Shape of the Hand

The Square Hand with Spatulate Fingers (*fig. 13*)

1) This is also a very good combination and the practical view point of the square type is added to energy, enthusiasm and originality displayed by the spatulate fingers.

2) Persons of this type are good engineers and also inventors.

3) Their inventions are based on material basis and they do not have vague or impractical ideas. They produce things which are useful and instruments which are necessary in everyday life.

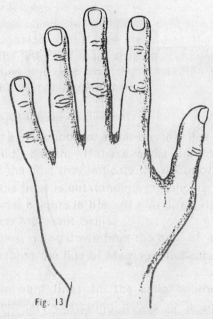

Fig. 13

The square hand with spatulate fingers (invention and originality)

4) They have a very practical view-point and love mechanical work.

5) They like to construct bridges and streets and dams which are of lasting value.

The Square Hand with Conic Fingers (*fig. 14*)

The readers will be surprised to note that the square hand can have conic fingers. It is also supposed that this type of combination is not a good one, since the characteristics of the square type are marred by those of conic fingers. But this notion is not quite true. Though the square type is incompatible with the conic one, the blending of these two types is very essential to produce a person with ability to make a concrete suggestion. Conic fingers denote an artistic nature and high imagination, but in order to bring those ideals into practice the hand must be a square one. A poet

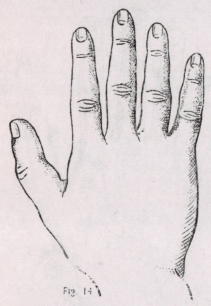

Fig. 14

The square hand with conic fingers   (method in art and poetry)

or a literary writer may have conic fingers which display his sense of art, but in order to bring poetry on papers, the poet must have method, system and regularity which are the characteristics of the square type. Thus, a conic type alone, that is without the support of the square type, will produce weird music and the person will live in his utopian ideas,

The Shape of the Hand

but if the conic fingers have the square type, the person uses his art and ideals on a practical basis and gives the benefit of his imagination and ideals to the world at large. Thus, we should not be surprised to note conic fingers to the square type, in fact, it is a necessity. (*case 3*)

Defects of this type

These people are susceptible to changing moods and they find it very difficult to take decisions. But once they take up the decision, their plans are solid and their material constructive.

The Square Hand with Psychic Fingers (*fig. 15*)

This is a very rare combination and at the same time very unfavourable. Psychic fingers are smooth and very long or

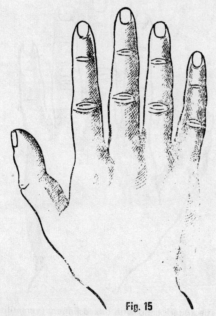

Fig. 15

The square hand with psychic fingers (clash between idealism and materialism)

pointed. Psychic fingers are very good to look at and they are also very attractive. By virtue of the psychic fingers these persons are too idealistic and aspiring for a very high motto which is beyond their reach. They have visions, hallucinations and day dreams. They are too emotional and sensitive. But, the square hand displays a nature which is exactly opposite to this. Naturally, there is always an inner clash between idealism and materialism. Both these instincts being very powerful, it reduces the vitality and energy of the person. That makes him very unsteady and shaky. The result is that such a person is miserable in life and cannot achieve anything.

The Square Hand with Mixed Fingers *(fig. 16)*

Sometimes we come across a hand which is square in its shape but the fingers are not of any particular type and they

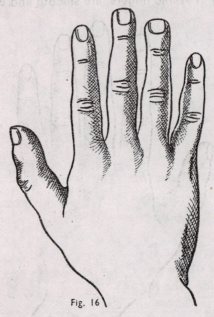

Fig. 16

The square hand with mixed fingers (versatility)

are of different shapes. In such a case generally, the first or the Jupiter finger is pointed, the second or the Saturn finger is square, the third or the Apollo finger is spatulate and the little or the Mercury finger is again pointed. These fingers generally exhibit versatility of ideas as shown by different fingers. The main characteristics are as under :

1) The person has many kinds of activities and he can discuss and be the center of many subjects.

2) He is very artistic as shown by the first finger which is pointed and he has his own ideas of religion.

3) He is very practical as shown by the Saturn finger. Saturn, by nature is practical and materialistic and square formation adds to its mundane philosophy.

4) The person is original in his ideas as pointed out by the third finger which has a spatulate formation.

5) He is very shrewd and business-like as shown by the pointed fourth finger.

In short, this person takes to many subjects but cannot concentrate on one. The result is therefore that he never rises to a high position since he lacks the tenacity to follow one trade. He is a Jack of all trades but master of none.

By now the readers might have got an idea of the combination of different types with different fingers and therefore hereafter I shall avoid such combinations. The readers should make their own combinations before they arrive at a conclusion.

The Spatulate Type (fig. 17)

Characteristics : The third type to be taken into consideration is the Spatulate type. This type is so called because of its formation like that of the spatula of the chemist. In this case, the shape at the wrist of the hand is very narrow, and the sides of the hand rise upward separating the distance between them. The figure will give a good idea. Similarly, the fingers are narrow at the bottom and broad at the top.

Nature and Temperament

1) This type shows originality and energy. This is the type which is found in the case of inventors, workers and

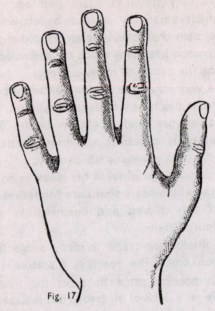

Fig. 17

The spatulate hand (originality, invention)

speculators. They generally invest all their energy in new ideas and like to avoid the beaten track.

2) They hate custom, tradition and regularity. They have on the contrary their own ideas of morality, methods and conduct. They take any course they please and care little about what others will say.

3) If the hand is hard and firm, it indicates a nature which is restless and excitable, but full of energy of purpose and enthusiasm.

4) If the hand is soft and flabby, it means a spirit which is restless but irritable. Such a person works by fits and starts but cannot stick to anything for long. Generally, the hand is large and its singular characteristic is the independence of spirit which the individual possesses in his development.

5) No matter in what grade or position in life these spatulate hands find themselves, they always in some form

strike out for themselves and assert their right to possess a marked individuality of their own.

6) They have intense love of action, energy and independence.

7) It belongs to the great navigators, explorers, discoverers and also the great engineers and mechanics.

8) It is doubtless the spirit in them which makes them depart from the known rules of engineering and mechanics to seek the unknown and thus become famous for their inventions.

If people have spatulate type of hands and if they follow the professions of doctor or preacher or actor, they will gain more fame in their trades since they will get an opportunity to exhibit their originality and spirit.

iv) **The Conic Hand** (*fig. 18*)

Characteristics : The conic hand is characterised by smooth fingers whose nailed phalanges assume the form of

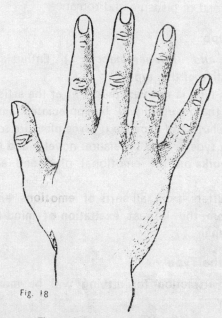

Fig. 18

The conic hand (an artist)

cones or of elongated shape. By smooth finger is meant the absence of knots between the joints of the fingers. The hand proper is broad at the base and the sides go on narrowing on both the sides making a narrow angle at the base of the fingers. The fingers also are broad at the base and pointed at the tip.

Three types of Conic Hands

There are three varieties of the conic hand and accordingly it betrays three different tendencies. In the first case the hand is developed in a moderate way but it is supple and the thumb is small. This type likes beauty of form and proceeds with enthusiasm. The second type of the conic hand is large, thick and short. It is more practical than the other two and runs after wealth, greatness and good fortune. This type is very shrewd and cunning. The third variety of the conic type is found when the hand is large and very firm. This is more or less cynical and has a tendency to fatalism. This type is fond of pleasure and romance.

The First Type

Nature and Temperament : 1) Enthusiasm is the principle motive of this type.

2) This type is not very much after the artistic value in a thing, but the beautiful will be appreciated simply for the sake of its beauty and because it gives pleasure to the eye.

3) This type is fond of leisure, novelty and liberty.

4) It works on the emotional plane and acts instinctively.

5) It suffers from all sorts of emotions and will pass suddenly from the loftiest exaltation of mind to the profoundest despair.

Defects of the Type

a) The attraction for a thing will be more than the sense of duty.

The Shape of the Hand

b) It is capable of command and still more incapable of obedience.

c) It does not understand the real value of a thing and runs after the superficial beauty of that thing. It leads to disappointment in the end, since the outer beauty is not of permanent value and fades in course of time.

The Second Type

Nature and Temperament : The second type is that of the large thick and short hand.

1) This type has its own idiosyncrasies and is more jealous of the three types.

2) It values money and wealth more than beauty. It is opulence that attracts it.

Poetry of the imagination is the characteristic of the first type, whereas poetry of mundane type is the characteristic of this second type. The first type will appreciate pictures of angels and of love, the second type will enjoy pictures of nature and landscapes and would like to keep them in exhibition where they will be sold out for a good value.

Defects of the Type

1) The first defect of this type lies in being lustful and its love for money.

2) It is envious of others and cannot be in love except for money.

3) This type is more hard-hearted and cruel than the other two.

The Third Type

Nature and Temperament : 1) This hand has a large appetite for sexual pleasures and lacks moral control.

2) It has no strength of mind and it is also incapable of conducting conversation based upon reason and logic.

3) It refuses to think and is swayed away by inspiration.

4) It hates serious talk and is troubled by thought provoking ideas.

v) The Psychic Type (fig. 19)

Characteristics: 1) It is the most beautiful hand of all and consequently the most scarce.

2) It is small and fine in relation to the rest of the body.

3) A narrow palm, smooth fingers, the outer phalange long and drawn out to the point, the thumb small and elegant is the description of this type.

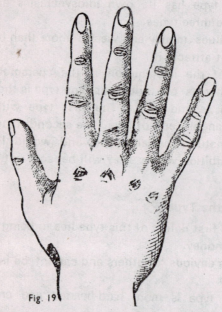

Fig. 19

The psychic hand (emotional and moody)

If this hand is large and the joints prominent, it shows force but it lacks ingenuity. The most beautiful but the most unfortunate of the seven types is what is known as the psychic type.

Nature and Temperament: 1) They have imagination which is difficult for the other types to appreciate.

2) They live in the remote idealistic world and people with square or spatulate type, who go after precision or method, find it impossible to follow the ideas of the psychic type.

3) Square and spatulate types are carried away by war and its results ; whereas the psychic type takes pleasure in the esoteric dreams of the soul, in contemplating intangible realities.

Defects of the Type

1) It has only a moediocre comprehension of the things of the outer world and of real life. It looks at them from too high a point to be able to see them well.

2) The talent of applied sciences is wanting in them.

Parents having such children do not know how to treat them. The strange thing is that they are often the offspring of matter of fact people.

vi) The Philosophic Hand (fig. 20)

Characteristics : 1) The philosophic hand is the one where the fingers are long and the joints of the fingers well developed. These types of fingers are also called knotty fingers because the knots are developed. This will be more clarified while dealing with the chapter on fingers. These fingers have a peculiar significance and the persons of this type are of the philosophical nature. The word 'philosophic' is derived from the Greek 'philos'-love and 'sophia'-wisdom.

2) The fingers are bony in appearance.

3) The palm proper is rather large and well-developed and the joints well marked in the fingers.

4) The top phalanges are half square and half conic, a combination producing on the upper joint a kind of egg-shaped spatula.

5) The thumb is large and indicates the presence of as much logic as will since both phalanges are of equal length.

6) The rest of the hand is either square, psychic or spatulate in appearance.

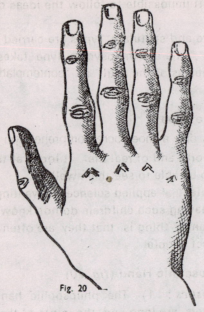

Fig. 20

The philosophic hand (a philosopher)

Two Types

There are two types of philosopher, the one is the sensualist and the other is the idealist. The former derives his ideas from external influence. This class comprises the philosophic hand with square or spatulate palm in proper. These philosophers think on the rational basis and produce such philosophy which is useful in everyday life. Examples of this type can be cited and we have Karl Marx who evolved the political philosophy of communism. Then we have modern philosophers like Bernard Shaw and Bertrand Russell who threw some light on ethical philosophy. There again is another class of philosophers who have philosophic hands in general and the psychic palm in proper. These are idealists and an example may be given of Dhyaneshwar of India. This idealist has his comparision with such great luminaries of the West as Plotinus, Augustine and Echkar. He can also be compared with Dante, whose vision, philosophic imagination and poetic melody are just a counter-part of the greatest Indian poet and mystic. Of the female philosophers in India, we have Muktabai and Janabai. Similarly in the West we have Julian of Norwich, Catherine of Siena and St. Teresa. These philosophers of the second type are usually known as the mystic philosophers.

We can have a third class of philosophers who are midway between the above two. This third class has combined ideal philosophy with practicality and as examples we have Buddha and Mahatma Gandhi. These philosophers have philosophic hands of the mixed type.

If we look to the formation of the hand and especially to the shape of the tips of the fingers, the square formation to the tip gives material aspect to the outlook which can be seen in social utility and practical ideas. Again, half formation of the tips is towards a conic one, which means love for beauty and art. These two formations tend to give the shape of a spatula which means usefulness. In short, if we combine all these three aspects of the fingers of the philosophic hand, we have a subject who loves the ideal and speaks the truth.

The joints of the fingers denote mental traits. We should notice whether the first or the second joints are developed. If the first joints are developed, the type falls in the second category of the philosophic type which has mystic philosophy as its aim or which deals in metaphysics. If however, the second joints of the fingers are developed, the person falls under the first category of the philosophic type and his philosophy is more materialistic than idealistic and more of the outer world than of the inner one. These hands denote calculation, more or less vigorous deduction and method. By the half conic formation of the tips, they have the intuition of a relative form of poetry and in general they have the inclination towards metaphysics.

Nature and Temperament : Thus, when we have the philosophic hand before us, we can conclude that the person likes to analyse things. He is absorbed in thoughts about the creation, evolution, existence and destruction of his own self and of the world at large. His ideas and beliefs are not borrowed from others but they are formed out of his own experimental experience. His thoughts are occupied with details and with mass, with the individual and with mankind, with the atom and with the universe.

As far as success in the form of wealth is concerned, it is not a favourable type to have. This type is a student throughout his life. He studies mankind and loves it. In character, he is silent and secretive, he is very careful over little matters, even in the use of words. He is proud of being different from others. He rarely forgets an injury but waits patiently for an opportunity to take revenge. When the development of the hand is in excess, the person is egotistic which is in keeping with the life he leads and also fanatical in religion or mysticism.

vii) The Mixed Shape of the Hand (*fig. 21*)

Characteristics : The last of the seven types of the hand is the mixed type of the hand. This is so called because it does not possess a particular type of shape but it is a mixture of two or more of the types described previously. This is a very difficult hand to read, because it is often very deceptive. Sometimes, we think that it is a combination of square and conic, but in fact it may have a different formation.

In this type, the fingers may take a different shape from the shape of the palm proper, or the fingers may also differ from each other in their formation. The palm proper may be either square, spatulate, conic or psychic, or a combination of two or more of these types. The fingers also may belong to different types, often one pointed, one square, one spatulate, one philosophic etc.

Nature and Temperament : 1) The mixed hand is the hand of ideas, of versatility and generally of changeability of purpose.

2) A man with such a hand is adaptable to both people and circumstances and is clever in the application of his talents.

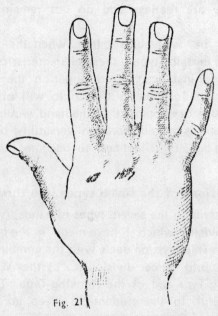

Fig. 21

The mixed hand (Jack of all trades)

3) He will be brilliant in conversation, the subject may be science, art or just gossiping.

4) He may play some instrument fairly well, may paint a little and so on, but rarely will he be great. When however a strong line of head rules the hand, he will, of all his talents choose the best and add to it the brilliance and versatility of the others. Such hands find their greatest scope in the work requiring diplomacy and tact.

5) They are so versatile that they have no difficulty in getting on with the different dispositions with which they come into contact.

6) Their most striking peculiarity is their adaptability to circumstances.

7) They never feel the ups and downs of fortune like others and almost all types of work are easy for them.

8) They are generally inventive and thereby relieve themselves of labour.

9) They are restless and do not remain long in any town or place.

It must be remembered that when the palm proper belongs to a certain type, these characteristics are much modified as for instance, mixed finger on the square, the spatulate, the philosophic or the conic will often succeed where the pure development of the hand would fail. When the entire hand is mixed, through versatility of talent and purpose, the subject is inclined to become the Jack of all trades.

6 Combinations of the seven types into three Groups

After describing the seven types of hands, we shall turn to the 5th division which I have made in the beginning of this chapter. This division deals with the combination of the seven types into three divisions: a) the Willing Type, b) the Feeling Type and c) the Thinking Type. This division is more useful to the student to keep in memory the characteristics of the seven types.

The elementary hand was the first of the seven types of hand. Its development is peculiar to that type only and the characteristics shown by that type are singular and cannot be mixed up with any other type. Similarly, the last type, which is the mixed type of hand, is also very difficult to combine with any other type. These two types are independent and stand as they are.

a) The Willing Type

This type comprises the square hand and the spatulate hand. The main reason why these two types are combined together is that these types exhibit a nature which is practical and useful. These two types are always original and have an aptitude to learn, study and analyse that which is tangible and belongs to everyday life. Both types have energy, patience and capacity to work hard. Both of them produce the product which is utilitarion and scientific. That is why they are conveniently grouped as the Willing Type.

b) The Feeling Type

Under this group come the Conic hand and the Psychic hand. Both these hands reflects more or less the same type of feeling with the difference that the psychic type is an exaggerated form of the conic type. Both are emofional and sentimental and both value things of the heart and of feelings more and live in their idiosyncracies. Thus, it is convenient to combine them in one group.

c) The Thinking Type

In this group comes the philosophic hand. The philosophic hand is the hand which revels in deep thinking and in problems which affect humanity at large.

These three types of people will give us three different pictures and once we are able to make a distinction between the three, our work will be very easy and we shall be in a position to grasp the working of the mind of the subject whose hands are under examination.

7. The Palm in General

After the above discussion it is very useful to study the palm in general. This general observation will convey to us certain important aspects of the person whose hands are under examination.

A very thick palm, full and soft shows sensuality, gross sensual instincts, excessive confidence and selfishness.

A thick and hard palm with short fingers indicates a primitive hand. This is the hand of an unskilled labourer who is not expected to improve his lot. If this is accompanied by a bad-looking thumb, it is the hand of a brutal criminal.

A thin, hard and narrow palm connotes timidity, meanness, poor intellect, absence of passive or active energy and a nervous, worrying, troubled nature.

A firm and elastic palm is indicative of quickness of intellect, equanimity of mind and energy.

8. The Indian System

In Indian palmistry, there are ten signs which indicate good and praiseworthy hands. They are :

1) warm to touch, 2) coloured like the sky before dawn, 3) no light would pass through the chinks if the fingers are closed together, 4) bright hands as if they are oiled, 5) full and thick, 6) medium sized, 7) copper coloured nails, 8) long fingered, 9) wide, 10) no sweat that is dry. A rich man has long fingers and good looking palms.

If the hands of a woman appear as charming as a lotus flower, she is fortunate and will lead a happy life. Women with thin, skinny hands with protruding veins, with a network of lines and signs are not destined to be happy.

A heavily lined palm signifies misery and troubles in life, sometimes a short life. If there are very few lines, it is a sign of poverty. A clear yellow palm means the person will lose his patrimony. A palm with a distinct hollow is a sign of poverty.

CHAPTER VI

The Division of the Hand

1 The Three Systems of Division

After considering the shape of the hand, the next thing to be noted on the hand is the division of the hand. In the previous chapter, we considered the hand as a whole that is, the hand from the wrist to the top of the fingers. We must first get an idea of the hand as a whole and that is why I took the shape of the hand first while dealing with the subject of hand-reading.

The hand is divided into different sections. There are different methods of dividing the hand. I will give a clear idea of the different systems of the division of the hand and if the readers have an idea of the whole system, they will be in a position to understand the psychology of the person whose hand is under examination.

The First System (*fig.* 22)

The hand is divided into three worlds. The fingers constitute the first world, this is known as the mental world. The second division is made from the base of the fingers to the imaginary horizontal line which runs from the top of the Mount of Moon to the top of the Mount of Venus. This is known as the material world. The third division constitutes the part from the horizontal line to the wrist of the hand. This is known as the basal world.

The Second System (*fig.* 23)

An imaginary line is drawn from the middle of the fingers of Jupiter and Saturn in a vertical manner which reaches

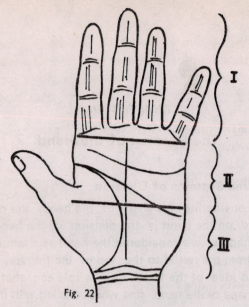

Fig. 22
Division of the hand—first system

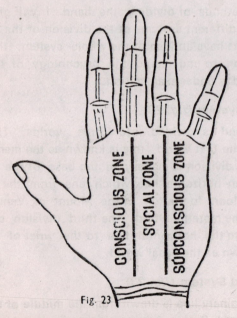

Fig. 23
Division of the hand—second system

The Division of the Hand

straight to the bottom of the hand. The portion comprises of the Mount of Jupiter, the positive Mount of Mars and the Mount of Venus. This is known as the conscious zone or the radial zone. The second zone is on the other side of the hand and an imaginary line is drawn from the middle of the ring finger or the finger of Apollo to the bottom of the hand. This second zone comprises of the latter part of the ring finger, the finger of Mercury and the portion below it, the negative Mount of Mars and the Mount of Moon. This is known as the subconscious zone or the ulner zone. The third zone lies between the above two zones and is known as the social zone.

The Third System (fig. 24)

In this system the hand is again divided into different zones. The first zone extends from the base of the fingers

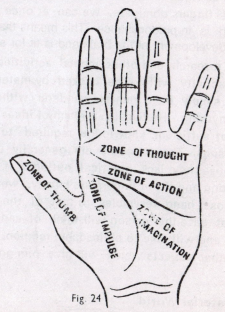

Fig. 24

Division of the hand—third system

upto the line of Heart. The figure will make it clear. This is known as the zone of Thought. The second zone lies between the line of Heart and the line of Head. This zone is known as the zone of Action. The third zone stretches inside the line of Life and is known as the zone of Impulse. The fourth zone extends from the line of Life to the entire Mount of Moon going to the percussion of the hand. This zone is known as the zone of Imagination. The fifth zone lies in the Thumb.

We shall study seperately these three different systems of the division of the hand.

2 The First System
i) The Mental World

According to this system the fingers constitute the mental world. When the hands are stretched before us for examination or when the hand impression is taken and when we find that fingers dominate, we can at once say that the mental wolrd is in predominance. This means that the person has a good development of the brain and is fit for such pursuits as studies, research and other mental activities. However, his mental activity will not be backed by material success and he will simply be a mental wanderer without actually achieving anything. He lives in a realm of ideas and exaltation without sufficient knowledge required to follow his mental pursuits. These people are generally unsuccessful in life because they lack practical outlook. If the mental world is strong and if the fingers are knotty, we shall have a subject whose hand resembles to that of the philosophic type. In that case the person will think of serious subjects and studies and will take to philosophy, religion, psychology and such other subjects which will give him good food for thought.

ii) The Material World

If the second world is more developed than the other two, the subject will be more practical in ideas and behaviour.

He takes to such studies and activities which will be materially useful to him or which will give him fame and money. The reason for this attitude is that the second world is composed of the Mount of Jupiter which gives ambition, the Mount of Saturn which gives wisdom and sobriety, the Mount of Sun which gives success, the Mount of Mercury which gives shrewdness and intellect, the positive Mount of Mars which gives dash and aggressive nature and the negative Mount of Mars which gives resistance. If all these mounts are well developed his main object in life will be to earn money. Subjects which develop the brain but which do not bring money out of them are of no value to the person of the material world. Naturally, he is not fit for any mental activity and he will rise in life only on sheer hard work and patience which are the characteristics of persons with a practical outlook. Thus, they are good for commercial pursuits, business, agriculture, war and politics.

iii) The Basal World

If however, the third world is developed, we can know that the person lives in basal ideas, that he has poor intellect and also poor common sense unlike the first and second worlds. He has developed lower type of passions and he is vulgar in his talk and action. He takes intense pleasure in gratifying his sensual pleasures and he has no other motive than to do this. He loves eating and drinking. He does not enjoy the delicious food but is satisfied with filling up his belly. Mind is not a guiding force with him and he does not like mental recreation. He is sometimes shrewd but with instinctive cunningness of the fox. He does not see how ridiculous he makes himself to men of elevated thought. He sees only from his earthly point of view and all his tastes and thoughts are coarse and vulgar.

The best development on the hand is when all the three worlds are well-developed and when we find difficulty in giving importance to any one world. In this case there is the balancing of all the qualities and the mental pursuits of the person are materialised by his practical viewpoint and at the same time he can fulfil all his desires. This type of combination is very rare to find in practice and what is more common is the combination of the two worlds.

iv) Combination of the three Worlds

Sometimes the first and the second worlds are in good combination with each other. This person will make a good success in life and will earn money by using his intellect and shrewdness. If he is a philosopher he will be successful in writing books and thus getting money and fame for his knowledge and ideas.

If the second and the third worlds are well-developed we have a combination of the material and earthly aspects in the individual. In this case the person will earn money but in a coarse way. He will run after cheap popularity and will spend his money in vices and in gratifying his lower senses.

If the first world is in combination with the third world, there will always be a clash between the higher ideals and the lower passions. This person will always aspire for high positions and ideals in life but his interests in the lower sense will always check his career. He will not be able to control his basal instincts and thus he will find it difficult to concentrate on higher studies. The result will be that he will be unsuccessful in life and with all his intelligence and talent he will not achieve anything in life. The main reason for this failure is the clash between two opposite types of emotions without the support of common sense and balanced judgement. This is therefore a bad type of combination.

3 The Second System of Division (*fig. 23*)

After the first system of the division of the hand, which gives a clear idea as to the working of the mind of the person, the hand should be studied from the second system of the division. This system is also equally important as the

The Division of the Hand

first one and it will give further insight into the working of the mind.

i) The Conscious Zone

In this second system the first zone comprises the finger of Jupiter and the whole portion below it extending to the wrist of the hand. This zone is known by three names, the Radial zone or the Active zone or the Conscious zone. The names active and conscious give a clear idea of the functioning of this zone. From this zone we can judge the working of the conscious and active mind of the person.

Why this zone is called by this particular name will be clear from the following. In this zone comes the finger of Jupiter and the thumb. These two fingers are the characteristics of the human being. If we look to the evolution of man, we will find that these two fingers are not developed on the hands of apes and monkeys. More information about the Jupiter finger and the thumb is given in chapters on them. Readers may please remember that these two fingers indicate the conscious activities of man which can be seen in matters like picking up of small things and writing and this is the main reason why this zone is called the conscious zone.

In this zone comes the Mount of Jupiter, the Positive Mount of Mars and the Mount of Venus. If we look to the development of these three Mounts and the Jupiter finger and the thumb, we can very easily see what ideas are ruling the person and whether he is over ambitious or lacks in ambition and whether he has dash and aggression or he is mild, whether he is strong in passions and action or sober and imbecile. Similarly, his ego and his will, logic and reason, as shown by the thumb, will indicate the functioning of his active mind.

Another aspect to be noted on the conscious zone is the pattern of the papillary ridges. On a normal hand, that is on the hand of a normal person whose mental development is normal and who does not suffer from any mental defect, this pattern is also normal in its development. Normal development of the pattern will be seen on the figure shown in the introduction.

If this pattern forms an abnormal development of the ridges it means that the conscious mind of the person is not developed, and the person is susceptible to suffer from some defect such as nervousness or fear or inferiority complex.

Thus, in examining the conscious zone, we have to take into consideration the Jupiter finger and the thumb and note their development or abnormality. Secondly, we have to look for the Mounts in the zone and observe the nature of their development. Lastly, the papillary ridges are to be noted. When the examination of these three aspects in the conscious zone is completed, it will fully reveal to us the working of the conscious mind of the person and his conscious activities.

ii) **The Sub-conscious Zone**

The second zone to be considered is on the other side of the conscious zone. This zone is known as the passive zone or the ulner zone or the zone of subconscious mind. This zone comprises of the little finger or the finger of Mercury, the latter part of ring finger, the Mount of Mercury, the latter part of the Mount of Apollo, the Negative Mount of Mars and the Mount of Moon.

I shall deal with the fingers and the Mounts later on while describing the chapters on fingers and Mounts. But mention may be made here that the ring finger and the little finger are more or less decorative and the act and talent shown by the ring finger is many times the working of the subconscious. The negative Mount of Mars shows resistance and it has the qualities which are in opposition to those shown by the positive Mount of Mars. The positive Mount of Mars is in the active zone and so it reflects activity whereas the negative Mount of Mars comes under the passive zone and thus reflects passivity. It shows defence unlike the positive Mars. Below the Mount of Mars there is the Mount of Moon. This Mount shows imagination, whims, ecstasy, fantasies and such function of the mind. Any deformity of this Mount will mean defect in the mental working. The little finger is also very important and its deformity means the sex and the gonadic troubles. The short little finger is often the result of the abnormal endocrine balance as has been pointed out in the introduction. These defects in the body cause faulty working of the brain and neurosis is the result. Thus, from this zone we can know the working of the inner world of the person.

The papillary ridges on this zone are also very important. By studying these two zones, we can know which of the zones is defective. It will help a doctor in diagnosing the mental defect of the person. If the person is a neurotic, the psychiatrist must know whether the defect created in the mind of the person is owing to the defect in the conscious mind or owing to some deep rooted cause in the subconscious. A student of palmisty can help the psychiatrist by examining the different zones on the hand.

iii) The Social Zone

The portion that lies between the two zones described above, is known as the middle zone which is also known as the zone of social conduct. The readers will be interested to note that this zone shows the person's social behaviour and social adaptability. In this zone comes the Mount of Saturn which shows sobriety, wisdom and materialism ; the first half of the Mount of Apollo which shows success in life. The line of Fate starts at the bottom of the hand in this zone and ends on the Mount of Saturn. This is an important line to be noted. By the development or the course of this line, we can judge the social adaptability of the person. It has been observed that this line is the most unstable line on the hand because there is always a change in man's attitude and behaviour towards his social mates. As he gains more and more experience of the world, his ideas go on changing and thus it affects his behaviour. It has also been found that this line is present in most of the cases and its absence shows lack of sociability. Our conduct towards other people is a complex phenomenon. It is largely determined by character and temperament, but it can be modified by education and especially by the innate impulse of the more developed individual to create a super-ego. Babies, criminals and mental defectives who lack this super-ego and social adaptibility are also lacking in this line of Fate.

As it has been noted already, this zone comprises of the Mount of Saturn. Saturn has the capacity to be practical. In order to acquire material success, social adaptibility is necessary. Thus, from the development of the Mount of Saturn also ; we can get a good idea of the material and practical ideas of the person. Thus, in this second system of the Division of the Hand we get the character reading of the person on a different level than that described in the first system. We have to combine the first system with the second system and then arrive at the conclusion. For instance, if the mental world of the first system is dominating and the conscious zone of the second system is powerful, we can say that the person has too much of mental activity and he is more conscious of his thoughts than of his actions. He has an active mind, good ambition, dashing and pushing nature and good expression. This will make him a successful man provided he has patience and a good line of success. In this way we have to combine the different aspects of these two systems and find out the resulting characteristic of a person.

After this, I shall deal with the third type of the Division of the Hand.

4) The Third System *(fig. 24)*
i) The Zone of Thought

This zone lies between the base of the fingers and the line of Heart. In this zone come the four Mounts—the Mounts of Jupiter, Saturn, Sun and Mercury. As this zone should be large, it is necessary that the Mounts should be well developed. When the Mounts are

The Division of the Hand

developed, this zone remains at a higher level than the portion below it. It shows a promising career for the person. But, often it is found that the portion between the Mount of Saturn and the Mount of Sun is depressed. When this portion is depressed, it shows lack of perseverance and tenacity to achieve the mission taken in life. Since the Mounts of Saturn and Sun are depressed, it means an opposition to the general success in life as shown by the Saturn and to the reputation in public life as shown by the Sun. This depression shows lack of concentration, physical suffering and unfavourable mental condition. It also shows unexpected difficulties, sorrows and opposition. However, if other signs on the hand are favourable, this depression may not produce very great effects and the person by his constant pursuit in his line may achieve success ultimately.

Sometimes we may encounter such hands wherein the zone of Thought is entirely lacking in its development. In this case, the zone is flat and the mounts are more or less in the same plane as that of the zone of Action (*fig. 25.*) This type of zone is found on the hands of persons who have no ambition and intellect and who do not work for reputation or for money. But, they simply pull on their lives which is of course very trying. In such cases, the chances of acquiring fame is remote and the desire for loneliness or reckless revelry is very strong. Such persons are usually self centred, reserved and narrow in their outlook.

ii) The Zone of Action

This zone lies between the line of Heart and the line of Head. This portion of the hand is also known by the name Quadrangle. The Quadrangle should be clear as far as possible. More information will be given while dealing with the Quadrangle. The important thing to be noted of the Fate line is its course through this zone of Action. A square or a triangle attached to the Fate line in this zone indicates good fortune and success to the individual. Ideally, this zone should be in one plane and the space between the line of Heart and the line of Head should be uniform throughout. This creates a balanced zone and the person is uniform in his actions. He has a desire for higher things and ideals in life. However, other signs on the hand must also be favourable

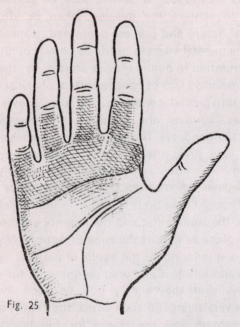

Fig. 25

Flat zone of thought (no ambition)

for this ideal to be achieved. If there are cross lines, bars and islands on the positive Mount of Mars and the Mount of Venus, there will be difficulties in achieving the ideals. This is because there would always be a clash between the high ideals and the gratification of physical passions which would be great owing to strong physical constitution. The result will be that the individual will find it difficult to concentrate on his studies and will find obstacles in achieving his aim in life.

Another thing to be noted regarding this zone is the formation of the line of Heart. Triangles attached to the line of Heart indicate periods of income and the individual will gain much during that interval. Similarly drooping lines from the line of Heart and ending in the zone indicate lack of jugdgement. The individual relies upon wrong persons and loses through them. He will also lose opportunity by keeping wrong company and, if the chances are not recurring, there are very few hopes for the individual to be successful in life. Breaks and islands in the line of Fate in this zone show financial setbacks, losses, disputes and disappointments.

In short, the things to be noted in this zone are the balance of the Quadrangle, the square or triangle attached to the Fate line and the Heart line, the drooping lines from the Heart line and the defects in the Fate line.

iii) The Zone of Impulse

This zone lies inside the line of Life. This zone is important because it relates to family influences, sexual equilibrium and pleasant atmosphere. If this zone is full of lines running parallel to the line of Life, it shows that the individual has many brothers, sisters, sons and daughters. It also means that he is very social and has many friends living and influencing his state of feeling and producing happiness. Naturally, one may expect the presence of sweetness, good humour, fellow-feeling and great family prosperity.

However, this condition is very rarely found on the hand and many times lines of opposition are seen crossing the line of Life. These lines are the indications of difficulties, obstacles in family happiness and mean sorrow and misunderstanding amongst the relatives. There is also the difference between the lines running from the Mount of Mars and crossing the line of Life and the lines running from the Mount of Venus and crossing the Life line. In the former case it means worries through enemies and in the latter case it means worries through loss of relatives and through the members of the family.

Thus, the things to be observed in this zone are the parallel lines to the line of Life, the horizontal lines showing opposition, the lines from the Mounts of Mars and Venus.

iv) The Zone of Imagination

This zone lies between the line of Life and the percussion of the hand. It includes the Big Triangle which lies in the area surrounded by the line of Life, the Mount of Moon and the Head line. The chapter XI dealing with the Hollow of the Palm and the figure will make it clear. The major portion of this zone is covered by the Mount of Moon which shows imagination and hence the zone is called by that name. From the development of the Mount of Moon, we get a clear idea as to the working of the mind and imagination of the individual. A good development of the Mount of Moon shows big ideals, love for the beautiful and love for travel and change. The Big Triangle shows the social atmosphere and general happiness of life. In this area the position and composition of Fate line is to be observed. A clear and flawless Fate line shows good social circle and happy environment.

Defects in the Fate line show lack of social adaptability and self-centredness.

v) The Zone of the Thumb

The thumb is the seat of the ego and from its examination, we can guess the conscious development, will-power, reason and logic and the social understanding of the person. I have dealt with the thumb in chapter IX and hence I will not discuss it here again.

Thus, the readers will know from the Division of the Hand and by the three systems the working of the individual's conscious and the subconscious mind and his social and family happiness. The Division of the Hand enables us to know whether the individual will achieve success or failure in his life and whether he has sufficient strength of character to back up his natural aptitude.

CHAPTER VII

Skin, Colour, Consistency, Hard and Soft Hands, Flabby and Elastic Hands, Flexibility of Hands

The next step to be taken in the examination of the hand is the skin, its colour, the elasticity of the hand and of the fingers and to note whether the hand is hard or soft. This examination will help us to know the intensity of the type indicated by the shape of the hand and the mounts on the hand.

Skin

Study of the skin can be done in three ways.

Firstly, we have to note whether the skin is fine, coarse or elastic. This is known as the texture of the skin. Secondly, we have to apply the characteristics shown by the different types of the texture and find out the nature of the person. Thirdly, we have to combine our findings with the shape of the hand and the mount on the hand to which the subject belongs.

Texture shows the natural refinement of the person. A fine textured man will indicate a refined person in thought and deed. His actions will be very pleasant and he will use his commonsense in every act of his and generally he will have good manners and etiquette. His skin is fine because it will give us smooth touch and the capillaries on the hand will be practically invisible. Even the growth of the hair is very little and the whole hand looks smooth and attractive. Such people talk very slowly, handle books very delicately and make very little noise. They do not like to disturb others and their behaviour shows quietness and patience. In short, the fine texture means delicacy of feeling, refined behaviour, polished manners, silence, quietness and pleasant talk.

Fine skin and the Type of the Hand

This fineness of the skin should be combined with the shape of the hand and the Mounts on the hand to which the person belongs. If we look to the traits shown by the Elementary hand, we find that it is not possible for that type to have refined thinking or development of the brain. Naturally, people with Elementary hands cannot have fine texture. Elevation of mind, high thinking and such other qualities of the mind are lacking in the Elementary hand and thus it also lacks in having a fine texture.

Fine texture will make a Spatulate hand more energetic, a Square hand more impressive, a Conic hand more idealistic, a Psychic hand more dreamy, a Philosophic hand more sensitive and the Mixed hand more enthusiastic.

Fine texture will make a Jupiterian less tyrannical, less domineering and more religious. It will make a Saturnian less melancholy, less moody and less cynical. Fine texture will elevate an Apollonian, will increase his talents and lessen his speculating nature. It will subdue a Mercurian and will make him more intelligent and less dishonest. A Martian with fine texture is less fighting and less pugnacious. Fine texture helps a Lunarian to lead his imagination into higher channels. Fine texture will increase the love of nature of the Venusian, will make him love the beauty and arts and will make him refined so that low passion will not dominate him. Fine texture will make a Neptunian less callous and would lessen his desire to shun the pleasures of life.

Coarse Skin

Incompatible with the characteristics of the fine skin is its opposite, the coarse skin. In this case the skin is rough, has big capillaries and the touch is unpleasant and coarse. An absolute type of this skin is very rare to meet with. It will modify all things in hand by coarsening them. It will make the Elementary hand more dull, will take away enthusiasm of the Spatulate type, will make a Square hand less practical, will lessen the artistic virtues of the Conic type, will make a Psychic type more cynical and lunatic, will make a Philosophic hand more coarse in his understanding and finally will lessen the versatility of the Mixed type.

Coarse skin will increase the gloom of the Saturnian, will make the Jupiterian more tyrannical, it will divert the talents of the Apollonian to wrong paths and will make a Mercurian more dishonest and a low-schemer. It will turn a Martian into a foolish aggressor by making him a vagabond and truant. It will make a Lunarian an idler reveling in low imagination. It will make a Neptunian a fanatic and will make a Venusian full of sore taste and crooked in his art.

In short, fine texture softens everything whereas coarse one animalises it.

The nature of the skin that is often found is the elastic skin. This is a development which is neither very fine nor very coarse. The skin will feel elastic, not soft, firm, not hard. Elastic texture shows the practical development of the person and therefore it is often found on the hands of men who are more practical in outlook and who have common sense and good judgement. Thus, this is found on the hands of doctors, pleaders, businessmen and clergymen. It will add proportionately to the natural tendencies shown by the shape of the hand and the mount on the hand. It will keep the person balanced and will never allow him to go to the extremes as shown by the fine skin and the coarse one.

Colour

Colour of the hand will give some hints regarding the natural force of the blood and thus of the physical constitution of the person. Circulation of the blood is an important factor in the function of the body and the colour of the blood will affect the colour of the hand which will inform us about the natural stamina of the person. However, one thing is to be borne in mind that the colour of the hand will not always give us the correct idea of the vitality of the person, for the simple reason that the colour changes according to the season in the year. In winter white pale colour of the hand is common, while in summer dry hands with reddish dark colour are expected. Therefore we should allow a certain percentage of misapprehension before arriving at the actual colour of the hand.

Red Colour

Red colour indicates strength, vigour and activity. The person who possesses it is intense in his desire and attempts to achieve his ends. This colour also, should be thought of in combination with the type to which the person belongs. By this time the readers might have followed the line of thought of combinations and therefore it will be better to delete the same hereafter.

Yellow Colour

Yellow colour shows the bilious type. It shows that the person has bile trouble and thus he cannot be joyous, bright and happy. This colour is peculiar to the Saturnian, though the Mercurian also shares it. Here we can know why the Saturnian is more gloomy and melancholy in outlook. The pale yellow colour of the hand shows his troubles which affect his mind and tendencies. The bile irritates the nerves and consequently he is not a pleasant companion. His brain is clogged by bilious poisoning and his views become poisoned. Like the coarse skin, the yellow colour will distort all the Mounts.

Blue or Purple Colour

Blue or purple colour does not necessarily mean a poor quality. We find that this colour is caused by improper circulation of the blood. It shows a sluggish condition of the circulation. It means the feebleness of the working of the heart and shows a dangerous stage. We should be pretty careful to note the hand and the mount and to combine this colour with that type.

Thus we have studied how the colour of the hand helps us to find out the natural health of the person and its effect on his temperament. Combination of the colour with the different types of hand has not been dealt with, because it would mean unnecessary repetition.

Consistency of the hand

The next thing we have to study on the hand is the consistency of the hand. Consistency is of four kinds, flabby, soft, hard and elastic. We can study the consistency by shaking hands with all customers when we can press their hands with uniform pressure. It is through practice only that we can find whether the hand is flabby, soft or hard. I would like to point out that hard developments on the mounts of the hand or at other places, due to games like cricket, hockey etc. or due to hazardous professions where certain portions on the hand become hard, should not be confused with hardness of the hand. Hardness or softness of the hand depend upon the resistance the hand gives us, when pressed under a particular pressure.

Flabby Consistency

We shall first study the hand with flabby consistency. On our receiving the client, we should hold his hand firm in our two hands and then start exerting pressure on his hand. We shall come to know whether his hand is resisting our pressure. In this particular case, there will be no resistence and we shall get the feeling that the client does not have sufficient energy to resist our pressure. The muscles are very loose and we do not find the presence of bones in the hand. This is the flabby consistency which shows mental lethargy and laziness. He is merely a dreamer and does not desire to bring into action his ambitions or ideas. He prefers easy and comfortable life. A hand with flabby consistency is therefore a lazy hand and it affects adversely on the qualities of the mounts by which a particular person is characterised. For instance, it will diminish the ambitious nature of a Jupiterian, increase the loneliness of a Saturnian, lessen the energy of an Apollonian and of a Martian, intensify the dreamy nature of a Lunarian, affect adversely the business of a Mercurian and finally diminish the zeal and artistic nature of the Venusian.

Soft Consistency

Next to flabby consistency is the soft consistency which looks like flabby consistency but which does not show as much laziness as that of flabby consistency. The difference between the flabby and the soft consistency is that but we do not get the feeling of any bony structure in flabby consistency, we can get that feeling in soft consistency. The intensity of laziness is therefore less in soft consistency and there is scope for the person having soft consistency to improve upon their inherent characteristics. Such persons have delicate mind and the will-power is lacking. They cannot resist anything in life and suffer much if the odds are too many. These hands also affect the characteristics shown by the different mounts on the hand but the intensity is not much as exhibited by the flabby consistency.

Elastic Consistency

This type of consistency shows energy, activity, vigour and enthusiasm. This is usually found on the hands of persons who are active in life and whose life is always busy. In this case there is a spring-like action as we press the hand and the mounts on the hand repel in a spring-like way. These hands are energetic and give ready response to our handshake. This is therefore a good type and it will add to the basic characteristics of the person as shown by the shape of his hand or by the mount most developed on the hand. The elastic consistency shows an intelligent brain working behind the energy of the person.

Hard Consistency

We may occasionally come across a hard consistency which is indicative of a brain which is not receptive but which finds it difficult to absorb new ideas. When we press this hand in order to find out the consistency of the hand, we find that this hand opposes pressure and we feel the resistance of the hand. This hard consistency also shows an active brain not of the intelligent type but the one which would prefer manual labour to mental activity.

Flexible Hands

In our study of the hand, we must also study the flexibility of the hand. A hand is either stiff or flexible. A stiff hand shows a mind which is not prepared to modify its ideas. This is the orthodox type and any innovations are not acceptable to him. Such a person is therefore very narrow in ideas, stingy and unhelpful. He is very selfish and can never understand the feelings of others. If we try to open his hand we get a resistance and the fingers refuse to open.

As against the above, we have normal flexibility where the fingers readily open and the hand becomes straight in position. This is the normal development. This person has an understanding of the human mind and can absorb the ideas in a normal way. He is receptive, intelligent, active and helpful. He will not go to extremes. Even if he wants to help others, he will not throw money and will always be restrained in his behaviour. This normal flexibility will add to the characteristics of the person as exhibited by the shape of the hand or by the most developed mount on the hand.

We have still a third type of flexibility which is extreme in nature (*fig. 41*). This person does not hold his own views on any subject and is changeable in nature. He is extremely emotional and adaptable to circumstances. He is brilliant, active and receptive but extreme flexibility is his drawback. When we hold this hand in our own and try to exert pressure we find that the hand does not resist and it bends back readily. Sometimes the flexibility is so much that the fingers bend back in such a way as to make a graceful curve.

Thus, we have studied colour, texture, consistency and flexibility of the hand in this chapter which will help us to understand the client's mind in greater details and small shades of his thinking power can be known by this study which will help us in finding out the psychological behaviour of our client.

CHAPTER VIII

The Fingers

Introduction

Fingers form a very important part of the palm. They are the instruments of the sense of touch and the means by which we obtain much of our information about the exterior world. In the evolution of man their place is striking as is shown by their length and by the development of complex and varied patterns of their papillary ridges. Besides their highly tactile sense, they possess a high degree of mobility of a kind, quite their own. The phalanges and length of the fingers enable them to perform a rich variety of movements. The most important function of the fingers is to receive the life's spark. The life current that runs through the human body is first received through the fingers.

1 Psychological Significance of the Fingers

In palmistry the fingers denote the mental world. When the fingers are well developed it means that the mind is elevated. Such a subject is fit for study and mental pursuits. But the other signs on the hand must back-up these mental faculties, otherwise, without such a backing the person becomes a mental wanderer and has no material aspect in him. This is why many literary men and others who possess good intellectual power are poor businessmen and they accumulate nothing and fail miserably in life. Fingers therefore are the instruments which translate the thought and the impulse into visible expression. They are the keys to the analytical gauging of character.

2 Smooth fingers with different tips (*fig. 26*)

Fingers are either smooth or knotty. Smooth fingers may have any shape or any tip. In such fingers the joints or the knots are not very well-developed which enable us to distinguish these fingers from knotty fingers. Since these fingers do not develop the knots they receive the ideas quickly and the waves of expression pass easily through these fingers into the brain. Naturally persons with smooth fingers are endowed with the faculty of comprehension. They always

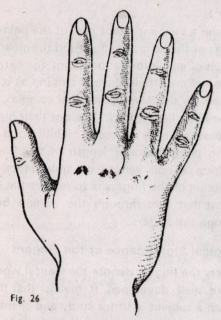

Fig. 26

Smooth fingers (inspiration)

proceed by inspiration rather than by reason, by synthesis rather than analysis. These fingers are also very graceful to look at and therefore grace, spontaneity and insight are the characteristics of these persons. Since everything slips out easily owing to the smoothness of the fingers, they are too passionate and too hasty. In love, in business and in everything else they often fail to attend their ends by aiming at them with too much vigour and expecting the wrong thing or a thing which is beyond their reach. Smooth fingered persons are wrong in their intuitive deductions. Their minds not formed in an analytical mould, are not able to cope with those who have knotty fingers on matters that require deep reasoning and analytical power.

In order that persons possessing smooth fingers should win in debate over those with knotty fingers, they should rely more on their intuitive faculty and imagination than trying to follow reasoning. In religion, they do not reason much but are carried away by the words of others and are scarcely sceptics though not agnostics. We find that smooth fingers are more agreeable and pleasant company because they are not provoking and trying to find faults in others which is the characteristics of the knotty fingers. Smooth fingers love those things which please the eye or appeal to the sense of beauty and have a taste in dresses and decorations at home. Persons having smooth fingers are carried away by emotional appeals and are swayed more by instinct than those having knotty fingers. In music and painting the persons who gain fame may have other types of fingers but smooth fingered persons will get applause in acting and expressing inner feelings. In delicate, emotional type of music smooth fingers are a necessity. Harsh music, marching songs may be sung and produced by less artistic minds, but the music to reach the heart must emanate from the heart. So it is the smooth fingers that music must turn to for its greatest exponents. Smooth finger with conic tips will produce weird and dreamy tunes.

Smooth fingers may have spatulate tips. Spatulate tips show energy, activity and originality. These characteristics of the spatulate tips when added to the smooth fingers produce persons who work hard and for locomotion and who have desire for corporeal exertion. Such persons act more upon the dictation of their organization than of their heads. They generally have fascination for such animals as horses and dogs and love hunting, agriculture and commerce. Persons with smooth fingers and spatulate tips are more talkers than workers, their brain is more particularly adopted for the evolution of theories than for putting those theories into practice which is the peculiarity of square tips.

Smooth fingers may also take the shape of a square at their tips. Persons who possess such smooth fingers with square tips are by reason of the square tip, didactic, analytical and dramatic. They love grammar, order and form. They have a good reasoning capacity and their arguments are based on practical utility and logic. Rhythm, symmetry and conventional attitude are their peculiarities. Such persons have moderate ideas, they appreciate and respect honesty, cultivation of virtues and good behaviour. Such persons have more brains and so they prefer what they actually see to what they imagine. They never endeavour for higher poetry which is the work of conic tips but their work is methodical with proper presentation. To compare the spatulate tips with the square tip, we can say in brief that the former has more simplicity but less politeness, more freedom but less elegance than the latter.

The third type is that of smooth fingers with conic tips. Conic tips indicate the natural love for music, painting, dancing and such other forms of art where intuition plays the most important part and the artistic piece is the result of emotion rather than of more methodical work. We have studied earlier in this chapter these characteristics of smooth fingers. So in combining these characteristics of smooth fingers and other of conic tips, we get such a marvellous subject who is a great lover of art. Such persons succeed in sculpture, monuments, architecture, poetry of the imagination and of the senses, romantic charm and social independence. They mostly live on their utopian ideals and are susceptible to phantasy. Such persons are full of idealism and lack the realistic view of life. Their home will be beautiful and artistic but not methodically arranged. In paintings, they do not like battle scenes or landscapes but prefer pictures which appeal to their imagination. Art to them means freedom from conventionality. In short, when we encounter a person with smooth fingers and conic tips, we at once think of art, quickness, romance, idealism, grace and we notice them as the ruling tendencies in the person rather than the desire for action, system, regularity and common sense which are natural to the person having square tips. The exaggerated form of this is the smooth fingers with pointed tips. If all the fingers including the thumb are conical, it is a sign of weak will and suggestibility. Pointed fingers are seen on the hand of feeble minded persons and imbeciles.

Strict observance of time and measure being the necessary precedent condition of musical rhythm, it is among subjects whose fingers are square that we find the most perfect musicians. Instrumentation is the special aspect of spatulate fingers and melody is the peculiar feature of the fingers with pointed tips.

3 Knotty fingers with different Tips (*fig. 27*)

Knotty fingers display the nature which is contrary to the smooth fingers. Knotty fingers are generally the characteristic of those who are mature in thought. Analysis, investigation, thoughtfulness and reasoning are the prominent qualities of knotty fingers. These people love truth and are more rightly called philosophers. They are not carried away by impulse and are seldom emotional. They act with their head and not with the heart. Knotty fingers, generaly belong to the scientists and historians who are studious and depend upon well-stored information, which they use when occasion demands. Such people will not rush to anything suddenly. They need something to think over and take time in doing so, but once they arrive at a conclusion they can abide by the results of their investigations. When their advice is sought, the problem should be put before them and they should be allowed and given time to think over it.

Sometimes the first knot alone is developed (*fig. 28*). This formation shows mental order. It indicates an intelligent person with systematic and careful thinking. Too much

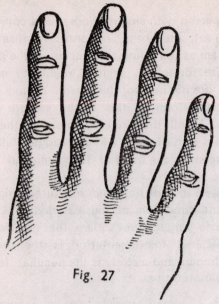

Fig. 27

Knotty fingers (maturity of thought)

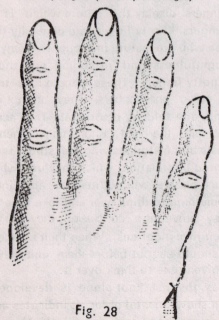

Fig. 28

Fingers with first knot developed (system and careful thinking)

The Fingers

pronounced knot shows excessive thinking exerting tremendous pressure upon the brain which may result in insanity.

When the second knot is developed (*fig. 29*), it is a sign of proper handling of things in material affairs. The subject, whose second knot is more developed than the first, loves order at home and likes to keep his things neatly and in order. He is methodical in his habits and in dressing.

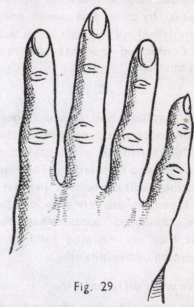

Fig. 29

Fingers with second knot developed (method and order in work)

Knotty fingers may have square, spatulate or conic tips. When square tips are found it shows system to an already methodical type. Such a subject observes strict discipline and whatever field he may be in, he will display fanatical red-tapism.

Persons whose first knot is developed and possess spatulate tips are obstinate. Knotty fingers with spatulate tips indicate an instinctive appreciation of real life, a talent for calculation, a tendency to cultivate physical power, inclination towards natural and experimental sciences, administration, jurisprudence and so on. This aptitude makes such persons obstinate in their thought and action. Since such persons have the talent of practical and mechanical sciences, they bring perfection to such studies as statistics and utilitarian architecture such as bridges, streets etc.

Knotty fingers with conic or pointed tips is not a very good combination to have. They lighten the intensity of the knots. System, order, method which are the virtues of knotty fingers are lessened by conic tips which denote idealism. Thus, neither materialism nor idealism is the outcome of such a combination. Conflicting thoughts and ideas make the mind elastic and unsteady.

Conclusion

In short, for spatulate and square fingers, prominent joints are an additional beauty, considering that they are by nature destined for cultivation of the useful arts which are those of combination and calculation. They are so bound to materialism that they will not believe in what they cannot see and touch. Thus, they are very sceptical. But for pointed or conic fingers, developed joints would be a deformity, considering that they are destined for liberal arts which depend upon intuition and inspiration.

4 Short fingers with different Tips

There are two types of fingers, long and short.

How to measure long or short fingers

If by covering the fingers on the palm, they reach the first bracelet on the wrist, the fingers are long (*fig. 30*). If the fingers reach just upto the middle Mount of Venus, they are of the normal length (*fig. 31*). If, however, they do not reach the middle Mount of Venus, they are short fingers.

Short fingered people have a quick mind. Their grasp of things is very easy and they judge the whole from the part. Their mind is very active and alert. People with short fingers usually succeed in visualising their ideas and they see

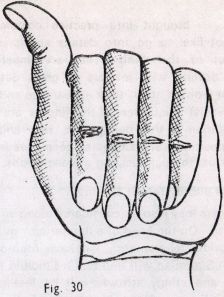

Fig. 30
Long fingers (slow and sensitive)

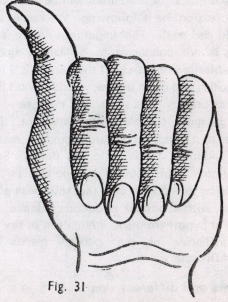

Fig. 31
Normal length fingers

their ideas brought into practice completely. Such people do not like to go into details and they take the broader-aspect of the thing. They are impetuous and impatient in dealing with matters of great details. Such people are not worried about their appearance and care very little about social etiquettes. If the fingers are thick and clumsy in addition to their being short, they show a selfish and cruel disposition. Short fingered people are in danger of falling into errors through jumping at conclusions.

Short fingers and different Mounts

Short fingers may also be considered along with the type they belong to. On the hand of a Jupiterian, qualities such as ambition, pride, religion etc., will have intuition working with them. A Saturnian will find that his morbid tendencies, superstitions and stingy attitude will be lessened by the virtue of short fingers. Since short fingers indicate activity, vigour and quickness an Apollonian will be more smart, intelligent and quick. A Mercurian will be alert and quick in whatever profession he is following. We know a Martian is hot-tempered and rash. The impetuous nature exhibited by short fingers is not conducive to a Martian since it would enhance the Martian qualities. If the person is a lunarian, he is dreamy, selfish and of an unsteady mind. Short fingers would make him less dreamy, less selfish but more sensitive and his mind would be more flexible and inconsistent. Short fingers on the hands of a Venusian would make him more energetic in his arts and more intuitive in his poetry. Such fingers would add vigour to his impulse and fire to his action.

It should be noted with care that shortness of the fingers is associated with abnormal endocrine balance as is shown in the cases of hypothyroidism, infantalism of sex glands and in under functioning of the pituitary glands (please see 'Fingers and Disease').

Short fingers and different tips

Square tips are the best for short fingers since they show material outlook and give practical common sense which check the hasty attitude shown by the short fingers.

Spatulate tips to the short fingers mean additional activity and originatity.

Conic tips to the short fingers are not desirable. Hopeless idealism and dangerous impulsiveness of the pointed tips would lead the short fingered type to grave danger.

5 Long Fingers with different Tips

Opposite to the short fingered people are those who have long fingers. Naturally these people have their attitudes, aptitudes, likes and dislikes which are contrary to those having short fingers. Thus, long fingered persons are slow going and slow talking. They are slow in movement, dignified and lack the rushing, dashing way of short fingered persons. They go into the details of the things and are particular about small things. They are suspicious and do not feel quite sure that seeming friends are true. They are extremely sensitive and are easily offended. They will check accounts for a month to discover a penny which has destroyed their balance. They show meddling disposition and are ever finding faults. It is interesting to note that sometimes they are cruel and if other aspects on hand are unfavourable their hands is the poisoner's hand.

The length of the fingers is related to the degree of intellectual development. Abnormally long fingers go with a too abstract intellectual development at the expense of vitality and instinct.

Long Fingers with smooth and knotty joints

If the long fingers are smooth, it will not take much time to grasp an idea but if the fingers are knotty, it means love of details with analysis and this class will always be slow. Such persons achieve success by labouring hard.

Thin Fingers

Thickness or thinness of long fingers is important. Thin

fingers accentuate long fingered qualities and form a more disagreeable estimate. People having such fingers are diplomats, deceivers and pick-pocketers.

Thick Fingers

The animal vitality belonging to thick fingers reduces the pushing tendencies of the long fingers and prevents them from going to an excess. So, they will indicate some of disagreeable qualities of the long thin fingers.

Longer fingers and tips of the fingers

A square tip to long fingers means regularity, practical insight, business or common sense duties. The square tip is too much bowed down by routine and custom to be original.

A spatulate tip shows activity and originality. Persons of this combination are inventors and careful explorers. This is the best sign to indicate originality.

A conic tip to long fingers indicates a love of art and the beautiful. Such a combination may be found in all classes of people. But each will have the faculty of looking after the trifles and little things in their lives. Ignorant people may also have this type of combination but they cannot be ascribed the creative artistic talent and yet they do love beauty.

6 Fingers and their lengths
Normal lengths of the fingers

We have discussed previously the normal length of the fingers. Therein I have stated that when the fingers reach the middle Mount of Venus, they are of normal length. But now we shall see the normal length of the individual finger in relation to fingers (*fig. 32*).

Jupiter Finger

To be normal in length, the Jupiter finger should reach the middle of the first phalange of the Saturn finger.

The Fingers

Saturn Finger

Normally this finger is longer than the Jupiter and the Apollo fingers.

Fig. 32

Normal length of fingers

Apollo Finger

Usually, this is equal in length to that of the Jupiter finger.

Mercury Finger

To be normal in length, this finger should reach the first knot of the Apollo finger.

We shall now study the individual finger in more details.

The Finger of Jupiter

The first finger is considered as the finger of Jupiter. The simple reason why it is named so is that it stands on the Mount of Jupiter. Naturally, this finger partakes all the qualities of the same mount and the finger is very important in judging the type of the subject. If the mount is slightly displaced, but the finger is strong and erect, the qualities of the mount which are lessened by its displacement may be enhanced by the firmness and the development of this finger. So in judging the type, we must take into consideration the mount as well as the fingers. Being the finger of Jupiter, it shows pride, honour, religion, ambition, dignity, honesty, sacrifice, command, love of nature and such other qualities of Jupiter.

Psychological significance of the Jupiter finger

There has been much anthropological and anatomical discussion on the specialisation of the Index finger in man, in whose evolution it plays an important part developing in him an independence of movement. The high degree of mobility of this finger goes with a pattern of movements quite incomparable with those of monkeys and it is no chance phenomenon that the typical postures and gestures of the index finger suggest the expression of conscious thought and persuasion. All monkeys have index fingers much shorter than those of man, generally not reaching beyond the middle phalange of the middle finger. In some Mongolian imbeciles, the same type of similar condition is noticeable.

Of all the fingers, the Index finger has been singled out by physicians, as having a special medical significance. Hypocrates discovered that this finger has direct connection with the lungs. Normally the Index finger should reach the middle of the first phalange of the Saturn finger.

When this finger is very long, it shows the excess characteristics of a Jupiterian type. When very long, that is to say, when it is as long as the Saturn finger, the desire for power will be great. If it is longer than the Saturn finger it shows tyranny. It also means a proud and dogmatic type of person. Such a person would resent being ruled by what he considers to be his social inferior. However, the person is very ambitious and also religious. If the Jupiter finger is equal to the Saturn finger in length and if the hands are soft, it reveals a person who is proud of himself, who is arrogant and a tyrant. Such a person however, enjoys the pleasures of the world. If this finger is longer than the first knot of the Saturn finger, the person is happy in his relation with his brothers.

Too short a finger of Jupiter

When this finger is shorter than the normal, for example, when it does not reach to the first knot of the Saturn finger, it will show that the subject is not a pure Jupiterian, even though he may have a strong mount, for there will be lack of ability to lead and this does not belong to the Jupiterian type. It also shows dislike for responsibility and lack of pride. Such a person fears public opinion and merely keeps up appearances. When the Jupiter finger is shorter than the normal, the person is very quick and active. Such a person will fail in his duties and will try to shirk responsibility. He will also be unhappy in his relations with his brothers.

Moderate in length

When this finger has a moderte length, that is, when it reaches the middle of the first phalange of the Saturn finger, the Jupiterian desire for leadership will not be excessive and indicates moderate love of rule and an active disposition. When the Jupiter finger is moderate in length the person is capable and of good character. He has a very good balance of mind and is very steady. He is a leader and possesses good and sweet tongue. Such a person is usually popular. He loves justice, prestige and craves for knowledge.

Conic tip to the moderate finger of Jupiter

If this moderate finger of Jupiter possesses a conic tip, it shows a man of high imagination and religious nature who loves reputation and who attains high position.

Square tip to this finger shows fidelity, sharp intelligence and a sweet tongue.

Spatulate tip to this finger shows a person who forgets things and commits mistakes.

Crooked finger of Jupiter

If this Jupiter finger is crooked, it adds to the shrewdness of the type and is not necessarily a bad sign, though it strengthens the mount very much. It shows that the person will systematically plan all his moves. According to the Hindu system, it means lack of honour and the person having this finger is a fool and does not deserve respect.

As regards the length of this finger, the Hindu system states that if the Jupiter finger is longer than the Apollo finger but shorter than the Saturn finger, the person is good by nature but he is slightly hot-tempered, very clear and sophisticated. He is also a very good advisor.

The Finger of Saturn
Psychological Significance

Next to the finger of Jupiter is that of the Saturn. By virtue of its position on the hand, it is generally the longest of all the fingers. It is called the balance wheel because Saturn gives this finger, wisdom, sobriety and a balanced mind. Naturally the development of this finger is very important. By the shape of this finger and its standing on the Mount of Saturn, we shall know how far this finger has absorbed the qualities of the mount underneath. This finger shows gloom, carefulness, check in activities, common sense and wisdom.

Physiological Significance

This finger is probably related to the abdominal viscera which would account for the belief that a long middle finger indicates melancholia since faulty abdominal condition is known to induce depression in a marked degree. This finger has also special relation to the liver and its deformity shows liver troubles (see fingers and disease). When this finger is

The Fingers

thicker and broader than the rest, the person marries more than once.

Very long in length: When this finger is very long, it shows a morbid, gloomy, melancholy person, pessimistic and stingy.

Moderate in length: When this finger is normal in length, it indicates prudence. It gives great accuracy concerning the power possessed by the subject to hold undue enthusiasm in check. It keeps the Jupiterian, the Apollonian, the Martian and the Venusian from going too fast and from being carried away by their excessive spirit.

Short in length: When the finger of Saturn is shorter than the normal length, it means lack of balance and untrustworthiness and also frivolity.

Crooked finger of Saturn

When the Saturn finger is crooked, it reveals hysteria and murderous instincts. It shows twisted and complicated nature of the person which gives him a peculiar vindictive and revengeful attitude. When this finger is strong, broad and long, the person is timid, melancholy, mentally suffering and believing in fate. If however, the finger is thin and flat, the person is vindictive and jealous.

Tips and the Saturn finger

A conic tip to the Saturn finger means that the person is engrossed in family affairs and is not trustworthy.

A square tip: with strong joints of the Saturn finger makes the person love mathematics.

A spatulate tip: to the Saturn finger makes the person inventive, enthusiastic and a lover of science and literature.

The finger of Apollo

Next to Saturn finger is the finger of Apollo. This finger indicates eloquence, brilliance, enthusiasm and a sense of beauty. A good development of this finger reveals a refined character. The development of the knots and the tip will give a fair idea as to the development of the finger. An abnormal development of this finger will show either excessive or diminishing characteristics of the subject. Normally this finger should reach the middle of the first phalange of the Saturn finger.

Long finger of Apollo

If this finger is longer than the Saturn finger, the person will have no control over himself and will be losing foolishly in gambling. According to Hindu school, it shows the art of acquiring money. If however this finger is as long as the Saturn finger, the person will have speculative tendencies and will be taking great risks in life. According to this school, with this length, if the second phalange of this finger is good and the Mount of Moon developed, the logic of the person is most developed and he is fond of lottery. If, in addition, the Mount of Mercury is developed, the person is a first class gambler and does not care for the future.

Moderate length of the finger

If the finger of Apollo is equal to the Jupiter finger in length, there is a good combination of brilliance and ambition. If this finger is dominant, artistic tendencies will prevail. According to the Hindu school, it means that the person has talent and loves to gain fame, honour and money through machinery.

Short length of the finger

Persons with this type of finger will lack in the sense of beauty and artistic notions.

Crooked finger of Apollo

When the Apollo finger is crooked in nature, we shall have a tricky gambler, a person who uses his art for a wrongfull purpose. According to the Hindu school, a crooked finger of Apollo means a person who loses his success which he has practically gained. The person builds up everything but fails at the eleventh hour. His natural virtues are useless. He is not capable of foresight and is prejudiced. He does not care much for the moral character and is careless about everyday life.

A conic tip to the Apollo finger represents a person who is impractical, whimsical and likes artificial things and pomp.

A square tip to this finger shows a person who is not very courageous but is determined. He learns things by his own experience and by his intellectual capacity.

He is self-supporting and finds out his own profession. If this tip is thin and flat, the person is skilful and systematic. If the Mount of Moon is developed, the person is fond of dramas.

A spatulate tip to the finger indicates that the person is a lover of speculation and is engrossed in lottery, racing and gambling. If the shape of the finger is also spatulate, the person is original in his ideas and brings about revolution in the ideas of other persons also. He is a great orator and an actor.

The finger of Mercury
Psychological Significance

Lastly comes the finger of Mercury. Of all the fingers the Mercury is a peculiar one. The best of talent in business and shrewdness in life is shown by this finger. Its development indicates either good or bad qualities of the mount underneath. A bad Mercury finger reveals a shrewd rogue or a wise criminal. This finger has a special reference to the hand in relation to criminology.

Physiological Significance

This finger is a good indicator as regards health factor. It shows the gonadic trouble with the person. A deformed finger of Mercury shows sex trouble.

Length of the finger : The normal finger of Mercury reaches the first knot of the finger of Apollo.

Long finger of Mercury : When this finger is very long, it shows literary ability, fluency in speech and writing. It also shows crafty instincts. According to Hindu system, very long finger indicates infidelity. If this finger is broad and and strong, the person achieves success in spite of many difficulties. If this finger is longer than the base of first phalange of the Sun finger, the person enjoys all comforts in life and enjoys the love of mother and of her relations. He is fond of sweet dishes and also adores women.

Moderate length of the finger

When the finger is moderate in length, it shows versatility and desire for general improvement. If this finger is equal to the first phalange of the Saturn finger, the man loves studies and learning. He loves scientific research. When it is as long as the Jupiter finger, it reveals philosophic attitude. (the hand of Mahatma Gandhi)

Short finger of Mercury

A short finger of Mercury indicates lack of discretion and inability to judge matters. Such persons arrive rapidly and hastily at conclusions and a lack of tact as well as stupidity is indicated. Such persons however, grasp things very quickly. Mercury finger and longevity : see seperate chapter at the beginning of this book.

Crooked finger of Mercury

The crooked finger of Mercury is notorious and is known for its hypocrisy. If the finger is properly developed, the crooked shape adds to the diplomacy and the subject will be cautious in his dealings. This type of finger is often seen on the hands of thieves and robbers.

A pointed tip to the Mercury finger makes the person very cunning and he deals in secret arts and occultism.

A square tip to the Mercury finger shows a good teacher. He loves fancy and is very neat and knows the art of dressing. He is a sophist and likes discourses on scientific subjects.

A spatulate tip to the Mercury finger denotes a mechanic or an engineer.

General Remarks

After discussing the length of the individual fingers, a general remark may be passed that fingers which are evenly set on a line above the mounts indicate success. An absolutely even line is seldom met with. Any finger set below loses some of its power. When the Jupiter finger is low set, it gives social awkwardness. The Saturn finger is hardly displaced, but when so found it loses the balance of the hand. Similarly, with the Apollo and the Mercury fingers, we find that they lose their power when placed at a lower level than the normal. A person who possesses mixed fingers (that is when the first is conic, the second realistic, the third energetic and the fourth idealistic) is a man of great versatility. He appears to the outside world as a man somewhat whimsical and unstable in mental disposition, but he may be persistent in his action and sometimes remarkably succesful as a diplomat, politician or a literary critic. He is generally a Jack of all trades and master of none.

7 Space between the fingers

The space between the different fingers gives a valuable information regarding the development of the mind of the person and his action.

Space between the thumb and the Jupiter finger

The thumb shows the will of the person. If the thumb is away from the finger of Jupiter, it must set low on the hand (*fig. 33*). This thumb does not lie close to the sides of the hand and thus leaves a great space between itself and the finger of Jupiter. When the thumb is naturally away from first finger, it will show a nature full of human qualities which are of a higher plane. As this thumb is low set, it takes all the qualities of the Mount of Venus and thus creates a mind which shows warmth, sympathy and generosity. Such a subject loves independence, freedom and liberty. He is always willing to help those in distress, though he may not be helpful from monetary point of view.

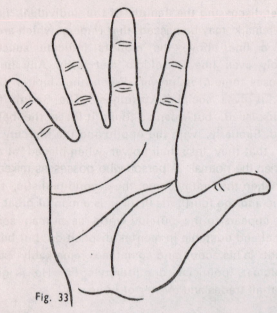

Fig. 33

Space between thumb and Jupiter finger (sympathy and generosity)

Space between the Jupiter and the Saturn fingers

If the space between the Jupiter and the Saturn fingers is wide (*fig. 34*), it means that the Jupiter finger is leaning towards the thumb and in doing so, it partakes the qualities of the thumb which are strong in will-power and independent character. Thus, the pride of Jupiter combined with the will-power of the thumb produces a person who is independent in character. Thus, the pride of Jupiter combined with the will-opinion and is not logged down by the views of others.

Space between the Saturn and the Apollo fingers (*fig. 35*)

While in keeping a wide space, the Apollo finger does not partake the qualities of the Saturn finger which have

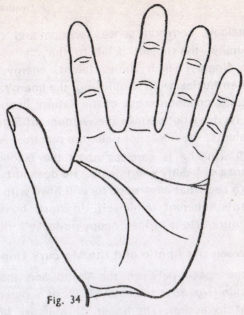
Fig. 34
Space between Jupiter and Saturn fingers (man of thought)

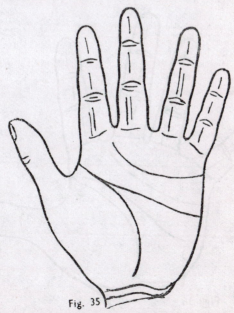
Fig. 35
Space between Saturn and Apollo fingers (carelessness about future)

practical outlook, common sense, wisdom and balance of mind. Naturally, the subject is left to the characteristic of the Apollo finger, which shows talent, energy, sense of beauty and enthusiasm. In employing the energy, he does not possess the common-sense of the Saturn, in appreciation of beauty, he does not partake the wisdom of Saturn and in using his talents, he does not gain the practical view point of the Saturn. Thus he is careless about the outcome of his energy, sense of beauty and talents. He does not peep into the future to see what advantage he will have with the qualities and merits inherent in himself. In short, he is careless about the future. He is of the "happy-go-lucky" disposition.

Space between the Apollo and the Mercury fingers

When the space between the Apollo and the Mercury fingers is wide (*fig. 36*), we shall know of a person who is independent in action. The finger of Mercury being away from the hand, it shows Mercurian qualities which are

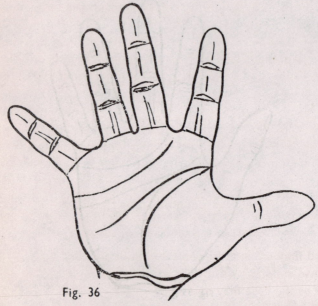

Fig. 36

Space between Apollo and Mercury fingers (man of action)

The Fingers

shrewdness, energy and judgement. He is very energetic and therefore a man of action. He has sound judgment and relies upon his skill. Since he has the faculty of expression he can best exhibit it in action.

Equal spacing between the fingers

When the fingers are keeping equal space in between them, every finger will have the freedom to exhibit its qualities (*fig. 37*). A person with such equal spacing of fingers does not follow conventionality. He is a person independent in thought as well as in action. He will be easy to approach. According to the Hindu school of thought, large spacing between the first and the second fingers, between the second and the

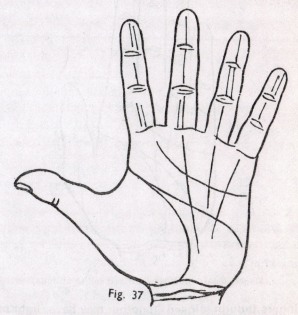

Fig. 37

Equal space between the fingers (balanced nature)

third fingers and between the third and the fourth fingers shows constant sorrow in young age, middle age and old age as the case may be.

Fingers closed together with no light passing through them

Sometimes we encounter hands wherein the fingers are held very close together and the person finds difficulty to separate them from each other (*fig. 38*). Fingers may be so close to each other that no light passes through them. It means that the knots of the fingers are smooth and we have a subject with smooth fingers. Unlike the smooth fingered person, he is selfish and mean in attitude. According to the Hindu school, it shows riches.

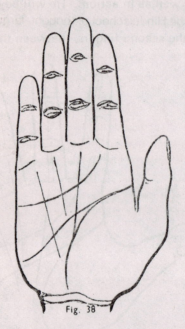

Fig. 38

Fingers closed together (stiff and selfish attitude)

Fingers though closed together may have light passing through them. This is possible when the knots are developed. While dealing with knotty fingers I have explained that the knots show order, analysis, method and inquisitiveness. Therefore these fingers show a person who is philosophical and inquisitive.

8 Leaning of the fingers towards each other

When the first finger leans towards the thumb, it keeps wide space between the first and the second fingers which means independence in thought. When the finger leans towards the second finger, it gets the morbid tendency of the second finger. This morbidity combined with the pride of Jupiter produces morbid pride. The ambition of the person would be more Saturnian and also hidden or concealed.

Second Finger : When the second finger leans towards the first, it indicates superstitious sadness. The second finger exhibits its melancholy nature and in leaning towards Jupiter, it reduces the true aspect of religion which is inherent in Jupiter. So religion misunderstood, the person believes in superstitious aspects and the Saturn makes him sorrowful and depressed. When this finger leans towards the third finger, it loses some of its bad aspects and absorbs the characteristics of the third finger. Thus, it indicates less morbidity. When both the fingers, (the second and the third) are leaning towards each other, it shows a secretive disposition (*fig. 39*).

Third Finger : When the third finger bends towards the second, the vanity of the third finger gets the tinge of morbidity. The talent of the person shows crooked tendencies. When this third finger leans towards the fourth finger, it shows that the sense of beauty and the artistic talents in man have a monetary object in view.

Fourth Finger : If the fourth finger bends towards the third finger, it indicates a marvellous combination of the two fingers. The business aptitude as shown by the fourth finger will have artistic blending and the shrewdness of the finger will have additional talent and eloquence of the third finger (*fig. 40*).

9 The flexibility of the fingers

The next aspect to be taken into consideration is the flexibility of the fingers.

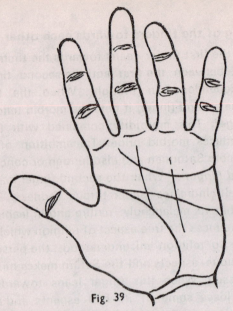

Fig. 39
Saturn and Apollo fingers leaning towards each other (secretive disposition)

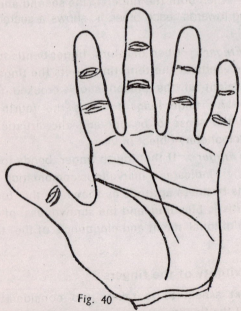

Fig. 40
Mercury fingers leaning towards Apollo finger (talent in business)

Three Rules: 1) A flexible object can adapt itself to a greater variety of conditions. 2) A flexible object bends under pressure, a stiff object under the same amount of pressure breaks or remains immobile. 3) As the fingers reflect the condition and quality of the mind, flexible fingers show a flexible mind and stiff fingers a stiff mind.

If we fix in our mind the above three rules, we can have an accurate estimate of the psychological development of the person by judging the intensity of the flexibility of his fingers. A subtle distinction may be made here between bent and flexibility. A bent is a natural position when the subject does not know that he is observed. Flexibility is only judged by touch. Generally women have more flexible mind than men.

When the fingers are stiff and cannot bend backwards, the person lacks flexibility or elasticity of mind and manner. He is narrow in his ideas and stingy in his ways but succeeds with his hard work.

Moderate flexibility of fingers

When the flexibility of fingers is moderate, the person is moderate in his ideas and understands the practical view of life. He has common-sense and does not go to extremes. He is self-contained, listens readily and understands it. He is neither held back by old fogism nor impelled into rashness or over-enthusiasm. He takes a bird eye view of things and can appreciate the difficulties of others. He is thoughtful, broad minded, earnest, sympathetic, yet all this within bounds.

Extreme flexibility of fingers

Lastly, we may confront persons whose fingers have the greatest flexibility *(fig. 41)*. These fingers seem mobile. Such a flexibility shows a mind that is elastic and a brain that is susceptible to receiving keen impressions. This person is adaptable and versatile. Since this person can make himself suitable to any trade, his versatility would affect his concentration in any one trade. He is extremely sympathetic and generous. Such flexible fingers are capable of wonderful achievements. Such a hand is as extreme in prodigality as the stiff hand is in economy.

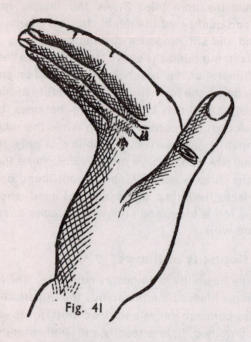

Fig. 41

Flexible fingers (adaptability)

10 The phalanges (*fig. 42*)
Psychological significance of phalanges

The next aspect to be taken into consideration is the phalanges of the fingers. The best example to prove the relation of the hand to the development of the brain is that of phalanges. The third or the basal phalange of finger shows the material world and its thick development shows a desire to satisfy sensual things and gratification of physical desires. It is best seen on the hand of a new born baby who has no other motive than to eat and sleep. Thus, the baby's mental development is only seen towards the gratification of sensual desires and to satisfy its hunger. Naturally, the third phalange of the fingers is thick. As months pass the child develops other aspects and develops the mental power, gradually other phalanges also show their growth in proportion to the growth of the mind.

Order of phalanges: The phalanges are considered from the tip of the finger towards the base, the upper phalange being the first, the middle, the second and basal as the third.

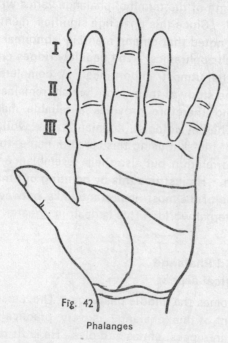

Fig. 42
Phalanges

The First Phalange
Psychological Significance

If we notice that the first phalange is most developed we have a subject whose mental faculty is more developed than the practical one. He lives in his mental world, is idealistic in views and has marvellous schemes for his life. This phalange should be considered along with the finger on which it is found. On the finger of Jupiter, the man will have more respect for religion and will think of achieving success in mysticism. On the finger of Saturn the first phalange will show more wisdom and studious nature. On the finger of Apollo, it indicates high intellectual activity and ideal love and on the finger of Mercury it reveals interest in law and pursuits in scientific studies.

Physiological aspect

The length of the terminal phalange varies with the type of the hand. Since this phalange signifies mental developments, it is noted that among mentally abnormal people, it is longer in schizophrenics. The papillary ridges on the finger tips are of the utmost importance. A complete science is based on the study of their form which remains unchanged till death and therefore provides a reliable mark of identification. The physiologist, Kollman in his work has called them gyri of the skin using this cerebral name to stress not just their correlation but also their resemblance to the cortex of the brain. He justifies this by pointing out that the tactile sense is one of the most important links between the brain and the external world. This is dealt in greater details later on.

The Second Phalange
Psychological aspect

Next comes the middle phalange. The person with the development of this phalange is very practical and counts everything in rupees, annas and pies. He is fit for commerce, politics, war, agriculture or for anything which is entirely practical. Getting money is his primary desire and he lives in the world of material affairs. The development of this phalange on the Jupiter finger signifies ambition, pride and vanity. On the Saturn finger it shows love for agriculture, extreme caution in business and love of mathematics. On the third finger, it means common sense blended with talent and on the fourth finger, a developed second phalange reveals an aptitude for science and inventions. Excessive development of this phalange on this little finger shows talent used for criminal purpose.

As regards the diseases shown by this phalange, I shall deal at the end of this chapter while describing "Fingers and Diseases".

The Third Phalange

When the third phalange of the fingers is thick and long, the person lives on the lower plane, does not possess high intellectual capacity. He does not follow high ideals. He does not care for money since his middle phalange is not developed. His desires are for eating and sensual things. He loves the pleasures of the world and hunts after them. If he has money he will spend it in buying comforts and pleasures. This phalange should also be considered from the point of view of the finger on which it is developed. If the third phalange of the Jupiter finger is developed, it means the desire to rule and love for power are carried too far. If it is found on the Saturn finger, it means economy and avarice. If it is most developed on the Apollo finger, it shows foolish display. On the Mercury finger, the third phalange reveals business talents and sometimes the disposition of thieves.

Physiological aspect

When the third phalange is thick, it shows endocrine make-up and the susceptibility to hyperthyroidism. According to the Hindu school of palmistry, following is the significance of the phalanges of the different fingers and the signs on them.

The Finger of Jupiter

If the first phalange of the Jupiter finger is longer than the first phalange of the Mercury finger, it shows a person who is religious and pious and who gives discourses on religious matters and who is fond of philosophic talk and high thinking.

If the third phalange of the Jupiter finger is longer than the third phalange of the Mercury finger, the person is very ambitious. He is also very proud of himself and loves to inflict lawful punishment.

If the first phalange of the Jupiter finger is as short as the length of the nail, the person marries a widow.

The Finger of Saturn

If the first phalange of the Saturn finger is long, the person is melancholic and credulous. If this phalange is very long, the person thinks of death and desires it. If the second phalange is long and the fingers are smooth, the person acquires the occult practices and is good at mesmerism, hypnotism, yoga, mantra shastra, astrology and palmistry. If the second phalange is long and the finger is knotty, the person is a good mathematician. If the third phalange is long, he gets fame and popularity.

The Finger of Apollo

If the phalanges of the Apollo finger are hard to touch, the person is skilful. If the second phalange is long, it reveals the person's concentration in trade and his aptitude for painting. If such a phalange is found on the hand of an artist, he writes the history of art.

If the third phalange of the Apollo finger is long, the person loves pomp and artificial beauty and has vanity.

The Finger of Mercury

The first phalange of the Mercury finger is very important because it reveals many important characteristics of the person.

If this phalange is long, it shows that the person is clever in speech and has eloquence. If it is very long, it shows that the person is methodical but is a liar. If the phalange is as long as the other two, the person is very regular and if the Head line has branches, the person is capable of acting as a political agent or as an ambassador.

If the second phalange is long, the person is a good writer as well as a good businessman. He is very learned and likes to teach others also. If this phalange is square and strong, the person is good at accounts.

If the third phalange is long, the person is practical, intelligent and a statesman. If this phalange is very long, he is very clever, cunning, dishonest and tricky.

I give below in short, the good qualities and the bad qualities of the different phalanges of the fingers.

Finger	Phalange	Good Qualities	Bad Qualities
Jupiter	I	Ambition, high moral sense, pride in religion, prestige, position, mysticism.	Dictatorship, vanity, false pride.
	II	Dignity, courage, love for humanity	Tyranny, vulgarity, timidity.
	III	Practical religion, simplicity, happiness.	Sensuality, gluttony, dishonesty.
Saturn	I	Sober, independent nature, authority, wisdom.	Superstition, melancholia, fatalism.
	II	Research, mathematics, order, system, studiousness, occultism.	Secrecy, backbiting, treachery, envy.
	III	Solitude, economy	Cold nature, dislike for opposite sex, misery.
Apollo	I	Talents, art, versatility, brilliance.	Avarice, gambling
	II	Reputation, love for wealth, integrity.	Infidelity, unsteady mind.
	III	Liberty, gaiety, freedom.	Audacity, stupidity.

Finger	Phalange	Good Qualities	Bad Qualities
Mercury	I	Intelligence, diplomacy, activity, law, scientific pursuits.	Crookery, swindling.
	II	Business, law, invention.	Scandal, mockery.
	III	Shrewdness	Cheating, Robbing.

11 Hair on the Fingers

This is not a very important aspect to be taken into consideration. But, sometimes a little attention to it may be useful. Many times the hair on the hand is not found or the growth is so scarce that it can hardly be seen with naked eyes.

The psychological aspect of Hair

Black Hair: Black hair shows heat and warmth. If these persons do not find an outlet for their vigour, then they will love sensual pleasures and indulge in sensual activities. They are restless and unsteady.

Grey Hair: People with grey hair are moderate in temperament and their vitality and energy is sufficient to keep them fit. It is worthwhile noticing that the grey colour may be the effect of mental worries or old age.

White Hair: White hair indicates lack of iron pigments in the body. Such people are calm, easy going and less sensual. They may suffer from head-aches and may have less vigour and enthusiasm.

Red Hair: Persons with red hair are excitable and engage in quarrels. The texture of red hair is important. Fine texture indicates fits of anger which are momentary. Coarse texture means violent nature, brutality and revengeful attitude.

Golden Hair: The most beautiful hair to be seen is the golden hair. It is a combination of warmth and passion. Heat is added to this from the redness of the colour. If the

The Fingers

subject on whose fingers it is found, is of a bad type, we should at once note that the warmth is only superficial and underneath there is fire.

Hair on Phalanges

Hair on the hand of a woman indicate the instincts of a man. When the growth is moderate, it shows prudence, energy and self possession. Hair on the thumb indicates inventive genius. Hair on the two lower phalanges of the fingers show stiffness of demeanour and lack of simplicity. When hair are found on all phalanges, they reveal a person who is ardent and has an easily aroused disposition.

12 Fingers and Diseases

The last factor to be considered is the medical aspect of the fingers. It might have been clear to my readers that the fingers have a psychological as well as a physiological aspect. Fingers are a very good index in disclosing the defects in the health of the person, and medical research, (though inadequate in this field), has revealed that physical defects may be noted on the fingers.

The shortness of the fingers is associated with abnormal endocrine balance which can be seen in cases of hypothyroidism infantilism of the sex glands and in under functioning of the pituitary glands.

Waisted fingers (*fig. 43*), where the development of the joints is normal, indicate lack of tubercular resistance of the body. When the fingers are all very smooth with a pink, reddish skin, it is an indication of some acidity, generally of intestinal origin.

Hippocrates discovered that the first finger shows the defects of the lungs. Any abnormal development of this finger will show diseases such as laryngitis, asthma, pneumonia and such other defects of the lungs.

The second finger has a connection with the abdomen and its deformity means troubles with the liver. Faulty abdominal conditions produce a deformed second finger and liver disturbance is prominently signified.

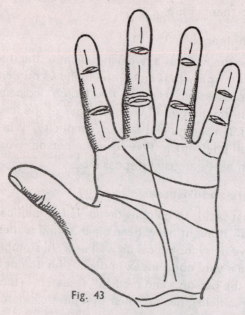

Fig. 43

Waisted finger (critical nature)

The third finger or the finger of Apollo has a connection with the kidneys and defects in the functions of the kidneys are many times noticeable on this finger. In this case the finger looks very weak and is generally long and thin.

Lastly, the fourth finger reveals the gonadic and sex troubles. I have noticed this trouble on the hands of women who have been suffering from the troubles of the ovaries and the womb.

Phalanges of the fingers are also very important from the point of view of diseases.

First Phalange

The first phalange, if abnormally long, indicates mental defect and the person is susceptible to hysteria, insanity and such other psychological defects where the mind of the person is affected seriously. Many times, long first phalanges are noted on the hands of schizophrenics.

Second Phalange

The second phalanges is very thin when the person is suffering from tuberculosis. In case of tuberculosis of the lungs, the middle phalange of the first finger is more affected. In other consumptive illness, the middle phalanges of all the fingers are affected.

Third Phalange

The third phalanges of the fourth finger is affected more when the person is suffering from gonadic troubles. Earlier, in dealing with the fourth finger, I have mentioned that it has a special significance in relation to the sex glands and gonadic functions in particular and therefore the third phalange of this finger should be observed with care.

Another aspect to be noted on the fingers for detecting the health defects of the person is the pattern of the papillary ridges on the finger tips.

Loops : Loop type formation on the finger tips indicates nervous trouble (*fig. 44*). It also shows defective digestive system and poor action of the heart.

Tented Arch : This type of formation indicates a higher degree of nervousness (*fig. 45*).

Arch : The third type of the pattern of the papillary ridges on the finger tips is the arch type. It reveals faulty blood circulation and defects in digestive system. It also shows marked tendency to infections and malignant conditions (*fig. 46*).

Whorl : The fourth type is the whorl. It indicates troubles with the nerves and faulty action of the heart. In this case however the intensity is not as much as that of the second type. (*fig. 47*).

Composite type : The fifth type is the composite type. (*fig. 48*). It is the type of the glutton. The natural health development is fatty and it shows all health troubles which

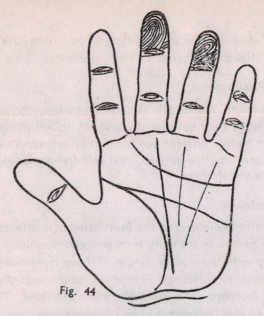

Fig. 44
Loops on finger tips (nervous trouble)

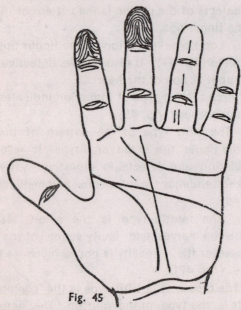

Fig. 45
Tented arch (nervousness)

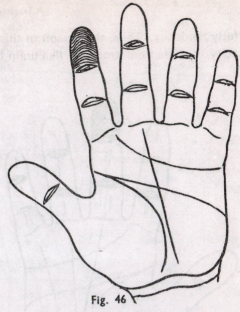

Fig. 46

Arch type formation of papillary ridges (faulty blood circulation)

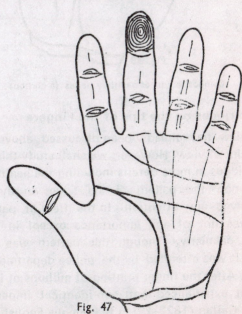

Fig. 47

Whorls on finger tips (heart troubles)

are due to fatty tendency. Thus, the person of this type lacks mental capacity, suffers from troubles like brain fever, dullness etc.

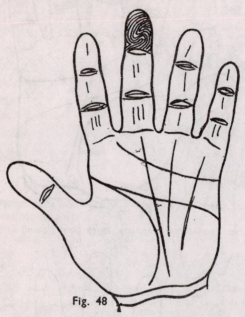

Fig. 48

Composite type of papillary ridges (a glutton)

13) Skin ridges on the tips of the Fingers

This view has already been discussed above from the health point of view. However, we shall study this pattern of papillary ridges in more details including the health aspect.

Uptil now the pattern of the ridges on the finger tips never received any attention. In the field of palmistry the pattern was not of any importance except in the Hindu school of palmistry. Though this pattern was ignored in palmistry, it was attended by the police department all over the world. After the finger printing of millions of individuals, it has been experienced that two identical finger prints do not exist. Galtan (1822-1911) the famous English anthropologist who has given finger printing its scientific foundation,

The Fingers

calculated that 64,000,000,000 different patterns were possible *i.e.* about four times the number of fingers existing in the world.

Finger prints are formed in the fourth month of pregnancy. During further growth as well as after birth, the patterns enlarge but no changes take place in the number of arrangements of the friction ridges. The pattern is not influenced by illness except by leprosy. Recent attempts of criminals to alter or destroy the skin on the fingers by plastic operations have also proved unsuccessful. The friction ridges disappear only after death by the decomposition of the body. It can truthfully be said of them that they are an indelible signature which we carry with us from the cradle to the grave.

It is also a matter of observation that these papillary ridges exhibit a vital psychological significance. They show hereditary characteristics upon which the individual character is founded. These basic psychological factors determine the elasticity of the individual and supply information as to the manner of its action within these psychological boundaries.

The fingers may all bear the same type of pattern or they may be mixed in all sorts of odd ways. There is an endless variety of finger print constructions, but there are only five types of prints.

First type : The first type of the pattern of these papillary ridges is the loop (*fig. 44*). In this type, the apex is a sloping loop. This may run from left to right or right to left. In this case, the person on whose finger tips it is found, is very intelligent and is varsatile in activities. His is a high mind which possesses a high degree of mental and emotional elasticity. He is very active and gives ready response to environment. Since he is versatile in activity, it becomes difficult for him to stick to one thing and therefore lacks concentration. He finds it difficult to control emotional impulse and if other signs on the hand are also unfavourable, such diversity of interests is most destructive to the individual efficiency.

Health : There are also certain health defects of this type which we have already discussed. Since this type is more intelligent than the rest, it exerts greater pressure to the brain and leads to nervous trouble. When the brain is engaged all the while, the blood rushes to the brain and the digestive system is disturbed as it gets a lesser supply of blood. Thus, nervous trouble and faulty digestive system are the main defects of this type. Sometimes excessive mental strain may affect the heart also.

Second type : This is the tented arch type (*fig. 45*). In this case, the apex is perpendicular. This type reveals a still higher degree of nervous activity than the previous one. The person on whose hand this pattern is seen possesses a nervous system that is sensitive and highly strung, a nervous system that is too readily responsive to emotional stimulation. Naturally, he is affected by musical tunes and is very idealistic so he expects too much of people and of life itself. He is restless and terribly anxious to live. The danger with this type is that his far reaching emotional impulse may destroy all his directional effort.

Health : His health defects are practically the same as that of the first type since the second type is one step ahead of the first in quality and intensity. But the main trouble with this is that of the nerves. Naturally, it reveals a highly strung disposition and nervous disorder.

Third type : This is known as the arched type (*fig. 46*). In this case the apex flows across the finger and the ridges make an arch-like formation. This type reveals a character which is secretive. The emotions and sentiments of this person do not give way to, and consequently they have been repressed. Thus, though outwardly he appears to be a man of strong will, we should know that he has other side also and his emotions have found a deep seat in his subconscious mind. He is therefore uncertain, bewildered and hesitant. The sub-conscious mind works under the pressure of the dormant emotions and it therefore exerts an inhibitionary effect. This repressive tendency often produces an accentuation of the normal will-power and it causes the person to be obstinate and rather mulish. He is resentful of his own short-comings and deficiencies and these instinctive defensive mechanisms make him obstinate and awkward.

Health : The health weaknesses of this type are mainly of the digestive system producing faulty blood circulation. It has a marked tendency to infections and malignant condition.

Fourth type : The fourth type is the whorl (*fig. 47*). This type is the most important as it reveals a definite independence of both thought and action. This pattern can always be connected with originality of thought. Persons on whose fingers tips the whorls are seen are original in ideas and they resent dominance of others. They are self-confident and depend upon their own whims. They are eloquent and lucid in expression, but they are more of listeners than of talkers. They have a secretive disposition and they keep their secrets to themselves.

Health : This type suffers from the nerve troubles and faulty action of the heart. It is very difficult to argue why this type should suffer from nervous disorder since it is so strong a type. However, it can be stated that the tips of the fingers always indicate the nervous disposition and, if small sensitive pads are found on the tips, it is a sure sign of nervous disorder. Thus, it will be noticed that any type of pattern on the tips exhibits nerve trouble. The intensity is however, to be judged by the particular pattern. In the case of the whorl, it can be stated that the intensity is not as much as that of the second type.

Fifth type : The last is the composite type (*fig. 48*). This pattern is formed by two apexes, running in loop formation in inverse directions as is shown in the figure. This is the practical type. It resembles in many respects the type shown by the square finger in its characteristics. But the main difference between this type and the square fingered type is that while the latter is practical and is backed-up by common sense and sound judgement, the former one is practical but lacks common sense. This person values everything in rupees, annas and pies but he does not take into consideration the emotional side of the life. Another defect with this person is that he lacks mental ability. He cannot understand the ideal views on life or ideal schemes in life. He is in short, a man of the basal world and third phalanges will make him a man of the world without high elevation of the mind. This composite type is the symbol of a marked lack of mental elasticity, it is the sign of narrow limitations everywhere.

Health: Since this type loves things of the world, it has a love for eating and many-times it leads to gluttony. The natural health development for the person of this type is the fatty one and he suffers from all health troubles which are due to fatty tendency. Since he lacks mental capacity, troubles like brain fever and dullness are common in him. His inability to work in the intellectual field makes him malignant and mental disorders resulting from malignant disposition are the natural outcome.

The Hindu System: These papillary ridges play an important part in the Hindu school of palmistry. The interpretation of these ridges on finger tips is based on experience. In the Hindu system, there are only three patterns of these ridges and not five as described above.

The first type is the *Shankh*. It is similar to the loop type. The ridge formation may run from right to left (*fig. 49*) or from left to right (*fig. 50*). the following is the significance of this type.

If the Shankh appears on—
    one finger only, the person is happy,
    two fingers, it is an unfavourable sign,
    three fingers, also is a bad sign,
    four fingers it is not a good indication,
    five fingers, it is not an auspicious sign,
    six fingers, the person has prowess,

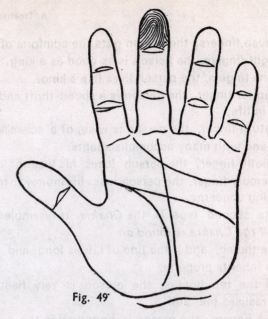

Fig. 49

Loop formation turning to the left

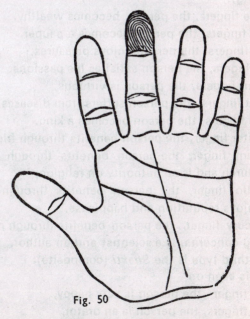

Fig. 50

Loop formation turning to the right

seven fingers, the person gets the comforts of a king,
eight fingers, the person is as good as a king,
nine fingers, the person lives like a king,
Jupiter finger, the person is a spend-thrift and unsteady in life,
Saturn finger, the person is wise, of a scientific outlook and with many accomplishments,
Apollo finger, the person loses his wealth in business
Mercury finger, the person loses his money in manufacturing concerns.

The second type is the *Chakra*. It resembles the whorl type. *If the Chakra is found on*

the thumb, and if the line of Life is long and good, the person inherits property,

all the ten fingers, the person is very happy and he realises the 'Self',
two fingers, the person is honoured in the courts of the king,
three fingers, the person becomes wealthy,
four fingers, the person becomes a pauper,
five fingers, the person enjoys pleasures,
six fingers, the person satisfies his passions,
seven fingers, the person is virtuous,
eight fingers, the person suffers from diseases,
nine fingers, the person becomes a king,
Jupiter finger, the person benefits through friends,
Saturn finger, the person benefits through religion or church and is an authority on religion,
Apollo finger, the person benefits through trade and enjoys reputation and happiness,
Mercury finger, the person benefits through manufacturing concerns, is a scientist and an author.

The third type is the *Shakti* (composite).
If it is seen on

one finger, the person is very happy,
two fingers, the person is an orator,
three fingers, the person is very rich,

four fingers, the person is virtuous,
five fingers, the person is a vedantin (philosopher),
six fingers, the person is of a high level of thinking,
seven or more fingers, it is a sign of success in life.

14 The Signs on fingers
The Jupiter finger

If there is a line encircling the first joint of the Jupiter finger, the person loses his vitality and has a scar on his skull. If there is a cross line on the second joint, the person is harmful and dishonest. If the cross line is seen on the third joint, the person acquires money from other people.

The Star

If there is a star on the first phalange, the person travels wide and in the end gets honour and fame. This person is very lucky and wealthy. If this star is seen on the second phalange, the person is very bold and courageous but he is very obstinate and forms rigid opinions. If the star is seen on the third phalange, the person is immoral.

Lines : Four vertical lines each on the second and the third phalanges of the Jupiter finger show a person who is virtuous and happy. If there are three vertical lines on the third phalange and a star on the bracelet, the person gets the money from others. If a line starts on the Jupiter finger and ends on the first joint of the thumb (*fig. 51*), the person is accused of crime and is found guilty and sentenced to death.

If the line at the root of the finger is broken, the person who has been appointed to perform the religious duties will rob him of his things.

The Saturn finger

Lines : If a line starts at the root of the Saturn finger and goes up to the first phalange of the finger (*fig. 52*) the person is very learned, gains victory and is wealthy. If however, the above mentioned line is not straight, the person dies in war.

The vertical lines on the middle phalange of the Saturn finger indicate success in difficult enterprises and also riches.

Few lines from the root of the finger up-to the first phalange indicate success in business connected with minerals.

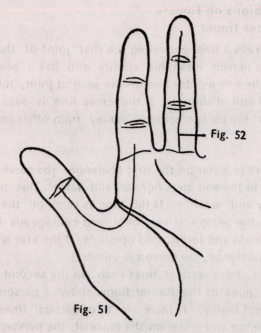

Fig. 51. Line from Jupiter upto thumb (Death sentence)
Fig. 52. Line from base to the top on Saturn finger (a scholar)

Vertical lines on the first phalange indicate a jealous person.

Vertical lines on the third phalange and very near the root of the finger indicate a person who is unlucky.

Star on the Saturn finger

If two stars are found on the third phalange with a break in the Head line under the Mount of Saturn, it means death. If found on a woman's hand, it means suicide in water.

A star on the first phalange denotes unhappiness.

The Fingers

A star on the third phalange denotes death through weapons or poison.

A star at the root of the finger denotes the sterility of the wife.

Triangle on the Saturn finger

A triangle on the first phalange denotes a person who will go to any extent to accomplish his selfish motive. A triangle on the third phalange denotes immoral character.

Spot on the Saturn finger

It denotes theft by one in his own family.

A spot on the third phalange indicates loss of money through women.

Island or Yava on the Saturn finger

An island on the second joint of the finger brings wealth, either through adoption, lottery or heredity.

Sign of an Angle

On the second phalange, it indicates a gambler. He can as well be a good conversationalist.

Sign of a Trident

On the third phalange it means a person who is surrounded by difficulties. He is tempted to commit theft and suffers from suffocation. This is however, a good sign if found on the Mount of Saturn.

The Finger of Apollo

Lines : Lines starting at the root of the finger and going up-to the first phalange indicate a person who is very lucky, wealthy and even an owner of mills. If there are many such lines, the person spends lavishly for his fiancee.

Vertical lines on the first phalange indicate a learned and a wise person. If any one of these lines is bending towards the sides of the finger near the knot, he acquires fame and reputation.

If there is any line which crosses the third knot, the person will come out successfully through all difficulties and impediments.

Star on the Apollo finger

It shows a person who is a spend-thrift.

Cross on the Apollo finger

On the first phalange and on a woman's hand, it indicates chastity.

The Finger of Mercury

Lines : If a line starts from the bottom of the finger and reaches up-to the first phalange, the person is a scientist and has a noble heart. If the lines are three in number, the person is a dreamer.

If there are strong vertical lines on the first phalange, the person is not healthy.

If there are two or three vertical lines on the middle phalange, the person pursues occult subjects. If however, these lines are broad and wavy, the person loses all bonds of morality.

A straight line from the bottom of the finger to the second phalange signifies an orator. If this line is not straight, the person is obstinate and follows his opinions rigidly.

Cross on the Mercury finger

A cross on the first phalange of the Mercury finger shows the person may not marry.

15 Zodical Signs on fingers (*figs. 53 and 54*).

The Zodiacal signs and the months shown by the different phalanges have great importance in preparing the horoscope from the hand. The readers will be surprised to know that according to Hindu system, there are certain definite methods of calculating the exact day, the month and the year of birth from an examination of the hand. By the adoption

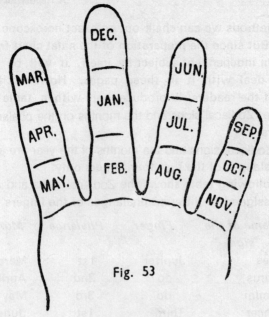

Fig. 53

Fingers and months

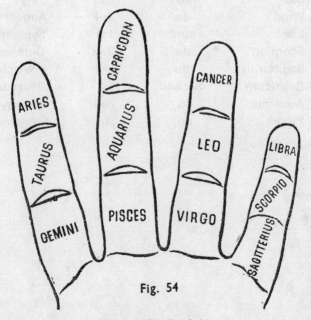

Fig. 54

Fingers and zodiacal signs

of such methods we can chalk-out an exact horoscope of the person. But since the preparation of the natal chart from the hand, is an independent subject by itself, it will be out of place to deal with it in these pages. However, for the interest of the readers, I produce here-with a table which shows the Zodiacal signs and the months on the phalanges of the fingers.

The Zodiacal signs and the months of the year are assigned to the phalanges of the first four fingers only.

The following table shows the Zodiacal signs and also the months assigned to different phalanges of the fingers.

No.	Name of the sign	Finger	Phalange	Month
1	Aries	Jupiter	1st	March
2	Taurus	do	2nd	April
3	Gemini	do	3rd	May
4	Cancer	Third	1st	June
5	Leo	do	2nd	July
6	Virgo	do	3rd	August
7	Libra	Fourth	1st	September
8	Scorpion	do	2nd	October
9	Sagittarius	do	3rd	November
10	Capricorn	Second	1st	December
11	Aquarius	do	2nd	January
12	Pisces	do	3rd	February

CHAPTER IX

The Thumb

Introduction

In all the books on palmistry, the thumb is considered as the most important part of the palm. References are made regarding the examination of the thumb alone and it is said that ancient Hindu and Egyptian systems based their entire work on the thumb.

In religion and history, the thumb has been used to signifty the will and the decision of the person. Ancient Romans used the word "pollice truncatus" to mean a cowardly citizen who cut his thumb to obviate his possibility of being sent to the war. This is recorded of a Roman citizen at the time of Augustus Caesar, who cut off the thumb of his two sons so as to keep them at home. The Chinese have a most minute and intricate system based solely on the capillaries of the first phalange. Cherio has given very interesting information of how the thumb secured its high place in religion. The Romans in their gladiatorial displays raised their thumbs and the combatant struck down received his life. If they lowered the thumbs, he died.

Evolution

In the evolution of man we find the existence of the thumb in monkeys. But there also the thumb is not fully developed. Sir Charles Bell has in his works called attention to the fact that in the paw or the hand of the Chimpanzee, which is the nearest approach to human being, the thumb, although well-formed in every way does not reach the base of the first finger. The deduction therefore is that the longer and better formed is the thumb, the more the man has developed beyond the brute creation. In the case of the monkey's thumb, we find that it is very weak and high set. It also lacks the ability to oppose the fingers. It is found mostly on the hands of man only. It shows the development of the will-power and the ability of the brain for higher thinking.

Psychological significance of the thumb

If we observe the position of the thumb under different situations, we shall be convinced of the psychological aspect of the thumb and its direct relation to brain. The main characteristic exhibited by the thumb is logic and reason which is the speciality of man only. The man can think and plan many years in advance, a faculty which is peculiar to him only. In the animals, it has been found that they can visualise a thing or think of an object only a few minutes in advance. The development of the will-power is indicated by the development of the thumb. The carriage of the thumb is a good indicator of individuality. A thumb closer to the hand shows lesser development of the will-power and of the individuality than when it is away from other fingers. It is very interesting to observe the thumb of a newly born baby when the thumb remains closed in the hand and other fingers cover it. It shows undeveloped individuality and will. After a few weeks the thumb gradually comes out of the fingers which is a symptom showing the beginning of development of the Will. Similarly, we can observe the reverse process when the man is on his death-bed. In this case, the thumb gradually starts coming in the folds of the fingers, a symptom indicating loss of the Will. As long as the thumb is outside the hand, we can know that the Will is fighting the illness, but the moment it is completely closed by other fingers, we can be sure that the Will to survive is lost and the person will succumb to his illness.

Thus a relation is being established between the thumb and the development of the Will, logic and reason. We shall now proceed with the study of the thumb in greater details.

Large and Small Thumbs

There are two types of thumbs, large thumbs and small thumbs.

Large Thumbs

People with large thumbs are governed by their head and are more at ease in an atmosphere of ideas than of sentiments. They judge things better by reflection than on the spur of the moment. Persons who have large thumbs are masters and they do not allow them-selves to be ruled by others. They have principles which form their laws. This characteristic of the large thumb often makes such persons powerful and they are susceptible to despotism. Large thumbs indicate trustworthiness and high intellectual ability. Sometimes a large thumb is considered as a sign of remarkable aptitude for the occult sciences. Thus whenever a large thumb is seen, it should mean strong will-power, determination, reason, love of history and force of character.

Small Thumbs

Small thumbs exhibit such characteristics which are incompatible with those of the large thumbs. Naturally, persons with small thumbs are ruled by sentiments and emotions. These persons are attracted towards the ideal and poetical imagination. They are governed by their hearts and are more at ease in a atmosphere of sentiments than in one of ideas. They appreciate things more at a rapid glance at them than on reflection. A thumb, which is small and weak, means an irresolute mind and a wavering disposition in those things which require the reasoning power. Such people are impressionable, sensual and dominated by their innate tendencies, but they are at the same time impartial, tolerant, naturally amiable and able to accommodate themselves to all characters with whom they are thrown together.

Comparison between large and small thumbs

After studying the above characteristics of large and small thumbs, a comparison between the two will be useful.

1) Large thumbs show a powerful character, small thumbs the reverse of it.

2) Large thumbs have attraction towards mathematics, small thumbs have fancy for poetry.

3) Large thumbs are guided by reason, small thumbs by emotions.

4) Large thumbs go in for the practical and useful things, small thumbs go in for artistic and decorative things.

The result is that the persons with small thumbs find it very difficult to get on with persons with large thumbs. They lack logic and reason and are unable to convince others.

Women with large or small thumbs have an interesting personality. Large thumbs make them more intelligent than sensitive and small thumbs make them more sensitive than intelligent. For pleasure and consideration for others, we must look for a large-thumbed woman. Love under her clear sighted guidance attains its end without scandal, her passion which she follows without consulting her head, has more root in her senses than in the heart. Leave her alone and trust her skill, at the right moment she will come to the assistance of your timidity, not because she has much sympathy with your torments, but in the interest of her own pleasures. Besides complete security, her many graces of mind will add to the joy of winning her.

Women with small thumbs are not endowed with so high a degree of sagacity. Their whole science is to love and they do not find equal delight in any-other thing.

After studying the large and small thumbs a difficulty may arise as to how to judge a large thumb and a small thumb. The thumb is of normal length when the tip of the

The Thumb

thumb reaches the middle of the third phalange of the finger of Jupiter.

Position of the thumb

After noting whether the thumb is large or small, the next thing to be noted is its position on the hand. There are three positions of thumb (i) high set (ii) low set and (iii) medium set.

i) High set thumb (*fig. 55*)

If we compare the human thumb with the simian thumb, we find that the thumb of a monkey is very high set and the

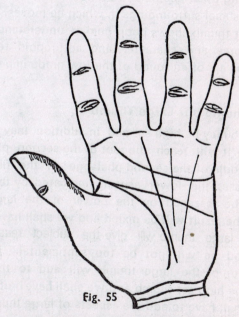

Fig. 55

High set thumb (mean minded and selfish)

carriage of the same is very close to the hand. The thumb of a monkey is very stiff and it does not have the capacity to oppose other fingers which is the characteristic of the human thumb. Thus, when we find a high set thumb on the hand of a man, we can say that the person has not developed his mental plane and is nearer the brute creation. His ideas are simian, his attitude is brutish and his likes and dislikes are of the basal world, that is to say, they are poor, in a crude form and those concerning only the satisfaction of the lower desires. The person is mean-minded, very selfish and looks to his own self only. He does not have generosity, does not know the good and higher aspects of human life and is crooked in his ideas and behaviour.

By its high position on the hand, the thumb does not have the capacity to stand away from the hand and thus, it is carried very close to the hand. It shows lack of independent thinking and social adaptability. This person is incapable of understanding other people and cannot mould himself according to the social surroundings in which he moves. In short, this high set thumb shows poor human understanding, lack of moral force and character and anthropoid tendencies. Such thumbs are often found of the low grade imbeciles and idiots.

High set Thumb but Large Thumb

A thumb may be high set and in addition may be large. In that case it will reach the root of the second phalange or even the middle of the second phalange of the first finger. In such a case, the lower aspects indicated by the high set thumb will be lessened by the power of the large thumb. However, the result will be mxied and we shall have a typical subject. A large thumb will give the subject reasoning and capacity and he will not be too sentimental. But strong determination of the large thumb will add to the sensual nature of the high set thumb and we shall have brutal tyranny. Thus, we shall have to add the aspects of large thumb to the high set thumb and make comprehensive judgement.

High Set but Small thumb

This is the worst type of combination since the lower aspects of the small thumb will be added to an already bad type of thumb. The subject will become more sensual, weak

The Thumb

and eccentric since he will completely lack the moral character and force of mind. He behaves like an animal and exhibits all the traits of the monkey. This is certainly not a good combination to have.

ii) Low Set Thumb (*fig 56*)

When the hand is stretched before us we can at-once recognise the low set thumb by its low position on the mount of Venus and much away from the finger of Jupiter. This thumb is a symbol of a very high level of mind which is full of sympathy, generosity and love which are the characteristics

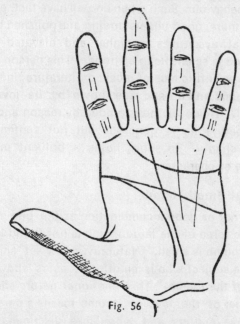

Low set thumb (sympathy and generosity)

of the Mount of Venus. By its position on the Mount of Venus, this thumb partakes all the good qualities of that mount and we have a subject whose heart has warmth, whose reason is backed by understanding and whose behaviour is full of sincerity. Such a person is more practical and is ruled by his common-sense, unlike the subject with a high set thumb, who is guided by his sentiments and emotions. Since this thumb absorbs the qualities of the mount of Venus, the subject has a sense of beauty and appreciates the more artistic and fine things in nature.

Low set but Large Thumb

A thumb though low set on the hand may be a large thumb. This is a best formation for the hand to possess. (case 3). Good qualities of large thumb together with good qualities of the low set thumb, will make a subject of exemplary behaviour. Such a person will have tact, eloquence, elegant manners, good understanding and polished behaviour. The person always strives for higher and elevated things in the world and is scientific in attitude. This person will look more to the scientific side of music or literature indicated by the large thumb and artistic side shown by its low position on the hand. However, he is guided by reason and does not throw sympathy, he is generous but not sentimental and careless in charity. In short, he is a brilliant man with a strong force of character.

Low set but Small Thumb

This is not as good a combination as the one mentioned above. The force of the large thumb is not found in the case where the thumb is small. Naturally, a low set small thumb will create a subject who is emotional, as is shown by the smallness of the thumb. This emotional nature added to the sensual side of the low set thumb means a person who is hasty in love matters and who lacks discrimination. The small thumb indicates selfish nature and though the low set thumb shows generosity, the person is generous but he expects something in return for his generosity. He will not help others out of charity, but with a motive to benefit out of such a help. In short, this thumb though good in its way does not exhibit such elevated characteristics as the one mentioned previously.

The Thumb

iii) Medium set Thumb (*fig. 57*)

This is the thumb which is not too high or too low on the hand and which by its medium position gives good shape to the hand. This is the thumb of the practical man who is reasonable in ordinary matters in life and who is also sentimental on proper occasions. He has good understanding and can know the feelings of others. This thumb gives a balanced mind and shows a hand which exhibits commonsense, materialism, practical outlook and enthusiasm.

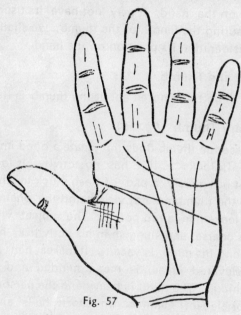

Fig. 57
Medium set thumb (balanced mind)

Length of the Thumb

My readers might confuse large thumbs with long thumbs. The large thumb is long in addition to its being big in shape. The shape of the thumb is dealt with in the next paragraph. But mention should be made here that a large thumb is a combination of a long thumb and a big thumb. How we have to judge a big thumb is also dealt with in the following paragraph.

A thumb to be normal in length must reach the middle phalange of the Jupiter finger. A thumb longer than this is generally considered as a long thumb and a thumb that is shorter than this length is supposed as a small thumb. The word 'generally' is used because the length of the thumb will again depend upon the setting of the thumb. A thumb which is low set may not reach the normal level of the Jupiter finger, but still it may not be a short thumb because by its low position on the hand, it may not have its usual level. Thus, in measuring the length of the thumb, we shall have to take into consideration its position on the hand.

The Shape of the Thumb

The next thing to be noted about the thumb is its shape.

i) Elementary Thumb (fig. 58)

In this case the thumb does not create a good impression on our mind. It looks as if it has no activity. It looks dull and dead. It has merely a pad of flesh stuck to the hand. The joints of the thumb are not visible and the phalanges are uniform. It looks like a red potato. The subject who holds this thumb is coarse, and sluggish in his activities, he has no enthusiasm and his mind is vacant. It makes him indolent. He has no elevated ideas, is mean minded and slow to understand things. The mind is heavy and the person has no grace, tact or elegant manners. In short, he is animal-like and brutal. It is brutal force in will, brutal force in reasoning and brutal passion in love. It is the manifestation of ignorant obstinacy, operated in an unreasoning way.

ii) Strongly developed thumb (fig. 59)

This is the thumb, the shape of which is attractive and has grace with its position on the hand. This thumb when observed from nail side has the strong appearance and we can judge its power to oppose the fingers. In this case the

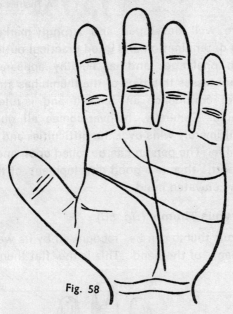

Fig. 58

Elementary thumb (dull intellect and blunt nature)

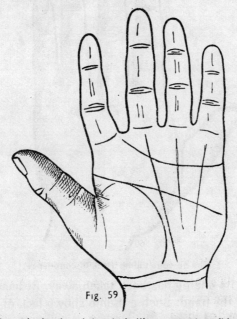

Fig. 59

Strongly developed thumb (will power and confidence)

phalanges are well developed and strongly marked which shows strong determination and good practical outlook. It is broad in both phalanges and has healthy appearance. The person who possesses this type of the thumb has strong will-power, perfect confidence in himself and is ruled by his reason and logic. Generally, he over-comes all obstacles in his way and ultimately wins over the difficulties and becomes successful in life. The person can be relied upon and is trust-worthy. In short, this is a good development of the thumb and shows the elevated mind.

iii) **The Nervous Thumb** (*fig. 60*)

The nervous thumb can be recognised by its weak position and carriage of the hand. This is the flat thumb and it

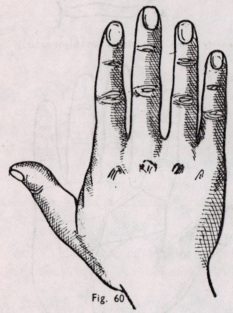

Fig. 60

The nervous thumb (lack of confidence)

looks as if all its energy has been taken away. It hangs loose by the side of the hand. Such a thumb shows lack of nervous energy and lack of force. The subject is nervous and does not have the capacity to bear the shocks of the ordinary day-to-day life. He has no mental strength and is unable to arrive at decisions. In fact, he is carried only by his nervous energy and is merely driven forward by his nervous activity. He finds it difficult to keep his nerves under control and he is likely to suffer from all sorts of nervous diseases. Such thumbs are usually seen on the hands of persons suffering from feeble-mindedness. In short, this thumb shows lack of self-confidence, lack of will-power and lack of determination. This thumb is usually accompanied by a fluted nail which means additional weakness to the already existing type. This person may be intelligent, he may have originality which can be judged by a good formation of the Head line, but he will not be able to use his intelligence and talents. He will always fear public rumours and scandals and will think that others would not take in proper spirit what he speaks to them. Naturally, these persons carry a solitary life and lag behind.

iv) The Diplomatic Thumb (fig. 61)

This is the thumb which is uniform throughout and the phalanges are well-developed. The tip of the thumb is usually strong and the whole thumb looks attractive. This thumb does not have the strength of the strong thumb or the weakness of the nervous thumb. But, when it opposes the fingers, it looks firm and artistic. This is the diplomatic thumb. This person does not like to criticise others and keeps everything to himself. He will never disturb others and even if he differs from them he will never attack them. But he will influence all those who come in his contact and his presence in his circle is so compelling that others may find it difficult not to grant his wish. Thus, this person gets what he wants but at the same time he never burdens others. He is very social, but at the same time keeps-up his originality. He mixes in all circles of people but is firm in his opinions and ideas. He has tact, refinement and elegant manners. In short, this is the beautiful thumb which attracts others towards its owner, and fills the lives of all others around him with beauty.

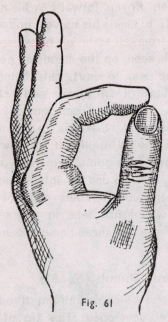

Fig. 61

The diplomatic thumb (tact of diplomacy)

v) The Clubbed Thumb (fig. 62)

Every student of Cheirosophy has heard about the clubbed thumb but I think very few of them might have seen one. The clubbed thumb has been marked as the murderer's thumb because it has been observed on the hands of many murderers. But that does not mean that all those who possess it will commit a murder. Since the hand reflects the psychological bent of the person, it can truthfully be said of such a thumb that the person has cruel and murderous instincts, which may be dormant in him. These instincts may not show themselves even for the whole life, because of the environment, if it is good, it will not give an opportunity to the person to show off his characteristics. *I very well remember the visit*

The Thumb

of one of my clients who had this clubbed thumb and who disclosed to me during our discussions, that many times he thought of killing his wife. He also explained that there were no specific reasons which made him think so, but occasionally he was moody and during those moods he used to feel like killing his wife.

Fig. 62

The clubbed thumb (cruelty)

As we know that the hand also reflects hereditary qualities, this clubbed thumb is often found in families. But the murderous instincts according to the modern criminal investigation are not hereditary. Authorities on criminology do not believe that men are born as criminals. However, I would like to point out to them that though their observations are right to a certain extent, the clubbed thumb is usually a characteristic showing heredity.

The peculiarities of this thumb are that it is very thick and broad in the first phalange. The nail is short and coarse. The thickness of the first phalange shows obstinacy and shortness indicates violent temper. As has been said above the clubbed thumb may not exhibit its characteristics throughout the life, but, if it is found on a bad hand, the person is very dangerous to keep company with.

When we come across such a thumb, we should be careful to note other signs on the hand before we pronounce the judgement.

Red colour will show ardour, texture will show refinement, consistency will show energy, flexibility will show elasticity of the mind, the Mount of Venus will show love. All these aspects when properly considered and understood will assist us to estimate this most difficult and dangerous indication.

vi) Paddle-shaped thumb (*fig. 63*)

This thumb at first sight resembles the clubbed thumb. But if we carefully note the development of this thumb we

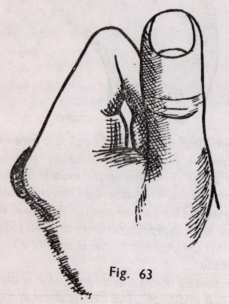

Fig. 63

Paddle shaped thumb (determination and tenancity

shall find a great difference between this thumb and the clubbed thumb. The similarity between the two thumbs is regarding the breadth. Both the thumbs are broad in shape. Both the thumbs have this breadth in the first or the top phalange. But the difference is as follows : the clubbed thumb is short in its first phalange and thick in addition to its being broad. But the paddle-shaped thumb is only broad and is not very thick. Another difference is that the clubbed thumb is usually found on the hand of a person who possesses robust health whereas, the second type of thumb is found on the hands of men who generally are weak in constitution.

After observing the above difference between the clubbed thumb and the paddle-shaped thumb, I am sure that the readers will be able to distinguish the one from the other. To go ahead, the paddle-shaped thumb shows strong determination and tenacity of purpose. If the development is excessive, It will mean that the person will go to any extent to achieve his ends and may use brutal force and tyranny is the result. The person has weak health but the development of the first phalange of this thumb shows that the person is backed by strong nervous force. This force is in operation as long as the aim is not achieved but once he gets out of the emergency by his constant will-power he loses his control over his nerves and his energy breaks down.

vii) The Waist-like thumb (*fig. 64*)

Occasionally we confront a thumb which is waist-like in its formation. The thumb is narrow in its second phalange and it looks as if it is twisted. The figure shown will give a clear idea of the shape of this type of thumb. This is one of the good formations of the thumb and the owner of this thumb has tact in him. He knows very well how to approach others and is very good at manners. He has talents and can influence others by his talk. He is intelligent and can partake in the discussions. He is elegant and refined. In short, he has all the necessary virtues in him which are necessary to achieve success in society and the ends in view. This person on the strength of his tact, refinement and elegant talk can win the good-will of all those with whom he comes in contact and, without disturbing others in the least, will get from others what he wants.

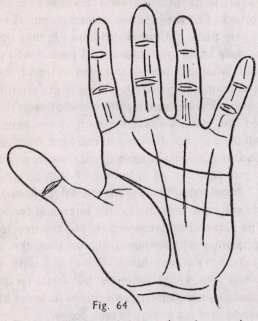

Fig. 64

The waist-like thumb (talents and good manners)

Since the second phalange of the thumb shows logic and reason and since it is twisted in the waist-like formation of the thumb, it means shrewdness. The logic of the person is cunning and the reasoning is very shrewd. He has lips which would please others. In the end however he gets what he wants and others also shower him for generosity and goodwill. In short, persons with waist-like formation of the thumb are good companions to meet with.

Phalanges of the thumb

The first phalange shows will-power and determination, the second phalange shows reason and logic and the third one which is known as Mount of Venus shows love and sympathy.

If the first phalange of the thumb is longer than the second phalange, the person has strong determination and strong will-power. He is very powerful in his actions and, unless it is backed by a good Head line or second phalange of the thumb, the subject is likely to take such steps which prove wrong in the long run. The lack of reason and logic invites hasty steps and thereby the subject suffers intensely. When long in length, the first phalange shows tyranny and foolish obstinacy. In such a case the person is stubborn and will fight out his way to the last. He will first act and then think over the matter. He is impetuous and hard to be convinced. This is the type which shows how the good qualities in man, if led too far, make him unsuccessful in life.

If the second phalange of the thumb is longer than the first one, it shows a person whose logic and reason are more developed than his determination. He is a good reasoner and his logic is powerful. He is very intelligent and can grasp things very easily. His ideas are pertaining to the every-day world and he counts everything in rupees, annas and pies. He has sound judgement and can advice others on matters of importance. The great defect of this type is that the person is merely a reasoner and is sophistic but he will not bring his ideas and reason into practice. Since action requires strong mental force and determination, the person with good reason lags behind owing to the weakness of the first phalange. He is more a talker than a doer.

If the second phalange is very long, the person discusses everything to death, trusts no body and is paradoxical to a degree. If the phalange is short, it means lack of reasoning power. Too short in length, the second phalange shows lack of simple common-sense and the person does not like to think before he acts.

If the second phalange is long and also broad, it reveals good understanding of material things. But if it is short and broad, it shows primitive type of intellect since it resembles the ape type

Sometimes this phalange is slender in shape. It shows refinement in thought but nervousness affects the reasoning power.

Thus, in studying the phalanges of the thumb we should carefully note the following things, 1) length of phalanges, 2) their shape, 3) their thickness.

Let us now study the third phalange of the thumb. The third phalange of the thumb is the Mount of Venus. It is generally longer than the first two. The simple reason is that the ball of the thumb is formed by the bone which is in the metacarpus and which is longer than the bones in the first two phalanges. Generally the inner portion of the line of life shows the third phalange of the thumb excluding the Mount of Mars. According to our hypothesis, if this third phalange is longer, it should exhibit the characteristic of the Mount of Venus. Venus shows love, sympathy and generosity. These characteristics are usually found in different persons but they get no proper opportunity to show these virtues in them. In order that these characteristics should be seen in a person, his other two phalanges should also be taken into consideration. Unless his will-power and logic are sound, his generosity and sympathy have no value. So his first two phalanges should be well balanced so as to enable him to get the benefit of the third phalange of the thumb. If he lacks determination and good reasoning, he will only get the other side of the Mount of Venus which shows gratification of the basal desires. In short, the third phalange should be properly backed by the first two phalanges in order to have its full effect on the subject. More information about this will be found in the chapter on the Mount of Venus.

Tips of the thumb

Tips of the thumb must always be considered with the shape of the thumb. As is in the case of the fingers, the tips of the thumb either enhance or reduce the strength of the thumb. There are always four types of tips which are to be taken into consideration, square, spatulate, conic and pointed.

Square tip of the thumb

Square shape always denotes practical out-look, materialism, scientific attitude, love for history, good reason and calculating tendency. This shape may be of the hand proper, or of the fingers, or of the tips of the fingers and the thumb. Though its significance is the same, its location on the hand has a different interpretation. For example, a square tip to the Jupiter finger carries a different meaning from a square tips to the Saturn finger. Smooth fingers with square tips will carry a different significance from knotty fingers with square tips. Thus, the significance of the different tips should be combined with the characteristics of the individual fingers and then arrive at a decision.

Square tip to the first phalange

While studying the tip of the thumb, it is important to note which phalange of the thumb is more developed. If the first phalange is more developed and it bears a square tip, it shows a person whose ideas are more developed than reason and, are based on sound knowledge. This type of combination lessens the impractical side of the first phalange and a square tip makes up the deficiency.

Squre tip to the second phalange

When the second phalange of the thumb is more developed than the first and the thumb possesses a square tip, it gives the person more of reason as shown by the second phalange and it is strengthened by the virtues of the square tip. In such a case the person is a good speaker and his eloquence is backed by good logic and well-stored information. It is very difficult to convince such a person since he has his own judgement and sound common-sense. He is very practical and counts everything from a pecuniary point of view. The fault with him is that sometimes he is sophistic and pedantic.

Spatulate tip to the first phalange

If the first phalange of the thumb is more developed and if it possesses a spatulate tip, the characteristics of the spatulate tip will be added to the mental aspect shown by the first phalange. Thus, the subject will have original ideas and he will always be hunting for inventions. He will be a mental wanderer and he may look a fanatic to the outside world because he will have such ideas as will not be appreciated by others. They are mentally more active and are very enthusiastic about their achievements. Will-power and determination as shown by the first phalange when added to the mental vigour shown by the spatulate tip makes the subject obstinate. In spite of much opposition he tries to bring his ideas into practice, but often suffers intensely through bad luck.

Spatulate tip to the second phalange

If the second phalange of the thumb is developed and if it bears a spatulate tip, the person is more active in useful things, since materialism is shown by the second phalange and activity is shown by the tip. Such a person is interested in constructing bridges and roads which have permanent value, but at the same time he will have originality in constructing such bridges. For example he will not merely do the useful thing, but he will have new ideas which will keep his name alive for future generations. I know of a person whose thumb was developed like this. He had interest in constructing roads which would be straight only. He disliked curves and corners and he suggested to the Government that certain roads and high-ways should be very straight as far as possible. On one occasion he suggested that there was no necessity of any road round the hill and a long tunnel even of two miles should be constructed.

Conic tip to the first phalange of the thumb

A thumb may have a conic tip. If the first phalange is developed it means a mental wanderer who has idealistic views on life. Since he has strong determination and willpower, he tries to bring his ideas into practice but since he lacks common-sense, he meets with great failure. He is very obstinate and a strong headed person. He thinks that the world is full of foolish people who have no ambition and who are indolent. He thinks that if his plans are brought into practice, the world will be saved from many afflictions and sorrows.

Conic tip to the second phalange

If the second phalange of the thumb is developed, a conic tip to the thumb reduces to a great extent the materialism shown by the second phalange and the person is shaky in his ideas, has no confidence and takes up silly arguments.

Pointed tip

A pointed tip is an exaggerated form of the conic tip and is not a good thing to have. It destroys all the qualities of the thumb and the person is eratic, feeble minded and weak in his mental strength and logic.

Knot of the thumb (*fig. 65*)

Sometime a well-developed knot is found between the first phalange and the second. As has been stated while dealing with fingers, knots denote a natural barrier to the passing of current to the brain. It takes some time to grasp an idea or to send the message to the brain. But once an idea is grasped, it finds deep roots in the brain of the person. This knot shows a thoughtful nature, a slow thinking person and a brain well-developed in mental strength. It is therefore a good check for the mental wanderer whose first phalange is developed and also for the person whose second phalange is developed and who values everything from the material point of view. Thus, this knot gives a balancing power to the two phalanges and the person is saved from taking a wrong step or from going to extremities. It greatly strengthens a conic tip and adds force to all the other tips. It increases the reasoning of the second phalange by reducing the intuition of the first, making a hasty operation of the will, until thought and consideration have had a chance.

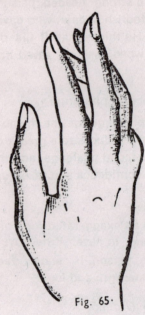

Fig. 65.

Knots of the thumb

Flexibility of the thumb (*fig. 66*)

The flexible thumb which is judged by the fact that it bends back at the joint, shows that the person is extravagant, brilliant, versatile and easily adaptable. He is very generous and sympathetic and also emotional. His moods vary, one day he is in a good mood, another day he is in a depressed mood. He has talent and versatility. He is most brilliant and happy natured, but often ruined by his brilliance. When we come across such a thumb, we should look for indications that may

The Thumb

hold in check the supple thumb qualities. Square tips, a good Head line and a good Mount of Saturn will do more than any other combination to hold them in balance. Spatulate will not help them nor will conic impulse.

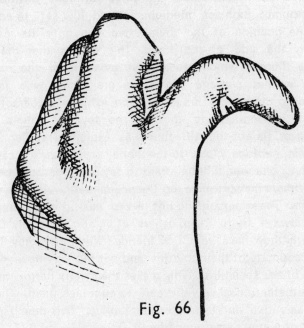

Fig. 66

Flexible thumb (extravagance and versatility)

The stiff thumb has all the characteristics which are incompatible with those mentioned above. This thumb has a tendency to carry itself erect and close to the hand as well as to be stiff in the joint. The stiff-thumbed subject is practical, economical, stingy and weighs everything carefully. Those who have it, possess a strong will, stubborn determination and are cautious, reserved and do not give or invite confidence. They save their money. They are steady not extremists, do not expect a great deal and are consequently in their way but it is in a quiet fashion. They have a sense of justice and great self-control. They do not go in for many things and attempt only a few but they succeed in their undertaking. If the stiff thumb is coarse and common, it will lower the qualities of all its attributes and makes a man stingy and hard hearted.

Carriage of the thumb

We have considered the three different positions of the thumb, high set, medium set and low set. In addition to the position of the thumb, we can note its carriage along the side of the hand. This means that there are some thumbs which are always away from the hand in their normal carriage and there are others who lie very close to the hand. This latter type exhibits a characteristic which is opposite to that of the low set thumb. This however, is not the stiff thumb as explained earlier. By its peculiar carriage close to the hand, it indicates a cautious person, one who will be afraid to say much because he fears that others may presume on the acquaintance and ask some favour. These persons do not like to mix-up with others and they always try to keep others at an arm's length. Consequently they have very few friends. Naturally, they have a high estimate of their abilities and get but very little experience of the social life. This makes them verry narrow minded and others find it very difficult to approach them. They are very secretive and lack the adaptability. This thumb shows want of warmth and sympathy.

Thumb in combination with other aspects on the hand

By now we have understood the importance of the thumb in reading the full character of the person. We shall now consider it in combination with other factors on the hand.

First, we should note the mount on the hand which is most developed. It would give us an idea of the working of the person's mind.

If the person is a Jupiterian, his pride, honour religion, ambition and other qualities will get a turn according to the development of his thumb. We should note which phalange of the thumb is most developed. If the first phalange is developed, his pride will be egoistic, his honour will be levelled too high, his religious ideas will be firm and his ambition very high. If however his second phalange is more developed, his pride will be reasonable, his honour based on material success, his religion of every-day life and ambition will have a pecuniary value.

If he is a Saturnian, he will have sober mind, philosophic attitude and melancholy thoughts. These we shall find if the first phalange of his thumb is developed. If however, the second phalange is developed, his reason will be powerful and logic very sound in all matters of day-to-day life. He will not aspire for too high a post in life but he will get his success through hard work because Saturnians are good workers.

The same logic and reasoning will be applied to other mounts on the hand.

Another factor to be taken into consideration is the colour of the hand. Red colour will make the will-power more rigid and the person will be obstinate. If the second phalange is developed, the red colour will mean impertinent arguments. Pink colour will show a balanced temper and the person will be approachable.

The third thing to be noted is the consistency and the texture of the hand. Fine texture indicates refined brain, and when added to the first phalange of the thumb, it means clear cut ambition and broad views. There is no muddle of ideas in the brain. The person has good outlook in life and knows very-well how to bring his ideas into action. If the second phalange is developed and the texture is fine, the person has elegant manners, can talk well and can understand the logic and reasoning of others

Another quality of the texture of the hand is the coarse one. If the texture is coarse and the first phalange is developed, the person's will-power and determination has brutal force behind the will. If the second phalange is developed, the arguments and reasoning of the person are very blunt.

In short, the thumb should be considered in combination with other signs and marks on the hand. In fact, lines on the hand should also be taken into consideration but since the lines are not considered in this volume, permutations and combination of lines with the thumb are deleted herewith. However, it is sufficient to know that every factor on the hand should be mixed with every other factor before the final word is passed.

The signs on the thumb

The last thing to be studied about the thumb is the signs on the thumb. Stars, crosses, squares, triangle and other minor signs are found all over the hand and their importance is located according to the place where they are found. The majority of these indications are, however, of a traditional or atleast of an empirical nature and it is not easy to connect them logically with what is called scientific cheirosophy. However, tradition has proved its worth and we experience its validity in our every-day practice. So without trying to probe into the scientific explanation of these signs, we shall study their significance which will be interesting and useful.

Signs on the first phalange of the thumb

Vertical lines on the first phalange of the thumb indicate will-power. But the number of such lines is restricted to three lines only. More than three lines mean obstacles in getting the success.

Small vertical lines near the nail show legacies (*fig. 67 A*).

A line from the first phalange to the line of Life shows death from a metalic weapon like a sword or a dagger (*fig. 67 B*).

Two lines running from the first phalange to the line of Life indicate riches and wealth. If these two lines run very near to each other, almost touching each other, the person loses all his estate in lottery and speculation.

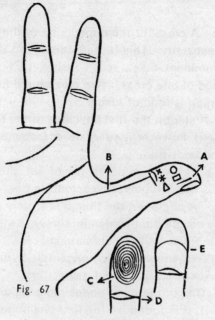

Fig. 67

Signs on thumb

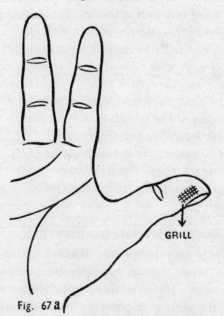

Fig. 67 a

Signs on thumb (danger to partner)

Cross : A cross at the upper side of the first phalange indicates unchastity. This is particularly so if the Mount of Venus is prominent.

If instead of one cross, two crosses are found, it shows that the person is fond of luxury.

Star : A star on the first phalange of the thumb indicates immorality. If however two stars are found the person is captious and fault-finding.

Triangle : If a triangle is found on this phalange, it concentrates the will-power on scientific field.

Circle : A circle on the thumb is a very good sign and its presence on the first phalange shows a steady person in determination who will get ultimate success.

Square : A square means concentration in one direction. Sometimes it shows tyrannical disposition.

Grill : One of the most undesirable signs on the thumb is the grill. If it is found on the first phalange and especially near the nail, it shows danger to the life partner of the person on whose hand this grill is found. The danger is even to the extent of death through the person himself.

Chakra (whorl) : In dealing with the signs on the fingers I have dealt with this type of sign. If this sign has a southward direction (see fig. 67 C), it is regarded as a lucky mark on the hand. If found on the hand of a woman whose middle portion of the thumb is big and round, it is a bad sign and it shows infidelity and immorality.

Island or Lotus : It shows legacy (67 D).

Rainbow : A sign like a rainbow on the thumb shows wealth and the person gets all the comforts and luxuries of life. (67 E).

Signs on the first joint of the thumb

If there is one prominent line on the first joint of the thumb and if this line is in a slanting position, it shows a wealthy person. If two or three vertical lines run down from this joint, the person is good at heart and of a lovable disposition.

The Thumb

If there is a line which encircles the thumb on the first joint, it shows that the person will end his life on the scaffold.

Signs on the second phalange of the thumb

Vertical lines : If there are two or three lines on the second phalange running downward, it shows sound reasoning power.

Cross lines : Cross lines show that the person has no sound judgment and reasoning. His reasoning is often false and lacks common-sense.

Cross : A cross indicates that the person does not have firm views and is often influenced by the views and opinions of others.

Star : One or two stars on the second phalange show that the person is susceptible to temptation and can easily follow the path to satisfy his vulgar desires.

Triangle : A triangle shows deep scientific, philosophical talents.

Squares : A square on this phalange of the thumb means logic that is firm. If the hand belongs to the bad category, this square means blind stubbornness.

Circle : Circle on the second phalange has the same meaning as the circle on the first phalange. It shows triumph and success in argument.

Grill : It shows lack of moral sense and of honest reasoning methods.

A line from the second phalange to the line of Life shows troubles in married life.

Signs on the second joint of the thumb

If a line starts from the second joint of the thumb and runs towards the line of Life, it shows wealth. Sometimes when this line is very thin and long, it shows inheritance and, if there are two or more lines, it means riches.

Vertical lines on the joint show the number of brothers and sisters. But if these lines are too thick and black in colour, they indicate the death of brothers and sisters.

A cross or a star on the second joint of the thumb of a woman is a good sign and it shows wealth.

Islands or Yavas, as they are called in the Hindu system, on the second joint of the thumb indicate the number of children.

CHAPTER X

The Nails

Most of the students of Palmistry ignore nails in their study of the hand. As a matter of fact, nails are also very important in delineating the temperament of the person in general and the health condition in particular. I will give below some information regarding nails and their significance.

1 Evolution

The evolution of the nails depends upon their functional role. In animals, they serve as organs of attack and of apprehension; in man, these functions have become atrophied. It is true our nails are still to a small extent, organs of apprehension, as for example, when we use them for picking-up pins or other minute objects, but in general they are little more than a shield to protect the finger tips. The nails are the first tissues of the body to appear as early as the ninth week of prenatal life. The embryonic nail, which is delicate and transparent and without moons differs from the adult nail also in texture.

2 Anatomy

In structure and substance they resemble the hair. Both hair and nails lose their shining quality in states of reduced vitality. Great difference in the size of the nails exist between individuals. The size depends largely on the form of the hand to which they belong. In long hands for instance, they are generally elongated, in the other types, especially the elementary, they are broad and short. The nail of the thumb is always the biggest, and that of the little finger the smallest. Weel Jones noted that in right-handed people the nails of the right hand develop faster than those of the left. The nail entirely renews itself in 130 to 160 days. After the age of thirty the rate of growth declines, a fact which in itself shows that general vitality and a full function of the main springs of health are reflected in the nails.

The normal development of the nail is even and smooth in surface and it is not composed of ridges or flutings. It must also look alive and elastic. It should be pliable and not brittle. Once we know the normal nail then we can distinguish other nails from the normal one.

3 Fluted Nails (*fig. 68*)

Sometimes it happens that the nail, instead of growing over the end of the finger in a protecting way, goes away from the flesh. It shows a serious condition of the subject. The white spots on the nails indicate a beginning of the loss of vitality and are nature's first warning of trouble ahead.

As the disorder increases, the white flecks first grow larger, then grow together and lastly cover the whole nail taking away the transparency and clearness. Following this condition the fluted nail manifests itself. By this time, the nail loses its graceful shape and turns high on one side and low on the other. At this stage there is a grave danger of paralysis. Thus, in this process from the mere warning conveyed by the white spots, through the stage of fluting to the brittle turning back nail, we can trace the degree of danger from nerve destruction in our subject. As the subject improves in health, the same nails gradually resume their normal texture and lose the fluted appearance.

There is another observation on this nail. If this nail is long, thin and curved with ridges, it is a sure sign of consumption. However nails showing tuberculosis have different shape and I shall deal with that nail later on.

The longitudinal ridges on the nail are a product of chronic infections and therefore remain as long as illness,

The Nails

which may continue for years (*fig. 68 a*). Colitis, which is common after middle life, indicates the presence of rheumatism, with a focus of infection either in the roots of the teeth or in the bowel. These ridges can be hereditary, indicating rheumatic tendency in the family.

The nails of a person suffering from nervous exhaustion lose their shining quality. the moons grow cloudy and the nail-plate becomes brittle, but the most common and most familiar nail symptom of this condition is the so-called white spots. They occur, at least in small numbers, in the hands of 85 per cent of men and 75 per cent of women. Physicians and cheirologists agree that they occur in weak, tired and nervous people and they disappear when the strain is removed.

White spots might well indicate a calcium deficiency in the organism as it so often goes with soft or brittle nails. They occur with significant frequency in children and adolscents, who are the chief subject of calcium deficiency in the cells. It thus seems clear that white spots indicate both a lack of calcium and of nervous resistance.

Character: After considering the health defects of the fluted nail, I shall give its significance with reference to the character. Ridges on the nail of a certain finger indicate a stronger devotion and aptitude of the subject to the particular art or profession which that finger specially represents.

4 Narrow Nail (*fig. 69*)

A person who is carried by nervous energy generally develops this type of nail. It is not indicative of any health defect but merely shows that the subject has no muscular strength but is carried by nervous energy. The colour of this narrow nail is generally white, yellow, blue or pink. Since this nail does not indicate any special disease, the health defect of the subject should be seen from the colour of this nail. This nail is many times found with a blue colour at the base. Blue colour always means poor circulation. If this nail is delicate, the constitution of the person is also delicate.

Brittleness or fluting may also be found on such nails and the significance of the fluted nails should be applied to this nail.

There are other characteristics of this nail. The nail can be narrow as well as short and curved *(fig. 70)*. This nail indicates spinal cord weakness.

A third type of this nail is that it is narrow as well as long and thin *(fig. 71)*. This nail shows the disposition of the person on whose hand it is found. It shows timidity and cowardice and it is often found on the hands of convalescing persons. This long, narrow, shiny nail with a large opaque moon represents hyperthyroidism. In the owners of such nails metabolism is accelerated causing a rapid growth rate resulting in a long nail with a big moon. It is interesting to note that this type of endocrine disturbance is often associated with a lively and even brilliant intelligence, a characteristic feature of the leptosome person.

5 Broad Nail

After the narrow nail I turn to the broad nail *(fig. 72)*. This is a nail which is found on all types of fingers and does not belong to any one type of the hand. This nail is quite distinctive in appearance and once seen can always be recognised. This is a small nail and regular in form. The end of this nail is a square and the lower side is slightly small in breadth but many times also of the same width as the outer end. The difficulty of such a nail is that of the heart. Person possessing such a nail is susceptible to heart trouble more out of an organic difficulty than lack of circulation. If in addition to the shape of the nail, blue colour is found at the base, it means pronounced heart difficulty. Since the colour is very important in looking for the heart disease, attention to it is very necessary. If the colour on the nail is blue and the subject is a female one, it is obligatory to see the age of the person. Women who are near the age of twelve to fourteen are passing from childhood to womanhood and always have some disturbance of circu-

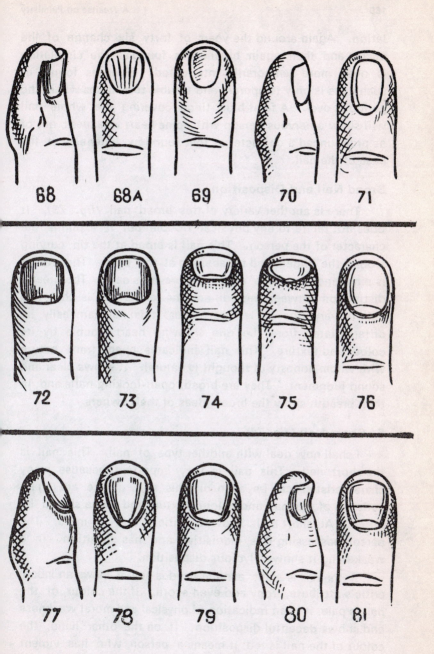

lation. Again around the years of forty six change of life occurs and then again blueness is found as the circulation is once more temporarily interrupted. Blueness found at such ages is only temporary and trouble terminates when the period is over. A faint blue tinge covering the whole nail will show a nervous person with some heart weakness, not of as pronounced a character as that found by blueness at the base of the nail.

Broad Nail and Disposition

There is another variety of this broad nail *(fig. 73)*. It does not relate to any physical trouble but it explains the character of the person. This nail is broad at the tip curving around the fingers and broadening at the base. The colour is pink and not blue as in the previous case. The greater distinction between this nail and the former one is that this nail is very fine in texture. Thus, this nail can easily be differentiated from the one showing heart trouble by its colour and texture. This nail indicates open, frank nature with whom honesty of thought is natural. It shows clear and sound judgment. They are broad, open-looking nails and in their breadth show the broad ideas of their owners.

6 Short Nail (*fig. 74*)

I shall now deal with another type of nail. This nail is the short nail. This nail is very important because many characteristics can be seen on this nail. There are again varieties of this nail and colour, texture and shape should be noted. All short nails show a critical turn of mind. The person possessing it is inquisitive and has intuition. In a weak hand it shows frivolous disposition.

If the nail is short and the hand is soft, it shows an inborn critic's attribute, irony and even scorn. If the colour of the nail is pale, it is an indication of physical and moral weakness and shows deceitful disposition. If, on the other hand, the colour of the nail is red, it means a person who has violent temper.

In general, it can be stated that short-nailed persons are more analytical, even of themselves and their own work. They are always inclined to logic and reason in direct opposition to the more visionary qualities of those who have the long type. They are good in debate, keen and sharp in their arguments and quick to make their points. But their weakness is that they are easily roused in temper.

A pronounced development of this short nail is the nail which is more broad than long (*fig. 75*). These nails indicate a quarrelsome, irritable disposition, one inclined to take offence at little things. This nail is very broad, covering the entire visible end of the finger and giving the top an exceedingly flat, blunt appearance. This nail gives almost a clubbed appearance to fingers. This nail goes with a vigorous constitution and active mind and a very critical, pugnacious, argumentative disposition. Such a person disagrees with you on subjects even when he knows perfectly well that others are right, simply for the delight it gives him to argue. The influence of this nail will be strong on any hand on which it appears. The critical mind is a factor in everything, love, literature, music, business or war. It must be noted that the short nail may also result from lack of vitality. This may be hereditary accompanied as it is usually by poor teeth and hair. But complete atrophy of the nails is another matter. It is very rare and appears in highly abnormal families. It has been reported only in cases of polydactilia, a symptom of degeneracy occuring in an extremely small percentage of cases. It has also been found in mental defective.

7 Throat Troubles (*fig. 76*)

There are nails which show throat affliction. These nails are large and round in shape. Illnesses such as asthma, laryngitis, bronchitis etc are always associated with this particular type of nail. This nail has a curved formation approaching the bulbous nail (see below), though in a very slight degree.

This nail may also be on any shaped tip, it is the curving alone that distinguishes it. It shows one who is exceedingly liable to colds at least and for whom sudden changes of temperature produce disturbance of throat and bronchia tubes. When this nail is long in shape it indicates trouble of the lungs.

8 Tuberculosis *(fig. 77)*

This type of disease is very well shown on the nail and medical practitioners often refer to nail for the symptoms of tuberculosis. In this case the finger as well as the nail play a part in the formation of it. It is bulbous nail and grows on a bulbous finger-tip.

In appearance the end of the finger thickens underneath until it forms a distinct bulb or pad. Over this bulbous tip the nail is curved forming a complete clubbed, blunt end, the top curved with the nail, the under part fleshy. The appearance is most striking and disagreeable. This nail shows the advanced stage of tuberculosis, sometimes of the spine, most often of the lungs. Medical authorities say that it is lack of nourishment that produces it. The lungs, which should be removing carbonic acid gas from the blood and filling it with oxygen, are so obstructed or destroyed that the blood is not renewed as it goes through them, but carries many of its poisonous qualities back through the circulation. Thus blood obstruction and impurity give these bulbous nails a marked blue appearance.

9 Paralysis *(fig. 78)*

Nails showing paralytic troubles have a formation of their own. They are flat and shell-shaped and narrow at the bottom. This danger will be still more accentuated if at the same time such nails are white and brittle and inclined to lift up at the edges. White spots like flocks on the nails denote an over-strung nervous temperament and there is danger of nervous prostration especially if there are no moons or very small ones. In this case we have mental paralysis.

10 Almond-shaped nails (fig.79)

When the nail has this type of formation and is naturally polished and is moderately long and thick, it denotes a happy nature and a satisfactory state of health. It has been observed with surprise that such nails are found on the fingers of conceited and selfish subjects, especially women. However, a person possessing this nail lacks forcefulness and clear perception.

11 Syphilis (fig. 80)

Syphilis, which goes with either hyperthophy or atrophy of the nails, is a frequent hereditary cause of epilepsy and mental deficiency. It generally produces a soft, short, nail with a concave profile called a spoon nail. Such type of nail is also seen in many mental defectives and in several cases the family history reveals syphilis.

Thus the under development of the nails is one of the most striking features in the hands of mental defectives. As mental deficiency is so often based on faulty heredity, naturally the dystrophies and atrophies of the nail, which are associated with syphilitic and hereditary endocrine illnesses, are likely to be found in the hands of these patients.

12 Cross-ridges (fig. 81)

Sometimes cross ridges are found on the nails. It looks as if one nail has stopped and another has grown over it. It shows that a serious illness has interrupted the health of the subject and that the illness was attended with grave danger. This nail always records a past event. It requires about six months to grow a new nail, so that in handling this indication we can tell how long the illness occured by noting how far the ridge has grown.

Thus I have shown how nails reveal certain diseases. Nail diognosis is still in its infancy and much interesting research work awaits physicians and psychiatrists.

I will give below a very interesting account of spots on nails based on Hindu system before I close this chapter

Though no scientific explanation is given for the following remarks, it will be of great help to the student of palmistry as the information below is based on empirical laws.

Spots on the Nail of the Thumb

Black spots on the nail indicate grief and sorrow. White marks on the nail indicate a reciprocated attachment. A star-shaped white mark indicates an illusion of life, unrequited love, self deception and a vain worship of things and persons one cares for.

Black spots on the nail of the thumb indicate crimes caused by passion.

Spots on the Nail of the first Finger

A white mark on the nail of the Jupiter finger shows gain, a black mark shows loss.

Spots on the Nail of Saturn Finger

A white mark on the nail indicates foreign travels. Yellow spots indicate worry, loss of brothers or wife. Black spots denote incoming danger.

Spots on the Nail of Apollo Finger

A white spot on the nail denotes honour and wealth, whereas, a black mark means loss of reputation.

Spots on the Nail of little Finger

A white spot on the nail denotes success in business and a black spot signifies a business failure.

Thus we notice that in the examination of the hands a careful investigation of the finger nails should be made and all possible information gained as to their texture, shape and colour. The nails reveal not only secrets relating to health but also give information about the temperament of the person concerned.

CHAPTER XI

The Hollow of the Palm

1 The position of the Hollow on the hand (*fig. 82*)

The next aspect of the hand that helps in character reading is the hollow of the palm. The only portion of the palm proper that remains after deducting the Mounts on the hand is the hollow of the palm, which is also known as the Plain of Mars. This is called as the Plain of Mars because it connects the lower and the upper Mounts of Mars. This is to be studied along with our knowledge of the two Mounts of Mars. The lower Mount of Mars shows aggressiveness and the upper Mount shows the courage of resistance. The flat or the bulging aspect of this plain indicates the absence or the presence of the combative tendency and that is why ancient cheiromants gave the name 'Cross of Battle' to the large cross which is occasionally seen in the middle of the plain.

The hollow of the palm occupies a space in the Big Triangle which is formed by the line of Heart at the top, the line of Mercury and the line of Life. The figure 82 will make it clear. The intensity of the Hollow will depend upon the development of the Mounts of upper Mars, the lower Mars, the Venus and the Moon. If the mounts are well-developed, the Hollow will be deep and if the mounts flat, the Hollow will also be flat.

As a general rule, a far deep Hollow is not a good sign to possess. It signifies misfortune. The person has to meet with disappointment. If the Hollow is more towards the line of Fate, it fore-tells misfortune in business, money and worldly affairs. If the Hollow inclines towards the line of

Head, it indicates brain trouble. If it leans towards the line of Heart, it means disappointment in love affairs.

The Hindu palmists regarded the Hollow as a mark of

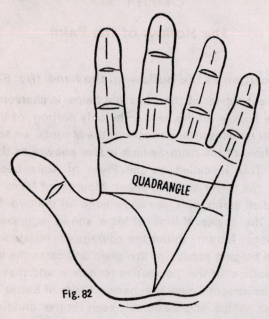

Fig. 82

indigence. A clearly hollow palm means that the person will lose his patrimony. A palm with a distinct Hollow is a sign of property. Varahamihira said that such a palm betrays a tendency to be hard hearted and pitiless.

2 The division of the Hollow

This Hollow is divided into two parts. The first part is known as the Quadrangle and the rest is known as Triangle. These two divisions give a very interesting account of the personality of the individual. The readers so far have seen the hand as a biological and also a psychological significance. Here also by studying the Hollow, the readers will be in a position to know more about the psychology of the individual and his character.

3 The Quadrangle
i) The position of the Quadrangle on the Hand

It occupies the space between the line of Head and the line of Heart. In the Big Triangle, it takes the upper portion of the Triangle. On the side of the first finger, the Quadrangle lies between the Mount of Jupiter and the lower Mount of Mars, neither of these Mounts being included. On the side of the percussion it occupies a space below the Mount of Mercury and above the Mount of Moon and does not include the upper Mount of Mars.

The Quadrangle is the zone of action which I have discussed in chapter V. The only difference is that the zone of action contains all the space enclosed in between the lines of Head and Heart including the upper Mount of Mars. This Quadrangle is also called the Mount of Uranus which is separately dealt with in the chapter on Mounts.

In order that the Quadrangle should be well-formed, the lines of Heart and Head should be parallel to each other as far as possible, with a slightly wide space towards the percussion. Normally the line of Heart and the line of Head go away from each other when they reach the Mount of Sun.

When the Quadrangle is formed in the normal way as described above, it shows a calm, easy and loyal disposition. The Quadrangle should be free from lines, otherwise it indicates a nervous disposition.

ii) The development of the Quadrangle

The width of the Quadrangle is to be observed. The width is a) very narrow, b) narrow, c) normal, d) broad or e) very broad.

a) Very Narrow: When the Quadrangle is very narrow and has the appearance of a waist, it denotes prejudice, injustice and bigotry. This is a remarkable sign on the hands of a religious person.

b) Narrow : When the Quadrangle is narrow, it shows narrow ideas, smallness of thought in regard to religion and morals.

b-1) When it is narrow on account of the line of Head rising towards the Heart line, it indicates narrow-mindedness. In such a case feelings dominate reason and often cloud it. This shows that the Heart line is powerful and that is why the feelings are powerful and that the Heart line by its strength has pulled the Head line towards it, making the latter poor in its force.

b-2) The Quadrangle may be narrowed on account of the Heart line lowering towards the Head line. This shows that the Head line is powerful and that it has attracted the Heart line towards itself. This means that reason as shown by the Head line is more powerful than sentiment, emotion and affection shown by the Heart line. Thus, we conclude that the head rules over the feelings and the person is mean in his attitude and wanting in generosity.

b-3) The Quadrangle may be narrow and in addition the line of Mercury is also very poor. It shows asthmatic trouble and hay-fever.

b-4) Sometimes, we encounter hands wherein the fingers are bending inside and the Quadrangle is also narrow. In this case, we have a person who is unsocial and stiff in his behaviour. It also shows a miserly disposition.

b-5) If the Mount of Jupiter is in excessive development, the narrowness of the Quadrangle means excessive religious ideas and asceticism. One would expect such Quadrangle on the hand of a blind fanatic.

b 6) If the Mounts of Mars and Mercury are in excessive developments, the significance of the narrow Quadrangle is that the person is unfair in his dealings with others. If in addition, the Heart line is short, it shows cruelty because the shortness of the Heart line is a symptom of a lack of kindly feelings.

b-7) Sometimes it is possible that the Quadrangle is narrow in both hands. If it is so and the Mount of Mercury is badly marked like grill, it shows that the person is very narrow minded and selfish and is given to lying. In short, it shows infidelity.

b-8) The Quadrangle may sometimes be narrow under the Mount of Sun. This formation diminishes the intellectual brilliance of the individual.

c) Normal : Sometimes the development of the Quadrangle is normal. It means that the lines of Heart and Head are running in a normal way and the Quadrangle is well-formed keeping slightly wide space at the end. When this type of the Quadrangle is free from tiny lines which show nervous and worrying nature, it is a good development and shows a calm, steady and loyal disposition. It also indicates straight-forwardness.

d) *Broad* : When the Quadrangle is broad with a good line of Head and a well-formed second phalange of the thumb, it shows broad mindedness. Here reasoning is seen at its best.

e) Very Broad : When the Quadrangle is very broad throughout, it shows an independent thinking even to a fault. It also denotes want of order in the brain, carelessness in thoughts and ideas, an unconventional nature and imprudence in everything. This is a serious indication and no other favourable sign on the hand is sufficient to counter-balance it.

In this case the line of Heart rises very high and the line of Head runs very low in the hand. High rising of Heart line denotes extreme jealousy and sensuality and the low running of Head line denotes ill-balanced reasoning power.

e-1) When the Quadrangle is broad under the Mount of Jupiter or Saturn and narrow at the other end, it shows a change in the temperament from the generosity of views and broadness of mind to narrowness and prejudice. It shows an exaggerated sensitiveness about other peoples' opinions.

e-2) If the Quadrangle is broader under the Mount of Sun than under the Mount of Saturn, it shows that the person is careless about his name, position or reputation as shown by the Mount of Sun.

iii) The Signs in the Quadrangle (fig. 83)

Cross : The cross must be absolutely independent and not formed by the main line. If such a cross is found in the Quadrangle and if it touches the Heart line (*fig. 83*), it means that there will be great influence on the subject by a person of the opposite sex. If this cross does not touch either the Fate line or the Sun line, this influence will be favourable.

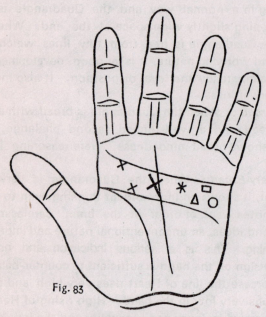

Fig. 83

Signs in the quadrangle

If however, a cross is found touching the Head line and not touching the lines of Fate and Sun, it means that the individual will impress himself more on other person in matters of love or friendship.

A cross under the Mount of Saturn touching the Fate line shows a fortunate and lucky life. It also shows one's religious attitude and this is found on the hands of religious preachers.

If this cross under the Mount of Saturn is poorly formed, it is not a good sign and it reduces the good effects of the mounts on the hand and also precipitates the qualities of the mounts. Thus if the person is a Jupiterian, this cross will give him extravagant ambition. If he is a Saturnian, the cross shows morbid disposition. If he is an Apollonian, it shows excessive vanity and avarice. If he is a Mercurian, it means deceiving and even thieving instincts. If he is a Lunarian, the cross means insanity. If his Mount of Venus is developed, it shows lasciviousness to the point of mania. And finally, if his lower Mount of Mars is developed, the cross under the Mount of Saturn and in the Quadrangle shows cowardice.

A cross, which is most favourable in the Quadrangle, is the Mystic Cross or St. Andrew's Cross. This is generally found under the Mount of Saturn and in Quadrangle. Whenever this cross is found it shows an aptitude for abstruse subjects and a love for occultism. This cross must be distinct and beautiful.

The Star : A star in any portion of the Quadrangle is an excellent sign, particularly if it be under some favourable mount. Under the Mount of Jupiter it promises pride and power. Under the Mount of Saturn it shows success in worldly matters. Under the Mount of Sun, it means success in science and research. A well-formed star shows good and true subject at the mercy of a dearly loved person of the other sex. This sign is found to be located generally between the line of Life and the line of Fate in the Quadrangle. This sign is often accompanied by a broken line of Heart.

The Square : A square in the Quadrangle is a good sign and it shows a quick grasp of things and the person possesses a kind and sympathetic heart. If the square touches the main lines it is to be taken as a protection against the imperfection of the particular line.

The Triangle : A triangle in the Quadrangle (*fig. 83*) shows a love for deep studies. It also protects the defects of the line to which it touches.

The Circle : One circle in the Quadrangle shows eye trouble. If three circles are found touching each other under the Mount of Saturn, they show epilepsy.

The Grill : A grill shows madness.

Lines : Many small lines which have no particular significance show a weak and nervous mind and restlessness.

Dots : Red dots in the Quadrangle show murder or serious wound. The general character of the hand will tell whether the subject is the guilty party or the victim. White dots indicate general weakening of the system.

Sometimes it may happen that the Quadrangle is entirely absent in the hand. This will happen if the line of Heart or of Head is absent. If the line of Heart is absent, it shows a cruel and cold nature. If, however, the hand is of a good type, the absence shows poor circulation of the blood or poor functioning of the heart. If the Head line is absent, it shows a poor intellect and lack of understanding. This person is very dull and acts by instinct and not by reason.

4 The Triangle on the hand (*fig. 84*)
i) The Position

The Triangle is enclosed by the lines of Head at the top, Life line on one side and the Mercury line on the other. If any of these lines is missing, there is no Triangle in the proper sense. However, in such a case an imaginary line should be taken in place of the absent one. Generally, the line of Mercury is absent and an imaginary line of Mercury should be drawn and the Triangle should be completed. Sometimes the place of the Mercury line is taken by the line of Sun.

ii) The Development of the Triangle

Broad : If the lines of Head, Life and Mercury form a broad and well traced Triangle, it indicates benevolence and a finely balanced nature. If the lines are of good colour, the Triangle shows a good understanding.

Large : If the Triangle occupies a larger space in the palm and is of good character and good colour, it is a sign of good luck, long life and courage.

If, it is very large, it would be influenced by both the Mounts of Mars and the person is dominated by the idea of energy and has audacity.

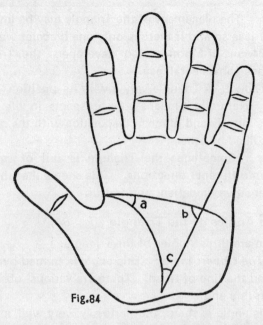

Fig.84

The big triangle consists of lines of life, Head and Mercury

Narrow : The Triangle may be narrow in its formation and the lines may be poorly developed. It indicates timidity of spirit, meanness and cowardice. Such a man would always go with the majority even against his principles.

When in the above formation of the Triangle, it has for its base the line of Sun, the subject will have narrow ideas but great individuality and strong resolution. Such a sign, from the very qualities it exhibits, contains within itself the seeds of worldly success. If the Triangle is narrow through a poor line of Head which inclines towards a poor line of Mercury, it shows failure in business.

Flat : When the Triangle is flat in both the hands with a low Mount of Saturn, it denotes an insignificant life.

Bulging : If it is bulging in both the hands, it shows an aggressive temperament and a spend thrift disposition. If it is bulging in one hand only, it is a sign of generosity and bravery.

Low : The placement of the Triangle may be low on the palm. If it is so and if there is only one bracelet well traced and the Mount of Moon is also developed, the Triangle in such a case shows catalepsy.

Very Low : A Triangle very low in its position indicates lethargy. Naturally it means poor prospects in life. Such a subject is miserly and of mean disposition with the result that he is not liked by others.

Lines : Sometimes the Triangle is full of small lines running in different directions. This shows that the person is very sensitive, impatient and fretful.

iii) The Angles of the Triangle (*fig. 84*)

There are three Angles of the Triangle.

a) The Upper Angle : This angle is formed by the line of Life and the line of Head. There are various observations regarding this angle.

If this angle is sharp, that is to say, very well marked, it shows a mind which is of high quality and sound common sense. It gives a good balance to the Head line and also to the Life line which shows a good understanding and practical outlook on life.

When this angle is wide, that is to say, when the Life line takes a short curve and the Head line is straight, this indicates a blunt nature. If the Head line is short, it indicates a dull intellect. If it is long, it shows little appreciation of others' feelings and of art.

Sometimes this angle may be very wide. This is possible when the Head line is rising towards the Heart line. It shows miserly habits because the Quadrangle is small. The person is also very indifferent.

It may happen that the angle is wide owing to the Head line separating from the Life line at the beginning. The independent rising of the Head line shows an independent disposition. This independent nature, if not backed by good signs on the hand, shows recklessness even to the point of danger.

b) The Middle Angle : The second angle in the Triangle to be taken into consideration is the middle angle, which is formed by the Head line and the Mercury line. There are various degrees of this angle all of which deserve careful consideration.

When this angle is well-defined and clear, it shows quickness of intellect, vivacity and good health. If this angle is very sharp, it shows ill-health, and nervousness.

This angle may have an obtuse formation. This is possible when the Head line is dropping down and the Mercury line is rising on the Mount of Moon. If so, it shows an extremely nervous disposition.

If the Head line is long and the Mercury line is rising on the Mount of Moon towards the percussion, the middle angle is formed on the Mount of Moon itself which shows catarrh or epilepsy or mental paralysis. Nails will confirm it. If this is found on a child's hand, every care of the health of the child is necessary and secondary importance may be given to the studies.

If the middle angle is broad and heavy and if the Heart line is poor and the Quadrangle very narrow, it denotes an uncharitable disposition.

c) The Lower Angle : The third or the lower angle is formed by the Life line and the Mercury line. This angle is rarely formed.

If the angle is very narrow, it shows ill-health and feeble-mindedness. It is not a good sign for the Mercury line to touch the Life line.

When this angle is well-formed, that is to say, when it leaves some space between the Life line and the Mercury line, it denotes good health. With this angle if the Mount of Mercury is developed, it shows wit.

If this angle is good as mentioned above and the Mercury line goes upto the Mount of Mercury, it indicates success in business.

This angle may also be obtuse in its formation. When it is so, it shows a strong position. With this obtuse angle, if the first phalange of the thumb is weak and the Mount of Venus exaggerated, it denotes faithlessness.

The angle will be either too widely opened with poor lines of Head and Mercury or the line of Mercury will be connected to the line of Life. In both the cases it is a sign of neuralgia or even palpitation of the heart and fainting fits.

The angle may be formed by lines which are broken whereby it denotes a bad nature, both rough and incurably lazy.

This third angle may be formed by the line of Sun and the Life line. If it is very acute, it gives individuality but a narrow view of things. But if the angle is obtuse, it shows a broad and generous mind.

iv) The signs in the Triangle

Cross : A cross in the centre of the Triangle indicates troubles from others brought about by the quarrelsome disposition of the subject. If this cross is found in both the hands, it is one of the strongest indications of murder of the subject.

A cross in the Triangle and under the Mount of Saturn with long fingers and the first knots strongly marked shows scepticism.

A badly formed cross in the centre with a badly formed Mount of Saturn shows a series of misfortunes.

Many crosses in the Triangle indicates continuous bad luck. A cross inside the upper angle of the Triangle indicates law-suits. Generally these law-suits are of a criminal nature. If the branches of this cross touch the main lines, the suit will be lost, otherwise it will be won.

Star : An independent star in the Triangle shows riches obtained after great struggle. When it is seen in both the hands with other indications on the hand, it shows violent death.

A star touching the line of Mercury indicates blindness. A badly formed star shows trouble in love, resulting in some act of violence.

Square : An independent square in the Triangle is a very serious warning of danger.

Triangle : A triangle between the lines of Life and Fate shows military renown.

Circle : Circle in the Triangle denotes trouble from a person of the opposite sex. If the Mount of Moon is exaggerated, the circle signifies captiousness.

Grill : It shows a shameful death. If the hand is good, it indicates hidden enemies

Crescent : A crescent inside the Triangle, if it touches the line of Mercury, shows good health. It also foretells good luck and success. If the crescent touches the Head line, it is not a good sign since it indicates violent death due to a fault of judgement or a foolish act of the subject. A crescent in the lower angle which is obtuse indicates infidelity.

Dots : Red dots indicate pregnancy, white spots indicate anaemia and a tendency to fainting fits.

Lines : Many lines with a short or drooping down Head line shows insanity.

CHAPTER XII

The Right Hand and the Left Hand

A few words on the right and the left hands will prove useful to the readers. There is an age-old theory amongst ancient palmists that the right hand for man and left hand for woman should be studied. The reason is that they considered the right hand as the active hand and the left as the passive hand. Men play an active part in life, that is to say, they work for their livelihood and bring home their day's wages to feed their wives and children, they also do the most laborious work and look to the protection and maintenance of their family. Since most of man's work is done by the right hand, it has become the practice to study his right hand only.

On the contrary, ladies remain at home and do the household duties. They are by nature submissive and passive. They are not expected to have an independent life as such and they have to depend entirely on their husbands or the male members in the family. As such, the left hand of ladies should be studied, since it would portray the woman as she is. The right hand shows what the person will do in life, with his merits, strength and abilities. But since these virtues are suppressed in the case of ladies, their right hand will not indicate a future of their own. Thus the theory, right hand for men and left hand for women has been evolved.

According to the Hindu system, indication of marriage of men is to be read on the left hands and that of women on the right hand. Also it is stated that left hands of children upto 14 years should be studied.

The above theory was improved upon and developed in further generations and it stated that left hand indicated man's mind. It revealed his inner sentiments and desires and the right hand showed the possibility of the fulfilment of his desires.

The theory was further developed and it stated that handedness, right or left, is a product of evolution. We find that apes and monkeys are ambidextrous and the same atavistic character was observed in the primitive man. Amongst children also we notice that upto the age of about two they use both the hands, a state which shows the early stage of evolution.

Amongst twins we find that left handedness is a common phenomenon. But this may be due to the position of the child in the uterus. Normally the left hand is fixed to the back which enables the right hand to have free movements. However, the left-handedness may be due to the faulty position of the child which is more likely in the case of twins where the left hand may be left in a better position to get more freedom.

After the above discussion it may be pointed out that throughout the generations, right-handedness was considered to be a normal thing whereas left-handedness was thought of something abnormal. Modern discoveries also support this theory and we draw the conclusion that the right hand shows the mental development and the intellectual level, whereas the left hand shows the inner world of the person, his subconscious mind, his hereditary characteristics. Modern science has proved that the left hemisphere of the brain shows the conscious behaviour of the person and this portion of the brain is heavier than the right hemisphere and also this left hemisphere shows all the important centres of cognition such as reading and writing. This left hemisphere is connected with the right hand.

On the contrary, the left-handed-people show abnormal traits. This hand is connected with the right hemisphere of the brain which indicates the subconscious working of the person. Left-handedness is found very common in the case of persons who lack average intelligence. It has been observed that many of the left-handed children have difficulty in reading and memorizing letter and numbers.

However, we cannot make a rule that all left-handed persons have low intelligence. There are so many cases wherein we find that left-handed persons have created the most exalted works in history. Painters, sportsmen, actors and writers, who are left-handed, show a speciality of their own which would become a wonder for others. However, there is also some explanation for this speciality of such persons. It is a psychological fact that a child who has a physical defect in him feels inferiority complex and he all the time feels that something is wrong with him and that others are getting a better advantage because of his debility. It makes him more conscious of his weakness and to hide this weak point in him he tries to concentrate his energies in something else which would bring fame and honour to him. He thereby tries to attract the attention of others to his skill and ingenuity and thus tries to overcome his inferiority complex. This may be the reason why many of the left-handers show extraordinary merit in certain trades.

The question of the right and left hand may also be studied from another point of view. The crease lines found on the hand give a good clue to the understanding of the functions of the two hands. The assumption of some of the opponents of the study of palmistry that crease lines are formed according to the manual labour of the hand is not so correct. For in that case a labourer would possess the largest number of crease lines on his hands as his hand is likely to have more of muscular movements. But in fact we find that a person, who is very rich and need not do any manual labour, possesses the largest number of crease lines. Thus, we conclude that the developments of the crease lines is due to the mental development of the person and they show his emotional behaviour. Since the left hand is the receptive hand, it has more net-work of crease lines showing the emotional feelings of the person. Such crease lines on the right hand are comparatively less and they show the action or the decisions or the conscious efforts of the person to face life.

It will also be a matter of great interest to the student of palmistry to study the papillary ridges on both the hands. In the case of mentally defective persons, the left hand shows a very complicated net-work of the papillary ridges. This means that the right hemisphere of the brain, which shows the subconscious developmet of the person, has some disturbance affecting the mental blance of the person. In feeble-minded persons, who do not have a steady outlook on life, the papillary ridges on the ulner zone of the right hand shows queer formations. In the study of the division of the hand, we have studied that the hand is divided into different parts wherein we have observed that the ulner zone on the hand shows the subconscious mind. Naturally any malformation of the papillary ridges on this zone means the abnormal development of the brain.

In conclusion, we can say that the left hand shows the subconscious development of the brain. It shows the hereditary characteristics and the natural instincts of the person. Any diversion from the normal formation of the crease lines of the papillary ridges means some type of weakness of the subconscious make-up of the person. On the other hand, the right hand will indicate to us the capacity of the person to fulfil his desires and ambitions as well as the development of his conscious get-up. Thus the old conception, though not altogether discarded has now been explained scientifically, and naturally they have received more attention that has hitherto been given to it.

CHAPTER XIII
The Mounts on the Hand

1 Introduction

The study of the Mounts on the hand is very important to a student of palmistry. At the same time this study is most difficult and complicated. It is a matter of patient study, perseverance and sound grasp of the subject. No other aspect on the hand is more difficult to locate, more difficult to understand and more difficult to interpret than the Mounts on the hand. However I have arranged each mount in such a way that every aspect of the mount has been codified in suitable sub-headings. This arrangement will definitely help the readers to grasp the various characteristics of a mount. This is the main reason why I have taken this chapter at the end of this book.

Uptil now only seven mounts on the hand have been recognised by all the authors on this subject. Mars is split up into two and thus the number is made to eight. But even after the discovery of the planets Neptune and Uranus, they have not been assigned any suitable place on the hand though their influence on human life is considered in Astrology. However, these planets have been properly placed on the hand in this book and the study of the hand in relation to these mounts will bear testimony to the proper place alloted to them. I hope this will be very illuminating and interesting to the advanced students of palmistry.

2 Psychological aspect of mounts

Mounts are the flabby pads which rise up high on the hand. They are sensitive pads which consist of a network of nerves. The centre of these nerves is called the apex of the mount. This apex is of great importance in locating the correct position of the mount. The hand-print will give us a clear idea of the right development of the mount. The tissues that are just below these pads have various degrees of elasticity and the mounts become more or less sensitive depending upon the tissues underneath.

Theory of Vibrations

It has now been recognised that the whole of our body has vibrational waves. The vibrations of the body are thrown away and these vibrations have their own effect upon other persons. Without going into details of this vibrational theory, I wish to emphasise here that these vibrations of the body find certain outlets and the mounts on the hand are one of these outlets. Powerful vibrations make these mounts more sensitive and they respond quickly to the outside world. The hand of a hypnotist is a good example of this. Hand and finger gestures known as 'passes' enable the hypnotist to use his vibrational power into a definite purpose. By the constant use of his practice, his finger tips as well as the mounts on his hand feel the vibrational force and the hypnotist can send away these vibrations on the person whom he wants to hypnotise. Thus, these vibrations can be felt on the mounts in which case the mounts will be more or less sensitive depending upon the vibrational force.

These mounts also have the same psychological significance as the shape of the hand. As the shape of the hand depends upon the shape of the brain centre, similarly the development of certain mounts on the hand depends upon the development of different sensitive centres in the brain which control the health and mind of the person. That is why different mounts indicate different health types and personalities.

3 Pathological significance of the mounts

In pathology there are different blood groups. These groups exhibit certain characteristics of the blood. In the case of blood transfusion, it is necessary to find out the blood group. Different groups cannot be mixed up and the blood to be transfused should be of the same group as the blood of the person to whom the blood is to be transfused. These blood groups can best be represented by the mounts on the hand. They indicate a particular trait of the blood group which is responsible for building up the basic characteristic of the person.

4 Psychological aspect of the mounts

It is a matter of great thought and observation as to why the particular mounts on the hand were allotted particular places only. It seems that our ancient scholars on the subject, who were also the masters of astrology, found that the persons who have Jupiter powerful in their horoscope have a powerful mount developed under the first finger which they called the mount of Jupiter and the finger of Jupiter. In this way persons having powerful planets have certain places more developed on the hand which were named after those planets.

The mental behaviour of the person, his characteristics, the development of his mind, his ideas, his ambition, his sub-conscious mind and such other things which form the psychology of the person are thus determined from the particular type of mount to which he belongs. Mounts which are in combination with other mounts make a person of a mixed nature and his personality becomes of a more mixed type than if he belongs to one specie only. There is not the least doubt that the planets exert their influence on human life. In palmistry these planets are seen in the form of mounts on the hand. These mounts represents the basic facts of character and personality. The nine mounts whose influences are seen on the mankind are as under.

The Mounts on the Hand

1	Mount of Jupiter	Pitru Sthana	Father
2	Mount of Saturn	Matru Sthana	Mother
3	Mount of Apollo	Vidya Sthana	Education
4	Mount of Mercury	Jaya Sthana	Wife
5	Mount of Mars :		
	Negative	Dharma Sthana	Religion
	Positive	Shatru Sthana	Enemies
6	Mount of Moon	Kalpana Sthana	Imagination
7	Mount of Venus :		
	Upper	Bhratru Sthana	Brothers
	Lower	Bandhu sthana	Relatives
8	Mount of Uranus		
9	Mount of Neptune		

The chart (*fig. 85*) will show their positions as well as their symbols.

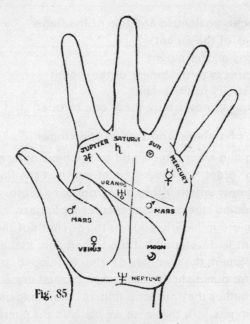

Fig. 85

The mounts on the hand

By the study of the mounts, we shall be in a position to fix-up our subject in one of the nine types. Once we decide type of the mount, the principal mount as well as the subordinate mount, it will enable us to know the several aspects represented by that mount such as his i) nature, ii) health, iii) financial position, iv) marriage, v) vocation etc.

It is very difficult to fix-up the mount type of the individual because pure specimen of the type is rarely met with. In older days it was possible because Roman Race, Aryan race were available and these were governed by particular mounts. However, as races were mixed-up, pure specimen became rare. In order that the students may find it easy to locate the prominent mount, I give below some valuable tips.

5 Valuable tips for locating the prominent mount

Mounts on the hand may be either developed, flat or under-developed. In order to accurately judge the development of the mount, we shall have to apply the following tests.

1. Finger, phalanges and tips of the finger
2. Apex of the mount
3. Signs on the mount
4. Hardness or flabbiness of the mount
5. Elasticity of the mount

We shall now study these one by one.

1 Finger, phalanges and tips of the finger

Strong and erect fingers add to the development of the mount. In order to know the strength of the fingers, we must first know whether they are of normal length. We have already studied them in our chapter on fingers. A finger, normal or more in length, adds to the strength of the mount. If the mount is developed but the finger on that mount are under-developed, the qualities of the developed mount are lessened and diminished. Fingers in general are also to be studied, whether they are long fingers, short fingers, smooth or knotty fingers. In that case we can add the characteristics of these fingers to the qualities of the mount which is developed. After the fingers, we can study the different tips and know more about tip of the finger on the developed mount.

The Mounts on the Hand

Conic, pointed, square and spatulate tips will add to the qualities of the mount. Similarly the phalanges will show which world is governing the Mount.

2 Apex of the Mount

The apex of the mount helps us to locate the position of the mount. A mount is in its normal position if the apex is in the centre of the mount. Further, in order that the mount should be in its normal position, it should also be exactly below the finger to which it belongs.

The apex is the core or centre of the ridge pattern. All the finger tips bear the apex. Similarly, at least the four mounts beneath the four fingers bear apexes. These apexes are the skin ridges running in a definite pattern to a central point which may be of a circular or a triangular formation.

If the apex is exactly in the centre of the mount, that makes the mount of a normal position. If the apex is shifted to any other side it means that the mount is displaced.

If the apex is towards the finger, it elevates the qualities of the mount.

If the apex is nearer the base of the mount, it lessens the qualities of the mount.

If the apex is leaning towards other mount, it gives out its qualities and takes the qualities of the mount towards which the apex leans. Thus, the position of the apex will add or diminish the qualities of the mount.

3 Signs on the Mount

There are good or bad signs which can be seen on the mount.

A) Good Signs

i) A single vertical line is a good sign and adds to the qualities of the mount. Even on a flat mount, this vertical line gives equal prominence with the higher development.

ii) Star, triangle, square, circle etc. are considered to be auspicious signs and they add to the qualities of the mount.

B) Bad Signs

i) Cross lines, grills and two or more vertical lines diminish the qualities of the mount and they show hindrances in acquiring the qualities of the mount.

ii) Island, dots and spots are considered as inauspicious signs on the mounts and they exhibit dangers, accidents, lossess and troubles.

4 Hardness or flabbiness of the mount

Hardness of the mount adds to the strength of the mount. A hard mount, even though it is less developed, will add strength to that mount and in our study of the mounts, we may find that this mount gets more marks than the one which apparently looks more developed but which is actually flabby.

5 Elasticity of the mount

Finally, we should study and observe the elasticity of each and every mount. In order to find out the elasticity of the mount, it is better if we take a brand new pencil which is not sharpened and press it on the mount. We have to exert homogeneous pressure. We shall notice that the mount when pressed comes to its original bulging in a rebounding way. It has a springlike action. We have to study this spring-like action of each mount. A mount which rebounds back to its original position in a quick and consistent manner can be supposed to have good elasticity. A mount which has a good elasticity adds to the qualities of the mount.

6 Arithmetical formula

After studying the above aspects, we shall be in a position to know the most developed mount on the hand. In order to make this judgment accurate, I have invented an arithmetical formula. The order of marks is given according

The Mounts on the Hand

to preference we should give in estimating the strength of the mount. The maximum marks that can be given are ten. The following table will be useful.

1) **Fingers** Maximum marks allotted 5
   a) Finger if fully developed   5 marks (full marks)
   b) Finger if normal   3 marks
   c) Crooked finger   2 marks
   d) Under-developed finger   −2 marks

2) **Apex** Maximum marks allotted 2
   a) Apex if centrally located   2 marks
   b) Apex if displaced   −1 marks
   c) Apex leaning towards the finger 1 marks

3) **Signs** Maximum marks allotted 1
   a) Good sign   1 marks
   b) Auspicious sign   1 marks
   c) Bad sign   −1 marks
   d) Inauspicious sign   −1 marks

4) **Hardness or flabbiness**
   Maximum marks allotted 1
   a) Hard mount   1
   b) Flabby mount   −1

5) **Elasticity of the Mount**
   Maximum marks allotted 1
   a) Spring-like   1 mark
   b) Slow   −1 mark

In studying the mounts, we can prepare a chart as follows and start giving marks according to the merit described above. Below is given an example which will show the strength of the mounts. The five points mentioned above are taken in one line and the marks are given below them.

	Finger	Apex	Signs	Hardness	Elasticity	Total
Mount of Jupiter	3	−1	1	−1	−1	1
Mount of Saturn	3	2	1	−1	−1	4
Mount of Apollo	5	−1	−1	1	1	5
Mount of Mercury	−2	2	1	−1	1	1
Mount of Venus	−2	2	−1	1	1	1

With the above information, we find that the mount of Apollo gets the highest marks. Then come the mounts of Saturn, Jupiter, Mercury and the Mount of Venus follows thereafter. There is no finger attached to the mounts of Mars, Moon, Uranus and Neptune. It is also very difficult to locate the apex of these mounts. Therefore the total number of marks which are ten, are to be distributed as follows as far as these mounts are concerned.

Signs— 5 marks, Hardness—3 marks, Elasticity—2 marks. I am sure that with the above method it will be very easy for the students to find out the mount type to which the person belongs. With this method we can also know the principal mount and the subsidiary mount. We can also know whether the person is a combination of two or more mounts.

Each mount has its good qualities as well as its bad qualities. Any excessive development is bad. Every mount indicates the following peculiarities.

a) Physical peculiarities : In this we shall know the physical structure of the person, his colour, the type of his eyes, nose, height etc.

b) Mental peculiarities : By the study of the mount, we shall be able to know the ambition, desire, abilities, capabilities, likes, dislikes, etc., which will help us to know the working of the person's mind.

c) Health peculiarities : Each mount is liable to certain health weakness. By our study we shall be able to guide our subject as regards his health difficulties.

7 Categories of mount

The nine mounts are divided as regards their power, influence and functioning into four categories.

a) Good mounts which are clear and supported by good main lines.

b) Bad mounts which are over-grown, red in colour and full of bad signs.

c) Deficient or poor mounts which are of bad influence though slow in action.

d) Flat mounts which are neither good nor bad by themselves. They may be used to strengthen or enfeeble the good or the bad qualities of the subject.

Important

The special characteristics and traits governed by a pure type of mount is very rare. Majority of persons are directed through their lives and destinies by two or more different mounts. Thus, every individual is a combination of, more or less, good and bad forces which have the greatest influence upon his whole being. Therefore while studying the mounts on the hand, the combination of the principal mount and the subsidiary mount is very important. We have already seen how we can allocate marks to the individual mount and thereby find out the most well developed mount on the hand. We can call this mount as the principal mount and the mount which stands next to it according to the marks, is the subsidiary mount.

After the above discussion we shall start with our study of the individual mount on the hand, one by one.

The Mount of Jupiter
1 General

When the mount of Jupiter is found to be well-developed with the apex centrally located and the finger of Jupiter long and strong, it shows that the person is a Jupiterian (*fig. 86*). A good example of this type is Napolean Bonaparte.

Cheirosophically, Jupiter is the mount of morality, pure love and justice with mercy and is known as the greatest benefactor and the uplifter. The vibrations coming through this mount are essentially harmonious and their use leads to real sympathy and untiring effort to do good to all, devoutedly religious and of true dignity. The abuse of the same vibrations causes the stimulation of Jupiterian virtues leading to hypocrisy, especially in religious matters. The good nature is marred by excess in many directions.

People with Jupiter in prominence and well-aspected in their hands are known to be lucky. Vibrations radiating through them attract all that is good to them and their affairs prosper as a consequence. The judge who gives sane decisions and merciful sentences, the physician and the church dignitary are Jupiterian types while the world's teachers and philosophers also come largely under the influence of Jupiter.

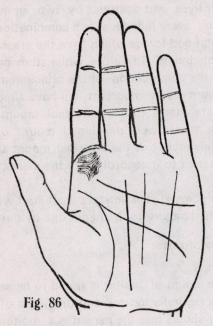

Fig. 86

The mounts of Jupiter (ambition, dignity, honour, prestige, religion)

The Jupiterian is a good type. He is confident about his ability. He is self-reliant and takes his own decisions. He has a habit to talk loudly. He is fond of show and likes to observe form, order and law. He is jovial in spirit and cordial in manner. His passions are healthy, spontaneous and without inhibitions. He is free in his expressions.

2 Physiological Significance

A Jupiterian has a peculiar psyique and from his structure we can judge him as a Jupiterian. If we try to study him from the top to the bottom, we shall see that in general he is of a medium height. He is well-built and strong. He is dignified and aristocratic. He has a large forehead which often perspires and has abundance of hair. His arms and legs, though short, are in good proportion and well-shaped. His eyes are brilliant and large and he has a steadfast look. His skin is smooth and fine in texture. His nose is prominent and his face shows a dignified and confident personality.

3 Psychological Significance

A Jupiterian takes an active interest in sports and outdoor activities from his earliest youth. He has tremendous enthusiasm in life and he is not at all self-centered. His intellect is of a very high quality, his nature foreseeing and practically imaginative. He has a kind of vision that understands the world and loves it for what it is and not for what it ought to be. He is a broad minded person, tolerant, humorous and truthful. He is open hearted with good understanding and entirely lacking in malice or petty jealousies.

A low grade Jupiterian is boastful and there is no limit to the varieties and colours of the life he can invent. If he is promoting an illicit scheme, no story is too fantastic for public consumption.

There is another class of Jupiterians who love the unknown and the mysterious. They are devoted to the studies of occult and esoteric fields of imagination. They also believe in the truth of the phantom world.

4 Development of the mount

The development of the mount may be normal or in excess or sub-normal. This we can find with our standard rules described earlier in the chapter.

i) If the mount of Jupiter is developed in a normal way, it shows, a) high religious ideas, b) lofty pride, c) pride in everyday life, d) pride in great enterprise. The person has an attractive personality and powerful looks. He enjoys a luxurious and happy life. He is very popular, attains distinction with kings and princes. He is generous, lucky, courageous, straight-forward, noble, calm and strong. He gains victory over his rivals. He is religious and remains busy in his own activities.

ii) If the mount is developed in excess the person has, a) arrogance, b) boasting, c) vindictiveness, d) criminal jealousy, e) tyranny, f) superstition. He is also egoistic, selfish and shrewd.

iii) If the mount of Jupiter is lacking, it means, a) absence of veneration, b) vulgarity, c) lack of self-respect. He will lack ambition and will not take steps to improve his lot in life. There will be no self-respect or pride in him. He will feel nervous, shy and awkward in presence of strangers.

5 Placement of the mount

The mount of Jupiter has five positions of placement. They are judged by the position of the apex.

i) When the apex of the mount leans towards the first finger it shows egotism and vanity.

ii) If the apex leans towards the mount of saturn, it means that Saturn will influence the Jupiterian ideas and sobriety and sadness will hold down the Jupiterian ambition. This will make him self-conscious.

iii) If the apex leans towards the outer edge of the hand, it will mean a selfish motive and pride in one's family.

iv) If the apex leans towards the line of Heart, it shows pride in affection and ambition for the loved ones. Such a person is lucky, benevolent, rich and religious.

v) If the apex leans towards the line of Head, the Jupiterian ambition will be towards intellectual pursuits and pride in intellect.

6 Texture, Flexibility etc.

While studying the mount, we have to take into consideration the skin texture, flexibility, the consistency and the colour of the hand. The texture of the hand will indicate

The Mounts on the hand Jupiter Mount

whether the Jupiterian qualities are fine or coarse. Flexibility of the hand will mean whether the adaptability will lead the Jupiterian to gain success or whether his stiff demeanour will obstruct his ambition. Consistency will help us to know the energy behind his ambition. Finally we have to study the colour of the hand. White colour will make the Jupiterian a cold man and less attractive. Thus, he will not be able to lead men and his success in life will be limited. Pink colour is good. In this case, he is bright, active and vivacious. He is loved by his friends and admired by his enemies. He is the idol of the masses. Red colour shows excessive enthusiasm and ardour.

7 Mount and Fingers
Finger of Jupiter

If this finger is as long as the Saturn finger, the desire for power will be great. If this finger is longer than the Saturn finger, the person will be a tyrant. A crooked finger of Jupiter adds shrewdness and the person will plan his schemes very systematically.

Smooth fingers

Smooth fingers to a Jupiterian will add to the intuition, impulse and inspiration. They mean brilliant thinking.

Knotty fingers

Knotty fingers develop organising capacity, orderliness and discipline and such type of Jupiterians will be good office managers.

Long fingers

Long fingers are not advisable to a Jupiterian as they will make him slow in thinking and reduce his quickness. However, these long fingers will assist the Jupiterian to go into details and will make him studious.

Short fingers

Short fingers show quickness and alertness and that will

increase the brilliance of the Jupiterian. Short fingers show a desire to go in for big things. Such a person can be head of the department or promoter of a big company.

8 Phalanges of the Jupiter fingers

This we have already covered while studying the phalanges. However, for elucidation, I may state that the developed first phalange will give intuition to the person. If the second phalange is more developed, it shows the business side of the Jupiterian. If the third phalange is more developed, it will give him good taste and makes him a glutton.

9 Tips of fingers

They are also important. We know that square tips and spatulate tips are stronger than the conic or pointed tips.

Square tips to the normally developed mount of Jupiter show high religious ideals. To the excessively developed mount, they mean superstition, whereas they indicate absence of veneration when the mount of Jupiter is lacking.

Spatulate tips to the normal mount of Jupiter show pride in great enterprise. They mean boasting and arrogance when the mount is excess in development and they indicate vulgarity if the mount is lacking.

Conic and pointed tips to the normal mount mean lofty pride and religious ideals, to the excessive mount they mean artistic concept and superstition, to the lacking mount they mean lack of respect for others and absence of veneration.

10 Bad Jupiterian

Even though the Mount of Jupiter is developed, it is not necessarily a good type as described earlier, but it can also have the bad characteristics.

A bad Jupiterian can be recognised by the red colour of his hand and a crooked finger of Jupiter. His phalanges are thick, his skin is coarse and fingers stiff. There are grills, cross bars, islands or dots on the mount.

A bad Jupiterian also has ambition and love for command but he does not have the ability to lead men and also does not have the personality to attract men. He is a sensualist selfish and a debauche. He is unsuccessful in life. Since he cannot dictate large crows, he imposes his will on his family members and becomes tyrannical. He is weak and mean and becomes miserable in life.

A bad Jupiterian has a big mouth and short nose. His lower lip is large and thick which indicates brutal appetite. He does not believe religion. He shows apparent contempt to his parents and family and often leaves his wife and children to depend on others. His tongue is very sharp and his heart wicked. His anger can be easily aroused and he often resorts to quarrels. Poor and distressed women and girls show love to him for fear of threat and injury. He leaves his victims to their fate after satisfying his hungry nature. The main characteristics of a bad Jupiterian are vulgarity, dishonesty, timidity and immorality.

Dangers : A Jupiterian is susceptible to certain accidents such as fire, falling from a horse or a tree or from the top of the building.

12 Character and the mount of Jupiter

The main characteristics of a pure Jupiterian are: i) ambition, ii) leadership, iii) religion, iv) pride, v) honour, vi) love for nature, vii) enthusiasm, viii) generosity, ix) respect, x) reverence.

Once we understand the above characteristics we shall be in a position to elaborate them.

A born Jupiterian is ambitious and also leader of men. He will show his command and ability in various fields. In army he will lead men. In judicial line, he will be strict and a man of principles. In business he will be ambitious and will try various enterprises. He loves luxury and in eating he has taste and eats rich food. He has respect for law and established customs. He believes in his own religion and observes religious practices with faith. He is inherently religious.

A Jupiterian hates cheating and deceit and has contempt for meanness and miserliness.

A Jupiterian is warm-hearted and has a fellow-feeling for humanity. He is proud of himself which gives him confidence. He likes to hold positions of honour and respect and commands respect His love for nature, enthusiasm, generosity makes him an excellent personality which enables him to create confidence in others too.

13 Health and the mount of Jupiter

Physically this mount has chief influence over the blood, arterial system and liver. Jupiter governs the sense of smelling. A Jupiterian is liable to suffer from chest and lung disorders, throat afflictions, gout and apoplexy and sudden fevers. He may also suffer from tonsilitis, sore throat, diphtheria, adenoids, pneumonia, plurisy and tuberculosis of the lungs.

A developed mount of Jupiter but with grill or cross lines will mean skin disease.

The third phalange of the Jupiter finger when well-developed shows a strong desire for eating and often makes him a glutton. Naturally he suffers from all the troubles arising from over-eating. It is a menace to health. He has ruined his stomach and has become a dyspeptic, suffering from stomach disorders of various kinds.

A bad Jupiterian suffers from bile and liver, blood diseases and leprosy.

14 Finance

A Jupiterian is a lucky type. He is apt to spend money too freely. There is a saying that a Jupiterian is early out of puberty and poverty.

15 Marriage and the mount of Jupiter

As a general rule, a Jupiterian attains puberty at an early age and marries early. However, as he is ambitious, his ambitions also make him expect to many things from his wife and thus he becomes disappointed. He desires to have a wife of whom he should be proud of. She should have attractive personality, commanding presence, charming manners and intelligence. It is always better for him to choose a Jupiterian or a Venusian as his life-partner.

A Jupiterian wife is the best companion to her husband. She is not an intruder but takes active interest in the business of her husband. She is efficient in house-keeping and has sympathetic and balanced outlook on her children. Her passions are healthy and joyous and her approach to physical love is highly refined and inspiring.

A Jupiterian husband is most loving, thoughtful and considerate. His passions are adventurous and demand immediate satisfaction.

A bad Jupiterian is a debauche and sacrifices his wife and children to his vile habits and very soon becomes a weak and degraded object of general contempt.

A combination of Jupiter and Apollo makes him appreciate and love beautiful women and his fate also brings him across many lovable women. This makes his married life unhappy.

16 Vocation and the mount of Jupiter

His love for position and command makes him a politician. I have observed certain Jupiterians as occupying very high post such as ministers or their associates. They are gifted for public life, statesmanship, high offices etc. It may be in the army or in the church. They are good preachers as well as teachers. They are good educational masters. In order to know the details of vocations, we shall have to consider the mount of Jupiter in combination with other mounts.

Jupiter-Saturn

A Jupiterian, with Saturn as the subsidiary mount, will be successful in the field of research in minerology, soil and food analysis and in scientific pursuits. He can equally be a good teacher of philosophy and literature. The fine grade of

Jupiterian will make him an executive. He can also be fit for jobs such as blasters, blowers, moulders, etc. If the texture of his hand is of second grade, the combination of Jupiter and Saturn is good for employment in factories engaged in marbles, stones, lime, cement, fertilisers, paint and varnish.

Jupiter-Apollo

A combination of Jupiter and Apollo mounts creates good managers and administrators who judge people owing to their merits and talents. The artistic qualities of an Apollonian are added to the Jupiterian qualities and we have an interior decorator, a designer, a sculptor and a painter. He is also fit for jobs engaged in tapestries, embroideries, furniture making etc. In lower grades, he can be occupied in departmental stores, jewellery store, gift shops, ladies tailors shops etc.

Jupiter-Mercury

The shrewdness of the Mercurian will make a Jupiterian a good businessman. This combination is good for salesmanship. Many Mercurians are doctors and lawyers and a Jupiterian can be successful in these lines also. Jupiter-Mercury combination will make the person successful in insurance trade, banking trade and in ready-made garment industry. Fine texture will make him a high executive, whereas rough and coarse texture will make him a clerk or a worker in these industries.

Jupiter-Mars

Usually, upper Mars is seen in combination with Jupiter and the qualities of Mars will make the Jupiterians excellent soldiers, explorers, diplomats and missionaries. The power of resistance and courage as shown by Mars will create tenacity in the Jupiterians. They are successful in automobile industries and engineering industries such as marine, bridge construction, railway, communications, etc.

A combination of Jupiter and lower Mars is not a very favourable combination, and the combative nature of Mars will reduce the qualities of Jupiter. The fiery and aggressive nature of Mars will have adverse effect on the diplomatic disposition of Jupiter.

Jupiter-Moon

Moon shows high imagination which will give a Jupiterian literary talents and he will be a story writer. He will be successful in advertising line, news-papers, library and allied lines where he will get scope for his imagination.

Jupiter-Venus

A Jupiterian with Venus as the subordinate mount will be successful in vocations connected with arts, crafts, hotels, cinema houses etc.

17 Mount of Jupiter in combination with other Mounts

We shall now study the various combinations of the mount of Jupiter with other mounts. Here we presume that the mount of Jupiter is the principal mount on the hand and the mount in combination is either equally important or a subsidiary mount.

a) Jupiter-Saturn

This is a good combination and it means excellent luck ahead. Saturn's check to Jupiter creates a more balanced and practical Jupiterian. The remarkable patience and perseverance of Saturn will check Jupiter's enthusiasm. Before arriving at any decision, the Jupiterian will first study the problems and probe their depths. The extravagance of the Jupiter will be checked by the economy of the Saturn.

This combination exhibits good ability and perseverance displayed in the pursuit of worthy objects and studies which bring good reputation to the subject. He is a person of high moral character and is happy, learned and generous. He is a terror to his enemies. His mind is always engaged in works of humanity.

A woman with this combination is virtuous, amiable and of helping nature. However, she has few children.

A combination of Jupiter and badly developed Saturn will produce a person of an irritating temperament and of an uneven balance of character. Sometimes he looks bright and gay and often sad and morose.

b) Jupiter-Apollo

The combination of these two mounts is a favourable sign and it shows success in life. It means fame, wealth, and fortune. The person is endowed with talents. Everything that he desires is given to him. This combination creates the best managers and administrators who judge people correctly. He has good memory for recalling events, names and persons after a long time. He has great love and appreciation for everything that is beautiful. Because of his repeated love affairs, he is usually faced with serious troubles at home. He comes across many different lovable women whose temptations he cannot resist. His married life is not happy. A combination of Jupiter and badly developed Apollo makes the person unscrupulous. He loses his money in gambling and accepts bribes to cover his expenses. He is impulsive and short sighted. He needs no advice and creates around him hosts of enemies who undermine his career.

c) Jupiter-Mercury

In this combination a man loves scientific pursuits and attains positions in scientific, medical, literary and business fields. A person with this combination is intelligent and attentive. He is gifted with fluency, oratory and first-rate administrative and business capacity. This combination creates successful diplomats and skilful businessmen and legislators who are only interested in laying down practical laws and doctrines. It is a good combination for reformers, lawyers, judges, philosophers and statesmen.

A combination of Jupiter and badly developed Mercury makes the Jupiterian realise his ambition through cheating.

According to him every method is lawful as long as it suits his ends. His transactions and deeds often conceal some ambiguous clauses which enables him to put his customers under his mercy. He attacks his rivals on all sides using every method to ensure their defeat. He usually begins by creating a foul atmosphere amidst them and then destroys them one by one. He also takes pride in deceiving and robbing others.

d) Jupiter-Mars

This is an ambitious man who seeks fortune and fame through military deeds. Qualified generals who display in battles a spirit of endeavour and courage are under the control of these mounts. Once provoked, they will maintain fight and refuse to accept any defeat until they achieve complete victory. Being endowed with physical and mental powers they will never hesitate to shoulder any responsibility. They are always proud of their struggles and victories. In love affairs, they give their heart its full dues, but they never mix love with duty for which the utmost consideration is paid.

A combination of Jupiter and badly developed Mars makes the Jupiterian go the wrong way. He tries to be acquainted with bad women or misguided wives and husbands in order to scare them by scandalous threats. Scandal mongers and slanderers who write anonymous letters to husbands and parents defaming their wives or daughters are controlled by these two mounts.

e) Jupiter-Moon

This is a good combination. It means a religious person with high moral sense, who adheres to tenets and precepts. The Mount of Moon shows lethargy and hatred for struggle. Therefore, the combination of Jupiter and Moon makes the person contented and satisfied. The chastity and integrity of the Moon will check Jupiter's luxury and pleasure. This combination makes the person a humanitarian and philanthropist.

A combination of Jupiter and badly developed Moon checks the Jupiterians ambition by imaginary fear and illusion. He gets many chances in his life but he loses them on account of hesitation and lack of determination. An interesting thing about this type is his fear for domestic animals especially dogs. He has a fear for darkness.

f) Jupiter-Venus

One of the best combinations to possess is the combination of Jupiter and Venus. Persons with this combination are honest. They have pure love and unselfish devotion to women. They are generous, sincere and have a taste for selecting beautiful things. Being very true and shrewd, they can know your inner self. However, they try to conceal the same. A good word or a gentle smile on their part will win over others.

A combination of Jupiter and badly developed mount of Venus makes these persons lazy and effeminate. The smallest contact is sufficient to arouse their bad emotions. They will be satisfied with a kind word or contented with oral promises. However once their anger is aroused, they will use every foul means to attack their opponent.

Important : Since the mounts of Uranus and Neptune are not mounts in the sense we know the other mounts, we cannot have a person who is solely dominated by Uranus or Neptune. Therefore, these mounts do not combine with other types to create new types. However, prominence of these mounts helps other mounts to accentuate or diminish the force of other mounts.

Uranus actuates Jupiter to consistent action. There will not be any stagnation or unexpected result that can upset Jupiterian pride. Neptune gives to Jupiter concrete and inspiring visions of a world of international stability and ntensifies supernatural element in life.

Signs on the mount of Jupiter

Good signs on the mount of Jupiter are a star, a cross, a circle, one vertical line, a triangle, a square, the ring of solomon.

Bad signs on this mount are a spot, a bar, a grill, a ladder-like formation, an island, capillary cross lines and a spring.

i) Star : a) A star on the mount of Jupiter is an excellent sign. It is indicative of realisation of ambition and fame. It also shows sudden rise in life. The period of rise in life can be calculated by studying whether the star is at the bottom of the mount in which case it means rise in early life. If it is in the middle of the mount, it shows success in the middle of life, *i. e.* between 30 to 45 years, and if the star is found on the upper side of the mount, it indicates success in old age.

b) Two stars on the mount of Jupiter mean distinction attained twice in life.

c) If the star is found on the outer edge of the mount of Jupiter, it shows accident through fire. If there is a square around this star, it gives protection against danger.

d) If there is a star at the edge of the mount which touches the line of Life at its beginning, it shows the loss of mother after the birth of the person.

e) If the above star does not touch the line of Life, it indicates that the person is an illegitimate child.

f) When a branch of star on the mount of Jupiter is continued by a line which cuts the line of Apollo on the mount of Apollo, it shows that a revengeful enemy has interfered with the ambition of the person.

ii) Cross : A cross on the mount of Jupiter shows a happy married life. A cross and a star show a happy union in love as well as position. The person is very popular amongst ladies and when in difficulty he is also helped by ladies. If the cross is under the finger of Jupiter, he marries a wealthy woman but he is not happy in begeting a child.

iii) Circle : A circle is very rarely seen on this mount. However when found it shows success. It also means that the person remembers his previous birth.

iv) Vertical lines : A single vertical line when bright and uncrossed by other lines shows success.

A strong red line separating the first and the second finger shows weakness of the intestines.

If there are five vertical lines between the mounts of Jupiter and Saturn, it means that the person has many friends as well as enemies.

Two vertical lines on the mount of Jupiter show divided ambition of the person.

v) Triangle : It is a good sign and gives the possessor a diplomatic cleverness. It is the mark of a politician.

vi) Square : It means protection from scandal and preservation from social failure. It gives the possessor a sober sense which guides his ambition.

vii) Ring of Solomon : A line placed at the root of finger and in a semicircular shape, which encloses a portion of the mount, is known as the ring of Solomon (*fig. 87*). As the name signifies, it shows knowledge and wisdom. It is a symbol of occultism. It gives one prophetic vision.

viii) Spot : A black or red spot on the mount shows misfortune and loss of reputation.

ix) Bar : A cross bar denotes failure and difficulties. The difficulties may be due to ill-health.

A bar crossing a branch of the line of Heart indicates misfortune through love. It also means unfortunate ending of love.

x) Grill : A grill pulls down the virtues of the mount. It destroys the efficiency of the mount. It also turns qualities into defects and vices. It means loose morals and superstition.

xi) Ladder : A ladder-like formation shows a poor life suffering losses.

xii) Island : An island indicates the ruin of an ambitious career by the conduct of a close relative or a friend.

xiii) Capillary cross lines : These lines show a wound to the head.

xiv) Spring : A sign like a spring shows apoplexy.

xv) Sign of Jupiter : It enhances the good qualities of the mount.

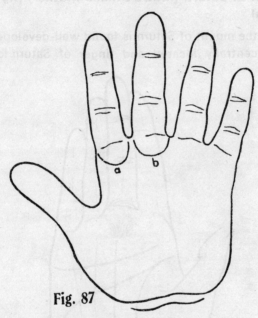

Fig. 87

a) Ring of solomon, b) Ring of Saturn

xvi) Sign of Saturn : It mean caution. It also means love of occult studies.

xvii) Sign of Sun : It gives the the possessor eloquence and love of fine arts.

xviii) Sign of Mercury : It shows administrative abilities and statesmanship.

xix) Sign of Mars : It shows honourable position in army.

xx) Sign of Moon : It shows imagination leading to fanaticism.

xxi) Sign of Venus : It represents dignity and shows consistency in love.

xxii) *Sign of Uranus* : It shows readiness to push one's ideal in the face of opposition.

xxiii) *Sign of Neptune* : This is a good sign and indicates realisation of ambition.

The Mount of Saturn (Matru Sthana-Mother) *(fig. 88)*
1 General

When the mount of Saturn is found well-developed with the apex centrally located and finger of Saturn long and

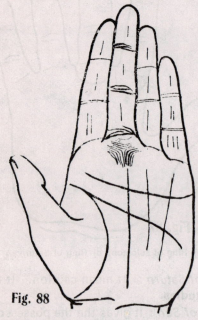

Fig. 88

The mount of Saturn (philosophy, melancholiness, soberness, balanced mind)

strong, it shows that the person is a Saturnian. A good example of this type is Dr. Sarvapalli Radhakrishnan, Ex-President of India. A good mount of Saturn shows extreme sense of discipline and it represents steadfastness, constancy and dutifulness. He will have a sober and solitary personality. He is a very conservative person and does not do anything hastily. He is a lover of classical music but mostly of melancholy type. He is also a lover of art but he loves landscapes, natural scenery and flowers.

His melancholic nature has a depressing effect upon others also. He lacks imagination and is sceptical. Even though he is passionate, he has no capacity to appreciate the good qualities of his life partner and thus he is unsuccessful in his married life.

The good qualities of the Saturnian are endurance, politeness, system, method, wisdom and sobriety.

The vibrations from Saturn will be continuously binding and limiting. The highest states signified by the vibrations of Saturn in the physical world are physical purity and justice which produce the virtues of chastity, economy, thrift, industry, perseverance, veneration and love of truth.

2 Physiological significance

A Saturnian has a peculiar physique and from his structure we can judge him as a Saturnian. If we try to study him from top to bottom, we see that in general he is the tallest of all the types and his Saturn finger is the longest on the hand. Since Saturn is a bilious type, his colour is pale and yellowish. His hair is dark black, rough and thick. His skin is rough and dry. He has a long face and bony cheeks. His eyebrows are thick and grow over the nose. His eyes are black and deep-set. We find that the ears stand away from the head and are very large. He has a thin, sharp nose with stiff and rigid nostrils. He is a man of large mouth with thin lips. His teeth are good but they decay early. Coming downwards, we find him with a lean neck. His voice is unpleasant. He has high shoulders with long arms. On the whole, a Saturnian is anything but graceful.

3 Psychological significance

A Saturnian is considered to be a balance wheel to the character. A Saturnian has an aptitude to look at the other side of life. He can control the ambition of a Jupiterian, enthusiasm of an Apollonian and excessive spirit of a Venusian and a Martian. A Saturnian is a prudent person, wise and sober amongst all the types. He is never over-enthusiastic and is more or less gloomy and melancholy. Usually, he does not have the capacity to look at the bright side of life. Thus, he is a pessimist. He is a lover of solitude and prefers loneliness to company. He shuns society rather than courts it. with the result that he repels the opposite sex rather than attracts it. He is cautious about the future and he takes decisions very carefully on matters which pertain to mundane affairs. A Saturnian is also ambitious and persevering. He is capable of enormous efforts towards the attainment of desired objects. He will never take any important step without profound deliberation and unless he is sure of the result he is sceptical and analytical. Constant work and industry is a mania to a Saturnian.

4 Development of the mount of Saturn

The development of the mount may be normal or in excess or below normal. This we can find out from the standard rules described in the earlier chapter.

i) If the mount of Saturn is developed in a normal way, it shows a) suspicion, b) conservatism, c) prudence and d) caution. It shows a studious person, especially in abstruse subjects such as science, astrology, palmistry and mysticism.

ii) If the mount is developed in excess, it shows a) morbidity, b) melancholia, c) pessimism and d) stingy nature. The exaggerated prominence of this mount shows the wrong side of the good qualities of the mount. Love of solitude and seclusion are converted to intense dislike of society, even to the extent of hatred of mankind. There will be extreme selfishness and avarice. The exaggerated mount of Saturn can be destructive and even though he may be a good friend, he is dangerous as an enemy. Excessive development of this mount shows a tendency to commit suicide and secretive temperament will not disclose the method employed in doing this.

iii) Saturn is considered as a balance wheel and when its mount is absent on the hand, it means want of harmony in the balance of personality. Such a person will be callous and he has to work very hard with a suppressed sense of misfortune. He has to face public mistrust and undergo corporal punishment. He is vicious and unreliable.

5 Placement of mount

The mount of Saturn has five positions of placement. They are judged by the position of the apex.

i) When the apex of the mount leans towards the Saturn finger, it intensifies the qualities of the mount which shows intense love of solitude and conservatism. It also shows extreme shyness and repulsion for the opposite sex. Such a person would lack grace. He would be awkward in his manners and be tactless.

ii) If this apex leans towards the mount of Jupiter, it partakes the qualities of Jupiter and makes the person morbid in pride. He suffers from brothers and relatives. He has danger from the head of the nation. He is always worried and sad. However, after his middle life, he enjoys the company of his children and spends life in good company.

iii) If the apex leans towards the mount of Apollo, it partakes the joyfulness of the mount of Apollo and makes him less melancholy and less gloomy.

iv) If the apex moves towards the line of Heart, it shows anxiety for the loved ones and sincerity in love.

v) When the apex is centrally located, it means that the person is a Saturnian in its real sense and is the balance wheel as described earlier.

6 Texture, flexibility etc.

Fine or medium texture is the best for the Saturnian since it would make him sensible in his thinking and he can be more refined in his behaviour with others in society. This fine texture will lessen his shyness and he will have the ability to mix in society.

Coarse texture will add to the bad qualities of the Saturnian which will make him rough, arrogant and curt. It will increase his hatred for mankind.

We have also to take into consideration the flexibility of the hand. Normally, a flexible hand of a Saturnian will not readily yield to gloom, despondency or bad instincts as shown by the stiff hand. A flexible hand will make the Saturnian enjoy the society of his fellowmen whereas a stiff hand will make him hate mankind intensely. Flexible hand will elevate the good qualities of the Saturnian whereas the stiff hand will make him more selfish.

We have also to study the consistency of the hand. If the Saturnian has a flabby consistency, it will make him more lazy and useless. Being lazy, he will simply have tall talk and will be a man of words rather than a man of deeds. On the contrary, soft hand will be of better use to the Saturnian. This person will not be as lazy as the one having flabby consistency and he will have better ideals.

Elastic consistency is the best since it will give him proper amount of energy and will reduce his gloomy and morbid tendencies.

The colour of the hand also is a good indicator of the character. Yellow colour is expected of a Saturnian. It shows distorted views, irritability, intense nervousness and even criminal behaviour. Sometimes we also find white colour which makes him cold, repellent and unattractive. He will not be popular in society. A cold Saturnian is a picture of misery.

Pink colour will make him better in health and more cheerful. For such a person, everything will not be hopeless. The pink colour is likely to drive away the gloom which always dominates a Saturnian. Red colour is also good. Blue colour is not desireable since it would indicate health defects of a Saturnian.

7 Mount and finger

We have now to take the finger of Saturn in combination with the mount of Saturn. If the finger of Saturn is straight and of normal length, it adds to the good qualities of the mount and we have a pure Saturnian. We have to consider this finger according to its development in relation to the type of fingers we have considered earlier. For easy reference we may take a few points for discussion. We already know that the fingers are either smooth or knotty, long or short.

Knotty fingers

If the finger of Saturn has the first knot developed, it shows the development of the brain and the person is engaged in mental pursuits. This knot will make the Saturnian systematic and methodical in his behaviour and he will succeed in scientific pursuits where perseverance and tenacity are required. He can become a better writer on scientific subjects. The knotty fingers will make the Saturnian qualities more prominent and add to his seriousness. This will make him more careful and slow and there will be nothing like impulse or sentiment within him.

It is also possible that we may come across a Saturnian with the second knot developed which would make him orderly in practical affairs. He will try to create a philosophy which is mundane and which will be useful to the world at large. He can therefore proceed in research work in subjects like economics, history and mathematics.

Smooth fingers

If the fingers in general are smooth, we know that such a person is capable of grasping and absorbing things quickly with the result that this Saturnian develops an intuitive faculty which would help him to draw conclusions more quickly and easily. It will also reduce his shyness and retiring disposition.

Long fingers

We may also come across a Saturnian with long fingers. According to the description (we have already studied while discussing long fingers), this type of fingers will make the Saturnian slow in thinking and he will be successful in studies where research is needed for a long time. The mental faculties of the Saturnian work slowly. In order to accomplish something he must be free from excitement and confusion. Laboratory and soil analysis are good jobs for him.

Short fingers

A Saturnian with short fingers is a rarity, but the short fingers would make him more critical and sceptical and less analytical. This will add to his loneliness and his nature to jump to conclusions would deceive him in life.

Saturnian with deficient finger of Saturn

If the finger of Saturn is very deficient with a conic tip, the person will be led away by events and will have no mental stamina to face the circumstances. In this case, the balance wheel is entirely lacking. Even a good thumb will not help the Saturnian to keep up the balance of mind.

8 Phalanges

The development of the phalanges shows the type of the world which is developed. If the first phalange of the finger is developed, the person will be a thinker and inclined to occult subjects and superstitions. If the second phalange is developed, that would create interest in critical and scientific investigations such as physics, chemistry, mathematics, etc. The second phalange shows the business side of the Saturnian. If however, the third phalange is the longest, the base attributes will be more pronounced and the Saturnian will be a money worshiper. He will count everything in terms of money and would be a miser.

9 Tips of fingers

We have also to consider the tips of fingers while studying the mount of Saturn or a Saturnian person.

a) *Conic tips* : These tips to the Saturn finger are not advisable as they would disturb the characteristics of the balance wheel. If however tips of all the fingers are conic, it would not throw the Saturnian out of balance.

A conic tip to the normally developed mount of Saturn will make him morbid in tendency, whereas the conic tips to the excessively developed mount of Saturn will make him more sad in life and conic tips to the underdeveloped mount of Saturn will make him a lover of art.

b) *Pointed tips* : These tips to normally developed mount of Saturn will give him poetic melancholy* whereas they will increase morbidity if the mount is excessively developed. If the mount of Saturn is lacking, pointed tips will make him careless about life.

c) *Square tips* : Square tips to the normally developed mount of Saturn will add to his love of mathematics and solitude. These tips will make him more calculating and materialistic. Square tips to the excessively developed mount will create hatred for mankind as it will intensify his loneliness. Square tips, if found on the badly developed mount of Saturn, will make him lacking in scientific approach towards any subject and it will also create in him chronic indifference towards others.

d) *Spatulate tips* : Such a tips to the Saturn finger will add to the love for agriculture which is a part and parcel of the nature of a Saturnian. This type of tip makes him active in his occupation if the mount is normally developed.

Spatulate tips show energy and individuality and will create aggressive hatred for others if the mount is in excess development. If however the mount is lacking, spatulate tips will make him work hard and he will care little for others and for society.

10 Bad mount of Saturn

A bad mount of Saturn shows a premonition to commit suicide. Such a person will throw himself from a high place or choose a gas to commit suicide. A bad mount of Saturn makes the person cold-blooded and he becomes dangerous to society. Prisons are full of Saturnians who are also poisoners. The main characteristics of a bad Saturnian are secrecy, superstition, mutiny, envy and pessimism: When the vibrations of Saturn are perverted, they show miserliness, meanness, envy and extreme selfishness.

11 Dangers of the mount of Saturn

As described above, a bad Saturnian is a danger to society and he will achieve his selfish ends through any means, even to the point of going to extremes and at the cost of others' lives. He is most unscrupulous and, if he is crazy about money, he will go even to the extent of killing persons to acquire their wealth and estates. An illustration has been cited by Cheiro in his book of one Dr. Mayer who used to poison his patients in order to acquire their wealth. These bad Saturnians adopt shrewd methods to achieve their ends and it is very difficult for the police department to investigate crimes committed by them.

12 Saturnian characteristics

The main characteristics of a pure Saturnian are cynicism, wisdom, superstition, sadness, gloom and sobriety. The Saturnian is a cynic and looks upon life as an unpleasant experience. He is a profound student of life and his dominant characteristic is wisdom. His second characteristic is superstition. Saturn is a mystic mount and persons governed by this mount are interested in occult sciences and mystic studies. These subjects make him believe in all sorts of superstitions. He has strange ideas about religion and has an insight into the working of miracles.

Sadness is his next characteristic and as stated earlier, his writing and music is melancholic, since sadness always empowers him. He fears death and the fear of death makes him gloomy which is his next characteristic. He is very sober in his nature and his other characteristics rarely make him smile and he seldom jokes.

From the above, the readers are likely to feel that the Saturnian is a bad type. But it is not always so. Some of the greatest figures in history were Saturnians. Saturn is a mount giving monetary stability and success to the individual. He has ability to work hard and concentrate on his studies. He will not leave his subject, however strenuous or critical it may be, till he finds out his results or completes the work. Regularity and responsibility are his inborn elements.

13 Health

A Saturnian is predisposed to certain health defects and his main defects are nervousness, irritation, troubles with legs, teeth and ears, paralysis, rheumatism, etc. A Saturnian is a bilious type and many times suffers from chronic melancholia. It is very interesting to note that the delaying characteristics in the life of a Saturnian are also observed in his sickness. The ailments he suffers from also take a long time for his cure. Ear troubles including deafness are very common to a Saturnian. He is also prone to suffer from knee joints, lower limbs and spinal column. Among the accidents, he is liable to falls, affecting his limbs. As already stated above, this is purely a bilious type. However, his liver trouble is not of temperary nature but remains a structural defect.

Varicose veins and haemorrhoids are a common tendency of a pure Saturnian.

14 Finance

Saturn is mainly a planet giving monetary stability to the individual and a prominent mount of Saturn with a strong line of Fate will make a Saturnian achieve good financial stability in life. Such persons usually succeed in life due to their work and patience. On the contrary a flat or under-developed mount will make the person strive hard for money. But he faces set-backs in life resulting in his worst financial condition.

15 Marriage

Basically, a Saturnian does not have a desire to get married. As described earlier, he prefers loneliness and likes to be left to himself. He has less attraction for the opposite sex. So he tries to postpone his marriage with the result that, if at all he marries, it is at a very late age. He also finds it difficult to make a choice of his wife. As he prefers seclusion to gathering, he often makes his married life miserable. He is very orthodox in his views and does not allow his wife to adopt modern ideas in dress, at home or in public places. The natural result is disappointment on the part of his wife and hatred for her husband. If however he has a desire to be successful in married life, he should prefer a person who is also interested in deep and serious studies and likes to devote himself to philosophy and occult subjects.

A Saturnian does not allow much freedom of action to his wife so much so that even if he is a rich person, his wife is not free to spend. Sometimes he is tyrannical, obstinate and unreasonable laying down laws for the family routine which may be wholly unsympathetic to a happy home. His passions are strong but quick, he considers it entirely animal to satisfy and dispose them off without the development of delicacy.

A Saturn wife is a masculine personality. She is capable and systematic. She enjoys her family life and likes to sacrifice for her children and for the ambition of her husband. The fault is that she lacks feminine warmth, sentiment and delicacy.

16 Vocations

Subjects suitable to a Saturnian are occult sciences, chemistry, physics, medicine and even higher mathematics. In order to study the particular aptitude of a Saturnian, we must study the division of the hand. If the mental world of the Saturnian is developed, we can be sure that he would be successful in medicine. He may be either a general practitioner or a specialist in ear, nose and throat or even an eye specialist. He can also be successful in pathology and biological research. He can as well be a good writer and can write on the subject of astronomy. If his middle world is developed he is suitable for positions in business and he can occupy a good post in rail or road management.

If the lower world is developed, he is likely to be successful in construction companies such as bridge construction, dam construction etc.

17 Combination of mounts
a) Saturn-Jupiter

If you find on the hand of a Saturnian, that Jupiter is the next mount most developed, then we have a combination of Saturn and Jupiter. In this case, the mount of Jupiter inclines towards Saturn or sometimes only the finger of Jupiter inclines towards the finger of Saturn. In this case, the Jupiterian ambition is added to the Saturnian one and the Saturnian, instead of studying the subject for its own sake, will work hard in order to achieve money and reputation. The Jupiterian desire for leadership will also make a Saturnian less shy and the Saturnian characteristic of leading a secluded life will be lessened to that extent. If the Saturnian is interested in music, his music will be less melancholy. His love for nature will grow. With Jupiter as a secondary mount, a Saturnian is less sober, less sad and less gloomy. The Jupiterian secondary type will add the spontaneous qualities to the Saturnian and, if the Saturnian is a writer, he will write popular articles on scientific subjects. He can teach philosophy and psychology in a popular way and get success in being a good teacher.

b) Saturn-Apollo

If the hand shows that the mount of Apollo is the

secondary mount on a Saturnian's hand, the hand will show a Saturnian-Apollonian combination.

The nature of these two mounts is opposite to each other. Apollo means light, whereas Saturn means darkness. Apollo shows enthusiasm, benevolence, optimism, success and opulence, whereas Saturn indicates melancholia, stinginess, nervousness, failure and hardship. Even then, this is a good combination and the Apollonian characteristics of enthusiasm, activity and energy will lessen the Saturnian seriousness and love for occult and superstitious subjects. This combination will help a Saturnian to socialize in society. The Saturnian will partake the artistic qualities of the mount of Apollo and his art will have a back-ground of sadness. According to Hindu palmistry, he will have only one son and he will achieve success and fame through this son.

c) Saturn-Mercury

A combination of the mount of Saturn and Mercury will increase the Saturnian love for scientific research and occultism. As both these types are bilious types, they produce a remarkable person and sometimes a very undesirable one. The Mercury is primarily noted for shrewdness and succeeds in business where other types fail. A Mercurian has sixth sense which tells him when to buy and when to sell. This will therefore make the Saturnian achieve good results in agriculture which is one of the main interests of the Saturnian. The combination of Mercury with a bad Saturnian will create the tendencies of 1) cheating instincts, 2) loss of status, 3) hysteria and 4) melancholia.

d) Saturn-Mars

The combination of Saturn and Mars is not very favourable but the characteristics of Mars such as courage and resistance will be added to the Saturnian features. Mars is a warrior and fighter and these characteristics, if added to the gloomy Saturnian, will make him a useless fighter and will create unnecessary enemies.

e) Saturn-Moon

A Lunarian has a vivid imagination and this when added to a Saturnian will make him a lair. This combination will help a Saturnian to write better technical books or descriptive subjects. He can write good articles in news-papers or in magazines on philosophy or religion. Moon is the mount governing the mind of a person. This makes him highly imaginative and emotional. This will create suicidal tendencies if the mount of Saturn is badly developed. According to Hindu palmistry, a combination of Moon with a bad Saturn means loss of wealth due to one's foolishly spending on enjoyment. He will not get his mother's love.

f) Saturn-Venus

As has been stated earlier, a Saturnian is not very much in favour of marriage or in finding out a partner of the opposite sex. However, his combination with the mount of Venus will make him love the beautiful things of the world and he will have adoration and attraction for the opposite sex though in a serious way. He will be thoughtful and will appreciate art in a scientific way. He will enter into arguments with the opposite sex on subjects of natural beauty.

18 Signs on the mount

As single signs or in combination, a triangle, a square, a single vertical line, a circle etc., strengthen the mount of Saturn. On the other hand, a cross bar, grill, island or cross will lessen the characteristics of the mount.

Star : a) A Star means distinction. If it is added to a strong line of Fate on the mount of Saturn, it is a sign of some mysterious force working to raise the Saturnian to greater heights but only to pull him down to suffer the worst fatality.

b) Star on the mount of Saturn also indicates paralysis and an incurable disease. If it is strongly marked on both the hands, it means death on the scaffold.

c) If a star is found in the middle of a double or triple girdle of Venus, it shows terrible venereal diseases to be followed by death.

d) If a deep line of Fate is entering into the mount of Saturn and has a star either at the end of the Fate line or on the mount, it shows danger of assassination. The same sign with a bad Saturnian implies murderous tendencies.

e) A star between the mounts of Saturn and Sun shows danger from electricity, lightning and snake biting. However, a square will show protection.

ii) *Cross* : A cross on the mount of Saturn shows tendencies to misuse occult subjects. It also means childlessness. This cross also shows death on scaffold. Hindu palmistry has a different interpretation and according to it, a cross on the mount of Saturn is a sign of wealth and happiness.

My experience shows that both the above interpretations are correct and whenever I have seen such a cross on the hand, I have noticed that the person had no child but at the same time he was a rich and happy man.

iii) *Circle* : A circle on the mount of Saturn is a good sign. It will increase the spiritual attainments of a Saturnian. A circle is a favourable omen and it will save the Saturnian from many calamities. We have however, to study the exact location of this circle.

a) If it is at the root of the Saturn finger, it is not considered as a good omen.

b) If it is towards the line of Heart, the person has to struggle in life, but he comes out successfully with the assistance of others. He is also likely to suffer from Heart trouble.

c) A circle in the centre of the mount is the best and such a person will be successful in mineral trades.

iv) *Whorl or loop* : According to Hindu palmistry, a whorl-like or loop-like formation or a flag on the mount of Saturn means a person who is learned, religious, popular, benevolent, courageous, outspoken and virtuous.

The Mounts on the hand Saturn Mount

v) *Vertical lines* : A single vertical line on the mount gives prominence to the qualities of the Saturnian. It shows satisfaction in life and indicates a successful and happy old age. It also means good luck.

If two lines are found, the one on the side of the mount of Jupiter and the other on the side of the mount of Apollo, they show (on a woman's hand) happy maternity. If the lines are clear, they indicate a son. Many lines on the mount of Saturn reduce the qualities of that mount and the person faces a hard life. Small and very thin lines descending from the mount indicate rheumatic disposition. Such lines along with a star indicate paralytic condition. If, however, these lines touch the line of Heart, we can be sure that rheumatic indications are hereditary.

A ladder-like formation of small lines going towards the mount of Jupiter shows gradual success in life.

vi) *Triangle* : A triangle on the mount of Saturn indicates success in scientific pursuits. It also means deep insight into occult and mystic subjects.

vii) *Square* : A square on the hand shows protection. On the mount of Saturn it means protection from bad effects of the mount. It will therefore save the Saturnian from fatality. This sign will even reduce the intensified qualities of a bad Saturnian.

viii) *Ring of Saturn (fig. 89)* : The ring of Saturn is not a favourable sign, it will enhance the bad qualities of Saturn. It means delay and difficulties in the career of the person.

ix) *Spot* : The presence of a spot on the mount of Saturn shows evil influence.

x) *Bar* : A bar on the mount of Saturn is not a good sign. It indicates unavoidable misfortune.

xi) *Grill* : A grill is also an unfortunate sign and shows ill-luck to the person on whose mount of Saturn it appears. It shows an unscrupulous and untrustworthy person. He can be a culprit and will undergo imprisonment.

xii) *Island* : An island anywhere on the hand shows trouble. On the mount of Saturn it weakens the qualities of the Saturnian. It also shows trouble and misfortune if found at the end of the Fate line. However, according to Hindu

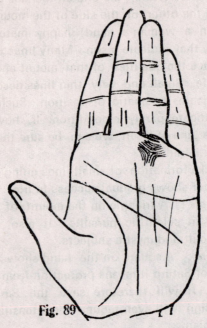

Fig. 89

The mount of Apollo (art, success, originality, oratory)

system, a Yava (island) between the mounts of Saturn and Jupiter shows a learned person who will achieve fame in life. An island on the centre of mount shows loss of memory or deafness.

xiii) *Capillary cross lines* : Many hair-like lines across the mount of Saturn indicate wound in the chest.

xiv) *Sign of Jupiter* : This sign will increase the ambition of a Saturnian in his pursuits of philosophy and psychology and will give him a faculty of understanding human personality.

xv) *Sign of Saturn* : The sign of Saturn on this mount is an excellent sign and it will give the best results for the endeavours of the Saturnian. It means devotion to the study of the occult and the supernatural. It shows intelligence, thoughtfulness and a person well-versed in hypnotism.

xvi) *Sign of Apollo* : This sign creates artistic outlook in the gloomy Saturnian and he will have better capacity to study human personality.

xvii) *Sign of Mercury* : As already described earlier, the Mercurian is also a billious type like a Saturnian and the business qualities of the Mercurian added to those of the Saturnian will make him more cunning and shrewd. He can develop subjects like astronomy and mathematics.

xviii) *Sign of Mars* : A Martian is outspoken and a warrior and also a non-believer in unscientific matters. This sign therefore will make the Saturnian believe in religion and philosophy only in a scientific way.

xix) *Sign of Moon* : This sign on the mount of Saturn will increase the fatalistic tendencies of the Saturnian which may result into insanity.

xx) *Sign of Venus* : As a Saturnian shows dis-inclination to artistic life and natural opposition to the opposite sex, a sign of Venus on the mount of Saturn will create clashes between the aptitudes for solitary life and the romantic life of the person.

xxi) *Sign of Uranus* : It adds to the love of mystery. Sometimes it also accentuates fatality.

xxii) *Sign of Neptune* : It is a good sign on the mount of Saturn and it helps the Saturnian to attain the highest distinction in occult sciences.

xxiii) *Sign of Trident* : This is an auspicious sign on the mount of Saturn and it means riches.

The Mount of Apollo (Vidya Sthana)
1 General

The third mount on the hand for our study is the mount of Apollo (*fig. 89*). This is also called as the mount of Sun. When the mount is found well-developed with the apex centrally located, the finger of Apollo long and strong, it shows that the person is an Apollonian. This mount however does not have the bulge like Jupiter or Mercury and the bulge may be on one side, more probably on the Mercurian side. But this does not mean that it is not a developed mount. We can identify an Apollonian if the finger of Apollo is straight and when other fingers are leaning towards the Apollo finger. If however we find a single deep vertical line on the mount, we can positively confirm that he is an Apollonian.

Apollonian qualities are found in many persons, but a pure specimen of the type is very rare. The development of the mount of Apollo (Sun) also shows the prominence of Sun in the horoscope and the astrological attributes of the Sun are applicable to the Apollonian. The planet Sun is considered as the originator of the solar system and thus it shows originality and energy. He also has the capacity to pass on his energy to others.

This mount has always stood for art and brilliance. These persons are spontaneous in their outlook, they respond to nature and have the capacity to enjoy life. They are usually successful in life due to their active nature and capacity to mix in any society, as they have easy adaptability. An Apollonian has a taste for everything and we find two types of Apollonians, the one who is capable of creative art and the other who merely loves the beautiful and tasty things in life. This distinction can be seen on the hand and we have an Apollonian with creative power and not with merely a love of the beautiful, when we find a deep, vertical line or a star on this mount. An Apollonian knows very well how to get on with others and how to get things done through others. This is a pleasant type to handle because it is a good type. The mount of a Apollo stands between the mount of Saturn on the one side and the mount of Mercury on the other. Even when this mount is nearer the mount of Saturn, it throws back the dark side of the life as depicted by the mount of Saturn. But at the same time the vicinity of Saturn mount is necessary for the Apollonian to have a check on over-enthusiasm shown by him.

We have studied earlier that a Jupiterian is engrossed in in his ambition and religion whereas a Saturnian is filled with gloom and studies and philosophy. The role of an Apollonian is to give life, energy and enthusiasm to the world at large. An Apollonian is an artist and has many talent but they are all spontaneous in nature. He has liking for attractive dress, beauty at home and out-side and active life in business and in every walk of life. He enjoys life in the real sense and also helps others to enjoy. With the mount of Mercury standing nearby, an Apollonian also absorbs the qualities of business, as shown by Mercury and with his energetic and enthusiastic capacities, he usually becomes successful in business. An Apollonian has a style and a grace which influence others and attracts people to him with his natural brilliance and versatility. He has taste for everything and chooses always the beautiful. He is gifted with intuition and he hardly studies any subject by going deep into it. Even then, he can influence others with his knowledge and flash. These characteristics make him a hero of the drawing room. The inherent characteristics of this mount develops quick friendship with persons of both sexes. In short, an Apollonian shows a good understanding of nature and has a positive attitude towards life though sometimes uncertain.

2 Physiological significance

An Apollonian has a handsome personality. He is very attractive and magnetic. His physique is moderately developed. He is neither too fatty nor too lean. His form is graceful, shapely and athletic. He has a fair complexion with rosy cheeks. His height comes in between the height of the Jupiterian and that of the Saturnian. His face is radiant and has an expression of frankness and honesty. His eyes sparkle with brilliance and change to sweetness and sympathy when the emotions are in play. His eyes are almond-shaped having a brown or blue colour and with long lashes. He has a straight nose and the nostrils have a good shape. His ears, teeth, chin and neck are all in proportion. His chest is nicely developed and thereby gives a volume to the sound. His voice is musical. The hands and feet are all in good proportion and his walk has a spring-like action. From every point of view he is an attractive person and intelligence, brilliance, enthusiasm and energy are reflected through each of his movements.

3 Psychological significance

He is an intuitive type and, as explained earlier, he has a quick grasp of any subject and can participate spontaneously in any conversation. This has made him confident with the result that he is never afraid to express his views or speak his mind freely. He has a religious attitude but not in a fanatic or a superstitious way. He also learns occult sciences and does wonders with his natural gift of intuition. By nature, he is cheerful, happy and bright and his outlook on life is very optimistic. He does not harbour any grudge and has the ability to win over his enemy at least for some time. He is changeable and is not constant in his friendship. He is honest and acknowledges his faults. However, he desires celebrity for his honesty. Sometimes he gets angry quickly but also cools off at once. His most ardent wish is to celebrate his name both for fame and esteem. He is not egoistic and does not have vulgur ambition but has intense thirst for reputation.

4 Development of the mount

We have also to see the development of this mount and study whether its development is normal, exaggerated or abnormal. If the mount is developed in a normal way, it shows enthusiasm, eloquence, oratory and life full of energy. Such persons are also dreamers and idealistic artists.

If, however, we find that the mount is excessively developed, it shows the wrong side of the Apollonian attributes and indicates vanity, ostentation and a passion for wealth and luxury. His talents and brilliance may result into insanity. He is over-talkative and has a craze for showing his talents to others. But his superfluous knowledge of any subject exposes him soon and he often becomes the subject of abuse.

If we find that this mount is under-developed, the usual enthusiasm and energy are lacking and art has no place even in his dreams. He may be clever but is not truly gifted. He has no attraction for the intellectual enjoyment and is merely showy.

5 Placement

The aspect we have to study next is the placement of the mount. There are four positions to be studied in this respect.

a) When the mount of Apollo is leaning towards the finger of Apollo, it shows love for the public life.

b) If the apex is leaning towards the mount of Mercury, it means that the shrewdness and the business qualities of the Mercurian are absorbed by the Apollonian and he can make money out of his talents. It also shows love for children and animals, especially domestic pets.

c) If this mount is leaning towards the mount of Saturn, it denotes an Apollonian with selfish attitude and sometimes diffident about his abilities.

d) We may also find this mount leaning towards the line of Heart in which case he is sentimental and emotional and his talents and talk have a personal and emotional touch.

6 Texture, flexibility, consistency, colour etc.

a) *Texture* : As we have studied earlier in the chapter on texture, we can gather much information about the nature of a person by studying the texture of his hand. Normally smooth texture is expected of an Apollonian, as it shows refinement of the character. An Apollonian is on the whole a good type and therefore rough and coarse texture is an abnormality. If however we find a rough skin on an Apollonian's hand, we can immediately know that the Apollonian characteristics of enthusiasm, ability, instinctiveness and intuition are reduced to a great extent and his adaptability is lessened.

b) *Flexibility* : We can expect a little more fexibility than the normal in the case of an Apollonian because he has an aptitude to mix in the crowds and take the lead. If the hand is stiff, he will find it difficult to go with the masses and that will naturally have a check on his natural talents.

c) *Consistency* : There are two types showing the consistency of the hand. Hands are either flabby or soft.

i) Flabby hands show laziness and therefore flabbiness is not expected on the hand of an Apollonian. If we find flabby hands, we may conclude that the Apollonian is a lazy person who merely talks of talents without doing any concrete action.

ii) Soft hands are therefore normal with an Apollonian and they indicate the development of the natural talents in him.

d) *Colour* : Pink or red colour is good for an Apollonian since these colours indicate vigour, strength and consistency. Pale colour will make him bilious and that will lessen his good qualities and will make him a bad Apollonian. This is mere possibility if the apex or the finger of Apollo is leaning towards the mount of Saturn. White colour shows a weak constitution and in-spite of the good talents in the Apollonian, his health will not permit him to exhibit his talent in a proper way.

7 Finger of Apollo

If this finger is longer than the Jupiter finger, it will show enhanced characteristics of the Apollonian. He will be over-enthusiastic and vain. If it is longer than the Saturn finger, he will have no control over himself and will lose foolishly in gambling. He will have speculative tendencies and thus will have to face great risks in life. According to Hindu palmistry, it shows that he will be fond of lottery. If this finger is crooked, it shows a tricky gambler. He will use his talents for a wrong purposes.

Knotty fingers : If the first knot of this finger is developed, it will create an artist who will be endowed with high ideals. If he is a writer, he will write on mental pursuits and novels depicting the intellectual side of the human being. If the second knot is developed, we shall have an author who will delineate the practical side of human nature. If he is an artist, he will develop his art in instrumental music, dancing, and such other arts which involve physical activity.

An Apollonian with either of his knots developed will be studious and thoughtful.

Smooth fingers : If on the contrary, the finger of Apollo is smooth *i.e.* without knots, he will have easy grasp over any subject but will try to make a show of the little knowledge he acquires.

Long and short fingers : The Apollo finger may be either long or short. We know the characteristics of long and short fingers. In the case of an Apollonian, a short finger will make him more critical and he will be cautious about his dialogues, expression of views and the liberty he is taking in public life. He will all the while think how far he is being appreciated by the public. Long fingers will make him a little slow in action, whatever talents he may exhibit.

8 Phalanges

If the first phalange of the Apollo finger is developed, we shall have a mental wanderer who will only dream of high ideals. If the second phalange or the middle phalange is developed, we shall have a more practical type of the Apollonian and he will have better understanding of human life. If the third phalange is found more developed, we shall have an Apollonian of the basal world who will enjoy life only for the sake of enjoyment. He will have friends for the sake of company only and there will not be any sincerity in his friendship.

9 Tips of the fingers

A conic tip adds to the artistic nature of the Apollonian

whereas a square tip makes him more practical. A spatulate tip to the Apollo finger means an original thinker who will have good oratory and command on his language. He will find it very easy to influence others by his originality, but at the same time, he will not very much like to mix with the ordinary people who are not intelligent enough to come up to his rank.

10 Bad mount

We may have the mount of Apollo badly developed in which case we do not have a person with the fine qualities described above. He will have the qualities of an Apollonian, but in a coarse way. He will be boastful and will be fond of show and display. He will crave notoriety and will misuse his brilliance. Such a person will be as follows: He will have thick third phalanage, crooked fingers and short nails. His complexion will not be fair. His eyes may not be clean and probably may be crossed and his face will not give us an impression of his intelligence. In this bad type, the weaker attribute of his character become harmful, both to himself and to others. He is egoistic and indulges in ruinous display of his talents. He is also arrogant and over-estimates himself.

11 Dangers

The person having the mount of Apollo prominent if considered as a good type and his presence to others will normally be elavating and energising. But a badly developed mount and bad characteristics of the Apollonian are likely to be dangerous to others. Such a type may think all the while that others are conspiring against him and he may create bitter and revengeful attitude towards others. He will try to be conspicuous and will commit any folly to produce these results. Though he is seldom a criminal, he may act spontaneously to take his vengence.

12 Characteristics

An Apollonian has basically the following characteristics.
a) He is artistic, b) He is brilliant, c) He is dashing,
d) He is enthusiastic, e) He is of a happy disposition.

His artistic temperament is noticed in his love for nature, grace and decoration at home. He is passionately fond of music which is generally melodious. He expresses his love for beauty in all his actions, even in his eyes and his smile.

His brilliance is exhibited in the way he absorbs any subject quickly. His manner of expression in giving out his thoughts is also brilliant. He shows mastery over language and his flashes of wit can be felt his at every stage.

His dashing spirit is wonderful and it shows his confidence to mix with any class of people. His little knowledge of many subjects pushes him forward wherever he goes.

He is found enthusiastic in every walk of life, in music, sports, at home and in public life. His enthusiasm is so much that he will also make others more active and will make them give-up their lethargy and sluggishness. His company is always lively and everybody enjoys his presence.

It is quite natural that with all the above characteristics he should be a person of happy disposition. He takes things very lightly and is hardly aggrieved. He appreciates criticism and hardly feels offended when he is attached in arguments.

13 Health

Even though an Apollonian is a happy-go-lucky fellow and is normally of good health, he is also susceptible to certain health defects and has to be very particular about the following diseases.

Heart trouble : It has been observed in modern research on heart troubles that there is a malformation of papillary ridges under the mount of Apollo and near the line of heart. With the Apollonian, the heart trouble is a structural deformity and this can be observed even in childhood.

Weak eye-sight: Another trouble with the Apollonian is the eye-sight. We have studied that the Apollonian has good magnetic eyes but it is an irony of fate that he suffers from poor eye-sight, sometimes even to the point of blindness.

Over-exertion: The most common trouble to be found with this type is over-exertion and an Apollonian should always be on his guard and see that he is not exerting himself too much out of over-enthusiasm. His straining too much will weaken his constitution and he is likely to be susceptible to fevers.

Sun-stroke: Sun-stroke is also a common thing with him.

14 Finance

We can say that an Apollonian is a lucky person as far as his financial status is concerned. Even though he is extravagant due to his over-enthusiastic personality, he also earns sufficient to maintain his ostentatious disposition in life. He may not amass wealth but his personality and behaviour will convey to others that he is a rich person. As previously discussed, if the finger of Apollo is long as the finger of Saturn, the Apollonian is a gambler of the highest rank and in such a case, it is possible that he may lose his money in vices.

15 Marriage

An Apollonian husband is generous and desires his wife to shine in society. He wants his family members to dance to his tunes and will not tolerate disrespect. He has a kind and loving disposition and a great heart.

An Apollonian wife is aristocratic by temperament and attracts people to her home and commands great respect. She needs a virile husband who can supply her with the romantic outlets that her passionate nature requires.

An Apollonian is therefore predisposed to marriage and he is always fond of his help-mate, provided his life partner is also of equal enthusiasm and has a love of beauty and of dress, at home and in public. It is however often seen that he hardly gets a companion of his choice, with the result that he is often disappointed in his married life. In his marriage relations he is not uniformly successful. He finds it difficult to go in for a life partnership with a Mercurian, a Saturnian or a Lunarian.

16 Vocations

Before we find out a suitable vocation for an Apollonian, we have to study the type of the world he is governed by.

a) If the mental world is developed, he will be best fitted for occupations where his mental powers can be brought into play. He is therefore suitable for advertising concerns, and newspaper business, especially in the editorial department. He can also be a good cinema producer and can be successful in theatrical performances.

b) If his middle world is developed, he can be successful in materialistic pursuits and show his art as an interior decorator. He can equally be successful in banking business. Salesmanship will be an advantage to his fine appearance, his rich mellow voice and his magnetic personality. With his charming personality, he may also get opportunities to choose his vocation which will have relations with foreign countries, such as a political ambassador or a trade dealing in foreign commodities.

c) The lower world if developed, he will have more of the basal ideas of vocations. He will not be fit for occupations which require mental efforts. He can be successful as a hardware merchant or he can show his salesmanship in dealing with heavy machinery, laundry machines or printing machines. If he is occupying service in a cinema theatre, he can best be a stage manager.

17 Mount of Apollo in combination with other mounts
a) Apollo-Jupiter

If the hand shows Apollo as the primary mount and the

Jupiter as the secondary mount, we shall have a good combination of enthusiasm coupled with ambition and high ideals in life. The Apollonian energy will be creative and the Jupiter will always keep some ideal which an Apollonian will also try for. Thus there is a goal in life to be attained and the brilliance, energy and enthusiasm of the Apollonian will achieve the desired end.

b) Apollo-Saturn

A combination of Apollo and Saturn is also quite good and the over-enthusiasm of the Apollonian will have a natural check of Saturn. The Apollonian will have practical outlook towards life and his art will have a materialistic touch. His writing or creative art will be seen in landscapes and literature of everyday life. This philosophical aspect of Saturn will be brought into play by the materialistic tinge that an Apollonian will get from Saturn. In such a case, an Apollonian will not merely be admired by others but his philosophical outlook will also make others follow him. He will not merely be an idealist in sports, arts and in his tastes but he will have the benefit of the practical and utilitarian view points shown by the mount of Saturn.

c) Apollo-Mercury

Mercury is the mount of business and its assistance to the Apollonian will make the Apollonian a shrewd as well as a cunning person. He will not merely run after popularity but will try to turn his talents towards business. Mercury also shows scientific approach and the writing of the Apollonian will be on scientific subjects such as medicine.

d) Apollo-upper Mars

Upper Mars shows resistance and tenacity. Though it has a dashing spirit, it is always on the defensive. These characteristics of the upper Mars will assist the Apollonian in his oratory when he will make statements which will not be aggressive. His talk will have a dash but he will not offend others. He will have the capacity to resist public scandals as well as prolonged diseases. Mars will make the Apollonian more energetic as a Martian has a natural strength of mind. Martian, by constitution, is a hot-tempered person and this when added to the temperament of an Apollonian, is likely to make him upset and irritable for slight opposition.

e) Apollo-lower Mars

This is not a very healthy combination as it would make the Apollonian an arrogant person. Arrogance, vanity and false pride are the outcome of this combination and an Apollonian is likely to have enemies rather than friends when in combination with Mars.

f) Apollo-Luna

A combination of Apollo and Luna is not a very favourable one as that will make an Apollonian imaginative. The mount of Moon shows dreamy nature and, when added to an already artistic talent of the Apollonian, it will create a person of mere dreams and impractical in his ideals. The cold nature of the mount will make an Apollonian less responsive to social life and his literary career will create fairy tales and stories or novels of fantastic events. This combination however, will make the Apollonian travel a lot and he can be known as a humorist and can achieve fame in producing dramas, paintings etc., whereby he will create funny characters.

g) Apollo-Venus

This is a combination which will enhance the characteristics of the Apollonian. An Apollonian, by nature, is a talented person, has good many arts in him and has a desire to exhibit his talents in various ways. Venus is also a mount of art and Apollonian coupled with Venus will be more attractive, more graceful and handsome but his figure will be feminine. He will always be found in the company of the fair sex and will be surrounded by beautiful women and persons with highly artistic talents. He will pass on his conversational characteristics to those who surround him and he will make the Venusian more energetic and enthusiastic. He will succeed in trades such as jewellery and can earn reputation as an expert jeweller. Money will be easy for him and he can deal in all trades which are concerned with art and beauty. This is also a lucky combination and an Apollonian will always make others feel his absence.

18 Signs on the mount of Apollo

i) *Star* : A star is an auspicious sign on the hand and especially on the mount of Apollo. It shows distinction and accession to wealth. It means a distinguished name acquired in the field accepted by the Apollonian and his efforts would be rewarded. With a vertical line of Apollo, or with several other vertical lines, a star shows a high social standing and great wealth. A star without the support of the line of Apollo is indicative of a life of risks but with a successful end.

ii) *Cross* : A cross is also a good sign on the mount of Apollo. If accompanied by an Apollo line, it means success in life. But a cross without the line of Apollo means disappointment in the desired pursuits. It also indicates difficulties and obstacles in the path of success. It is probable that there is too much intellect standing in the way of practical realisation. According to Hindu system a cross indicates a learned person. On the hand of a woman it means an avaracious woman who is unscrupulous.

iii) *Circle* : A circle on the mount of Apollo shows the strength of the mount as the circle is itself a sign of the Sun. However, if the line of Apollo is poorly developed and the circle is towards the line of Heart, it shows heart trouble as well as eye trouble.

iv) *Vertical line* : A deep, straight vertical line is indicative of domestic happiness. It also means health and fame.

v) *Triangle* : A sign of a triangle on this mount will direct the talents of the Apollonian towards the specific direction which will result in his acquiring reputation.

vi) *Square* : The presence of a square will protect the Apollonian from jumping to unwarranted activities and will also protect him from bad results due to over-enthusiasm. That will also keep his gambling in check and it will save him from disrepute. According to Hindu palmistry, he will be successful in his business and will expand it.

vii) *Spot* : A spot on the mount of Apollo indicates some evil influence and it will keep the Apollonian in troubles. The nature of evil influence can be studied from the other signs on the hand. But if we find such a spot, we have to warn the Apollonian and ask him to be more careful in his talk in choosing his friends and in mixing with the crowds due to his over-enthusiasm.

viii) *Bar* : A bar on this mount lessens the chances of success and creates difficulties in enterprises.

ix) *Grill* : The presence of a grill on this mount will create vanity and he will be satisfied with his little knowledge he has on various subjects. There is little possibility of his developing talents and achieving success in life.

x) *Island* : An island is indicative of some danger probably to the health of the person and we have to see other indications on the hand, especially with the health troubles shown by the mount of Apollo.

xi) *Many hair like lines* : These lines across the mount of Apollo indicate abnormal constitution, showing physical weakness. Such a person is uneasy, changing, unlucky and dull.

xii) *Sign of Jupiter* : This sign will give ambitious outlook to the enthusiastic Apollonian.

xiii) *Sign of Saturn* : The sign of Saturn will pull down the gambling nature of an Apollonian and will also make him realise the values of practical life.

xiv) *Sign of Apollo* : This will give the same result as given by the circle described above but this sign will add to the personality of the Apollonian. It will make him more attractive and cheerful.

xv) *Sign of Mercury* : The sign will make the Apollonian business-like and he can make money with his talents and arts.

xvi) *Sign of Mars* : This sign will help the Apollonian to write novels on battles and wars as well as on subjects of war histories.

xvii) *Sign of Moon* : It will make the Apollonian more imaginative in his art, and with an exaggerated mount of Apollo, the sign of Moon may create a hopeless dreamer and even a lunatic.

xviii) *Sign of Venus* : This sign will add to the poetic nature of the Apollonian and will add to his taste of music and art. It is a good sign and he will enjoy his domestic and social life.

xix) *Sign of Uranus* : With this sign on the mount of Apollo, we will have literature depicting man's progress through revolution.

xx) *Sign of Neptune* : This sign will give more fame than money to the Apollonian.

The Mount of Mercury (Jaya sthana-Wife)
1 General

This is the fourth mount for our study (*fig. 90*). It is a peculiar mount in its characteristics and we have to be very careful in making our judgment about the good or the bad development of the mount. As usual, we can use the same knobs in determining the development of this mount. The apex should be in the centre of the mount and the Mercury finger straight and well-developed. This mount is likely to deceive our judgment and we have to be very cautious in making our predictions. On its good side, it is one of the best and most successful of all the types, but at the same time, the greatest swindlers, cheats or liars can be found in this type only.

Mercurian is a very active and quick type and this does not pertain to physical ability only but also to the mental side as well. He is very skilful and has intuitive faculty. He is equally proficient in games where he uses both his hands as well as his brain. He has the capacity to judge the ability of his opponents in games and knows very well how to take advantage of the weak points of his opponents. He is fond of oratory and eloquence in expressing himself. He is ener-

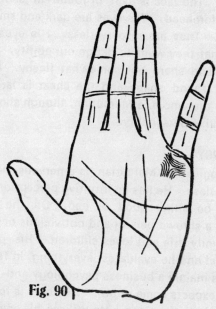

The mount of the Mercury (shrewdness, cunningness, business-ability, love of science)

getic, constantly working and is adroit and crafty and a constant schemer. He has the capacity to pursue his objectives and knows very well how to plan for achieving his ends. He is not at all indolent, and industry is his basic characteristic. As a result, he hardly loses any opportunity and strains every hour to account. He is deeply interested in occult subjects and has a fancy to master all the intricacies of such abstruse subjects. He is a lover of nature and is very much fond of animals like horses and dogs. He is also interested in reading books not on romance, but his subjects are likely to be scientific.

2 Physique

The stature of the Mercurian is short and somewhat flabby. His colour is yellowish since he has a bilious constitution. His skin is smooth and fine and the general texture is attractive. The face is oval or round in shape with high and bulging forehead. The eyes are dark and small but have a sharp look. They are also restless. His eyes give us the impression that they want to gauge our ability. The nose is not straight and sharp but somewhat fleshy. His arms and legs have a round shape and the chest is large and well muscled. On the whole, a Mercurian, though short in stature, has an attractive personality.

3 Psychology

Psychologically a Mercurian is a nervous person. He is therefore restless. He has an intuitive perception and has the capacity to be either good or bad. On the good side, a Mercurian is a shrewd person and not vicious or criminal. He is fond of family life and loves children. His pleasures are mainly mental and he evaluates everything in terms of business. His is mainly a business psychology and for whatever he does he expects some return. His love is for study and for scientific investigations. He utilises his energy in order to get some reward out of them. He is very calculating and is strong in mathematics. He is not a sensualist and not an amorous type. He has definite outlook on his married life, friends and the circle he has to mix with. His intelligence is quick and he grasps the ability of others instantaneously and has a desire to extract the maximum from others. He is also quite capable to do this due to his natural capacities. When he is a good type, he does not like to play upon the credulity of others, but would definitely like to take advantage of the attraction that others have for him. Even though he is a good type, he is sometimes tempted to overcome others by his natural shrewdness and outwit his fellowmen. Sometimes, the temptation is so much that he cannot resist it and once he acquires success in his tactics to outwit others, he often betrays his conscience and descends to the bad type. Though we are going to study the bad type later on, mention may be made here that a good Mercurian may degenerate and may follow a line of a criminal or a liar or a thief.

4 Development of the mount

The mount, if normally developed, shows intelligence, occult aptitude, diplomatic shrewdness, legal profession, oratory, talents, dexterity, love for travel and experiments, eloquence and intuitive faculties.

If the mount is over-developed or exaggerated, it brings into prominence the bad side of the Mercurian. In such a case, the Mercurian will try to impose his desires on others and may practise deceipt, hypocrisy and dishonesty. He is likely to be callous and criminal. He is a dangerous schemer. His natural biliousness is likely to be intensified and he will suffer from nervous troubles. He is also likely to be a gambler, who will lose all his wealth in gambling. This is more true, if there is a cross on this developed mount. If, however, we find that the mount of Mercury is under-developed, we shall have the negative aspect of the Mercurian talents and he will have failures in personal, social and domestic life. He will be superstitious and will have indiscretion. All this will result in a great handicap to his life. His power of eloquence will be handicapped by some physical or mental defect.

5 Placement

a) If the apex of the mount is in the centre, we shall have a Mercurian with balanced qualities. Such a person will be reasonable in all his dealings and will have normal emotions, feelings and discretion.

b) When the mount of Mercury is leaning towards the finger of Mercury, it shows eloquence and humour.

c) If it leans towards the mount of Apollo, it will add enthusiasm in the field of business and a life more dominated by energy but less by Mercurian shrewdness. According to Hindu system, the leaning of the mount of Mercury towards the mount of Sun, on the hand of a woman, shows widowhood and a vicious husband.

d) If the mount is towards the percussion, it will add to the commercial side of the Mercurian and he will get success in business through perseverance and industry.

e) If the mount is inclined towards the negative mount of Mars, that will create hypnotic powers and will give the Mercurian self-confidence. Such a person loves to enjoy life and he does not know sorrow. He will never shed tears nor will he care for others' miseries.

f) Sometimes we may find this mount leaning towards the mount of Uranus, which lies between the line of Heart and the line of Head, and the Mercurian will have agressive spirits.

6 Flexibility, consistency, colour etc.

a) Flexibility : It shows the elasticity of the mount and the flexible hand of a Mercurian means a brilliant person. The aspects of the flexible hand can be studied on the hands of the persons in different trades. For instance, a Mercurian lawyer, with flexible hand will be unusually shrewd and brilliant, who will devise many loopholes to save his clients. On the hand of a doctor, flexibility means new remedies.

As against a flexible hand, we may come across a stiff hand which delineates the characteristics which are just opposite to the ones described above. Such a person will follow old fashions, traditions and notions. For *e.g.*, a doctor., he will be rigid in his diagnosis and will not apply modern methods. If he is a businessman, he will follow old techniques and conventional methods.

b) Texture : The study of the texture will give us an idea as to what class or grade the Mercurian belongs to and what are the underlined forces governing him. A fine texture will give intuition to a doctor, sound arguments to a lawyer and refined manners to a businessman. We can expect a fine texture on a well-developed mount of Mercury, which will add to the natural abilities of the Mercurian such qualities as judgement and common sense.

A coarse texture, on the other hand, can be expected on a bad mount of Mercury and this will add to the evil characteristics shown by a bad mount in his criminal acts. A Mercurian with coarse texture will use rough methods and he will exhibit his callous tendencies at the time of committing crimes.

c) *Consistency* : The consistency can be either elastic, hard, soft or flabby.

Elastic consistency indicates energy, which is an advantage to the Mercurian and it will make the Mercurian sharp in his thinking, arguments and advocacy.

Flabby consistency is not normally expected on the hand of a Mercurian, but if found, it shows a check to the Mercurian shrewdness. Flabby consistency means laziness. In such a case, the normal brain powers of a Mercurian are reduced due to dullness of the brain.

Hard consistency is expected on a bad mount and a hard hand with coarse texture means a scoundrel who will not stop at anything in order to achieve his aim.

Soft hands will lessen the ability of the Mercurian to judge others and he will be less intuitive.

d) *Colour* : Red colour will add to the natural qualities of the Mercurian and will make him more successful in his business, as he will have good health and energy and strong will to execute his plans.

Pink colour is also not bad on the hand of a Mercurian which will make him ardent in all his activities

Pale or white colour shows weakness and the white colour will create a cold Mercurian. He will be hard-hearted, selfish and extracting.

Yellow colour is natural for a Mercurian which means biliousness. This is more often found on the hand of a bad Mercurian.

7 Finger of Mercury

If the finger of Mercury is longer than the normal, *i.e.* if it is longer than the first phalange of the finger of Apollo, we have a strong Mercurian. If, in addition to its being long, it is also straight and erect, we shall have a person with strong will-power and independence of action. It shows literary ability and fluency in speech and writing. According to the Hindu school of palmistry, a person with such a long finger enjoys all comforts in life and also enjoys maternal love.

The normal length of the finger will show versatility and a desire for general improvement.

A short finger of Mercury indicates lack of discretion and inability to judge matters. Such persons are hasty and jump to conclusions. The most important thing to be noted about the finger of Mercury is to see whether it is a crooked finger. This is a notorious finger and is known for its hypocrisy. If we come across such a finger, we have to be very cautious in dealing with such a subject because he will approach us with much diplomacy. If the first knot of the Mercurian finger is developed, we shall have a subject whose mind is scientific and who is working on idealistic lines in scientific pursuits of the higher sort. Such subjects are inventors. If, however, we find the second knot of the Mercurian finger most developed, we shall have a person with materialistic outlook and his writing, thinking and scientific pursuits will be towards the materialistic things. He will invent things which will be useful to ordinary men in life.

A smooth finger will add to the intuitive ability of the Mercurian and he will have easy and quick understanding of his fellow beings.

8 Phalanges :

If we notice that the first phalange of the Mercury finger is developed most, we have a subject whose mental faculty is more developed than the practical or material side. Such a person lives in his mental world. It reveals law-mindedness and pursuit of scientific side. It also shows that the person is clever in speech and has eloquence. If it is very long, it means a methodical person but a liar. If the first phalange is as long as the other two, the person is very regular and if the Head line has branches, the person is capable of acting as a political agent or an ambassador.

If the second or the middle phalange is found more developed, the Mercurian will be very practical and will count everything in rupees, annas and pies. He is fit for commercial positions. It also shows aptitude for science and inventions. Excess development of this phalange on this little finger exhibits talent which is used for criminal purposes. If the second phalange of this finger is developed, it creates a good writer as well as a good businessman. He is very learned and is also good at accounts. When the third phalange of the finger is thick and long, the person lives on the lower plane and does not possess high intellectual capacities. If the Mercurian has money, he will spend it in buying comforts and pleasures for him. On the hand of a bad Mercurian, the developed third phalange shows disposition to crime.

9 Tip of the finger

i) *Pointed tip* : A pointed tip on a Mercurian finger gives psychic powers to the Mercurian and he can have good intuition. He will be highly imaginative and will indulge in flights of fancy.

ii) *Conic tip* : A conic tip indicates an artistic nature and that will create a Mercurian artist. Such a person will be able to make money from his arts. Such a person hardly does well in occupations which require studious approach.

iii) *Square tip* : A square tip to the Mercurian finger will make a businessman who is methodical and practical. He will have good common sense and reason.

iv) *Spatulate tip* : A spatulate tip shows originality and energy to an already energetic Mercurian and it means great success.

10 Bad mount

As disscussed previously, the Mercurian is capable of exhibiting his bad nature and qualities and, if the mount has bad signs on the hand, that will make a bad Mercurian. These people have all the characteristics of a good type, but others cannot find out what is actually in the minds of these bad Mercurians. This type with the qualities of eloquence and effective speech can capture his prey and take undue advantage of the confidence reposed in him by others. In such a case, a Mercurian will go down to any level, even upto committing murder to achieve his ends. He however, does not have steady look in the eyes and his eyes are restless which cannot face you squarely. This bad type has a crooked finger which is sometimes even twisted. It is indicative of cold heart and criminal tendencies. A visit to prison will convince us of a number of criminals who are bad Mercurians. They are bank robbers, pick-pockets and dishonest gamblers. Bad Mercurians are without any conscience and we find humbug clairvoyants and fortune-tellers belonging to this type.

11 Dangers

The main danger of the Mercurian is that he finds it very difficult to draw a line of margin beyond which he should not descend. In his eagerness to play upon the credulity of others, he often turns himself to a charletan and creates troubles for himself In such a case, he cannot use his discretion and is mainly swayed by the small successes he gets in fooling others.

12 Character

The main characteristics of the Mercurian are as follows: a) shrewdness, b) quickness, c) scientific pursuits, d) business ability, e) industry, f) intuition, g) diplomacy.

a) *Shrewdness* : A Mercurian is very shrewd and he has the capacity to go deep into the mind of others and grasp the situation. This capacity makes him overcome his rivals.

b) *Quickness* : Quickness is the speciality of the Mercurian. He is quick not only in thinking but also in action. He takes good decisions and makes quick movements and sometimes his movements are so swift that before his opponents can apprehend what he is doing, he would have overcome them by that time.

c) *Scientific pursuits* : A Mercurian has a scientific mind and he is successful in medicine. We can have very good doctors and surgeons among Mercurians.

d) *Business ability* : Business is the constitution of a Mercurian and he is not required to make any special efforts as to how he should run an industry. His natural tact and talents make him a businessman.

e) *Industry* : Hard work is the basis for a Mercurian and we shall not find a Mercurian who is merely idling away his time or who is lazy. His success in life is mainly due to his industry which brings him fame and fortune.

f) *Institution* : He is a highly intuitive type and intuition is a gift to a Mercurian. It is also possible that we may find a line of intuition on the hand of a Mercurian. This intuition helps him in all walks of life, whether he is a businessman, an artist, a doctor or even a criminal.

g) *Diplomacy* : As already stated earlier, a Mercurian can be a good diplomatic agent or an ambassador and, if he has fine texture, he will have very pleasant manners and he can extract the information he wants from others very diplomatically.

13 Health

There are peculiar diseases which affect a Mercurian. A Mercurian's basic health defect is biliousness and nervousness. However, his liver trouble is different from that of a Saturnian and his biliousness has close relation with his psychological disturbances. Experience shows that his biliousness increases with the increase in tension and the same is reduced or disappears when his nervous trouble is also under control. In the case of a Saturnian, liver trouble is a structural defect. If a Mercurian suffers from nervous troubles, he may get paralytic trouble, mostly in his arms or upper portion. We have also to study the line of Mercury on the hand of a Mercurian and the intensity of his biliousness can be judged by the wavy position of this line. Before we give a judgement on his nervousness or nervous troubles, it is essential to study his nails. We have studied earlier in the chapter on nails that fluted nails exhibit a nervous constitution, and if we come across such nails on the hand of a Mercurian, we can at once consider this as a serious case of nervousness. If the nails are brittle and bending back, we may warn the subject to use his energy sparingly. The colour of the nail is also very important in diagnosing the trouble of the Mercurian. Blue or yellow colour means poisoning of the blood. The mount of Mercury governs the brain, the spine and the upper part of the body. His nervousness may also affect his digestive system and it may also have effect on the function of his kidneys. Mercury governs speech and a bad Mercurian may create stammering and impediments in speech.

14 Finance

Since Mercury is a business planet, we can expect opulence with a Mercurian. With his shrewd characteristics, he is capable of developing his industry, carry out his plans systematically with the result that he gets good returns for the efforts he has put in. He is a practical person and has a fancy to amass wealth. A good Mercurian without chinks in between the fingers can hoard wealth. On the whole, the Mercurian is a lucky person as far as his financial position is concerned.

15 Marriage

A Mercurian is also a lucky and successful person in his married life. His selection is good and usually he selects a person of his own type. He loves his partner. He expects neatness and cleanliness from his partner and also desires that his partner should accompany him in the enjoyment of life. Such a man, would like his wife to be stylish and full of fire and life. He is proud of his wife and likes to see her well-dressed. In return, he proves himself to be a good husband. A Mercurian loves his children and he is very much fond of home. Even if he travels long, he is very much attracted towards home and is eager to return early and be amongst the members of his family. A Mercurian is very fond of marriage and family life and he often finds a match among his friends. He loves his family so much that he is very liberal in spending on clothing and other wants of the members of his family and furnishes his house with taste.

A Mercurian wife has interest at home as well as outside. She has many activities and manages them well. She likes tidiness and, though she seldom does her own work, she gets it done through her commanding personality. If the mount of Mercury on the hand of a woman is inclined towards the mount of Sun, her husband is a vicious person. She also becomes a widow.

16 Vocations

A Mercurian is adaptable to the role he has to play in the drama of life. With his adaptability he comes in contact with various classes of people and becomes successful in whatever he accepts in business. Banking is a good business for a Mercurian. If we find medical stigma on the mount of Mercury, we shall have a good doctor or a surgeon who will achieve name and reputation in his trade. The mount of Mercury also exhibits powers of brain and such a person will have the capacity to argue his points and convince the people. In that case, he can be a good lawyer. He can occupy important positions such as controller of accounts, credit manager or analyst and statistician. He can also be successful in departmental stores and also as a personal secretary to high executives.

17 Mercury in combination with other mounts
a) Mercury-Jupiter

If we find on the hand of a Mercurian that Jupiter is the secondary mount, we have a combination of Mercury and Jupiter. In such a case, the Mercurian will be able to restrain himself from misusing his shrewdness and diplomacy due to the combination of Jupiterian scrupulousness. When gifted with Jupiterian ambition, Mercurian industry and quickness will be intensively utilised to achieve the desired ends. Thus, Mercury-Jupiter is an excellent combination, as Mercurian drawbacks will be made up by Jupiter's assistance. He will have prestige in society. He will have capacity to guide others. He takes delight in writing and will take life easy.

b) Mercury-Saturn

This is not a very favourable combination since both the types are bilious. This will intensify the bad characteristics of the mount of Mercury. A shrewd Mercurian, when backed by Saturn, will be all the more unscrupulous and will have capacity to harm others. A businessman of this type will have an inclination to deceive others in his trade. This combination will also intensify the nervous troubles of the Mercurian and will affect his health seriously. If we come across such a combination, we should always to be on guard and be very cautious in delineating the life of such a person. He will not be frank and would not admit the truths we have predicted. It is however necessary to point out to him his pitfalls and warn him against the disastrous effects he may have to confront owing to his cheating and lying. If in addition to this we find a ring of Saturn, we can positively warn him of imprisonment.

c) Mercury-Apollo

Both Mercury and Sun are lively mounts. The quickness and alertness of the Mercurian with the energy and enthusiasm of Apollo will be a brilliant combination and such a person will achieve great success in life and in every walk of life he enters in. He will be a renowned scientist, an intuitive writer and a brilliant diplomat.

d) Mercury-upper Mars

The tenacity of Mars will help a Mercurian to sustain business losses, if any. It will also assist the Mercurian to pursue his trade tenaciously. The upper Mars shows self-defence which will always make a Mercurian to be on his guard and take cautious steps in his plans. According to Hindu interpretation, such a person is capable of mixing with young and the old. He will enjoy the company of all types of people. He loves his brothers and is very religious. He may create a charitable institution.

e) Mercury-Luna

Moon is considered to be a highly imaginative mount giving love for travel. Mercurian is also fond of travels and this combinaton will be beneficial to a Mercurian in whatever trade he may be. If he is a surgeon, he will be known for his skill. If a writer, he will get the reputation in writing fairy tales or detective stories. He will make extensive tours for his business. According to Hindu system, if the mounts of Mercury and Luna are developed, and if there is a grill on the mount of Mercury or a cross on the mount of the Moon and if the line of Head is divided, we shall have a person who is deeply interested in philosophy and mysticism and who will have acquired good mystic powers. If such a sign is seen on the hand of a child, his parents should give him good education to make him a saint.

f) Mercury-Venus

Though a Mercurian is not a sensualist, he appreciates beauty and well-dressed women. This particular combination enables him to mix more with the fair sex. He can be popular by his quick actions and intellectual fits. If he is in business, he can deal in articles such as cosmetics, jewellery and crafts which have artistic and decorative value. He is fond of children and good exercise. He dislikes medicines. He takes delight in philosophical discussions.

g) Mercury-lower Mars

Lower Mars is an aggressor and a warrior. On the hand of a Mercurian, it means dash and courage in his trade. With this combination, a Mercurian can try for very high schemes. He can develop industries where he can produce weapons and appliances for military or can set up a scientific laboratory where he can explore his scientific talents for military aids. According to Hindu palmistry, such a person takes care of his dependents and does successful business in trades of articles which are found in water, such as pearls, sand conch, shell etc.

18 Signs on the mount of Mercury

i) *Star* : A star is a good sign on the hand and it shows sense in business, eloquence and science. It also indicates unexpected luck. A star in combination with a transverse island indicates mental shock due to some fatal event. On a bad mount, it means persistant dishonesty and a mania for stealing.

ii) *Cross* : A cross is also a good sign on the mount of Mercury and it adds to talent and diplomacy as exhibited by the mount of Mercury. On a bad mount, it means dishonesty and deceiving disposition. A number of small crosses on the mount indicate unnatural vices. On an over-developed mount, a cross implies a gambler.

iii) *Circle* : A circle, even though it is considered to be a good sign on the other mounts, is not so on the mount of Mercury and it indicates danger from water and poisoning.

iv) *Vertical line* : A vertical line indicates enhanced qualities of the mount and, even though a mount is depressed a single vertical line on the mount will indicate the prominence of the mount. It is therefore a good sign and it means unexpected accession to wealth and good fortune.

A number of vertical lines on the mount of Mercury are called medical stigma and a Mercurian possessing such lines has a natural inclination to medical studies. We can recommend a Mercurian with these lines to go in for any medical profession. Such lines, if found on a woman's hand, indicate that she is likely to marry a medical person and she will prove to be an excellent nurse. If such lines are found along with a prominent mount of Mercury, we shall have good doctors who can cure real or imaginary ailments.

Many mixed lines on this mount lessen the qualities of shrewdness and scientific aptitude. If several such lines reach as low as the line of Heart, it means unwise generosity in spending money.

v) *Triangle* : The triangle adds to diplomacy and cleverness of a Mercurian.

vi) *Square* : The square will save the Mercurian businessman from financial losses and from dangers arising out of the restless temperament of the Mercurian.

vii) *Spot* : A spot indicates accidents or illness and sometimes even major failures in business. If it is connected with the line of marriage on the mount, it shows troubles in married life.

viii) *Bar* : A sign of bar on the mount bringes troubles and obstacles in business. It also means loss through theft.

ix) *Grill* : A grill shows temptation to commit suicide after a crime is committed by the Mercurian. Saint Germain had an occasion to see this sign on the hand of a cashier who committed suicide on being discovered to be an embezzler of a large amount.

x) *Island* : An island means betrayal of trust by the subject.

xi) *Many hair-like lines* : These on a woman's hand show chattering habits.

xii) *Sign of Jupiter* : Fame achieved through one's efforts.

xiii) *Sign of Saturn* : It means talent tinged with sadness.

xiv) *Sign of Sun* : Appreciation of natural philosophy, admiration of God's creation and interest in astronomy.

xv) *Sign of Mercury* : It intensifies the natural qualities shown by the mount of Mercury.

xvi) *Sign of Mars* : It shows a positive and dashing approach towards any undertaking. On the hand of a bad Mercurian, it shows violence and theft. Such a person can be a highwayman.

xvii) *Sign of Moon* : High imaginative disposition giving intuitive judgement to the Mercurian. He is also arrogant, full of pride and destructive by nature.

xviii) *Sign of Venus* : It shows sensible love and desire for lasting companionship.

xix) *Sign of Uranus* : It shows an author on scientific subjects or a scientist.

xx) *Sign of Neptune* : It creates a writer of childrens' stories.

The Mount of Mars

 i) Negative Mars—Dharma Sthana—Religion
 ii) Positive Mars—Shatru Sthana—Enemies

1 General

There are two positions for the mount of Mars on the hand (*fig. 91*). One of them is located below the mount of Mercury and above the mount of Moon on the side of percussion. This mount is called the upper mount of Mars or the negative Mars. The other position is situated inside the line of Life above the mount of Venus. This is called the

The Mounts on the hand Mars Mount

positive Mars or the lower Mars. These positions of Mars were located on the hand at a very late stage in the study of palmistry and, before they were discovered, the study of the hand was concentrated on the plain of Mars in order to find out the influence of Mars on the individual. The plain of Mars as we have studied earlier, occupies the position bet-

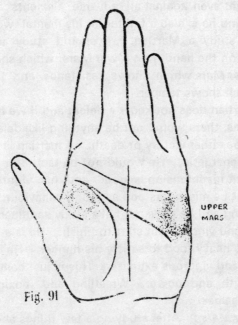

Fig. 91

The mount of Mars (dash, courage, energy, activity, hot temper, errotic)

ween the Head line and the Heart line. It was also thought earlier that, if there is a hollow in the hand, the individual was considered to be unlucky and miserable in life. But later on during the study of the hand, it was observed that what we call the plain of Mars can best be explained as the mount of Uranus and the locations described above for the lower and the upper Mars were found more suitable in diagnosing characteristics of Mars on the hand of an individual. In order to find out the exact places, readers are requested to refer to (*fig. 1*) explaining the map of the hand.

To start with the positive Mars or the lower Mars, we can say that it shows aggression and the Martian is considered as a fighter. This does not mean that all soldiers are Martians, but a Martian can be a good soldier. He is called a fighter because he is always positive and aggressive in all his acts and will not stop till he achieves his end. He has the capacity to fight even against all adverse elements and circumstances, and he is also a fighter in his mental world. If we want to study a Martian, we should study all the three positions on the hand, *i.e.*, lower Mars, which shows aggression, upper Mars which shows resistance and the plain of Mars which shows temper.

A Martian does not know a defeat and if we have an army of Martians, there would not be anything like defeat for them. It would be either victory or death. A martian is very active, brisk and energetic. He would not be tactful or delicate in his talk but his intension is good and his vigorous manner should not be misunderstood as rough behaviour. He is fiery and dashing and he does not have sickly sentiments. He has audacity and vigour from start to finish. He is a heavy eater and needs heavy food to satisfy his hunger. He is also fond of games and vigorous exercise. This is just compatible with his strength and power. Wrestling and boxing are his favourite games.

Upper Mars : After studying a few things about aggressive Mars, we shall now study the upper Mars, or the negative Mars which shows self-defence and passive nature. This mount also shows fighting qualities. Here we can have a distinction between the qualities of the lower Mars as already studied above and of the upper Mars which is under study now. There are two types of fighters. The one is aggressive and forces the issue and the other is on self-defence or resists the pressure brought on him. The upper mount of Mars is cool under all circumstances unlike the lower Mars and does not get discouraged if things go against him. He has the power of perseverance and he will not give up fighting even when he knows that he would lose the battle. This power of resistance makes the Martian successful over every obstacle. If however this mount is absent, it is likely that a person would be easily discouraged, giving up his efforts when hard pressed. A Martian with upper mount developed will not force fighting but will be content with his resistance to opposition and will wait till he overcomes the obstacles.

All Martians have strong sexual passions and they are naturally attracted towards the opposite sex. They are prepared to go through any ordeal to gratify their desire. However, there is a great difference between the approach of a positive Martian, who will not wait for the consent of the other person and will exert his force, and the negative Martian who will not take any step without the consent of the other person.

Thus, we have seen the general aspects of both the types of Martians and in our study we have to find out which of these two mounts is prominent on the hand.

2 Physiology

A Martian has a good height and as a whole his personality depicts figure with energy and enthusiasm. His face is round and even the head is a little small in proportion to the body and the lower back portion of the brain is heavy. He has sharp eyes and ears though not touching the head but still nearer to it. He has a strong chest and broad shoulders and his hands and legs are rather short in proportion to the body. But his built is strong and he always takes a pose which is aggressive. His colour is reddish. His chest is broad and it has strong lungs which send forth a big commanding voice, full of resonance and power. In short, a Martian by his very appearance shows his character *i.e.*, aggressiveness both mental and physical with a strong and robust constitution.

3 Psychology

A Martian is a brave person to whom conflict does not

bring the thought of danger. He is exceedingly devoted to his friends and will fight for them. He is very generous, magnanimous and devoted friend. He has sympathy and consideration for the weak. He loves children and animals. He takes delight in showing mercy to others. He likes the healing profession. Like a good soldier, he does his duty and cost is no consideration for him. He is backed by self-control, moral courage and the power of forgiveness. His psychological aptitude is remarkable and under all circumstances he proves his strength of will and exhibits courage.

Psychology of upper Mars

The brave spirit of the Martian is also experienced with this mount but he is cool to opposition and faces emergencies with courage and is not at all discouraged if things go against him. He will fight to the last even against all odds.

4 Development of the mount
The upper Mars

a) When the mount is developed in a normal way, it will show the courage of a soldier, a martyr or a patriot.

b) When it is developed in excess, it will exhibit a violent temper.

c) If the mount is lacking in development, it will mean a coward. It shows absence of resistance and surrender to fate. He will be easily discouraged and will not seize opportunities. It also shows a suicidal tendency.

The lower Mars

a) If we find the development of lower Mars in normal proportion the Martian is seen to be a resigned person, a stoic and careless about fears.

b) If the development is in excess, he is likely to be hard-hearted.

5 Placement of the mount

This mount does not have an apex but we can find out

the development from the bulging it has. If the positive Mars is leaning towards the mount of Venus, it shows the power of endurance through affection and attachment. It also means that the vigour of Mars gets an outlet in the company of an opposite sex and shows polygamy.

If the mount is deflected towards the thumb, it will give the power of endurance and determination. If the mount is inclined towards the interior of the palm, it will partake the qualities of the mount of Uranus. It shows unexpected changes in life an upheavals due to the aggressive nature of the Martian.

If, however, the mount is inclined towards the line of Head, it will mean a combination of intellectual strength and discrimination.

Placement of negative Mars

If the upper mount of Mars is inclined towards the mount of Mercury, it will make the Martian a businessman who has the power of resistance and who will not be discouraged in emergencies.

When this mount inclines towards the middle portion of the line of Heart, he will show courage and patience in his affairs of love.

When it inclines towards the mount of Uranus, it will make the person highly intelligent and energetic.

If this mount is leaning towards the mount of the Moon, it will protect the subject from laziness and dreaming. It will also give the Martian hypnotic powers.

Lastly, if the mount is seen bulging towards the percussion, it means that the qualities of the negative Mars are intensified.

6 Texture, flexibility, consistency, colour etc.

a) *Flexibility* : A medium type of flexibility is expected on the hand of a Martian, which is a balance between an elastic mind and a stiff mind. Normally, great flexibility is not expected with this type for the simple reason that they do not think as quickly as other types. However, a very flexible hand will mean elevated thinking and that will make the subject more versatile. Flexibility of the hand will show the elastic mind behind a Martian.

The stiff hand will make the Martian more obstinate, quarrelsome and a person with fixed ideas

b) *Consistency* : i) Flabby hands are most unsuitable for a Martian as they would reduce the qualities of a fighter and will make him less aggressive and less provocative. Such a Martian will only visualise fights and will dream of bravery, but will achieve nothing in practice.

ii) Elastic hands will be best suited to a Martian as he will be backed by energy and will therefore be able to push his strong qualities within reasonable limits. He will never be lazy and will have developed masculine and Martian energy.

iii) Hard hands show a coarse nature and less adaptability to new conditions. It is a very bad combination on the hand of a Martian with lower mount developed.

c) *Texture* : A fine texture will lessen the coarseness and brutality of a Martian. This Martian will be more delicate in his approach. A Martian can be seen in all professions and a very fine texture will make him a person with refined character and behaviour. Such a texture, if found on the hand of a wrestler, will make him cool and level-headed and not brutal.

Medium texture will be found on the hand of a Martian who moves in good society. If the upper mount of Mars is developed, a medium texture means refined resistance under disappointment.

Coarse texture on the hand of a Martian will make him a disagreeable fellow.

d) *Colour* : Red colour is expected of a good Martian which shows a strong heart, rich blood and a great amount of vitality. If there is too much of reddishness, it is a dangerous sign for a Martian to have as he will not be able to control his vigour and may cross his limits. If he belongs to a bad type, he will commit even crimes to achieve his ends. These are the men who commit murder out of jealousy.

Pink colour is also suitable to a Martian as he will keep under control his hasty nature, vigour and intense temper.

White colour is hardly seen on the hand of a Martian, but when found, it will diminish the qualities of the mount and reduce its strength. Coldness is the opposite of the qualities shown by the red colour. The white colour will not give the strength to the Martian either to fight or to resist.

Yellow colour, if found, will show nervousness underneath the Martian qualities. Yellow colour also indicates biliousness and that will make a Martian a quarrelsome person as well as a criminal Martian.

We can also take into consideration the nails of the Martian and use our discretion in combining the various types of nails in order to find out the fine shades of the character of the Martian.

7 Mount and fingers

Here also we have to combine four types of fingers with the mount. We shall take them one by one as follows :

Long fingers : Such fingers on the hand of a Martian will make him plan his campaign with utmost care and he will look after the equipment of his men. He will be neat in his dress and will also expect these things from others. Such a Martian is not impulsive and likes to take his decisions cautiously and slowly. He will be very particular in attending to minute things and that may lessen his aggressiveness.

Short fingers : These fingers will make him very active, impulsive and quick in his decisions. The impetuous nature of the short fingers will make the Martian commit blunders.

Smooth fingers : Such fingers indicate quick grasp on the subject and that will add to the intuitive faculty of the Martian. He will therefore grasp the situation in a very short time and will take his decisions to over-come his opponents. There is also a possibility of making a Martian thoughtless and we have to observe his line of Head very carefully.

Knotty Fingers: It is necessary to study whether the first knot is developed or the second. The first knot will make him unusually intelligent and will give him order in his plans. The second knot will make him tidy and neat in his dress and regular in his work and profession. If both the knots are developed, it will create an analyser who is not motivated by impulse.

8 Phalanges

If we find that the first phalanges of all the fingers are well developed, we shall have a Martian who has developed his mental faculties. As already described earlier, he is a courageous as well as a dashing person, and with the first world more developed he will be absolutely fearless and sometimes fanatic in his aggressive moves. He will be more intelligent and will have good mental qualities to make him a successful personality.

If the second phalange of all the fingers is in prominence, such a Martian will possess enthusiasm for practical affairs, will have courage in public life and have the power of resistance in all practical odds.

The development of the third phalange will make a vulgar Martian who will try to satisfy his animal desires only. He will only be a sensualist, a heavy eater and will hate mental pursuits.

9 Mount and tips
a) Upper mount of Mars and the tips

Pointed tips: If the mount is normally developed, these tips will show courage. If it is developed in excess, the tips will mean violence. If the mount is lacking, we shall have a coward.

Conic tips: These tips will indicate a patriot with normal development of the mount. On an excess mount, they show vanity.

Square tips: They add to the courage of the Martian if the mount is normal in development. If the development is in excess, the square tips indicate the violence of a disappointed schemer. If the mount is lacking, they exhibit a coward in everyday life.

Spatulate tips: To the normally developed mount of Mars, these tips mean an explorer. Such type of tips when added to an excess mount, produce a rough Martian. These tips on a lacking mount means a coward on the battle field.

Lower mount of Mars and the tips

Pointed tips with normal development of the mount indicate resignation. With excess development they mean hard-heartedness. Such tips on a lacking mount show a sensitive soul.

Conic tips: To a normally developed mount, these tips mean a stoic. These tips on an excessively developed mount mean a blunt nature. On the mount which is lacking, such tips make the Martian easily offended.

Spatulate tips: When the mount is normal in development, spatulate tips show carelessness about the future. if it is developed in excess, they exhibit active cruelty and when the mount is lacking, they denote a coward.

Square tips: On a normal mount, they show patience. On an excessively developed mount, they mean passive cruelty and if the mount is lacking, they indicate physical or mental pain.

10 Bad mount

The Martian has a bad side also. On his bad side. he becomes a drunkard, lascivious and sometimes even a criminal. A Martian is not bad by birth, but he is made so because he is not able to control the bad elements which tempt him more. In this case, the skin is very coarse, the hand is very stiff and with red colour. Fingers are short and the third phalanges are more developed. The plain of Mars will be unevenly developed with many cross lines. Sometimes a large single cross is also seen in the plain of Mars which indicates uncontrollable temper.

The physique or the appearance of this Martian is also very typical. He will be short in stature. His face will be red with spotted skin. He will have bold, red coloured eyes. He lives only to gratify his passions and he will be brutal in his actions. In committing murder, he uses only peculiar weapons such as a knife or an axe. If he is disappointed in love, he will take pleasure in exhibiting his wickedness and will murder the person in a most nasty way.

11 Dangers

A Martian, if he is not backed by good signs on the hand, is likely to be a great danger to society. His natural qualities of courage, enthusiasm and dash will have perverted motives and he will lose control over his emotions and sentiments and will go to any extent to gratify his desires.

He is liable to accidents connected with the earth, *i.e.* falling from a high place or from a tree. He may suffer from a bite of reptiles and domestic animals. He is also prone to accidents from fire.

12 Character

The main characteristics of the Martian are as under: a) Aggression, b) Resistance, c) Courage, d) Coolness, e) Calmness, f) Quickness.

Basically a Martian is a fighter. He always takes the aggressive moves. He does not know defeat. In excessive development he has either victory or death. This characteristic is mainly shown by the lower mount of Mars. In opposition to this characteristic, the upper mount shows the quality of resistance and this Martian in his capacity to resist an aggression or opposition hardly knows as to when and how he is being defeated. Resistance is his guard and he protects himself with courage behind him. Thus the third characteristic of courage comes in. Courage actually assists an upper Martian to prolong resistance and ultimately makes his opponents lose temper and commit blunders.

Coolness is another characteristic of the upper Martian. We can observe it when we find him controlling his temper even though circumstances are against him.

Calmness of the Martian is the outcome of his power of resistance and this faculty will assist him in taking decisions which are not to be taken hastily but need time. A Martian with smooth fingers take quick decisions and that leads him to success.

13 Health

The main health defect of a Martian arises from heat and he is susceptible to troubles such as piles, fevers, small-pox, etc. He is also likely to suffer from kidney or bladder stone. Throat trouble, bronchitis, laryngitis are also common to a Martian. These troubles are mainly shown by the grills or cross bars on the upper mount of Mars.

14 Finance

A Martian, usually being in hazardous occupations such as army, navy, airforce etc. earns far more than an average man. He is also liberal while spending. He spends much especially to please his sweet-heart or for other pleasures in life such as drinking etc.

15 Marriage

A Martian is vigorous by health and has strong circulation of blood which makes him more passionate and enthusiastic about married life. He is fond of a beautiful wife and likes her to be submissive and passive to his sexual desires. He is fond of family children and likes to have a good house. He usually leads a good married life in spite of his hot-tempered nature and eccentricities. He has a romantic mental picture of what he wants in his wife. This mental picture demands perfection. He desires a beautiful, clever and a very good wife. The most difficult thing in the married life of a Martian is to satisfy his romantic conception of physical love. He has a voracious appetite and his wife with her devotion can harmonize with him physically. Usually, we find a Martian suspicious about his wife and can hardly have a harmonious married life.

Martian wife : A Martian lady will make a wonderful wife for an ambitious man. She is a witty and clever conversationalist with wonderful social presence. She will assist her husband in his business. She may also start her own activity and add to the family income. She will be happy if married to a passionate and possessive man.

6 Vocations

A Martian is found in all walks of life but he will be more suitable for army and professions where there is full scope for his aggression and courage. The best profession for a Martian would depend upon the combination he will have, with other types of mounts on the hand. For instance, a Jupiter as a secondary type is a powerful combination and the desire for leadership as shown by the Mount of Jupiter will make the Martian successful in any field. In military, he will rise to high positions, in politics he will be eminent and in business he will exhibit his dashing and pushing nature. A Martian-Saturnian combination will make a good agriculturist.

A Martian-Apollonian is good for a salesman. He will be successful in selling the finer lines of merchandise such as jewellery, luxury articles etc.

If the mount of Mars is in combination with the mount of Mercury, it will not be difficult to imagine what the effect will be. When we add shrewdness, industry and the business ability of the Mercurian to the aggressive nature of the Martian, it will create a force which will be very active and untiring. Such a person will be successful in clothing industry, ready-made garments industry etc.

We can combine the Martian in a similar way with a Lunarian or a Venusian and find out the right type of vocation for the Martian.

17 Mars in combination with other mounts

a) Mars-Jupiter

The combination of Mars and Jupiter is a healthy combination. We shall have an aggressive personality coupled with ambition and high motives in life. Such a Martian can reach great heights in his profession and courage will endorse his personality to help him to rise to any position in life. With his calm approach to the circumstances around him, he will slowly gain honour and prestige exhibited by the mount of Jupiter and will have pride and dignity in life.

b) Mars-Saturn

A good Martian combined with a good Saturn will have balancing qualities of Saturn and such a Martian will hardly go to extremes, either in his courage or aggression. It is not as bad a combination as it is usually considered to be. This is however not a favourable combination if both Mars and Saturn are afflicted. The favourable combination will help a Martian to follow customs and traditions of the society he lives in.

c) Mars-Apollo

The agressive nature of the Martian and the successful salesmanship of an Apollonian will make a pleasant Martian, who will be more accomodative, adjusting and less quarrelsome.

d) Mars-Mercury

If we find this combination, we have to be very cautious in studying the development of both these mounts. This is necessary as both these have an equally bad side. A bad Mercurian, as we know, is a criminal, and bad-tempered nature as exhibited by a Martian will make this type a dangerous criminal. This is only a precaution we have to take in studying the combination of these mounts. The combinations in our discussions are normally of the good type and if both these mounts have fine qualities, we shall have a Martian who will have shrewdness and patience in achieving his ends. He will wait till the opportunity is given to him and then with his dash and courage he will take the fullest advantage of the opportunity given to him.

e) Upper Mars-lower Mars

This will be one of the best combinations for a Martian to possess. It will be a good blending of aggression and resistance, courage and patience, dash and coolness. This combination will make a Martian level-headed and he will neither go to extremes nor will he remain unaffected by circumstances. This type of combination will make a perfect soldier who is bound to get victory.

f) Mars-Moon

It is difficult to find this type of combination on the hand, for the simple reason that Mars is too powerful to accept Moon as a subordinate and Moon is also too weak to go with a powerful Martian. If, however, we come across such a combination, the mysticism and fancy of the Lunarian will have adverse effects on the Martian qualities and in exhibiting his aggressive temper, he will be a fanatic and will expect only success, even though his actions and decisions are wrong. He will be motivated by fantasy.

g) Mars-Venus

A Martian combined with a Venusian will add to his personality and he will be more attractive and amorous. Others will be fond of his company. His talk will be amusing. His dash will be pleasing and his vigour, strength and enthusiasm will have a natural outlet in the company of a Venusian.

18 Signs on the mount of Mars

a) *Star*: A well-formed star on a good mount of Mars shows military honour and gain as a result of patience and tolerance. It will also make him bold. If a line rises from the star to the mount of Apollo, it denotes a distinguished military service.

On a bad mount, a star denotes danger in strife, even a murder. On an exaggerated mount, it shows murder committed by the subject through jealousy or anger.

b) *Cross* : Normally it shows danger of bodily harm. On an over-developed mount, it indicates danger through quarrelsome and stubborn nature.

c) *Circle* : This is a bad omen. This may also cause wound in the eye.

d) *Horizontal line* : A single horizontal line, rising from the line of Life and going into the positive or negative Mars, shows severe illness, sorrow or death. An independent horizontal line on the mount is also a bad omen.

e) *Triangle* : It shows military skill, also aptitude for and gain from mining and geology.

f) *Square* : It shows control over violent temper and protection from any danger shown on the mount including bodily harm.

g) *Spot* : It shows wound in a fight. On an over-developed mount, it shows a self-inflicted wound.

h) *Bar* : It shows enemies who will stand in the way of success.

i) *Grill* : It shows violent death and murderous instincts. When it is connected with the upper part of mount of Luna or is extended towards it, it shows serious and chronic intestinal troubles, even tuberculosis of the intestines and catarrh of the stomach.

j) *Island* : It is not a good sign and it shows obstacles in life. On the upper mount, it shows obstacles from friends and on lower mount from relatives.

k) *Many hair like lines* : These lines are bad on the hand of a Martian and they stand in the way of success. They also show violence of temper and brutality in love.

l) *Sign of Jupiter* : On a good hand, it means an insatiable conqueror. On a bad hand, it can be the sign of a lady-killer.

m) *Sign of Saturn* : An unhealthy sign showing morbidity and murderous tendencies especially with revenge in the background.

n) *Sign of Apollo* : It is not useful for wordly benefits. It shows childish vanity and showiness.

o) *Sign of Mercury* : It shows dashing and successful plunges into big business for making quick money.

p) *Sign of Mars* : It intensifies the merits of the mount.

q) *Sign of Moon* : This sign indicates tendency towards violent insanity. Other signs for insanity should be present for actual insanity.

r) *Sign of Venus* : It means violence in love matters.

s) *Sign of Uranus* : It signifies a revolutionary with high ideals.

t) *Sign of Neptune* : It shows travels in far away lands.

The Mount of Moon (Luna)   (Kalpana sthana-Imagination)
1 General

The next mount under our study is the mount of Moon. (*fig. 92*). This mount is located under the upper mount of Mars and is the biggest mount on the hand. As it occupies a vast portion of the hand, this mount has been divided into three sections : a) Upper mount, b) middle mount and c) lower mount. This division is useful in order to study the health defects of the Lunarian which is another name for the mount of Moon.

The mount of Moon shows high imagination, idealism and dreamy nature. It is necessary for every individual to possess this mount and its growth to a certain extent at least. The power of imagination is the natural faculty of a human being and, if it is withdrawn, our life will have no charm. A person who lacks the mount is a very dull person

Moon Mount

spending his life in a routine way but without having any lively spirit or enthusiasm or idealism. A Lunarian has fantasies and he lacks the practical side of life. He lives in his own dreams and therefore shuns society. He does not

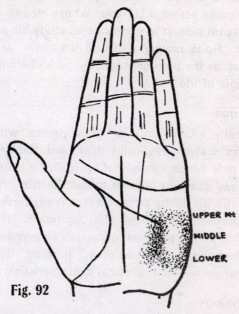

Fig. 92

The mount of Moon (imagination, moodiness, love of travel, a dreamer)

like to enjoy the comany of others as he finds them too ordinary for his imaginary world. While considering this power we have to take into consideration the other signs on the hand especially the line of Head. If the line of Head is also dropping down, we shall have a person who does not have mental strength to cope with the hurdles of life and he is prone to commit suicide.

A Lunarian loves natural and beautiful things in life such as the sea, flowers, scenery and the vastness of the sky. He takes pleasure in spending hours in the company of the high tides of the sea or in rivetting his eyes to the galaxy of stars in the sky.

A Lunarian is very unsteady, fickle-minded and a lover of change. He therefore has a fancy for travel, especially long travels which would satisfy his natural urge or imaginary things. Such travels would keep him engaged in his imagination and he will go on building castles in the air.

If we come across a Lunarian whose mount is bulging to the percussion side, it is necessary to study his psychological behaviour. He is mainly a mental wanderer without either the mental or the physical capacity to withstand the everyday struggle of life.

2 Physique

Basically, a Lunarian is a flabby person with oval face, round and watery eyes and thick and flabby neck. His colour is pale which shows that basically he is of weak constitution and does not possess robust health. He is tall in stature but with flabby arms and legs. His flesh is soft and spongy unlike the solid flesh of a Jupiterian. He has a big and bulging abdomen which gives him an awkward look. His hair on the head is soft and silky. In short, flabbiness and pale colour are his main physical characteristics.

3 Psychology

A Lunarian is not a very attractive person and does not possess magnetism. As a result of this, he finds pleasure in seclusion and remains in his own mental world. He is of a psychic type and material happiness or success is subordinate to his mental pursuits. He is introspective and loves mysticism. He is very fickle-minded and does not have the capacity to stick up to one thing. He is always changing and is fond of travel. He is a moody person and therefore most unreliable. His nature is cold and therefore he is also selfish. He is highly imaginative and superstitious. Since he lives in his mental world mostly, he is a very lazy person. He often suffers from melancholia and nervousness. He is effeminate in behaviour as well as in thinking.

Moon Mount

The mount of Luna is divided into three parts; the upper Moon, the middle Moon and the lower Moon. The upper Moon when more developed makes an eccentric person who is liable to suffer from mental disharmony, feeble-mindedness and nervous breakdown. If the middle Moon is more developed, his thinking will have practical side and he will be less dreamy. The lower Moon, if more developed, will make him more sensual and his imagination will work on the lower level making him vulgar.

4 Development of the mount

If the mount is developed in a normal way but on the lower side towards the wrist, it indicates that the subconscious and the subtle mind of the person is active and he will have the power of foretelling the events. This power will be further accentuated if there is a vertical line on this portion of the mount. We have also to study the formation of the line of Head in connection with the development of this portion of the mount. If the formation of the line of Head is such that it is connecting this lower mount of Moon and the mount of Jupiter, we have a good combination of the Jupiterian idealism and Lunarian imagination. If, on the other hand, this line of Head has no connection with the mount of Jupiter, the Lunarian imagination will be much distorted.

The vertical lines on the mount show the strength of the mount, but if these lines are not directly connected with other powerful lines on the hand, it shows that the mental energy and psychic forces are wasted and that there is a conflict between materialism and idealism. This person therefore becomes helpless and disappointed. His energy therefore has adverse effects on his health and he suffers from nervous troubles.

Another powerful indication to be seen on the lower mount of Luna is a prominent line across the mount separating the lower mount from the rest of the mount. This line shows the powerful mental qualities of the Lunarian. It shows the strong development of the sub-conscious mind.

Such a person secludes himself and does not like to interfere in the affairs of the world. This is a case for serious study to the psychiatrist and this indication is a warning of the serious disturbances in the sub-conscious mind. Such a person is susceptible to various alergies and allopathic drugs are not useful to him. Such a person is too much nature-conscious and probably his cure may be from natural methods. This horizontal line across the mount is a warning against indulgence in alchoholic drugs. If the warning is not heeded, this Lunarian is likely to develop alchoholism even to the extent of fatality.

Middle mount of Moon

If the middle mount is more prominent with a bulge towards the percussion, it suggests a strong creative urge which in a good hand will bear excellent results. This development will have at least a partial reconciliation to the outside world. Even though such a person is restless, he will have a desire to move along-with other persons. This is the mount which basically shows a desire for travel and vertical lines on this mount will indicate a long travel. These Lunarians are also moody and believe that the most impractical affairs are easily practical.

Upper mount of Moon

The development of this portion of the mount shows the highest type of imagination, but this will not be as bad a development as that of the lower mount. This is because the upper mount of Luna comes in contact with the upper mount of Mars and the Martian courage and practicability will be added to this mount. In short, the three worlds of the mount of Luna will exhibit the inner ego and the sub-conscious development of the mind. When the mount is nicely developed, it shows idealism, refinement and the power of imagination which is a gift peculiar to this mount. This person will have a good style of expression, may be through poetry or drama or music and he will depict the subtle beauties of nature. This mount is also indicative of benevolence, understanding, intuitive power and sympathy.

A good development of the mount of Luna also means a liking for luxury and fancy. He will have strange experiences due to his intuitive faculty.

Over-developed mount

Excessive development of this mount is a danger and it means extreme sensuality. It develops hysteria, insanity and nervousness. The mystical imagination develops into a superstition. The over-development of the mount will weaken the character and such a person will be addicted to dreams and severe drugs.

We may sometimes come across the development of the mount which is only by way of a narrow strip along the percussion. This development gives a good power of meditation and concentration but it means more seclusion and lack of mental force.

The development of the mount of Moon in a general way may also be taken into consideration from a different angle, when it is found more developed on the hands of women. With women who are suffering from troubles, this developed mount of Moon will indicate disturbance of mind, with the result that they become gloomy. The trouble is intense, especially during the monthly periods. Under such circumstances, their minds get clouded and they imagine all sorts of odd things. They may feel that their relatives or husbands are not looking after them carefully and others are growing less affectionate towards them. These are the periods when they think of committing suicide and their relatives especially the husbands, have to be very careful in handling them.

Under-development of the mount

The deficient mount of Moon lacks imagination and such a person becomes very cynical. If in addition to this, we find a girdle of Venus or a deficient mount of Venus or a chained line of Heart, we can be sure that such a person has developed secret vices resulting into nervous disorders, hysteria and insanity.

5 Placement of the mount

When the mount of Moon leans towards the rascette, it adds to the power of meditation, and thoughts on abstract subjects can be concentrated.

If the mount leans towards the mount of Venus, the Lunarian will imbibe the artistic qualities of Venus and will imagine of things more beautiful and idealistic. This will however make the Lunarian more effeminate.

If the mount of Moon leans towards the plain of Mars or the mount of Uranus, it will produce drastic results and the person will have to suffer from the greatest blows of life. If towards mount of Mars, it is a healthy combination, the Lunarian will have automatic check on his foolish ambition and imagination.

If the mount inclines towards the percussion, it enhances the creative power of the Lunarian.

6 Texture, flexibility, consistency and colour

a) *Texture* : The next thing we take into consideration is the texture of the Lunarian. Medium texture is most suitable for the highly imaginative nature of the Lunarian. This will make him think of practical idealism and will prevent him from going to insanity or extreme sluggishness, which are the characteristics shown by fine texture and coarse texture respectively.

b) *Flexibility* : Flexibility shows the elastic mind and it adds to the Lunarian imagination. This will create a person with extreme views and moods which change from time to time. These people are brilliant but due to their sluggishness they do not achieve anything and hate to exert much. They are versatile and good conversationalists. It is therefore better to have the common type of flexibility for a Lunarian.

The Mounts on the hand Moon Mount

c) *Consistency* : Flabby consistency is expected of a Lunarian as it depicts idealism, fancy, dreaminess and laziness.

Elastic consistency will make the person intelligent and one not bound down by rules. That will reduce his lethargy and this is likely to give him success in life.

Hard consistency is not expected for a Lunarian to possess: If found, it will make him selfish and restless. Hard consistency brings for a Lunarian distorted views on religion and all matters of life. They are always discontented and are fond of travelling, seeking change or excitement.

Stiff hand will mean lack of intelligence. He will have developed the lower qualities of the mind and he will be miserly, lacking in sympathy. He will have fears and will be very difficult to approach.

d) *Colour* : The complexion of the Lunarian is pale and white and if we find a pink or red colour, it will mean that the heart is strong and there is rich blood flowing in him. This will make him less mystical and more practical in his ideas. He will be less selfish and restless.

We may also come across a Lunarian with yellow colour. This is the worst colour for a Lunarian to have since it will indicate gout and rheumatism and even poisoned blood.

7 Mount and fingers

Smooth fingers : These fingers easily receive ideas and the wave of expression passes easily through these fingers into the brain. Smooth fingers, therefore, show inspiration rather than reason, synthesis rather than analytical knowledge. They exhibit a hasty and passionate nature. Such formation on the hand of a Lunarian will make him more intuitive and revelling in fancies. They will make the Lunarian spontaneous, believing in superstition.

Knotty fingers : Knotty fingers, by their characteristics, show an analytical mind. This will therefore be an advantage to a Lunarian as he would get the power of reasoning and analysis. In such cases, he will even try to analyse his idealistic concepts and thus realise their practical implications.

Long fingers : These fingers show a slow grasp and they will make the Lunarian dull and indolent. These persons will always find it difficult to give expression to their thought and feelings.

Short fingers : Short fingers are critical in nature and they have a habit to jump to conclusions. A Lunarian who possesses such short fingers will have wrong judgement about others' behaviour and he will misunderstand them. He will imagine that others are talking and discussing about him only. He will, however, have no courage to go and mix with them and will suffer from seclusion.

8 Phalanges

If the first phalanges of the fingers are prominent or more developed, we have an excess development of the Lunarian imagination and such persons will have fantasies and hallucinations. They will imagine themselves to have a direct contact with things which are beyond this world, such as talking to ghosts or spirit or relations in the ethereal world.

The middle phalanges when developed will add to the logic of the Lunarian and make him a creative thinker.

When the basal phalanges are developed, we shall have a Lunarian who will indulge in lower emotions and sensual gratification.

9 Tips of the fingers

i) *Conic tips* : Conic tips to smooth fingers will make a Lunarian hysterical. Such a person will find it very difficult to control his sensual mind and will always suffer from hysterical fits.

ii) *Square tips* : This will be an asset to check the unwanted emotional nature of the Lunarian and we can expect a practical person with a good power of imagination. Such persons can be good poets or writers and can have healthy idealism.

iii) *Spatulate tips* : These tips are not expected on the hand of a Lunarian since they indicate an opposite nature to that of a Lunarian. This is therefore not a good thing to possess and that will create many conflicts and contradictions in the mind of a Lunarian.

iv) *Pointed tips* : Such tips do not show a healthy combination and such formations may indicate feeble-mindedness, madness and schizophrenia.

10 Bad mount

The mount of Moon also has a bad aspect and a badly developed mount of Moon illustrates a person who is short in stature with white and spotted skin and watery grey eyes. He is often very talkative but untruthful. He is very selfish and cowardly. He is very cold and takes pleasure in gratifying his imagination. He is deceitful and a hypocrite. In combination with a bad mount of Saturn, he will be the worst type exhibiting mental degeneration and criminality.

11 Dangers

The main danger of a Lunarian is excessive indulgence in imagination which may lead him to insanity. There are various stages of madness and the Lunarian in order to protect himself from extremes must try to mix with friends and lessen his love for solitude. The greatest danger of a Lunarian is his tendency to commit suicide. A sloping line of head, a grilled mount of Moon and a badly developed mount of Saturn are the worst formations to meet with and it is highly necessary to take every precaution to keep such Lunarians in the proper social and family environment so as to avoid calamities and misfortunes in their lives.

12 Characteristics

The main characteristic of a Lunarian is high imagination. Imagination is a gift given to human being and it is necessary to have the faculty of imagination. Without it, our life would be dull and meaningless. It is therefore advisable to have the development of this mount on every hand, at least, it should not be totally lacking. However, a pure Lunarian is endowed with the gift of imagination to a great extent even to the point of danger. Imagination is a mental faculty and it works at its highest when one is in solitude and seclusion. This is why a Lunarian loves loneliness and enjoys his being alone.

The second characteristic of the Lunarian is his coldness which is the natural outcome of his weak health. As he lacks the warmth of sympathy, he is cold and dry to his friends and others. This again intensifies his love for mental wandering.

The natural outcome of the above two characteristics is selfishness. He will all the while go on thinking about himself only and he will lack the appreciation or the understanding of the feelings, sorrows and grievances of others that he comes across in life.

His other characteristic is his fancy for mystic subjects. His fancy often takes him to impractical heights of imagination which may ultimately end in lunacy.

13 Moon and health

The mount of Moon is divided into three parts and each of them reflects certain health defects. Grills, wavy lines, chained lines, dots, islands are indicative of bad health and the defects notified on this mount should be confirmed by other signs on the hand such as nails, colour, Life line, line of Mercury etc.

The white complexion of the Lunarian is a sign of weak action of heart and may mean anaemia, kidney trouble and dropsy. He is susceptible to many diseases due to poor circulation of blood.

The health difficulties notified on the mount of Moon are of special importance with women, since they are directly concerned with maternity, temper and happiness. We should also be able to distinguish between travel lines and sickness lines. Short and powerful horizontal line indicates travel whereas thin and obscure line shows health defect. Similarly, short vertical line shows travel, whereas wavy line shows

The Mounts on the hand Moon Mount

health defects. If the entire percussion is lined with cross lines, it indicates delicate health.

The upper mount of Moon shows the throat and bronchial troubles, intestinal inflammation and blood disorders. These defects are shown by cross lines and troubles like appendicitis are also indicated by these lines.

The middle mount of Moon shows troubles such as gout and rheumatism. This indication will be confirmed if we notice another line descending from the mount of Saturn and touching the line of Life.

The lower third line of the mount of Moon reflects troubles such as kidneys and bladder and sometimes dropsy.

We may sometimes observe a cross line running upto the line of Life which is a signal of serious danger to life. This line also indicates female troubles and this will be confirmed if there is a star on the line of Mercury and near the line of Head. This sign gives premonition of difficulties in maternity and presupposes defects in child-bearing. This is the spot we have to concentrate upon when we get cases of childlessness. This shows a basic defect in the reproductive organs and a woman having these defects should not expect children.

The diseases described above are positive and experience shows that they are true in most of the cases.

14 Finance

A Lunarian is a lethargic fellow and is not capable of doing any hard work. He also does not have physical capacity to stand the strain of everyday life. The outcome is a mediocre financial status. He however can improve his financial condition, provided he is able to make the best of his talents and develop his natural ability to create art of his imagination. He may be a good author or a painter who can create novels and weird paintings and earn a good livelihood. However, his unstable mind often drags him away from the routine work which artistic creation involves, and this creates uncertain source of income. A Lunarian therefore is not a very lucky person as far as finance is concerned.

15 Marriage

A Lunarian is a cold person and he does not have the fire of passion. He is therefore incapable of strong affections and he is not happy in his married life. He is also weak physically and his capricious nature is also responsible for making him unhappy in his married relations. He is whimsical, unstable and fond of change and cannot make proper choice of his wife. Sometimes, he may select a partner who is either far older or younger than himself. A Lunarian is restless and fickle-minded and is poor husband or a wife.

Lunarian husband : He has natural love and attraction for home than any other type. There are two types of Lunarian husbands. The one is dominating and exacting. He is fault-finding and nothing satisfies him. The other type is passive, lazy and indulgent. He will marry for the sake of money so that he may ultimately get comforts.

Lunarian wife : A Lunarian wife is also sympathetic, affectionate and devoted. She is satisfied with anything her husband provides her with. However, she is also moody, changeable and sensitive.

16 Vocation

The high imaginative power possessed by the Lunarian will help him to be a good composer of music or a writer of fiction stories or romance. He can as well be a good artist and can create works of everlasting value. Immortal paintings, dramas and celestial poems will be the outcome of highly developed mount of Moon. As Lunarians have the greatest vocabulary and linguistic capacities among all the types, they can be successful teachers or professors of various languages. They can also be good translators and editors.

A further detailed study of the vocations can be done by combining the mount of Moon with other mounts, the different vocations already studied by us earlier can be combined with the high imaginative power, mystic idealism exhibited by the mount of Moon. For instance, a combination of Jupiter and Moon will make a good writer on religious subjects. He can as well be a good political correspondent. A combination with the mount of Saturn will create a writer on occultism and such other subjects.

17 Mount of Moon in combination with other mounts

a) Moon-Jupiter

The combination of Jupiter with Moon will create foolish ambition for a Lunarian. The quality of leadership shown by Jupiter will make the Lunarian dream of false leadership. The Lunarian will also develop fantastic ideas about religion which is an aspect of Jupiter. The mount of Jupiter also exhibits love for nature, and that will add to the already existing characteristics in a Lunarian. It will therefore intensify his love for nature. Jupiter also shows pride and when added to a Lunarian it will mean false pride.

b) Moon-Saturn

This is a peculiar combination and it will mean a check on a Lunarian in creation of his characteristics, but it also intensifies certain unwanted developments in the Lunarian.

Wisdom is the main characteristic of a Saturnian and, when it is added to Lunarian, the Lunarian will have practical idealism, which means a good check on his building castles in the air. A Lunarian is a shy person and, when added to the sobriety of a Saturnian, it will create more loneliness in the nature of a Lunarian. Sadness and superstition are the other characteristics shown by a Saturn-Lunarian, will make him more superstitious, gloomy and sadistic.

A bad Lunarian combined with a bad mount of Saturn will be the worst combination and we shall have a person who is mean-minded, tricky, dishonest and even a criminal.

c) Moon-Apollo

A Lunarian exhibits artistic nature which is also a characteristic of an Apollonian and both in combination will produce a real artist with powerful imagination, who is capable of depicting dramas or paintings showing love and romance. Fanciful imagination of the Lunarian, if added to the dashing nature of an Apollonian, will create a person who will have high ideas about his capacities and will be a great failure in life.

d) Moon-Mercury

Shrewdness is the basic characteristic of a Mercurian and this is the exact thing which is lacking in a Lunarian. Since Lunarian loves to wander mentally, he can never acquire the shrewdness and business ability shown by a Mercurian. Industry is another aspect of a Mercurian which is again against the nature of a Lunarian. In short, the characteristics shown by a Mercurian are exactly opposite to those of a Lunarian, and a combination of these two mounts will create greater conflict in the mind of a Lunarian and thus he is likely to be more miserable.

e) Moon-Mars

This is somewhat a favourable combination as Mars is capable of checking the bad elements of a Lunarian. Courage and resistance will enable a Lunarian to face the frustrations confronted by him and a basically cold Lunarian will be calm and quiet even in adverse circumstances.

f) Moon-Venus

This is another combination which is likely to aggravate the natural qualities of love, art and idealism as shown by a Lunarian, since these are also the characteristics of the mount of Venus. By the natural position of these two mounts on the hand, they are found side by side and it is quite natural that these two mounts have their influence on each other.

We can therefore expect a real artist who will have patience for art and who will always live in his mental creations and hallucinations. Such a person can create wonderful art which can be lasting and will keep his name behind for centuries. (see also lines of influence on page 618)

18 Signs on the mount of Moon

a) *Star* : A star, when small and well formed, is a good sign. With the line of Apollo and Saturn, it shows success through imaginative faculty.

A star on the lower Luna and connected to a line of Voyage from the line of Life shows great adventures and mysterious experiences.

A star on the middle Luna and connected with the line of Head shows fame through imaginative power. If the same is found on the upper Luna, it shows capacity for brilliant reasoning. A star on Luna on a very sloping line of Head shows danger from over-imaginative nature. The same on an exaggerated mount along-with an afflicted mount of Saturn shows suicide by drowning. Both hands must confirm this, accompanied by other indications. A star that is not small and well-marked also shows death by drowning.

A star on the voyage line from percussion shows danger from voyage and ship-wreck.

A star connected with an influence line from the mount of Venus or from the line of Life shows hysteria or insanity of an erotic nature.

b) *Cross* : A cross shows a superstitious and dreamy nature. Moreover, a cross on the upper mount shows intestinal trouble, on the middle of mount it shows rheumatism and on the lower mount it shows bladder, kidney and womb troubles. A large cross shows an unreliable and deceiving nature.

c) *Circle* : A circle on Luna shows danger by drowning.

d) *Vertical line* : A single vertical line is bad omen. If it is on the down portion of the mount and a short one crossing it in the middle of the mount, a tendency to chronic rheumatism and gout may be predicted.

Long, clear vertical lines from the rascette show long travels. Many short vertical or slanting lines on the lower Luna show excitable, over-fanciful and uncontrollable nature. Very often it is an indication of hysteria. When these lines are confused, the result is visions, insomnia and nightmares.

When the confused lines are accompanied by cross lines, they show bladder troubles, nephritis and diabetes. They show troubles peculiar to women such as troubles with the organs of reproduction.

e) *Horizontal lines* : A strongly marked horizontal line, cutting across the mount in the middle and present on both the hands of a man, shows chronic disease of the partner. If the same is lower down the mount cutting the lower portion, it shows allergy to allopathic drugs and injections. It is called a poison line.

Horizontal lines from the percussion into the mount especially in the middle portion show voyages. When this line reaches the line of Heart and ends there in a star, the subject will leave all material comforts for the sake of a long voyage, probably in the company of a sweetheart.

f) *Triangle* : This is an excellent sign on the mount of Moon showing a high imaginative faculty used with understanding and good sense.

g) *Square* : A square shows protection from the dangers arising from the bad signs or the over-development of the mount.

h) *Spot* : It shows danger from drowning. With an afflicted line of Head, it may even show hysteria or madness.

i) *Bar* : A bad sign resulting in a weak, inconstant and unreliable nature.

j) *Grill* : A grill gives tendency to worry and discontent. It also shows melancholic and nervous troubles or trouble with womb and bladder. With a star on the mount of Saturn, it shows paralytic strokes and apoplexy.

But on the hands of a genius, it may show good indications. With a good line of Apollo, it shows flights of poetic imagination and literary capacity.

k) *Island* : An island shows worries, obstacles and dangers from voyage, shipwreck and drowning.

l) *Sign of Jupiter* : It shows dreams of power and high positions.

m) *Sign of Saturn* : It indicates insanity arising from religious mania.

n) *Sign of Apollo* : It means folly arising out of wealth and extreme artistic and poetic nature.

o) *Sign of Mercury* : It shows financial ruin through unwise financial speculation.

p) *Sign of Mars* : It shows raving mania and tendency to brain fever.

q) *Sign of Venus* : A strange combination of vitality and imagination is shown by this sign. It means yearning for strange and new sensations.

r) *Sign of Uranus* : It indicates moral leadership in mass revolutions.

s) *Sign of Neptune* : In a good mount, it shows spiritual elevation. In an afflicted mount, it shows delusion and religious mania.

t) *Sign of Moon* : It indicates diseased imagination, nightmares and insanity. It is a bad omen.

The mount of Venus

Upper—Bhratru sthana—Brothers
Lower—Bandhu sthana—Relatives

1 General (*fig. 93*)

The seventh mount in our discussion will be the mount of Venus. This is also a large mount to be found on the hand. This is an interesting mount for our study. A Venusian is the most beautiful and attractive person to meet with. He is always governed by love, sympathy and adoration. We have to be very careful in pronouncing our judgement for the character of the person as we are likely to be mislead by the passions and sex vigour exhibited by a powerful Venusian. It is true that he has good vigour with the result that we may expect good blood force and warmth of passions. But it does not necessarily mean that a Venusian is only fond of sex and passion. He is a born artist and love for art and

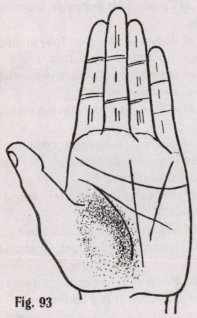

Fig. 93

The mount of Venus (love, art, beauty, compassion, sex)

beauty in life have an attraction for him. We must not misinterpret his love for nature and beauty as his zeal for passion.

There is however, a strong biological reasoning as to why the mount of Venus should exhibit sexual desires. We have studied in the introductory chapter and also in the chapter on the thumb about the development of this mount and its relation to sex. We have therefore sufficient ground to prove that the mount of Venus shows vigour and strong passions.

A Venusian is a pleasant personality to meet with. It is always charming to be with him. His company is full of enthusiasm, energy and charm. His talk is interesting and lively. We may sometimes be required to keep aside our ideas of morality and social conduct in understanding and appreciating his feelings and discussions.

This mount is also capable of indicating the family life of a person and according to Hindu palmistry, vertical lines on the lower part of the mount of Venus indicate the number of family members. Further details about these lines will be studied while dealing with the signs on the mount.

Venus stands for beauty and health, vitality and warmth, attraction and above all love. Venusians are gifted with all these aspects. They are fond of music, dancing and poetry. They love to have a life full of ease and luxuries, money and happiness. They prefer spending to saving. They will have rich clothes, jewellery, perfumes and all sorts of beautiful things. They are good at house-keeping and succeed in leading a happy family life.

They do not have the ambition and dominating nature of Saturnians and the Martians, nor do they have scholarship of Jupiterians or practical wisdom of Mercurians. Even then, they are the most popular among all the other types. This is because they realise the importance of love in human life.

2 Physique

In appearance, a Venusian is attractive and beautiful. He has grace and ease in manners. His is more of a feminine type than masculine. He is of medium height with graceful curves. He has fine and soft texture and the complexion is usually fair. His face is usually oval or round in shape and his other features are proportionately set. The eyebrows are well marked with graceful curves and they are sharply outlined. The eyes are round or almond shaped and usually black in colour with long, silky lashes curling upward at the ends. His hair is silky, soft and shining. On the whole, he has a very graceful and symmetrical figure.

3 Psychology

We can understand the psychology of a Venusian if we compare him with a Saturnian or a Lunarian. A Saturnian is a much restrained fellow who likes to desert company and who has a sort of hatred for others. A Lunarian is a cold person who lacks warmth of sentiment and also dislikes others. A Venusian however has an outlook towards life which is exactly contrary to the types explained above. A Venusian is an embodiment of love, warmth and beauty. He always imagines that life is full of love and romance and he hates quarrels. He therefore desires that the company in which he moves should also be optimistic with a sense of enjoyment in life.

He is necessarily a loving type and he has a feeling of kinship and humanity. He will therefore not desert his friends and always likes to understand the grievances and difficulties of others with a considerate approach. He prefers joy to gloom and has the capacity to bring others along with him to participate in the moments of enjoyment. His outlook is bright and vivacious. Due to his loving nature, he develops the ability to forgive others. He is not fickle-minded as a Lunarian and likes to remain honest and truthful to his love and friendship. To him, love is not merely a pleasure or an unimportant thing as to a Saturnian, but it is the highest value in life to be developed with refinement and delicacy. He endures everything for the sake of love. If necessary, he does not hesitate to forego money, position or ego for the sake of love. Love is a gift of the Venusian to human race and it rules and sustains the world.

4 Development of the mount

We have to consider the development of the mount separately in the case of a man and of a woman. Venus is basically a feminine mount and the main characteristics apply to a female than to a male. The basic characteristics of love and beauty are more predominant in the case of a female and, even though a man exhibits these characteristics, he will not have the same degree of delicacy which would be found in the case of a woman. We may therefore have this distinction at the time of considering the development of the mount.

Excess development of the mount

The excess development of the mount on the hand of a woman means sensuality and inconstancy. On the hand of man it shows vicious thinking. On the hand of a woman, it means sympathy to a fault, whereas it shows selfish motive behind sympathy on the hand of a man. Excessive development means feminine aptitude of a man whereas it means extreme delicay and sensuality in a woman's hand. Excessive development may create a criminal in a man whereas in the case of a woman it shows immorality and profligacy.

Normal development

On the hand of a woman, it means honest love for family and an artistic aptitude having attraction for beautiful things at home. She will have a fancy for beautiful clothes and for stones such as diamonds and pearls, etc. A normal mount for a man shows love for music, grace and passion. The normal development of the mount on the hand of a woman indicates a desire for wealth, popularity, luxuries, jewellery, perfumes, and rich clothes. On the hand of a man, it denotes generosity, love of social life and healthy attitude to life.

Under-development

A woman lacking in the mount of Venus shows an artist who is foolishly wedded to an art. She is cold to the opposite sex and she finds her existence as encumbrance. In the case of a man, it shows indifferenc to the charms of the other sex. In the case of a man, it means coldness and self-centeredness, whereas in the case of a woman it shows weak and miserable disposition.

5 Placement

a) When the mount leans towards the positive Mars, it is an indication of aggressiveness in love matters and a purely sensual nature.

b) When the mount is leaning towards the thumb, it will add logic and reasoning to the artistic talent and we shall have a balanced personality with regard to love. Such a person is more realistic in life and utilises his talents so as to gain reputation and money by his arts.

c) When the mount leans towards the rascettes, in a woman's hand it means trouble in child-bearing.

d) The leaning of mount towards the mount of Moon is indicative of highly imaginative love and impractical thinking of the individual. He is more sensual and foolishly involved in love affairs.

6 Texture, flexibility, consistency, colour etc.

Texture: Fine texture on the hand of Venusian is normal since it exhibits a high standard of art and refined behaviour with others. An already loving Venusian will have a natural understanding and appreciation of the feelings of his colleagues and friends. He will also be capable of creative arts such as music, painting and sculpture. He will always be depicting the beautiful side of life in his crafts. Coarse texture is indicative of a person with basal development in his passions and he will indulge in vices and even commit crimes for fulfilling his selfish and vulgar passions. A medium texture will add to the natural talents of the Venusian and will make him engaged in music or arts which will be appreciated by the masses.

Flexibility: A Venusian usually has flexible hand which shows flexibility in ideas. He will therefore have a knack to develop his ideas all the time and he will not be rigid in his ideas regarding the arts known to him.

Stiff hand, on the other hand, will create an artist with rigid and fixed ideas who will think that his art is of higher quality and others do not appreciate it. His art will contain the same motive hroughout and as such it will be monotonus to others.

Consistency

Flabby : It shows indolence and an inactive mind. A Venusian with flabby consistency will be a lazy artist who will not develop his art but will remain in the world of his high imagination, beauty and art. He will merely be a vain talker and not a man of action, without achieving anything for himself.

Soft : This consistency is normal with a Venusian but it is rather difficult in the case of woman to distinguish between flabby hands and soft hands. But by using the technique of finding out the flabbiness, we can know the difference with a little practice. Soft hands will make the Venusian more energetic and will make his idealism practical and he will achieve success in life with his artistic talents. He will be more charming and will be attracted to the fair sex, not out of passion but for the real appreciation of beauty. A Venusian woman will have grace and refined manners and she will have a knack to attract the opposite sex towards her.

Elastic : This type of consistency is still better for a Venusian and that will add energy, enthusiasm and moral responsibility to the charming and flirting nature of the Venusian.

Hard : This is not expected for a Venusian, but if found, it will diminish love and sympathy which are the main characteristics of a Venusian. Such a person will be cold in his passions and will be rough and arrogant in his approach to the opposite sex.

Colour : Pink colour is natural for Venusian and in order that the Venusian enthusiasm be developed, pink colour is essential. Such a person will have intuitive faculty in his art and he will be capable of mastering the subjects which he is interested in. With this pink colour we shall have a Venusian with his qualities of vivacity and gaiety developed in a normal way. Here we shall find a perfect Venusian as far as colour is concerned and he will be more refined in developing his higher qualities.

When red colour is found on the hand of a Venusian, we have to be very cautious. If the mount is fully developed with deep red colour and with grill on the mount, it indicates extremity and a Venusian will not stop at anything to accomplish his desires. Such type of formation is sometimes seen on the hands of criminals who murder either their wives or husbands or relatives for the sake of selfish passions. These acts are perpetrated in certain fits of jealousy.

White colour as we know shows a weak hand and it runs counter to the hand of a Venusian who is a healty person by nature. If however the white colour is seen on the hand, we can judge that the warmth of passions is lacking in him and he is not capable of enjoying life to the extent to which a pink coloured Venusian is. This white colour indicates extraction of energy which may lead a Venusian to suffer from anaemic condition.

Yellow colour means bilious nature which will destroy the lovable nature of a Venusian. It will also create bad temper and nervous trouble.

Blue colour on the hand of a Venusian will mean difficulties with the heart. This colour is also usually seen on the hand of a Venusian and, in order to confirm our readings about heart trouble, we have to look to other signs on the hand such as nails, Heart line, especially under the mount of Sun.

7 Mount and finger

Smooth fingers : These fingers will give an insight to the Venusian in his arts and he will have quick grasp of the subject. Smooth fingers are graceful and therefore the grace of the Venusian will have added strength. These will also increase the spontaneity of the Venusian. Such a Venusian is often correct in his first impressions and is seldom wrong in his intuitive perception. Smooth fingers are too hasty and passionate and their addition to a Venusian means added impetuosity towards his approach to the opposite sex. These fingers however add to the romance, grace and idealism of the Venusian.

Knotty fingers : These fingers will give to the Venusian love for his arts and also an analytical mind, system and method in his profession. He will not suddenly fall into love and will weigh the qualities of the person whom he wants to love.

Short fingers : They indicate a nature which is impetuous and hasty and they have tendency to jump to conclusion. A Venusian with short fingers will therefore be hasty in his arts and will not have the patience to go into the details of his studies and will therefore never master any art. In his love, he will always be changing and fickle-minded. He will never be successful in his love and profession.

Long fingers : On the other hand, long fingers show an inclination to go the root of a subject, and have an ability to study it into details. A Venusian, if he is an artist, will show the details of the leaves of a tree, will portray the small shades on a face and will paint landscapes with the utmost care. These persons are exceedingly sensitive and sometimes very cruel. With excess development of the mount, long fingers sometimes mean a poisoner's hand.

8 Phalanges

Phalanges will show in more details the characteristics of a Venusian.

The first phalanges of the fingers, when developed, will mean that the person has developed the higher faculties of his mind and has a finer shade in his approach towards his love, art, sympathy or profession. He will have an ideal love, platonic as it is called and he will not have vulgar passions or selfish nature as shown by the lower side of his mind. A Venusian, with the first world developed, will have mastered creative art, may be music or painting, for the sake of art only. He is therefore the real artist and exhibits all the qualities of a Venusian in proper perspective.

If the second phalanges are developed, we have a person whose pragmatic thinking is more developed and such a Venusian artist will create mundane art, landscape, and natural scenery. He will think as to how he can earn with his art and will be more businesslike in presenting his art. He will therefore be a successful artist and will have a more balanced life than any of the other two types.

When the third phalanges are developed, we shall have a person who has animal passions, who is merely selfish and who desires gratification of his lower passions. He is not intelligent and does not have the intuition required for an artist. He will live a dull life without any appreciation of beauty.

9 Mount and tips

Pointed tips : These tips with normal development of the mount of Venus mean ideal love. With the excess development of the mount, they mean vicious imagination. These tips will also create a mad lover if the mount is lacking.

Conic tips : Such tips to the normal development of the mount exhibit material love and poetical character. With the excess development of the mount, they mean inconsistency in the pursuit of art. If the mount is lacking, they mean an artist wedded to his art.

Square tips : They show a practical and level-headed person. A normal Venusian with square tips will be a successful artist and will also achieve his ambition in realising his arts. With excessive development of the mount, square tips mean a clash between practicality and idealism. If the mount is lacking, the square tips mean indifference to the charms of life.

Spatulate tips : These tips to the fingers of Venusian indicate a good husband or a good wife who will create erotic passion in the life-partner. He will adore the grace and artistic outlook of his partner and will encourage the development of the artistic faculty in the partner. With the excess development, spatulate tips show a flirting and debaucherous nature. When the mount is lacking, he does not like the company of the opposite sex.

10   Bad mount

There is a bad side to every mount and the same is experienced in the case of a Venusian also. A Venusian is basically a healthy person with vigour, stamina and strong sexual passions. When he is of fine grade, he has refinment, grace and fine manners. His approach to others is on a higher plane. He tries to convert his energy into useful arts. But when we come across a bad Venusian, we shall have a personality who is contrary to the one described above. In the first place, a bad Venusian is not an attractive person. He is short with a flabby body and prominent abdomen. His mind is all the time engaged in gratifying his desires. He has animal passions and low thinking. He is cold-blooded, cruel and selfish in his outlook. Unless there are other good signs to give him control over his mind, he will be a criminal who will commit murders in order to satisfy his hunger.

11   Danger

The main dangers to a Venusian are from his bad health and his vices. He is liable to suffer from venereal diseases. He has also to guard himself against evil thoughts which may finally lead him to commit murder or be a criminal.

12   Characteristics

Basically a Venusian is an artist. He finds beauty everywhere in life and likes to depict that beauty in his art. Being an artist, he loves music, painting and the more beautiful things in life. In this search for beauty he begins to develop higher level of emotions and sentiments with the result that he begins to love all the things he comes across. Thus to love is another characteristic of the Venusian which is the outcome of his fundamental outlook on life.

Due to his loving approach towards everything, he himself becomes a lovable personality. He is very amiable and is capable of creating cheerfulness in the company he mixes which is from all walks of life. Due to his magnetic personality and affectionate nature, people like to come close to him and express their grievances and difficulties. By his keeping in touch with such people, he develops sympathy. Sympathy is therefore the third characteristic of the Venusian.

The sympathetic nature of the Venusian enables him to come in contact with a number of people and especially with the opposite sex. This results in arousing his passions and passion is the next characteristic of a Venusian. His passions can be seen in many of his activities. These passions may not necessarily be of a lower type and he may sublimate them into art. Thus he begins as an artist and ends as an artist.

13 Health

On the whole the Venusian is a healthy person and bad health is not expected of him. We can suspect health defects of this type only if we come across a white or yellow or blue colour with a grill on the mount of Venus. These indications show something wrong with the blood. They are therefore susceptible to epidemic fever and influenza. They do not have any particular weakness as such but they suffer from general ailments which are common to all men. Occasionally, they are prone to nervousness but not in a chronic way.

14 Finance

A Venusian is not attracted towards money and accumulation of wealth is not his aim in life. All his interest is directed towards attaining pleasures and gratifying his desires. He therefore spends his earnings on whatever thing that attracts him. He also never repents for having spent his money on his art which may not ultimately give him monetary rewards. Opulence therefore is a rarity with a Venusian but he somehow has the knack to make both ends meet. He may also sometimes be lucky in getting windfalls.

15 Marriage

People of this type are very much fond of marriage and they usually marry early in life. He expects his partner to be neat and have charm and grace. His is usually a large family with many children. He loves his children and home. He is very kind, generous and devoted. Though he creates a lively atmosphere in the house, he somehow finds it difficult to fulfil all the necessities of the members of the family. This may sometimes create unpleasantness in the family and make the Venusian a little unhappy in his married life. Art is everything to him and he remains impractical in not understanding the material values of a successful life. He can therefore be happy in his married life only if his partner is also of a Venusian type.

A good Venusian wife never resorts to divorces and endures extreme hardship rather than desert her mate. She is a devoted mother and loving wife, satisfied with her husband's efforts in her behalf. She loves domestic life and is a perfect house-maker.

16 Vocations

In order to find out the vocations for a Venusian, it will help us if we find out the subsidiary mount and combine its characteristics with those of the artistic Venusian.

The mount of Jupiter will engage a Venusian in honourable professions where the latter will get an opportunity to exhibit his artistic talents. He will therefore be engaged in the profession of an interior decorator or in departmental stores in the ladies wares. He will also be engaged in the business hotel, cinema theatre and jewellery.

The mount of Saturn will endow a Venusian with the faculty to write books on history or will make him a writer who will write on subjects which will contain universal philosophy. He may also be engaged in mines of precious stones, especially diamonds. He can as well be a salesman in cosmetics shops or in book-stalls.

The mount of Apollo is a suitable subsidiary mount for a Venusian. There are some points common to both, namely energy, enthusiasm and originality. Such a Venusian will be successful as a composer of music, a manager of beverage hotels or of night clubs. He can also be a successful executive in an industry, manufacturing decorative or luxurious articles.

The mount of Mercury will add shrewdness to the musical talents possessed by a Venusian. He will therefore be successful in his business as an artist. Mercury shows scientific pursuits, but since science is not the field of a Venusian, he will not be able to take the advantage of this Mercurian ability. He can however be successful as a broker, estate broker, stock broker or as commission agent. Mercury will impart its practical qualities to the Venusian and the Venusian may be able to turn his art into a profitable business.

The mount of Mars when combined with the mount of Venus, will create a subject who will feel courageous and will pursue his trade without diffidence. Such a Venusian will be energetic and dashing and he will achieve success in trades such as a club secretary, intermediary in conciliations who can use his charm as well as dash in bringing two parties together and settle the issue.

The mount of Moon will add to the imagination of the Venusian artist and this artist will be more successful in trades where his artistic talents coupled with imagination will be brought into play. He will therefore be successful as an interior decorator, music composer for picture movies, dramas etc. He can also be a good ladies' tailor, where he will invent fashions in dresses. The mount of Moon will add vocabulary and expression to the Venusian and we can expect authors who will write on subjects such as music, painting, dancing, drapery, decoration etc.

17 Combination of mounts
a) Venus-Jupiter

A Venusian, who normally does not hold any ambition,

may feel that he should have some ideal before him and that he should direct his efforts in that direction. He may therefore plan his programme and may practise his art everyday with the aim in view. The religious aptitude of a Jupiterian will tempt the artist to study ancient music, draw mythological paintings and portray historical figures. The Jupiterian love of nature will also make the Venusian spend hours in painting landscapes. The Venusian will take pride in presenting his art and he will be a great artist.

b) Venus-Saturn

The charming nature of the Venusian will be lessened with the qualities of Saturn and the Venusian will become thoughtful and sober. Saturn shows materialism and that will make the Venusian realise the value of money. The Venusian is careless about money and Saturn will put a check on this tendency. The Venusian love will be wise as a result of the effect of Saturn and the Venusian will be realistic in choosing his love-mate. Saturn also shows monetary comforts and this combination will help the Venusian to get the enjoyment of life which he often seeks.

There is however the possibility that the Venusian will be affected by the bad qaulities of Saturn in which case he will be mean, tricky, dishonest and even a criminal.

c) Venus-Apollo

This is a happy combination and a happy Venusian will partake of the energy and brilliance of Apollo. The Venusian, therefore will be more original in his paintings, music or art and the artistic faculty of the Apollonian will be added to the born Venusian artist. When this is the case, the Venusian will be more graceful, more charming and more attractive. The complexion will be very alluring and he will be an emblem of love and beauty. He will be conscious of his beauty and will try to influence others with his power of expression. He will succeed in any field of life and his talents, speech, art, grace, etc. will make his life more lively and happy.

d) Venus-Mars

This is not a very favourable combination and the aggression of a Martian will tempt a Venusian to bring his thoughts into action which may land a Venusian into troubles. Such a Venusian will think all the time of gratifying his passions, and his mind will work in finding out ways and means as to how to fulfil his lower passions. Since passion is the basic factor with a Venusian as well as a Martian, its hunger is so strong that the Venusian may not be in a position to partake of the other qualities of a Martian such as perseverance, courage, resistance etc. If a Venusian can take advantage of these qualities of a Martian, he will achieve greater success in life and will have a better chance in presenting his talents.

e) Venus-Mercury

Mercury is a shrewd mount whose characteristic is entirely lacking in a Venusian. However, a Venusian will never partake this quality of Mercurian, and it will not be acquired by a Venusian. A Venusian is fond of charm and a comfortable life without much industry. He therefore will acquire the business aptitude of a Mercurian and earn money in his art, music or painting.

f) Venus-Moon

Lunarian imagination, when added to a Venusian, will create a dreamy artist who will not think of anything else but his art. His art will be everything for him and he will forget all other things in life. In fact, he is a genuine artist, but he does not care for recognition whether he earns money or not. He is an emblem of art and it is a misfortune that his name is known to others only after his death. The love for seclusion of Lunarian will make the artist live in places away from cities and society. Such a combination may create lunatics who lose their sense of all practical living. They are mystics to others and can never be understood even by their closest friends. They will always be regarded insane by those who surround them. However they are capable of producing weird music and their art will affect the spectators through paintings of frustrated love, sculptures of isolated lovers and stories of exciting sex life. In short, Venus-Moon combination will make the subject a great sufferer in life.

18 Signs

a) *Star*: The result of this sign on this mount varies according to its placement.

i) A star on the centre of the mount shows success in love.

ii) On the side of the mount and nearer to the thumb, it shows love with a person of distinction.

iii) Between the reason phalange of the thumb and the mount, it shows unhappiness caused by the opposite sex.

iv) At the outer side and far removed from the rascette, the star will produce the same result

v) At the base and near to the rascette, it will show successful, unopposed and distinguished love. But such a star with a very sloping line of Head will show a diseased imagination.

vi) A star in the lowest section of the mount with a line of influence or a thin line from it to the other lines shows a female enemy.

b) *Cross*: It shows great trial to one's affections. If it touches the line of Life, it shows trouble with relatives. A large cross shows an only love.

c) *Circle*: It shows chronic ill-health.

d) *Vertical line*: A single vertical line going up to the mount of positive Mars shows a love-affair. Two vertical lines show inconstancy in love.

e) *Horizontal line*: A single horizontal line from the second phalange of the thumb to the line of Life shows troubled married life or faithlessness or death of the lover.

f) *Triangle* : It shows prudence and calculating attitude in love affairs.

g) *Square* : It means protection from the troubles brought about by passion. If it is near the line of Life, it loses its significance. Two squares in the upper part close to each other show litigation.

h) *Spot* : It indicates frustration in love and trouble from relatives.

i) *Bar* : It is scarcely found on this mount, but when seen, it shows obstructions in getting hereditary property.

j) *Grill* : It shows lasciviousness, morbidity and unhealthy curiosity.

k) *Island* : It means susceptibility to love affairs. When placed cross-wise or connected to the Heart line it shows missing of an advantageous opportunity of marriage.

l) *Sign of Jupiter* : It means love of flattery, partially for those who cater to one's vanity.

m) *Sign of Saturn* : It shows unnatural kind of love and morbidity.

n) *Sign of Apollo* : It indicates platonic love.

o) *Sign of Mercury* : It signifies mercenary love.

p) *Sign of Mars* : It means exaggerated Venusian qualities. Higher and finer aspects in love are degraded to animal passions.

q) *Sign of Moon* : It shows extreme erotic imagination.

r) *Sign of Venus* : It emphasises the qualities of the mount favourably in a good mount.

s) *Sign of Uranus* : It means extreme self-denial.

t) *Sign of Neptune* : It shows love for a mental rather than physical companionship and an unconventional fairyland feeling about the home.

The mount of Uranus and Neptune

Uptil now the above mounts were not allotted any space on the hand and their influence on hand was also not observed. However, after the discovery of these planets and their influence on human life, it was necessary to study whether these planets also showed their importance on the hand. It was, therefore, observed that what is called the Quadrangle on the hand represented the mount of Uranus and the portion near the wrist, between the mounts of Venus and Moon, represented the mount of Neptune.

Even though these planets influence human life, they do not present us any distinctive personalities as we have in the case of other mounts, such as Jupiter, Saturn etc. We therefore, do not have a Uranian or a Neptunian as a personality and we have to bear this fact in mind.

Though they do not place before us any individuality or distinctive personalities, their influence on hand is none the less significant. The presence of these mounts and their development on the hand elevate the importance of other mounts, and the development of these mounts can be considered according to the mount type represented by the hand. Thus, a developed or depressed mount of Uranus will affect the Jupiterian, Saturnian, Apollonian, etc., and when we study the other mounts, we have to take into consideration the development of the mounts of Uranus and Neptune. The mounts of Uranus and Neptune have a subtle and magical influence on the activities of other mounts. These mounts show progress, elevated ideas and interest in spiritual life. After this general information I shall deal with the individual mount.

The Mount of Uranus

The portion covered by this mount is the Quadrangle described earlier in this book and we can see the development of this mount by the bulging of this portion or by sign of Uranus in this Quadrangle.

The mount of Uranus shows revolution and unexpected happenings in life. Usually, the changes that take place are for the better and the mount represents the higher faculties of the mind. The mount shows activity and intelligence engaged in the reconstruction or the betterment of human life. The peculiar nature of this mount is that it constantly aims at changes in life and society and is after the liberation of mind from the bondage of environment and society.

Psychological significance

This mount is mainly dominated by the two lines, the line of Head and the line of Heart. It therefore signifies the intellectual nature on the one side shown by the line of Head and the emotional nature on the other side as shown by the line of Heart. On the opening sides of the Quadrangle, there is the mount of Jupiter and the negative mount of Mars which give the intuitive faculty. If the Quadrangle possesses the sign of Uranus, it will give occult powers to the owner.

Development of the mount

When the mount is developed in a normal way, without any signs or lines in the Quadrangle, it shows a person who has a clear understanding and a steady mind. A rather more developed mount shows love for money and a tendency to amass wealth. But this wealth will be lavishly spent. An under-developed mount shows a stingy nature.

Bad mount

If there are many cross lines or there is a grill type formation on the mount of Uranus, we may consider it as a bad mount. When the mount is badly developed, the person is very selfish and does not have any control on his emotions. He therefore goes to extremes and naturally suffers from the ill effects. He is eccentric and constantly changes his attitude toward his family and society.

Vocations

There are certain vocations suitable for a Uranian and he will be more successful in trades such as transport, electricity and all sorts of machinery.

Signs on the mount of Uranus

The mount of Uranus is represented by the Quadrangle on the hand and we have already discussed the various signs in the Quadrangle.

Thus we have studied the mount of Uranus and since it does not stand by itself, we can study its importance in relation to other mounts most developed on the hand.

The mount of Neptune

This mount lies between the mount of Venus on the one side and the mount of Moon on the other side and above the rascette. This mount has similar characteristics to that of Moon and as Moon governs the mind, this Neptune also has control over the mind of the person. This is also a mystic mount similar to that of Uranus and a person with this mount prominent on the hand has to undergo a number of experiences in life and he often is a rolling stone which gathers no mass. Even though there are many changes in life, the person does not take them seriously and every failure is considered as a stepping stone to success. When the Life line goes upto this mount, it shows longevity.

This is a spiritual mount and Supreme Consciousness is developed in this individual. He is like a free bird and likes to break the traditional bondage and restrictions. It is possible that the greatest of the prophets and spiritualists may have this mount well-developed on their hand.

Neptune shows love for travel, especially, sea-travel and change in life. Persons with this mount developed are restless, uneasy and whimsical. Their behaviour is a mystery to others and they are many times absent-minded. Their thoughts are engrossed elsewhere and they prefer to lead a life of sacrifice and renunciation.

Neptune is tempted to speculate and gamble and the trades suitable for him deal in chemicals and liquids. Laundry business is also suitable for a Neptunian.

If the mount is badly developed, it shows idle imagination and disappointment in achieving the aim. In this case, disappointment is bound to take place, since stability and consistency of mind is the lacking factor. As already stated in the beginning, the mounts of Uranus and Neptune add to the qualities of other mount types and they do not have their own personality as such. However, what has been described above, will help the readers to know more about the clients with the study of these two mounts.

I may state once again that the chapter on mounts is the most important in this book and we can combine the characteristics of different mounts after studying the colour, texture, consistency, nails, fingers etc. The next chapter will assist the readers as to how we have to prepare a chart of the hand before we start hand-reading.

CHAPTER XIV

Epilogue

I think this volume would not be complete, unless I write a few words by way of conclusion. I am sure that this chapter will assist the students of palmistry to understand the study of palmistry in its proper perspective.

As already stated in the introductory chapters, the study of the hand has a biological and psychological significance and it is capable of understanding the personality of the individual, his behaviour, his likes and dislikes, his basic characteristics, his vocations, his success in life, his psycology and the basic constitution of his health. This study will therefore definitely help the doctors to diagnose the disease of the person, either physical or psychological. It will also help the educationists in finding out the proper course of study for the children. It will equally assist in finding out the delinquent children and giving them the proper treatment. Several physical sicknesses are due to psychological disturbances and several psychological sickness are due to physical defects. The study of palmistry helps us to find out the root causes of the ailments, so that remedial measures can be applied.

A good palmist must necessarily be a good psychologist and he must develop a personality to win the confidence of his client.

The study of palmistry, as described Uptil now , is called the study of Cheirognomy and in order to go deep into the client's personality it is necessary that we are in a position to combine the various factors on hand successfully. The success of hand-reading depends upon the combinations of various aspects on hand and in order to study the hand in a scientific way, I produce herewith a chart, which when completed will give us a complete picture of our client.

The hand reveals different phases of life and a palmist can specialise himself in anyone or more of these phases. As we have a general medical practitioner as well as a specialist, such as a T.B. specialist, a Heart specialist, and E.N.T. specialist, etc. we can also have a general palmist, who can read the hand and life in a general way, or even a specialist who may study this subject from the specific angles of marriage, vocations, health, finance, psychological ailments, etc. If one wants to master any of these phases, one has to be conversant with the art of interpreting various combinations on the hand. The chart reproduced here will be of immense help in this respect.

I have tried my best to explain the study of the hand in as much details as possible and I have not omitted any aspect of the study. In fact, I have taken into consideration all the possible details and have explained the signs from the Hindu point of view also. The chapters have been arranged in such a manner so that the student will grasp the subject without much difficulty. *The main idea in writing this book is to gather all available material on this subject so that one may not go in for any other book on this subject.* I have no doubt that the readers will appreciate my efforts to handle this subject in a most scientific way and also imparting the knowledge in a systematic way. Regular study of methods and systems is the keynote to success and I have carefully handled this subject giving finally a chart which will comprise all our observations of the hand in a nut-shell.

In the next few pages that follow, I have tried to explain the hand of President Nixon of America, whose photograph of the hand is also reproduced for the guidance of the readers

Epilogue

The Model Chart

1) The shape of the hand.
2) The division of the hand :
   - a) First division :
     - i) Mental world :
     - ii) Material world :
     - iii) Basal world :
   - b) Second division :
     - i) Conscious Zone :
     - ii) Sub-conscious zone :
     - iii) Social zone :
   - c) Third division :
     - i) Zone of thought :
     - ii) Zone of action :
     - iii) Zone of impulse :
     - iv) Zone of imagination :
     - v) Zone of the thumb :
3) Skin :
   - a) Fine :
   - b) Medium :
   - c) Coarse :
4) Colour :
   - a) Red :
   - b) Pink :
   - c) Blue :
   - d) Yellow :
   - e) White :
5) Consistency :
   - a) Flabby :
   - b) Soft :
   - c) Elastic :
   - d) Hard :
6) Flexibility :
   - a) Stiff :
   - b) Normal :
   - c) Excess :
7) a) Fingers :
   - a) Smooth :
   - b) Knotty :
   - c) Short :
   - d) Long :
   b) Finger tips :
   - i) In general : Square :
     - Spatulate :
     - Conic :
     - Pointed :
   - ii) Jupiter finger :
   - iii) Saturn finger :

			iv)	Apollo finger :
			v)	Mercury finger :
	c)	Length of finger :	a)	Normal :
			b)	In relation to each other :
	d)	Space between the fingers :		
	e)	Leaning of fingers :		
	f)	Phalanges :	Jupiter finger : 1st–2nd–3rd	
			Saturn finger : –do–	
			Apollo finger : –do–	
			Mercury finger : –do–	
	g)	Signs on fingers :		
8)	Thumb			
	a)	Small :		
	b)	Large :		
	c)	Position :	i)	High set :
			ii)	Medium set :
			iii)	Low set :
	d)	Length of the thumb		
	e)	Shape of the thumb :	i)	Elementary :
			ii)	Nervous :
			iii)	Strong-willed :
			iv)	Diplomatic :
			v)	Paddle-shaped :
			vi)	Clubbed :
			vii)	Waist-like :
	f)	Phalanges :		
	g)	Tips :	i)	Square :
			ii)	Spatulate :
			iii)	Conic :
			iv)	Pointed :
	h)	Knots :		
	i)	Flexibility :		
	j)	Carriage : a) close b) Away		
	k)	Signs on the thumb :		
9)	Nails : a) fluted, b) narrow, c) broad, d) short, e) almond-shaped, f) throat trouble, g) tuberculosis, h) cross ridges, i) spots			

Epilogue

10) Mounts : a) Which is principal mount
              b) Which is subsidiary mount
              c) Placement of the mount
              d) Signs on the mount

CHAPTER XV

The Hand of President Nixon

I shall now take the hand of President Nixon for our study (*fig. 94*). The photo-print reproduced here had appeared in one of the magazines. From the photo-print, we

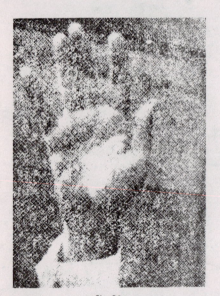

Fig. 94
The Hand of President Nixon

would not be able to fill in our model chart in all respects. We would not be able to find out the following things in particular. 1) Skin, 2) colour, 3) consistency, 4) flexibility and 5) nails. However, the chart can be completed in all other respects. This will be only a model example of hand-reading from the rules of cheirognomy stated throughout this book.

If we go on filling the chart, the picture of the chart becomes under :—

1) The shape of the hand : Spatulate
2) The division of the hand.
   a) First division : Mental world
   b) Second division : Conscious zone
   c) Third division :
     a) Zone of thought is developed haphazardly throwing out the mount of Jupiter.
     b) Some of the action is narrow under the mounts of Saturn and Sun.
     c) Zone of impulse is developed.
3) Fingers : Smooth : Jupiter and Mercury fingers.
         Knotty : Saturn and Apollo fingers.
         Long : Fingers are long in general.
         Tips : Tips of all the fingers are square.
         Length : Apollo finger is longer than Jupiter.
         Spacing : Jupiter and Mercury fingers are away. Saturn and Apollo close together.
         Leaning : Saturn finger is leaning towards Apollo.
4) Phalanges : Jupiter : All phalanges are equal.
              Saturn : Third phalange is longer.
              Apollo : All phalanges are equal.
              Mercury : All phalanges are equal.
5) Thumb : a) Size : Medium.
        b) Carriage : Close to the thumb.
        c) Position : Medium set.
        d) Length of the thumb : Normal.
        e) Shape of the thumb : Diplomatic.

f) Phalanges	:	Long first phalanges.
g) Tips	:	Conic.
6) Mounts	:	All the mounts except Apollo and Moon are well-developed on the hand. Mount of Saturn is shifted towards Apollo.

Now, we shall discuss each item one after another and see the result.

1   The shape of the hand : Spatulate

We find that the hand of President Nixon has a spatulate shape. This hand therefore shows originality and energy. It shows inventors, workers and speculators. President Nixon must be inventing all his energy in new ideas and he would like to go out of the way of conventional pattern. He hates customs, traditions and regularity. He has his own ideas of morality, methods and conventions. He prefers to take any course he pleases and cares very little for what others say. Individualism is his main characteristic and he has love for action, energy and independence.

His confidence is supreme and he aims at abundance and not merely at sufficiency.

This is a restless type. That which does not astonish him does not please him. He likes structures and bridges which may or may not be beautiful but which will convey an idea of muscular effort and mechanical industry.

The spatulate hand has played an important part in the history of America. President Nixon is an inventor. He loves risk and speculation and is versatile but his chief fault is changeability.

2   The division of the hand
First division

According to the first division, the mental world of the President's hand rules. That means his fingers dominate the hand. The development of the mental world shows that he is fit for mental pursuits, studies, research, etc.

Second division

According to the second division of the hand, the conscious zone of the President's hand is more developed. In this zone lies the fingers of Jupiter and the thumb. These two fingers form the characteristics of the President. The development of this zone shows the development of the conscious mind and the President is conscious of his actions and has a wider outlook.

The third division

It is very interesting to study the development of different zones according to the third system. The zone of thought, as covered by the line of Heart, is haphazardly developed and the mount of Jupiter is thrown out of the zone. It means that the honour and prestige as shown by the mount of Jupiter will be at stake and the President will have to face occasions where he will find it very difficult to protect his honour and prestige.

His zone of action is narrow under the mounts of Apollo and Saturn. That means that these two mounts have greater influence on him as far as his actions are concerned. As we know, the mount of Saturn is a philosophical mount. It shows serious thinking and gloomy and melancholy outlook on life. There might have been several mounts in the President's life when he would have felt lonely and depressed.

The mount of Apollo is an active mount and its dominance on the hand means over.activity and sometimes over enthusiasm. The President therefore would suffer from physical exertions due to his many activities. The third division also shows the development of the zone of impulse as shown by the mount of Venus. This development is indicative of his love for art and for the fair sex. The President would therefore have many pleasant occasions in his life.

3 The next thing to be studied on the hand is the development of fingers. We find from the photo-print that the fingers of Jupiter and Mercury are smooth, that is without

knots. Smooth fingers, as we know, show quick grasp of things and a free flow of thought. The President is therefore endowed with the faculty of comprehension. He will proceed by inspiration rather than reason, by synthesis rather than analysis. Since everything slips out easily owing to the smoothness of the finger, he is too passionate and hasty. Smooth-fingered persons are always guided by the first impressions and seldom are wrong in their intuitive deductions.

4 Tips of the fingers

We have now to combine the tips of the fingers with smooth fingers. We find from the photo-print that the President's fingers have square tips. This indicates that the President is analytical and methodical. He loves grammar, order and form. He appreciates and respects honesty, trust and good behaviour.

5 Long fingers

We find that the fingers are in general long and the characteristics of long fingers will be applicable to him. Thus, he is fond of going into details especially of small things. He is suspicious and does not feel quite sure that seeming friends are true. Long fingers also show meddling disposition.

6 Length of the fingers

We find from the photo-print that the finger of Apollo is longer than Jupiter. When it is so, it shows speculative tendencies and the President will be taking great risks in life.

7 Spacing between the fingers

Jupiter and Mercury fingers are away which shows that he is a person of independent thought and action. Closing together of the fingers of Saturn and Apollo means that he is careless of the future.

8 Leaning of the fingers

We notice that the Saturn finger is leaning towards the Apollo finger which is indicative of the fact that the Saturn mount is losing its power to a certain extent, thereby lessening its gloom and melancholia and partaking of the characteristics of Apollo, which are energy, enthusiasm and risk.

9 Phalanges

All phalanges of Jupiter, Apollo and Mercury fingers are equal. Such a formation shows a balanced mind and a practical nature. Jupiter's equal phalanges show a modern approach to religion, dignity and happiness. Apollo's equal phalanges indicate talent and brilliance, reputation and love for wealth, liberty, gaiety and freedom. Equal phalanges of the Mercury finger indicate intelligence, diplomacy, invention and shrewdness.

In the case of the Saturn finger, we find that the third phalange is longer than the other two. It shows love for solitude.

10 Thumb

After discussing the fingers, I shall discuss the President's nature from the development of the thumb.

a) The size of the thumb is medium. The characteristics shown by the medium thumb are love of history and romance.

b) *Carriage of the thumb* : The carriage of the thumb is close to the hand. It exhibits a nature which is cautious, who will be afraid to say much because he fears you may presume on the acquaintance and ask some favour. The President has a high estimate of his abilities.

c) *Position of the thumb* : There are three positions of the thumb, high set, medium set and low set. In the case of the hand under study, we find that the thumb has a medium setting. This is the thumb of a practical man who is reasonable in ordinary matters in life and who is also sentimental at proper occasions. He has good understanding and can know the feelings of others. This thumb gives a balanced mind and shows a hand which exhibits commonsense, materialism, practical outlook and enthusiasm.

d) *Length of the thumb* : The length of the thumb is normal and it means good logic and reasoning.

e) *Shape of the thumb* : The shape is that of a diplomatic thumb described earlier in this book and the President deserves to be a good politician. He will not like to criticise others but keeps everything to himself. He will influence all those who come in his contact and he dominates his political circle so much that others may find it difficult not to grant his wish.

f) *Phalange* : The first phalange of the thumb is developed, meaning thereby that he has strong will-power and determination. He is very firm in his action. He is likely to take hasty steps which may later on land him into troubles. The first developed phalange has made the President impetuous and hard to be convinced.

g) *Tip of the thumb* : The tip of the thumb is conic and, when added to the first developed phalange, it makes the President idealistic in his views. He sincerely thinks that if his plans are brought into practice, the world will be saved from several dangers and catastrophes.

The chart in the beginning shows that all the mounts of the President, except the mounts of Apollo and Moon, are well-developed. We have therefore to find out what aspects will be lacking on the hand due to the absence of these two mounts.

We know that the mount of Apollo shows originality, activity and energy. Now if this mount is lacking, it will mean the absence of these characteristics. However, in the beginning we have studied that the hand has a spatulate shape which exhibits all the above characteristics. We have therefore to combine our first observation with the lack of the mount of Apollo.

However, the finger of Apollo shows good development and thereby gives strength to the mount. It will therefore mean that even though the President will not get all the benefits of the mount, it will help him to a certain extent. The spatulate hand, therefore, with the somewhat strength of Apollo mount, will reduce the intensity of the President's energy, as shown by the spatulate type and he may experience moments of exhaustion and fatigue due to over-activity and over-enthusiasm.

The undeveloped mount of Moon shows that the President will not have powerful imagination to visualise the results of his actions or decisions.

We may now consider in short the aspects of the developed mounts on the hand.

The mount of Jupiter : It shows honour, prestige, religion, command, dignity, authority.

The mount of Saturn : It shows philosophy, sadness, melancholia, mysticism, method, regularity, studiousness, practicality.

The mount of Mercury : It shows shrewdness, quickness, scientific pursuits, business ability, industry, intuition and diplomacy.

The mount of Mars : It is a symbol of aggression, resistance, courage, coolness, calmness and quickness.

The mount of Venus : By virtue of the development of this mount, the President loves art and the beautiful things in life and nature. He is capable of creating cheerfulness in the company he mixes with. Sympathy and passion are his other characteristics.

Thus, we are in a position to describe the characteristics of the President with the help of the *model chart* and we can describe them in more details depending upon the eloquence and imagination of the student of palmistry. We have given this description from our study of Cheirognomy described in this book, and I am sure my readers will appreciate the necessity of filling the model chart, which enables us to know the different phases and shades of the individual's mind and thinking. We could have gone in more details, if we could know the skin, colour, texture, nails, etc. We can also study in details about his finance, vocations, marriage, health, etc. from our study of his hand, but I have purposely not dealt with these aspects for sake of brevity. The readers, therefore, may put down their own observations and complete the reading of the President's life. Whereever we find opposite results, we have to weigh the strength of each and every item and then pronounce our judgement.

I am sure that the method explained above of delineating the characteristics of the individual from the *model chart* will be of great help to the readers and they will also adopt the same method when interpreting the development of the hand.

CHAPTER XVI

The Lines on the Hand

Introduction

After discussing Cheirognomy, which covers the first volume of this book, we shall proceed further to discuss the other part, which is known as Cheiromancy. This part deals with the lines on the hand and has a prophetic aspect. As already explained in the third chapter, lines have a psychological significance and they are capable of indicating the working of the conscious mind of the person. However, basically the science was evolved to peep into the future of man's life. This subject is also known by the word 'Cheirology' or 'Palmistry'. This subject is as much fascinating as it is popular. Every line on the hand has a purpose and a meaning. However, it should not be considered for a moment that each line can be read independently at all times. It is necessary to read the line in combination with other lines or other marks on the hand and also in relation to the mount by which the person is governed.

a) **Theory behind the lines**

The scientists in the world believe that every detail in the human body has a purpose and nothing has been created without any motive. During their research, there may still be some parts, the function of which is still not known to the medical world. We have therefore to believe that the lines have some function to perform and the discussion below will give us the clue to the function.

b) Biological significance of the lines

The main lines are the direct result of the muscular activity of the hand and the arm and they are found where the skin folds. They are located in relation to the joints but the quality and thickness of the underlying tissues causes individual variation in their position.

c) Psychological significance of the lines

It has been observed that the lines change and new lines come-up where originally there were none. New off-shoots appear or parallel lines make their appearance and strengthen or weaken the original main lines. All this happens because the lines have a psychological significance. The lines show the conscious and the sub-conscious behaviour of the person and the lines are formed according to the changes that take place in the psychological process of the mind. Thus it has been observed that the mind controls, produces and alters the lines on the hand.

When profound changes occur and incidents take place in the life of the person, strong enough to affect the behaviour of the person, these changes are recorded on the lines. Another example may be cited to prove the influence of the mind over the lines. In paralysis, the brain loses control over some parts of the body and in some cases it looses control on all the body. It has been observed that in such a case the lines on the hand disappear. However, the lines do not disappear in all cases of paralysis. In some cases life continues without the end of the sickness and the mind remains alert. In such cases, the lines merely become dull and dim but they do not vanish. In the process of the decay of the brain, the lines are affected proportionately and the lines completely disappear when the mind ceases to work. Thus, there may be the brain but it will not control the lines unless there is the mind behind it.

We find similar relation between the mind and the lines in the case of lunatics. If the lunacy is from a lack of mental balance, we find strong lines on the hand. However, if it is due to cellular brain destruction, we may find absence of lines.

In addition to the main lines, there are the accessory lines which are not in proportion to the manual activity of the owner. On the contrary, lazy hands are the richest in these creases. The more sensitive a person is, the greater is his desire for self-expression and the richer his vocabulary of gestures. These gestures involve a high degree of mobility of the hand and cause many accessory creases. The meaning of gestures is wholly psychological. It is profoundly allied with nervous and emotional reactions.

d) Prophetic significance

The most significant part played by the lines on the hand is their relation to future events. We have seen above how the lines can show the past events but it is a matter of great surprise that they are also capable of foretelling the events.

We have two minds, the conscious mind and the sub-conscious mind. It has been experienced that the sub-conscious mind has the capacity to peep into the future and that if it is tapped, we can know what is going to happen in future. As we have seen above, the mind has control over the lines, similarly this sub-conscious mind produces lines giving us the knowledge in advance about the future course of life.

e) Pre-destination and free-will

Often a question is asked, that if the lines tell us our past, present and future, what is the use of our knowing it in advance, that if we can change or alter the future, why any importance be given to the lines and that if the mind produces and alters the lines, what is the use of our knowing the future, because we can create our future according to our will-power. These are the various questious which often confront us. The answer is very difficult. It is true that we have a predestination and it is also true that we can change our future. As it has been studied already the left hand shows what we are born with *i.e.* it shows our predestination, our hereditary characteristics, whereas the right hand shows what we are going to do. As there is a natural position on the face for the nose, the ears, the eyes, etc. similarly there is a natural position on the hand for different lines and marks. Therefore, if any line takes the unnatural position on the hand, it shows some abnormal characteristics. There is a natural course through life that every person would follow and the lines form a map of his natural life's course. If no change takes place in his mental or physical attitude and no accidents occur, this course would be followed.

We do not find two hands exactly alike because no two individuals are exactly of the same temperament and character. Since these two persons differ from each other in some respects, their hands also show the variation in the formation of the lines. It has however been discovered that persons with similar characteristics have similar lines indicating their nearness of temperament. That is why we find hereditary characteristics on the hands of parents and their children.

f) Study of lines

A hand may have a few lines or many lines. Few lines do not mean that there are no important events in the life of the person and that there is nothing special which we can tell to the person. Similarly a number of lines or a complicated pattern of lines does not mean that the life is full of events. We may experience the opposite. However, if we find that the entire hand is covered with irregular lines running in several directions, the lines exhibit a worrying nature and nervous temperament.

Different hands show different markings and formation of lines. If the same pattern of lines is found on two different hands, it does not mean that the interpretation is the same. This is because we have to interpret the lines in relation to the other aspects on the hand. Similarly, there is a difference in the pattern of lines on the left hand and the right hand. In case there is no difference, we can conclude that the person is lethargic and that he is happy with what he has and that he has no dynamism. Such a person is averse to progress.

As regards the formation of lines and the defects in them, it is always better and advisable to study both hands before we pronounce the judgement. We may find a break in the line on the left hand but it may be bridged over on the right hand. This means that the danger shown on the left hand has not been shown on the right hand and the person may not meet with the difficulty shown on the left hand. It means that the intensity of the danger is reduced. However, if the danger is shown on both the hands, we may be sure of the event that is to take place.

Basic facts about the lines

Before studying the lines, we have to study the basic facts of the lines and observe certain rules.

1) We have to observe whether the lines are in proportion to the hand. On a large hand we expect deep and large lines whereas on a small hand we expect delicate lines. If this proportion is not maintained, we may expect ill effects of the formation of lines.

2) We should study each line in detail, its starting position, its course and the ending position. Similarly, we should study the defects on the line and how much importance we should give to those defects.

3) It is better to follow a method in studying the lines and we should start from the Life line, then the Head line, the line of fate etc.

4) If we find that the main lines on the hand are clear and strong and the chance lines are very few, we may say that the person is even-tempered and he will follow the natural course of his life. If however the chance lines are

many and cross the main lines in various ways, it shows that the person is drawn in many directions and will change his natural life's map.

5) We should also study the natural character of the lines in order to have pure formation of the line. The line should be neat and very clear. It should not be too thin or too broad and should not look very pale. It should also be free from all defects such as breaks, islands, forks, etc. We have therefore to study the formation, the colour and the defects of the line, etc. We shall study them one by one.

g) Defects in the line (fig. 95)
Islands (fig. 95-1)

An island anywhere on the line weakens the line. It shows difficulties and losses till the island lasts. However,

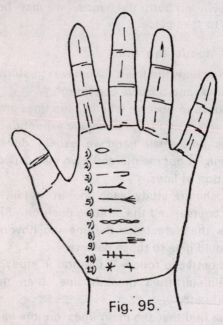

Fig. 95.

Defects in the line: 1) Island, 2) Break, 3) Broken end turning back, 4) Fork, 5) Tassel, 6) Dot, 7) Chained line, 8) Wavy line, 9) Capillary lines, 10) Cross bars, 11) Star and cross.

this is not an independent sign but it is often misunderstood. It is produced by splitting of a line and the return of the splitting. If however, two different lines cross each other in such a way as to form an island, it does not convey the meaning of an island. A true island should be formed from the splitting of a line. The operation of an island is to divide the current flowing along the line. It is therefore an obstruction in the course of the line. The size and the length of the island show the extent of obstruction and its duration.

Breaks in the line (*fig. 95-2*)

They denote obstacles and troubles, depending upon the line on which it is found. A break means stopping of the force running through the line. If the break is small, there is the possibility of joining the line again and the obstructed force will once again join the regular course. If however, the break is big, the danger is serious and we have to find out whether there is a sister line over-lapping the break which would lessen the intensity of the danger.

An alarming position of the break is when the broken end turns back to its source (*fig. 95-3*). If there are no other signs or lines which would repair this break, such as the sister lines or over-lapping lines or a square it shows disaster. Such a break is a warning either for health, life or career.

Fork (*fig. 95-4*)

A fork at the end of the line indicates the diversified force of the line on which it is found. It is not a good indication except on the line of Head, where it shows talents. On the line of Life it shows loss of energy and vitality.

Tassel (*fig. 95-5*)

It means several forks. It dissipates the qualities indicated by the line. Tassel generally means the end of the usefulness of the line.

Dots (fig. 95-6)

A dot or dots on the hand indicate obstruction to the flow of energy. Sometimes we find strong dots sufficient to make a ditch in the line. It is observed that usually such dots appear after a serious illness. The significance of a dot or dots at various places and on different lines has a different meaning and we shall study it while studying individual lines.

Chained lines (fig. 95-7)

If islands are placed one after the other, they form chained lines. These chained lines also show disturbed flow of energy. They weaken the natural quality of the line. On the line of Heart, it shows changeability and weakness of affections and also the weak action of the Heart. On the Head line, it means weak mental power and lack of decision. On the Life line, it means weak constitution. The chains are usually formed on these three lines only and they are not found on the other lines.

Wavy lines (fig. 95-8)

It obstructs the force of the line and creates troubles occurring to the line which has this formation.

Capillary lines (fig. 95-9)

These lines are hairlike lines running by the side of the main line, sometimes joining it, sometimes falling from it. They indicate weakness.

Cross-bars (fig. 95-10)

A bar on the line completely obstructs the natural flow of the energy of that line. If there is a break after the bar, it is a serious warning and the effect of that line will be lost.

Star and Cross (fig. 95-11)

A star or a cross anywhere on the line indicates danger and difficulties.

h) Good signs on the hand
The Square and the Triangle (fig. 96-1)

After studying the above defects found in the line, we have to see whether that defect has been protected by a square or a triangle. If a break in the line is protected by a square or a triangle, (fig. 96-2) the intensity of the break is lessened. If an island is encircled by a square or triangle, the result shown by the island is lessened.

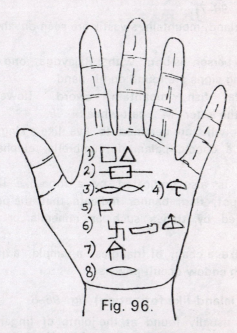

Fig. 96.

Good signs on the hand : 1) Square and triangle, 2) A break protected by square, 3) Two fish, 4) Umbrella, 5) Flags, 6) Swastik-sword-bow, 7) Temple, 8) Yava.

Signs on the hand

According to Hindu system there are several signs on the hand and these signs are described briefly as under.

1) Two fish type formation on the hand shows a benevolent person (fig. 96-3).

2) Signs like an umbrella, a palanquin or a lotus if seen on hands speak of those who lead a luxurious life and live like a king (*fig. 96–4*).

3) Flag, pot, trident, are indications of a very rich life (*fig. 96–5*).

4) Swastik, sword, bow, show military position of a very high rank (*fig. 96–6*).

5) A sign like temple, throne or a lake means a religious person (*fig. 96–7*).

6) Garland, mountain, swastik are seen on the hand of a Mahatma.

When a person is born with a Rajayoga, one or more of the following signs are found on his hand.

Umbrella, fish, mountain, sword, flower, circle, palanquin, the letter 'M', cart-wheel.

Persons, who are destined to live like a king, have on their hand a conch, palanquin, umbrella, elephant and a horse.

Wealth is also indicated by a rope-like line; lines forming a pot, flag, banner indicate that the person will be benefitted by trades such as minerals or petroleum products.

Signs like a chain of triangles, a temple, a quadrangle, a pair of fish endow occult powers.

Yava : (an Island-like formation) *fig. 96–8*

This is usually found at the joints of fingers, on the middle or base of the thumb and at the rascette. It is a sign of happy existence.

1) Yava at the base of the thumb signifies the birth of a son.

2) At the base of the Fate line, it signifies mysterious birth or death of parents.

3) Yava at the centre of Fate line shows love-intrigue.

4) Yava on the Head line means influence from some other class of society.

5) Yava in the Heart line under the mount of Jupiter shows death at a holy place.

Fish: The sign of a fish is a fortunate sign or mark. It bestows wealth, prosperity and a comfortable life. It indicates that the native will be religious, wealthy, a charitable man of power and authority. On a woman's hand, it indicates a lady of good disposition, wealthy, blessed with a son and having a good husband commanding respect from her. Unless there are adverse circumstances and other unfavourable signs, found on her hand, the husband will outlive her. It is said that if the fish sign has its face pointed to the side of the fingers, one enjoys happiness and prosperity throughout one's life, otherwise benefits will come late in life.

Conch: This is a rare mark and such a person will be a famous millionaire. It indicates all the comforts of life, greatness, purity of life and a spirit of renunciation.

Other important signs are circle, angle, grill, star, star of Shiva, Sun, Moon, Mars, Mercury, Venus, Jupiter, Saturn and Kite:

i) Formation of lines

In appearance the lines should look lively, active and energetic and such lines show a happy disposition. On the contrary, dull and dismal lines indicate a non-active and lethargic life.

The lines should be uniform throughout the course in their appearance, depth and width. Sometimes we come across lines which are shallow and feebly marked. Such lines show a nervous constitution and low vitality.

At the first glance of the hand, the lines should create an impression that their pattern is normal with the usual number of main lines and also the accessory lines. However, if the hand shows the bare three lines, which are also poor and dull, it shows dull and dry life. In contrast, the pattern should not be too complicated which means tension and sensitivity. A much-lined hand shows ill-health and a neurotic. In this case, the nervous system is mal-functioning and usually the basic cause is repressed emotions.

j) Lines on different types of hands

The same type of formation of lines on different types of hands has a different meaning. For example, a sloping Head line on a conic hand or psychic hand is a natural position, whereas it is abnormal on a square hand. Similarly, a multiplicity of lines on a square hand is a matter of serious concern than when it is found on a conic hand.

k) Rising and falling lines

Sometimes we may find that a line rises from the main line. It shows periods of uplift and accentuates the power of the main line. Falling lines or descending lines from the main lines show the opposite. These lines have importance on the line of Heart while studying the problem of marriage. Rising lines show affection and harmony in marriage whereas descending lines show failure in married life.

l) Colour of lines

The next thing we have to study is the colour of the lines. Normally, the colour should be transparent and should be slightly deeper in shade than the colour of the palm. Very dark lines indicate a life of hardship and poverty. Pale lines indicate lack of vitality and anaemia.

Red colour : It shows robust health, activity, a healthy and energetic mind and hopeful disposition. However, very deep and dark red lines indicate abnormal physical vigour which is dangerous. Sometimes we find such dark red lines in the case of an insane person.

Yellow colour : Lines with yellow colour show a self-contained, reserved and proud nature. It shows uncompromising attitude. It also shows the wrong functioning of the bile and a jealous disposition.

Black colour : They show a pessimistic and melancholy nature. Such persons are revengeful, vindictive and unforgiving.

The lines on the Hand

m) General observations of the lines

1) Deep and shining lines indicate a wealthy life.
2) Shallow and faint lines indicate misery.
3) Thin, deep and attractive lines show a wealthy life and charity.
4) Distracted and broken lines indicate loss of health and wealth.
5) Lines with off-shoots show worries and difficulties.
6) Lines, which are not uniform but which are thin for some length and are thick thereafter and the lines which do not follow their normal course but divert from the natural course, indicate unusual life, loss of money and troubles.

n) Map of the hand (fig. 97)

There are six important lines on the hand and eight lesser important lines. The important lines are as under.

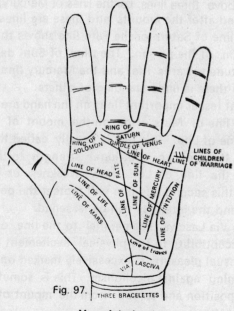

Fig. 97.

Map of the hand

1) The line of Life which embraces the mount of Venus.
2) The line of Head which crosses the centre of the hand.
3) The line of Heart which runs parallel to that of the Head line at the base of the fingers.

The above three lines are present in all the hands with a few exceptions. Sometimes we find one line across the hand which may be a combination of the Head and Heart lines. These three lines usually start from the region of Jupiter and they exhibit the three basic principles, the spiritual, the mental and the physical.

4) The line of Mercury which starts from the mount of Neptune and goes to the mount of Mercury.
5) The line of Sun which rises generally on the plain of Mars and ascends to the mount of Sun.
6) The line of Fate which starts from the wrist and goes to the mount of Saturn.

The above three lines, i.e. the lines of Mercury, Sun and Fate are called after the mounts and these are lines of inspiration. The line of Saturn or the Fate line shows the sorrows or satisfaction of the person. The line of Sun denotes the brighter attitude towards life and the Mercury line shows a life in which there is understanding of others.

The eight lesser important lines on the hand are as under:

1) The line of Mars rises on the mount of Mars and within the line of Life. This line is usually called the Double line of Life. It gives an additional strength to the line of Life. When the line of Life shows weakness or breaks, or accidents, this second Life line will protect the person from the danger and the intensity will be lessened.

2) The Via Lasciva lies parallel to the line of Mercury. It shows susceptibility to the physical excitement and indulgence in sensual pleasure. If excessively marked on the hand, it gives warning against alcoholism. This is sometimes seen in a curved position and spreads from the mount of Moon to the mount of Venus.

3) The line of Intuition, which extends like a semi-circle from the mount of Moon to the mount of Mercury, strengthens the spiritual aspect of the sub-conscious mind and normally it is a healthy sign on the hand. However, in a weak hand, it shows superstitions and fanciful mysticism.

4) The line of marriage is the horizontal line on the mount of Mercury. This line is found in all the hands with a few exceptions. It shows marital relationship and abilities to live in sex partnership.

5) The Girdle of Venus, lying above the line of Heart and encircling the mount of Jupiter and the mount of Mercury, shows activity, enthusiasm and sex. It is a good line on a good hand and a bad line on a bad hand. To be good, it must be well traced and full. To be bad, it must be broken and poorly formed.

6) The three bracelets found on the wrist. They relate to longevity.

7) The lines of children seen on the line of Marriage and elsewhere on the hand.

8) The lines of travel found on the mount of Moon.

Other minor lines

In addition to the above main lines and the lesser important lines, there are a number of minor lines. They are the lines of influence. We shall deal with them in details later on, but a few may be mentioned here.

1) The Ring of Solomon is found on the mount of Jupiter in a semi-circular way and is representative of wisdom.

2) The ring of Saturn is found on the mount of Saturn and it enhances the Saturnian characteristics. It also shows motherly wisdom and is good on the hand of a woman.

3) Other lines of influence found all over the hand often appear and fade and show the hope that rises in the individual and also the frustration which he has to face. The influence lines show the events with amazing accuracy.

o) The time factor on the hand (fig. 98)

The most difficult part of the hand-reading is calculating the exact age or the period on the hand. The hand may show foreign travel or uplifting of periods of promotion in life, but it is difficult to find out the exact age at which the incidents may take place.

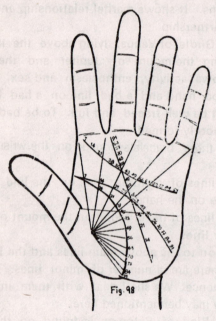

Fig. 98

Time factor

Most of the learned authors on this subject with long experience state that an approximate period with two years' variation on either side is possible and we should not exaggerate our accuracy further than that. We can approach the nearest period with our knowledge of numerology and a good palmist must be conversant with that study. However, numerology being entirely a different subject, as palmists we should be able to fix-up the periods in life with our own method of calculation. There is a method of seven and we shall abide by that method. The number seven is considered as a mystic number and the importance of this number is explained in several ways such as the seven wonders of the world, the seven heavens, the seven seas, the seven days of the week and the seven planets, etc. In the first place we shall draw a straight line from the second joint of the thumb, from where the mount of Venus starts, upto the middle portion of the percussion. The map of the hand will make it clear. The point where this line intersects the line of Life is the 35th year read on the line of Life. Then from the percussion side beneath the little finger or the finger of Mercury, we have to draw a line which will cut the point on the line of Life and continue upto the middle mount of Venus. From this middle point on the mount of Venus we shall draw lines towards other fingers as shown in the figure. These lines, where they intersect the line of Life will show the years on the Life line. The basic line drawn from the Mercury finger will also intersect the line of Head and the line of Fate. The point of intersection will also indicate the 35th year on the Head line and also on the Fate line. The periods on other lines will be as shown in the figure.

CHAPTER XVII

The line of Life

Introduction

The line of Life is the Map of the natural course of man's life. It is the first line that is developed in the embryonic life. It usually shows the vitality and energy of the person. The length, the depth and the continuity reveal the quality of the vitality. This line also has great psychological aspect. If this line does not take a graceful curve and comes down in a somewhat straight way (*fig. 99*), it shows a cold, unresponsive nature and lack of natural human warmth. These people may be sensuous but they are cold. This formation is often associated with faulty endocrine balance. A short, shaky and interrupted line of Life indicates nervous constitution.

From the length of the line we can know the span of life. According to Hindu system, before we start reading the hand, we must first find out the longevity of the person which we can know from the Life line, which indicates not only the vitality of the person or the psychological aptitude of the person but also his span of life. Since this line shows the existence of man, we can never expect this line to be absent. However, one of the authors on this subject has stated that he has seen a hand without a Life line. In such a case, we can say logically that even if the person survives and is living, he does not have the spirit and energy that is required to sustain the life but he lives on his nervous energy and is susceptible to nervous breakdown.

In such a case, we have to study the thumb and the Head line and the Heart line also. It is said that even the line of Mercury, if found on the hand but not touching the Life line,

The line of Life

is sufficient to sustain life. This line can make-up the loss shown by the absence of Life line.

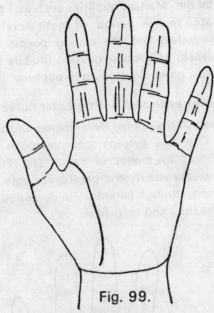

Fig. 99.

Straight line of Life (cold nature)

As a general proposition, we may consider that longer the line of Life, longer the life and shorter the line of Life, shorter the Life. But this is not true always. Occasionally, we find a long line of Life but actually the person died at a much earlier age than is shown on the Life line. It may also happen that the Life line is short but the person enjoys a long life. This is because we have to take the other lines and signs on the hand into consideration before we pronounce any judgement. A defect may not be shown on the Life line but it may be shown on the Head line or the Heart line. Thus, we have to study the various lines and signs on the hand and no specific inference can be drawn by judging a single line or a sign.

If we study the route of the line of Life, we find that it first encircles the positive mount of Mars, then the mount of

Venus and then the mount of Neptune. It therefore partakes all the qualities of these mounts. For the first few years, it is governed by the Martian qualities such as, dash, vigour, enthusiasm, etc. In the period of youth it is governed by Venus indicating love and the mating period. At the end, the spiritual aspect of Neptune governs the Life line. This is how the changes go on developing in our life.

Mount of Venus encircled with greater curve

1) Instead of the normal development of the line, if we find that the Life line sweeps into the palm enclosing a greater portion of the mount of Venus (*fig. 100*), it is an indication of excess vitality and greater sex urge. The person enjoys happiness through parents. He descends from a high family and is healthy and long-lived.

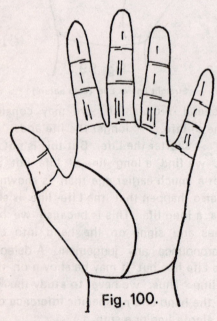

Fig. 100.

Life line covering greater portion of the mount of Venus (excess vitality and greater sex urge)

2 Position on the hand

This line rises from the lower edge of the mount of Jupiter, encircles the lower mount of Mars and the mount of Venus and goes down the hand. Usually this line is in between the mount of Venus and the mount of Moon. But for all practical purposes, we can consider that the mount of Venus is all within the line of Life.

3 Normal development

Normally, this line should form a graceful curve and should look lively. It should be even throughout its course. It should be long, narrow and deep without any breaks or crosses. The colour should be deeper than the skin, transparent and lively. Such a formation promises a long healthy life and an optimistic outlook. Such a person lives with good ideals and appreciates life even upto old age.

Deviation from the normal formation

If the line runs closer to the second phalange of the thumb and if there is a star at the intersection of the lines of Head and Mercury, it shows childlessness and difficulty in child-bearing (*fig. 101*). Such a formation reduces the size of the mount of Venus and checks the operation of that mount. This makes the person cold, unsympathetic and lacking in sexual desire. This is an important formation we have to take into consideration at the time of studying the married life of a person.

4 Starting position

a) If the line starts well high on the mount of Jupiter, it shows a very ambitious nature and if it starts still higher on the mount, it shows dictatorship and cruelty (*fig. 102*). Here comes the question of combining the characteristics of the mounts with the line of Life. We must know what type of ambition will govern the subject if the Life line starts on the mount of Jupiter. The logical explanation is as under.

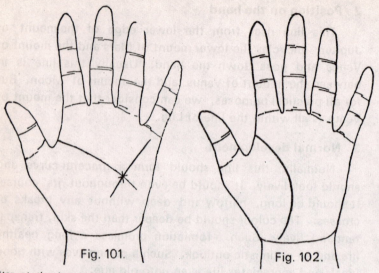

Fig. 101. Star at the intersection of Head line and Mercury line (childness)

Fig. 102. Life line starting high on the Jupiter mount (ambitious nature)

If he is a Jupiterian, his ambition will be for learning and high position. If he is a Saturnian the ambition will be for acquiring occult powers or in developing medicine, science, mining, farming, etc. If he is an Apollonian, he will crave for success and fame in public and also as an administrator, or even as an actor or artist. If he is a Mercurian, his ambition will be for business or in scientific pursuits. We can apply the same logic in case he is governed by other mounts.

A good start for the Life line is from the bottom of Jupiter mount quite independent of the line of Head but still very near to it. The starting point of the line should be sharp and slightly pointing to the mount of Jupiter. Such a formation will give the line all the good aspects of the Jupiter mount, such as honesty, honour, prestige, etc. The closeness of the Life line with the Head line will give clarity of mind, good reasoning and understanding and the life of the person will be governed by these qualities. This also indicates the child's upbringing in a healthy and happy family. This formation also shows the happy life of the parents.

The line of Life

b) If the Life line starts from the positive mount of Mars, it indicates struggle and hardship. It shows poor health and few opportunities in life (*fig. 103*).

c) If the Life line at its start is closely connected with the Head line, it is a good formation and it shows good logic and reasoning, even though he is somewhat sensitive. It also speaks of caution and prudence in practical life. The person is interested more in intellectual pursuits than in physical work (*fig. 104*).

d) If there is a small space between these two lines, it shows an independent nature and the person is free to carry out his plans and ideas. It also shows good energy and dash (*fig. 105*).

e) If the space is wide (*fig. 106*), it shows too much of independent nature and the person is not guided by reason or intelligence. He is too impulsive and hasty and commits mistakes. This defect can be counter-balanced by a well-developed second phalange of the thumb and knotty fingers.

This wide gap between the lines of Life and Head on a hand with a girdle of Venus shows an irritable nature and ill-luck in profession. This wide gap shows vanity, envy and falsehood. If the colour of the line is red, it shows cruelty and great love of money. Sometimes this wide space indicates violent death. It means unhappiness in married life and a temptation to have some close friend of the opposite sex.

f) If the lines of Life, Head and Heart join each other, (*fig. 107*) it is an unfortunate sign and the person lacks perception and creates difficulties and dangers for him. It also means sudden death. Such a formation means that no line can have a free hand to show its characteristics, either moral, mental or instinctive. Such persons are extremely nervous and are sincere in their duty. They have a peculiar temperament and thinking. They are enthusiastic about love but usually they love a wrong person and finally meet with frustration. They, all the while, imagine that their life is a tragedy and somehow tragedy prevails in their life. From the health point of view, such a formation shows rheumatism.

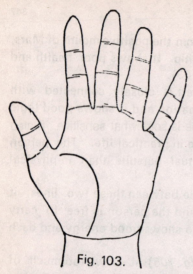

Fig. 103.

Life line starting from the mount of Mars (struggle and hardship)

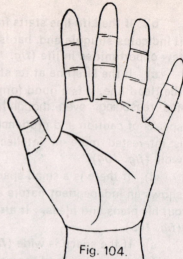

Fig. 104.

Life line and Head line connected at the start (good logic and reasoning)

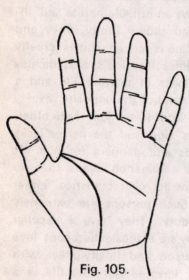

Fig. 105.

Small space between Head and Life lines (independent nature)

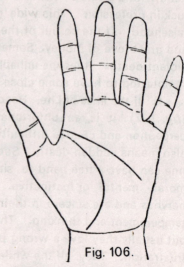

Fig. 106.

Wide gap between Head and Life line (hasty and quarrelsome nature)

g) If the Life line is connected with the Head line and forms a sharp angle, it means prudence. For such angles between the Life line and Head line, please refer to chapter on Triangle and Quadrangle.

h) If the Life line is joined to the Head line and both the lines run together for sometime (*fig. 108*), it shows extreme sensitivity, diffidence and timidity. In order to avoid these results, the thumb should be powerful and should counter-balance the defect.

I know of a boy who was in love with a girl but his diffidence never allowed him to express his love and remained unmarried throughout his life. His hand showed the Life line joined with the drooping line of Head and with a Girdle of Venus.

i) If the Life line is connected with the Heart line and if the Head line is poor or short (*fig. 109*), it always indicates accidents or sickness. The nature of the accident will depend upon the mount of the person by which he is governed. If he is a Jupiterian, the trouble will be of high blood pressure; if a Saturnian, it will be with legs; if an Apollonian, it will be with the eye; if a Mercurian, it will be with the bile, and so on.

j) A fork at the start of the Life line means a sense of fidelity and justice (*fig. 110*).

k) A long fork deep into the mount of Jupiter shows realisation of the ambition and a successful life (*fig. 111*).

l) Two or more forks at the beginning but below the line of Head and under the mount of Jupiter (*fig. 112*) indicate honour to the parents which ultimately benefit the person. If however these forks are crossed, they mean law-suits.

m) An island at the beginning shows mystery of birth (*fig. 113*).

5 Course of the line of Life

The next thing we have to study about the line of Life is it's course. As already stated, normally the line should be of even thickness throughout the course. However, if we find

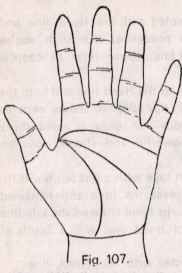

Fig. 107.
Joining of Life, Head and Heart line
(sudden death)

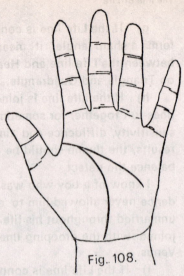

Fig. 108.
Life and Head lines run together
(sensitivity, diffidence and timidity)

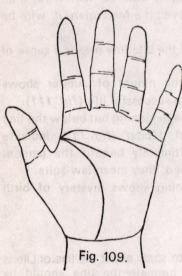

Fig. 109.
Life line joined to the Heart line with
short Head line (sickness or accident)

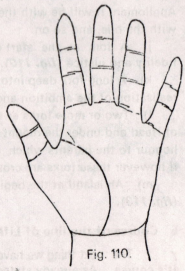

Fig. 110.
Fork at the start of the Life line
(fidelity)

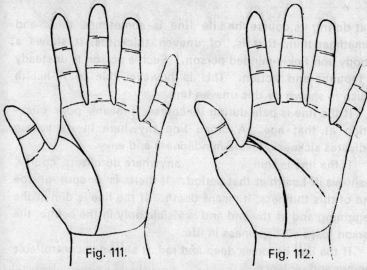

Fig. 111.
Life line starting with a deep fork on Jupiter (successful life)

Fig. 112.
Two or more forks at the beginning below the line of Head (honour to the parents)

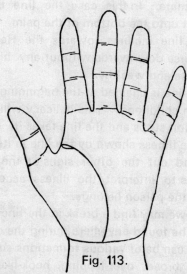

Fig. 113.
Life line starting with Island (mystery of birth)

that during its course the Life line is sometimes thick and sometimes thin, that is, of uneven thickness, it shows a moody and fickle-minded person. Such a person is unsteady in thought and action. This is however due to ill-health which is shown by this uneven line.

If the line is pale during its course, it means poor circulation at that age. A broad line anywhere in its course indicates sickness, feeble-mindedness and envy.

If the line is thin anywhere during its course, it shows ill-health at that period. If there is a spot at the end of this thinness, it means death. If the line is dim at the beginning and at the end and is visible only in the centre, the person loses all happiness in life.

If the line becomes deep and red, it shows uncontrollable temper and violence.

If the line of Life is very deep throughout the course, it is an indication of exertion for the nervous system which is terribly affected. This abnormal depth of the line is a warning of the coming paralysis due to over-work.

If the line is clear, evenly traced and thick, the person is good and fortunate. In this case the line is round and descends straight upto the bottom of the palm. If during its course the Life line inclines towards the Head line, then continues its course downwards without any hindrance, the person is fortunate and wealthy.

Usually, the line is chained at the beginning which shows delicate health in childhood. This delicacy will be over after the chain formation stops and the line takes its usual course. In finding out the illness shown by the line in its course, it is necessary to find out the other signs on the hand and the most important is to interpret the illness according to the mount to which the person belongs.

Sometimes, we may find a break in the line of Life (*fig. 114*). This can be found anywhere during the course of the line. The break can be of various formations such as a break that is narrow, broad, over-lapping, hook-like, etc. Every formation has its own meaning. We may also find a bar, a dot or a hole in between the break.

Break

The break indicates change in life. It may be caused by accident, sickness, or through some shock. The exact cause can be ascertained from other signs on the hand.

a) *Over-lapping* : If we find a break in the line and if the lower part of the broken line begins before the break on the upper side, we may say that the break is over-lapping (*fig. 115*).

If the break is seen in one hand only, the over-lapping position safeguards the danger. However, if it is found in both the hands, it is a warning of incoming danger. The over-lapping position may however mean recovery from the danger.

b) *Hook-like* : If we find a break in the line and if the upper line or the lower line turns inward into the mount of Venus, the accident is likely to be fatal (*fig. 116*).

If after the break the Life line has ladder-like formation, if means a period of prolonged and continuous ill-health (*fig. 117*).

A break in Life line with a break in the line of Fate at the same time of age, is most dangerous and shows danger to one's longevity.

All breaks indicate a check or danger to the health and consequently to the life of the subject. These dangers come either from illness or accidents. It is difficult to predict accidents, but in a healthy hand a break in Life line should be read only as an accident.

c) *Square on the break* : A square anywhere on the hand shows protection from danger. Danger shown by the break is protected by the square outside the break (*fig. 118*). However, if a line descends from the mount of Saturn and touches the square, it means that the protection is from an accident and not from an illness.

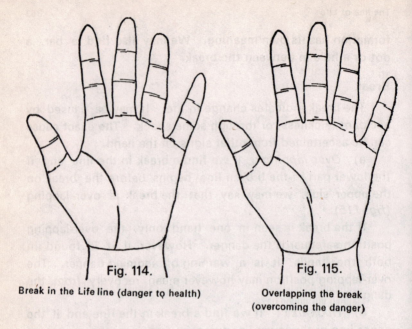

Fig. 114.
Break in the Life line (danger to health)

Fig. 115.
Overlapping the break
(overcoming the danger)

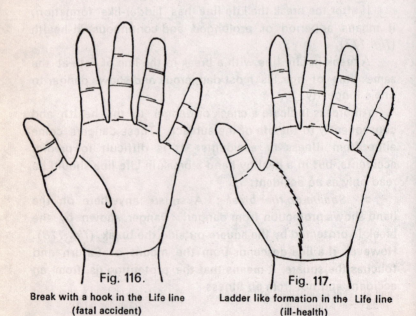

Fig. 116.
Break with a hook in the Life line
(fatal accident)

Fig. 117.
Ladder like formation in the Life line
(ill-health)

The line of Life

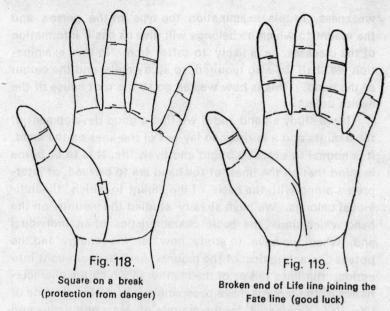

Fig. 118.
Square on a break
(protection from danger)

Fig. 119.
Broken end of Life line joining the
Fate line (good luck)

d) *Bars* : A bar in between the break has the same meaning as over-lapping line and it shows recovery from the danger.

e) If the Life line is broken and if the broken end is joined to the Fate line (*fig. 119*), it shows good luck due to which danger is avoided.

f) A black spot at the end of broken line is the worst sign and shows sudden death or assasination.

If we see a good formation of the line after the defect, the person will have a strong constitution as soon as the delicacy shown by the line is over. If however after the defect the line is thin and continues so to the end, it indicates poor health. If after the defect the Life line is broad or shallow or chained, the person will never be strong and will always suffer from weak constitution. He will always experience periods of good health and ill-health and all this can be ascertained from the character of the line during the course of the Life line. Once we notice a period of weak constitution, we should try to discover the cause behind the weakness. In this examination the type of the person and the mount to which he belongs will give us basic information of the diseases he is likely to suffer from. In this examination we shall be also required to study nails and the colour of the hand. This is how we can go to the root cause of the health defect.

If we study a hand and if we find a good development of the mounts and a fairly good lay-out of the lines on the hand, it is normal to expect a bright and lively life. It is to be borne in mind that all the lines of the hand are to be read or interpreted along with the basis of the mount to which the individual belongs. We have already studied the mounts on the hand which show the basic characteristics of an individual and, when we have to study how far the energy and the potent characteristics of the mounts have been brought into action, the lines tell us of the manner in which the characteristics of the mounts have been employed. As for the line of Life, it is dominated by the mounts of Mars and Venus and Neptune. It has also a connection with the mount of Jupiter.

During the course of the line of Life, we find branches or sprouts either rising or falling from the Life line. This indicates the active development of the personality, whereas the descending lines denote wastage of energy and abuse of it. The rising line can also absorb the energy and potentialities of the developed mounts and use these resources for advantage.

Rising and falling lines from the line of Life
Rising lines

During our study of the Life line we shall observe that certain lines go down from the Life line and certain lines rise from the line of Life (*fig. 120*). These lines may be called split lines. We shall first study the rising lines. Whenever these rising branches are seen, it shows good health, realisation of ambition and riches and a change for the better. If the rising line goes to the mount of Jupiter (*fig. 121*), it promises success and realisation of ambition. It is also an

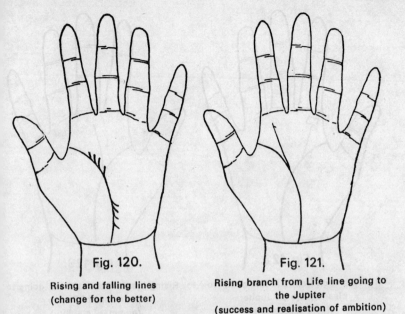

Fig. 120.
Rising and falling lines
(change for the better)

Fig. 121.
Rising branch from Life line going to the Jupiter
(success and realisation of ambition)

indication of egoism showing that such a person will be reserved and afraid to show his reactions to great joy or sorrow experienced by him. It shows freedom of life in earlier ages and the person will lead a freer life. He may lead an independent life either in a boarding house or college hostel or may continue his studies abroad. If such a line goes to a clear square on the mount of Jupiter (*fig. 122*), it gives the subject lucid expression often required for a good teacher.

If we find a line rising from the Life line and going to the mount of Saturn (*fig. 123*), it shows marital success and financial stability. The success is due to personal efforts and not luck. If we find a rising line going to the mount of Apollo (*fig. 124*), it promises success, glory and wealth. If however we find a line from this rising line going to the mount of Jupiter and also a line rising from a line of Fate and going to the mount of Apollo we have a distinguished person enjoying honour and success as a diplomat or a politician. If a rising line goes to the mount of Mercury, it means success in scientific pursuits and or in business (*fig. 125*).

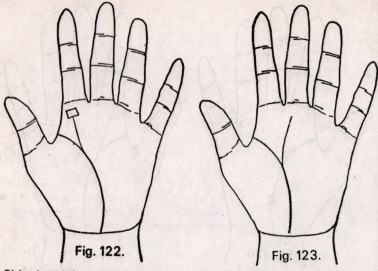

Fig. 122.
Rising branch from Life line going to clear square on Jupiter (lucid expression)

Fig. 123.
Rising branch from Life line going to the mount of Saturn (monetary stability)

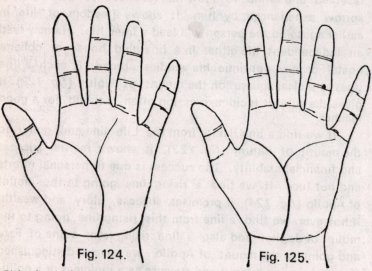

Fig. 124.
Rising branch from Life line going to the mount of Sun (success, glory and wealth)

Fig. 125.
Rising branch from Life line going to the mount of Mercury (success in business)

If the rising line goes to the mount of Uranus, it shows general success in life (*fig. 126*). We may sometimes find that these rising lines do not reach any mount. In that case, they indicate only efforts without any success.

If the rising branch is connected by a line from the mount of Venus, joining each other on the line of Life, it shows great attachment to family life (*fig. 127*). If the rising branch goes upto the line of Fate but does not touch it or cross it, it shows honour or riches. If however the line is stopped by the line of Head under the mount of Saturn, it shows wrong judgement and mistake in career. If this rising line is stopped by the line of Heart (*fig. 128*), it means wrong judgement in one's affections. If any of the rising lines is cut by a line from the Mercury line, it indicates loss of enterprise on account of bad health (*fig. 129*).

Sometimes we find that these rising lines are crossed by the lines from the positive Mars or Venus mounts. The indication is unhappiness. It may also mean judicial separation from the married partner or a law-suit to that effect. The success or failure of the suit will depend upon the way the cutting line behaves towards the line of Saturn and Apollo.

We may come across occasionally rising lines from both the sides of the Life line (*fig. 130*). They indicate riches, realisation of ambition and good health.

Falling lines

We may also come across lines drooping down the Life line and they show a meaning opposite to that of the rising lines. They often indicate the inability of the subject to cope with the circumstances due to deficient energy. They also indicate loss of money due to sickness.

Sometimes we find falling lines or splits joining the other main lines. If it joins the line of Fate (*fig. 131*), it has a happy indication as regards health. Usually the falling offshoot shows the weakening of the nervous system. But in such cases it assumes a new role and helps to revitalise the health of the person. In case the Life line is shortened or

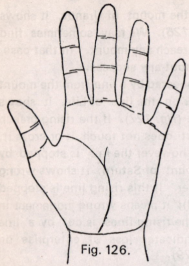

Fig. 126.

Rising branch from Life line going to the mount of Uranus (success in life)

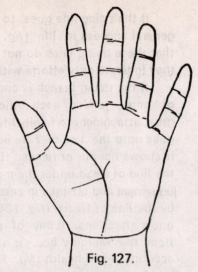

Fig. 127.

Rising branch from Life line connected by a line from Venus joining each other on Life line (family attachment)

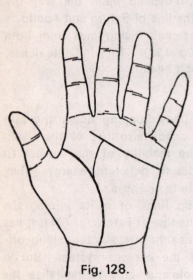

Fig. 128.

Rising branch stopped by Heart line (misjudgement in affection)

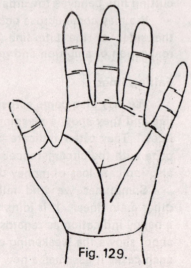

Fig. 129.

Rising branch cut by a line from Mercury line (loss of enterprise)

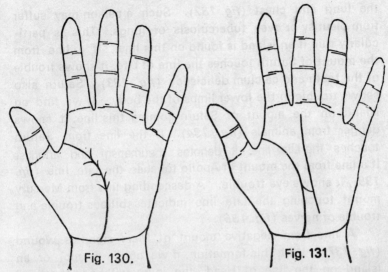

Fig. 130. Rising lines from both sides of the Life line (riches and good health)

Fig. 131. Falling sprout from Life line, joining the Fate line (regaining health)

stopped and the split line joins the line of Fate, it indicates that the function of the Life line is handed-over to the line of Fate. Thus the effect of the short Life line is nullified. Such a formation is seen on a few hands. Such people are rescued by these falling lines. They can live upto old age and enjoy better health than those who merely depend on a long and strong line of Life.

Sometimes this split runs along the line of Life as a double line. This reduces the vitality during the period of the split. Though it does not indicate any positive weakness, sometimes these falling lines are just like hair lines and they do not affect the size of the Life line. These are seen on a deep Life line and they consume the vigour and strength shown by the deep line.

We have studied above the advantage of the lines rising from the Life line. However, we may come across some fine lines from the mounts descending and touching the line of life. It is not a good sign to have such a line. A line from the mount of Jupiter touching the Life line shows troubles of the lung and chest (*fig. 132*). Such a person may suffer from pleurisy or even tuberculosis of lungs. This is particularly true if an island is found on this line. If a line from the mount of Saturn touches the line of Life, it shows trouble of the teeth and calcium deficiency (*fig. 133*). Saturn also shows trouble in the lower limbs of the body. If we find an island on the mount of Saturn joining this line, it shows danger from animals (*fig. 134*). If the line from Saturn touches the Life line, it denotes rheumatism and arthritise. If a line from the mount of Apollo touches the Life line (*fig. 135*), it shows eye trouble. A descending line from Mercury mount touching the Life line indicates bilious trouble and trouble of nerves (*fig. 136*).

A line from negative mount of Mars signifies wound (*fig. 137*). With this formation, if we notice a spot or an island on the line of Head, the injury will be to the head (*fig. 138*).

If a line is seen rising from the plain of Mars and touching the Life line or cutting it, it means an accident (*fig. 139*).

It is very interesting to note that if two parallel lines from the mount of Uranus cut the Life line, it speaks of strange and unexpected favourable happenings (*fig. 140*).

Branches from the Life line

a) We may occasionally come across a Life line in which a branch starts from the beginning of the Life line and ends at the rascette (*fig. 141* and *case 7*). This indicates severe headache. In this case, we have to study the line of Head also so as to arrive at the right decision. If however the Head line is strong and good, the intensity of the trouble will be reduced.

b) Sometimes the branch may start after the middle age which means loss of vitality. On the hand of a woman this is usually seen during the period after forty when there is a biological change.

c) Sometimes the branches may go towards the mount of the Moon which means restlessness, forgetfulness and

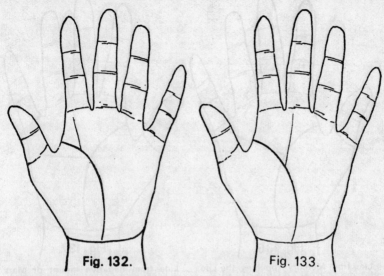

Fig. 132.
A line from Jupiter touching the Life line (lung and chest troubles)

Fig. 133.
A line from Saturn touching the Life line (tooth trouble)

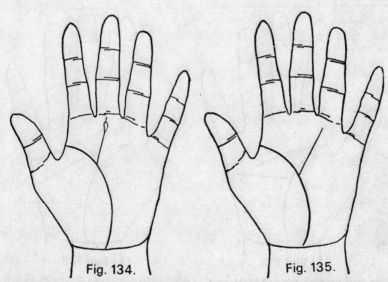

Fig. 134.
Island on Saturn on the line joining the Life line (danger from animals)

Fig. 135.
Line from Sun touching the Life line (eye trouble)

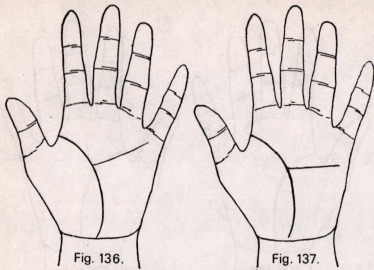

Fig. 136.
Line from Mercury touching the Life line (bilious trouble)

Fig. 137.
Line from negative mount of Mars touching the Life line (wound)

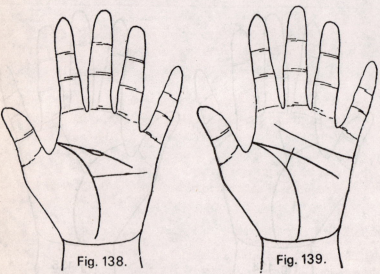

Fig. 138.
Line from negative mount of Mars with island on head (wound to the head)

Fig. 139.
Line from plain of Mars touching the Life line (accident)

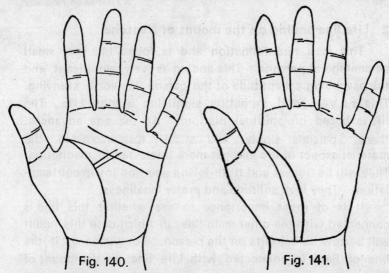

Fig. 140.
Two parallel lines from Uranus cutting the Life line (strange and unexpected favourable happenings)

Fig. 141.
Branch from the beginning of the Life line upto bracellet (severe headaches)

erotic nature. If in addition the hand is soft, flabby and with a sloping line of Head, it shows that the person will take to vices and will revel in those pleasures.

d) If a branch starts from a black spot in the Life line, it means chronic complaints (*fig. 142*).

6 Ending position

The next thing we have to study is as to how the Life line ends. Ending of the line of Life is equally or perhaps more important than the starting of the same. The Life line may end at one of the four following places *viz*., the mount of Venus, the mount of Neptune, the mount of Moon or the Rascette. We shall study these positions one by one.

1 Life line ending on the mount of Venus

This is a happy termination of the line and it denotes a happy married Life and a big family. The person is a good husband and also a good father. He will enjoy healthy life and will get co-operation and understanding from his wife.

2 Life line ending on the mount of Neptune

This is a rare formation and is found in a very small percentage of persons. This ending is very significant and the psychological aptitude of the person is worth studying. This is a very good formation signifying a long Life. The life is based on spiritual platform. As the age advances, these persons slowly and steadily lose interest in the material aspect of life and get more interested in meditation. They will be honest and truth-loving and find joy in contemplation. They love solitude and prefer loneliness.

It is of great importance to see whether this line is connected with the other main lines in which case this mount will bestow its benefits on the person. For instance, if the line of Fate is connected with Life line on the mount of Neptune, the person will be benefited by the material aspects of Saturn (*fig. 143*). If the line of Apollo touches the Life line, the person will emanate peace to others.

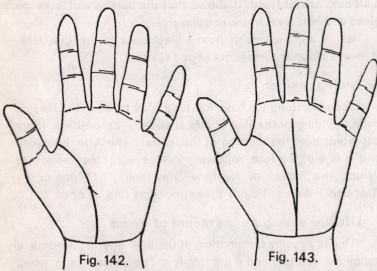

Fig. 142.
Falling branch from a black spot on Life line (chronic complaints)

Fig. 143.
Fate line touching Life line on the mount of Neptune (success & fortune)

The line of Life

3 Life line ending on the mount of Moon

Sometimes the Life line may run in a normal way and after the first half, it may take a turn on the mount of Moon, running deep into the mount and reaching the rascette (*fig. 144*). In such a formation the life will be dominated by the characteristics of the mount of Moon. The person will be fond of travel and will love to live near the sea or reservoir of water, such as a lake. It also shows the possibility of leading the life in foreign country for most of the time. He will always look for a change. Mentally, he will be unsteady. On the hand of a woman, this life line going to the mount of Moon shows gonadic trouble and trouble in child-bearing.

A Life line suddenly going at right angles on the mount Moon indicates epilepsy (*fig. 145*).

4 Life line ending on rascettes

Sometimes we may come across a Life line which is long

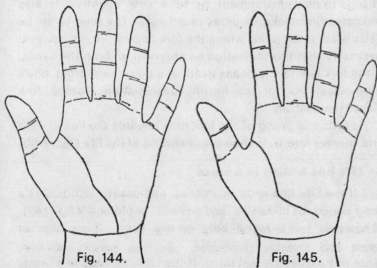

Fig. 144.
Life line taking a turn on mount of Moon and reaching rascettes (love for travel)

Fig. 145.
Life line suddenly going at right angles on the mount of Moon (epilepsy)

enough to touch the rascettes at the bottom of the hand. Such a line indicates a long life. But on a woman's hand with a rayed mount of Venus and vertical lines on the mount of Saturn, it shows troubles of the generative organs.

In short, the end of Life line shows either the death or illness or change in life. The life of the person is largely influenced by the way the Life line ends on the hand.

5 Life line ending in a fork

a) If the Neptunian line of Life ends in a fork and if one branch of the fork goes on the mount of Venus, it is an indication of clash between the married partners (*fig. 146*). The person is governed by Neptune, who loves loneliness and spiritual life, whereas the partner is a Venusian, who runs after material pleasures. Naturally, there is no harmony between the two and the married life is not happy.

b) Usually, Life line ends in a fork. The termination of the line with a fork shows a general weakening of the system, change to new environment or to a new country. It also indicates financial difficulties in old age. The time is to be calculated at the point where the fork begins. It is however necessary that this indication be observed on both the hands. If the fork is wide, it means death at a place away from one's birth place. As for the health consideration, such a fork shows rheumatism.

c) If one prong of the fork runs towards the line of Fate and merges into it, it shows dull ending of the life (*fig. 147*).

6 Life line ending in a cross

If the Life line ends in a series of crosses, it indicates a long period of ill-health and poverty in old age (*fig. 148*). If however this is found only on one hand, it is a sign of talent and loveable disposition. Such a person, however, does not succeed in anything. If the Life line ends in a cross, it is a sure sign of sudden death. The cause of death should be seen elsewhere on the hand.

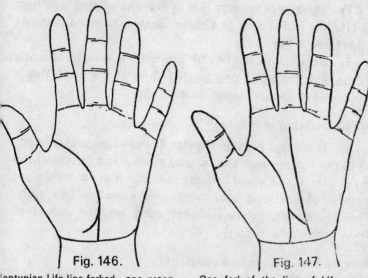

Fig. 146.
Neptunian Life line forked—one prong to mount of Venus (clash between married partners)

Fig. 147.
One fork of the line of Life merging into Fate line (dull ending of life)

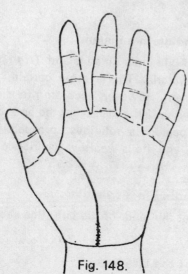

Fig. 148.
Life line ending in series of crosses (poverty in old age)

7) Sometimes we may find a fine line coming out from the Life line and ending in a star. Such a formation shows sudden death (*fig. 149*).

8) Sometimes the line of Life may terminate abruptly and we may find short and parallel lines at the end. This is also an indication of sudden death.

Life line ending in a tassel

9) If the line ends in a tassel, it shows general weakening of the constitution and loss of money and trouble at the end of life. If the tassel is badly formed, it indicates violent death and sometimes even murder or execution (*fig. 150*). If one branch of the tassel goes deep into the mount of Moon, it foretells insanity.

10 Life line ending in a cross-bar

If the Life line ends in a cross-bar or a dot, it signifies sudden or unexpected death. The dot may indicate death by accident or violence (*fig. 151*).

11) The mole at the end of the line has the same meaning as above.

12 Life line ending in an island

If the line of Life ends in an island (*fig. 152*), it shows a tendency to hysteria. This is more certain, if the line of Mars is also present. However, according to Hindu palmistry, an island is called a fish and fish at the end of the Life line means that the person is religious, prosperous and leads a comfortable life and he is wealthy, charitable and a man of power.

13 Life line ending in a triangle

A triangle at the end of the Life line shows falsehood (*fig. 153*).

7 Character of the Life line

In the study of the Life line, the character of the line is

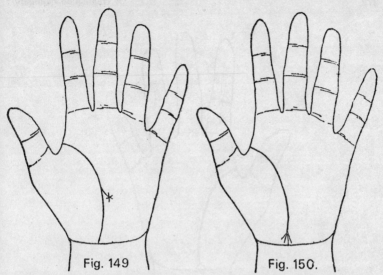

Fig. 149
Cross at the end of the line coming out from the Life line (sudden death)

Fig. 150.
Life line ending in Tassel (violent death, or murder, or execution)

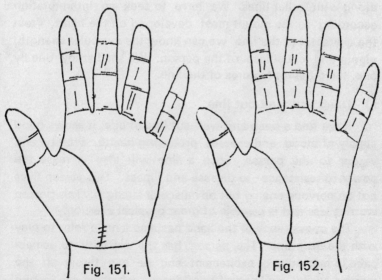

Fig. 151.
Life line ending in cross bar (sudden or unexpected death)

Fig. 152.
Life line ending in an island (hysteria)

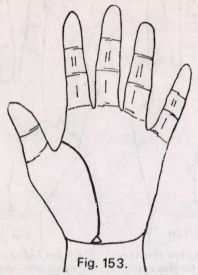

Fig. 153.
Triangle at the end of Life line
(falsehood)

very important and sometimes we have to compare this line along with other lines. We have to seek an interpretation according to the mount most developed on the hand. From the character of the line, we can know the muscular strength, vigour and robustness of the person. We shall study one by one, the different features of the line.

a) Deep and well-cut line

If we find a deep and well-cut line of Life, it shows good supply of blood and ensures promising health, vitality and vigour to the person. Such a line will also increase the power of resistance to disease and illness. This person lives not on nervous energy but on muscular strength. This person worries less and is capable of great physical exertion.

The consistency of the hand has also a main role to play with the deep line. The person has the capacity to remain calm in moments of excitement and he can throw off the worries easily. He has self-confidence, which he can inspire in others also. We may find a deep line which is also long and it indicates robustness throughout life. In short, ardour, self-confidence, energy, vigour and ability are the main attributes of the deep and well-cut line of Life.

We can combine these aptitudes with the qualities of the mounts to which he belongs. If he is a Jupiterian, with the third phalange of the Jupiter finger developed, he may lead a merry life and his ideal will be to drink, eat and make merry. The main danger to the Jupiterian is from apoplexy. We can similarly combine this line with another mount and interpret it accordingly.

b) Narrow and thin line of Life

We may come across a narrow and thin line which indicates less resistance, less robustness and less vitality. This is incompatible with the deep line studied above. Here also we can study the proportion of the line with other main lines on the hand, *e.g.*, if other lines are deep and well-cut but the Life line is thin, such a person will overstrain and will suffer from ill-health. This thin line does not necessarily indicate nervousness. But in comparison with the other main lines, he will feel the tension on his health. If we have to combine this line with a Jupiterian, we may state that the excess shown by the deep line will not be experienced by this thin line. Similarly we can combine this line with other mounts on the hand and the qualities of the mounts will either increase or diminish the nature shown by the thin line.

c) A broad and shallow Life line (*fig. 154*)

Such a formation is not healthy and it shows lack of resistance to disease. Such persons are not robust and they are susceptible to any disorders. They are diffident and lack dash and push. Due to the weak constitution, they do not have the stamina for active life required in day-to-day world. They always suffer from small complaints and never feel well. They require to be looked after either by relatives or friends. They are merely carried by nervous force and lack aggression. They can only do the routine work without higher responsibilities.

While in comparison with the other line, which may be good, the shallow and broad line indicates an unsuccessful and sickly person. Here also we can interpret the line according to the mount which the subject belongs to. For instance, to a Saturnian who is already melancholy and gloomy, the shallow formation of the line makes more it gloomy and wretched. The prominence of the mounts will also give us the indication as to the health defect of the person. It is more dangerous to have such a formation on a hand where the lower third of the mount of Moon is badly affected. On a woman's hand it indicates self-destruction.

d) Ladder-like line of Life (*fig. 155*)

Such a line indicates repeated illnesses. The health of the person is very unstable and the person experiences intermittent periods of physical suffering.

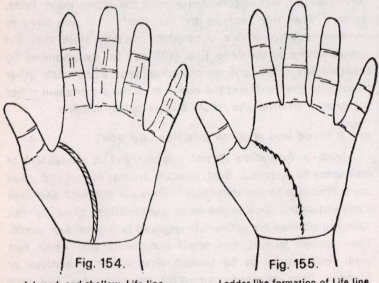

Fig. 154.
A broad and shallow Life line
(lack of resistance to disease)

Fig. 155.
Ladder like formation of Life line
(repeated illness)

e) **Life line formed by small lines** (*fig. 15g*)

We may come across a Life line which is composed of several fine lines instead of one continuous line. Such a formation shows intense nervousness and great delicacy of health. These small lines diminish the pushing and active character shown by the natural Life line. In order to locate the sickness of the person, we have again to refer to the mounts on the hand.

f) **Chained line of Life** (*fig. 157*)

This formation also signifies disturbing health and the period will continue as long as the chain formation lasts. Thus this formation aggravates the delicacy shown by the broad and shallow line.

g) **Wavy line of Life** (*fig. 158*)

A wavy line lessens the power of the Life line and the person will suffer from ups and downs in his health throughout the life.

We have studied above the character of the line in a general way only. We have to study the Life line in detail from its source to termination. It is by this method that we shall be able to find out from the Life line periods of ill-health or delicacy and to read at what age they occur. From the character of the line, we can read the constitution of the person and tendencies of various degrees. However, we have to refer to various signs and influences of lines by which we can know the temporary sickness of the person, which is not his constitutional health defect.

8 Defects of the line of Life

a) *Island*. If we come across an island at the beginning of the line of Life and also find an island at the end of the Head line, and if the Life line has been cut by many bars and worry lines, it shows a person who is deaf and dumb (*fig. 159*). Normally an island on the line of Life indicates

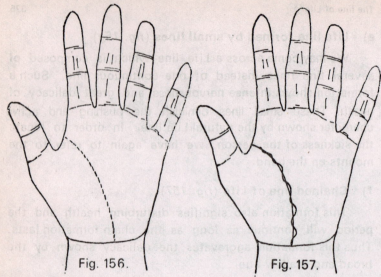

Fig. 156.
Life line formed by small lines
(intense nervousness)

Fig. 157.
Chained line of Life (disturbing health)

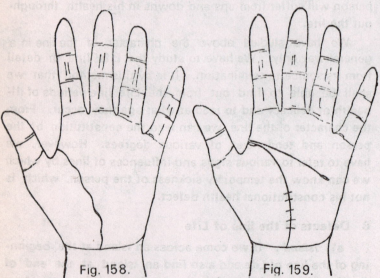

Fig. 158.
Wavy line of life (ups and downs in health)

Fig. 159.
Island at the beginning of Life line and also at the end of head line with many bars in the Life line (deafness and dumbness)

The line of Life

serious health trouble, the cause of which will have to be seen elsewhere. It may also mean trouble of the digestive system.

A small island means a small period of sickness and we can look for the indication on the mounts and on the lines of Head, Heart, Mercury and chance lines. We may also refer to the nails, colour of the hand, etc. If there is a series of islands, it operates in a chain-like formation and denotes continuous sickness. During this formation of islands, if the size of the island increases, it means an increased sickness and vice versa. The island indicates a chronic state of illness rather than acute attacks. If we come across a hand filled with cross lines and island on the Life line, such a hand will show great nervousness (*fig. 160*). We shall now proceed to the interpretation of the island with other signs on the hand.

i) An island in the Life line with small bars in the Head line indicates severe headache. The headache is due to the island on the Life line which speaks of delicate health. However if a similar island is seen on the line of Head, the cause of headache is some mental disturbance.

ii) If the island is in the Life line accompanied by the dots in the Head line, it means brain fever. If the dots are seen in the Heart line, heart trouble is indicated. Nails and colour will confirm these indications.

iii) If a wavy line of Mercury is seen with an island on the line of Life, the delicacy of the health will be due to biliousness.

iv) If this Mercury line has a ladder-like formation, it shows dyspepsia, indigestion and stomach trouble.

v) If an Island line from the mount of Saturn joins the island in the Life line and if another line from the middle mount of Moon also joins the island in the Life line, it is an indication of gout or rheumatism (*fig. 161*).

vi) If a line starts from a grill on the mount of Saturn and joins an island in the Life line and simultaneously the Head line has a dot or an island under the mount of Saturn,

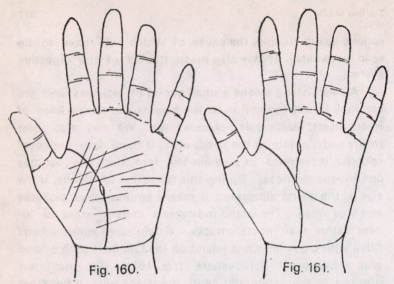

Fig. 160.
Island on Life line and hand full of cross lines (nervousness)

Fig. 161.
Island line from Saturn joins on Island on the Life line and another line from middle Moon joins the island (gout and rheumatism)

we may consider such information as an indication of paralysis (*fig. 162*).

vii) A line joining a red dot on the Jupiter mount and an island in the Life line indicates tendency to apoplexy (*fig. 163*).

Thus, we have interpreted the troubles shown by the Life line with the island by taking into consideration the way the island is connected with other signs on the hand. As already discussed, an island is usually found on the hand of a woman at about the age of 40 to 46. This generally shows a change in her life. We have to study this island in more detail and also the development of the Life line on the hand of a woman at her particular age. For instance, if we notice a grill on the lower mount of Moon, the female weakness will be an added impediment to the change that is to take place. In such a case we can guide the person well in advance that she should take proper care or medical treatment to avoid danger. If after the island the line is shallow and broad, it means that the change has weakened the constitution. If this shallow

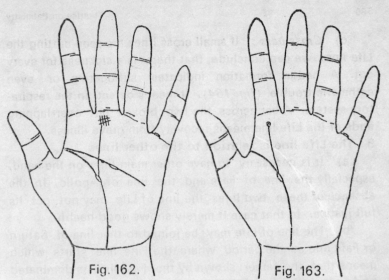

Fig. 162.
A line from a grill on the mount of Saturn joining an Island on the Life line with dots or Island on the head line (paralysis)

Fig. 163.
A line joining a red dot on Jupiter and an island on Life line (apoplexy)

formation continues to the end of Life line, it means that there will be no recovery till the end of life. The weakness that has taken place after the island can be located on the Head line or the Heart line whereby we can warn the person about the mental weakness or the heart trouble that is to come.

b) *Dots* : Occasionally, we may find dots in the Life line which also indicate health trouble. We have to study the size and colour of the dot and also the way it is connected to the other signs on the hand. Each dot shows some trouble. A number of dots show unsatisfactory health. The dots are harmless and they are also to be interpreted with the same logic we have followed in the case of an island. Crimson and purple dots are indications of fevers like typhoid or malaria. A deep black dot indicates dangerous wound or a serious trouble. A blue dot denotes self-administered poison. If however the spot is not right on the Life line but very close to the Life line, it means poisoning by an enemy. Red dots indicate feverish disposition.

c) *Cross bars* : If small cross lines are seen cutting the Life line, we can conclude that there is a sickness for every cut. A hedge formation indicates suffocating or even asthmatic trouble (*fig. 164*). It means defect in the respiratory system. A bar across the two broken but over-lapping ends of the Life line means recovery from grave illness.

9 The Life line is relation to the other lines

a) It is necessary to have other main lines on the hand, especially the line of Fate and the line of Apollo. In the absence of these two lines the line of Life may not get its full justice. In that case it merely shows good health.

b) The line of Life may be joined to the line of Saturn or Fate line at the period where the Fate line starts which means that the career shown by the Fate line is dominated by family influence. We may also occasionally find a Fate line joining the Life line at any period later in Life. The period at which the Fate line joins the Life line shows the dominance of the family on the individual.

c) If the line of Apollo is joined to the Life line at the starting point of the former, it is an excellent sign and shows success in art, music and literature. It also is an indication of brilliant fortune.

d) If the Life line is short and ends abruptly by capillary lines and if these capillary lines are joined by Saturn line rising from rascette, the person is saved from the defects of the short line of Life. The great danger to Life will be averted by good luck (*fig. 165*).

e) Sometimes we may come across a line from the mount of Venus which joins the line of Apollo on the Life line itself. It shows so much popularity, reputation to the wife as to the husband (*fig. 166*).

f) Joining of line of Mercury to the line of Life is a dangerous thing ; it shows health trouble, biliousness and sometime the end of life. If the Mercury line joins the line of Life and at the same time the Heart line makes a narrow quadrangle, it indicates fainting fits.

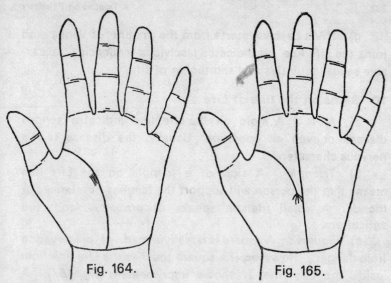

Fig. 164.
Hedge formation on Life line (Asthma)

Fig. 165.
Short Life line ending abruptly by capillary lines and these capillary lines joined to Fate line starting from rascettes (danger to life avoided by good luck)

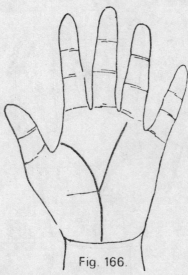

Fig. 166.
A line from mount of Venus meeting the Sun line on the Life line (popularity and reputation to wife)

g) If Via Lasciva starts from the mount of Venus and joins the Life line, it indicates lascivious tendencies, excessive sexual activities and shortening of Life.

10 Signs on the line of Life

a) *Mole* : A mole on the Life line indicates serious disease or even an operation. Usually, the disease is of a nervous character.

b) *Triangle* : A sign of a triangle on the Life line means that the person will support the families of relatives or friends. A small triangle speaks of property, land and agriculture.

c) *Square* : A square is usually a mark of preservation from danger. However, if a square touches the Life line from inside the Life line, it shows imprisonment (*fig. 167*). A square enclosing a cross on the line of Life shows protection from sickness. A square on the Life line shows healing power.

d) *Cross* : A cross on the Life line is a bad indication and it indicates law-suits. A cross towards the end of Life

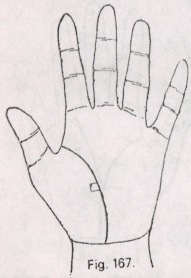

Fig. 167.

A square touching Life line from inside
(imprisonment)

line means that the person's character and ability are threatened with poverty and ill-health during the closing year of old age. Two crossess at the beginning of the Life line on the hand of a woman speak of immodesty.

e) *Star*: A star is a more serious sign on the hand than a cross. It signifies fatality or serious accidents. If the star is found right on the Life line, it means suicide. A star on the side of the mount of Venus and touching the Life line shows trouble from members of the family or close friends.

f) *Circle* : One circle on the Life line shows susceptibility to blindness of one eye. Two circles indicate total blindness.

g) *Cresent* : A cresent or a small curved line across the line of Life and the ends of the curve pointing upward is indicative of serious and sudden illness.

h) *Grill* : A small patch of grill formation on the mount of Venus but touching the line of Life alongwith a grill formation in the line of Head and touching the line of life indicates change of religion.

11 Lines of influence

While studying the line of Life, we have to take into consideration the importance of lines of influence, which are seen inside the line of Life. These influence lines are either vertical or horizontal.

The Hindus have an elaborate system of interpreting these lines and depend upon them for a large part of their work. The lines usually show the influence of family members or very close friends either for good or evil. The lesser the number of influence lines, the more self-contained is the person. Such a person has few friends and even the close relations do not influence him much. The absence of lines show coldness and non-receptivity to the warmth of affection and attachment. It indicates a self-centred man. When the lines are deep and strong and well coloured, they show the power of influence. If however they are thin, shallow, chained or broken, they indicate that their influence is not so strong. If any influence line is deep in the beginning, then slowly becomes thin and fades away, it shows that it has lost its influence. We can come across the reverse marking also in which case the influence will gradually grow strong. Vertical lines are not impediments or hostile to development. On the contrary cross lines show obstacles and worry us.

a) Vertical lines

1) These vertical lines start either on the mount of Venus or on the mount of positive Mars. A line starting on the mount of Venus and from the commencement of Life line shows the influence of the parents or even governess (*fig. 168*).

2) If the line of influence begins from the Life line at a later date on the hand, it shows the influence of the opposite sex or a love affair.

3) The influence of the other person will continue as long as the line of influence is seen and the influence vanishes when the influence line fades. In this case it may also mean separation by the death of the influencing person.

4) If the influence line turns away from the line of Life towards the mount of Venus, the influence will become less strong and will drift away from the person (*fig. 169*).

5) If we find an island in the influence line, it means that the influence is not beneficial and it shows distinct disadvantage.

6) If we find an influence line receding towards the mount of Venus and if another influence line shows its existence between the first influence line and the Life line, it means that with the power of the middle influence, the influence shown by the first influence line has been lost.

As stated above, we may notice the lines of influence rising from the positive mount of Mars.

i) An influence line from the positive mount of Mars on the hand of a woman shows the influence of the man over her (*fig. 170*).

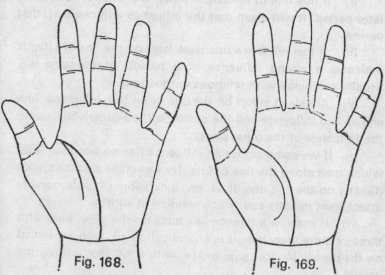

Fig. 168.
A vertical line of influence from beginning of Life line (influence of parents)

Fig. 169.
A vertical line of influence turning away from Life line (withdrawal of influence)

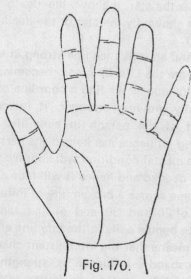

Fig. 170.
A vertical line of influence on positive mount of Mars (influence of a male)

ii) If this line of influence joins the line of Life at a later period it will mean that the influence will cease at that period.

iii) If this influence line rises later on the line of Life, it indicates a strong influence of a person of the same sex, usually combined with religious enthusiasm.

iv) An island either on the Life or on the influence line shows bad influence and the person will be completely under the influence of the other person.

v) If we come across an influence line on positive Mars which runs along the line of Life for sometime and then ends directly on the Life line, it is an indication of unfavourable attachment in early age which resulted in sorrow.

vi) If such an influence line ends on the Life line with three or more branches, it is an indication of worries forced on the person by the passionate nature of the influencing person.

vii) If an influence line rising early ends in a star and has another line by its side but away from Life line which grows shorter after the star, it shows the death of father or mother at the age shown by the star or the death of a distant relative (*fig. 171*).

viii) If we find an influence line strong in the beginning but going away from the Life line and becoming thinner or weak and if simultaneously we find a poor line of Head at its start and gradually growing stronger, it indicates a weak mental condition of the person in early life. During this period some strong influence has helped the person. It further means that as the mental condition will improve the influence will no longer be needed and hence it will fade away.

ix) If we come across a broken line of influence starting between the age of 20 and 30 and at the same time find another line which begins early in the Life line and continues uninterrupted, it means that the intermittent character of the wife's or the husband's influence is strengthened by the constant influence of the mother or father. Often, such a marking will unite the ties of a broken marriage.

The line of Life

x) If a line of influence is cut by a strong cross line and if the influence line has an island after the cut and then ends in a star, it is an indication of some disaster showing probably the death of the influencing person.

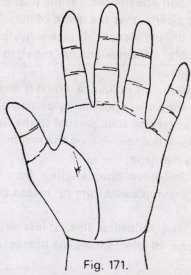

Fig. 171.

If an influence line rising early on positive Mars ends in a star, and has another line by its side, but away from Life line which grows shorter after the star (death of father or mother)

xi) A line of influence on the mount of Venus connected at the start to the line of Life, is a sign of marriage. If in addition, a line of Marriage is seen under the mount of Mercury, the significance is confirmed.

If there is an island in the Marriage line, the marriage will take place without the sanction of law and convention.

xii) If a small line is seen connected from the influence line to the mount of Saturn, mental trouble connected with the influencing person is indicated. If both the influence line and the small line are surrounded by an island, there is disgrace and scandal.

xiii) An island on the influence line on the mount of Venus and an island on the influence line on the mount of Moon show the bad character of the influencing person.

xiv) Islands both on the influence line and on the line of Fate show bad attachment. If the island is only on the Saturn line, it means that the death of the marriage partner has reacted on the individual. It means hysteria.

xv) A double influence line on the right hand is a sign of happy marriage.

xvi) A faint line of influence which is thrown away from the line of Life shows less possibility of marriage.

xvii) If a sister line runs parallel to the Saturn line, the presence of the influence line on the mount of Venus also indicates happy marriage.

xviii) An influence line, starting from the line of Life and suddenly curving away from it, means broken engagement.

xix) A broken influence line at intervals, which runs close to the line of Life, shows the illness of the marriage partner.

Signs on the vertical influence lines

a) *Square :* A square on the influence line shows restrictions, self-imposed or otherwise. It may mean unsocial behaviour, bed-ridden sickness or seclusion in a hospital or asylum. It may also mean imprisonment.

If an influence line enters a square and comes out of it from the other side (*fig. 173*), it indicates imprisonment of the influencing person. It also means that during the period of the square the person stays apart from the influencing person.

In case the influence line ends in a square, it shows the death of the influence in a hospital due to an accident.

If there is a line from this square going to the mount of negative Mars, it relates to death of the influence in battle.

If the square on the influence line is connected to a square on the line of Life at the same period, the individual himself is involved in an accident but not injured. If however

The line of Life

the square on the line of Life is found over a break on that line, the individual is also injured in the accident.

b) *Island* : Islands in the influence lines on the mount of Venus indicate either sickness or infidelity.

A long island at the beginning of the influence line shows a change in the attitude or relationship of the influencing person.

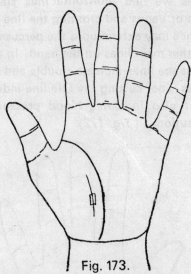

Fig. 173.
An influencing line on mount of Venus entering a square and coming out of it from other end (imprisonment to influencing person)

An island at the termination of the line of influence gives prolonged illness to influence ending in fatality.

c) *Star:* Star on the influence line indicates sudden and shocking experience connected with the influence. A star at the end of the influence line shows the disappearance of the influence due to death in some tragic manner. The age is calculated on the line of Life opposite the star.

Star at the termination of the influence line, which turns away from the line of Life, means that the person will not feel or be affected by the tragic death of the influencing person.

A star, at the end of the influencing line connected to a star on the mount of Moon, and the influence line, receding from the line of Life, means the death of the influence which took place abroad.

b) Horizontal influence lines from the positive mount of Mars

Many times we find horizontal lines starting from the mount of Mars or Venus and crossing the line of Life. These lines of influence may extend upto the percussion of the hand and may cut other main lines on the hand. In all cases, these horizontal influence lines indicate trouble and worry.

1) A cross line cutting the Life line indicates ill-health or accident. It also indicates blood pressure and hot and chronic constitution. (*fig. 172*)

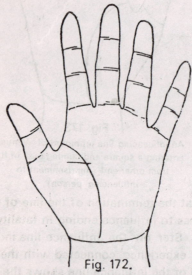

Fig. 172.
Cross line on the mount or Mars cutting the Life line (blood pressure)

2) A strong line across the hand and sloping down after crossing the lines of Saturn and Apollo indicates a bad influence of the opposite sex.

The line of Life

3) If however at the end after the slope it turns upwards, it indicates spiritual inclination.

4) If this crossing line turns upwards towards the mount at the base of the fingers, it shows favourable and helpful influence.

Lines going to other mounts

5) A line from positive mount of Mars going to the mount of Jupiter indicates success and ambition and egotism. This indication is strengthened if there is a star on the mount of Jupiter. It receives less power if this line ends in a cross or a bar.

6) If the line goes to the mount of Saturn, it indicates an accident from a vehicle. However if this line ends in a fork, the accident will be fatal. If this line goes deep into the root of the Saturn finger, it indicates trouble of the womb and danger in child-bearing. If a line from positive mount of Mars going to the mount of Saturn acts like a sister line to the line of Fate, it means increase of wealth, due to efforts made by relative or close friends.

If a line first goes to the mount of Jupiter and then turns to the mount of Saturn, it indicates a deep religious feeling.

Horizontal influence lines from the mount of Venus

These influence lines have great significance in the life of the person concerned depending upon the way the influence line cuts other major lines. Small lines, running from the base of the thumb and crossing the Life line but not going further in the hand, indicate worries, losses and reverses in the life of the person.

1) Such a line, cutting the Life line only, means obstacles caused by the interference or the opposition of the influencing person.

2) If this line just cuts the Life line and does not go further in the hand, it shows the interference of the relatives usually connected with home affairs.

3) If this line cuts the line of Saturn, it shows loss due to the interference of the influencing person (*fig. 174*).

4) If this cross line cuts the line of Head, it shows interference with plans and ideas (*fig. 175*).

5) If it cuts the line of Heart, it shows interference with one's affection (*fig. 176*).

6) If this line ends in a star or a spot, it shows sickness due to anxiety.

7) If this cross line, cutting the line of Heart, has an island within itself, it shows a disgraceful liaison (*fig. 177*).

8) If this line crosses the line of Apollo, it indicates loss of position, scandal and disgrace.

9) If this line just reaches the line of Apollo, it shows loss of money. However alongwith this indication if we find that the line of Apollo is broken or has an island, it also means loss of position and disgrace.

10) When this crossing line crosses the line of Mercury, it shows loss of health due to domestic worries.

11) If this line from the mount of Venus touches the line of Marriage, it means an unhappy married life, which may even end in separation (*fig. 178*).

12) If however there is an island in this line or if this line cuts the Marriage line, divorce is the result.

13) If any of the above cross lines have an island, the person who causes the trouble is scandalous.

14) We have studied that the rising branches from the Life line indicate an upward tendency. However if these rising branches are cut by the cross lines, it shows an impediment and or a check in the career, or upward tendency. This cross line starting from the influence line indicates that the influence has caused a check.

15) If the cross line starts from a star at the end of an influence line and cuts the rising branch from the Life line, it indicates that the death of a relative has hampered the rising career of the person (*fig. 179*).

16) If an influence line ends in a star and is connected by a cross line which ends in an island on the Head line, it

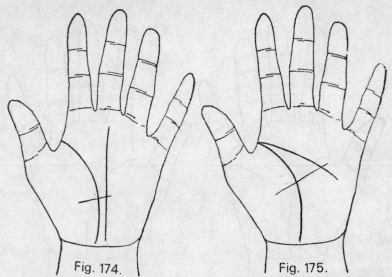

Fig. 174.
Horizontal line from Venus mount cuts line of Life and the Fate line (loss)

Fig. 175.
Horizontal line from Venus cutting the line of Head (interference in plans)

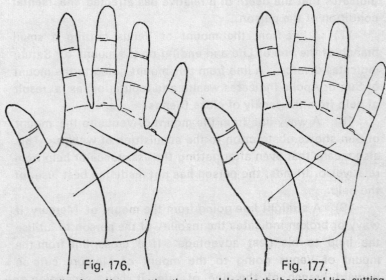

Fig. 176.
Horizontal line from Venus cutting the heart line (interference in love)

Fig. 177.
Island in the horizontal line cutting heart line (disgraceful liaison)

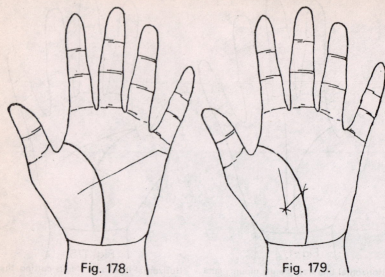

Fig. 178.
Horizontal cross line from Venus tonching the marriage line (unhappy married life)

Fig. 179.
Cross line from Venus starting from a star at the end of influence line and cutting a rising branch on Life line (death of a relative obstructs career)

indicates that the death of a relative has affected the mental condition of the person.

17) A line from the mount of Venus cutting a small branch of the line of Life and ending on the mount of Saturn indicates divorce. A line from this mount going to the mount of Sun or Apollo indicates wealth and reputation as a result of help from the family of close friends.

18) A wavy line from the mount of Venus to the mount of Sun shows obstruction to the acquisition of wealth. This also means that even after getting the assistance or help from relatives or friends, the person has not made the best use of the help.

19) A straight line going from the mount of Mercury if wavy or broken indicates the inability of the person to utilise the help to his best advantage. If a cross line from the mount of Venus going to the mount of Mercury cuts an upward branch of the line of Life, it shows separation or divorce.

The line of Life

20) A cross line cutting the lines of Fate, Head and the Sun and ending on the upper mount of Mars (*fig. 180*), indicates wound on the date marked on the Fate line. This may also be due to a relative or a friend.

21) A line from the mount of Venus going to the mount of Moon and cutting the lines of Fate and Life shows misfortune through interference of the opposite sex.

22) A line from the Venus mount, crossing the line of Life and merging into the line of Fate, shows interference of relatives or friends (*fig. 181*).

23) A line, cutting the line of Life and also cutting the line of Fate, indicates that the relatives will oppose the person in business or career and often force him to take up the career he is not fit for.

24) A cross line from the mount of Venus ending at the line of Head indicates interference and opposition to the freedom of thought of the person.

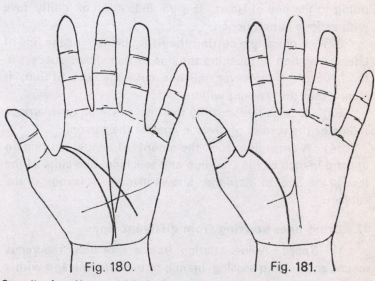

Fig. 180.
Cross line from Venus cutting the lines of Fate, Head, Sun and ending on upper mount of Mars (wound due to relative or friend)

Fig. 181.
A line from Venus mount crossing the Life line and merging in Fate line (interference in career)

25) If this line also cuts the line of Head, it indicates mental trouble due to act of relatives.

26) If the line from the mount of Venus cuts the line of Life and terminates on the line of Heart, it means heart trouble due to unfaithfulness of a close friend.

27) If the above line also cuts the line of Heart, it indicates interference of relatives in the affections or love of the person.

28) If this cross line cuts a rising branch from the Life line and also intersects the lines of Head and Heart, it signifies trouble in married life and even a legal separation. If this line cuts the line of Marriage, it is a sure sign of divorce.

29) If this cross line ends on the Heart line in a fork, it also means separation or divorce.

30) In addition to the above indication, if there is an island in the Fate line, it shows guilty intrigue resulting in scandal or divorce.

31) If however there is an island in the cross line itself going to the line of Heart, it is an indication of guilty love with serious consequence.

32) A cross line cutting the rising branch of the line of Life and ending or touching the line of Sun shows success in the law suit. If however this line cuts the line of Sun, it means that the law-suit will be lost.

33) A cross line cutting the line of Union or Marriage indicates the verdict of divorce against the person.

34) A cross line from the mount of Venus, cutting an upward branch of the Life line and touching one side of the fork in the line of Marriage, shows divorce in favour of the subject.

12 Cross lines starting from different signs

1) *Spot* : A line, starting from a spot from the Venus mount and cutting a rising branch of the Life line and with a cross on the Jupiter, is an indication of love marriage ending in separation.

The line of Life

2) *Star* : A cross line starting from a star and cutting the line of Life, shows the death of a close relative or a friend. The date is to be confirmed on the line of Life.

If the above line ends in a fork on the mount of Saturn it shows an unfortunate marriage. It may mean the death or insanity of the partner (*fig. 182*). If this line goes to the mount of Sun, it indicates quarrels.

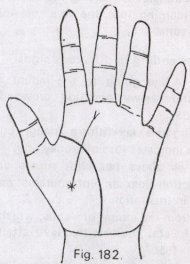

Fig. 182.

Cross line starting from a star on mount of Venus and ending in Fork on the mount of Saturn (death or insanity of the partner)

If the above line merges into the line of Fate, the quarrel will end in amity.

A line, starting from the star on the mount of Venus and cutting the line of Fate, indicates obstruction to the career due to the death of a relative or close friend.

The same as the above line but crossing the line of Apollo indicates loss of money due to the death of a friend or a close relative.

A line from a star, cutting the short upward branch of the line of Life, means law-suits due to the death of a relative or a close friend. If this line cuts the line of Sun, the law-suit is lost. If however this line merges into the line of Apollo it means winning of the law-suits. Such law-suits usually are the result of quarrels about the estate left by the deceased.

3) *Island* : A line starting from the island on the mount of Venus, which ends under the mount of Mercury, indicates loss of prospects due to wicked intrigue.

A line from an island, crossing the upward branch of the Life line and merging into the line of Apollo, indicates success in law-suits.

13 Cross lines ending in different signs

a) *Star* : A line going to the mount of Jupiter and ending in a star shows ambition crowned with brilliant success (*fig. 183*).

A line ending in a star within a Triangle but after crossing the line of Fate indicates loss of money (*fig. 184*).

The same as above but with square around the star indicates protection from an unfavourable marriage or love affair resulting in frustration.

Two lines from the mount of Venus, which meet in a star on the line of Fate, indicate two love affairs resulting in frustration (*fig. 185*).

If we come across a line from the mount of Venus, which ends in a star on the Head line, it shows serious brain trouble due to a relative or a close friend.

A cross line from the mount of Venus, cutting an upward branch from the line of Life and terminating in a star on the line of Apollo, shows scandal and loss of law-suits.

If this cross line ends in a star on the line of Heart, it shows heart trouble caused by the conduct of a relative or friend.

b) *Island* : If a cross line from the mount of Venus ends in an island on the mount of Jupiter, it indicates severe illness of respiratory organs.

If a line from the mount of Venus cuts the line of Apollo and terminates in an island, it indicates scandal due to intrigue.

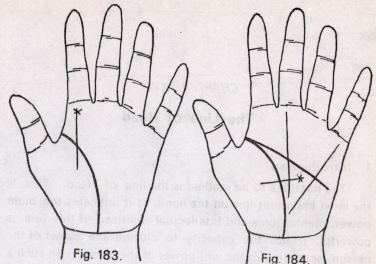

Fig. 183.
Cross line ending in a star on the mount of Jupiter (ambition crowned with success)

Fig. 184.
Cross line ending on a star in the Triangle but after crossing the line of Fate (loss of money)

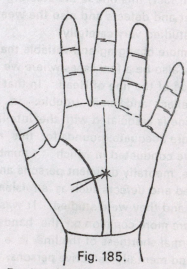

Fig. 185.
Two lines from mount of Venus which meet in a star on the line of Fate (two love affairs and frustration)

CHAPTER XVIII

The Line of Head

1 Introduction

The next line to be studied is the line of Head. This is the most important line on the hand, as it indicates the brain power, mental force and intellectual abilities. If this line is powerful, it has the capacity to change the career of the person, according to the will-power of the person. In such a case, the meaning attached to the signs and development of the lines can be altered according to the strong desire of the person. We have therefore to be very careful in estimating the value and importance of this line in relation to the person's life. In fact, this line is the steering wheel of life. The development and defects and also the weaknesses of the line have to be studied very carefully.

This line is more changing and variable than the line of Life. There may also be a few cases where we may find the complete absence of the line of Head. In that case, it signifies a dull intellect and brain trouble. In the study of palmistry, this line is associated with the intelligence of the person. There are adequate grounds for this reason. Some experiments were conducted in which number of hands of college students, mentally deficient persons and schizophrenics were studied and defects such as an island and breaks etc were found and they were studied. It was observed that such defects were more common on the hands of abnormal persons. Abnormal shortness of the line is a very common feature in low and mentally defective persons. It is however not possible to relate this line to any special faculty of intelligence.

The line of Head

The formation of the character of the line is to be studied in relation to the type of the hand, the mounts on hand and the fingers. For instance, a particular formation of the line on a square hand has a different meaning from the same formation found on a psychic or conic hand.

This line divides the hand into two parts. The upper part shows the mental development and the lower part shows the material development. From the position of this line, we can find out the way the hand is divided, whether the upper or the lower hemisphere is prominent in the hand. In case this line is found on the upper side of the hand, it means that the material world has greater sway and the person is more brutal and animal-like in his desires.

This has been observed on the hands of criminals. Whether such people murder one or many is not the question but it points out to the abnormal tendencies for the crime. In a few cases, the line of Head leaves its proper place on the hand and rises much high on the hand and sometimes even goes beyond the line of Heart. The interesting thing in this connection is that we can sometimes predict in advance the year of death of a person. For example, if the Head and Heart lines meet under the Saturn mount, the period is 25 years; if it is between Saturn and Sun, it is 35; under the mount of Sun, it is 45 and so on.

This line of Head should not be too much pronounced in comparison with the other lines on the hand. In short, it should maintain a balance of strength in relation to other main lines on the hand. This line has the responsibility of maintaining the balance of the hand. In case, there is no balance, that is to say, if the line is too much on the upper side or on the lower side of the division of the hand, it will not show co-ordinatination between the mental aspect and the material aspect, shown by the two hemispheres, but it will show complete disharmony between them.

The line of Head indicates the strength or weakness of the mind, the power of memory and concentration. The weakness shown by the line of Head can be a moral weakness, or it means weakness of health or mental or physical trouble. It may also denote accidents that generally affect the brain or the head. It is generally observed that the incidents of accidents will have corroborative markings on other parts of the hand, especially on the lines of Life, Fate or Mercury. However if we do not find corroborative signs, the indication shown in the defect of the Head line will relate more to character than to health.

As already stated above, the Head line shows the power of the mind and also its working. However, it is very difficult to find out the intensity of the power of mind. The brain structure is so delicate and sensitive that its physical examination is very dificult. Even the closest microscopical examination fails to differentiate between the brain of a highly intellectual person with the brain of a criminal of the most brutal type. This has been verified in hundreds of postmortem examinations. Uptill now at least, the working and functioning of the brain has been found to be most complicated, so much so that it is very difficult or practically impossible to locate the good or the evil aspects of the mind.

However the study of line is capable of explaining the small shades of the mental behaviour and the study is capable of finding out the good traits as well as the traits of various types of criminals. We can also judge with great accuracy the mental sickness and also the sickness due to psychological upset.

II Position on the hand

This line usually starts from the line of Life and goes to the other side of the hand in a slightly downward curve. This formation indicates a combination of calculation and imagination (*see fig. 97*).

III Normal development *(fig. 186)*

A good line of Head should be long, even and with attractive curve. The colour should be natural, that is

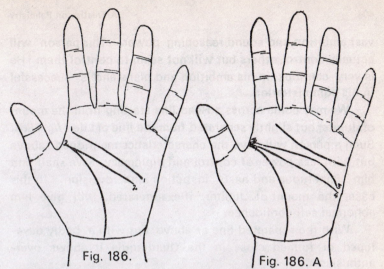

Fig. 186.	Fig. 186. A
Normal development of Head line 1) Starting slightly below the mount of Jupiter 2) Touching the line of Life	3) Slightly going up towards the Heart line 4) Ending between upper Mars and upper mount of Moon

slightly deeper than the colour of the hand. It should be neither too broad nor too narrow, neither too deep nor too shallow. It should be without any defects such as breaks or islands. The line of Head should look as if it has divided the whole palm into two hemispheres, giving apparently a balanced outlook. It should normally start from below the mount of Jupiter and slightly touch the line of Life at its beginning. It should then go slightly towards the line of Heart under the mount of Saturn and then curve down and end between the mounts of negative Mars and the upper portion of the mount of Moon.

IV Starting position

There are various starting positions for the line of Head. Basically there are three positions as under :

a) From the mount of Jupiter b) from the line of Life c) from inside the line of Life.

a) If the Head line starts from the mount of Jupiter but touches the line of Life, it shows a powerful mind (*fig. 187*). It gives energy, determination and talent. This gives a vast ambition and sound reasoning power. This person will actually control others but will not seem to control them. He is very cautious in his ambition and plans and is successful in his administration.

We may come across a Head line starting from the mount of Jupiter but slightly separated from the line of Life (*fig.188*). Such a person will have the characteristics mentioned above but with less power of control and diplomacy. We shall find him impetuous and hasty in action and decision. In this case, the mount of Jupiter, if exaggerated, will give him abnormal self-confidence.

With the separated line as above but with a badly developed or formed cross in the Quadrangle, it shows over-enthusiasm.

If the distance between the Life line and the Head line is too much at the start (*fig.189*), it denotes fool-hardiness and over-confidence. It also means recklessness and conceit. If however the line is short, it shows lack of intelligence (case 5).

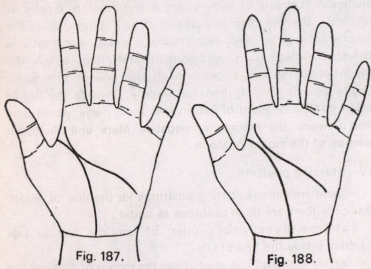

Fig. 187.
Head line from Jupiter but touching Life line (powerful mind)

Fig. 188.
Head line from Jupiter but slightly separated from line of Life (impetuous and hasty nature)

The line of Head

If the line of Head starts from the mount of Jupiter but does not touch the line of Life and steps down to the mount of Moon (*fig. 190*) with the broad and short first phalange of the thumb, we have a person with great obstinacy and quarrelsome disposition.

The space between the Life line and the line of Head is important. A small gap between the two is beneficial. It denotes splendid energy, promptness and self-confidence. This is useful for actors, barristers and preachers.

If the gap is too wide, it shows fool-hardiness as stated above. It also means egoistic character. Such people usually hurt orhers by their fault-finding nature.

A Head line, with open formation at the beginning and sharply bending down from its commencement, is an indication of a purely imaginative and romantic type. Such persons are most impractical. Such a line is usually found on the hand with numerous fine lines, which indicate a highly strung and nervous disposition. A Head line, with a curve under the mount of Jupiter at the beginning and going right

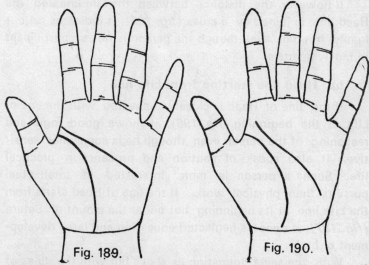

Fig. 189.
Wide distance between Life and Head lines (Foolhardiness and over confidence)

Fig. 190.
Head line from Jupiter away from Life line and sloping to the mount of Moon (Obstinacy & quarrelsome disposition)

across the palm without touching the Life line, shows extravagance and conceit *(fig. 191)*.

A Head line, which is separate from the life line and which slopes down to the mount of Moon with a poor line of Heart, the first phalange of the thumb being short and broad, is indicative of obstinacy and quarrelsome disposition.

This also shows restlessness and sensitivity. It also means unreasonable behaviour leading to danger. Such persons are usually unhappy in their married life.

A Head line starting from the mount of Jupiter shows leadership, dignity, ambition, ability and quick memory. If a line from the mount of Jupiter joins the line of Head, it shows a desire to become great *(fig. 192)*.

A Head line starting from the mount of Jupiter but touching the line of Heart on the mount of Jupiter indicates a balanced mind and harmony in love and duty *(fig. 193)*.

If we come across a Head line, which does not touch the Life line but is connected by minor lines or branches, it shows evil temper *(fig. 194)*.

If however the distance between the Life line and the Head line is joined by a cross *(fig. 195)*, it indicates serious family trouble, even though the person is not a participant in family quarrels.

b) Head line starting from Life line

If the line of Head is closely connected with the line of Life at the beginning *(fig. 196)*, it shows good logic and reasoning of the person even though he is somewhat sensitive. It also speaks of caution and prudence in practical life. Such a person is more interested in intellectual pursuits than physical work. If the line of Head starts from the Life line at its beginning but under the mount of Saturn *(fig. 197)*, it denotes neglected education and late development of brain.

With the same formation as above but with the lines of Life and Heart short, it means danger of sudden death.

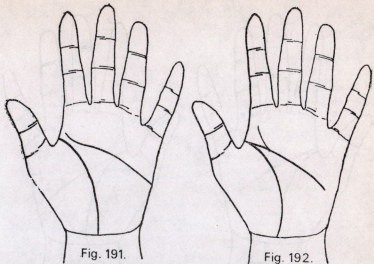

Fig. 191.
Head line with a curve under the mount of Jupiter and going right across the hand without touching the Life line (extravagance and conceit)

Fig. 192.
Line from Jupiter joining the Head line (desire to become great)

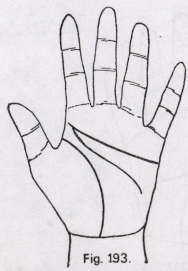

Fig. 193.
Head line from Jupiter, touching the Heart line on Jupiter (harmony in love and duty)

Fig. 194.
Head line, not touching the line of Life but is connected by minor lines or branches (evil temper)

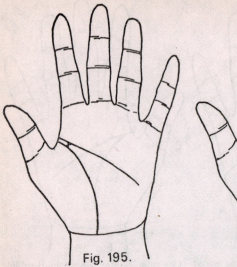

Fig. 195.
Cross joining the head line and the Life line (serious family troubles)

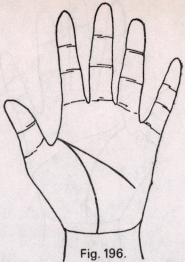

Fig. 196.
Head line closely connected to Life line (sensitive nature)

Fig. 197.
Head line starting from Life line but from under the mount of Saturn (neglected education)

If the line of Head is connected with the Life line and also the line of Heart at its beginning, it shows sudden death *(fig. 198)*.

A Head line closely connected with the line of Life and running together for sometime indicates a negative aspect of free-will *(fig. 199)*. Such persons are influenced by the parents or by family members and their dominance will be to such an extent that these persons have no capacity to think and act independently. They do not have free expression and have fear complex. They under-estimate themselves, distrust their own judgement and dislike responsibility.

c) Line of Head starting from inside the line of Life

The third position starting of the line of Head is from within the line of Life or the positive mount of Mars *(fig. 200)*. Amongst the three positions for the line of Head this is one of the unhealthy formations. This shows great timidity, shyness and lack of confidence. A person with this formation does not have the courage to voice his opinions and he thinks that others are better than him.

This formation is an outcome of inferiority complex. It indicates a worrying temperament and inconsistency in thought and action. Such a person is always in conflict with his neighbours and is also sensitive and irritable.

If the line of Head starts from within the line of Life and crosses the hand in a winding and wavy way, we have a person with a violent but changing mind *(fig. 201)*.

If the line of Head, which starts from within the line of Life has a branch which goes to the mount of Venus, it indicates impatience and intolerance and lack of foresight *(fig. 202)*.

If the Head line has a bunch-like formation at the start on the mount of positive Mars *(fig. 203)*, it means lack of clear ideas and thinking. It also shows lack of confidence and the person seeks advice of his friends in all matters.

If the line from the mount of Jupiter touches the line of Head, which starts from within the line of Life, it signifies

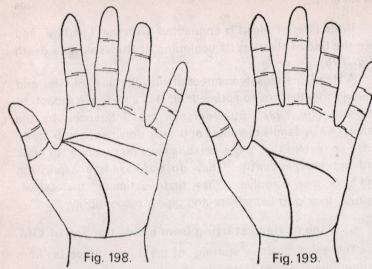

Fig. 198.
Life line, Head line and Heart line connected to each other at the start (sudden death)

Fig. 199.
Head line closely connected to Life line and running together for sometime (family dominance)

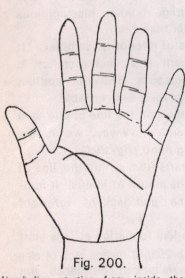

Fig. 200.
Head line starting from inside the Life line or from the mount of Mars (timidity and shyness)

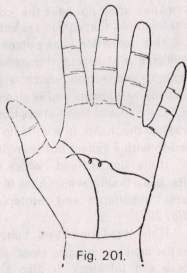

Fig. 201.
Head line starting from inside the line of Life and across the hand in a winding and wavy way (violent resolutions)

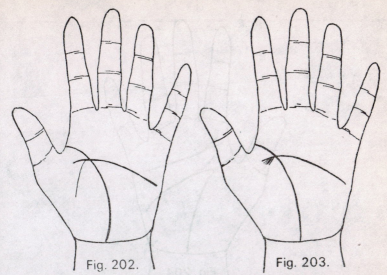

Fig. 202.
A Head line which starts from inside Life line having a branch which goes to the mount of Venus (lack of foresight and impatience)

Fig. 203.
A bunch like formation of the Head line at the start on the mount Mars (lack of confidence)

indifferent educational career and great hardships due to ill-health.

If the line of Head starts with a fork, one prong of which is joined to the line of Life and the other goes to the line of Heart but does not cut it, and if at the same time the line of Heart is also forked, it indicates good fortune *(fig. 204)*.

V Course of the line of Head

The next thing we have to study is the course of the Head line. As stated earlier, the normal Head line should run with a soft curve and go to the mount of Moon. The colour should be natural and the line should not be either too broad or too narrow. The line also should be free from all defects such as breaks and islands. A Head line without breaks or defects is a sign of happiness and prosperity.

1) **A Head line straight like a bar**

If the Head line is extremely long and straight going to

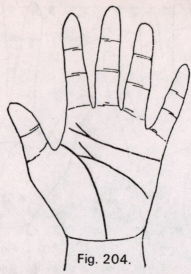

Fig. 204.

Line of Head forked at the start, one prong of which goes to the Life line, another to Heart line but not touching the Heart line, and the Heart line also forked (good fortune)

the other side of the hand *(fig. 205)*, it speaks of more than ordinary intellectual powers but the person is inclined to misuse these powers for selfish purposes. If this line turns up at the end, it shows avarice and a calculating and selfish nature.

This Head line, which is stretched across the hand, signifies aggressiveness in intellect put to practical account. This person likes to lead a life of his own and does not like to be disturbed by others. Such a person refuses to be impressed by anybody and loses respect.

If this straight line of Head originally starts from the mount of Jupiter, then descends to the line of Life and then goes straight across the hand, it shows boundless energy, and determination *(fig. 206)*. If the line of Head is straight but slanting, it shows cleverness *(fig. 207)*. If with this formation, a branch goes to the mount of Mercury, it gives talent to the person.

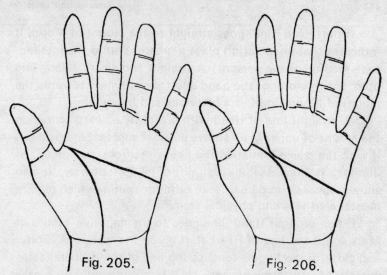

Fig. 205.
Extremely long and straight Head line like a bar (extra-ordinary intellectual powers)

Fig. 206.
A Head line that starts on Jupiter then descends to Life line and then goes straight across the hand (energy, and determination)

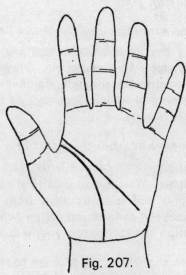

Fig. 207.
A straight Head line but slanting (cleverness)

If the Head line goes straight to the mount of Moon, it indicates that imagination plays a greater part in the intellectual faculty of the person. A straight and clear Head line upto the middle of the hand and then curving towards the mount of Moon signifies a luxurious and happy life.

A straight line of Head with a slightly upward curve on the mount of upper Mars shows unusual success in business. If with the same formation the line rises from the mount of Jupiter, it indicates unusual gift of mental power. It also shows success in games and outdoor sports which require mental alertness and physical stamina.

If the straight Head line goes to the negative mount of Mars and if the line of Heart starting on the mount of Jupiter and close to the fingers touches the line of Head, it indicates misfortune. A straight and clear Head line without breaks or defects signifies fascination for the opposite sex.

2) Head line running close to the Life line for a while

A Head line running close to the Life line for a while shows brain fever *(fig. 208)*

3) Head line running close the Heart line *(fig. 209)*

This narrows the Quadrangle which we have already studied in the chapter on Quadrangle. However, we may state here that a narrow Quadrangle signifies oppression, bigotry and meanness of moral tendency. As regards health, it shows asthmatic trouble.

Head line running away from the Heart line

On the contrary we may find a large gap between the Head and Heart lines. This is also a bad indication, more in respect of character and morality than from the point of health. This is a very serious indication which no other favourable indication can sufficiently counterbalance.

4) Head line slightly sloping down to the mount of Moon

Such a line indicates intellectual faculties influenced by

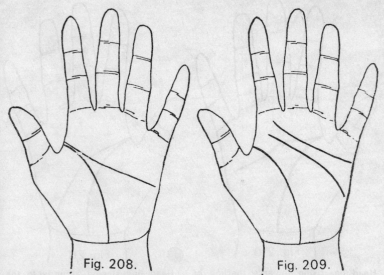

Fig. 208.
Head line running close to Life line for sometime (brain fever)

Fig. 209.
Head line running close to Heart line (Asthma, a bigot)

imagination. The quality of imagination will be influenced by the type of the hand. When such a line is sloping deeply on the mount of Moon, it indicates romance and idealism. If however it ends in a fork, it promises literary talent of the imaginative sort.

5) **Head line rising towards line of Heart under the mount of Saturn**

This is not a healthy formation and the person becomes miserable even to the point of insanity (*fig. 210*).

6) **Head line sloping abruptly to the mount of Moon with a star on second phalange of the Saturn finger**

This signifies insanity (*fig. 211*).

It can be stated as a general rule that the greater the downward curve of the Head line, the greater the degree of imagination.

7) We may come across a Head line, which sweeps down to the wrist which indicates abnormal imagination even to the point of hallucination. This also shows nervous

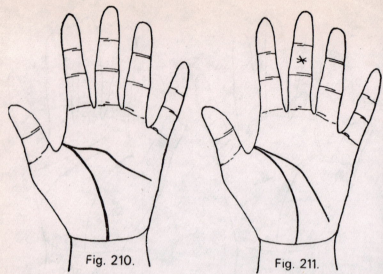

Fig. 210.
Head line rising towards the line of Heart under the mount of Saturn (insanity)

Fig. 211.
Head line sloping abruptly to the mount of Moon with a star on the second phalange of Saturn finger (insanity)

trouble and morbid spiritualism. If with this Head line, the second phalange of Jupiter finger is filled with lines, it indicates an aptitude for occult science. It also means superstition (*fig. 212*). If the Head line runs in a normal manner for sometime and then drops down sharply, it shows suicidal tendencies.

8) If during its course the line is found to be thin in the centre, it shows nervous or brain trouble, which lasts as long as the thinness extends on the line.

9) If the Head line is joined to the Life line at its beginning and then it rises towards the line of Heart and then comes down and resumes its normal position, it shows blind passion. It also means engagement or entanglement which never results in marriage.

10) A short and straight Head line *(fig. 213)*

Such a Head line shows a very practical and materialistic attitude. Such a person will lack the imaginative faculties.

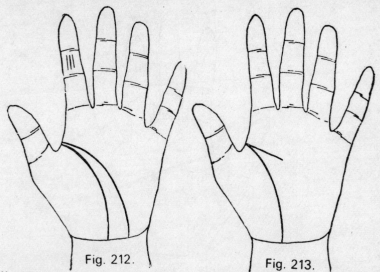

Fig. 212.
Head line sweeping down to the wrist with lines on the 2nd phalange of Jupiter finger (occultism and superstition)

Fig. 213.
A short and straight line of the Head (practical and scientific mind)

He will not believe in anything which is not scientific and which is not acceptable to logic and reason. If with this formation the mount of Mars is badly developed, it indicates want of spirit and courage.

If the Head line is short, we should carefully study the line of Life. The short Head line may indicate a short life and the Life line will guide us in this respect. If with the short Head line the Life line is also short, it means total death. If there is a star at the end of the short Head line, it indicates sudden death.

11.) **One straight line which is a combination of Heart and Head lines**

Occasionally, we may come across a hand where we find only one line straight across the hand (*fig. 214*). In this case, we may be at a loss to know whether it is a Heart line or a Head line. In such a case we have to find out the location of the line. If it starts from or near the line of Life

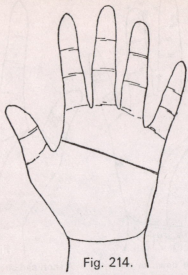

Fig. 214.
One straight line as a combination of Head and Heart lines (miserly and avaricious disposition)

and goes straight across the hand, we may read this line as the Head line. In this case therefore the line of Heart is absent. This one line formation shows a person who is cold, merciless, miserly and avaricious. If the colour of this line is red, it will make the person aggressive in his avarice. If the colour is yellow, he will be extremely mean in his acts.

Sometimes this one line may give us an impression that this line is a combination of Head and Heart lines. The collision of these two lines will result in a fusion of their strength. There is therefore a clash between the reason and the logic shown by the Head line and the emotion and sentiment shown by the Heart line. It is therefore difficult for such a person to discriminate between moral and ethical codes of conduct on the one hand and finer sentiment and emotion of life on the other. This person is very difficult to understand and is often misunderstood. He is very fickle in his moods and is sometimes very emotional and sometimes acts upon his reason and practical nature. He is therefore unreliable in his passion and love.

12) Branches

During our study of the line of Head we may come across several branches, either rising or falling from the line of Head. We shall first consider the rising branches.

Rising branches

We may come across a branch rising from the line of Head and going to different mounts.

1) If the branch goes to the mount of Jupiter (*fig. 215*), it shows realisation of ambition. If this branch terminates in a star, it shows brilliant success.

2) If this rising branch touches the root of the first finger, it indicates an ambitious nature. If in addition to this, there is a cross on the first bracelet, it shows wealth. If however this rising branch ends in a bar or is cut by a bar, it shows failure in realising the ambition (*fig. 216*).

3) If we come across three branches rising from the Head line and going to the mount of Jupiter, they indicate success and riches (*fig. 217*).

4) Occasionally, a rising branch going to the mount of Jupiter may turn to the mount of Saturn. It signifies vanity and religious fanaticism. It also indicates deep thinking in philosophy (*fig. 218*).

5) If the rising branch goes to the mount of Sun (*fig. 219*), it indicates success in talents. It denotes riches. It also means desire for notoriety.

6) If the rising branch goes between the third and the fourth finger, it shows scientific discoveries and achivements.

7) If one or two branches go to the mount of Mercury, they show business prosperity and commercial or scientific pursuits (*fig. 220*).

8) If the branch goes to the mount of Moon (*fig. 221*), it signifies mysticism, imagination and love for occult subjects.

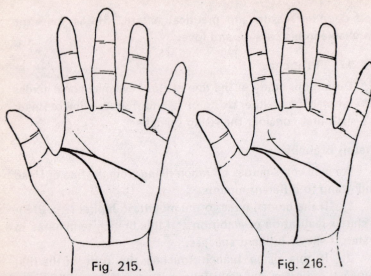

Fig. 215.
Rising branch from Head line going to the mount of Jupiter (realisation of ambition)

Fig. 216.
Rising branch from Head line going to mount of Jupiter but cut by a bar (failure in ambition)

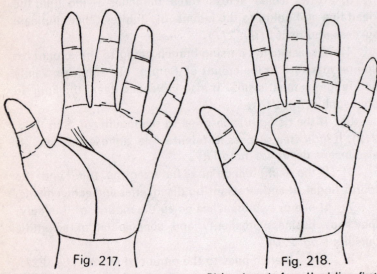

Fig. 217.
Three branches from Head line going to the mount of Jupiter (success and riches)

Fig. 218.
Rising branch from Head line first going to Jupiter and then to mount of Saturn (vanity and philosophy)

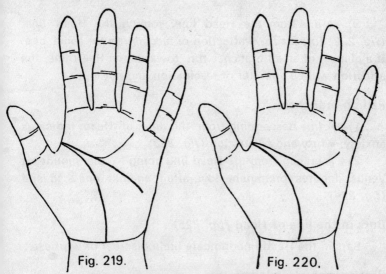

Fig. 219.
Rising branch from Head line going to the mount of Sun (success in talents)

Fig. 220.
Rising branch from Head line going to the mount of Mercury (business prosperity)

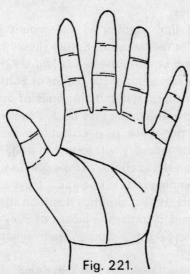

Fig. 221.
branch from Head line going to the mount of Moon (love for occultism)

9) A line from the Head line, joining the Heart line, (*fig. 222*) foreshadows affection or fascination for some one. If a number of small branches run towards the Heart line, the affection will be a matter of fascination and not love.

Falling branches

1) A line descending from the line of Head indicates anxiety, worry and frustration (*fig. 223*).

2) A branch from the Head line going to the mount of Venus denotes prominent love-affair against one's desire (*fig. 224*).

Bars in the line of Head *(fig. 225)*

Bars in the Head line indicate brain disorder or worries.

Breaks in the Head line

1) A break at the starting of the Head line shows a short life.

2) A break on the line (*fig. 226*) indicates a wound on the head. It also indicates mental trouble. Many breaks indicate headaches.

3) A Head line sloping to the mount of Moon and with a break under the mount of Saturn shows insanity. This is certain, if found on both the hands (*fig. 227*), (*case 4*).

4) If this break is under the mount of Saturn and if it is very distinct and sharp, without any signs of over-lapping, it means early death. The death may be due to serious accident of the head. If the break is over-lapping, we may expect partial or complete recovery. If found on both the hands, it indicates death on the scaffold. If the same as above is seen with the abrupt ending of Life line and a cross in the Triangle on both the hands, it also signifies death on the scaffold.

5) If the break is under the mount of Sun, it may mean trouble with the eyesight or danger from sunstroke or from hydrophobia.

6) A Head line broken at the beginning, in the centre and at the end shows a poor and unhappy life.

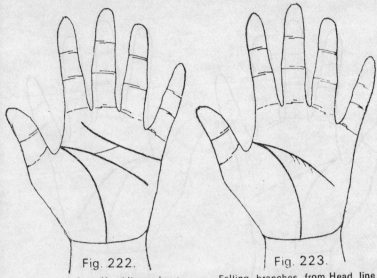

Fig. 222.
Rising branch from Head line going to the line of Heart (affection for some one)

Fig. 223.
Falling branches from Head line (anxiety and worry)

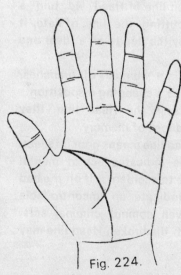

Fig. 224.
Falling branch from Head line going to the mount of Venus (forceful love **forced against one's desire**)

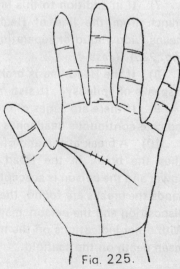

Fig. 225.
Bars in the Head line (brain disorder, worries)

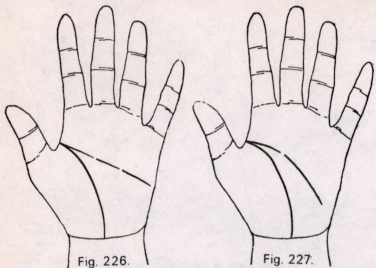

Fig. 226.
Breaks in the Head line (wound, mental troubles)

Fig. 227.
Head line with a break under the mount of Saturn, and going to the mount of Moon (insanity)

7) If in addition to this broken line of Head we find a branch from the line of Heart cutting the line of Fate, it means widowhood or separation by the death of a dear one (*fig. 228*), (*case 4*).

8) If the Head line is broken in a number of branches, it speaks of epilepsy. It also means a changing disposition.

9) If there are series of breaks in the Head line, they indicate continuous headaches and loss of memory.

10) A break at the end of Head line means poor intellect. Thus the break in the Head line indicates lack of mental power and the person is susceptible to accidents. If on the bad hands the breaks are found, they indicate an uncontrollable disposition and the person may even commit criminal acts. With other indications on the hand, the broken Head line may mean death on the scaffold.

Deflection of Head line towards different mounts

Normally, the Head line curves slightly above in the beginning in its course and usually the curve is between the

The line of Head

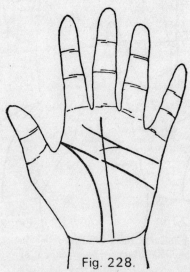

Fig. 228.
A break in the Head line and a branch
from Heart line cutting the line of fate
(widowhood)

mount of Jupiter and Saturn. However we may find that the Head line abnormally takes an upper curve during its course. This curve may be towards any of the mounts under the fingers.

This means that during that particular period the Head line is influenced by the mount towards which it is attracted.

a) If the line is attracted towards the mount of Saturn (*fig. 229*), the person will be influenced by the Saturnian qualities. In order to study the details of the characteristics of Saturn by which the person is influenced, we shall have to study the world by which he is influenced. For instance, if he is governed by the mental world, he will be attracted to the study of philosophy. If the second or the middle world is prominent, he may study mining or agriculture. If however the third world is dominant, he will think of saving money.

b) If the Head line is attracted towards the mount of Apollo or Sun (*fig. 230*), he will be influenced by Apollonian ideas. Here also we can apply the same logic and find out

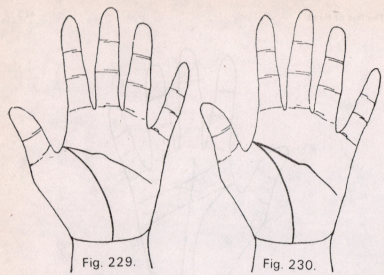

Fig. 229.
Head line deflecting towards the mount of Saturn (saturnian ideas)

Fig. 230.
Head line deflecting towards the mount of Sun (apollonian ideas)

his ideas which will be dominated by the prominent world shown on the hand. For example. if the mental world is ruling, he will be attracted towards pure art. If the middle world is powerful, he will strive for money-making. If the lower world is in domination, he will be more interested in display and show.

c) If the Head line is curving upwards under the mount of Mercury (*fig. 231*), his ideas will be governed by the Mercurian qualities. In this case he will be more business-like and will be efficient in scientific pursuits.

A Wavy Head line (*fig. 232*) shows inconsistency in thought and action. It shows changeability of purpose and lack of continuous mental efforts. This line is unstable and shows unstable ideas.

If during its course we find that the Head line is deflected towards the Heart line (*fig. 233*), we may conclude that the heart overrules the head. In such a case, the person is dominated more by emotions and sentiments than by reason and logic. If this deflection towards the Heart line is seen from the beginning of the Head line, it denotes that from the

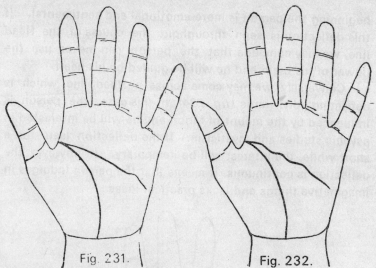

Fig. 231.
Head line deflecting towards the mount of Mercury (mercurian ideas)

Fig. 232.
Wavy Head line (inconsistancy in thought)

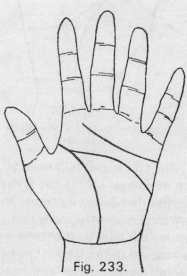

Fig. 233.
Head line deflecting towards the Heart line (emotions rule reason)

beginning the person is more emotional and sentimental. If this deflection is seen throughout the course of the Head line, we may conclude that the person can never use the power of his brain and he will be guided by his heart.

Conversely, we may come across a Head line which is deflecting downwards (*fig. 234*). In this case, the person is influenced by the mount of Moon and he will be interested in psychic studies and mysticism. If the deflection lasts for a short while, the interest will be temporary. If however the deflection is continuous, it means that the person indulges in imaginative things and lacks practical ideas.

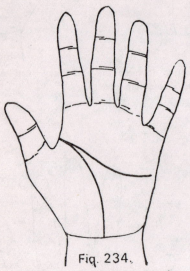

Fig. 234.
Head line deflecting downwards
(mysticism)

We should also study the thickness or thinness of the Head line during its course. If the line is deep in the beginning, then it becomes thin during its course and then chained upto the end, we can interpret logically that in the beginning the mind was strong but later on it became weak and nervous and finally was impaired to the last. If however we find the reverse condition of the course of the Head line, we can

The line of Head

interpret that at the beginning the mind was sick and defective but later on it developed to normalcy.

The beginning of the line shows the starting of the mental activity, the course shows the changes if any and the end speaks of the ultimate outcome.

VI Ending position of the line of Head

The next thing we have to study is the way the line of Head takes its position at the end. The ending of the line of Head is equally important and we shall study the various formation one by one.

1) Head line turning up at the end

We may come across a Head line, which turns up at the end on the upper mount of Mars *(fig. 235)* in which case it signifies over-confidence and egoism which results in serious trouble.

If however the line turns back towards the mount of Venus before reaching the upper mount of Mars, it indicates cowardice *(fig. 236)*.

2) Head line ending under the mount of Saturn

A short Head line which ends under the mount of Saturn indicates insanity or premature death. With badly developed mounts of Jupiter and Sun, it shows lack of intelligence.

If this line ends before touching the line of Fate, it shows a short and unhappy life. If this line ends in a tassel, it denotes paralysis.

3) Head line ending on the mount of Saturn

If the Head line ends on the mount of Saturn *(fig. 237)*, it shows death by a wound on the head. If however this line ends before touching the line of Heart, the wound to the head would not be fatal. If the Head line only turns up towards the mount of Saturn, it shows death by mental paralysis *(fig. 238)*.

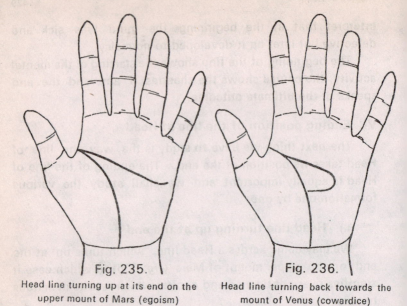

Fig. 235.
Head line turning up at its end on the upper mount of Mars (egoism)

Fig. 236.
Head line turning back towards the mount of Venus (cowardice)

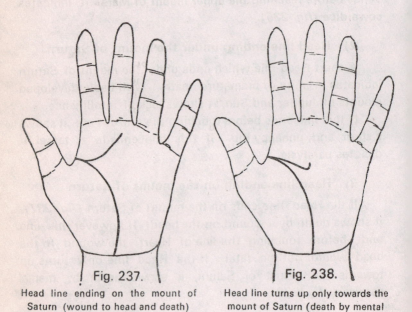

Fig. 237.
Head line ending on the mount of Saturn (wound to head and death)

Fig. 238.
Head line turns up only towards the mount of Saturn (death by mental paralysis)

The line of Head

4) Head line terminating on the mount of Uranus (fig. 239)

It shows prejudice towards industrial life and also shows interest in machinery. If however the mount of upper Mars is badly developed, it indicates lack of courage.

5) Head line terminating on the mount of Sun (fig. 240)

If the Head line turns towards to mount of Sun but ends before reaching the mount, the Head line gets the benefits of the characteristics of art and literature as shown by the mount of Sun. If this line ends on the mount of Sun, it shows success in literary activities and the person has a passion for fine arts. The person gets riches and fame with his intellectual capacity. It also shows complications and heart difficulty and mental disorder, probably apoplexy.

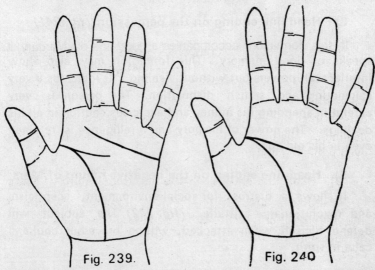

Fig. 239.
Head line ending on the mount of Uranus (interest in machinery)

Fig. 240
Head line ending before reaching the mount of Sun (love for art and literature)

6) Head line terminating between the Sun and Mercury fingers

This termination of the Head line brings success to the person in his scientific pursuits. He also has the capacity to apply his artistic aptitude in industry. If the Head line terminates on the line of Heart, it indicates fits of dizziness. In this case, the brain is affected by defective circulation. If the Head line is merged into the Heart line, it shows that the feelings overpower the judgement. It may mean criminality.

7) Head line terminating on the mount of Mercury

The person acquires tact and shrewdness which are the characteristics of Mercury. If however this line reaches only upto the line of Heart but does not touch it, it indicates the art of mimicry. On the health side it indicates bilious tendency, stomach disorders and nervousness. If this line ends in a star, it shows sudden death.

8) Head line ending on the percussion *(fig. 241)*

If this formation accompanies a good line of Mercury, it speaks of good memory. This formation may also show intellectual powers but without feeling. It indicates a very calculating and selfish disposition. The person is very careful in spending his money and exercises caution in all his dealings. The power of memory and intelligence is retained even in his old age.

9) Head line ending on the negative mount of Mars

It shows a distrust for social environment, scepticism and revolutionary attitude. *(fig. 242)* The subject will defend himself when attacked, will be brave but cool and calm in spirit.

10) Head line ending on the mount of Moon

When the Head line ends deep into the mount of Moon, it indicates fantastic imagination which may even prove harmful. If the drooping line ends in a star, it means insanity.

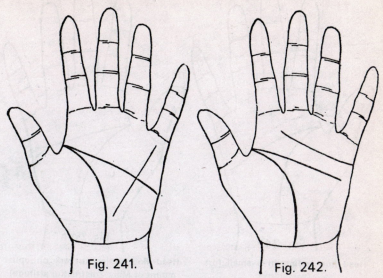

Fig. 241.
Head line terminating on the percussion with a good line of Mercury (strong memory)

Fig. 242.
Head line terminating on the upper mount of Mars (scepticism)

If it ends in a chain, it shows mental impairment. If it ends in an island or a dot, it shows danger of mental disturbance.

If at the end the Head line has a slight curve and then it ends on the mount of Moon, the person never falls short of any necessities of life.

11) Head line ending in a fork

a) If the Head line ends in a small fork, it shows versatility (*fig. 243*). This formation shows a combination of practical as well as imaginative sides. This is an asset for theatrical people to acquire success.

If the fork is slightly wide, it shows that the person has practical ideas and also equally strong imagination. With this formation, he is less inclined to be narrow and one-sided. By studying which prong is stronger, we can know which side will obtain the mastery.

The fork formation indicates a balancing of the practical and the imaginative qualities of the mind. However this

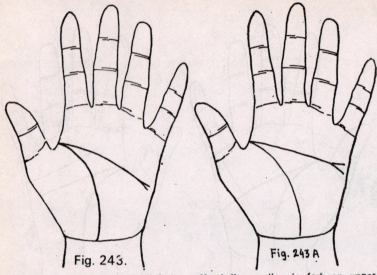

Fig. 243. Head line ending in a small fork (versatility)

Fig. 243 A Head line ending in fork on upper mount of Mars (distrustful attitude)

formation shows a hesitant and undecided disposition. Such people take quick but impulsive decision.

b) A small fork as above with a thick soft palm, a short thumb and the third phalanges of the fingers bulging inside the hand is an indication of untrustworthiness.

c) If the fork terminates on the mount of upper Mars, it shows a combination of critical mind and intuitive faculty.

d) If the Head line is normal and if one prong of the fork goes a little away down to the mount of Moon, it signifies cleverness. This is a good sign found on the hands of businessmen and successful lawyers, actors, etc. This also indicates enlarged imagination and the person may magnify the original idea, with the result that the fact becomes distorted.

e) **One prong going deep into the mount of Moon (fig. 244)**

In this case, the subject will deceive himself first and others afterwards. This type of fork also indicates doubledealing and hypocrisy. A large and uneven forking shows trickery.

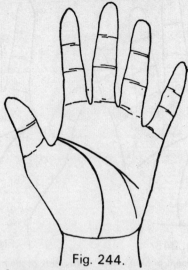

Fig. 244.
One prong of the Fork of head line
goes deep to the mount of Moon
(hypocrisy)

If both the prongs are strong, it shows the habit of falsifying. However the subject is not an intentional liar but tells things which are of his imagination.

f) If the fork on the mount of Moon ends in a star or cross or a dot, it means that the enlarged imagination will lead to insanity *(fig. 245)*, *(case 4)*.

g) A drooping line of Head with a fork on the mount of Moon, with mounts of Moon and Venus developed, indicates timidity, unscrupulousness, lack of a sense of responsibility and lack of patriotism. Such persons may even betray their country.

If with the same formation as above, one prong goes down to the mount of Moon, it shows talent, diplomacy and a gift of clairvoyance.

h) One of the forks of the Head line going to the mount of Moon and the other to the mount of Mercury *(fig. 246)*

It gives the power to hypnotise. It also indicates

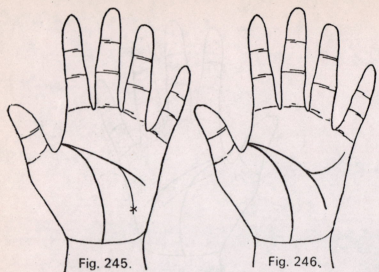

Fig. 245.
The prong on the mount of Moon ends in a star (Insanity)

Fig. 246.
One fork of the head line goes to the Mount of Mercury and the other to the mount of Moon (power to hypnotise)

application of imagination towards money-making. It also means a strong desire for riches that blinds the person to the sense of ethics.

i) **One prong going to the mount of Moon and the other touching the line of Heart**

With the formation the person will sacrifice everything for his affection. The same formation but with the line of Fate terminating on the line of Heart shows loss of career through affection or a love-affair.

j) A Head line ending in a fork, where both the prongs are sloping low on the mount of Moon, indicates a sense of romance, idealism and unconventionality in manners, morals and habits *(fig. 247)*.

k) **Fork ending in three prongs**

In this case, one prong goes straight, another curves down and the third one turns up towards the mount of Mercury *(fig. 248)*. This is a good formation and it shows harmony,

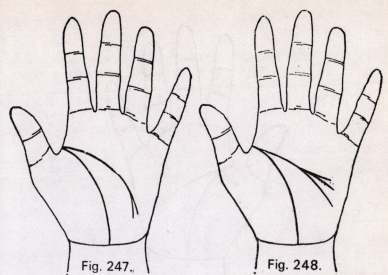

Fig. 247. Head line ending in a fork with both the prongs sloping low down on the mount of Moon (romance)

Fig. 248. Head line ending in the three prongs (mental harmony and power)

mental power, busineess talent and gift of imagination. It shows great diversity of intellect, adaptability and versatility. This formation shows success in life.

12) If the line of Head is joined to the line of Heart under the mount of Saturn, it indicates supremacy of Heart over the head resulting in fatal events.

13) If the Head line is joined to the line of Mercury, it shows suicidal tendencies, provided the line of Fate is poor, the Jupiter mount is exaggerated and there are many crossing bars on the line of Life.

14) If the Head line slopes down to the mount of Moon and ends in a star, it shows danger from drowning. It also signifies suicide by drowning.

15) An island at the end of the Head line (*fig. 249*) shows a tendency to weak memory in later life. It may also indicate loss of memory. A series of islands at the end of the Head line indicates a character very much given to extreme things. A large island at the end of the line of Head shows intestinal trouble.

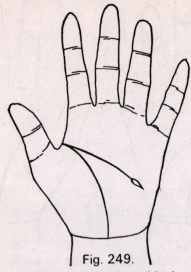

Fig. 249.
Head line ending in an island
(loss of memory)

16) If the Head line is short and ends in a star, it shows sudden death.

17) If this short line of the Head ends in a cross, it shows danger of death.

VII) Character of the line of Head

The next thing we have to study about the Head line is the character of the Head line. The character of this line shows the ability, the quality and also the power of concentration.

a) A deep and well-cut line of Head

This type of formation shows good memory, self-control, mental strength and health. Such a line shows one, who does not lose his head and has self-control. He is even-tempered and balanced and carries out his plans. A person with this formation may not take quick decision but he is very firm after he takes the decision. He pursues his aim and will collect all possible information necessary to execute his plans. A strong thumb will make him irresistible. A person with this deep and well-cut line of Head, accompanied by a strong thumb, will accomplish any task in life.

With this deep Head line, we shall have to study the characters of the other lines on the hand and their proportion to the Head line. If only the Head line is deep and well-cut and other lines are not so deep, we have a person who is a mental wanderer. If the hand and the lines in general are small but the Head line is deep and well-cut, it indicates great responsibility which the person cannot shoulder and naturally it shows grave danger.

The deep and well-cut line shows good health and such persons rarely suffer from headaches or mental disorder. If however we find excess development of this depth, we can fear trouble such as vertigo and fainting fits. It may also lead to insanity. This will be more certain, if the person is a Jupiterian with a thick 3rd phalange of the Jupiter finger.

b) Thin and narrow line of Head

A thin formation of the Head line indicates that the person is not mentally strong as shown by the deep line. He lacks vigorous brain power and is mentally delicate. It also shows weak mental stamina. He may be clever, but he finds it difficult to exert himself for a very long time and he soon gets mentally tired. He cannot stand mental tensions and also cannot concentrate on his subject for any length of time. Here also, we have to confirm his characteristics with other lines and also the type of hand. If the other lines are strong and the hands are large, they indicate the inability of the Head line to absorb or to bear great responsibilities which will involve the brain power. Such people should take sufficient rest and should not work, if they are tired and fatigued. Deep-cut formation on such a thin line gives us the period of danger. Stars, crosses and bars on a thin line of Head are a warning and a person should take proper care well in advance not to do any strenuous work. A thin and faint Head line with irregular line of Mercury shows chronic indigestion.

c) A broad and shallow Head line (*fig. 250*)

A broad and shallow Head line shows lack of force and intensity. It is not a vigorous formation and the person is not firm and resolute in his thought and actions. He also lacks courage, boldness and aggression. He has very poor memory and cannot influence other people. He is very lazy and not fit for intellectual work. If there is improvement anywhere, on this shallow and broad formation during the course of the line and especially at the end, we can expect better results from this person. If the left hand shows this broad

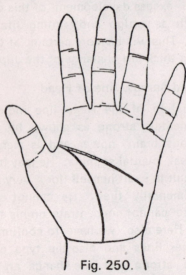

Fig. 250.
A broad and shallow head line
(lack of courage and force)

and shallow formation and we find breaks and splits on the right hand, we have a hopelessly weak and mentally retarded person. We can take this line into our first consideration while studying the mounts on the hand of the person. This weak formation will reduce all the mental attributes of the different mounts to which the person belongs.

For instance, the Jupiterian ambition will be diminished, the Martian aggression will be weakened, and instead, fear will prevail. It reduces the strength of every mount and the person will get a setback to all his mental abilites shown by the different mounts.

d) Chain-like formation of the Head line (*fig. 251*)

This formation has practically the same meaning as that of the shallow and broad Head line. It shows the serious mental strain but not necessarily the insanity. It also shows lack of concentration and inconsistency in thought. At times the person is extremely thoughtful and reasonable, while at other times his behaviour is illogical and emotional. (*case 5*)

e) Ladder-like formation of the Head line (*fig. 252*)

In this case, the person is fickle-minded and changing. He has continuous headaches and poor heath. With pointed tips, he is impractical and unreliable. It is necessary that he does not exert mentally and should take more rest and sleep. Otherwise, he will develop a nervous constitution which may lead to a nervous breakdown.

f) Wavy Head line (*fig. 253*)

A wavy line of the Head indicates lack of mental strength, perseverance and continuity of thought. If this line inclines towards the mount of Mercury, it shows morbid influence of the liver which creates melancholia and brain trouble. It also denotes nervous and bilious trouble.

A wavy Head line with a narrow Quadrangle and exaggerated mount of Mercury indicates dishonesty and shows a swindler or a thief (*fig. 254*).

A wavy Head line, slanting in an abnormal upward curve towards the Heart line under the mount of Sun or Mercury, shows insanity.

Colour: While studying the character of the Head line, it is necessary to study the colour of the Head line so as to

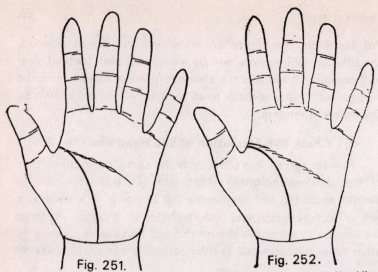

Fig. 251.
Chained line of the Head (lack of concentration)

Fig. 252.
Ladder like formation of the Head line (fickle mind)

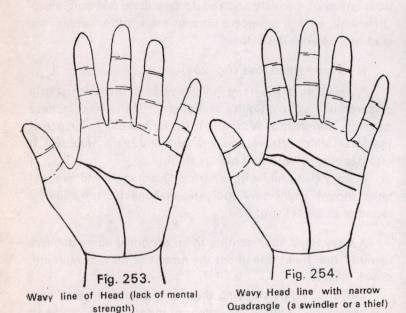

Fig. 253.
Wavy line of Head (lack of mental strength)

Fig. 254.
Wavy Head line with narrow Quadrangle (a swindler or a thief)

enable us to judge the intensity of the qualities exhibited by the Head line.

1) For a deep and well-cut Head line white colour is not usually seen. It will however add coldness and the person will be more calculating and avaricious and with little sympathy for others.

Pink colour : This colour to the deep and well-cut Head line will give added strength to the person. This will make him more energetic and active and he may suffer from overwork.

Red colour : It shows excessive mental strength and also too much blood and too much brain power, resulting into apoplexy. Red colour is therefore a menace to health.

Yellow colour : This colour to the deep and well-cut line of Head makes the person mean-minded.

2) Thin line of Head and colour

For a thin line of the Head *white colour* is not a good combination and it will make the line further weak.

Red colour : It will add strength to this thin line of the Head. However more strength shown by the red colour may not stand the thin line and overstrain may be the result.

Yellow colour : It makes the person nervous, unstable and narrow-minded.

3) Broad and shallow Head line and colour

White colour : This colour to a broad and shallow line is common, it shows poor blood supply.

Pink colour : This colour is better for such a line, which will reduce the weakness shown by the line.

Red colour : It is not a healthy combination for this line. This line will not be able to stand the vigour and strength shown by the red colour and it will make the person more nervous

Yellow colour : This colour will make the person more nervous.

We can apply the same logic to other characteristics of the Head line and draw the result.

VIII) Defects of the Head line

We may come across several defects such as splits, cross-bars, islands, dots, breaks, etc. We shall study them one by one.

1) Uneven line of Head

We may find that during the course of the line of the Head the line may be sometimes thick and sometimes thin. This may happen one or two times or even continuously. The thinness of the line whenever seen on the Head line indicates periods of weakness of mental behaviour. The period shows difficulties in standing the strain of the mind. The result is that the person is inconsistent in his behaviour.

If a star, cross or a dot is seen on this uneven line, it means paralysis, apoplexy or insanity. It is therefore necessary that this person does not exert much and avoids excitement. He should have plenty of sleep.

2) Splits in the Head line

We may come across small splits either rising or falling from the line of Head. These splits should not be mistaken for the forks already studied. These splits are small lines and they can be easily distinguished from forks.

Rising splits (*fig. 255*)

If the splits are small, they indicate an aspiration for one's rise and improvement. If the splits are large, the person is influenced by many things and he changes from time to time.

If the rising splits touch the line of Heart, they indicate that the sentiments and affections overrule the mind of the person.

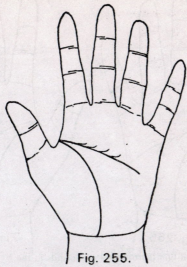

Fig. 255.
Rising splits in the line of Head
(aspiration to rise)

Falling splits (*fig. 256*)

These lines when found on the line of Head, makes a person easily discouraged. They indicate sorrow and disappointment.

3) Cross-bars (*fig. 225*)

These are short lines which are long enough to cut the line of Head. If these cross-bars are deep and short and also red, they indicate brain disorder, headaches and mental worries. Such bars are usually seen on the hands of the hyper-sensitive persons.

4) Islands (*fig. 257*)

Islands on the line of Head indicate brain fevers. It is also indicative of diminished mental force. It is a matter of interest to note that some people, who can act as spirit mediums, have such island formations on their Head line. Such people have got the confirmed idea that they could get

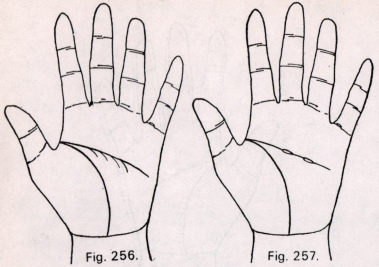

Fig. 256.
Falling splits in Head line (sorrow and disappointment)

Fig. 257.
Islands in the Head line (brain fever)

the power to get in touch with the spirits at the time the island formations are seen on the hand. However it is certain that the mind is not healthy and powerful during the period of the island. If the islands are deep and red in colour, they indicate fevers like typhoid. They also indicate extreme nervousness due to severe mental strain. In order to estimate the danger shown by the island we shall have to take into consideration other factors on the hand. For instance, a star or a cross after the island is a serious warning of mental health. If the Head line is islanded at the start, it shows hereditary brain trouble or trouble with the respiratory system.

5) **Dot** (*fig. 258*)

Another defect seen in the Head line is the dot. It indicates some bacterial infection affecting the brain. Acute dots indicate brain disorders and the intensity depends upon the size of the dot. If it is large and red, severe illness is indicated. If it is white or pink, the severity is lessened. We should study the line after the defects; if it is good, the sickness is temporary and so on.

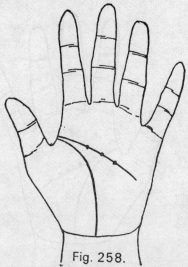

Fig. 258.
Dots in the Head line (brain disorder)

6) Breaks

We have already studied breaks in detail while studying the course of the Head line. They show lack of concentration and self-control. If after the break there is a split going to any mount, it shows the force that is responsible for the break.

7) Knot (*fig. 259*)

It denotes a tendency to murder.

8) A clear deep indentation shows slight injury to the head. It also indicates cruel neurolgia to last for some months.

We have studied above the various defects seen in the Head line. We have to study the seriousness of these defects. The sickness shown by the dot will be continued for sometime. If the dot is followed by an island, the duration of the delicacy will cover the period shown by the island. A dot followed by a cross or a star is a serious warning to the person about his health and it may mean fatal termination of his life.

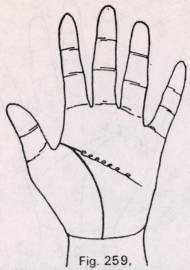

Fig. 259,
Knotted Head line (tendency to murder)

IX) Double line of the Head (*fig. 260*) (*case 7*)

It is rarely found on the hand, but when found, it indicates capacity to plan and carry out large undertakings with ease and success. Such persons usually have a magnetic personality. The double line of Head shows a tremendous mental power. Such people have versatility, great command of speech and a peculiar power of playing and toying with human nature. They have great will and determination.

The peculiarity of the double line of tha Head is that it shows a dual personality and the person can play a double role in life like Doctor Jackyle and Hyde with great mental strain. He has his own philosophy and ideals which may show contradictions.

The upper Head line shows logic, reasoning and a cold nature, whereas the lower line shows sentiments and emotions, which many a times control the person. Cheiro has mentioned a peculiar case of the double line of Head seen by him on the hand of one of his clients. Those who are interested may go through his autobiography.

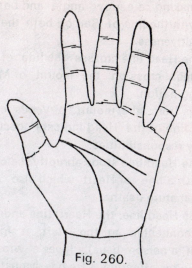

Fig. 260.
Double line of Head (Dual personality)

X) Line of the Head in relation to other lines

1) If the line of the Head rises towards the line of the Heart and at the same time if we find the line of Mercury touching the line of Life, it signifies fainting fits due to poor digestion.

2) A good Head line extending across the hand with a good line of Mercury shows good memory. A short Head line with a poor line of Heart and a triangle on the Life line at the end, shows talkativeness which is harmful.

In this case, the short line of Head shows the lack of intelligence and a poor Heart line shows a cold person. The foolish talk leads to scandals.

3) If the Head line is very straight with a poor line of the Heart, it means that the money will be spent for the family.

4) If the Head line is poor, the Heart line is absent and the line of Mercury is wavy, it shows a weak heart. This formation may also indicate irresolute nature which may lead to evil actions.

5) If the line of the Head is closely connected with the line of Life making a narrow angle and both these lines are connected with the line of Sun on both the hands, it shows extreme sensitiveness.

6) If the Head line crosses the line of Mercury making thereby a clear cross on the mount of Moon, it shows a diseased imagination.

7) Lines from the mount of Venus cutting the line of Life and the line of the Head indicate pecuniary difficulties due to family responsibilities.

8) If the Head line stops abruptly before it reaches the Fate line, with a line of Heart which also stops abruptly, it speaks of premature death.

9) If the Head line, the Heart line and the Life line are too closely connected at the start, it signifies premature death. Such a person usually loves a wrong person and is unfortunate in his affection. He has sympathy for the person he loves. He shows his affection for that person in the most difficult situations. If in addition to the above combination, the line of Fate starts from inside the line of Life, it shows tragedy in love affair.

XI) The line of the Head in relation to the type of hand

The line of Head is usually found in accordance with the type of hand on which it is seen. We can notice a practical line of Head on a square hand, an imaginative line of Head on a conic hand and so on. It therefore follows that the formation of the line contrary to its nature is more important than the characteristics indicated in accordance with the type of the hand.

1) Head line on the elementary hand

A short, straight and heavy Head line is expected on an elementary hand. If however we come across a long Head line going upto the mount of Moon, it will mean a superstitious tendency and the influence of animal nature. It signifies the fear of the unknown and superstitious dread.

2) Line of the Head on a square hand

The square hand is a practical hand and shows the development of logic and reason and all things pertaining to material development. On such a type of hand, a straight and long line of Head is expected. If we observe a drooping line of Head, it indicates contradiction in the original nature shown by the type of hand. In such a case, the person will not be able to execute his ideas to the full extent as he plans.

3) Line of Head on a spatulate hand

We have studied earlier that the spatulate hand stands for originality, activity, invention, independence, etc. Therefore the natural position for the line of the Head is long, clear and slightly sloping. If on the contrary we find a straight line of Head, we shall have a person with a combination of originality and practicality. The result is that such a person will be restless, irritable and dissatisfied.

4) Line of Head on a philosophical type of hand

The philosophical hand is thoughtful, sincere in the pursuit of wisdom and a lover of practical and mystical philosophy. The natural position for the line of Head on this type is long and closely connected with the line of Life and slopes down towards the mount of Moon. If we come across a Head line which is straight and high-set on the hand, we have an analytical and critical mind. Such a person will look to the faults and failings of his fellowmen and he will expose their fads and fancies.

5) Line of the Head on the conic hand

The conic hand represents the artistic and impulsive nature of the person. He is emotional and sentimental in his thought and action. On such a type of hand we can expect the sloping line of Head going deep into the middle of the mount of Moon. If we find a straight line of Head on such a hand, the person will utilise his art for money-making. He will use his talents according to the public demand.

6) Line of the Head on the psychic hand

The psychic hand exhibits a visionary or dreamy nature and we should expect an extremely sloping line of the Head on this hand. A straight line of Head is not usually found, but whenever seen it indicates a clash between idealism and materialism.

XII) The line of the Head in relation to the fingers

1) A straight Head line with square fingers indicates a very practical nature and a person who counts everything in rupees, annas and paise. It is very difficult to convince such a person. He does not believe in anything which is beyond logic.

A sloping Head line with square fingers gives a person imagination and he is capable of materialising his practical views and ideas with imagination.

2) Spatulate fingers with a straight line of Head is a good combination and the person can apply his original ideas and individuality which will bring the practical results.

A sloping line of Head with spatulate fingers gives imagination and originality to the person and this combination will create good architects and engineers.

3) A straight Head line with conic fingers is a contradiction and the person is likely to meet with failures in life unless he is backed by a good line of success.

A sloping line of the Head with conic fingers will create an artist who can employ his art with novel ideas and who can depict his feelings in his art.

4) A straight line of the Head with smooth fingers indicates a person who is sober in his thoughts and actions.

A sloping line of Head with smooth fingers will create a sentimental and emotional person.

5) A straight or sloping line of the Head with waisted fingers indicates a thoughtful disposition. Such a person is too careful and fastidious over details.

XIII) Signs on the line of Head

1) *White spots*: White spots on the line of Head,

The line of Head

under the mount of Sun and with cross bars on the line of Heart, indicates literary success.

White spots on the Head line under and close to the mount of Mercury indicate success in scientific pursuits.

2) *Black spots* : Black spots in the Head line, with a fork at the start in the Life line, indicate serious brain trouble. Only one black spot means typhoid.

Black spots indicate, tooth ache, if the mount of Saturn is powerful. However if the mount of Venus is powerful, they indicate deafness. A black spot with a line from upper mount of Mars to the mount of Jupiter also shows deafness.

If we find a black spot on the Head line and if the spot is joined by a line starting on a star from the mount of Venus, it indicates calamity and sorrow on account of the death of a loved one.

3) *Blue spot* : A blue spot on the Head line, which is on one side of the triangle, with Life and Mercury lines indicates a tendency to murder. In this case, the mount of the Mars should be powerful.

4) *Cross* : A cross on the line of the Head shows accident.

5) *Star* : A star signifies a wound to the head. If found on both the hands, it means fatality.

6) *Circle* : A circle on the Head line indicates blindness. If accompanied by a cross on the line of Mercury on the upper side, the indication is sure.

7) *Triangle* : A triangle on the line under the mount of Mercury shows success in scientific pursuits.

8) *Island* : An island in the line of Head under the mount of Saturn is a sign of deafness.

9) *Square* : Square shows protection from illness or accident.

10) *Bars* : Bars on the line of Head mean headache.

11) *Mole* : A mole at the starting of the Head line means a luxurious life. A mole at the end of the Head line shows acquisition of conveyance.

A mole at the beginning, at the centre and at the end of the Head line gives all happiness and an executive position.

CHAPTER XIX

The Line of Fate

I) Introduction

The next line to be studied is the line of Fate. The word fate is confusing and it is generally supposed that this line indicates fatality or predestination. Though it is true to some extent, it does not mean that all our life is predestined and that we have no choice regarding our future. On a scientific basis, we can say that this line indicates the course of our life from the standpoint of material success and shows whether we shall make our own way, whether we shall have a hard time or whether things will come in an easy way. Many times, we say that a particular person is very lucky in life and we attribute his success to his good luck. In such a case, the line of Fate only indicates that the person will have a comfortable and successful life. He however will have to work for his career and will have to put in his determination and ambition in order to get the success achieved by him. We come across people who say "others are lucky but I am not". In this case, they forget that others are hard workers whereas they are not. On a practical basis, we can say that luck consists in seizing the opportunities.

The line of Fate is a wonderful line and it reveals accurately the important events in life. From this line, we can find out the periods which are propitious. During such lucky periods we find in a subject the combination of good health, ambition and presence of mind. These combined qualities help the subject to take the advantage of the opportunities given to him.

The line of Fate

A strong line of Fate emphasises the Saturnian traits of wisdom, sobriety and the ability to see life from its serious side. Studiousness and the ability to think are the prominent characteristics of Saturn which will make a successful life. In many cases, we find the absence of this line. In that case, it indicates an insignificant life. Of course, this interpretation is not so accurate since the absence of this line has been noticed on the hand of some of the successful persons in life. The absence of such a line on the hand of successful persons only means that these people have worked hard to achieve success and it is not by sheer luck that they have achieved the successful career in life. The psychological interpretation of the absence of this line of Fate is unsociability. In other words, the line of Fate shows the social aptitude and behaviour of the person. It has been experienced that this line is more markedly observed on the hands of women than on the hands of men because women, in general, are more sociable than men.

The absence of this line indicates an uncompromising attitude. A sense of strong disagreement and dissatisfaction with the surrounding prevails without any cause or reason. This absence may sometimes mean a short life. In this case, life is seldom taken seriously. However a feeling of frustration will persist. There is no stability in life and there is always a craving for a change. The characteristics shown by the absence of Fate line can be counterbalanced by a good development of the mounts of Jupiter and Mars showing purpose in life. Sometimes the absence of the line is counterbalanced by the line of Sun or Apollo.

The line of Fate is also called the line of ego and also the line of environment. A study of this line will reveal that these different names represent the functional aspect of the line. The Fate line indicates, in general, the course of life in regard to worldy affairs. This line will tell us of the events in life, its success or failure in relation to the capacity of the individual to adapt to the outside environment. This line is a line of prudence, restraint, virtue and simplicity. The most significant indication of a good line of Fate is that the owner is deeply involved in material achievements, worldly success and family obligations occupy his mind.

II) Position on the hand

The line of Fate usually starts from the base of the mount of Neptune or from the centre of wrist, cuts its way upwards and terminates on the mount of Saturn. It should rise by itself without collaboration with any other line. The line should be normal in depth, colour and evenness. When the line does not show an even course, the strength or weakness shown by the line at different periods are indicative of the strength or weakness of the life of the person at that period. The line of Fate does not indicate any health defects nor any constitutional make-up of the person.

III) Normal development

The line should normally start at the base of the hand and should end either on the mount of Saturn or at the root of Saturn finger. This normal position indicates a will to do and energy to accomplish. This formation shows a steady but sure success in life. The person will get all his normal dues and will lead a normal and succesful life.

IV) Starting position

There are various starting positions for the line of Fate, but mainly it may start either from inside the line of Life or from the centre of the palm or from the mount of Moon *(fig. 261)*. Sometimes we may also find the line of Fate starting either from the line of Head or the line of Heart. In between the various positions described above, the line of Fate may take any position on the hand.

1) Line of Fate starting from inside the line of Life

If the line starts from inside the line of Life or the mount of Venus, it shows that the early life of the person has been

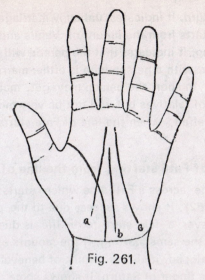

Fig. 261.

Three starting positions for the line of fate (from inside the Lifeline, centre of the palm, mount of Moon)

hampered by the influence of his relatives. In this case the career of the person is ruled by the family members. If this line continues as a weak line throughout its course, the relatives will have full control on his life. The relatives may be either parents or husband or wife. When the Fate line comes out of the Life line, that is the period when the person will break off the control of his relatives and exercise his own will. The period is calculated on the Fate line. This line, starting from the mount of Venus, is not necessarily a bad line and it may mean that the person is very much influenced by his relatives.

Since the line starts on the mount of Venus, his life will be influenced by the Venusian qualities and he will be a lover of music and art. His main interest in life will be to start his career as an actor, singer, writer or a painter. Such persons usually marry in haste and are sometimes unfortunate in love and marriage. They also have an outside love-affair, which creates a scandal for them. If this line ends in a fork on the mount of Saturn, it indicates unhappy marriage. When the line of Fate starts from the mount of Venus and if the line of Heart is sloping, it indicates that the person will be entangled in a love-affair with a person who is either married or is not free to marry. In short the person may get material success with the help of relatives but will not be very much successful in his love-affair, when the line of Fate starts from inside the line of Life.

2) Line of Fate starting from the line of Life

If we come across a Fate line which starts from the line of Life (*fig. 262*), it shows success due to the person's own efforts. However a fair start to his life is due to his own people. With the same starting, if the mounts of Jupiter and Venus are developed, it shows a spirit of benevolence. If this line runs to the finger of Saturn, it shows some danger. The more it goes to the finger, the greater is the danger. The danger is to be located elsewhere on the hand.

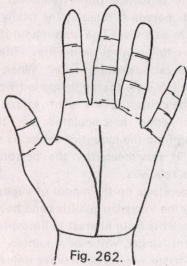

Fig. 262.

Fate line starting from Life line
(success)

3) Line of Fate starting from the wrist or the mount of Neptune

If the line of Fate rises from the wrist and proceeds straight to the mount of Saturn, it is a sign of fortune and success. The person will achieve success in life mainly by his own efforts. This also indicates a strong individuality but of the self-centred type.

If we find on a woman's hand a Fate line starting from wrist and going straight into deep mount of Saturn, it is a sign of well-to-do spinsters who have never married and are contented and satisfied with their own environment.

If the Fate line rises close to the Life line, it indicates the influence of relatives as long as the line runs close to the line of Life.

4) Fate line starting from the mount of Moon

When the line of Fate rises from the mount of Moon and runs on to the mount of Saturn, the person's success in life will be materially assisted by one of the opposite sex. Sometimes such marking is found on the hands of those whose wives have been of great assistance in the career of the persons. The Fate line starting from the mount of Moon will bestow average good fortune and a carefree life. A person with this starting likes speculative business and makes a success therein. He will be successful in the manufacture of luxury goods. They are generally restless and love to travel a great deal. He is often interested in occult sciences and hypnotic powers. If this line is found on the hand of a woman, it indicates an early marriage. If this line is very deep on the mount of Moon, the person is a public favourite. If the mount of Moon shows many voyage lines, the person will have success in foreign countries.

If the Fate line starting from the mount of Moon ends on the Heart line, it means heart trouble. It also means disappointment in love and also loss of career due to a love-affair.

If the Fate line starts from the base of the mount of Moon and if the fingers of Jupiter and Apollo are long and conical, it shows a gift of intuition.

5) The line of Fate starting from the first rascette

If the Fate line starts from the first rascette and penetrates into the third phalange of the second finger, it denotes an extraordinary destiny ; whether it is for good or bad will be seen elsewhere on the hand. Any way it is the strongest evidence of fatality. It is probably the only indication on the hand, which the will-power of the person seems capable to triumph over. This line also shows early responsibilities laid on the shoulders of the person.

6) The line of Fate starting from the third rascette

The line of Fate starting from the third rascette shows sorrows and natural trouble and some intense grief *(fig.263)*.

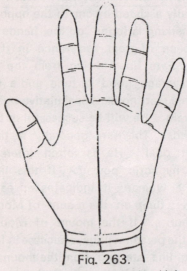

Fig. 263.
Fate line starting from the third rascette (sorrow)

The line of Fate

7) Fate line starting from the plain of Mars (*fig. 264*)

This is an indication of an uneventful early life. The starting of the line thereafter shows intelligence, shrewd planning and creative opportunities. If this line is supported by a well-formed cross on the mount of Mercury, it shows overcoming of the obstacles. If however this line penetrates into the third phalange of the Saturn finger (*fig. 265*), it shows a life full of unavoidable troubles and painful experiences.

8) Fate line starting from the upper mount of Mars

A crooked line of Fate, which starts from the mount of Mars and terminates on the mount of Saturn, signifies imprisonment (*fig. 266*).

9) Fate line starting from the mount of Uranus

This formation has practically the same meaning described in item 7 above. A person will have negative existence for the first half of his life. His best period will begin at the time the line starts. This line indicates that the destiny has really been shaped without much helpful influence from relatives or outsiders. If this line cuts the base of the second finger, it shows misfortune.

10) Fate line starting from inside the Quadrangle

It means difficulties in middle life, sometimes even imprisonment (*fig. 267*).

11) Fate line starting from the line of Head

This formation shows success in the middle of life and from the age of 35 onwards. If the mounts of Jupiter, Sun and Mercury are low set, the line shows dull intellect.

If the Fate line starts from the line of Head and takes a curve and then goes to the mount of Saturn, it shows a laborious life.

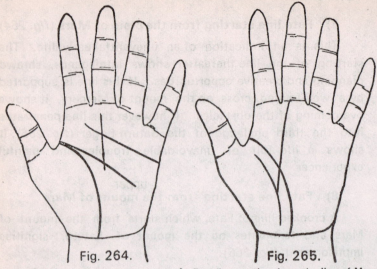

Fig. 264.
Fate line starting from the plain of Mars (intelligence, shrewd planning)

Fig. 265.
Fate line starting from the line of Mars and ending into the third phalange of the Saturn finger (troubles)

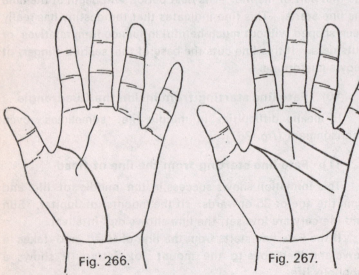

Fig. 266.
Crooked line of fate from mount of Mars, terminating in the mount of Saturn (imprisonment)

Fig. 267.
Fate line starting from the quadrangle (imprisonment or difficulties)

The line of Fate

12) Fate line starting from the line of Heart

A straight and good line of Fate starting from the line of Heart shows good fortune in old age.

13) Line of Fate starting from inside the Triangle (fig. 268)

A Fate line starting from inside the Triangle in both the hands shows favourable opportunities due to hard work and intelligence. If with this line a line of parental influence on the mount of Venus ends in a star, it means that the death of the parent has prevented a good start in the life of the person.

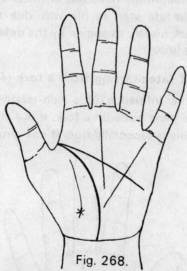

Fig. 268.
Fate Line starting within the triangle a
parental line ending in a star
(death of parent prevents good start)

From the above it will be noticed that when the line starts higher in the hand, the later period in life will be of smooth sailing. Special reference should be made that it is necessary to study both the hands in the case of the line of Fate. If the line begins low in the left hand but starts high in the right hand, we find that the natural course of life was favourable as shown in the left hand, whereas some difficulties altered the original plan. The difficulties may be due to health, or family or friends' influences. For the defect we must look elsewhere on the hand. The absence of Fate line in the beginning, where it should normally start, will often be explained by some accidents to the parents. Since the early period covers the childhood, it may not be through his fault that life started at a later age. As already stated, a parental influence line on the mount of Venus, ending in a star, indicates the death of the parent which has prevented a good start to the life of the person.

If with this late rising of the Fate line, we come across some defects either in the Head line or the Life line, we may conclude that the late start in life was due to the mental weakness or weak health, as shown by the defect either in the Head or the Life line.

14) Line of fate starting from a fork (*fig. 269*)

It shows the influence of a non-relative. If the line starts low in the hand but with a fork, it is a sign of adoption in early life. This is especially true, if one prong goes deep

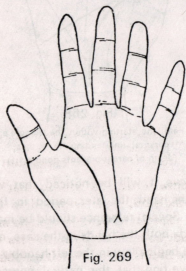

Fig. 269

Fate line starting from a fork (adoption)

The line of Fate

into the mount of Venus. This sign shows separation from parents resulting in a law-suit. This also indicates travels undertaken under the influence of one of the opposite sex. If this fork is wide apart, that is, one prong goes to the mount of Moon and the other to the mount of Venus, it shows the influence of one of the opposite sex or a great love that has inspired the person to work hard for success. But in this case, the progress is very much handicapped by wild imagination. In this formation, if the Fate line is not good, it shows disaster.

If one prong goes to the mount of Venus and the other to the centre of the hand (*fig. 270*), it indicates fatal influences of one of the opposite sex. If one prong goes to the mount of Venus and the other to the mount of Neptune (*fig. 271*), it shows the loss of married partner in early life. This is more true in the hands of men than that of women. In this case we shall have to study the line of Heart, which if

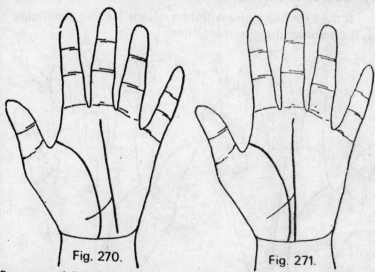

Fig. 270.
One prong of Fate line going to the centre of the hand and the other to the mount of Venus (fatal influence of the opposite sex)

Fig. 271.
One prong of the Saturn line going to the mount of Neptune and the other to the mount of Venus (loss of married partner)

powerful and good, will nullify the danger indicated by the fork.

If one of the forks goes to the mount of Neptune and the other to the mount of Moon, it signifies inspiration and imagination conflicting with the practical life, thus leading to great upheavels in the life of the person.

15) Fate line starting from a star (fig. 272)

A star at the beginning of the Fate line shows loss of fortune or great trouble to the parents of the person. If in addition there is another star on the mount of Venus, it indicates the death of one of the parents.

16) Fate line starting from an island (fig. 273)

It indicates the mystery of birth. If the Fate line is very poor, it shows illegitimacy.

V) Course of the line of Fate

If the Fate line starts with two islands forming the figure of '8', it shows the gift of intuition.

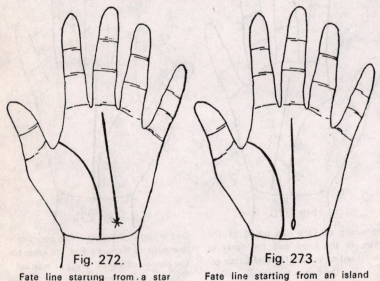

Fig. 272.
Fate line starting from a star
(troubles to parents)

Fig. 273.
Fate line starting from an island
(mystery of birth)

The line of Fate

If the line of Fate starts in the centre of the hand and if it is of a good character, it indicates good social habits. It also shows a receptive mind and great sympathy. We have already discussed in the introduction that the Fate line is more common on the hands of women than that of men. If this Fate line goes direct to the mount of Saturn and has branches rising upward, it is an indication of riches coming later in life. When the Fate line is marked uniform and clear on the mount of Saturn, it indicates great thinkers, inventors and mathematicians. They may not be rich but they are good, silent and profound.

If the Fate line shows its direction towards a particular mount for some length and then makes a curve to join another mount, it indicates a change of occupation. The nature of the change can be determined from the mount towards which it turns.

Sometimes we may come across a Fate line which runs close to the line of Life for sometimes, then takes a turn towards the mount of Saturn (*fig. 274*). This means that the person will shirk off his family responsibilities and go after worthless pursuits. If however this line goes to the mount of Sun, it indicates that the person will lead a spiritual life and will be least disturbed about his family commitments.

If the line of Fate starts from the mount of Uranus and goes in between the fingers of Saturn and Jupiter, it shows wound or diseases in the lower part of the abdomen (*fig. 275*).

If the Fate line is deep and red and cuts through the third phalange of the Saturn finger, it shows dishonourable death or imprisonment. This is particularly so, if there is a star on the first phalange of the Saturn finger (*fig. 276*).

A short line of Fate indicates a misfit in the community. The person has a destructive element.

If the line of Fate is chained where it crosses the line of Heart, it shows trouble in love (*fig. 277*).

The Fate line, if poorly traced as it approaches the middle portion of the hand, indicates trouble in the middle life. If

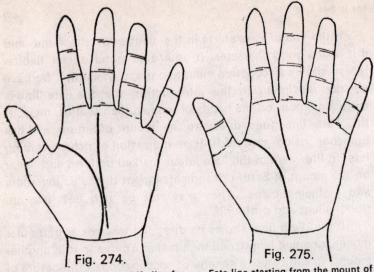

Fig. 274.
Fate line running close to Life line for sometime and then going to mount of Saturn (shirking of family responsibility)

Fig. 275.
Fate line starting from the mount of Uranus and going in between the Jupiter and Saturn fingers (wound in lower part of abdomen)

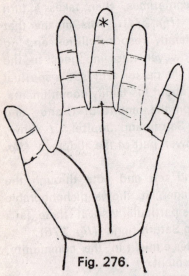

Fig. 276.
Deep and red Fate line cutting the third phalange of the Saturn finger, with a star on the first phalange of Saturn finger (dishonourable death or imprisonment)

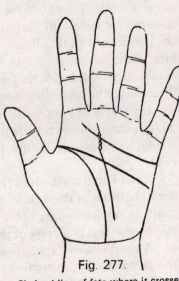

Fig. 277.
Chained line of fate where it crosses the heart line (trouble in love)

the line is faint in the beginning and becomes clear later on, it shows better ending of life, though there were troubles and difficulties in the early life.

If the Fate line, after rising for some length, turns backward into the hollow of the hand and towards the mount of Moon in a semi circular way, it threatens imprisonment (*fig. 278*).

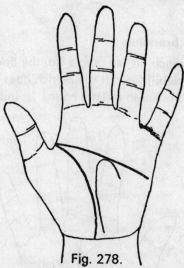

Fig. 278.
Fate line turning back in a semi-circular way in the hollow and towards the mount of Moon (imprisonment)

Branches

The line of Fate will be seen with little fine lines rising or falling from it. Rising lines show an upward tendency of the career and will add strength to the Fate line. Whenever a rising branch is seen that period will be filled with hope and ambition and will be more successful than any other period.

Falling branches indicate a hard life filled with discouragement and progress will be difficult.

Branches in the line of Fate are initiative lines. If the branch is thrown up, it shows new and successful achievement or a change in the career of the person. The nature of the branch will show whether the change is for better or for worse. The mount on the hand towards which the branch rises will tell the quality and the change in the career. Normally the new changes, indicated by the branches will be through one's personal merit and conscious action.

The branches may be upward branches and downward branches. Upward branches show good health and prosperity. Downward branches indicate losses and financial trouble.

a) Rising branches

A rising branch at an angle to the line of Fate shows increased responsibilities. If the branch goes to the mount of Jupiter (*fig. 279*) on an artistic hand, it indicates freedom

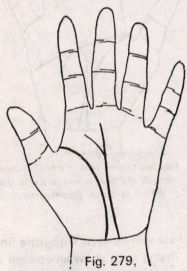

Fig. 279.
Rising branch of Fate line going to the mount of Jupiter (creative freedom in art)

in art and creative pursuits with energy and power. His success will be due to ambition and ability to command. This good formation is good for politician. If the branch rises to the mount of Sun, it indicates success in artistic or intellectual work. It also shows success and fame and glory in career. If the line of Fate is about to stop and at the same time another line starts from the same place, it shows prosperity in service and business. If the branch rises to the mount of Mercury, the person will get success due to shrewdness, business ability and good power of expression.

Rising branches from the Fate line to the Heart line, without touching the Heart line, indicate love affairs, which do not end in marriage. If however the line touches the line of Heart, union takes place. If the rising line cuts the line of Heart, it means an unfortunate union. A branch from the Fate line towards the Jupiter mount and joining the Heart line signifies a second marriage. However the usual line of Marriage on the mount of Mercury should be present.

b) Falling branches

A downward branch to the line of Fate gives a check to the career. The downward branch indicates periods of losses and difficulties in career. If with a downward branch the line of Fate is broken, it shows danger from faithlessness. If an island is seen either in the line of Head or the line of Head or the line of Heart at the same period where there is a downward branch from the Fate line, it shows mental trouble or heart disease, as the case may be. If there are indications of either rheumatism or gout or apoplexy on the mount of Moon, the downward branch shows difficulties in the career due to these troubles.

When the line of Fate is divided into a number of branches in the middle of the portion, it signifies different phases of the career.

VI) Ending position of the line of Fate

If the branch touches the line of Head, the person will have discretion and correct thinking in shaping the career.

a) *On Jupiter*: A Fate line ending on the mount of Jupiter indicates extraordinary success in life (*fig. 280*). It also means a brilliant union. If it runs through its usual course in the centre of the hand and ends on the mount of Jupiter, the success of the person will be the result of great ambition. When the Fate line is deep, rises from inside the Life line and ends on the mount of Jupiter (*fig. 281*), the influence of relatives coupled with great ambition makes the career a success. If this line is deep for a while and then becomes defective, the assistance of relatives lasts for a while but does not bring ultimate success.

If the line of Fate goes to the centre of the mount of Jupiter, unusual distinction and power is indicated. Such a person will climb up through his enormous energy, ambition and determination.

b) *On Saturn* : A Fate line going beyond the palm and cutting into the finger of Saturn (*fig. 282*) is not a good sign, and in such cases everything will go too far. For instance, if the person is a leader, his followers will not obey his wishes and orders and will most probably turn against and ruin him. A line of deep red colour and cutting the third phalange of

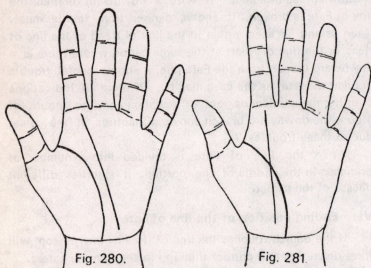

Fig. 280.
Fate line ending on the mount of Jupiter (brilliant union)

Fig. 281.
Fate line starting from the mount of Venus and ending on the mount of Jupiter (success due to relatives)

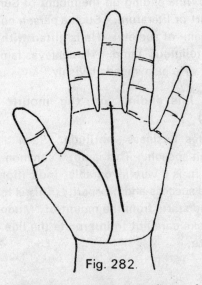

Fig. 282.

Fate line pushing into the finger of
Saturn (unfortunate happenings)

the Saturn finger means dishonourable death or at least imprisonment. A still more threatening indication is seen when there is a star on the first phalange of the Saturn finger.

The Fate line ending on the mount of Saturn gets strong Saturnian characteristics. With a long line so terminating, there is always some trouble to health. It may give constipation. If the line starts from the wrist, and is straight, steady and ends deep into the mount of Saturn, it indicates on a woman's hand a well-to-do spinster who has never married and who is contented with her environment. If the line of Fate terminates into the ring of Saturn, degradation and decline of prosperity is the result.

c) **Fate line ending in a cross**

If the Fate line ends in a cross and if there is a grill on the mount of Mercury, it indicates a violent death due to some evil action of the person.

d) Fate line ending on the mount of Sun (*fig. 283*)

The Fate line ending on the mount of Sun shows celebrity in fine art or literature. Such a person comes in contact with the cream of society. He is gifted with high culture, dignity and religious mind. He achieves fame and success in public life. He also spends lavishly.

e) Fate line ending on the mount of Mercury (*fig. 284*)

It indicates business aptitude. Such a person makes money through speech. This is not a common formation and when found it is a very favourable indication. It indicates great financial success and prosperity. This is more favourable when the line starts from the mount of Moon. In this case we have to take care not to interpret the line of Mercury as the line of Fate.

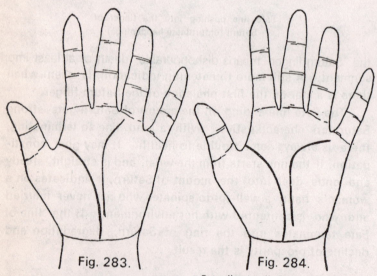

Fig. 283.
Fate line ending on the mount of Sun (celebrity in arts)

Fig. 284.
Fate line ending on the mount of Mercury (financial prosperity)

f) Fate line ending in a star

It indicates misfortune caused by wickedness or errors of others.

A star on the termination of the Fate line and another star at the termination of the Life line in both the hands indicate paralysis (*fig 285*).

g) Fate line ending on the upper Mars (*fig. 286*)

The Fate line ending on upper Mars means violence and love of conquest. It also means that the person achieves success from his leader-ship, power of resistance and courage.

h) Fate line ending on the Head line (*fig. 287*)

If the Fate line ends on the Head line, it shows loss of career through lack of discrimination. It also means a breaking away from an early environment. In case there is a new line beginning before the end of the first line, it means a change towards better conditions. If the Fate line stops at the Head line in both the hands, it signifies misfortune or check to career due to an error in judgement. If however the line of Life ends in a fork the loss is due to sudden shock and not through error in judgement.

i) Fate line ending on Heart line (*fig. 288*)

A Fate line starting from the first rascette and ending on the line of Heart shows serious trouble in love throughout life. In a bad hand, it indicates heart disease. If however the mount of Saturn is much lined, it means insane morbidity. If the Fate line starts from the mount of Moon and ends on the Heart line, it indicates extravagance and disappointment in love. However if this line, instead of ending on the Heart line, merges into the line of Heart, it shows a brilliant marriage (*fig. 289*). Normally, the ending of the Fate line on the Heart line indicates opportunities afforded by circumstances affecting one's affection. It also means loss of career due to a love affair or early retirement.

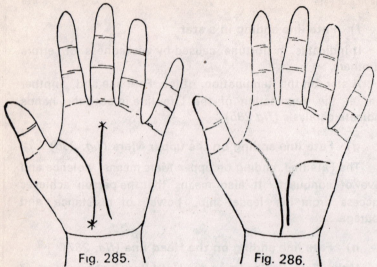

Fig. 285.
Fate line and Life line both ending in star on both the hands (paralysis)

Fig. 286.
Fate line ending on the upper Mars (love of conquest)

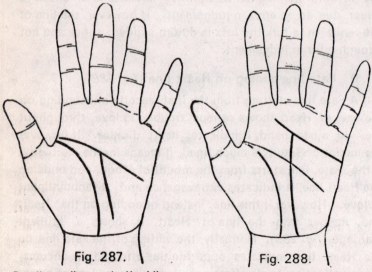

Fig. 287.
Fate line ending on the Head line (loss of career)

Fig. 288.
Fate line starting from 1st rascette and ending on heart line (trouble in love)

Fig. 289.

Fate line merging into the line of Heart (brilliant marriage)

j) Fate line ending in a fork

The ending of the Fate line in a fork is very important and we have to study the direction of the forks. The direction of the fork and their penetration into the neighbouring mounts will give the importance that is attached to the fork. If the Fate line has three prongs (*fig. 290*), one going to the mount of Jupiter, the other to the mount of Saturn and the third one to the mount of Sun, it gives an excellent combination. This shows a combination of ambition, prudence and brilliant intellect. It also means immense wealth, fame, property and all comforts of life.

If the Fate line ends in two powerful branches, one to the mount of Jupiter and the other to the mount of Apollo, it signifies two different and distinct careers existing side by side.

k) Fate line ending in an island

The ending of the Fate line in an island, with downward branches in the line of Life (*fig. 291*), indicates the end of life in unhappy surroundings. It also means loss af money and illness.

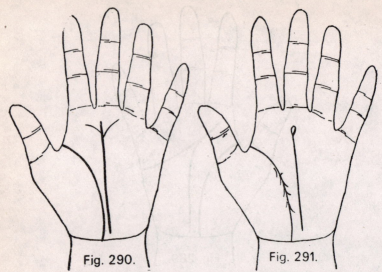

Fig. 290.
Fate line ending in three forks one going to the mount of Jupiter, the other to the mount of Saturn and the third one to the mount of Sun (wealth, fame and comforts)

Fig. 291.
Fate line ending in an island with falling branches in the Life line (unhappy ending of life)

I) Fate line ending on bars and crosses

If we find crosses or bars at the end of the Fate line, it denotes losses and trials in old age. If the bars are faint and do not cut the line of Fate. there are troubles and worries in old age. Great trials and misfortunes will harass the person.

VII) Character of the line

i) Deep line of the Fate

It indicates a believer in fate, who would not make any efforts to help himself. A very deep line denotes anxiety all through life. It also means perseverance in occupation. However, too much straining of will-power may result in paralysis.

ii) Thin and narrow line of Fate

It indicates easy success in undertakings.

iii) Broad and shallow line of Fate

This indicates a condition a little better than no line at all. If other lines are normal and only the Fate line is shallow, it signifies continued struggle. These troubles may be due to lack of healthy environment or inherited illness.

iv) Chained line of Fate (fig. 292)

It means misfortune due to hesitating nature. A chained line of Fate means a hard career. If it is chained during its entire course, the person will have continuous obstructions in his life.

v) Wavy line of Fate (fig. 293)

This formation shows unsteadiness of purpose resulting in a chequered career. It also means a changeable disposition and quarrel-someness.

If in addition to its waviness the line is uneven or defective in other ways, the person will have increased difficulties in his journey through life.

vi) Ladder-like position of the Fate line (fig. 294)

This formation shows continuous obstruction in the career resulting in monetary losses.

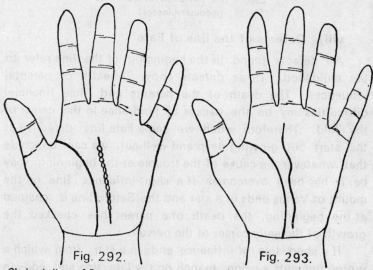

Fig. 292.
Chained line of Fate (misfortune, hard career)

Fig. 293.
Wavy line of Fate (chequrred career, quarrelsomeness)

vii) Poor line of Fate

A poor development of the line at the centre of the hand indicates trouble in one's middle life.

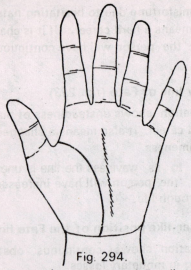

Fig. 294.
Ladder like formation of Fate line
(monetary losses)

viii) Defects of the line of Fate

All defects found in the beginning of the line refer to the childhood. These defects show ill-health of parental influences. The death of the parents and their financial difficulties my be the causes of hindrance in the career of the child. Therefore when we see a Fate line defective at the start but growing deep and well-cut, we can conclude that, whatever the cause of the trouble at the beginning may be. it has been overcome. If a short influence line on the mount of Venus ends in a star and the Saturn line is chained at the beginning, the death of a parent has checked the growth of the early career of the person.

If a short line of influence ends in a star, from which a worry line cuts a rising branch on the Life line and ends in an island on the line of the Head, it signifies that the death of a parent has brought on a check to the upward course of the person's life.

Usually, there are two places where the Fate line shows the greatest number of defects. The first is at the start and the second period is between 32 and 45 years of age, which is covered in the space between the Head and Heart lines. This is the critical time in business careers and is the formative financial period in life.

1) Breaks

a) Breaks in the line of Fate are not necessarily a bad formation and an unbroken line of Saturn indicates only a safe career for a person. It does not show success or brilliance. Similarly, a broken line of Fate need not be considered as a bad line ; on the contrary, a number of breaks indicates continuous changes and many times, change for the better. We may consider the break as a waiting period. It may mean financial difficulty through a loss of job or business or it may mean a serious change in life. If the break is over-lapping *(fig.295)*, the difficulties may not keenly be felt. A broad break in the line, below the line of Head, shows an entire change of surroundings.

If the line of Fate is broken and cut by many bars, the person experiences a succession of unfortunate incidents. However this deficiency of the line of Fate can be made up by a very good mount and finger of Saturn.

b) If the line of Fate is broken in the Quadrangle *(fig. 296)* and again starts from the line of Heart, it signifies that the fortune will be retrieved by the assistance of one of the opposite sex. This is more true if there is a good line of Apollo appearing at this period. This also indicates a hard life and physical and mental strain.

c) If the Fate line starts with a fork with one prong of the fork from the mount of Moon and the line itself is broken at the forking point, it is a sign of danger of death by drowning *(fig. 297)*.

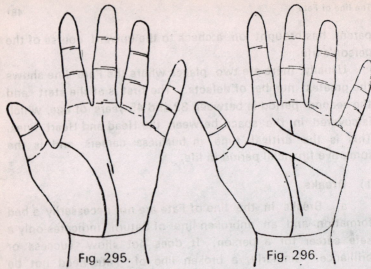

Fig. 295.
Overlapping break in Fate line
(difficulties overcome)

Fig. 296.
Fate line broken in the quadrangle and
again starting from the line of Heart
(fortune due to opposite sex, physical
and moral strain)

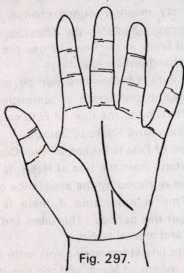

Fig. 297.
Fate line starting from a fork, one
prong from mount of Moon, and the
line broken at the fork (danger of
drowning)

The line of Fate

d) If we come across a break in the Fate line and the over-lapping line ends on the mount of Jupiter, it denotes a second union of the person on the date of the break (*fig. 298*).

e) A strong line of voyage on the mount of Moon with a break in the Fate line shows a career abroad.

If the line of Fate is broken and at the same time is wavy, it shows ill-health due to the abuse of some kind of pleasure.

2) Island

a) An island on the line of Fate, with a star on the mount of Jupiter, indicates a guilty love-affair with one in much higher position. If the star is on the mount of Sun, the loved person will be an artist or a literary man. If the star is on the mount of Mercury, the loved one will be a businessman or a person concerned with scientific activities.

b) An island in the line of Fate ending in a fork but between the line of Head and the line of Heart shows divorce

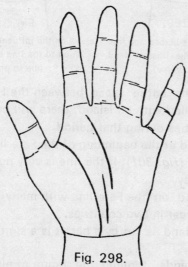

Fig. 298.
Overlapping line on the break in Fate line ending on mount of Jupiter (second marriage)

resulting from the person's leading astray an innocent girl (*fig. 299*).

c) An island on a line of influence from the mount of Moon to the line of Fate means misfortune resulting from the union (*fig. 300*).

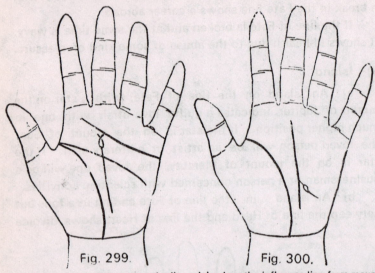

Fig. 299.
Island ending in a fork across the line of Fate and between the lines of Head and Heart (divorce)

Fig. 300.
Island on the influence line from mount of Moon to the line of Fate (misfortune due to union)

d) When the entire space between the Head and the Heart lines are filled with an island, there will be continuous financial difficulties during that period.

e) An island at the beginning of the Fate line shows the mystery of birth (*fig. 301*). If the line is very poor, the island shows illegitimacy.

f) An island on the Fate line with many short voyage lines shows interest in two countries.

g) If an island is cut by a bar, it is a sign of separation by death.

h) Two islands, forming the figure of eight '8' at the starting of the Fate line, indicates the gift of second sight (*fig. 302*).

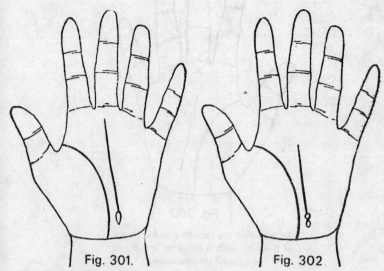

Fig. 301.
Fate line starting with an island (mystery of birth)

Fig. 302.
Fate line starting from two islands (figure of eight) (gift of second sight)

i) An island on the Fate line on the mount of Uranus, with a cross on the mount of Saturn (*fig 303*), signifies rigorous imprisonment.

j) An island on the higher side of the Fate line and towards the centre is an evil sign of unlicenced passion.

From the above, it will be clear that the islands on the Fate line have many different interpretations. Often it indicates a guilty intrigue or it may also mean marriage trouble or periods of anxiety. It also shows troublesome periods of loss of money or position.

3) Cross bars

If the Fate line is cut with cross bars, the person will meet with obstacles in his career. If the Fate line passes through these bars and severs them, the person will overcome the difficulties. Cross-bars always indicate obstructions. Each bar is a separate obstruction and by noting the depth of each bar we can know the seriousness of it.

Fig. 303.

An island on the Fate line on the mount of Uranus, with a cross on the mount of Saturn (imprisonment)

4) Uneven Fate line

If the Fate line is uneven that is if it is alternately deep and thin in character, the person will have intermittent periods of prosperity. This line indicates an unreliable and varying state of affairs.

IX) Double line of Fate

A double line of Fate is a good sign as it denotes two distinct careers which the person will follow. It indicates an eventful life or a career influenced by someone else. It signifies two distinct occupations. It also means a separate environment at home and in public life.

A double line of Fate in the middle of the palm shows good things for others and not to oneself. If the other Fate line starts from the line of Heart and is not clear or straight, it gives worry to the person.

If the other line of Fate runs close to the wavy and chained Fate line, there is unhappiness and misfortune due to the hesitating nature of the person.

The line of Fate

X) Fate line in relation to other lines

1) Deep lines from the line of Heart cutting the Fate line shows painful love affairs, which injure the financial prospects of the person. They also mean widowhood on the date the line of Fate is cut.

2) Deep lines from the line of Head cutting the line of Fate shows financial troubles due fo the law-suits.

If the Fate line starts late on the hand, with a defective Head line at the start, the person will have difficulties in early age due to brain weakness.

3) If the line of Fate starts from the mount of Moon and merges into a good line of Heart, it shows a brilliant marriage.

4) If the Fate line starts independently in the beginning and then joins the line of Life for sometime from which it is again separated, it signifies that the family circumstances prevent the independent action of the person but later on the person is left to his own decisions. Large space between the line of Fate and the line of Life shows success in life on account of direct contact with the public. It indicates individuality and an independent spirit.

5) The line of Fate when too much tied to the line of Life shows family surroundings which stand in the way of the career of the person. The nearer the line of Fate to the Life line, the person will have to share more responsibilities of the family.

6) A line from the mount of Mercury touching the line of Fate on the mount of Moon speaks of luck.

7) If the Fate line is deep and irregular in a much rayed hand, it is a sign of the constant irritability and extreme nervous disposition. The person will be vexed at the trivial things and his career will suffer due to his uneven temper.

8) If the Fate line is stronger than the line of Sun, the special talents and ideals of life remain undeveloped and unfruitful on account of adverse circumstances.

9) If a line from the mount of Moon crosses the line of Fate and proceeds towards the line of Life and at the same time two parallel lines start from the line of Fate (where the line from the mount of Moon crosses the line of Fate) and these two lines point towards the mount of Mercury, the person has to go on a foreign voyage.

10) When the Fate line after crossing the Heart line ends in a trident and if the Heart line is forked with one branch going to the mount of Jupiter, it is considered as a fortunate sign. Such a person has magnetic personality, romantic disposition and idealistic love.

With relevent marking on the hand and with a good line of Sun, the line of Fate will mean good fortune and achievements in one's career. With good mounts of Uranus and Neptune the line of Fate indicates spiritual heights and accomplishments in occult studies.

It is necessary to study both the hands in the case of the line of Fate. If on the left hand the line of Fate begins low in the hand but on the right hand it starts at a higher level in the hand, we may say that the natural course of the line was favourable but some difficulties have caused a late rise in the career of the person. The reason my be health, laziness of the family or friends influence. The absence of the Fate line at the place where it normally begins will often be explained as difficulties or accidents to the parents.

XI) Line of influence

A line of influence that cuts the line of Fate weakens the Fate line, whereas the one which runs along the Fate line strengthens the same.

1) Long and short lines running parallel to the Fate line show the influence of persons of the opposite sex on one's destiny. Whether the influence will be favourable or harmful will be determined by the course of the Fate line after the influence line. If the Fate line improves, it is favourable. If however there is an island in the Fate line, the influence is harmful. If the influence line itself is islanded, the influ-

encing person will have dishonour, disgrace or misfortune in his career. A good parallel line between the lines of Head and Heart indicates a brilliant marriage.

2) The line of influence may be either from the side of the mount of Moon or from the mount of Venus.

a) Influence lines from the mount of Moon

This line may have different interpretations. It may mean either a marriage or a foreign travel or a new start in life.

b) An influence line from the mount of Moon running as a sister line for a short time means financial gains in early life. It also indicates a favourable influence in partnership or a marriage which has benefitted the person's career. If this is found on both the hands, it conveys two careers followed simultaneously.

c) If the influence line starts high on the mount of Moon or from the negative mount of Mars and merges in the line of Fate, it shows vanity and not love. It may end either in intimacy or even marriage.

d) If the influence line from the mount of Moon merges into the Fate line and if the line of Marriage is marked on the hand, it means marriage in the case of woman and healthy influence in the case of man.

e) If the influence line from the mount of Moon cuts the line of Fate, it indicates broken engagement, a divorce or an unhappy union. If this influence line breaks on reaching the line of Fate and ends abruptly, it is a sign of misfortune in love affair or it shows a shock caused by the death or the accident.

f) If the influence line rises towards the Fate line but does not touch it, the love affair may not end in marriage. This is more true if there is no marriage line on the mount of Mercury.

g) If the influence line is more clear and stronger than the line of Fate, the person will be ruled by the one he marries.

h) If this line of influence is cut before it reaches the Fate line by an influence line from the mount of Venus, it signifies family opposition to the marriage.

i) An island on the line of influence on the mount of Moon is a sign of misfortune to the person as a result of the union.

j) If the influence line has a branch reaching the mount of Sun, it is an excellent indication of fame and fortune resulting from the marriage. This is more so if there exists a star or a cross on the mount of Jupiter.

k) If a line of Saturn is cut by a line from the influence line on the mount of Venus and the Saturn line is broken for the rest of the course, the influence will cause serious disaster. If from the influence line a chance line runs to the mount of Jupiter, the ambition of the wife or the husband will lead the person to the extravagance which he cannot afford. If the Fate line is defective thereafter, the person will never recover from the reverses.

l) If the Fate line is cut by a worry line from the line of Life, ill-health will be a bar to the progress of the person. If the Saturn line is defective thereafter, the person will never be able to get over it.

m) If a line of influence from the mount of Mercury cuts the Fate line on a bad Mercurian hand, the dishonesty of the person will bring him grief. (also see page 489)

The combination of these cutting lines will be infinite. In some hands we may notice several such influence lines. In these cases every cutting line is to be studied carefully. Many influence lines run towards the Fate line but they do not touch it. These lines are only influences which are possible menaces. If the Fate line is thin or defective in any way whereas the line of influence is deep and strong, it adds to the prosperity of the person and assists him to overcome his difficulties. If in the beginning a Fate line be chained or otherwise defective and a chance line merges into it after which it becomes deep, the influence which has come into the life has improved the condition of the person. If the influence line comes from the mount of Moon, it will bring some outside influence, whereas if it comes from the mount of Venus, it will have the influence of the close relatives.

XII) Signs on the Fate line

1) *Bars* : A number of bars on the mount of Saturn and crossing the line of Fate relate to obstacles constantly arising in life. If the line of Fate is good throughout, these obstacles will arise only late in life. It is to be noted that many of these important readings have a general application and are not limited to the period shown by the signs. Many bars in a ladder-like fashion indicate succession of misfortunes. They may also mean imprisonment. If the bars are enclosed by a square, the evil results will be minimised.

2) *Cross* : A cross on the line of Fate at its termination with a grill on the mount of Mercury is an indication of violent death due to some evil doing by the person.

A cross or a break on the Fate line shows the most critical change in the person's existence. A cross without a break shows disastrous change if found at the centre of the line.

A cross attached to the line of Fate inside the quadrangle with smooth fingers and the first phalange of the first finger well-developed, gives consolation from religious faith.

A cross near the line of Fate and between Fate and Life lines signifies an event which will affect a relative's life.

3) *Star :* A star on the Fate line is not a favourable sign and shows the danger on the date shown on the Fate line.

A star at the starting of the line of Fate means loss of fortune or great trouble to the parents. If in addition the star is found on the mount of Venus, it shows death of one of the parents.

A star at the termination of the Fate line with another star on the mount of Moon shows a tendency to suicide.

4) *Triangle* : A triangle touching the Fate line and in between the Fate line and the Life line with strongly marked mount of Mars shows a fight or military success (*fig. 304*).

A triangle on the Fate line indicates a monotonous life in which one is contented with one's lot (*fig. 305*).

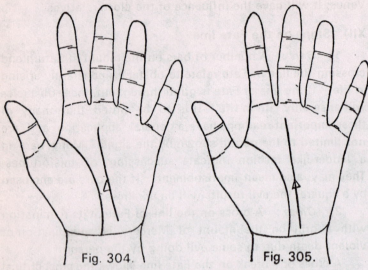

Fig. 304.
A triangle inbetween the Fate line and the Life line and touching the Fate line (military success)

Fig. 305.
A triangle on the Fate line (monotonous life)

5) *Square* : A square on the Fate line protects the person from loss of money or business. A square touching the line of Fate in the plain of Mars foretells danger from accidents. It will be in relation to home life, if the square is on the side of the Life line. It denotes danger in travel, if it is on the side of the mount of Moon.

CHAPTER XX

The Line of Heart

I) Introduction

The next line we have to study is the line of Heart. This is so named because it reflects accurately the condition and operation of the heart. There is no definite position for the starting or ending of this line. This line is also significant regarding the sentiments and affections of the person. Thus the Heart line represents the circulation of the blood and the functioning of the heart as far as health is concerned and the affections on the moral and mental world.

The line of Heart represents the human personality in its most subtle aspect. From it, we can know the inner conscience of man, his expression of human elements, his sense of morality and social conduct and also his reaction to the instinct of sex association. In all these aspects we can study not the behaviour but the attitude, not the action but the thought of the person. The line of Heart is capable of tracing the more abstract, the more incomprehensible and the more subtle faculties of the person which ultimately decide the character and the personality.

The line of Heart represents the higher qualities of the person, especially in its attitudes to the spiritual, the moral and the sexual impression. In the case of the line of Heart, the discriminating values of right or wrong, moral or immoral are more a matter of feeling than of reasoning.

The line of Heart reveals the qualities of love and attachment, affection and sentiment in greater or lesser degree. When the line reveals conflicting, destructive or negative characteristics, it must be accepted that love is repressed by hatred, attachment by repulsion and sympathy and sentiment by callousness.

The course of the line of Heart covers all the mounts at the base of the fingers. It has close contact with the upper mount of Mars and the line of Head. Therefore the Heart line acquires all the characteristics of these mounts as well as the line of Head. Thus the line of Heart acquires the ambition and the inspiration of the mount of Jupiter, the sobriety and the wisdom of Saturn, the energy and the intelligence of Sun, the wisdom of Mercury, the steadfastness of the upper Mars and the higher influence of the line of Head.

The length of the line of Heart shows the degree of the heart element present in the individual. Any shortness is indicative of a certain want in that direction. However it should not be misunderstood as heartlessness. It may be stated in a general way that too much of the line of Heart produces jealously to a fault. Too short a line indicates a material type of person which likes violence and not affection.

A Heart line devoid of branches through all its length, even though it may be well and clearly traced, speaks of want of affection and dryness of heart. Longevity and Heart line : see seperate chapter at the beginning of this book.

Absence of the Heart line

Absence of the line of Heart is rarely seen. We may occasionally come across a hand with only one line crossing the hand below the mounts and we shall be at a loss to know whether it is the Head or the Heart line. However if we consider that the lines are controlled by the brain and not by the heart, we have to presume that the Head line will always be present, being the indicator of the brain which controls and produces all the lines. When a single line is seen occupying a position which is relatively at a place where the Head line ought to be, it should be classed as the Head line and the Heart line is considered to be absent.

In order that this single line be considered as a Heart line and not the Head line, it must rise high towards the mount on the hand.

When the Heart line is absent, it speaks of a lack of sympathy and the affectionate disposition and warns us of one who is cold blooded and selfish and who desires personal success even at the expense of others. It is a bad marking which easily leads from mere selfishness into hypocrisy, deceit and positive dishonesty. The absence of the Heart line is to be interpreted in relation to other mounts and signs on the hand. On a bad Mercurian, it means a natural temptation towards dishonesty. If the finger of Mercury is crooked and twisted and the nails are narrow and short, the person cannot be trusted. He will lie, swindle, cheat, steal or do anything to get money. This is the hand of a typical cold-blooded brute.

On a Martian, the absence of the Heart line would mean unscrupulousness and cold-bloodedness. On provocation this type will become blood-thirsty and is very dangerous.

On a Saturnian the absence of the Heart line is a distressing indication. It will add to his natural hatred of mankind.

On the hand of a Jupiterian, the absence of the Heart line is rarely found, but if found, one of the traits described above will be prominent.

On the hand of an Apollonian, we may come across a defective Heart line but not an absence of it. The same is the case with the Venusian.

On a hand of a Lunarian, we may find the absence of the Heart line which will make him cold and selfish.

The absence of the Heart line, with the negative mount of Mars in prominence, shows cruelty. As health indicator, there will be susceptibility to haemorrage.

Absence of the Heart line is a grave warning of the character of the person. With other bad indications on the hand, it depicts a character completely devoid of feeling or sympathy for the opposite sex. It often develops into criminal acts of the most brutal nature. In a good hand things cannot be so bad.

II) Position on the hand

The line of Heart rises from some point under or near the finger of Jupiter and traces its way across the hand under the mounts ending on the percussion. It is not proper to say that this line has any normal place or normal ending place. This is because what might be normal with one person would not be so with another. So the line of Heart must always be considered in relation to individual on whose hand it is seen.

III) Normal position

A good line of Heart should start from the centre of the mount of Jupiter and should end on the percussion between the mounts of Mercury and Upper Mars. It should not be too closely associated with the line of Head nor keep too broad a space in between. The starting should be sharp and not blunt and the termination should not be abrupt. The line should be even in its course, even in breadth, depth and colour. Such a line of Heart speaks of a loveable personality, characterised by a happy and healthy attitude. It denotes the right type of emotional approach to persons and problems. It shows one who is conscientious, firm, reliable with a high sense of duty and unselfish devotion to love and friendship. He has strong sentiments and cares for others, as much as he wants others to care for him.

When the line of Heart is placed very high on the hand and close to the fingers (*fig. 306*), it absorbs the qualities of the Girdle of Venus which has its normal place where the present line of Heart is located. The higher placing of the Heart line reduces the qualities and energies of the mounts under the fingers. It will lead to violent passion and jealousy. A person with this type of Heart line is exceedingly calculating in love-affair.

If the Heart line is placed low on the hand, it does not absorb the qualities of the mounts *(fig. 307)*. This results in disturbing the mounts of Uranus and creates unhealthy closeness to the line of Head. Such a person is emotionally dull, indifferent cold and selfish.

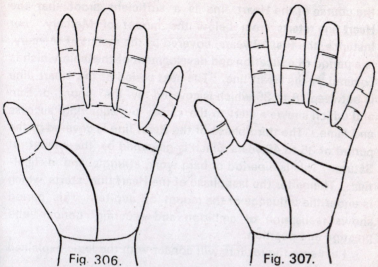

Fig. 306.	Fig. 307.
Heart line placed very high on the hand (violent passion and jealousy)	Heart line placed very low on the hand (cold and selfish nature)

When the Heart line is very low on the hand and with lines connecting it to the line of Head, there will be a mixing up of emotion and reason. In a bad hand the lower line of Heart will indicate avarice, duplicity and cruelty.

IV) Starting of the Heart line

There is basically a difference of opinion between the Hindu and Western scholars as to the starting position of the Heart line. According to the Western convention, the line starts on the mount of Jupiter from where it slopes down from beneath the mounts under the fingers and ends on the percussion under the mount of Mercury. According to the Hindu method, it starts under the mount of Mercury There are good many reasons to believe that the Hindu convention is correct. The arguments are as under.

1) Normally, the line at the start is thick and the same becomes thin during its course and at the end.

2) The changes, if any line take place only towards its termination point.

3) The period covered by the different mounts during the course of the Heart line is a sufficient proof that the Heart line starts from below the mount of Mercury. For instance, the first 18 years, covered by the mount of Mercury, is a period of education and development of the brain which is covered by the Heart line. The next period of the Heart line is between 18 to 35 which is covered by the mount of Sun and which shows a start to the career by acquiring success and fame. The third phase of the Heart line is covered by the period of 35 to 45 years which is governed by the mount of Saturn. This is a period of hard work, struggle and difficulties. Thereafter the last phase of the Heart line starts which is under the influence of the mount of Jupiter. This period shows realisation of ambition and securing honour and prestige and position.

I am sure the readers will concur with the logic explained above.

However it seems that the subject of palmistry is dominated by the Western thought. We shall therefore consider the origin of the starting point of the Heart line from beneath the mount of Jupiter and deal with the line accordingly.

1) There are various starting points for the line of Heart but there are three main positions from which the line starts.

a) Rising from the mount of Jupiter : This shows the development of the sentimental side to the affection. The person's love is ideal. To him, love is an adoration and to love a person in poverty is attractive.

b) Rising between the Jupiter and Saturn fingers : It shows affection which is practical and based on commonsense. Such a person is not carried away with sentiment but loves a person from the practical point of view. He does not believe in love in a cottage without plenty of bread and butter. He is strong in affection and is also sensible but not foolish.

c) Rising from the mount of Saturn : This shows sensualism in the affection for the one whose love is tinged with an idea of pleasure from sexual relation. This is infallible if the mount of Venus is large and of pink or red colour and with a strong line of Life.

When the line of Heart starts from all the above three points (*fig. 308*), we have a combination of sentiment, commonsense and passion. It means that the heart is the strongest factor in the making up of the person and a very fine Head line and a strong thumb must be present to prevent the heart from ruling the head. With this strong formation, we should try to find out which of the three lines is the deepest so that we can know whether sentiment, commonsense or the passion is the strongest force. This produces an affectionate person who has a warm heart and loves friends, relations and mankind in general.

2) We shall now study further the starting positions of the Heart line.

A) **Heart line starting from the mount of Jupiter** (*fig. 309*)

1) **From the third phalange of the Jupiter finger** (*fig. 309-a*) : It leads to lack of success in all the directions. This is because the person is over-emotional and he does not bring his reason and logic into play. This is typical of an exaggeration of a good line wherein the best qualities turn out to be a defect. This type of line represents the blind enthusiast who is so carried away by his pride that he can see no faults in the person to whom he is so much devoted or adores. Such people are the sufferers in the world of affections.

2) **Heart line starting from the base of the Jupiter finger** (*fig. 309 b*) : It gives one an ideal love without sensuality. This line can be seen to run almost straight without a deep curve which is noticeable in other types of formation.

3) **Heart line starting from the middle of Jupiter mount** (*fig. 309 c*) : This shows the highest type of love which is pure, deep and steady.

4) **Heart line starting from the base of Jupiter mount** (*fig. 309 d*) : The Heart line thus starting and going

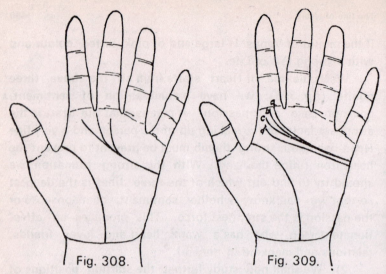

Fig. 308.
Heart line starting from all the three positions, *viz.,* mount of Jupiter, between Jupiter and Saturn fingers, and from the mount of Saturn (sentiment, common sense and passion)

Fig. 309.
Heart line starting from, a) 3rd phalange of Jupiter finger, b) base of Jupiter finger, c) middle of Jupiter mount, d) base of Jupiter mount

straight across the hand has a feminine touch with its mental or psychic approach. There is ideality and also jealousy. If this line is without any branches under Jupiter, it signifies poverty and misfortune. If the Heart line runs from the border of the mount of Jupiter, the person is very passionate and sometimes commits criminal acts of sex.

5) **Heart line encircling the mount of Jupiter** (*fig. 310*) : With this formation the person is jealous. The encircling is somewhat similar to the ring of Solomon, whereby love appears to be more ideal than sensual. It gives a marvellous faculty for occultism. If it is seen on both the hands, the person is religious and is blessed by a competent Master.

6) **Heart line curving downward on the mount of Jupiter at the start** (*fig. 311*) : In this case, there will be great disppointment in love and especially from those who may be trusted as friends. There may be treachery, cruelty and sometimes even death through the affection. Such people

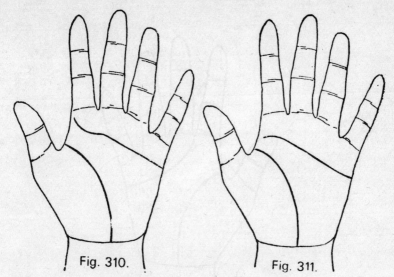

Fig. 310.
Heart line encircling the mount of Jupiter (jealousy, ideal love, occultism)

Fig. 311.
Heart line starting with a downward curve on the mount of Jupiter (disappointment in love)

often have their affections misplaced and seldom reciprocated. They lack the perception in knowing whom to love. They often marry below their status in life.

B) Heart line starting between Jupiter and Saturn mounts (*fig. 312*)

This shows commonsense and practical approach to the affection. Such a person is not carried away by sentiments but views love from a practical standpoint. Such individuals seem to rest between the ideality given by Jupiter and the passionate ardour given by Saturn. They are quiet and subdued in their passions.

In this case, where physical attraction has been placed in by the affection, the person suspects the character of the wife and is also an accuser of illicit contacts with other men. A Heart line without branches gives one the inability to adapt to the nature of others and the person prefers a lonely life.

C) Heart line starting from the mount of Saturn
1) The person will have more passion in his attachment

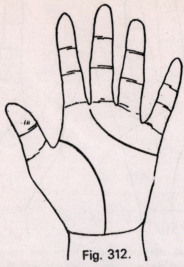

Fig. 312.
Heart line starting between Jupiter and Saturn mounts (common sense, practical love)

and will be more or less selfish in satisfying his ambition. At home, he is not demonstrative and expressive. The excess of the quality is shown when the Heart line rises very high on the mount of Saturn. This formation also shows the typical hypocrite. This is more prominent on the hand of women, who have no scruples in stimulating love and warmth of feeling in executing their designs on their men-victims. They design to lead men to ruin, without any way of feeling about it. Attachment may be strong but not pure. It is of the material type, selfish, sensual and bold. On a soft hand the qualities of this line are found in a greater degree.

If the line of Heart is pale in colour and with chained formation, there is contempt for the opposite sex.

The line of Heart starting from the mount of Saturn when short, indicates the premature death of the person. This is more so, if there is seen in addition a cross at the same time on the line of Heart.

2) **Heart line starting from the finger of Saturn** (*fig. 313*) : In this case, there is an exaggeration of passion, sensuality and selfishness.

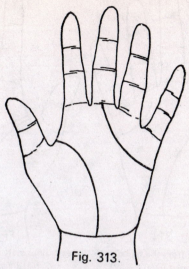

Fig. 313.
Heart line starting from finger of Saturn (passion and selfishness)

D) Heart line starting from the mount of Sun (fig. 314)

It shows the capacity for intense love, though outwardly jealous and selfish. If the Fate line is poor, the person is unsuccessful in love and life.

E) Heart line starting with a bent downwards

Sometimes the line of Heart inclines to fall towards the line of Head at the start. This shows that the Head line is powerful and when it comes to a choice between sentiment and utility, the head will rule the heart. This also indicates that the heart is in sorrow and faces misfortunes.

If the Heart line actually starts from the line of Head, there is pecuniary loss in commercial enterprises (fig. 315).

F) Heart line starting from the Life line

In this case it denotes a character with strong willpower and the person desires everything in his own way, be it good or bad. It reflects a strong sex impulse and the determination to gratify the same.

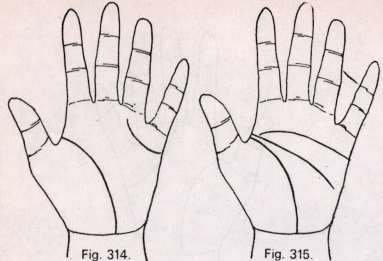

Fig. 314.
Heart line starting from the mount of Sun (intense love)

Fig. 315.
Heart line starting from the line of Head (monetary loss)

G) Heart line starting from Head and Life lines (*fig. 107*)

If the Heart line joins the line of Head and line of Life at its start, it is a very ominous indication of sudden and violent death to which the person is as it were driven by fate. No kind of precaution will be of any help against it. It indicates only fatality. If this joining of the Heart line is at a higher level of the hand and below the mount of Jupiter, it leads to great unhappiness through the affection. If in addition there is a cross on the line of Head, sudden death of a violent nature is confirmed. The date of the accident can be ascertained on the line of Life or on the line of Fate. If this indication is found on both the hands, the result is sure.

H) Starting from Head line only

It indicates deep grief due to misplaced love. It may also mean grief through the loss of a dear person. If a small line crosses the Heart line at the time of its touching the Head line, it is a sign of miserable marriage (*fig. 316*).

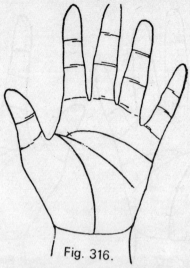

Fig. 316.
Small line crossing the Heart line at the time, the Heart line touches the Head line (miserable marriage)

A Heart line joining the line of Head under the mount of Saturn (*fig. 317*) is a sign of disaster due to unreasonable passion. It also means fatal events and great danger to life. A small bar crossing the Heart line at this juncture shows deep sorrow from misplaced affection or a wretched marriage.

I) **Heart line starting from the positive mount of Mars** (*fig. 318*)

A Heart line starting from within the line of Life and on the mount of Mars shows an irritable and quarrelsome person who tries to be perfect in all matters of affection and love.

J) **Heart line starting from a fork**

The line of Heart can have one or several forks and we have to study each formation separately.

Sometimes the line of Heart will start in several forks on the mount of Jupiter alone in which case it increases the sentimentality of a single line. The general principle is that a single line tends to make the affection more narrow and the person loves family and friends strongly but does not reach

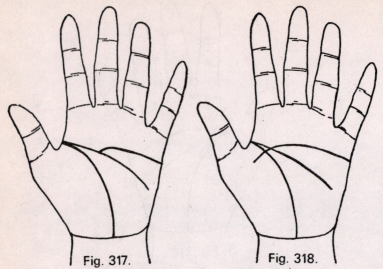

Fig. 317.
Heart line joining the Head line under the mount of Saturn (disaster due to passions, fatal events)

Fig. 318.
Heart line starting from the positive mount of Mars (quarrelsome and irritable nature)

out to everybody as does the one whose Heart line is forked at the start.

a) A fork on the mount of Jupiter signifies a successful married life. If one branch of the fork goes between the first and second fingers, it is a sign of a happy and tranquil nature, good fortune and happiness in affection. It indicates a home-loving nature and sincerity in affection conducive to happiness. The love that is bestowed is reciprocated.

b) When the fork is so wide that one branch rises on the Jupiter and the other on Saturn, it denotes a very uncertain disposition of one who is not inclined to make the marital relations happy due to his erratic temperament,

c) If the fork is at the edge of the mount of Jupiter with three prongs, it signifies good fortune (*fig. 319*).

d) The same formation as above but one prong going upto the mount of Jupiter shows happy love. If in addition there is a cross on the mount of Venus, it indicates the only one.

e) A fork at the start with one prong towards the mount of Saturn and the other towards the line of Head but

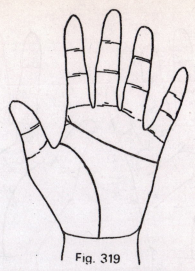

Fig. 319

A fork with three prongs at the edge of the mount of Jupiter (good fortune, happy love)

not touching it signifies self-deception. It causes many evils and losses (*fig. 320*).

    f) A trident like formation at the start of the Heart line on the mount of Jupiter (*fig. 321*) gives the power of control over others and depth of affection. It shows the capacity for organising humanitarian work. When the trident formation is on the line that starts between the fingers of Jupiter and Saturn, it signifies emotional outlook.

K) **Heart line starting from an Island** (*fig. 322*)

A Heart line starting from an island under the mount of Jupiter signifies throat and lung troubles.

V) **Course of the line of Heart**

During the course of the line of Heart we have to study the variations in the direction of the line. We have to study how the line is reflected, how long it runs in this course, the character of the line during the change in this course and the age at which it occurs. It is this minute analysis of the course of the Heart line that gives its complete history as

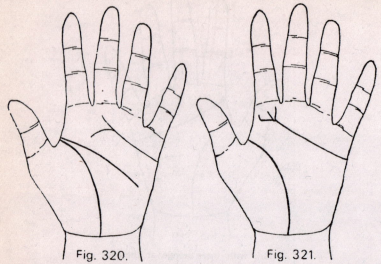

Fig. 320.
Fork at the start in Heart line, one prong going to the mount of Saturn and other to the Head line (self-deception)

Fig. 321.
Trident like formation of the Heart line, on the mount of Jupiter (power of control on others)

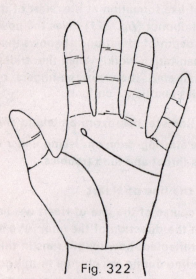

Fig. 322.
Heart line starting from an island under the mount of Jupiter (throat and lung troubles)

The line of Heart

applied to the person, the events that go with it, as well as the age at which they occur.

With the exception of Jupiter where it starts, the normal line of Heart takes its course from the lower boundary of the mounts of Saturn, Sun and Mercury ending just on the percussion. We shall now study the different courses the line takes.

a) Heart line rising towards the mounts : If in its course the line of Heart rises to any mount *(fig. 323)*, it shows that the attraction of the mount is very strong and that the person will love the qualities and friends belonging to that type of mount. We shall not often see the line rising to more than one mount and if it so rises under the mount, it indicates the age at which the strongest attraction will occur in that direction. If the person has attraction at other ages, they will be shown by a chance line leaving the Heart line and running to the mount to which it is attracted.

In case the line so rises to a particular mount and loses itself in the mount and ends there, instead of at its usual

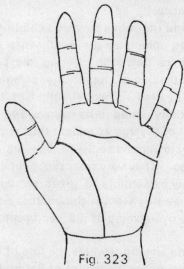

Fig. 323
Heart line rising to mount of Sun in its course (apollonian friends)

stopping place, it shows that the attraction has ended in affection and that the heart has surrendered completely. If it merely rises and then resumes its normal course, it shows that the attraction occurred but did not master the person. The deflection of the Heart line towards a particular mount indicates that the people of that type of mount attract the person greatly and exert a strong influence over him. These people form his ideal and we can describe the kind of persons one likes best and how they look, by describing the appearance of the type of the mount to which the line is deflected.

b) Heart line rising high towards the mounts : When the line of Heart rises far apart from the line of Head, it shows an obstinate nature and an extrovert, who treats the world wild with undue importance. He will grab things by force. We have already dealt with this formation while studying the line of Head. On the contrary we may find a large gap between the Head and the Heart lines. This is also a bad indication, more in respect of character and morality than from the point of health. This is a very serious indication which no other favourable indication can sufficiently counterbalance.

c) Heart line inclining towards the line of Head : In this case the head dominates the sentiments and reasoning and logic are more powerful. During the period the line deflects towards the line of Head, the person is avaricious selfish and cold-hearted. This deflection of the Heart line can take place at any period in its course. The point at which it begins will tell of the age at which this tendency begins. These deflection towards the Head line are in an infinite variety of degrees. They vary from slight curvings of the line which are scarcely perceptible to great swoops downwards. In whatever degree it is seen, it shows the pulling force of the head and the overcoming of the sentimental side of the person's nature.

The Heart line sinking towards the line of Head with an exaggerated curve under the mount of Saturn or the Sun and thus making a very narrow Quadrangle, creates a mean disposition. This is more so if the fingers are smooth and the tips are square. The Heart line, sinking towards the line as above and forming a very narrow Quadrangle and with a prominent mount of Moon, indicates duplicity. In this case imagination is added to a mean and selfish disposition which results in lying.

Inclining towards the line of Head as above, the line of Head connected at the start with the line of Life for a long time signifies stiffness and formality in manner and disposition. With a narrow Quadrangle, if the line of Mercury is poor and wavy, it leads to asthma and hay fever.

A small gap between the lines of Head and the Heart is a sign of unhappiness in affection.

d) Heart line cutting the line of Head (*fig. 324*) : There are cases where the line of Heart is deflecting downward and during its course cuts the line of Head instead of merging with it or going back to its original course. In this case serious injury or damage to the Head is indicated. At the time the cutting takes place, the person will have either

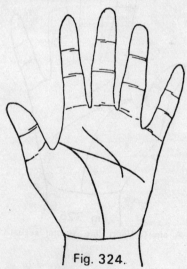

Fig. 324.

Heart line cutting the Head line (brain fever or death)

an unbalancing of the mental faculties or serious brain fever or death. This marking is a sure sign of disaster. It may also mean impairment of brain or paralysis. It will also be worth considering the mount of the hand to which the person belongs. A Jupiterian is disposed to apoplexy, a Saturnian to paralysis, the Apollonian to blindness and heart trouble and a Mercurian to nervousness and biliousness. A Lunarian and Venusian are not likely to have these markings. A Martian with excess blood supply is likely to have apoplexy. We may also study the line of Life and the line of Fate of the age shown on the Head line.

e) Short line of Heart (*fig. 325*) : A short and straight Heart line is a sign of brutal and selfish sexual tendency. If with this line, the will phalange of the thumb is strong, feelings will be under absolute control. The shorter the line of Heart the lesser the higher love works.

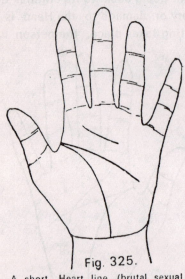

Fig. 325.
A short Heart line (brutal sexual tendency)

A short line of Heart stopping abruptly gives little affection for others. At the age indicated by the termination

The line of Heart

of the line, there will be a very serious difficulty and probably the heart may stop suddenly.

f) Long Heart line : A long line of Heart indicates an emotional nature. The longer the line the earlier is the sex development. If a long Heart line starts on the mount of Jupiter and if the Girdle of Venus is present, it means that a potential attitude will inspire one's profession or mode of life.

A long, clear and well-traced line of Heart gives lasting affection.

If the Heart line crosses the entire hand (*fig. 326*), it shows that the person has too much of heart and he will allow sentiments to guide him in every thing. In business, he will choose the employees not because they are best fitted to do the work but because they need a job. In all the walks of life he will be guided by sentiments. He is jealous and loves much but suffers if he does not get love in return. The desire for love will be an obssession and a tormenting influ-

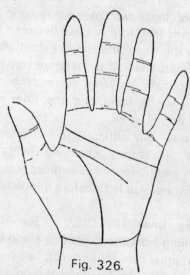

Fig. 326.
Heart line crossing the entire hand
(unhappiness and tyranny in love)

ence. There will be continuous unhappiness and tyranny in love.

When this straight line is stiff and stretched like a straight bar, it is still a bad sign.

If the Heart line crosses from side to side, with a developed mount of Moon, it signifies jealousy carried too far.

The Heart line, joined in a wavy termination to the line of Head under the mount of Mercury shows premature death.

We have studied above the course of the line of Heart and we find that every variation in its course means a change in the qualities for which it stands.

g) The lines of Head and Heart as one single line: The line of Heart and the line of Head forming a single line joined to the line of Life speaks us of a character both mysterious and puzzling, a nature difficult to accommodate and a person strong, stubborn, determined and inflexible in views. With a soft hand, we have a passionate and sensuous person. We have already studied this formation while studying the line of Head and we may refer to it again for immediate reference. The collision of these two lines will result in a fusion of their strength. There is therefore a clash between the reason and logic shown by the Head line and the emotion and sentiment shown by the Heart line. It is therefore very difficult for the person to discriminate between the moral and ethical codes of conduct on the one hand and the finer sentiments and emotion in life on the other.

This person is very difficult to understand and is often misunderstood. He is very changing in his moods and is sometimes very emotional and sometimes acts upon his reason and practical nature. He is therefore unreliable in his passion and love.

h) Falling lines (*fig. 327*) : Sometimes we come across lines falling from the Heart line along its course which indicates a perpetual conflict between heart and the head for mastery. These falling lines were read by old palmists as love ending in sorrow and disappointment.

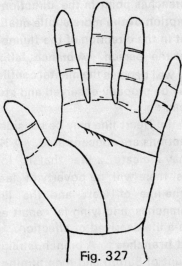

Fig. 327
Falling lines from the Heart line
(love sorrow)

Sometimes we see a large line which falls down from the Heart line and merges itself in the Head line. In this case the heart has surrendered to head and therefore is ruled by it.

Falling lines under the mount of Sun and in the Quadrangle mean versatility, seldom of much use to the person. Lines falling at other place show trouble from friends.

If these falling lines reach the line of Head but do not cut it, it is a sign that the life is greatly influenced by the opposite sex.

Drooping lines towards the mount of Uranus give financial setbacks and losses to the person and cause disputes and disappointments.

i) **Branches of the Heart line :** The branches constitute a natural feature of the line of Heart. They implement or strengthen the inherent qualities and basic character. From the direction, position and approach of the branches, it is possible to ascertain the direction of the growth and its susceptibility to outside influences both material and abstract.

When the branches point in the direction of the fingers there is an absorption of the more subtle qualities. Branches pointing straight in the direction of the thumb speak of riches and affluence of the person. A branch falling towards the line of Head very well denotes the mental conflicts and anxiety. Every branch may be properly observed and studied carefully in scope and meaning.

Branches of the Heart line may be considered as channels wherein the affections are concentrated. A Heart line without branches may indicate a life that is lonely. Without upward branches, there will be poverty of feeling and a dry nature. When the line of Heart and the line of Head are both without branches and lying far apart especially in the middle, it shows a life deprived of affection.

a) Upward branches : A branch, straight upward and reaching the mount of Saturn and then turning back abruptly, states misplaced affection. This is also an indication of some trouble in one's career due to a disastrous attachment (*fig. 328*).

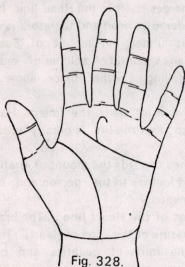

Fig. 328.
Rising branch from the Heart line,
going to Saturn and then turning back
(misplaced affection)

The line of Heart

Ray like-lines : These lines going to the mount of Saturn show religious thinking with Saturnian tinge. If a line from the mount of Saturn touches the line of Heart, there is misery in the family of the person. If in addition a branch goes to the mount of Mars, the person will suffer from blood pressure.

b) A descending line from the mount of Sun and touching the Heart line gives a high and unexpected rise in the position of the person. If a branch from the Heart line goes to the line of Sun, the person's affections will stand in the way of his success.

c) A branch from the Heart line to the mount of Mercury indicates failure in affection and love matters. A straight branch ending in a hook on the finger of Mercury is a sign of accident that will cripple the person (*fig. 329*). The accident will generally affect the legs.

If the line from the mount of Mercury touches the line of Heart, the person is either born in a rich family or the

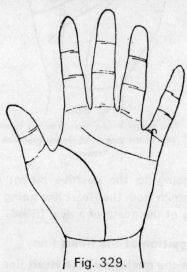

Fig. 329.

A straight branch from the Heart line on the finger of Mercury ending in a hook (accident to the leg)

financial position of the family will improve considerably after his birth.

d) A wavy branch down to the mount of Moon shows murderous disposition. A star at the end of the branch going to the mount of Moon indicates hereditary madness of the erotic type.

Two perpendicular lines from a poor line of Heart dropping straight to the mount of Moon show pressure on the nervous system (*fig. 330*).

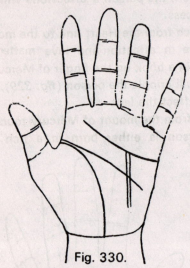

Fig. 330.
Two perpendicular lines from the Heart line to the mount of Moon (nervous tension)

A branch going to the positive mount of Mars shows calamity. A branch from the Heart line going to the Life line gives a warning of the death of a dear friend.

VI) Ending position of the Heart line

As we learn the qualities of the Heart line from its starting position similarly we learn their outcome from the ending position of the Heart line. For instance, if the Heart line rises under Jupiter and ends under Saturn, it shows that the

The line of Heart

Heart line which began with the right sort of affection soon changed into coldness and dislike of mankind peculiar to Saturn. Thus the warm nature in the beginning was soon changed to indifference later on.

The normal termination of the Heart line is on the percussion between the mounts of Mercury and negative mount of Mars. It is bad for the Heart line to end on the mount of Mars. If we have to compare the starting and the ending positions of the line of Heart and the line of Head, the termination of the line of Head is more significant than the termination of the line of Heart. But the starting of the line of Heart is more important than that of the line of Head. We shall now study the ending positions of the line of Heart, one by one.

1) Ending under the mount of Saturn: We have already referred to this ending in our general remark above, but in particular we may state that it indicates a short life span not even beyond 25 years. It also relates to heart and stomach troubles. When the Heart line is a succession of short lines under the mount of Saturn, it is an unfortunate formation and indicates hysteria.

2) Heart line ending in Head line *(fig. 331)* : The ending of the Heart line on the Head line shows overpowering of the head over the heart and reason is more powerful than emotion. The person is therefore dominated by his head. If the line of Heart after such a serious deflection regains its former course the affectionate disposition is again revived and head and worldly interests have not entirely mastered the heart. If the Heart line after its start, immediately runs and merges in the Head line, it means that the Heart has never run its proper channel but has merged its force in the Head line. It operates in making the person cold and heartless and should be read like an absent line of Heart. Such a person is very ambitous, as the line starts from Jupiter but will consider the welfare of no one when furthering his ambition.

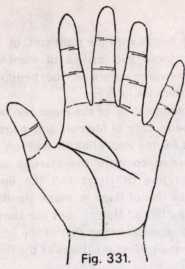

Fig. 331.
Heart line ending in Head line (more of logic and reasoning than emotions)

3) Heart line ending under the mount of Sun (*fig. 332*) : This formation shows that the Apollonian ideas of beauty and art strongly attract the person, who will be dissatisfied in marriage except with an Apollonian or the one approaching that type. If in this case the Heart line starts on the mount of Jupiter, it will give ideal love which added to that of the Apollonian character makes one indeed fond of beauty, love and grace. As one of the health defects of the Apollonian is heart disease, it is better to examine the character of the Heart line, the Life and the Mercury lines and also the nails to find whether the marking does or does not indicate heart disease.

4) Heart line ending on the mount of Mercury : It shows that the affections are largely influenced by finances. The Mercurian shrewdness guides this Heart line and it must always have money in sight before love is recognised. This is a good ending for an actor because it gives great creative power and excellent power of mimicry.

If the Heart line completely encircles the mount of Mercury at its termination, it shows an aptitude for occult sciences.

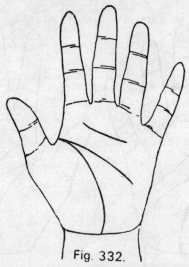

Fig. 332.

Heart line ending under Sun (attraction towards beauty and art)

5) **Heart line ending on the mount of Mercury but without any branch** : It signifies childlessness.

6) **Heart line ending on percussion** : With this ending of the Heart line, if the Head line is clear and upper mount of Mars prominent, it shows daring.

7) **Heart line ending on upper Mars** (*fig. 333*) : In this case the qualities of the different mounts under the fingers are not associated with the Heart line. In addition to this the constraint of the mount of Uranus must be added which gives a secretive disposition. The attraction will generally be for a Martian.

8) **Heart line ending on the mount of Moon** (*fig. 334*) : It makes the person extremely jealous because there will be too much of the heart backed by the imagination of the mount of Moon, which will magnify every act of one he loves into some form of unfaithfulness. This is a most unhappy formation. It shows jealousy aggravated by a wild imagination. Where there is no fault, fault will be seen. Small fault will be unduly magnified.

9) **Ending on the mount of Venus** (*fig. 335*) : This is rarely seen but when found it is a serious indication, since

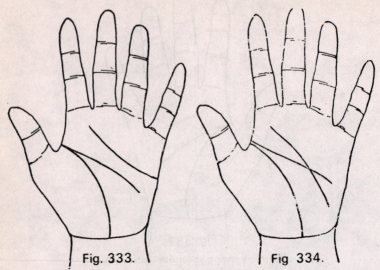

Fig. 333.
Heart line ending on upper Mars
(secretive disposition)

Fig 334.
Heart line ending on mount of Moon
(jealousy)

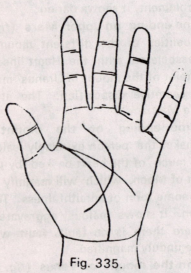

Fig. 335.
Heart line ending on mount of Venus
(danger to head or life)

it cuts both the line of Head and the line of Life. In this case we have to study the lines of Head and Life after they are cut by the Heart line. If they show weakness after the cutting, it means that the damage has been made either to life and the condition is serious.

10) Heart line ending on the plain of Mars (*fig. 336*) : In this case the Heart line will cut the Head line and it will be a serious menace since the plain of Mars is the seat of temper and excitability. This will create an irritable person who is changeable in affection and constantly seeking excitement. It is hard to get along with him.

11) Heart line ending in a fork (*fig. 337*) : A fork at the termination with one prong deep into the mount of Mercury and an island in the line of Saturn indicates divorce due to guilty intrigue of the person.

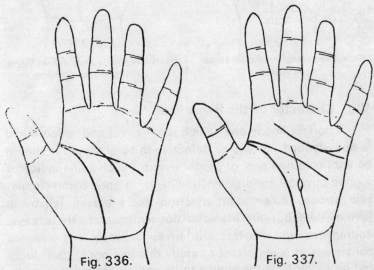

Fig. 336.
Heart line ending in the plain of Mars (irritable nature)

Fig. 337.
Heart line ending in a fork—one prong goes to the mount of Mercury, with an island in the Fate line (divorce)

12) Heart line ending in a tassel (*fig. 338*) : For every prong there is a love affair though of minor importance. It shows a very affectionate and prolific character.

13) Heart line ending in a hook on the mount of Mercury : It shows danger from elephant (*fig. 339*).

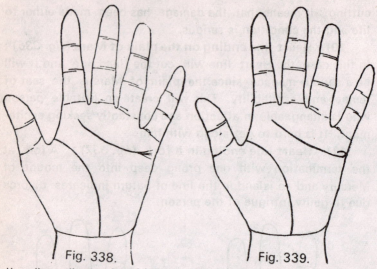

Fig. 338.
Heart line ending in a Tassel (many love affairs)

Fig. 339.
Heart line ending in a hook on Mercury (danger from elephant)

VII) Character of the Heart line

A perfect line is one which is deep-cut and smooth and is not islanded, broken or defective in other ways. It should be well coloured and of proper length. Such a line indicates a good physical condition of the heart, a good blood circulation, strong and constant affection and a person reliable in love matters but not frivolous nor sentimental. He is brave, courageous and fearless. He loves ardently and remains consistent. It is important to study this line not in its entirety but bit by bit from the source to its ending place.

1) Deep line of Heart : A deep-cut line of Heart, even and well coloured, lacks demonstrative kind of love. But the person is consistent in love affairs. This character of the line shows good constitution and there is very little possibility of any kind of heart disease. This deep line contributes to a happy nature and warmth of affection.

The line of Heart

A very deep and red Heart line, running stiff and clear across the hand with a similar line of Head and a strong mount of Mars, shows murderous tendencies. This line also shows the danger of apoplexy. The depth of the line when abnormal, always indicates a strain that may soon reach the danger point. When the line is deep and bright red, it denotes great violence of passion.

When the line is only deep and not red in colour, it gives confidence to the person whom he loves and a disappointment will affect him severely. Such a person does not pick up anyone and everyone making a great demonstration, but loves his dear ones and friends with a steady devotedness. This type of line therefore creates the strongest and most reliable affection.

2) **Narrow and thin line of Heart** (*fig. 340*) :. When the line is narrow and thin, the person cares very little for others. He is narrow-minded, cowardly, timid, unsympathetic and has no real affection for anyone. His display of love is for selfish ends. A very thin and long line shows murder-

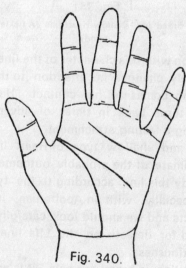

Fig. 340.
Narrow and thin line of Heart
(cowardly and timid disposition)

ous instinct. Thinness of the line is a great defect of the line of Heart.

3) Broad and shallow line of Heart (*fig. 341*) : If the line be broad and shallow, the heart action will be physically weak and the person is fickle-minded and senti-

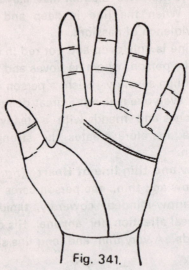

Fig. 341.
Broad and shallow Heart line (A fickle mind)

mental. A person with this character of the line falls violently in love but quickly changes his affection to the next attractive person who comes in his contact. He loves during prosperity but turns back in times of adversity. He is incapable of having a lasting attachment.

This broad and shallow type of Heart line is of great value in the estimate of the probable outcome of a marriage. We have to study this line according to the type the person belongs to. Especially, with an Apollonian, it will point out his health defects and we should look carefully for the colour of the nails and for defects on the Life line to judge the degree of its seriousness.

If the Heart line is broad but pale, it is an indication of a tendency to excess and shows a life of dissipation ending

The line of Heart

in complete weakness. It shows a nature which is indifferent, a character tired and sick of everything and even doubting whether life is worth living. He is tired of love and tired of life. He is dead to affection and passion. All this is due to poor blood circulation, poor heart action and a general weakness of the system.

4) **Chained line of Heart** (*fig. 342*) : This character of the line shows ups and downs in life. There is a strong flirting disposition. It also shows the imperfect action of the heart. If this line is rising towards the mount of Saturn, it is a sign of mental degeneration. It also shows contempt of the opposite sex and a strong tendency to unnatural vices. If the line is pale, broad and chained, it is a triple combination of evil indications.

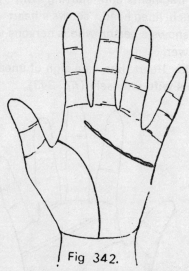

Fig 342.
Chained line of Heart (a flirt)

If the chained line of Heart is fretted by many small lines crossing it, we have inconstancy. In a soft hand with a weak thumb, it shows unreliable friendship.

If the Heart line is chained and the fingers are knotty or spatulate with a sloping line of Head and with a cross on the top phalange of the Saturn finger, there is a change of religion.

A poorly traced and chained Heart line with a similar line of Head and the mount of Venus exaggerated or much rayed shows that the person has unnatural sex ralationship, constant flirtations, guilty love intrigue and faithlessness (*case 5*).

When the line is chained at the time it crosses the line of Fate, the career of the person will be interrupted due to love affairs. It may also mean heart trouble.

5) Weak and poor Heart line : If such a line ends without any branch at the percussion, it shows childlessness.

A poor line of Heart, a double Girdle of Venus, a line of Fate in many fragments and starting away from the line of Life, with a much lined hand, shows a heart greatly affected by tobacco. It shows a person who is nervous with no memory and no will-power.

6) Rail-like Heart line is a sign of uneasiness but the person loves his wife intensely (*fig. 343*).

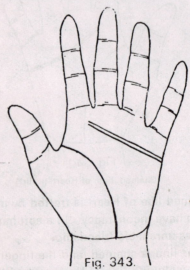

Fig. 343.
Rail-like line of Heart (intense love for wife)

The line of Heart

7) Colour of the Heart line : With every Heart line, colour plays an important role. While studying the line, it is better to press the line from its source to its termination and observe the blood that flows under this pressure. This will give us an idea as to the strength of the blood and will help us to ascertain the colour of the line. Sometimes the blood flows freely whereas at other times the whiteness under the pressure shows a weak blood supply. The colour of the Heart line tells us whether the person is warm or cold-hearted.

a) White colour does not indicate a good physical heart. In this case we have to look for the Heart line in both the hands. If the left hand shows good colour and the right hand denotes whiteness, it will indicate that the heart is originally strong but has been impaired and weakened. White colour of the line means weaker action of the heart.

It will be useful to study the mounts in the case of white colour of the line. We know that a Lunarian, a Saturnian and a Mercurian are naturally cold and therefore a white-coloured line will add to their coldness. On the other hand, a Martian, a Venusian and a Jupiterian are warm-hearted. Therefore the white colour of the Heart line will reduce the strength of their warmth.

White colour of the Heart line, on a thin and narrow, broad and shallow or a chained line, exaggerates the cold qualities and selfishness and fickleness will be the result.

b) *Pink colour* : This colour on a deep line of Heart will accentuate warmth, steadfastness and reliability of affection. This colour will make a thin line less selfish and narrow. It will also lessen the qualities of broad and shallow Heart line.

c) *Red colour* : It is a sign of rich and warm blood and endows the Heart line with intense love and affection. The red colour is rarely seen in a thin and narrow or broad and shallow or chained line of Heart. With the red colour we have also to study the mount to which the person belongs. It is a danger for a pronounced Jupiterian, where as for a Saturnian it is good because he yields some of his hatred for mankind. An Apollonian and a Venusian become too intense. whereas it will warm up a cold Lunarian. Red colour to a Martian is normal and will make him intense in his passions.

d) *Yellow colour* : Yellow colour spoils the functions of the Heart line and will create morbid affection. In this case we have a person who is suspicious of those he loves. It gives a pessimistic view of life.

A yellow Heart line on a strong Saturnian creates a mean-minded person who can also be criminal. With a Martian a yellow Heart line means a swindler. Thus the yellow colour of the line diminishes the good qualities everytime.

e) *Blue colour* : It shows congestion and sluggish movement of the heart. In this case also we have to study nails and also the Life line to find out whether the defect of the heart is serious.

The Heart line in general shows three main important aspects. Firstly, it relates to the function of the heart. Secondly, it indicates the thinking of the person and thirdly it points out to certain events in his life.

The Heart line is mainly concerned with the function of the heart and from its course we can know whether the heart has any functional defect. In this case also we have to study the other lines and marks on the hand, especially the line of Life and the line of Mercury. In case we do not find any health defects in these two lines, the defect shown in the Heart line may not be a functional defect of the heart.

Once we are convinced that the defect shown in the Heart line is not a physical defect, we can look for the psychological aspect of the Heart line. In that case the person may suffer due to excessive sentiment or emotion or affection. which may have affected either his career or his health. We shall also have to study the different mounts to which he belongs and then arrives at a conclusion.

The third thing that can be judged from the defect in the Heart line is the events in life. An island or a break or a dot or any such defect in the Heart line may show changes in the career of the person.

VIII) Defects in the Heart line

1) *Island* : All defects in the Heart line are more serious if they appear under the mount of Sun. Islands are obstructions to the flow of blood and weaken the physical action of the heart. The size of the island will show how serious it is. Islands under the different mounts will add to the defect of the mount under which it is found. We shall also have to consider the emotional part played by the Heart line, if the island does not show a physical defect. An island on the Heart line under the mount of Sun always shows a health defect and we should get it corroborated by the study of nails. The psychological significance of the island is as under.

a) For every island, there is a guilty intrigue.

b) An island under the mount of Saturn shows a love-affair which interferes with the prospective career of the person.

c) An island in the Heart line with an island on the Fate line shows guilty love that will stop at nothing.

d) An island under the mount of Sun indicates trouble with the eyes.

e) An island under the line of Heart shows indigestion.

A broad line of Heart formed by a series of islands starting under the mount of Saturn speaks of no love for the opposite sex. However it indicates unnatural desires.

2) *Dots* : Many dots in the Heart line is a sign of Angina Pectoris. Only a few dots show neuralgia affecting nerves. In the case of dots, we have to study the colour of the dots.

Red dots : Under the mount of Saturn they show fatality. Under the mount of Sun they show stupid pride. Between the Sun and Mercury mounts they indicate stupidity and avarice. Red dots mean sorrows out of love or troubles in general but an elongated red dot shows dangers of apoplexy.

Dark dots : They show love sorrows and pulpitations of the heart. A dark dot under the mount of Apollo is harmful to the person's ambition caused by a celebrated person. Under the mount of Mercury a dark dot means love-sorrows or troubles caused by a doctor, a scientist or a businessman. A deep dot with a poor and wavy line of Mercury shows a poor digestion and consequenty indicates palpitations of the heart.

Bluish dots : They indicate inflammatory type of rheumatism or grave malarial fever.

White dots : White dots on the Heart line is a good sign. They represent intellect and inventive genius. The location of the white dot is important. Under the mount of Jupiter the person will be attracted towards a Jupiterian, under the mount of Saturn towards a Saturnian and so on.

A tiny line running through a white dot on the lines of Heart and crossing the line of Head shows personal troubles.

3) *Cross bars (fig. 344)* : Cross bars cutting the Heart line are constant heart irritations. They show either illness or worries in the affection. Here also we have to study whether they indicate physical defect or relate to affections. If they are only small lines, they show temporary heart disturbances of a functional character. If they are very deep, they are more serious. Thus we have to note all these cross bars carefully to see how disastrous they will be in their results. If they do not relate to any disease, they may indicate disturbances in affections.

4) *Breaks* : They are noticed anywhere during the course of the Heart line but the place where the break is found is important. The breaks are serious and are significant indications of the sorrows and afflictions of the heart and also of acute health troubles that affect the heart and blood circulation. In combination with other signs on the hand, these breaks are capable of telling a lot about the person's mental and physical afflictions, his disappointments and sorrows.

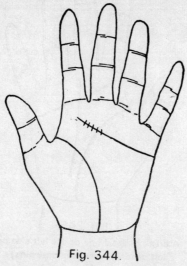

Fig. 344.

Cross bars in Heart line (illness or worries)

A break on the line of Heart generally indicates troubles with affections or a broken engagement. On the health side it shows weakness of the heart and heart trouble. When the break is only on one hand or the broken ends overlap, there is the possibility of reunion in affections and overcoming of the physical heart trouble.

A line of Heart, broken at the right side of the right hand, suggests danger from fire or poison. If the same break is found on the left side of the left hand, it shows danger from drowning (*fig. 345*).

A Heart line, broken in three places and with sphere-like formation at the termination of the line under the mount of Mercury, shows danger of drowning.

A much more broken Heart line indicates inconsistency, hatred of the opposite sex and a miserable married life. This also show constant recurrence of weakness in the heart action or broken love affair. If the break comes close together, he is likely to have heart failure.

A wide break is a sign of a violent, impetuous and interrupted affection. With contributary signs on the mount of Mars, a wide break means the tragic end of a love affair.

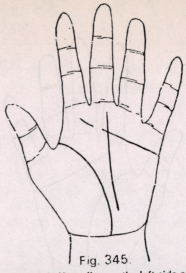

Fig. 345.
A break in Heart line on the left side on
left hand (danger from drowning)

A break in the Heart line under the mount of Saturn is a sign of broken love affair not due to the fault of the lovers but due to fatality. If after the break the line rises to the mount of Saturn, it indicates gout and rheumatism. It may also indicate rheumatism of heart.

If the break is between the mounts of Saturn and the Sun, it signifies a broken love affair due to one's own folly.

A break in the Heart line under the mount of Sun results in too much pride, often amounting to insane vanity governing the affections. The capricious conduct of the person may cause a break in the love affair. It is also a conclusive proof of health defect of the heart.

A Heart line having a break under the mount of Mercury indicates love of money and an avaricious disposition, which may lead to frustration in love. In seeking to discover if this break is a health defect, we have to take into consideration one's age. Usually the age under Mercury is near about 60 or so and it may indicate health trouble. It is always better to examine the character of the line after the break. If the line after the break is deep, the defect will be overcome. If it grows thin or chained, the defect shown will continue.

A Heart line broken at several places shows danger of falling from a high place.

The line of Heart   535

If the end of the broken line drops and cuts the Head line sharply, the thing which causes the defect, be it health or affection, will seriously impair the hand at the time the line crosses the Head line. If at the same time a star occurs on the line of Head at the same place, a danger to head is signified (*fig. 346*).

If an island is seen in the Heart line after the cut, the heart will be left in a delicate condition afterwards.

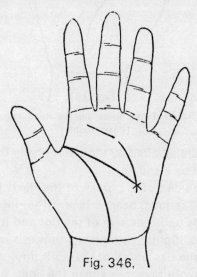

Broken end of Heart line, cutting the
Head line, and a star on the head line
(explosion of head)

If the break is in the Heart line and there is an island in the Heart line, the heart will be delicate during the time it is occupied by the island.

If in the break there is a star, the person will die suddenly or will have a serious attack of heart disease (*fig. 347*).

If the Heart line breaks and the ends of the broken Heart line are cut by cross bars, a sudden death by heart failure is indicated. If however there is a sister line joining the ends of the cross bars, the serious defects shown by the cut and

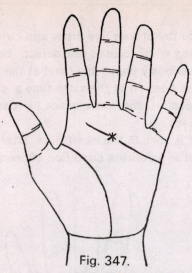

Fig. 347.
A star in the break on the Heart line
(Heart trouble)

the cross bars are repaired by the sister line. This defect also can be repaired by a square.

A dot at the end of the break of the Heart line is also an indication of a serious heart attack. The intensity of the trouble depends upon the size of the dot and its depth.

5) *Splits*: Splits will occur upwards or downward depending on the rise or fall of the split line. All the lines which rise are more favourable than the lines which fall from the Heart line. The splits may be a health defect or may indicate the character of the person. Split lines as health defect show a weakened condition of the heart and impaired circulation.

A rising split from the line of Heart under the mount of Jupiter will show that ambition will guide love and the person will be attracted towards a Jupiterian (*fig. 348*).

Similarly, a split rising either to Saturn or to Sun or to Mercury will mean that the person will have attraction towards a Saturnian, towards an Apollonian or a Mercurian, as the case may be. In this case also, we can study the world by which the person is governed. For instance, if the split is

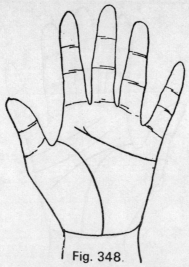

Fig. 348.
A rising split on Heart line, under the Jupiter mount (love guided by ambition)

towards the mount of Saturn and if the middle world is strongest, he will be attracted towards one who has farming, mining or horticultural aptitude or scientific talents. If on the other hand he is governed by the lower world, he will love one who has the saving disposition of the Saturnian. We can apply the same logic when the split is towards Sun or Mercury.

Minute splits on the line of Heart indicate a predisposition to smoker's heart. With a supple thumb it indicates an amorous disposition.

Splits drooping towards the Head line show health defects and weak condition of the heart. When the Heart line is made up of splits throughout, there is a conflict between the heart and the head. Falling splits are indicative of sentiments governed by calculation. The course of love does not run smooth and often there is sorrow and disappointment.

IX) Double line of Heart (*fig. 349*)

A double line of Heart gives the capacity for deep affection which will cause sorrow to the person. For men it

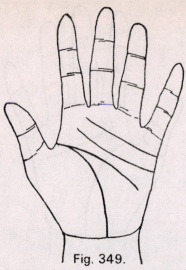

Fig. 349.
Double line of Heart (sorrow in love)

shows special vigour whereas for women it is exemption from female troubles.

A double line of Heart is rarely seen on the hand. It is a sort of sister line, running between the regular line of Heart and the base of the fingers. It may also partake the qualities of the Girdle of Venus. This has the force of a regular sister line just like the line of Mars to the line of Life. It has the capacity of repairing the defects of the original line.

When the double line of Heart is steady and long, great devotion both in friendship and even in love is indicated. It adds so much of sensitiveness that it often results in sorrow.

X) Heart line in relation to the other aspects

A well-traced and well-placed line of Heart, with a strong first phalange of the thumb, shows a changing disposition.

A good line of Heart with a good line of Head and a triangle near the termination of a good line of Life shows tactfulness,

A poor line of Heart and a poor line of Head, but with the same triangle at the end of the line of Life, indicates an unkind speech and foolish and harmful gossip.

The line of Heart

A well-developed line of Heart with exaggerated mounts of Venus and Moon is a sign of romantic disposition.

A long line of Heart with a Girdle of Venus and the mount of Moon much-lined shows insane jealousy, since imagination and not common sense rules over it. Such a person doubts the character of his wife and ill-treats her.

A poor line of Heart, with a Head line starting from the mount of Jupiter and separated from the line of Life, is related to misfortune in love and or love-affairs due to one's own foolish desire for a brilliant union. This type of Head line makes one reckless in behaviour.

A deep and red Heart line running stiff and clear across the hand from side to side, with a similar line of Head and strong mount of Mars, indicates a tendency to murder.

A pale and wide line of influence from the mount of Venus to the mount of Mercury or the upper mount of Mars indicates physical love and extreme sensuality leading one even to crime. This is more true if there is a broken Girdle of Venus.

A poor line of Heart with a poor line of Head shows faithlessness.

A chained or poorly traced line of Heart with a similar line of Head and an exaggerated mount of Venus indicates constant flirtations or even a guilty intrigue.

If the line of Heart is chained at its intersection with the line of Fate, the person has difficulties in his career due to love troubles. If a Fate line rising from the mount of Moon merges in the Heart line, which starts on the mount of Jupiter, it shows unexpected happiness due to the intense devotion of the loved one. It also shows a strong sentiment for one's country and community.

A line from the Heart line touching the broken line of Fate indicates widowhood or death of a dear one but not of a relative.

Connecting lines between the line of Heart and the line of Life are signs of illness caused by sorrow or by disappointment in love.

If a line joins the line of Heart and the line of Head with a high mount of Mercury, it shows the calculating spirit in love matters also.

If the line of Heart is longer than the line of Head, the person looks at others from an affectionate and symathetic standpoint and not from a practical or business viewpoint.

If the line of Head is forked at the start and there is a fork in the beginning of the Heart line also which reaches to the positive mount of Mars, it shows a separation which afterwards results in marriage. A couple deeply in love may be separated either by circumstances or by parental interference but it will ultimately triumph over all obstacles.

A Heart line, starting with a much elongated fork and a star at the beginning of the Life line with smooth fingers, shows a resigned attitude to Life due to religious belief.

The line of Heart, lying very close to the line of Head and joined to the line of Life for a short distance, shows passions and the lower instincts not under control.

A line from the negative mount of Mars meeting the line of Heart below the mount of Sun signifies a great writer.

If there is a parallel line to the line of Heart joining the mounts of Sun and Jupiter, the person will come into contact with great personalities who will hold benevolent views.

The line of Heart which is cut under the mount of Mercury by a cross on that mount shows business failure.

If a wavy or straight line from the upper side cuts the Heart line, death by drowning is indicated. A wavy crooked line below the Heart line and cutting the line signifies death by a snake bite or fire.

If the line of Heart is cut by a line on the mount of Jupiter, there is danger from falling from a horse.

XI) Signs on the line of Heart

a) *Triangle* : A triangle attached to the line of Heart in the Quadrangle denotes income and improvement in financial position. A triangle attached to the line of Sun and the line of Heart indicates a period of unusual enjoyment of wealth and reputation.

b) *Mole* : A mole on the line of Heart is a sign of failure and disillusionment. If a fresh line starts from the mole, faith will survive the disappointment. Small indentations indicate suffering from auto-stimulation.

c) *Square* : A square on or close to the line of Heart prevents physical harm and shows escape from love-sorrows.

d) *Cross* : Cross on the Heart line at the intersection of Fate line shows pecuniary troubles due to love matters.

e) *Star* : A star on the Heart line is a sign of sudden death from heart attack. It also means blindness. A star at the end of a branch from the Heart line going to the mount of Moon is a sign of hereditary insanity.

f) *Circle* : A circle in the Heart line shows weakness of the heart. If it is under the mount of Sun, it indicates optic trouble. A semi-circle on the Heart line resembling an island shows failures, distressess and complications in business or profession.

g) *Black spots* : They show weakness of sex activity.

h) *Bars* : A number of bars cutting the Heart line indicates repeated disappointment in love and the troubles of the heart and liver. A straight bar cutting the Heart line shows danger or injury from weapon: An oblique bar across the line of Heart on the mount of Jupiter is a sign of danger through horse riding.

i) Two vertical lines in the middle of the Heart line show danger of fall from a high place.

j) Red spots show a tendency to boils.

k) Dark dot shows danger from poisoning.

XII) The Heart line and the Mount

With all kinds of Heart lines, we have to study the type of the subject. A Jupiterian and Venusian will be expected to have the best kind of Heart lines. The Apollonian may have his health defect, which is heart disease, shown on the Heart line. The Martian will be expected to have a good

Heart line but it may be excessive in strength. A good specimen of the Mercurian type will have good Heart line but a bad specimen will have a thin line showing selfishness and disregard for others and the furthering of selfish ends. The Saturnian, if good, will have a good line ; if bad, he will have a thin line. The Lunarian, who is naturally cold and selfish, will be expected to have a thin or chained, shallow white line. If you find the thin line on the hand of a subject belonging to a type where it is abnormal, you should read the line properly, but do not give it all the emphasis that you would give to a type where it is expected. For example, a thin line found on a Venusian will not be read as strongly as the same line on a Lunarian.

CHAPTER XXI

The line of Apollo (Sun)

I) Introduction

The line of Apollo is the central of the three vertical lines on the hand. It is usually conceived that this line is capable of giving unexpected fortune and success more through chance or accident. But this chance and accident will always be backed by an inherent capacity, understanding, optimism and learning. There is always a talent behind this fortune or success. The presence of the line of Sun speaks of a gift of genius somewhere on the hand, which will unravel the mystery of chance or accident.

The line of Sun presents a happy personality without much labour or strain. To consider this line from the inward point of view, it represents the capacity to command circumstances that are favourable and happy. It shows confidence, a certain talent or a gift that would manifest itself in some sphere of activity of life.

The line of Apollo or Sun also shows financial prosperity without much labour. Acquisition of financial prosperity by hard work is the work of the line of Fate and acquisition of this prosperity by shrewdness, sagacity and intelligence is the function of the line of Mercury. In the case of the Sun line the prosperity is through luck only.

Apart from its gift for fortune, the line of Sun gives elevation of taste and the capacity for strong appreciation of higher values of life. It can give excellence in music and art, culture and learning.

The importance of this line will be more significant when we compare this line with the line of Fate. Whereas in the case of the line of Fate there is ordinarily a sense of surrender to the environment, it shows definite optimism and enthusiasm when the line of Sun is present.

A good line of Sun is undoubtedly an indication of possession of the characteristics of the Apollonian friends, money and reputation more easily than any other type.

The presence of the Sun line is an indication that the person has been endowed with exceptional talents for getting on in the world. However this line should be studied with other cheirosophic development of the hand. For instance, a fine line of Sun is spoiled by a flabby hand or a weak thumb and poor mounts of Jupiter, Mars, Mercury and Venus. In fact, these other factors are also equally important while studying any other line on the hand. On a hollow hand, the line of Sun loses all its power.

Usually, the lines of Fate and Sun are interdependent and in many cases one will be strong at a time when the other is weak. In such a case they act as sister lines and one repairs the damage of the other. The presence of a good line of Sun, with the Fate line absent, will compensate for the loss of the Fate line.

We may come across a Sun line which is sometimes present and sometimes absent. In this case the break in the Sun line shows that the talents are latent.

Absence of the Sun line

The complete absence of the line of Sun gives late recognition to the person even though he is talented and artistic. Even if he deserves honour and fame, he will hardly achieve it.

Even though the line of Sun is absent, a good line of Fate will compensate the absence of it and the good luck shown by the Sun line even though much reduced will not be wiped out completely.

It is absolutely incorrect to say that the absence of the line of Sun indicates bad luck in life but it is true that the presence of the line makes the success easier.

The line of Apollo

II) Position of the line of Sun on the hand

The line of Sun should begin more or less on a lower level on hand, directly under the mount and finger of Sun.

III) Normal position

The normal line of Sun starts between the mounts of Neptune and Moon and gets the qualities of both these mounts. Thus after getting the inspiration of the mount of Neptune and the imagination of the mount of Moon, the line cuts through the plain of Mars and enters the mount of Uranus which adds to the line the active qualities of energy, originality and ingenuity. It finally terminates on the mount of Sun at the base of the finger of Apollo. From the various qualities which the line of Sun absorbs, it is possible to get a fair idea of its significance in the moulding of the individual concerned.

IV) Starting of the line of Sun (*fig. 350*)

1) **Starting from the rascette :** It shows brilliant intellectual ability, fame and wealth.

2) **Starting from the line of Life :** It shows success in art and literature and also good fortune. Relatives will help this person considerably. This is more true if the line starts from inside the line of Life and from the mount of Venus. Rising from the line of Life, with the rest of the hand artistic, it denotes that the life of the subject will be devoted to the worship of the beautiful objects. It also promises success in artistic pursuits. The fortune may be either by inheritance or by merit. Success is shown in all fields, in profession, finance, marriage and health.

3) **Starting from the Fate line :** It adds to the success promised by the line of Fate and it begins from the date where it is marked. From that time onwards things will improve.

4) **Starting from the mount of Moon :** It promises success and distinction largely dependent upon the help of

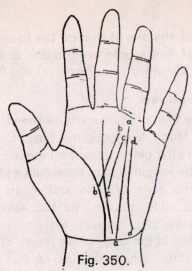

Fig. 350.
Line of Sun starting a) from rascette
b) from Life line, c) from Fate line,
d) from mount of Moon

others. In this case it is not a certain sign of success, being influenced by the fortunes of those with whom we come in contact.

If the Sun line starts from the mount of Moon but with a sloping line of Head, the person gets success in poetry, fiction and imaginative paintings.

Starting from the top of the mount of Moon, the person gets success and fortune connected with foreign countries. It may be through foreign trade. It may also mean that the success is achieved not in one's own country but abroad.

If the Sun line starts from the top of the mount of Moon but nearer the percussion, there is the display of imagination and power of language. If the mental world is developed, we have an author.

5) **Starting from the Heart line**: The love of art, music, literature, etc will not be much influenced due to serious love affair of the person. It merely denotes great love for art and artistic things showing distinction at the period shown on the Heart line. It also shows a noble heart and charitable activities. It may also indicate advantage from a

marriage late in life ; it may also mean a progressive educational career throughout, though it may not be marked by brilliant success.

6) Starting from inside the Triangle : It indicates success after serious struggle and due to the person's unaided efforts.

7) Starting from upper mount of Mars : It shows aggressiveness in the acquisition of fame or fortune.

8) Starting with an island : An island at the starting point of the line of Sun gives success due to a guilty love. It also shows brilliant future for the illegitimate child born of one in a high position.

9) Starting with a star : If the line starts from a star, it is a sign of success from the beginning. If such a line ends also in a star, the person will be brilliant and successful from birth to the end of his life.

10) Starting from the mount of Neptune : In this case the talent of the individual, more than anything else, leads him to fame and fortune. It is one of the best origins for the line of Sun to have. If it also terminates on the mount of Sun and at the base of the finger, it may give a carefree attitude to the one having the capacity and brilliance.

11) Starting from the mount of Uranus : It may mean either celebrity or notoriety. We have a dashing and aggressive personality in quest of fame and fortune. If however there is a double line, the bad side of the indication will be minimised. The person will achieve success due to his talents and powers of very high order.

V) Course of the line of Sun

1) The length of the line determines the extent of its influence. A line of Sun reaching from the wrist to the mount of Sun gives talents, which continue to develop during the life of the person.

In its course on the hand, the line of Sun must run to the mount of Sun, even though it may start from any point described earlier. There is the possibility of confusing chance lines as the line of Sun. In order to avoid this confusion, we must fix up a rule that while in its course through the hand, the line of Sun may deflect, may stop at any point, throw out branches or be met, strengthened or crossed by chance lines, the general direction of the line itself will be towards the mount of Sun.

a) Long and uncrossed line of Sun : This is a sign of riches, reputation and fame. It gives comfortable circumstances and easy money. With a strong and straight line of Head it shows love for position and power.

b) Deep line of Sun : A very deep line of Sun especially on an artistic hand is a sign of diminishing vital force which may lead to paralysis or heart trouble.

If the line is alternately deep and thin, the person is periodically active.

c) Strong on the mount of Sun : This shows a person achieving celebrity as an artist. He gets protection and favour from great personalities.

d) Broad line of Sun : The person acquires great powers of concentration.

e) Rising lines : Rising lines will increase the good effect of the line and, when seen on a good line, will make the success of the person more certain. His life becomes successful in overcoming obstacles that may come in his way.

f) Falling lines : Lines falling from the line of Sun are indicative of need for great efforts, if success is to be achieved. He will have an uphill pull and there will be times when the load gets heavy. He does not overcome obstacles easily and such a line bears no such promise of a brilliant life as when the branches rise.

g) Branches : 1) Two or more branches, rising from the line but becomming irregular, uneven or crossed by many bars, indicate failure in intellectual pursuits due to lack of concentration.

2) **Without any branch :** When there are no branches in the Sun line and when it goes straight to the mount of Sun, the person gets easy success in his career.

The line of Apollo

3) Branches to Saturn and Mercury : If the end of the line of Sun has one branch going to the mount of Saturn and one to the mount of Mercury, the person will have a combination of wisdom, brilliance and shrewdness which will lead him to wealth and renown (*fig. 351*).

4) Branches which leave the line of Sun and run to the other lines, signs or mounts will each have a special meaning which is to be read from the place where they terminate.

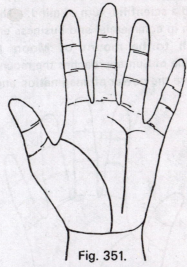

Fig. 351.

Sun line: One branch goes to Saturn
another to the Mercury mount
(wealth and renown)

A branch going to the mount of Jupiter

A rising branch going to the mount of Jupiter will show that in addition to talents, the person has a strong ambition and power of leadership. With this combination he will be successful and he is sure to win fame if not wealth. If in addition a star be seen on the mount of Jupiter, the ambition will be crowned with success.

5) A branch to the mount of Saturn : A rising branch to the mount of Saturn adds wisdom, sobriety and frugality. The scientific thinking and the balancing qualities of Saturn will increase the success of the person. If a star be seen on the branch of Saturn, the qualities of the mount will bring great success. Money is obtained from investments in land property and in agriculture. It also shows excellence in the occult sciences.

6) Branch to the mount of Mercury : In this case the qualities of the mount of Mercury will assist the person. He will have shrewdness, business ability, great power of expression and a scientific turn of mind. This combination is an indication in commercial and business enterprises.

7) Branch to the mount of Moon (*fig. 352*) If a branch of the line of Sun approaches the mount of Moon, the person will have the power of imagination and the ability to

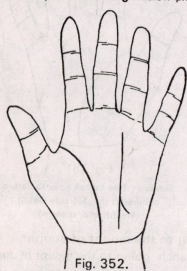

Fig. 352.
A branch from Sun line to Moon
(power of imagination)

express. As an author, he will be successful. If a star is seen at the end of the line, the person will achieve great renown from all these qualities. If cross bars or other defects are seen in this branch, he will make errors which will interfere with his reputation.

8) Branch to the upper mount of Mars (*fig. 353*):
A branch from the line of Sun leading to the negative mount of Mars enables the person to make his way through the world. He is confident, self-reliant and never discouraged. If cross, dots and bars are seen either on the mount of Sun or Mars, the person will have to face trials hard to overcome. If a sister line runs beside the line on the mount of Mars, he will have added renown.

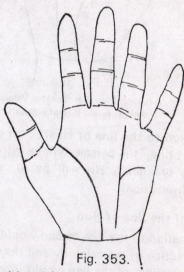

Fig. 353.
A branch from Sun line to upper Mars
(confidence and self-reliance)

9) Branch to the mount of Venus (*fig. 354*): If a branch from the Sun line runs to a strong mount of Venus, the person will be passionately fond of music of a melodious character. This will be accentuated, if the fingers be smooth and the tips conic or pointed. If the star be seen on the mount of Sun, he will achieve great distinction as a musician.

10) Branch to the line of Head: A branch from the Sun line touching a strong line of Head is a sign of clear mind, good judgement and self-control. A formation of a triangle at the point where the branch reaches the Head line is an indication of unusual mental power.

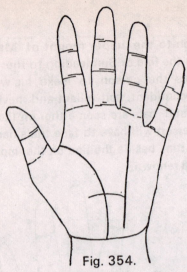

Fig. 354.
A branch from Sun line to Venus mount (great love of music)

11) Branch to the line of Heart : If a branch merges into the Heart line, the person will be gifted with warmth and goodness of heart. He will be of sympathetic and affectionate disposition.

VI) Ending of the line of Sun

The termination of the line of Sun would inform us of the source and direction of the celebrity and the field of success, whereas the starting of the line would give us more information of the nature of the aid and equipment to success. The line of Sun may terminate either as a single line or in multiple lines.

A healthy termination would be a clear straight formation of the line. Any tendency to curve deprives the line of its active goodness and may result in malefic significance.

1) Ending in a thin line (*fig. 355*) : If the line of Sun is deep at the start and grows thin until it gradually fades away, the wealth-acquiring capacity of the person will diminish as life progresses.

2) Ending in a dot : In this case the person will lose his reputation after a life of prosperity.

The line of Apollo

3) Ending in a star (*fig. 356*) : If the Sun line ends in a star, it shows brilliant success. If it ends in a double star, the career will be dazzling and he will achieve great fame. A star at the end also means success due to the assistance and goodwill of others.

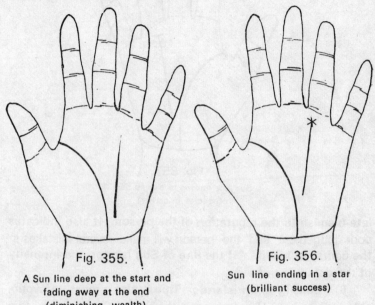

Fig. 355.
A Sun line deep at the start and fading away at the end (diminishing wealth)

Fig. 356.
Sun line ending in a star (brilliant success)

4) Ending in a deep bar (*fig. 357*) : A bar indicates insurmountable obstacles to one's career. This will be a decided check to career. In this case we have to study other signs and lines to locate the cause. For instance, if the line of Life is defective nearly at its end continues to be so, the ill-health and delicacy at that age will affect the prospects of the person. If an island or a star be seen in the line of Head, he will fail in mental power which will check his career and put a stop to his success. If a rising branch or split from the Head line runs to the mount, an error in calculation will check the career from which he will never recover.

5) Ending in a cross : A cross at the end of the line of Sun is a worse obstruction than a bar. It means an abso-

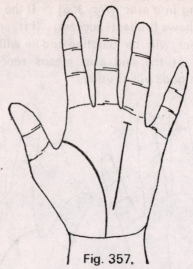

Fig. 357.
Sun line ending in a deep bar
(obstacles in career)

lute blemish to the reputation of the person. It also indicates poor judgement and the person will make several mistakes in the course of his life. If the line of Sun is poor, the intensity of the defect is more.

6) Ending in an island : This is also a most unfavourable indication. However good the line of Sun may be, this marking will cloud the latter days of the person and will end in loss of money and reputation.

7) Ending in a square : A square at the end of the Sun line protects the person from all sorts of evils.

8) Ending in a fork : If the line of Sun is forked at its termination on the mount of Sun into three prongs two of which are curved inwardly (*fig. 358*), it signifies the vast wealth of the person without yielding any earnings. These curved lines always indicate failure. Good opportunities are lost by weakness and defeat at the very critical point.

If the line is forked with two equal prongs, there are two different aspirations influencing the person. The result is bound to be unsatisfactory unless concentration is fully given to only one aspiration.

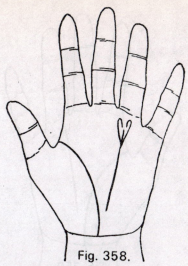

Fig. 358.
Sun line ending in three forks—two forks curving inside (opportunity lost and failure)

A single fork on the mount of Sun yields success only in one direction.

If the line is forked like the letter 'V' on the mount of Sun, power is neutralised by division and the desire for power is not realised.

9) **Ending in a trident** *(fig. 359)* : A well-marked trident at the end of the line of Sun is as good a marking as a star. It indicates celebrity and wealth from intellectual work

If the line is forked into a pointed trident starting above the line of Heart, fame and riches are due to personal merits. If this trident is found on the line of Sun which starts from the negative mount of Mars, the person will achieve success, fame and riches combined with meritorious distinction.

If three branches of the trident are even and of the same length and one goes to the mount of Saturn, the other straight to the mount of Sun and the third to the mount of Mercury, great fame and wealth are assured.

10) **Ending in furrows** : Three equal furrows stretching right to the base of the finger of Sun assure a great and universal fame.

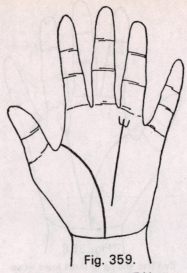

Fig. 359.
Sun line ending in a Trident
(celebrity and wealth)

11) Ending in a tassel : If the line ends in a tassel the person will scatter his efforts in so many directions that he will accomplish little. He has talent but too diversified.

12) Ending on the mount of Jupiter : This is a rare, indication and it shows power and successful leadership.

13) Ending on the mount of Saturn : This is not a very favourable indication because the talents shown by the mount of Sun will assume a gloomy character. Any inspiration given by the Sun will be clouded by scepticism.

14) Ending on the mount of Sun with several lines on the mount : This has the same meaning as the tassel and the person in spite of his talents, will not achieve anything. This can also mean unsuccessful efforts towards success.

15) Ending on the mount of Mercury (*fig. 360*) : This is a favourable indication and the Mercurian sense of utility and calculation will be added to the loftier and idealistic aspirations. To a person with practical ambition, this line gives complete success, may be in business or profession or in politics or literature or scientific inventions.

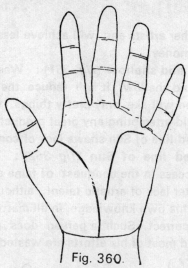

Fig. 360.
Sun line ending on mount of Mercury
(success in ambition)

VII) Character of the line of Sun

1) Deep : A very deep line of Sun on an artistic hand is the exaggeration of the vital force shown by the line of Sun. This may lead to probable fatal troubles of heart.

When the depth is not much, a deep line which is well-developed and well-cut gives beneficial qualities and indicates success in education. It also gives creative power in whatever sphere he operates and he will definitely achieve fame in the artistic field.

If the second phalange of the finger of Sun be longest with the first well-developed, he will still be an artist but will also have the ability to make money from his talents. The word artist may mean a painter, a poet, an actor, a singer or may refer to anybody who has mastered any form of art.

2) Long line of Sun : Long and uncrossed line of Sun is a sign of riches. If it is straight and strong on the mount of Sun, it indicates celebrity as an artist and confidence in the knowledge of one's own talents.

3) Narrow and thin line of Sun : In this case the person will not have the great creative power of the deep line, if he is an artist. He will be more guided by the effects produced by other artists and will achieve less celebrity and will make less money.

4) **Broad and shallow** (*fig. 361*) : When the line of Sun is broad and shallow, it will reduce the power of the line. The person will like only pretty things, will be fond of art but will avoid attempting any great production himself.

A very broad line of Sun shows lack of concentration.

5) **Chained line of Sun** (*fig. 362*) : This formation shows poor success in the conquest of fame and fortune. It indicates an utter lack of artistic talent, although the person may be sure of his own knowledge in all matters of art, most of which is incorrect. Such a person does not realise his shallowness and most of his efforts are wasted in talk.

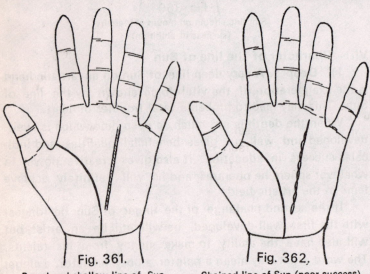

Fig. 361.
Broad and shallow line of Sun
(lack of concentration)

Fig. 362.
Chained line of Sun (poor success)

6) **Wavy line of Sun** (*fig. 363*) : A wavy line of Sun gives bad taste and shows lack of concentration. It also shows a vacillating career. He may be clever but will be erratic, unstable and unreliable. He may be versatile but wastes his brilliance and talents in several directions instead of pushing forward steadily in one direction.

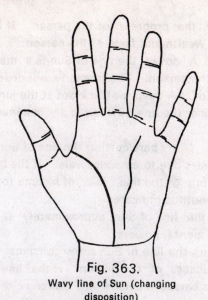

Fig. 363.
Wavy line of Sun (changing disposition)

If this wavy line ends in a star, the life of the person will be glorious and he will achieve reputation. Though unsteady in his talents his work will be crowned with success.

7) Colour of the line of Sun : a) Bright red colour shows a strong artistic vocation. b) Pale colour shows artistic aptitude but insufficient power of execution.

VIII) Defects in the line of Sun

a) *Island* : An island on this line means loss of position and name during the time the island lasts and generally such a loss will occur through scandal.

An island on the line with an indication of illness on the line of Life shows disease of the eyes.

The island shows a trial of some sort or other. It tells us of the time which is receding instead of proceeding. It can also mean temporary financial troubles due to the dishonesty of others. If an influence line from the mount of Venus joins the line of Sun before the island, the danger of scandal in domestic life is emphasised. An island is an obstruction in the progress of the person. If it is deep, it will affect the wealth and fame of the person.

b) *Dot* : A dot in the line of Sun is a menace to the reputation of the person. The intensity will depend upon the size of the dot. A deep or black dot at the junction of the line of Sun and the line of Heart is an imminent danger of blindness.

c) *Bars* : Many bars cutting the line of Sun horizontally hinder the career due to envious rivals. If the bars are seen at the beginning of the line, loss of fortune to the parents during one's youth is indicated.

A bar on the line of Sun, approximately at 50 years is a sign of failing mental powers.

Bars cutting the line of Sun show constant impediments during the success of the person. If the line of Sun cuts through these bars, the person will overcome the obstacles. If the bars cut the line, the impediments will seriously affect the career. If these bars are a few fine lines, they are only annoying interferences.

d) *Breaks* : Breaks in the Sun line indicate setbacks to the ambition and upward course of the person. These breaks destroy the utility of this line and its beneficial influences. With the breaks in the line we cannot expect more than an ordinary success.

If the line is broken inside the quadrangle and if it is connected with the mount of Venus by an influence line, series of misfortunes, in the struggle for recognition and success, are signified (*fig. 364*).

If the line is broken at the line of Head and if it resumes its course only from the line of Heart, the chances of success are good (*fig. 365*).

These breaks in the line of Sun are generally indicative of either temporary money losses or changes affecting one's private or domestic life. A repeatedly broken line may mean versatility but it will bring neither money nor fame. Breaks on the line in the left hand only mean money losses to the

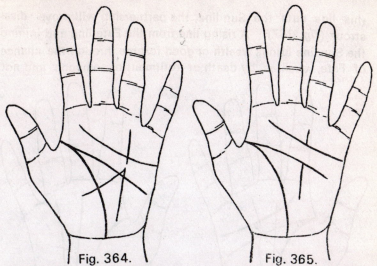

Fig. 364.
Sun line broken in the quadrangle, with an influence line from mount of Venus (misfortune)

Fig. 365.
Sun line broken at the Head line and continues only after the Heart line (revival of success)

family whereas only in the right they mean financial loss to the person himself.

If the line is broken on the mount of Uranus, with an influence line from the mount of Venus cutting the break, it would mean series of misfortunes suffered by the person in his struggle for recognition (*fig. 366*).

IX) Sun line in relation to other lines

The line of Sun and the line of Fate are complementary to each other in their nature and function. The relationship between these two lines, particularly in regard to their relative strength, gives significant value to the hand. If both these lines are well marked, it is a good combination, indicative of healthy circumstances that lead to a prosperous career. It usually means an inheritance together with an easy rise in career. We have to study which of the two lines is stronger on the hand.

a) A line from the line of Fate touching and not cutting the line of Sun will result in a successful partnership. But if this line cuts the Sun line, the partnership will prove disastrous (*fig. 367*). A rising line from the Fate line and joining the Sun line brings wealth or good fortune through the chance of Fate, such as by death or retirement of someone and not

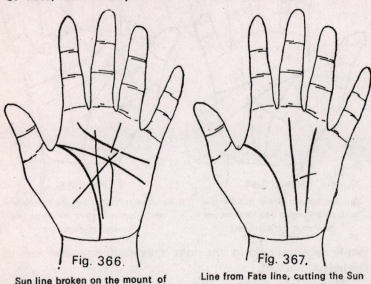

Fig. 366.
Sun line broken on the mount of Uranus, and an influence line from Venus cuts the break (series of troubles)

Fig. 367.
Line from Fate line, cutting the Sun line (failure in partnership)

through the efforts of the person. The date is to be read on the Fate line when the line rises. If on the contrary a line from the Sun line meets the line of Fate, there is money which will assist the career of the person. Sometimes it denotes marriage.

b) A straight and deeply marked line of Sun on the mount of Sun, with pronounced mounts of Jupiter and Mercury, gives wealth and fame due to exceptional talents. In this case intellectuality, shrewdness and ambition are the three strong elements of success.

c) A deeply marked Sun line on the mount of Sun, with pronounced mounts of Venus and Moon, shows an aptitude for fine literary work.

The line of Apollo

d) A pronounced mount of Moon and short nails with a deep line on the mount of Sun create a literary critic of distinction.

e) With a deep line of Sun and Jupiter mount developed on both the hands, the person develops friendship with people in high position.

f) A good line of Sun with a long line of Head indicates talents in the acquisition of wealth by speculation.

g) A good line in a hollow hand ceases to be effective in helping the person to fame and fortune.

h) The same as above but with twisted fingers, we have a person who uses his talents for evil purpose but with miserable failure as an inevitable end.

i) If the line of Sun is cut by a line of union or Marriage, the person loses position due to unsuitable marriage or disgraceful entanglement *(fig. 368)*.

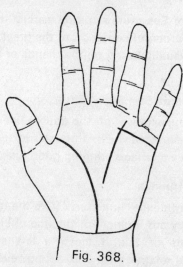

Fig. 368.
Sun line cut by the line of Marriage
(loss of position due to marriage)

j) If the line of Sun is touched, but not cut by an influence line from the mount of Venus, the person achieves success after many struggles and acquires wealth with the help of his own people.

k) If the above line cuts the line of Sun, it means loss of money generally through a relative and ill-luck.

l) A line from the Head line touching the line of Sun shows pecuniary success due to the person's intelligence. If this line cuts the line of Sun, it shows blunders committed by the person and loss of money.

m) A line from Mercury which touches the line of Sun assures artistic career with business ability. If this line cuts the line of Sun, cupidity of the person will interfere with his career. It means either loss of money or prestige or both. It also means money received from other people but not necessarily by legacy. It may be by gifts or rewards of some kind.

n) A prominent line of Sun on both the hands with a star on the mount of Sun signifies celebrity and immortal glory.

o) A line of Sun more strongly marked than the line of Fate has the burden of carrying on the great name of forefathers. It is usually found on the hands of sons who have famous fathers.

X) Double line of Sun (*fig. 369*)

A sudden appearance of the double line of Sun on the hand gives unexpected luck through lottery or shows a windfall or a love marriage bringing good luck.

XI) Line of Influence

1) If an influence line starts from the mount of Venus and cuts an upward branch of the line of Life and further touches the line of Sun, it means a law suit won by the person against a relative (*fig. 370*). If however this line cuts the line, it means that the law suit is lost.

2) An influence line running parallel to the Sun line for sometime indicates legacies (*fig. 371*). If this line starts on the mount of Moon, it means expected legacies. If it starts from above the mount of Moon, legacy comes from a relative.

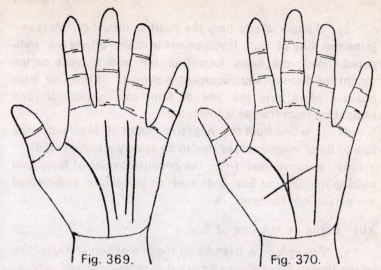

Fig. 369.
Double line of Sun (unexpected luck and windfall)

Fig. 370.
Influence line from Venus, cutting an upward branch in Life line and touching the line of Sun (law-suits won)

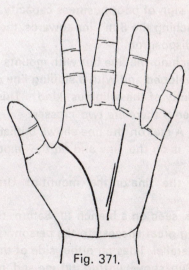

Fig. 371.
Influence line running parallel to Sun line (legacies)

3) If a line starts from the positive mount of Mars and joins the line of Sun, involvement in court affairs are indicated. With the same formation but with a cross on the mount of Saturn, imprisonment is shown. If this line from positive Mars cuts the line of Sun, loss of position and reputation from friends is indicated.

4) If a line from the negative mount of Mars cuts the line of Sun, money losses due to an enemy are indicated.

5) A curve line from the negative mount of Mars and cutting the line of Sun indicates an inordinate ambition of the person not realised.

XII) Signs on the line of Sun

a) *Triangle* : A triangle on the line of Sun and attached to the line of Heart shows a period of enjoyment and reputation in life. It also shows a comfortable life.

b) *Square* : It always shows protection and rescue from attacks on reputation or preservation from loss of money.

c) *Cross* : A cross touching the line towards the mount of Mercury is a sign of poor business capacity.

A cross touching the Sun line towards the mount of Sun shows a pious disposition.

A cross touching the line but with mounts of Saturn and Moon badly developed and with a sloping line of Head shows danger of insanity of the religious kind. This indication is more accentuated if there are two crosses.

d) *Star* : A star on the line shows brilliant and lasting success. If it is on the line and on the mount of Sun, it shows wealth.

A star on the line on the mount of Uranus shows a catastrophe.

If a star be seen on a branch to Saturn, the qualites of Saturn will bring great success to the person.

e) Two parallel lines on either side of the straight and deep line of Sun show untold fortune and glory. If these lines are wavy, they indicate misdirected genius.

CHAPTER XXII

The Line of Mercury

1) Introduction

In the previous chapters we have discussed five important and main lines and in this chapter we shall discuss the 6th and last important line, namely the line of Mercury.

This is the most controversial line on the hand. There are various opinions regarding the functions of this line on the hand. There are also controversial opinions regarding its starting position and its characteristics. We shall deal with them one by one.

1) There are some authors who state that the presence of this line is not a healthy indication. They prefer to have a hand without the appearance of this line. According to these authors, the line of Mercury shows delicate health and person and, according to some, it indicates success or

2) According to some other authors, this line starts from below the hand and runs up towards the mount of Mercury and according to others, this line rises on the mount of Mercury and approaches the line of Life.

3) There is difference of opinion regarding the function of the line also. This line shows the constitution of the person and, according to some, it indicates success of failure in business.

4) This line is also known by various names such as the line of liver, the line of health, the line of hepatica and the line of Mercury. These various names indicate the functions of the Mercury line. In our discussions of this line we shall consider all the aspects and the differences of opinion as stated above.

In fact this line signifies both the health aspect and the business aspect. It shows various health defects such as liver trouble, bile trouble, nervous trouble etc. At the same time it gives business ability and shrewdness which are the main characteristics of the mount of Mercury.

A good line of Mercury usually represents two primary factors of success and affluence through career or business and good health.

While considering the health factors, the line is more important in its association with the line of Heart and the line of Head. This line is also important during its course on the mount of Moon and the plain of Mars. Any defect in the line at these places may specify troubles with the lungs or gastric troubles, acidity and digestive troubles. Many of the troubles depend directly or indirectly on the function of the stomach and the liver, the kidneys or the bladder. Any defect in the Mercury line is a sure sign of one or the other type of disease. On the contrary, a good line of Mercury assures general good health and longevity.

The line of Mercury is invaluable in conjunction with the line of Head in estimating mental strength and balance. A good line of Head will be much disturbed by a poor Mercury line and a defective condition of the Head line may be accounted for by the bad Mercury line. Similarly, this line plays an important role in the defective functioning of the Heart and the root cause of the heart trouble may be located on the line of Mercury.

This line also has a great psychological significance. The presence of this line shows biliousness and many bilious types are criminals. Bad types of Mercurians prefer the criminal way in their life.

Absence of the line of Mercury

According to some authors, the absence of the line on the hand shows an extremly robust and healthy disposition and constitution. It also denotes a quick mind and an alert disposition. If the line is absent, with hard hand and square

The line of Mercury

fingers, it also indicates activity. When the line is absent, the developed mount of Mercury shows vivacity.

It has been observed that there are few lines on the hand when the Mercury line is absent. Such a hand with few lines is less nervous. In short, we can say that when the Mercury line is absent on the hand, the person does not suffer from the inevitable diseases or digestion and no disorder of the liver is found.

II) Position on the hand

It starts low on the mount of Neptune and close to the bracelet and cuts across the path in straight course terminating on the mount of Mercury. In a large number of cases, it starts from the Saturn on Life line, or from the centre or base of the hand. It is better that the line starts between the Saturn line and the percussion than between the Saturn line and the line of Life.

III) Starting position of the line of Mercury

a) Starting from the bracelet *(fig. 372)* : It shows an excellent business success, a good digestive power and a long life. If the line does not touch the line of Life, it indicates frequent travels and a busy life.

b) Starting from near the percussion : It signifies a changeable and extremely nervous disposition. It also gives the gift of clairvoyance.

c) Starting from the line of Life : If the line starts from the Life line and if the Quadrangle is narrow due to the line of Heart curving towards the line of Head, the person suffers from fainting fits due to bad digestion.

The touching of the Mercury line to the Life line tells of some kind of delicacy undermining the health and constitution of the person. If this line is as powerful as the line of Life, their meeting point will be the point of death *(fig. 373)*. The period is to be calculated on the line of Life. It also shows a hereditary family weakness which may reach a crisis at the age indicated on the Life line.

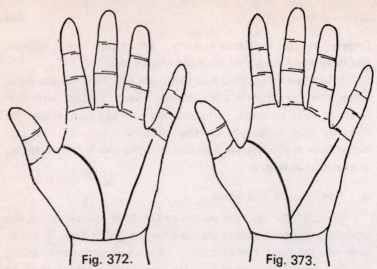

Fig. 372.
Mercury line starting from rascettes (long life)

Fig. 373.
Mercury line touching the Life line (death)

The joining of the Mercury line to the Life line at its start is indicative of self-earned money due to one's own business ability and labour.

d) Line of Mercury starting from the mount of Venus : A wavy line of Mercury starting from the mount of Venus and ending on the mount of Mercury shows immorality due to excess passions (*fig. 374*).

It also indicates love and fortune and the person is exceptionally lucky in business.

e) Starting of Mercury line from an island : Mercury line starting from an island indicates somnambulism (*fig. 375*).

f) Starting from the mount of Neptune : In this case the person spends his wealth in charity. This is particularly so, if the line ends on the mount of Mercury.

IV) Course of the line of Mercury

1) A good line of Mercury well developed represents physical and mental equilibrium. It shows the capacity to enjoy life and also a detached attitude to environment. It indicates robust health and vitality and good digestive system. It equally shows longevity.

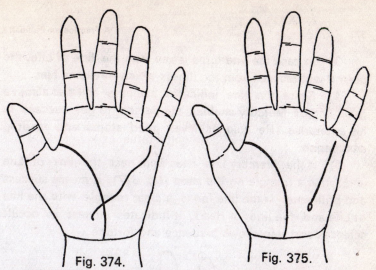

Fig. 374.
Wavy Mercury line, starting from the mount of Venus (immorality)

Fig. 375.
Mercury line starting from an island (somnambulism)

2) If the line first points to the mount of Apollo and then takes its course towards the mount of Mercury from near the line of Head, the person earns wealth but has to incur great expenditure (*fig. 376*).

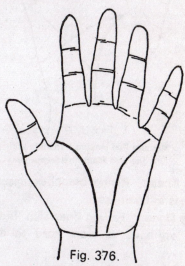

Fig. 376.
Mercury line first pointing towards the mount of Sun and then turning to mount of Mercury (good earning but equal amount of spending)

3) In case the line turns away from the line of Life, the person will recover from the illness which threatens him.

4) Since the line indicates business abilities also, a good line of Mercury enables the person to get success in his enterprise. He also achieves good status and merit in occupation.

5) If the Mercury line rises from near the line of Life and forms a triangle on the hand (*fig. 377*), it means success and brilliance. If the line forms a clear triangle with the line of Life and the line of Head, it indicates interest in occult sciences and also shows prudence and fortune.

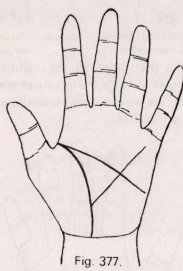

Fig. 377.
Mercury line making a triangle with
Life line and Head line (occultism)

6) **Rising lines :** Rising branches assure good health and great success in business.

7) **Falling lines :** Falling lines also indicate success but the person will have to work hard to accomplish the results.

8) **Branches :** Branches of the line of Mercury are generally good and indicate success and good health. The ascending branches denote changes.

The line of Mercury

a) A branch to Jupiter (*fig. 378*) will give success in business, assisted by the ambition and ability to lead and control men. If a star be seen in addition on the mount of Jupiter, influential friends will be helpful. This rising branch also produces an occultist.

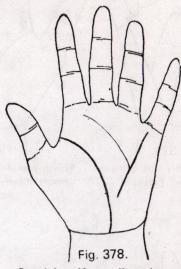

Fig. 378.
Branch from Mercury line going to Jupiter mount (success in business)

b) A branch to the mount of Saturn (*fig. 379*) signifies sobriety, frugality and wisdom and gives success. However if the branch cuts the line of Saturn the career is impaired.

c) A branch to the mount of Sun (*fig. 380*) shows a successful career due to shrewdness, brilliance and an aggreeable manner. If a branch from the line of Apollo joins the line of Mercury, it indicates wealth.

If the line of Mercury is connected with the line of Sun by a line, not cutting the Sun line, it is a sign of wealth (*fig. 381*). If this line cuts the line of Sun, it shows financial losses. It also means success ruined by an excessive love of the opposite sex.

d) A branch from the Mercury line running into a break on the line of Life shows danger from death (*fig. 382*).

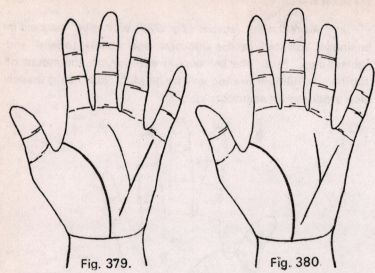

Fig. 379.
Branch from Mercury line going to the Saturn mount (wisdom)

Fig. 380.
Branch from Mercury line going to mount of Sun (shrewdness and success)

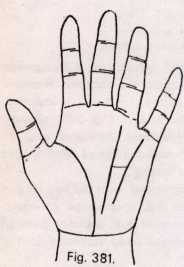

Fig. 381.
A line connecting the line of Sun and the line of Mercury (wealth)

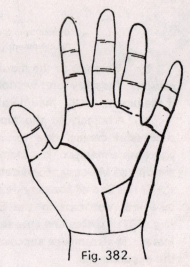

Fig. 382.
A branch from Mercury line touching a break in the Life line (danger of death)

The line of Mercury

e) A branch from the Mercury line reaching the mount of Venus after cutting the line of Life gives a warning of thieves or a fraud by those who intimately move with the person. It also means deceit from enemies (*fig. 383*).

f) If the Mercury line throws a powerful branch towards the mount of Moon, things will take place according to the will of the person giving him satisfaction (*fig. 384*). It gives a judicial mind and amiable manners. If the branches are unequal and make unusual formations, unhappy position is indicated. They show dangerous sea travels and for ladies they indicate frequent sorrows and difficulties in child-bearing.

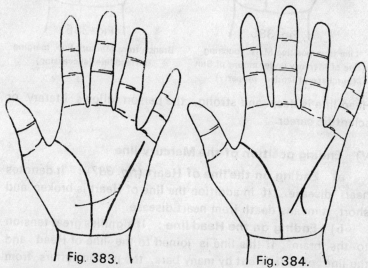

Fig. 383.
A branch from Mercury line going to the mount of Venus (warning against theft and deceit)

Fig. 384.
Branch from Mercury line to mount of Moon (satisfaction in life)

If a line from the mount of Moon touches the line of Mercury, the point of contact forms a lucky point.

g) A line from the positive mount of Mars, touching the line of Mercury under the mount of Sun, shows purchase of landed property (*fig. 385*).

h) A branch from the Mercury line, merging into the Head line, indicates succession due to will (*fig. 386*). If the

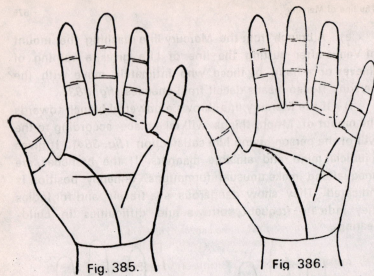

Fig. 385.
Line from positive Mars, touching the line of Mercury under mount of Sun (purchase of landed property)

Fig 386.
Branch from Mercury line, merging in Head line (succession)

Head line is deep and strong, the person follows literary or scientific career.

V) Ending position of the Mercury line

a) Ending on the line of Heart (*fig. 387*) : It denotes heart disease. If in addition the line of Heart is broken and short, it means death from heart disease.

b) Ending on the Head line : It signifies great tension to the brain. If this line is joined to the line of Head and the line of Life is cut by many bars, the person suffers from brain disease often brought about by a diseased liver.

If the Mercury line is forked at the termination so as to form a triangle with the line of Head (*fig. 388)*, the person loves honour and power and has great aptitude for occult sciences.

c) Ending on the mount of Sun : In the line ends on the mount of Apollo and there exist three rascettes which are well marked and complete, there is great wealth and successfully-built business.

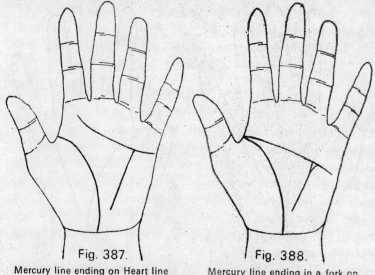

Fig. 387.
Mercury line ending on Heart line
(heart disease)

Fig. 388.
Mercury line ending in a fork on
Head line (love of honour)

d) **Ending on the Mount of Mercury:** In this case the person forms friendship with famous people.

e) If this line ends in a fork, it is a sign of deterioration of health and weakness mostly in old age (*fig. 389*). The person will divide his energy in achieving many things and will not achieve as great a success as would have been possible by concentration.

f) If the line of Mercury ends in a star on a powerful mount of Mercury and if it starts from the mount of Venus, it is one of the happiest formations on the hand.

g) **Ending in a bar:** The bar hampers the career of the person. If the type of the hand is bad, the deceitful or tricky qualities of a bad Mercurian will bring about a failure.

h) **Ending by intervening lines:** It denotes poverty in old age (*fig. 390*).

i) **Ending in a grill** (*fig. 391*) : It indicates failure in life either due to poor health or dishonesty.

j) **Ending on a cross :** It means a disturbed career.

k) **Ending on a tassel :** In this case the efforts are scattered and therefore no great success can be achieved.

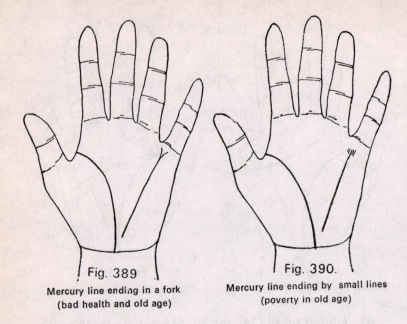

Fig. 389
Mercury line ending in a fork
(bad health and old age)

Fig. 390.
Mercury line ending by small lines
(poverty in old age)

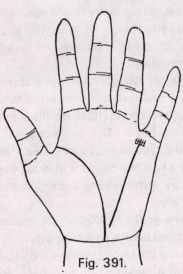

Fig. 391.
Mercury line ending in a Grille
(failure due to poor health)

VI) Character of the Mercury line

1) Deep line : A deep line of Mercury is a good asset but an abnormally deep line is a warning to life. It shows exuberance of animal vitality which leads to severe consequences. A deep Mercury line, which is absent in the Quadrangle but which touches both the lines of Heart and Head, shows danger of brain fever.

2) Thick line : A thick development of the line of Mercury, which is short and does not even reach the negative mount of Mars, discloses an impaired digestion in old age. It also shows poor and deteriorating health.

3) Vertical line : If the line of Mercury is more vertical a wiry kind of vitality is present.

4) Broad and shallow : It denotes a delicate stomach. The liver is unsteady in its operation and secretes its bile in unequal qualities. It results in sudden and violent headaches, heart-burn and dyspepsia.

5) Straight and thin : It signifies stiffness of manner.

6) Thin and narrow : In this case the person has good digestion, proper action of liver and general success in business.

7) Thick and short : It signifies impaired digestion in old age.

8) Chained line of Mercury (*fig. 392*) : It is invariably an indication of poor success in business. As regards health, it is equally a bad indication. It also indicates the inflammation of gall duct. The chained line not only shows trouble of the liver but it also shows great mental depression. The person is pessimistic, suspicious and intensely nervous. He is a burden both to himself and to his family or friends.

9) Twisted line of Mercury : It shows a thief and a cheat and one with evil conscience (*fig. 393*).

10) Ladder-like formation of the line of Mercury (*fig. 394*) : It is a sign of severe liver trouble and shows a succession of business losses. It also shows colitis. It also indicates gastric fever, catarrah of the stomach or intestines or inflammation of the bowels.

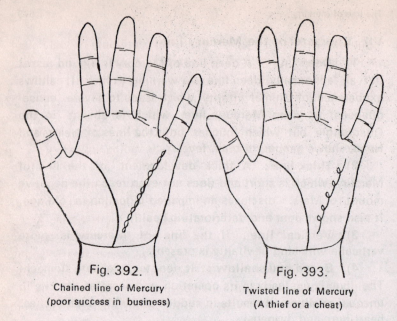

Fig. 392.
Chained line of Mercury
(poor success in business)

Fig. 393.
Twisted line of Mercury
(A thief or a cheat)

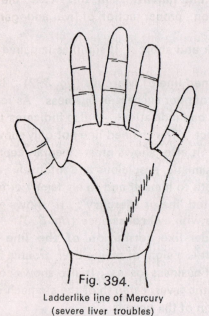

Fig. 394.
Ladderlike line of Mercury
(severe liver troubles)

The line of Mercury

11) A broken line, running parallel in a series, denotes lung trouble. If the line is made of little pieces and is approaching nearer to the line of Head, it means mental strain and even paralysis.

12) If the line is netted in its formation, it means loss of hair.

13) **Wavy line of Mercury** *(fig. 395)* : The line of Mercury indicates biliousness and when wavy it is a worst sign. On a bad hand it shows poor success in business and also dishonesty. When this line is twisted and irregular, it adds liver complaints and biliousness.

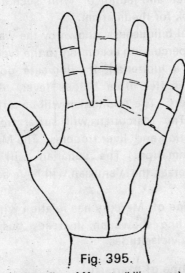

Fig. 395.
Wavy line of Mercury (biliousness)

A wavy line if long, starting from inside the mount of Venus, means immorality and a debauchee. It also means that the life is shortnened by excess.

A wavy Mercury line, with a poor line of Head and absence of line of Heart, shows tricky and unreliable business ways. This formation means a physically weak heart.

A long and wavy line of Mercury in combination with a wavy line of Fate and with second phalange of fingers long, gives bad breath due to bad teeth.

A wavy and broken line of Mercury terminating on the mount of Sun indicates serious fever in tropical countries. This is more so if there is a black spot or a dot or a star on the base phalange of the Sun finger.

If this wavy line is short and branched and if the mount of Mars is exaggerated, the person suffers from extreme nervousness leading to restlessness. He is very difficult to be pleased.

In short, a wavy line of Mercury indicates chronic biliousnes. The person will get attacks of bilious fever. malaria and various liver complaints ending in an enlargement of the liver and jaundice. With such a wavy line, one should also look for rheumatism.

The original biliousness shown by the wavy Mercury line will have its repercussion according to the type of the person. On the hand of a Jupiterian, it will create gout trouble. The Saturnian will suffer from bilious fever, rheumatism and nervous disorders. The Apollonian will be affected by heart derangement. The Mercurian will suffer from indigestion, nervous disposition and liver troubles. The Martian will have intestine inflammation. The Lunarian will have gout or rheumatism whereas the Venusian will have acute attacks of bilious fevers.

Since the line of Mercury has relation with the business career, a wavy line shows an unsteady business which is subject to many vicissitudes.

Colour of the line of Mercury

The colour of any line usually depends on the person. A Jupiterian, an Apollonian, a Martian or a Venusian, even with pronounced biliousness, rarely has any colour but pink or red, though blue is sometimes seen. The Saturnian, the Mercurian and the Lunarian will usually have a yellow colour.

a) **Red colour of the line at the start :** It shows a tendency to palpitations of the heart, especially connected with the line of Life. These palpitations will be due to poor digestion.

The line of Mercury

b) **Red colour throughout :** This is a sign of brutality and inordinate pride.

c) **Thin and red in the middle portion :** It shows tendency to bilious fevers.

d) **Red colour at the end :** It means chronic headaches.

e) **Of various colours :** It signifies apoplexy.

f) **Yellow colour :** It shows serious liver troubles.

g) **Pale in colour :** It means poor action of the heart.

h) **Darkly coloured and deeply cut :** It shows nervous disorders.

VII) **Defects of the line of Mercury**

A defect in the Mercury line may be due to islands, dots, bars, etc. and whenever found they lessen the power of the Mercury line. In such cases misfortune may come due to personal incapacity or through outside agencies. These misfortunes are usually unexpected and uncontrollable. They may be due to animal passions, health troubles, from over taxing of the brain or due to defective functioning of the digestive system.

1) *Island* : An island shows financial difficulties and affliction of the vocal organs. It also shows tumour or even cancer. If the line of Saturn or the line of Sun is broken or cut by a deep bar, the island shows bankruptcy.

If the island is wide and long, it shows lung trouble. If on the contrary the island is short and narrow, bronchial troubles are indicated. If the island is very short, weakness of bronchial tubes is observed. An island with filbert nails indicates tuberculosis.

An island on the line of Mercury between the line of Head and the line of Heart with a grill is a sign of operation.

Long island formations on the line of Mercury with a break on the line of Saturn at the corresponding age is a sign of epilepsy. An island on the Mercury line above and below the line of Head shows delicacy of the chest and lungs.

2) *Dots* : Dots on the Mercury line indicate acute attacks of bilious or stomach troubles at the age at which they occur on the line. If red, they indicate fever, if white, some disorder arising from a chronic disease. Here also one can look to the type of hand and then decide the measure of sickness.

3) *Bars* : Deep cross bars indicate as many sicknesses as the number of bars. They also indicate business reverses. If the bars cut the line of Mercury diagonally, they mean malarian fever.

4) *Breaks* : Breaks are a sign of chronic indigestion. They also mean poor health or incompetence in business.

If a small bar is seen across the break, it denotes fall in business.

If the line broken and a square covers the break, the person will suffer from typhoid fever.

A clear break in the middle of the hand, having bar lines at two ends of the break, show a possibility of a surgical operation.

If the break is encircled by a square and if there is a star in the square, it denotes cancer.

If the break is under the mount of Apollo and the line continues well after the break, there is a change in the manner of life. If this break is under the mount of Saturn, it shows a change in life which will increase longevity.

5) *Small lines crossing the line of Mercury* : These small lines weaken the health. They indicate headaches. If the line of Head is also crossed by small lines, congestion of the lungs or pleurisy is the result.

VIII) Mercury line in relation to other lines

1) A long, narrow, clear and straight line of Mercury, with a long line of Head across the hand, signifies good memory.

2) A long and fine line of Mercury, with a short line of Life, makes up for the insufficiency shown by the short line of Life.

The line of Mercury

3) A very narrow and highly coloured Mercury line with a broken line of Life and dark spots on the line of Head is a dangerous sign and the person suffers from fever.

4) If the Mercury line is irregular or wavy and the line of Head is poor and narrow, it denotes indigestion and inferior business capacity.

5) A poorly traced Mercury line with a narrow Quadrangle due to the line of Heart curving towards the line of Head, is a sign of asthma.

6) In case the line of Mercury is poor and all other lines are also poor, it is a sign of paralysis.

7) A poor line of Mercury, with a poor line of Head and a cross near the termination of line of Life, shows poor health, especially in old age.

8) If the Mercury line forms a cross with the line of Head on the mount of Moon, it is a sign of over-excited imagination.

9) If the line forms a clear triangle with the lines of Head and Life which is open at the base, it indicates great aptitude for occult sciences.

10) If the line forms a cross in both the hands with the line of Head on the upper mount of Mars, it gives talents for occult sciences.

11) If the line of Mercury forms a small triangle with the line of Head and the line of Life, it shows aptitude for occult sciences. It may also give the gift of intuition and clairvoyance.

12) When there is a clear line of Mercury, with the upper third mount of Moon more pronounced, the person has mesmeric and hypnotic powers.

13) A line from a powerful mount of Saturn, touching the line of Mercury under the mount of Sun, is an exceptionally lucky sign in regard to money. It shows success in races, lottery and share market (*fig. 396*).

14) A strong line of Mercury with a good line of Fate creates a successful business magnate.

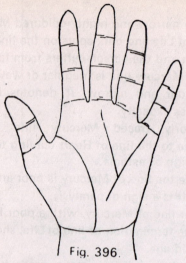

Fig. 396.
Line from Saturn mount touching the line of Mercury (luck in race or lottery)

15) A straight line of Mercury joined to the line of Life with a well-formed first rascette gives longevity.

16) It is better to have the line of Mercury separated from the line of intuition.

If they are mingled with each other, there is a warning of impairment of health due to one's excessive application to the study of esoteric subjects.

17) A poor line of Mercury, with the presence of intuition line with many crosses on it, creates humbug clairvoyants and fortune tellers.

18) The line of Mercury cut by Via Lasciva is a sign of grave liver troubles (*fig. 397*).

19) Fine cross bars crossing the Mercury line and also fine bars crossing the Head line indicate great suffering from nervous, bilious or sick headaches.

IX) Double line of Mercury

A double line has often the force of the sister line when they run parallel to each other. It would then indicate more than one business, inheritance, unprincipled avarice and

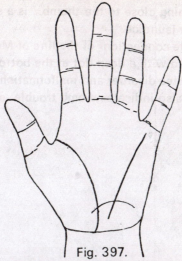

Fig. 397.
Line of Mercury cut by Via Lasciva
(liver troubles)

strong animal aptitude. If the double line appears only, in sections it does not create any serious illness. If a part of the line is divided into long and parallel line formations, they mean liver complaints.

X) **Signs on the line of Mercury**

a) *Triangle* : It represents illness which has quick recovery.

b) *Circle* : It denotes minor misfortunes during hunting or driving.

c) *Cross* : A cross near the line but not on it indicates serious changes in life. A cross on the line is a warning of coming danger. A cross towards the termination of the line of Mercury with a circle on the line of Head shows blindness.

d) *Star* : It denotes unexpected luck. It also means not more than one child.

A star close to the line of Mercury and inside the Big Triangle indicates blindness.

A star on the line of Mercury, especially at or close to the connection of the line with the line of Head and with the line of Life running close to the thumb, is a sign of sterility, childlessness or jaundice.

A star at the connection of the line of Mercury with the line of Head, and with a deep dot at the bottom of the mount of Moon, indicates disorder and malformation of the generative organs. It also indicates womb trouble causing sterility.

CHAPTER XXIII

Double line of Life or the line of Mars

I) Introduction

Though this is one of the minor lines, it has a great importance in relation to the life of the person in various ways. This line signifies resistance, vitality and divinity. It is also called the sister line of Life. The presence of this line certainly gives good health and material wealth. There is no difficult situation from which the person is not protected. He can venture in life and will be successful in climbing great heights.

If a defect is noticed in the line of Life and at the same time the line of Mars is powerful, the delicacy or the danger shown by the Life line will not prove fatal.

This line is also called by various other names such as the line of Mars, the inner vital line, the line of resistance, the line of stimulation etc. These various names tell in a general way the function and importance of the line.

When the line of Life is in itself strong, the line of Mars endows its owner with the power of great energy, robust health and stamina. This line is an insurance against ill-health.

The ardour and the energy shown by the line of Mars creates a state of auto-stimulation. It develops a taste for alcholism and a tendency to indulge in them. This creates an over stimulation of the nervous system which affects the heart adversely.

There are some bad effects arising out of this double line of Life. They create lack of patience, irritable nature and the person is constantly involved in quarrels. But their faults are compensated by their courage and confidence in the most difficult situations. They have the masterful spirit and the force of will. Their vital energy combined with their inherent culture endows them with magnetism and forcefulness.

The person is usually involved in love affairs very early in life and he is also fortunate in his married life. With magnetic power the line adds to the personality and also the caution it bestows, the line helps to attract the best and choose the right.

The possessor of the double line of Life has his traits also. The person, being extremely irritable and passionate, finds it difficult to control. In old age he develops a sour temperament. On the material side, the double line gives prosperity. It is also a gift to the person in his spiritual awakening. The person has his power of intuition strongly developed and experiences significant dreams. He has strong faith in what may be called divine help in time of urgent need. Slowly they may turn from materialism to spiritualism.

This double line of Life also indicates one's rise to positions of authority and command.

II) Position of the Hand of the double line of Life

Normally the line of Mars runs close and parallel to the line of Life on the lower mount of Mars and the mount of Venus. It starts on the mount of Mars and travels upto the wrist. It thus covers the two mounts, namely the mounts of Mars and the Venus, which impart the qualities of sympathy, kindness, steadfastness and love. This line is usually absent on the hand and it denotes lack of vitality.

III) Starting position

1) The starting point of the line of Mars is significant. It denotes the beginning of a great love affair at the time it corresponds to the line of Life.

If the line starts from the line of Life *(fig. 398)*, the above significance is more potent and the other partner is

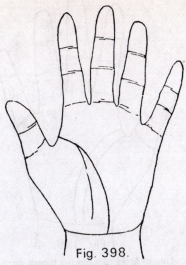

Fig. 398.
Line of Mars starting from Life line
(love affair)

governed by the Martian qualities. This origin of the line also has another meaning and emphasises the spiritual implications of the line.

2) If the line starts from a fork, it shows love affair in an early age.

IV) **Course of the double line of Life**

1) **Running quite parallel to the line of Life**, just like a rail track, shows brilliant life terminating in exile. If this is more marked in the later part of life, the person's death takes place away from one's country.

2) **Running too close to the line of Life :** It develops an irritable temperament. The person is prone to quarrels and disputes. It may also show a love of litigation.

3) **Running full length to the line of Life** *(fig. 399)*: The person enjoys a good life and comforts.

It has a very significant meaning regarding the marriage partner. The marriage partner will be in more affluent circumstances than the person concerned. This is more true on the hands of males.

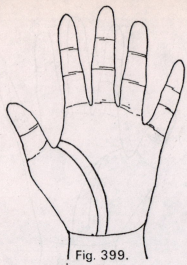

Fig. 399.
Line of Mars running full length to the Life line (good health)

4) If this line of Mars recedes away from the line of Life, its progress deprives the natural resistance shown by this line of Mars.

5) **Running only for a short time as a sister line to the line of Life :** The influence of this line is for the period calculated on the line of Life. The divine force and support also stops when the line comes to an end.

If the line covers only the mount of Mars and does not continue to the mount of Venus, the better forces shown by the mount of Venus are deprived of. In that case it becomes a line of anxiety only. It represents a reaction of certain repressed qualities of the mount of Mars. There is concern for health, safety and material well-being. They are often disturbed with a haunting fear that they are not destined to make a success in life either materially or spiritually. There is a constant lack of faith in the safety of life.

6) **The line of Mars seen only at the final portion of the line of Life** *(fig. 400)* : If this line is seen on a hand indicating violent nature, the line shows a tendency to murder. This is confirmed, if the line is deep and red in colour.

The line of Mars

7) The line of Mars touching the line of life both at the beginnig and at the end *(fig. 401)* : If the line of Mars makes a figure of strung and bow after touching the line of Life at the beginning and at the end, the life of the person will be as it were strung up and apt to be very much influenced by the person placed in very affluent circumstances. It may also mean that the husband may live in the home of the wife.

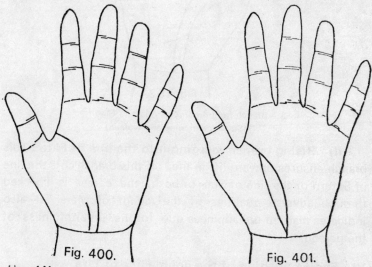

Fig. 400.
Line of Mars seen only at the end of Life line (tendency to murder)

Fig. 401.
Line of Mars touching Life line at the beginning and also at the end (husband living in the house of wife)

8) Branches : a) **Branch to the mount of Moon** *(fig. 402)* : This branch is seen on the hands of travellers who indulge in wine and women. They are often rash and heedless of danger. The age at which the line cuts the line of Life is a danger point.

b) **Rising branch :** It shows rise in Life. If it cuts the line of Life, it shows constant efforts to rise in life.

c) **Rising line merging in the line of Head :** There is accentuation of mental strength. If this branch cuts the line of Head, overstrain injures the brain power.

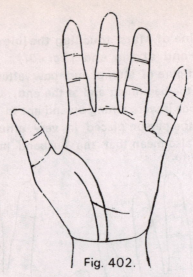

Fig. 402.
Branch from the line of Mars to Moon
(indulgence in wine and women)

d) **Rising branch merging into the line of Fate :** This branch ensures upward lift in life. If this branch cuts the line of Saturn or the line of Sun or both, the career is checked through adverse qualities of the mount of Mars. It also indicates married unhappiness due to the unfaithfulness of the person.

V) **Ending position of the double line of Life**

a) If the line of Mars ends in a fork and one branch goes to the mount of Moon, it indicates intemperance and brutal insanity.

b) If the line ends only in a fork, it shows a tendency to murder *(fig. 403)*.

c) If one of the prongs or the fork ends on the mount of Moon and in a star *(fig. 404)*, it means alcoholic intemperance. If there is a black spot in the Head line, it shows death from delirium or alcoholic insanity.

VI) **Character of the double line of Life**

a) *Deep* : If this line is as deep and strong as the line of Life, it speaks of tremendous vitality and aggression. If

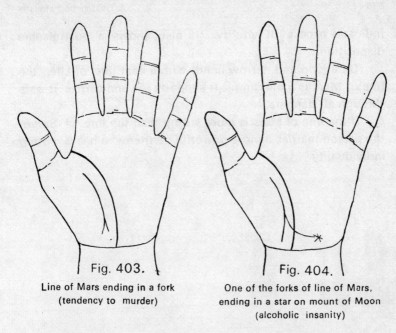

Fig. 403.
Line of Mars ending in a fork
(tendency to murder)

Fig. 404.
One of the forks of line of Mars,
ending in a star on mount of Moon
(alcoholic insanity)

in addition he is a Martian, he will be a fighter and consequently a good soldier. His greatest danger is of exerting the surplus energy in rioting and drinking.

b) *Short and thin* : The line of Mars, if found much shorter and much thinner in the right hand than the left, shows that the weakness in health is checked by proper care and treatment.

c) *Colours* : 1) A line with a deeper pink colour of the skin denotes decision and perseverance.

2) A line with a red colour indicates success in war.

VIII) **Double line of Life in relation to the type of the hand**

In order to study the defects of the line of Mars, the line should be treated more as a sister line to the Life line. The meaning of these defects on both the lines is the same.

VII) **Defects of the double line of Life**

The line of Mars on a square hand or a broad hand

indicates excess of vitality. It also shows a quarrelsome disposition.

On a long and narrow hand, with a neat line of Life, the line of Mars is a blessing. It supports life and carries it safe through all dangers.

If the line of Mars is more strong than the line of Saturn the person marries a more powerful partner who has a strong individuality.

CHAPTER XXIV

The line of Via Lasciva

I) Introduction

There are two positions of Via Lasciva on the hand *(fig. 405)*.

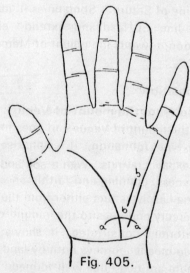

Fig. 405.
Two positions of Via Lasciva

1) Sometimes it starts as a parallel line to the line of Mercury. In that case, it works as a sister line to the Mercury line. In case there are faults or defects in the Mercury line, they are repaired by the presence of Via Lasciva. A wavy line of Mercury will not indicate bad results from biliousness if the Via Lasciva is present. Similarly, a broken line of Mercury will not have serious troubles of the stomach. If the Via Lasciva runs only a part of the way alongside of

Mercury line, its strength will be exerted during the time it continues.

2) It also sometimes starts on the mount of Venus and goes to the mount of Moon in a semi-circular way. In this case, it shows the lower instinct of man and animal appetite. It is a menace to the career of the person.

II) Position on the hand

It is generally supposed to occupy a slanting position rising from the inside of the base of the mount of Moon and terminating on the lower part of the upper mount of Moon near the percussion. It may also start from the line of Mercury or the line of Saturn. Sometimes it may start from the region of the line of Head and extend either towards the mount of Moon, towards the mount of Mercury or towards both the mounts.

III) Starting position

a) Starting from the mount of Venus : In case the line starts from the mount of Venus and goes to the mount of Moon, in a loop-type formation, it emphasises the coarser instincts and sexual cravings. With a soft and flabby hand it means lasciviousness, cunning and faithlessness.

b) If the Via Lasciva starts either from the line of Saturn or the line of Mercury and goes to the mount of Moon, unbroken and uniformly constituted, it shows healthy brain qualities. It also means journeys both by land and sea. This is more so, if there are two lines well-formed

The above formation with a very good mount of Venus shows favours from women.

c) If the Via Lasciva starts from the plain of Mars and runs parallel to the line of Mercury, it indicates sensuality and a passionate thirst for money.

IV) Course of the line of Via Lasciva

1) When the line starts in the region of the Head line and extends in the direction of the Mercury mount, the

person is enthusiastic and has a talent in science and eloquence.

2) If this line extends to the mount of Moon and goes downwards into it, the talent of the person is of imaginative sort. There will be useful and fortunate journeys.

3) A long and unbroken Via Lasciva ending on the mount of Mercury and running parallel to the line of Mercury shows a long life and an uninterrupted happiness.

4) If the Via Lasciva cuts the line of Mercury, the person will have serious liver troubles. This line will also mar business qualities and business success.

V) **Ending of the line of Via Lasciva**

1) If it ends on the mount of Mercury, it shows zest in business and profession. It may also mean a clever politician. It gives luck and eloquence.

2) If the Via Lasciva is formed at the end, there is a slow waste of energy due to excess. It also indicates impotence.

VI) **Character of the line of Via Lasciva**

a) A deep and clearly marked Via Lasciva will undoubtedly have a strong tendency to lower the person in some direction. He will be apt to think evil, even if he does not practise it and temptation will cause him to fall.

b) A deep and strong Via Lasciva on a soft hand with a full mount of Venus will make the person devote himself to pleasure and pursue it at any cost.

c) A wavy Via Lasciva shows inconsistency and lack of success due to disintegration. If this wavy line starts from the mount of Venus, it often means immorality and a short life.

d) **Branches :** 1) If a branch runs and cuts the line of marriage which ends in a fork, the lasciviousness of the person will rule his married life.

2) If a branch cuts the line of Sun, the lascivious tendency will ruin the success of the person.

3) If a branch from Via Lasciva crosses the line of Life, it will injure the health of the person.

4) If a branch runs to a dot in the Life line, the excess will cause severe illness at the age which the dot indicates.

5) If several branches run across the line of Head, the person will suffer from headaches and the brain power will be much impaired. If after crossing this, there are bars, breaks, or crosses in the Head line, the person will have an attack of brain fever. If with such combination a star be seen on the Head line, the person may become insane due to excess.

VII) The line of Via Lasciva in relation to other lines

a) If the Head line has a defect, the presence of Via Lasciva shows the lessening of the brain power.

b) The presence of the Via Lasciva with islands on the Fate line will indicate financial embarassment due to pleasure-seeking motive. If in addition a dot or a cross is seen on the line of Apollo or the mount of Sun, the intensity of the motive will ruin his reputation.

c) If a well-marked Via Lasciva is seen with a strong line of Mars and all the lines are deep and red with a big mount of Venus, the person will be a debauchee. If in addition he has a thick or clubbed thumb, he will commit rape, brutal murder or any crime to accomplish his desire.

d) If in addition to the existence of Via Lasciva, there is a Girdle of Venus also present, there will be a decided immorality and a craving for drugs and liquors. In its worst form when the Via Lasciva ends on the mount of Moon, the person will indulge in reckless conduct, in wine and women.

e) The Via Lasciva connected to the line of Apollo by a line that cuts the line of Sun shows a heavy financial loss. If the Sun line is not cut, it indicates wealth.

VIII) Signs on the line of Via Lasciva

Star : It is a sign of both success and riches.

CHAPTER XXV

The Girdle of Venus

I) Introduction

The Girdle of Venus is usually associated with highly sensitive and intellectual persons who are changeable in moods, feel easily offended and touchy over small things. The Girdle of Venus denotes a highly strung and nervous temperament and, if unbroken, it certainly gives most unhappy tendencies towards hysteria and despondency.

Persons possessing this mark are capable of rising to the highest pitch of enthusiasm over anything that engages their attention but they are rarely twice in the same mood.

The presence of this line on the hand has more psychological significance but it is not a very happy indication. It indicates those vicious habits which are generally developed at the time of puberty. These habits have always been considered as arising from nervous or hysterical troubles.

The Girdle of Venus speaks of the gravest troubles of the generative organs. The presence of double or triple or broken Girdle of Venus tells of natural vices, such as poisoning of the blood or even an erotic insanity of the worst character.

In a large percentage of hands in which the Girdle of Venus is found, the palm will be crossed by innumerable lines running in various directions. This proves that the person is intensely nervous and has nervous excitability.

II) Position of the Girdle of Venus

The Girdle of Venus is a broken or unbroken kind of semi-circle rising between the first and the second fingers and ending between the third and the fourth fingers (*fig. 406*).

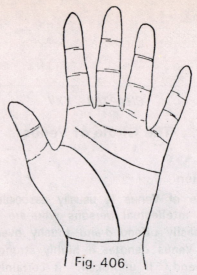

Fig. 406.
Girdle of Venus (passionate nature)

A single line of Girdle of Venus shows a natural inclination towards the opposite sex. It also shows sensitivity, energy and restlessness. The person is also interested in spiritualism and occult sciences. If the Girdle of Venus is present only on one hand, it means a happy marriage through the faithfulness and affection of the married partner.

III) Course of the Girdle of Venus

1) When the line connects the mount of Jupiter and the mount of Mercury, it indicates refinement of passions and occult wisdom.

2) When it is partially traced and is more evident under the mount of Sun, the person's energies will be directed more towards the heart.

3) If the Girdle of Venus is more prominent on the mount of Saturn, the lower qualities of the Girdle of Venus will become evident.

4) When it is found in bits, one at the starting and the other at the terminating point, a very emotional and sensitive nature is indicated.

5) If the Girdle of Venus is stronger than the line of Sun while cutting it, misuse of faculties and opportunities in a

most extraordinary manner is indicated which is detrimental to the person's career.

6) If the line of Sun is stronger, it shows favourable development in one's destiny, occurring in an unexpected way, giving fame, fortune and success to the person.

7) If the Girdle of Venus crosses both the line Fate and the line of Sun, inordinate passion and pursuits of sensual pleasures may stand in the way of success *(fig. 407)*.

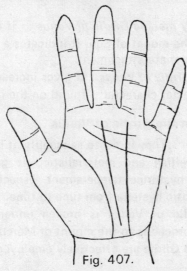

Fig. 407.
Girdle of Venus, crossing lines of Fate and Sun (sensual pleasures bar success)

IV) Ending position of the Girdle of Venus

1) **Touching the Marriage line:** When the Girdle of Venus goes over the side of the hand and by so doing comes in contact with the line of Marriage, the happiness of the marriage will be marred though the peculiarities of the temperament. Such a person is exacting and hard to live with and he will expect many virtues in his wife.

2) **Terminating on the mount of Mercury:** The person will have unusual, though unhealthy, nervous energy and orderliness in every undertaking.

V) Character of the Girdle of Venus

a) *Very deep* : A very deep and a red Girdle of Venus, cutting through the lines of Fate and Sun as if to obliterate their best characteristics, indicates that the intellect of the person is gravely impaired by the vicious tendency finally affecting the career.

b) *Thin* : If a strong and good line of Fate or line of Sun cuts the thin Girdle of Venus, the person has wit and love for literature.

c) *A finely marked Girdle of Venus* : If it is cut by a bar line under the mount of Sun, it indicates a life spoiled on account of passionate attachment.

d) *Thick Girdle of Venus* : It gives increased momentum to whatever special character is found on the hand.

VI) Defects in the Girdle of Venus

1) *Breaks* : They indicate sensuality at its worst. The person is very selfish and materialistic. It gives a retiring disposition and hysterical temperament. Especially in women, there will be erotic hysteria from time to time.

If the Girdle of Venus is broken under the mount of Apollo or then proceeds to the mount of Mercury, all energies indicated by the Girdle are effectively employed in the pursuit of art.

2) *Bars* : If the Girdle of Venus is cut by small lines and if the mounts of Moon and Venus are exaggerated, there is a tendency showing the presence of hysteria of the erotic nature.

VII) Double Girdle of Venus *(fig. 408)*

Sometimes we may come across a double or even a triple Girdle of Venus, which is indicative of intensified qualities of the Girdle. It shows invariably lust and intemperance.

VIII) Girdle of Venus in relation to other lines

a) If we find a star or a cross or a dot or an island near the termination of a sloping line of Head, and if there are

The Girdle of Venus

several lines on the hand and the Girdle of Venus is also broken, the person is in grave danger of insanity as a result of nervous disposition.

b) If there is a cross on the mount of Saturn with a dot or an island in the Head line under Saturn, a broken Girdle of Venus will mean danger from paralysis.

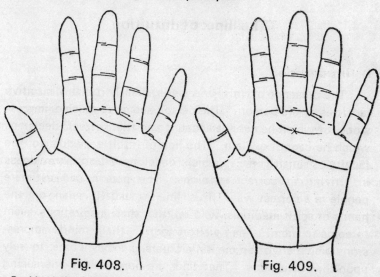

Fig. 408.
Double girdle of Venus (lust and intemperance)

Fig. 409.
Cross on girdle of Venus under the mount of Saturn (suicide by poison)

c) When the Girdle of Venus is badly formed and there is a presence of a Via Lasciva, there may be a strong tendency to indulge, in some form or the other, in the artificial stimulation of the nervous system which may lead to the worst forms of nervous exhaustion and nervous debility. It may even show premature death.

IX) **Signs on the Girdle of Venus**

a) *Star* : A star on a double or multiple Girdle of Venus is a strong indication of venereal disease, from which there will be no recovery.

b) *Cross* : A cross on the Girdle under the mount of Saturn shows suicidal tendency by poisoning *(fig. 409)*.

CHAPTER XXVI

The line of Intuition

I) Introduction

The presence of this line adds greatly to the intuitive faculties of the person. The person seems to receive impressions for which he cannot account and the correct decisions which he cannot explain. The line of Intuition adds to the faculty of sensitiveness, which develops adroit shrewdness in arriving at correct opinions. The person can estimate people in a correct way. This line is usually seen on the hands of spirit mediums, who tell that their inspirations seem to come to them. Their visitors form in their minds impressions which are often mental pictures and they come to rely upon their intuitions. They find the impressions increasing in number and in accuracy. Persons with this line of Intuition create fascination about themselves. They have culture, imagination, understanding and power of mind and thought. It gives a very impressionable nature, susceptible to vivid dreams and presentiments. They may have a gift of mesmeric and hypnotic powers and an aptitude for clairvoyance.

This line is usually found on the psychic and conic hands. On a square hand it exhibits day-dreaming in respect of coming events. On a Mercurian hand, the presence of this line creates a tricky and deceptive person. He may exploit intuitive faculties to make money.

If in addition to the line of Intuition, there is a mystic cross on the hand, the person has unusual aptitude for occult science.

The line of Intuition

II) Position of the line of Intuition

This line is seen in a curved form and rises on the mount of Moon and goes towards the mount of Mercury. It occupies the same position as the line of Mercury but it is distinguished from it by its curve formation. A good line of Intuition starts from the lower mount of Moon near the percussion and goes upward in an accentuated curve to the mount of Mercury but near the percussion.

III) Starting of the line of Intuition

1) The higher it starts on the mount of Moon, the more the intuitive faculty will be under the control of the person.

2) *Starting from an island* : It shows the gift of clairvoyance and also somnambulism.

IV) Course of the line of Intuition

a) If during its course the line cuts a sloping line of Head, imagination spoils mental faculties.

b) If it makes a triangle with the line of Head and the line of Saturn, a strong aptitude for occult sciences is indicated *(fig. 410)*.

c) If during its course the line is crossed by an influence line from the line of Life *(fig. 411)*, there will be opposition to the study and practice of the occult subject by the person from his close relatives or friends. These occult studies interfere in the career of the person.

d) *Branches* : 1) A rising branch from the line of Intuition to the mount of Jupiter will make the person ambitious to achieve something with his intuitive faculties.

2) If a branch rises to the mount of Sun, the person will achieve renown in the exercise of the intuitive faculties.

3) If the rising branch merges into the line of Fate, the exercise of the intuitive faculties will assist the career of the person.

V) Ending position of the line of Intuition

1) *Ending in a star* : It indicates great success from

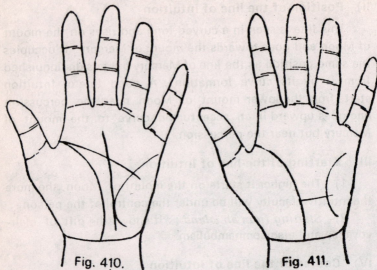

Fig. 410.
Line of Intuition making a triangle with the lines of Head and Fate (occultism)

Fig. 411.
Line of influence, from Life line cutting the line of Intuition (opposition to the study of occultism)

the exercise of the intuitive faculties. If in addition the line of Mercury is very strong, the person will make money from this gift of intuition.

2) *Ending on the mount of Moon* : It shows a change in the course of life and also a caprice.

3) *Ending on the mount of Mercury* : The person has intuition of a high order and has the gift of prophecy and attraction towards the occult sciences.

4) *Ending on the negative mount of Mars* : This formation shows a remarkably high hypnotic power.

5) *Ending on the Heart line* : In this case the person is much under the influence of vague imagination and lacks practicality.

VI) **Character of the line of Intuition**

1) *Deep* : This adds greatly to the intuitive faculties.

2) *Wavy* : A wavy line with an exaggerated mount of Mars creates an extremely nervous or restless disposition.

VII) Defects of the line of Intuition

1) A broken line of Intuition will show limited powers.
2) Islands in the line will bring poor success out of the intuitive faculty.

VIII) Signs

A cross on the line with a badly marked mount of Mercury indicates a humbug clairvoyant and charlatan.

CHAPTER XXVII

The Bracelets

I) Introduction

Bracelets on the hand are not of much importance except in the Indian Palmistry. They are traditional indications handed down to the posterity without much logical significance. However in the Hindu system they have been given much importance as showing longevity and good luck. There is usually one bracelet on the hand which is nearer to the wrist. But occasionally we may come across two or three or even four bracelets on the hand. They are also called Dragon's lines. In their usual position they are clear and separated by equal distance. If there are three bracelets, they are called the Magic Bracelets. If there are four such bracelets, they are called Royal Bracelets. Of all these bracelets it is the first one which is nearer to the palm, which has greater importance. A star on this bracelet is identified as the Dragon's Head. A clear line running from the second bracelet into the mount of Venus is the Dragon's Tail.

The effects of the bracelets are of greater importance in the later life of the person, when he experiences tranquillity, easy life and riches.

When a bracelet is placed higher on the hand and closer to the palm, it is an auspicious indication. It means noble aspirations and nobler and elevated ideas. If the bracelet is on the lower side of the hand, which descends away from the palm, it shows worldly ambitions and desires of an inferior character.

The presence of three bracelets of good colour indicate tranquillity of mind, with good health and wealth. These three bracelets will even compensate a short line of Life.

The Bracelets

If the first bracelet on the hand of a woman curves too much inside the palm, it shows difficulties in child-bearing (*fig. 412*).

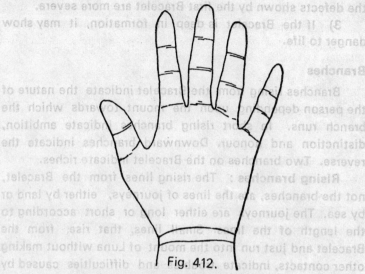

Fig. 412.
First bracelette, curving inside the palm (difficulties in child-bearing)

II) Position of the Bracelet

It is found below the palm and near the wrist. According to the Hindu system, each bracelet speaks a life of about 30 years.

III) First Bracelet

Its presence on the hand confirms a strong constitution.

IV) Course of the first Bracelet

1) If the Bracelet rises in the centre, it indicates delicacy of the abdomen in women. It shows difficulties of procreative organs and constitutes danger in maternity. If there is any other reason of female weakness on the lower mount of Moon or in the line of Mercury, the bulging Bracelet has strong confirmatory information. These are

valuable as pre-marriage indications and are good guidelines for a fruitful marriage.

2) If the second Bracelet is also arch-like in formation, the defects shown by the first Bracelet are more severe.

3) If the Bracelet is deep in formation, it may show danger to life.

Branches

Branches rising from the Bracelet indicate the nature of the person depending upon the mount towards which the branch runs. In short rising branches indicate ambition, distinction and honour. Downward branches indicate the reverse. Two branches on the Bracelet indicate riches.

Rising branches : The rising lines from the Bracelet, not the branches, are the lines of journeys, either by land or by sea. The journeys are either long or short according to the length of the lines. Small lines, that rise from the Bracelet and just run into the mount of Luna without making other contacts, indicate troubles and difficulties caused by private enemies. If the lines are checked or distorted, the troubles are more serious and the enemies more wicked.

a) **Rising to the mount of Jupiter :** A line from the Bracelet going to the mount of Jupiter is a sign of rise in life, success in law and high position. It also indicates a long journey. If this line goes from near the percussion and to the Jupiter mount, it indicates a long voyage. If this line changes its course at the end and goes to the mount of Saturn but does not reach the mount, the person will not return from his voyage.

A rising line which goes straight to the mount of Jupiter, with a cross or an angle or a star on the Bracelet, indicates wealth due to success in journey.

b) **Line rising to the mount of Saturn :** It shows elevation to some high position connected with science or religion. Two lines from the Bracelet to the mount of Saturn crossing each other on the mount indicate two travels but the person will not return from one of the travels.

c) **Line rising to the mount of Sun :** A single or double line, running to the mount of Sun, shows riches, honour, literary success and fame. It also shows good reputation through people in high position. It may also mean travels in tropical countries. If this line goes to the mount of Mercury, the person has various capacities.

d) **Line rising to the mount of Mercury :** A straight line to the mount of Mercury from the Bracelet gives sudden and unexpected wealth and industrial success and life in a foreign country.

If this rising line is broken in the middle and does not reach the mount, the person is untruthful and discontented.

e) **Rising line to negative mount of Mars :** It shows difficulties which overwhelm the person.

f) **Line rising only upto the plain of Mars :** It is a sign of wealth and honour through the influence of powerful friends.

g) **Line going to the mount of Moon :** This line is indicative of travels and voyages. It also indicates a wandering life. If there are two such lines, which go across the mount of Moon, a profitable but dangerous journey is indicated. If the lines from the Bracelet just reach the mount of Moon, private enemies and adversities are shown.

h) **Line rising from second Bracelet and going to the mount of Venus :** This is the Dragoon's Tail and shows adversities and difficulties from relatives or married partner.

V) Character of the Bracelet

a) If the Bracelet is poorly marked, the constitution of the person is not very strong. It also shows extravagance.

b) A chained first Bracelet shows a life of hard labour but with good fortune at the end.

c) A broad and shallow and even chained Bracelet speaks of a poor constitution.

VI) Defects of the Bracelet

A broken and badly formed Bracelet indicates troubles.

The third Bracelet formed like a series of small islands shows delicacy of the intenstines.

VII) Bracelet in relation to other lines

a) If a line from the Bracelet goes to a vertical Venus line and thence extends upto the mount of Jupiter, it indicates a rich marriage or wealthy alliance. If there is a cross on the mount of Jupiter, the marriage will be a happy one.

b) If the above line instead of going to the mount of Jupiter extends to the mount of Saturn, the person marries an old person.

c) If the above line goes to the mount of Sun, he will marry a person with artistic taste.

d) If the line goes to the mount of Mercury, the marriage will be with a merchant or a businessman.

e) If the line from the Bracelet crosses the mount of Moon and terminates on the line of Life, it shows death in a voyage.

f) If the line of Saturn cuts the Bracelet, it indicates sorrow and trouble.

VIII) Signs on the Bracelet

1) *A clear angle* : It shows unexpected wealth by inheritance and position and honour in old age.

2) *Cross* : A cross on the Bracelet, preferably in the centre of the first Bracelet, indicates a hard life which ends in tranquillity and fortune. Unexpected gains through legacy are also denoted.

3) *Star* : A star in the centre of the first Bracelet is the Dragon's Head and indicates fortune by inheritance in old age.

4) *A triangle with a cross in it* : Such a sign on the first Bracelet indicates large fortune through inheritance.

CHAPTER XXVIII
Line of Travel and the lines on the mount of Moon

I) Introduction

We come across several lines from the mount of Moon which have different functions. The lines go in various directions and from the nature of the line we can distinguish its function.

The lines on the mount of Moon mainly have three functions :

1) They show the travels or the voyages.
2) They indicate the diseases according to the place on the mount of Moon where they are found.
3) They show the influence of other persons in the career of the individual.

We shall discuss below the above aspects one by one.

1) Travel lines

We have already discussed under the chapter 'Bracelet' that the lines rising from the Bracelet and going upto the mount of Moon indicate travel or voyages.

Certain lines on the mount of Moon also show such voyages or travels. Horizontal lines or cross lines from the centre of the mount of Moon generally indicate travels or voyages (*fig. 413*). Such lines usually start from the percussion and run towards the interior of the palm and, if the line is longer, the person will go on a long voyage and vice versa.

A line falling out from the Life line and going to the mount of Moon is also a line of Travel.

(Also see page 612 for travel lines.)

Signs on the travel line

a) An island on this line of Voyage (*fig. 414*) shows danger from water.

b) A star on this line (*fig. 414*) shows a fatal accident during the voyage.

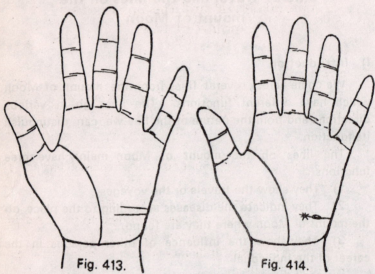

Fig. 413.
Travel lines on the mount of Moon

Fig. 414.
An island and a star on the travel line (danger from water)

c) A square, as we know, is a sign of preservation and the person is protected from danger if any during the journey.

d) A cross shows disappointment in journey.

If the above signs are seen on both the hands, the danger is sure but if they are seen only on the left hand and not on the right hand, they indicate only the possibility of such dangers. With a square on the line of voyage on the right hand, the person is sure to be saved and protected from the danger, even though he is liable to meet with an accident.

Ending Position of the line of Travel

a) If the voyage line turns up at its termination and shows direction towards the mount of Jupiter or the mount of Sun or the mount of Mercury or to the mount of Mars, the person will gain an advantage by the voyage (*fig. 415*). The nature of the advantage is shown according to the mount towards which the line points.

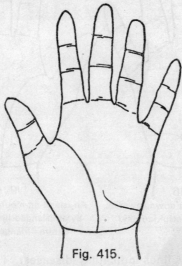

Fig. 415.
Line of voyage turning up towards mounts (Advantage through voyage)

b) If the line points out to the mount of Saturn, the voyage will seldom bring advantages.

c) In case the line of Voyage turns up and joins the line of Heart, the person will come across one who will influence his affections.

d) If the line of Voyage turns up and joins the line of Head, the influence will be of a business nature.

e) If the line of Voyage turns down and joins the line of Life (*fig. 416*), the journey will end in disappointment or even fatality.

If there is an island on the mount of Moon, which is joined by an islanded line from the mount of Saturn, there is great danger from water (*fig. 417*).

2) **Lines on the mount of Moon showing diseases**

We have already studied in the chapter on the mount of

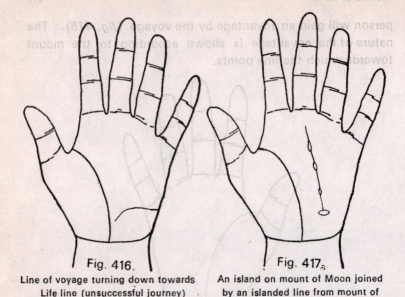

Fig. 416.
Line of voyage turning down towards Life line (unsuccessful journey)

Fig. 417.
An island on mount of Moon joined by an islanded line from mount of Saturn (danger from water)

Moon the various lines indicating diseases. For ready reference, we may state in short that 1) lines on the upper mount of Moon show apendicitis and bowel troubles, 2) lines on the middle portion show rheumatism and intestinal troubles and 3) lines on the lower part of the mount of Moon show kidney troubles and gonadic troubles.

3) **Lines of Influence on the mount of Moon** (also see page

Lastly the lines on the mount of Moon show other influences in the life of the person.

a) If a line of influence rising on the mount of Moon touches the line of Fate, it shows the influence of the opposite sex or the marriage of a foreign influence. This influence is beneficial to the person (*fig. 418*).

b) If this line crosses the line of Fate and turns down to the line of Life, the marriage may not take place.

c) If there is a break in the line of Fate after touching the line of influence, the career is adversely affected due to the influencing person.

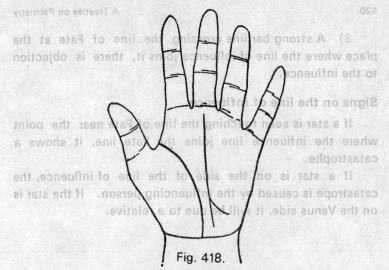

Fig. 418.
A line of influence from the mount of
Moon, touching the Line of Fate
(influence of opposite sex)

d) If the line of influence continues upto the line of Head, it will create anxiety to the person.

e) If it runs upto the line of Heart, the affections will suffer.

f) If the influence line joins the line of Voyage, the influence is from abroad.

g) If the influence line joins a small friendship line which runs close and parallel to the line of Head, a beneficial marriage will take place.

h) An influence line joining the line of Sun will bring money through foreign influence.

Defects in the line of influence

1) An island in the line of influence shows that the character of the influencing person is not good. If in addition the line of Saturn is broken at the point of juncture, the above reading is more certain.

2) If there is an island in the influence line and at the same time there is an island on the vertical line of Venus, it means bad character of the influencing person.

3) A strong bar line crossing the line of Fate at the place where the line of influence joins it, there is objection to the influence.

Signs on the line of influence

If a star is seen touching the line of Fate near the point where the influence line joins the Fate line, it shows a catastrophe.

If a star is on the side of the line of influence, the catastrope is caused by the influencing person. If the star is on the Venus side, it will be due to a relative.

CHAPTER XXIX

Rings of Solomon and Saturn

The Ring of Solomon

This is a rare line seen on the hand. It is a semi-circular line covering the mount of Jupiter or part of it. This line is usually seen between the fingers of Jupiter and Saturn and goes down towards the upper portion of the line of Life and towards the percussion. This line is named after the King Solomon, who was famous for his wisdom, generosity and his knowledge of the occult sciences.

Sometimes this line is also seen by way of small lines from towards the end of the hand and running under the mount of Jupiter. In this case it looks like the same line as the union or the Marriage line found on the mount of Mercury.

The possessor of this line is deeply interested in occult sciences and also in psychology. He acquires much in the psychic field. Such a person usually has square or spatulate tips with knotty joints. The ring of Solomon also indicates inclination towards spiritual life. If there are two strong lines close to each other or the line gets a shape of a square or triangle, it is a good indication. A star attached to it is a mark of greatness.

The Ring of Saturn

This is also another rare sign seen on the hand. This line forms a semi-circle under the mount of Saturn. Since this line obstructs the course of the Fate line, it indicates troubles and unhappiness in the career of the person. Such individuals usually lack continuity of purpose with the result that they get poor success in life.

Some students of the study of the hand found this sign on the hands of prisoners. This sign also indicates a tendency to suicide. The ring of Saturn creates a defect in the mount of Saturn and the person lacks the qualities of the mount of Saturn which are wisdom, seriousness and balanced attitude. He therefore develops as a bad Saturnian and with lack of continuity becomes a criminal.

The presence of the ring of Saturn with a slope in the Head line on the mount of Moon, which is large, makes the person extremely imaginative, restless and changeable and will make nothing of himself. When the ring of Saturn is composed of two lines, which cross each other on the mount of Saturn, it must be read in the same manner as a large cross on the mount of Saturn. This also means suicidal tendencies.

Even though the above bad qualities are attributed to the ring of Saturn, it has much better and happier significance on the hand of women. The mount of Saturn is considered as the mother mount and that is why the significance of the ring of Saturn is partial to women. The ring of Saturn invests in women the typical motherly attributes of sobriety and plainness as opposed to showy glamour. Children in the women group with the Saturn ring face obstacles and obstructions in life in a serene manner and with an intelligence borne out by experience and intuition. They have the gift of intelligence, refinement and grace.

In practical life persons with the ring of Saturn are unfortunate in friendship and are often misunderstood.

If there is a star on the ring, the person may find interest in seclusion as a monk or he leads a philosophical life.

A cross on the ring and a cross on the mount of Moon indicate death by drowning or by accident.

If the ring throws out a branch to the line of Sun, it is a sure indication of imminent misfortune that may cause loss, depression or sorrow to the person. It may be the death of a near relative or loss of reputation or a financial setback. In whatever shape the ring of Saturn may be found, it is a mark of sorrow through fate.

CHAPTER XXX

The line of Marriage

I) Introduction

This is the most important line amongst the minor lines. The marriage factor is a vital one in everybody's life and much of the happiness in life depends upon harmony in married life.

Everybody is curious to know about the nature and character of his life partner, whether the partner will be from a rich family, whether their love will continue to the end, etc. It is therefore necessary that this aspect of marriage should be carefully studied from the hand. The line of Marriage is one of the indications on the hand showing marriage relations and this line should be combined and studied in relation to various other factors on the hand, which indicate life-partnership or union.

The importance of the Marriage line is more marked because, in many hands, it is the only line that speaks about an individual's marriage or safe partner relationship. In most of the hands this line complements, confirms or explains the information that may be available from other sources on the hand regarding marriage and life. This line has not received the attention it deserves. Much research has been done on the Venus and Moon lines and also on the line of Fate (Saturn) and the line of Heart and their influence on man's married life or his life partnership. But the Marriage line has not been attended to regarding its subtle vagaries.

This Marriage line is also called the line of Affection or the line of Union. We have to interpret this line in its limit and in combination with other signs on the hand. If we use this line as indicating marriage and make it a hard and fast rule, it will lead to constant error. This is because marriage does not affect every person in the same way. Some persons are not impressed by the marriage aspect and they may consider it as an ordinary routine of daily life. On such hands we may not notice any marriage line. To use the word "marriage" in connection with this line is also misleading and therefore the use of words as "the line of affection or the line of union" is more appropriate. Such lines are often seen on the hands of those who are not married but who love their mates as fondly as if they are tied in wedlock.

Absence of the line of Marriage

The absence of the Marriage line does not mean that there is no sex relationship for the person. It often means a cold determined nature of one who has little faith in the higher responsibility of sex life.

Age factor

The spacing of the Marriage line in relation to the line of Heart and the finger of Mercury can give a fair idea of the time of marriage or a particular attachment. The distance between the line of Heart and Mercury finger can be considered as a span of 50 years. The centre point therefore is 25. This age factor, however, may differ from place to place or country to country, since the notion of early marriage or late marriage varies in different parts of the world. The nearer is the line to the line of Heart the earlier is the marriage and vice-versa.

II) Position of the line of Marriage on the hand

The line of Marriage lies on the mount of Mercury and runs from the percussion towards the inside of the palm. This line is horizontally placed between the line of Heart and the base of the Mercury finger. This is a fairly thick line and has the intensity of the secondary line. Usually, it stretches upto the middle mount of Mercury. It may be a short or a long line. There may be only a single line or a number of lines.

The line of Marriage

a) *A single line* : A single line of Marriage, running straight and parallel to the line of Heart, indicates a happy and healthy married life or partnership. In this case the two individuals are strongly attached to each other with good understanding and co-operation. They are willing to make a sacrifice, if it is for the common good.

b) *Two lines* : If two Marriage lines are seen and, in addition, a small line from the line of Fate joins the line of Heart on the side of the mount of Jupiter, it quite often indicates a second marriage (*fig. 419)*. If these two lines run parallel to each other, the person has two affairs with equal intensity. In this case the line nearer to Heart line shows the earlier affection and the upper one shows the latest one.

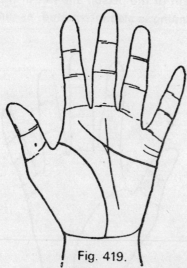

Fig. 419.

Two lines of Marriage and a small line
from Fate line joining the Heart line
on the side of Jupiter
(second marriage)

c) *Many lines* : These lines indicate susceptibility to attachments. The longer and deeper ones are the stronger and the more sustained are the love affairs. If these lines are deeper at the end, the earlier affairs have not gone out of the person's life.

The longer the line of Marriage, the longer the affection continues. When a number of lines are seen, the duration of each affair may be estimated by the length of each line. By this method we can know the strong attachments and their length of period.

III) Starting position of the line of Marriage

a) Starting with a fork (*fig. 420*) : It means delay in marriage brought about by financial difficulties, ill-health or travel in other lands. It also means strong attachment out of the earlier troubles and trials. If there is a separation, it is due to the fault of the person and not of the partner. This fork at the beginning is also interpreted as unusual strength of love.

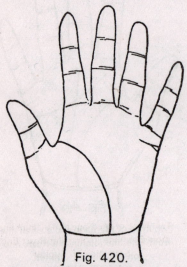

Fig. 420.
Marriage line starting with a fork
(delay in marriage)

b) Fork at both ends : It shows a period of separation due to travels, which may cause concern, anxiety and pain. This is not indicative of legal separation (*fig. 421*).

c) **Starting with an island :** It means illegitimate relationship or troubles before marriage. It can also mean delay in marriage or, separation of the couple at the commencement of the married life. If the line continues well thereafter they may have a happy life later on.

IV) **Course of the line of Marriage**

1) **Pointing towards the line of Heart** (*fig. 422*) : It means married life characterised by constant quarrels and

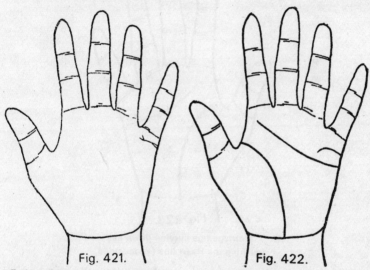

Fig. 421.
Forks at both ends of Marriage line
(separation due to travels)

Fig. 422.
Marriage line pointing at Heart line
(quarrels in married life)

disunity. But with the line of Fate starting from the mount of Moon, the disunity and quarrels will be lessened and there is the possibility of a happy married life. In this case the defect of the Marriage line is rectified by the line of Fate.

When there are two separate lines of Marriage pointing towards the line of Heart, the single line is rectified and there is a happy union instead of the one characterised by discord and quarrels. If these two parallel lines are of equal length, the interval of separation by the death of the partner is small and the death occurs in happy circumstances. It also means that both the partners live upto old age. If the line nearer to the line of Heart is the shorter one, the partner dies first in old age. If this line is longer, the person dies first.

2) **Marriage line turning to the line of Heart and resting on it**: It signifies widowhood. If there is a small bar on the line of Marriage, the death is sudden (*fig. 423*).

Fig. 423.

Marriage line curving down and touching the Heart line (widowhood)

If the curve is casual and not abrupt towards the line of Heart, the last illness of the partner is a lingering one.

If the sloping line crosses the line of Heart and terminates on the mount of Venus, there is either separation or divorce and not the death of the partner.

3) **Line of Marriage strongly drooping towards the line of Heart and with an island on it**: There is great sorrow resulting from the death of the partner through illness or serious accident.

4) A **broken and frayed line of Marriage** indicates disaster.

Branches: Rising branches from the line of Marriage indicate rise in position after marriage. Falling branches indicate sorrow and disappointment.

The line of Marriage

a) A branch going to the mount of Sun shows a brilliant marriage. It shows marriage with one of distinction and exalted position. If there is a star at the termination of the line of Sun, it means an exceptionally brilliant union. If however there is a downward branch of the line cutting the line of Sun, the person loses position through marriage.

b) Fine lines from the Marriage line crossing the entire palm indicate a struggle to get freed from the married life and to effect divorce. These fine lines mean that there is seldom hope for reconciliation.

c) Small capillaries or small capillary lines from the line of Marriage falling towards the line of Heart show illness or ill-health of the partner which causes anxiety.

V) **Ending position of the line of Marriage**

a) **Ending in a fork :** If the line of Marriage ends in a fork, the affection between the partners becomes less strong and the marriage may end in divorce. If the fork is not very wide, the estrangement is not very serious. It also means a broken engagement. This fork also means married happiness destroyed through the interference of others. In a less serious way, it signifies temperamental differences between the partners predisposing separtion.

If this forking of Marriage line is connected to the line of Heart, which curves downwards towards the line of Head at its start, a very unhappy marriage with a very serious and fatal involvement is the result. This is due to a very exacting and callous nature of the person.

In addition to the fork at the end of the Marriage line, if the line from the fork goes to the line of Sun and forms an island on it, there is a separation accompanied by a scandal, disgrace and loss of position (*fig. 424*).

b) **Marriage line ending in a hook :** If the line makes a hook at the end, the person will lose his affections which will not be regained (*fig. 426*).

c) **Line of Marriage curving upwards** (*fig. 425*) : In this case the person is not destined to marry. The give and

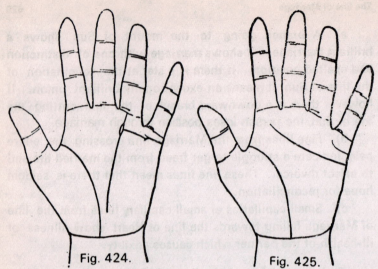

Fig. 424.
Marriage line ending in a fork. A line from the fork ends in an island on Sun line (scandal and separation)

Fig. 425.
Marriage line curving upwards (no marriage)

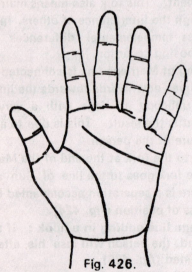

Fig. 426.
Marriage line ending in a hook (loss of affection)

take, the mutual concessions and sacrifices, necessary for the married life are foreign to him and his attitude. He often remains a bachelor throughout his life.

d) **Marriage line ending on the mount of Sun :** It shows prosperity after marriage. If the marriage line terminates at the line of Sun, not cutting it, the person marries one who has fame and riches. If the line goes downwards and cuts the line of Sun, it shows loss of position and riches through marriage.

e) **The line ending on the mount of Saturn in a distinct cross :** It means that the person may seriously injure or kill the marriage partner for some selfishness. If the line of Fate is also stopped by a cross on the mount of Saturn, the person will end his life on the scaffold for murdering the partner.

f) **Marriage line ending on the Heart line :** It shows the hyper-sensitive nature of the partner which hampers their married life. It also means that the person predeceases the partner.

g) **Marriage line ending on the mount of Venus :** If the marriage line droops down and terminates deep and clear on the mount of Venus on the left hand only, it shows inducement and intention for a divorce. If shown in both the hands, it means divorce.

h) **Marriage line ending on the palm :** If the marriage line bends in a long curve and ends on the palm without forking, the partner is quarrelsome, uncompromising and unreasonable, which leads to unhappiness in married life. If such a line ends in an island, the partnership ends in a scandal.

i) **Marriage line ending in a cross :** If the line ends on the negative mount of Mars with a cross at its end, uncontrolled jealousy injures fatally the marriage partner.

j) **Marriage line ending in an island :** It means that married life ends in disaster and separation. When there is an island at the termination of the line with another island at the base of the reason phalange of the thumb, marriage takes place between near relatives.

k) **Marriage line ending in a trident :** It shows utter dissipation and frittering away of the affections.

VI) Character of the line of Marriage

A long, clear and deep line reaching farther on the mount of Mercury shows longer life to the partner than to the person. If the line runs right across the full length on the mount of Mercury, the affection is more of a craze than an attachment. With a cross on the mount of Jupiter, it indicates a happy marriage.

A deep and well-cut line, with good colour, shows harmony in married life. If the line is strong and deep at the start but thin and faint later on, the attachment is gradually lost.

A very thin line makes the partner unhappy. It shows a cold and indifferent nature.

A short marriage line indicates a short engagement which may not end in marriage.

A broad or shallow or chained line of marriage shows indifferent nature.

Colour of the line

1) White colour will add coldness to the nature of the man.

2) Pink or red colour will strengthen the affections.

VII) Defects on the line of Marriage

1) *Island* : If an island appears on the line of marriage, there will be some unhappiness during the course of the island. If the line of marriage is composed of islands, the person will never have affection strong enough for the one whom he marries.

2) *Splits* : Splits in the line of marriage show divided interests of the partner. The two partners may live under the same roof and be happy in spite of divided interest. If a line

from the mount of Mars crosses this split, it is a bad indication.

3) *Cross bars* : They show unusual complications in married life.

4) *Breaks* : Breaks show interruptions in married life. They may also show divorce or separation. If a healthy marriage line is broken abruptly, some fatality is indicated. If the line is broken but with two parts overlapping, separation is followed by reunion. The person may marry the first partner after separation. The same result is shown if the line breaks into two and the terminal part continues straight and clear.

If the break is enclosed by a square, the reunion will take place.

VIII) **Marriage line in relation to other lines**

a) The marriage line connected to a Venus line shows the influence of one of the same sex which will interfere with the marriage.

A Venus line across the hand that goes towards the marriage line, signifies the interference of some other person in the marriage. If this line has its origin on the mount of positive Mars, the interference will cause quarrels. The date can be read on the line of Fate, when they cross each other.

b) A line from the positive Mars, which runs into a downward fork of the marriage line, indicates divorce.

c) If an influence line starts from the plain of Mars and cuts a forked line of marriage, it signifies divorce. If there is an island in this influence line, there is guilty intrigue on the part of the person.

d) A line from the mount of Mercury, which cuts the marriage line, indicates objections and obstacles to the marriage. If the marriage line is strong and healthy, one can overcome the opposition.

If the marriage line is joined to the Mercury line, there is delay in marriage or no marriage at all. There is much opposition both in domestic and social life.

e) A bar line across the drooping line of marriage shows a sudden death of the partner (*fig. 427*). A short bar cutting the marriage line shows great obstacles, which may prevent marriage or cancel engagement.

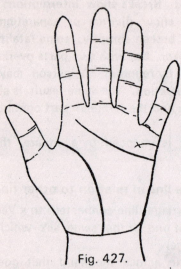

Fig. 427.
A bar line cutting a dropping line of Marriage (sudden death of partner)

f) If there is a grill on the mount of Venus with a line of opposition on the mount of Venus, there is physical disparity between the husband and the wife.

g) Red dots in the Heart line or falling splits in the Heart line going towards the little finger, or a cross on the Venus mount, indicates sorrow in married life.

IX) Signs on the line of Marriage

1) **Dots** : a) *Dot* : It indicates impediment in love.
   b) *Black dot* : It means death of the partner.
   c) *A dark red or yellow spot* : It shows poor health of the partner.
   d) *Many spots* : They show constant illness of the partner.

e) *A single dot with a cross* : An accident or a surgical operation which deforms the partner is indicated.

f) *Black spot not on the line but on the mount of Mercury* : It shows conjugal misery.

2) *Cross* : It shows difficulties in the attachment. A cross at the place, where the line of marriage drops down to the line of Heart, shows a sudden death of the partner. A cross above the line indicates abortion.

3) *Island* : An island on the marriage line shows quarrels and troubles as long as the island lasts. If there are many islands, they show unhappiness.

If the marriage line is attached to an island, there is unhealthy criticism and comment about the marriage. In this case the marriage might have taken place in spite of social or family opposition.

A large island on the line shows intimacy with a close relative.

4) *Square* : A square shows protection from any difficulties regarding marriage.

5) A star on the line of marriage shows shock through the death of the partner. A star on the line that turns upwards shows disillusionment of attachment.

CHAPTER XXXI

The lines of Children

I) Introduction

To tell accurately the number of children from the hand requires more careful study than is usually given to the pursuit of the hand reading. In the first place, a thorough knowledge of all portions of the hand that can touch on this point must be acquired. For instance, a person with a very poor development of the mount of Venus is not so likely to have children as the person with the mount full and large.

II) Position on the hand

The lines of children are the fine upright lines on the line of marriage (*fig. 428*). Sometimes the lines from the base

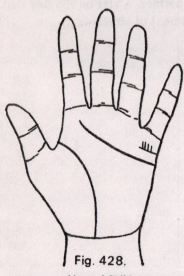

Fig. 428.

Lines of Children

of the finger of Mercury descend on the line of marriage. Many times the lines are so fine that they cannot be seen with naked eye and a powerful magnifying glass is necessary. From the position of these lines and by their appearance, we can make out accurately whether such children will play an important role in the life of the person. It will also indicate whether the children will be strong or delicate, whether they will be male or female.

III) Character of the lines of children

In general, we may state that broad lines denote males, whereas fine and narrow lines indicate females. Strong lines denote strong and healthy children whereas faint and wavy lines show the reverse.

Straight lines show sons whereas delicate and leaning lines show daughters. Thus, the structure, the depth and the height of the lines and their spacing can give us information regarding the sex and the characteristics of the children and the years between them.

IV) Signs on the lines

An island, a black spot, or a star on the line shows the delicacy of child's health. If these marks are found at the termination of the line, they indicate the death of the child.

If one of the lines is outstanding, it shows the rise of the child to great heights in life. If two lines rise from the same point, they represent twins.

Vertical lines, going down from the base of the Mercury finger and touching the line of Marriage, indicate the number of children.

Faint downward lines in the neighbourhood of the Marriage line indicate chattering habits or even gossiping. These lines on the hand of a woman show miscarriage in the later period of pregnancy.

The number of children is to be read from the percussion side towards the inside of the palm.

On a man's hand the lines are often as clear as on the woman's hand. They mean that the man will be exceptionally fond of children and will have an extremely affectionate nature.

V) Other places on the hand showing children

a) If a line of Heart is forked at the end and on the mount of Mercury, it shows that the person will have children.

b) A woman with the sign of a fish clearly marked on the hand will have children.

c) Men and women, with a broad palm and all the principal lines clearly marked and traced, will have children.

d) A sign like an island on the joint of the thumb indicates a child. The number of big islands refer to the sons and small ones to daughters.

e) Small lines on the mount of upper Mars between the lines of Heart and Head indicate children.

f) Falling lines from the line of Heart on the upper mount of Mars indicate children.

g) A rising branch from the first bracelet and from the percussion side of the hand indicates that the person will be blessed with children and grandchildren.

h) The lines of children on the hand of Yogis and Sadhus or monks indicate disciples and on the hands of nuns they mean monasteries and holy places where they reside.

i) A line on the second phalange of the Mercury finger and on the second phalange of the Saturn finger indicates the number of children.

j) Vertical lines on the first phalange of the thumb indicate children. Strong lines show sons and weak lines show daughters. Broken lines mean either death or miscarriage.

k) On the hand of ladies, a clear vertical line on the first phalange of the Jupiter finger or the Sun finger signifies a child. A clear and bold line means a son and a thin line means a daughter.

l) Red lines on the hand of women indicate the possibility of children.

m) A single sign like a trident, a pot, a lotus or a fish shows children.

CHAPTER XXXII

Case Studies

CASE 1

This is the hand print of a woman suffering from mild type of asthma. Please note a whorl like formation between the second and the third fingers which shows asthma.

A whorl between the third and the fourth fingers indicates gonadic troubles.

A whorl on the middle Mount of Moon is a sign of kidney troubles.

The woman was taking a homeopathic treatment on her asthmatic trouble. She was also suffering from gonadic troubles. However the doctor did not know about her kidney trouble. Later on, when the woman visited for her treatment, she confirmed that she had kidney trouble over 12 years, but she was thereafter operated and was relieved of it. During my discussion with the doctor, he confirmed that the kidney trouble could be the root cause of her asthma. Thereafter he started giving her treatment on kidney trouble and surprisingly her asthmatic trouble disappeared in a short time.

Other indications on the hand

1) Two lines of Marriage cut by a vertical line showing disturbed married life.
2) Presence of Via Lasciva.
3) Cross line from the Mount of Mars cutting the lines of Life, Fate and Head is a sign of family troubles, troubles in career and anxieties.

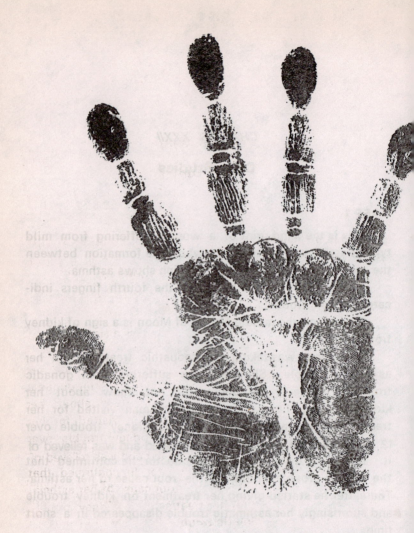

Case 1

4) Square hand with equal spacing between the fingers indicating a balanced mind and control over mind.

Conclusion : In spite of family and health troubles and troubles in career, the woman could maintain her balance of mind.

CASE 2

This is the hand print of a person of about 35 years old. He had come to me with the following problems.
1) He felt insecurity in his job.
2) He was suffering from rheumatic trouble.
3) He did not have a peaceful married life.

After studying the hand print from the point of view of the above difficulties, the following signs would be noticeable.

a) Fate line is stopped by a cross line starting from the Mount of Mars and going upto the line of Head. This shows troubles in career. Another Fate line starts at a short distance which is again stopped by the Heart line. It shows a gap of about two years in service and the person remained unemployed during this period. The other Fate line shows a new start to life, but this line is also stopped by the Heart line which means loss of career due to influence of the opposite sex. The period shown is at his age of about 48 for which we have to wait and see.

b) A cross line starting from the Mount of Mars and going to the Mount of Saturn shows rheumatic troubles especially to the teeth. Another small horizontal line on the middle Mount of Moon shows rheumatic troubles.

c) The shape of the hand as well as of the fingers is square and the line of Heart is straight. This shows a very practical person ruled by the head and not by the heart. The straight Heart line shows that he is less sentimental. The drooping down of the Marriage line shows that he is not very much attached to family life. Branches at the end of Heart line shows extra marital relations, and a powerful Mount of Venus confirms his vitality and enthusiasm in this direction. It is therefore natural that he should not have a peaceful married life.

The square hand shows a person measuring everything with a twelve inch rod, who sometimes shows foolhardiness.

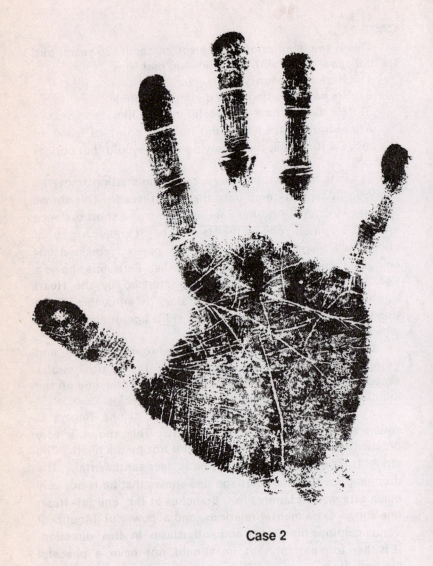

Case 2

He, being too materialistic, does not pay much attention to his family relations and he reasons out his behaviour for extra marital relations. Thus, he alone is responsible for his failure in married life.

Though the Life line is short, the course of the Fate line shows as if it is overlapping the Life line. In this case the continuation of Life line in the Fate line is showing a long life.

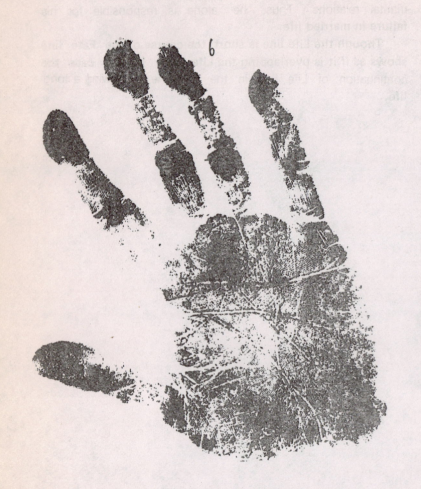

Case 3

CASE 3

This is an example of a low set thumb. This is the hand print of a social worker. The low set thumb shows his generous nature. The shape of the hand is square which means his thinking is on the practical plane and he will not throw his generosity for unfruitful things. The straight Head line and the parallel Heart line show a level headed person. The fork at the beginning of the Fate line shows that he was not attached to his family since childhood and he developed an independent attitude and later on got engrossed in social work.

A vertical line on the Mount of Mercury crossing the Marriage line shows unhappiness in married life. His wife could never come upto his level of intelligence and could never understand his ideal.

The line of Apollo is good, showing fame and reputation and success in his undertaking.

The wide gap, between the first and second fingers and the third and the fourth fingers, shows a man of thought as well as of action.

The first phalanges of the fingers are shorter than the other two, indicating practical and materialistic ideas.

The Big Triangle on the hand consisting of the Head line, the Life line and the Mercury line is incomplete because the Mercury line reaches only upto Fate line. It indicates missing of the person's good luck. However, a small Triangle formed by the Head line, Mercury line and the Fate line compensates for the missing good luck.

The person will reach the peak of his success at the age of fifty five when the line of Apollo appears strong.

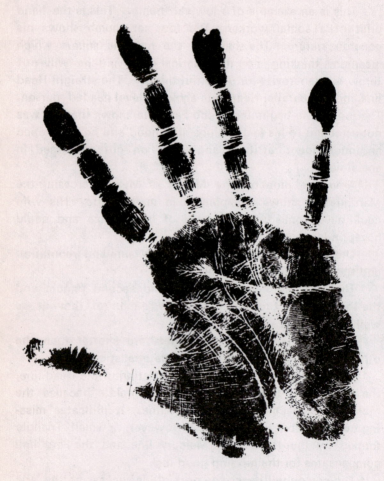

Case 4

CASE 4

This is the hand print of a woman. Please observe the following formations :

1) The Head line is forked at the end and one prong ends in a cross on the Mount of Moon indicating insanity.

2) Break in the Head line and the Head line sloping to the Mount of Moon shows insanity.

3) The line of Marriage bending down shows unhappiness in married life.

4) The Head line is broken and a branch from Heart line cuts the Fate line at the point of the break which means separation from husband.

5) A number of cross lines from Positive Mount of Mars cutting the Life line indicate family troubles.

6) A whorl between the third and the fourth fingers shows gonadic troubles. The woman got operated and removed her womb.

The first two items above indicate an abnormal mental behaviour. It shows a changing and unsteady mind. The lady is very moody and whimsical and left her husband on account of her misjudgement. She has been staying separate from her husband since 1972.

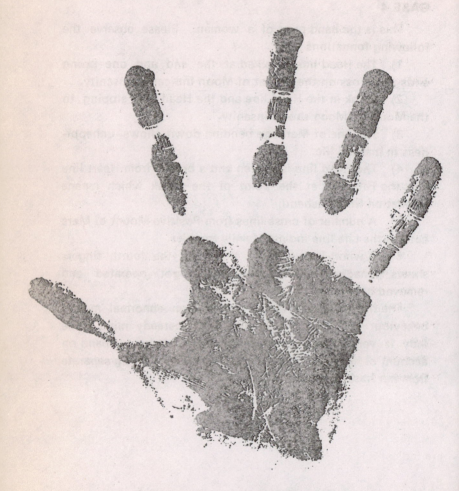

Case 5

CASE 5

This is the hand print of a boy of about 16 years. This boy in mentally under developed and is defective in his speech. After studying the hand print, the following developments of different lines were observed.

1) **Short line of Head with various defects**

The Head line is short as well as away from Life line. It shows recklessness and lack of intelligence. Short Head line means lack of imagination. The line has chain-like formation which indicates lack of concentration and inconsistency in thought.

2) **Very weak line of Life**

The Life line is weak and, when combined with a short Head line, shows danger to life. He got through serious illness on two occasions and his health is so weak that he cannot stand the strain of everyday routine.

3) **Numerous lines in the Hollow of the palm**

These lines, when combined with a short Head line, show insanity.

4) **Cross lines on the Mounts of Saturn and Apollo**

Many cross lines on the above Mounts, a short Head line stopping under the Mount of Saturn and a weak line of Life are indications of short life.

5) **Chained line of Heart**

A poorly traced and chained Heart line, with a poor line of Head and an exaggerated Mount of Venus, shows unnatural sex life.

The combined result of the above observations is in creating a mentally defective person with a defect in speech.

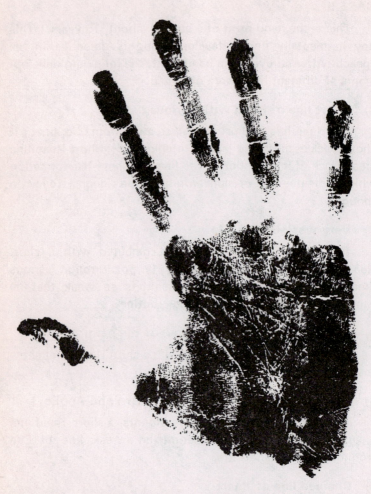

Case 6

CASE 6 : A hand showing heredity

This is the hand print of a girl of about twenty years. She is the sister of the boy in case no. 5. This is a typical example showing heredity. Please note the following similarity in both the hands.

1) Considering the age of the two children, their hands are large in size.
2) Fingers are long.
3) The Heart line is islanded in both the cases.
4) The Head line is also defective.
5) Life line is weak.
6) There are a number of lines in the Hollow of the palm.
7) Head line is separate from the Life line.
8) Life line covers a greater portion of the Mount of Venus.
9) Lower Mount of Moon is displaced.

The above nine points are common to both the cases, a typical case showing hereditary weakness. This girl is equally short-tempered, disturbed and mentally below average though not to the extent of her brother in case 5.

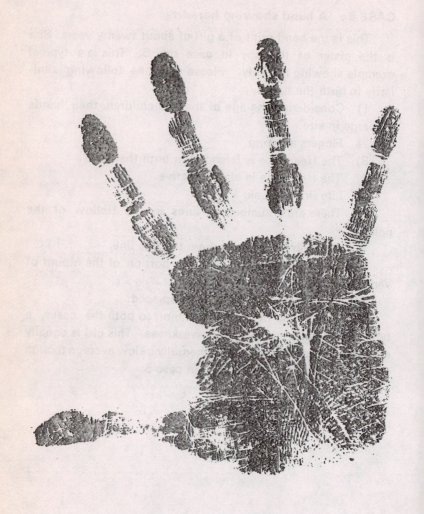

Case 7

CASE 7

This hand print belongs to a woman of about 40 years. She is unmarried and is working as a lecturer in a college. This is a good case for the study of psycho-analysis and a case showing internal psychological clash.

Please note the following developments on the hand.

1) The shape of the hand is square, showing interest in worldly affairs and an aptitude to reason out things.

2) Wide distance between the second and the third fingers indicates carelessness about the future.

3) Wide gap between the third and the fourth fingers shows a person of action, whether right or wrong.

4) **Double lines of Head :** The upper line of Head starts much away from the Life line showing an independent and erratic nature and an egotist. The second line of Head starts from the Life line and turns upwards towards the Mount of Apollo and crosses the upper line of Head. This means that the person is very sensitive and is very ambitious.

These two Head lines shows a mental clash. At times, the person is strong headed and sometimes very sensitive, sometimes very ambitious but sometimes very much depressed. This creates an internal clash and the person becomes moody and uneasy.

5) The line of Heart is uneven, shallow and with branches at the end. It means the person is very shaky in her affections and sentiments are not attached to any one person.

6) Three lines of Marriage and a cross above the second Marriage line are noticeable. Similarly, an island in a cross line from the Mount of Mars, which joins the line of Apollo just above the fork in Heart line, is seen. There are indications showing scandal and insincerity about marriage.

7) Several Cross lines on the Mount of Moon, a grill formation on the Mount of Venus just below the thumb, cross

lines in the Big Triangle indicate uneasiness, disturbed mind and indecisive disposition.

The result of the above points is a mentally upset person who has several moods and at the same time a great ego resulting in a quarrelsome and fault-finding disposition.

After forty years of lonely and disturbed life, the person had approached me to find out whether she could succeed in spiritual development and get the higher type of experience. This desire of hers was born out of frustration.

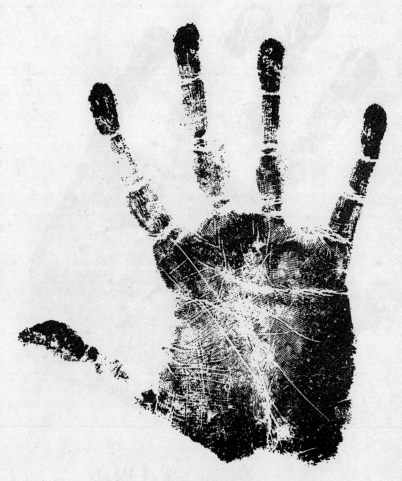

Double line of Head

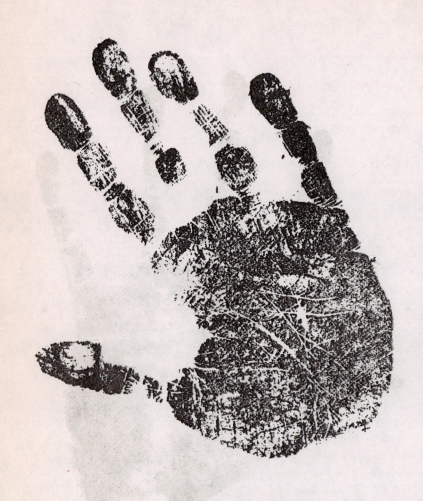

Double line of Head

Appendix I

Signs on the Hand

Cross

1) *Cross on the second phalange of Jupiter finger* : Rich friends.

2) *Clear cross on the mount of Jupiter* : a) Love for one person only, b) Wealthy marriage, c) Happy marriage.

3) *Cross on the mount of Saturn* : a) Childlessness, b) murder or assassination, c) misuse of occult power, d) ill health, e) sterility.

4) *Cross on the first phalange of Apollo finger* : a) on a woman's hand : Chastity, b) on man's hand : Celibacy

5) *Cross on the mount of Apollo* : a) Financial troubles b) Reverse of fortune.

6) *Cross on the first phalange of Mercury finger* : The person may not marry.

7) *Cross on the mount of Mercury* : a) Financial troubles, b) Wound on leg, c) Liar, d) Taking undue advantage of everything, e) Syphilis.

8) *Cross on the upper mount of Mars* : Stealing.

9) *Cross on the lower mount of Mars* : Suicidal tendency.

10) *Cross on the plain of Mars* : Death by execution.

11) *Cross on the mount of Venus touching the line of Life* : Troubles from relatives.

12) *Large cross on the mount of Venus* : Love for one person.

13) *Cross on the middle mount of Moon* : Rheumatism.

14) *Cross on the lower third of the mount of Moon*: Bladder and kidney troubles.

15) *Cross on the mount of Moon*: a) Superstition, b) Danger from drowning, c) Diabetes, d) Gout.

16) *Cross in the Big Triangle*: a) Murder by somebody b) A burglar, c) Change in life, d) Quarrelsome nature, d) Combativeness, e) Brutality.

17) *Cross inside the upper angle of the Triangle*: Involvement in law suit.

18) *Cross inside the lower part of the Triangle*: Late success.

19) *Cross in the Quadrangle under the mount of Saturn*: a) Fortunate and lucky life, b) **Priesthood**, c) Occultism, d) Clairvoyance.

20) *Cross on the upper side of the first phalange of the thumb*: Lack of morality.

21) *Cross on the Life line*: Law suits.

22) *Cross at the end of the Life line*: a) Ill-health, b) Poverty during closing years of life.

23) *Two crosses at the beginning of Life line, on the hand of a woman*: Immodesty.

24) *Cross on the line of Head*: Accidents.

25) *Cross on the line of Fate at its termination with a grill on the mount of Mercury*: Violent death due to some evil doing by the person.

26) *Cross on the break in the line of Fate*: Critical change in the person's existance.

27) *Cross at the centre of the Fate line*: Disastrous change.

28) *Cross near the line of Fate and between the Fate line and the life line*: An event which will affect a relative's life and comfort.

29) *Cross on the Heart line at the intersection of the Fate line*: Pecuniary troubles due to love affairs.

30) *Cross touching the Sun line towards the mount of Mercury*: Poor business capacity.

31) *Cross touching the Heart line but with mounts of Saturn and Moon badly developed and with sloting line of Head* :   Danger of insanity of religious kind ; more accentuated if there are two crosses.

32) *Cross near the Mercury line but not on it* :   Change in life.

33) *Cross on the Mercury line* :   Warning of incoming danger.

34) *Cross towards the termination of the line of Mercury with a circle on the Head line* :   Blindness.

35) *Cross on the line of Intuition with a badly marked mount of Mercury* :   A humbac clairvoyant and a charlaton.

36) *Cross in the centre of the first bracelet* :   a) Hard life, b) End of life in tranquillity, c) Unexpected gains or fortune through legacy.

37) *Cross on the line of Marriage* :   Difficulties in attachment.

38) *Cross at the place where the line of Marriage droops down to the line of Heart* :   Sudden death of the partner.

39) *Cross above the Marriage line* :   Abortion.

Star

1) *Star on the mount of Jupiter* :   a) Accident from fire b) Public honour, c) Fame and name, d) Wealthy marriage, e) Family troubles.

2) *Star on the outer edge of the Jupiter mount* :   Accident from fire.

3) *Star at the edge of the Jupiter mount but not at the line of life or touching the line of life* :   Illegitimate birth.

4) *Star at the edge of Jupiter mount and touching the line of Life* :   Loss of mother.

5) *Star on the first phalange of Jupiter finger* :   Travels.

6) *Star on the mount of Saturn* :   a) Paralysis, b) Ill-health, c) Poverty, d) Spinal cord troubles, e) Accident or misfortune, f) Suicidal tendency, g) Childlessness.

7) *Star on the mount of Saturn at the end of the Fate line* :   Assassination or murder.

8) *Star on the mount of Saturn on both the hands :* Death on scaffold.

9) *Star on the first phalange of Saturn finger :* Unhappiness.

10) *Two stars on the third phalange of Saturn finger with a break in Head line under the mount of Saturn :* Death. On woman's hand it means suicide in water.

11) *Star on the third phalange of Saturn finger :* Death from metalic weapon.

12) *Star at the root of the Saturn finger :* Sterility of wife.

13) *Star between the mounts of Saturn and Apollo :* a) Danger from electricity, b) Danger from snake bite.

14) *Star on the second finger :* Death by execution.

15) *Star on the second phalange of the second finger :* Insanity.

16) *Star on the mount of Mercury :* a) Stealing, b) Forgery, c) Loss by theft or treachery, d) Unexpected luck, e) Embezzler or Highway robber.

17) *Star on the upper mount of Mars :* a) Death in war, b) Military honour.

18) *Star on badly developed mount of Mars :* a) Murder by somebody, b) Murderous tendency, c) A burglar.

19) *Star on the mount of Venus :* Troubles in love.

20) *Star in the centre or at the base of the mount of Venus :* Success in love.

21) *Star on the mount of Venus near the thumb :* a) Love with a person of distinction, b) Influence of opposite sex.

22) *Star in the middle of double or triple Girdle of Venus :* Syphilis.

23) *Star on over developed mount of Moon with a sloping line of Head :* Suicidal tendencies.

24) *Star on the middle mount of Moon and connected to the line of Head :* Fame.

25) *Star on lower mount of Moon :* a) Mysterious life, b) Alcoholic insanity, c) Hysteria.

26) *Star on the mount of Moon on both the hands:* Hydrophobia.

27) *Star on the lower mount of Moon and connected with voyage line from line of Life:* Adventure.

28) *Star on the mount of Moon:* a) Dropsy, b) Danger from drowning, b) Jaundice, d) Paralysis, e) Romantic madness, f) Illness, g) Suicidal tendency.

29) *Star on the Voyage line from percussion side on the mount of Moon:* Danger from drowning or shipwreck.

30) *Star in the Big Triangle touching the line of Mercury:* Blindness.

31) *Star in the Triangle on both the hands:* a) Violent death, b) Disappointment in love, c) Great struggle in career.

32) *An independent star in the Triangle:* Riches.

33) *Star in the Quadrangle:* a) Success, b) Accident.

34) *Star at the upper side of the first phalange of the thumb:* Lack of morality.

35) Star of Tragic Fate is found at the base of the second finger.

36) Star of unusual faculties is found on the tips of the fingers.

37) *Star found right on the Life line:* Suicide.

38) *Star touching the line of Life on the mount of Venus:* Troubles from family members or close friends.

39) *Stars on the influence lines:* Sudden and shocking experiences connected with the influence.

40) *Star at the end of the influence line:* Vanishing of the influence due to tragic death of the influencing person.

41) *Star at the termination of the influence line which turns away from the line of Life:* No affection for the dead person.

42) *Star at the end of the influence line if connected to a star on the mount of Moon and if the line of influence recedes from the Life line:* Death of the influencing person in a foreign land.

43) *Star on the Head line:* Wound to the head.

44) *Star on the Head line in both the hands:* Fatality.

45) *Star on the Fate line:* Danger at that period.

46) *Star at the starting of the Fate line:* Loss of fortune or great troubles to parents.

47) *Star at the starting of the Fate line and an additional star on the mount of Venus:* Death of one of the parents.

48) *Star at the termination of the Fate line with another star on the mount of Moon:* Tendency to suicide.

49) *Star on the Heart line:* a) Sudden death from heart attack, b) Blindness.

50) *Star at the end of the branch from the Heart line going to the mount of Moon:* Hereditary insanity.

51) *Star on the line of Apollo:* Brilliant and lasting success.

52) *Star on the mount of Apollo:* Wealth.

53) *Star on the line of Apollo on the mount of Uranus:* Catastrophe.

54) *Star on a branch from Head line to mount of Saturn:* Qualities of Saturn will bring great success.

55) *Star on the line of Mercury:* a) Unexpected luck b) not more than one child.

56) *Star close to the line of Mercury and connected to line of Head and a line of Life running close to thumb:* a) Sterility, b) Childlessness, c) Jaundice.

57) *Star at the connection of the line of Mercury and the line of Head and with a deep dot at the bottom of the mount of Moon:* a) Disorder and malformation of the generative organs, b) Womb troubles causing sterility.

58) *Star on the line of Via Lasciva:* Success and riches.

59) *Star on the Girdle of Venus under the mount of Saturn:* Suicidal tendency by self-poisoning.

60) Star in the centre of the first Bracelet is the Dragon's Head and indicates fortune by inheritance in old age.

61) *Star on the line of Marriage:* Shock through the death of the partner.

Lines

1) *Very small lines on the mount of Jupiter* : Wound to Head.

2) *Line from Jupiter finger upto first joint of the thumb* : Death by accussion.

3) *Line circulating the first joint of the Jupiter finger* : Scar on the skull.

4) *Wavy line from the root of the Saturn finger going upto first phalange of Saturn finger* : Death in war.

5) *Wavy drooping line on third phalange of second finger:* Melancholia.

6) *Straight line from the root of the Saturn finger going to the first phalange of the finger* : Learned person.

7) *Two vertical lines on the middle phalange of the Saturn finger* : Success in difficult enterprises and riches.

8) *Line descending from the mount of Saturn and touching the line of Life* : a) Suffering from rheumatism, b) Suffering from pleurisy.

9) *Many lines on the Apollo finger from the root going upto first phalange:* a) Riches, b) Spending lavishly for fiance.

10) *One straight line on the third phalange of the Apollo finger:* Happy career.

11) *Line crossing the third knot of Apollo finger* : Success through difficulties.

12) *Line on Mercury finger from the bottom upto the first phalange:* Scientific approach.

13) *Line from the bottom of Mercury finger upto the second phalange:* Oratory.

14) *Very small line from the upper mount of Mars to the mount of Apollo* : Over ambition.

15) *Line from upper mount of Mars* : Wound in a fight.

16) *Line rising from the mount of Venus and going upto the mount of Saturn* : Accident with animals.

17) *Clear, straight and uncrossed line from the mount of*

Venus to the mount of Mercury: Happy love and skill in love making.

18) *Two parallel lines from the mount of Venus to the lower mount of Mars:* Many love affairs.

19) *Line starting from a star on the mount of Venus and going to the line of Heart and ending in a fork:* Happy marriage.

20) *Line from the Bracelet to the mount of Neptune and thence to the mount of Venus:* Marriage with an old person.

21) *Line from the upper part of the mount of Venus to the mount of Saturn:* Danger in maternity.

22) *Line from the Bracelet to the mount of Venus and thence to the mount of Mercury:* Marriage with a trader.

23) *Many lines in the Big Triangle:* Sensitiveness.

24) *Two lines from the first phalange of the thumb going upto the line of Life:* Riches.

25) *Line from the second joint of the thumb to the line of Life:* Riches.

26) *Line rising from the line of Life and going upto the mount of Saturn:* Accident of a motor car.

27) *Line from the Quadrangle to mount of Mercury:* Friendship of powerful people.

28) *Two parallel lines on either side of a straight and deep line of Sun:* Untold fortune and glory.

Vertical lines

1) *Four vertical lines on the second and third phalange of Jupiter finger:* Happy and virtuous life.

2) *Vertical line just above the root of the Jupiter finger:* A life of about 28 years.

3) *Vertical line on the back side of the Jupiter finger and on the third phalange:* Atheism.

4) *Vertical lines on the mount of Saturn:* Happy old age.

5) *Two vertical lines on the mount of Saturn, one on the side of Apollo and the other on the side of Jupiter:* a) Happy marriage, b) Male offspring.

6) *Vertical lines on the third phalange very near to the root of Saturn finger ;* Ill-luck.

7) *Vertical lines on the first phalange of Saturn finger:* Jealously.

8) *Thick vertical line on the middle phalange of Saturn finger and at the lower side:* Sanctity and holiness.

9) *Two or three vertical lines on the middle phalange of Mercury finger:* Occultism.

10) *Strong vertical lines on the first phalange of Mercury finger:* Ill-health.

11) *Two clear cut vertical lines on the fourth finger:* Profession of a nurse.

12) *Single vertical line on the mount of Venus going upto the mount of positive Mars:* Involvement in love.

13) *Vertical and confused lines on the mount of Moon:* Insomnia.

14) *Vertical and confused lines with a cross on the lower mount of Moon:* Suffering from diabetes.

15) *Short vertical lines near the nail of the thumb:* Legacy.

16) *Short vertical lines on lower mount of Moon:* Hysteria.

17) *Vertical lines on the second joint of the thumb:* Brothers.

Horizontal Lines

1) *Cross line on the third joint of Jupiter finger:* Tendency to acquire other's property.

2) *Cross line on the second joint of Jupiter finger:* Dishonesty.

3) *Cross lines from the line of Life to the mount of Saturn:* Rheumatism.

4) *Cross lines on the mount of Sun:* Lack of concentration.

5) *Cross lines on the third phalange of third finger;* Envy.

6) *Cross lines on the Upper mount of Mars:* a) Bronchitis, b) Blood disorder, c) Interest inflamation.

7) *Prominent line across the lower mount of Moon separating this lower mount of Moon from rest of the mount of Moon:* a) Alegry, b) Alcoholism, c) Dropsy, d) Kidney troubles.

8) *Horizontal line rising from the line of Life and going either to the Positive or Negative mount of Mars:* a) Illness, b) Sorrow, c) Death.

9) *Cross lines on the middle of the mount of Moon:* Gout and Rheumatism.

10) *Cross lines on the middle of the mount of Moon from the side of the percussion:* Voyage.

11) *Cross lines on the upper mount of Moon:* a) Appendicitis, b) Bronchitis.

12) *Cross lines on the entire percussion on the mount of Moon:* Delicate health.

13) *Horizontal line from second phalange of the thumb to the line of Life:* Unsuccessful married life.

14) *Cross line on the first phalange of thumb:* Obstacles.

15) *Wavy cross lines on first phalange of all fingers:* Danger from drowning.

16) *Cross lines on the mount of Mercury:* a) Deceitful disposition, b) Disappointment in ambition.

Grill

1) *Grill on the mount of Jupiter:* a) Loss, b) Convent career, c) Bondless egotism, d) Matrimonial unhappiness.

2) *Grill on the mount of Saturn:* a) Ill-health, b) Culprit, c) Misfortune, d) Prison life.

3) *Grill on the mount of Apollo:* Visionary idealism.

4) *Grill on the mount of Mercury:* a) Suicidal tendency, b) Embezzler, c) Dishonesty, d) Highway robber.

5) *Grill on the mount of Upper Mars:* a) Sudden and Violent death, b) Murderous tendency.

6) *Grill on the mount of Moon:* a) Nervous troubles, b) Life of anxiety, c) Melancholia, d) Paralysis.

7) *Grill on the mount of Venus:* Danger of imprisonment.

8) *Grill in the Big Triangle:* Enemies.
9) *Grill in the Quadrangle:* Madness.
10) *Grill on the mount of Venus and a grill on the line of Head, both touching the Life line:* Change of religion.

Spots

1) *Spot on the mount of Jupiter:* a) Loss of reputaion, b) Misfrortune.
2) *Spot on the third phalange of Saturn finger:* Loss of money through women.
3) *Black spot on first phalange of Saturn finger:* Malerian fever. Theft by one in his own family
4) *Dark spot on the mount of Mercury:* a) Wound on legs, b) Accident leading to paralysis.
5) *Spot on the Upper mount of Mars:* Wound in fight.
6) *Spot on the mount of Venus:* Frustration in love.
7) *Spot on the mount of Moon:* a) Danger from drowning, b) Jaundice, c) Liver trouble.
8) *Spot on the nail:* a) Nervousness, b) Grief and sorrow.
9) *Black spot on the* thumb: Crime caused by passion,
10) *Black spot in the Quadrangle:* Ashthma.
11) *Black-bluish spot on the nails:* Blood poisoning.
12) *White spot on the line of Head under the mount of Sun with a cross bar on the line of Heart:* Literary success.
13) *White spots on the Head line under and close to the mount of Mercury:* Success in scientific pursuits.
14) *Spot on the Head line with a fork at the start in Life line:* Serious brain troubles.
15) *Spot on the Head line:* Typhoid.
16) *Spot on Head line with mount of Saturn developed:* Tooth ache.
17) *Spot on a line from the Upper mount of Mars to the mount of Jupiter:* Deafness.
18) *Spot on Head line with powerful mount of Venus:* Deatness.

19) *Spot on the Head line joined by a line which starts from a star on the mount of Venus:* Calamity and sorrow due to death of the loved one.

20) *Blue spot on the Head line, and the Head line makes the Big Triangle with lines of Life and Mercury, and a powerful mount of Mars :* Tendency of murder.

21) *Spot on the Heart line :* a) Weakness of sex activity, b) Danger from poisoning.

22) *Red spots on Heart line :* a) Tendency to boils, b) Sorrows in married life.

23) *Black spot on Marriage line :* a) Death of the partner, b) Impediments in love.

24) *Many spots on Marriage line :* Constant illnes of the partner.

25) *Spot not on the line of Marriage but on the mount of Mercury :* Conjugal misery.

Circle

1) *Circle on the mount of Jupiter :* Remembrance of previous birth.

2) *Circle on the mount of Saturn towards the line of Heart :* Heart trouble.

3) *Circle on the mount of Mercury :* a) Danger from water, b) Danger from poisoning.

4) *Circle on the mount of Mars :* Wound to the Eye.

5) *Circle on the mount of Venus :* Ill-health.

6) *Circle on the mount of Moon :* Danger from drowning.

7) *Three circles touching each other in the Quadrangle ;* Epilepsy.

8) *Circle in the Quadrangle :* Eye trouble.

9) *Circle in the Big Triangle :* Troubles from opposite sex.

10) *One circle on the Life line :* Susceptibility to blindness of one eye.

11) *Two circles on the Life line :* Total blindness.

12) *Circle on the Head line :* Blindness.

13) *Circle on the Heart line :* Weakness of the Heart.
14) *Circle on the Heart line under the mount of Sun :* Eye trouble.
15) *Semi circle on the Heart line resembling an island :* Failures, distress and complications in profession.
16) *Circle on the Mercury line :* Minor misfortunes durin_ hunting or driving.
17) *Circle on the first phalange of Apollo finger :* Intelligence and argumentative skill.

Quadrangle

The space between the lines of Heart and Head is known as Quadrangle.
1) *Narrow Quadrangle with excess development of Jupiter finger :* Inclination towards asceticism.
2) *Narrow Quadrangle with a poor line of Mercury :* Asthma.
3) *Narrow Quadrangle with Mars or Mercury mount developed :* Cruel nature.
4) *Very narrow Quadrangle :* a) Bigotry, b) Cruelty, c) Vindictiveness, d) Immorality, e) Excessive, f) Hey fever.

The Big Triangle

This is formed by the lines of Life, Head and Mercury.
1) *Flat Triangle with low mount of Saturn :* Insignificant life.
2) *The middle angle of the Triangle formed on the mount of Moon :* a) Catarrh, b) Epilepsy.
3) *Low position of the Triangle with mount of Moon developed and with only one bracelet :* Catalepsy.
4) *Narrow Triangle :* Cowardice.
5) *Broad Triangle :* Benevolent character.
6) *Bulging Triangle :* Bravery.
7) *Large Triangle :* Good luck.
8) *Great Triangle intercepted by two wavy lines giving appearance of a Cross :* Poverty.

Sign of a triangle

1) *Triangle on the mount of Jupiter :* Diplomatic career.
2) *Tringle on the mount of Saturn :* Occultism.
3) *Triangle on the third phalange of Saturn finger :* Immoral character.
4) *Triangle on the mount of Sun :* Success in Science.
5) *Triangle on the mount of Mercury :* Diplomat.
6) *Triangle on the Upper mount of Mars :* Military mind and honours.
7) *Triangle in the Plain of Mars :* Military mind.
8) *Triangle on the mount of Venus :* a) Prudence and calculative attitude in love, b) Worldly wisdom.
9) *Triangle on the mount of Moon :* Power of intuition.
10) *Triangle on the Life line :* The person will support families of relatives and friends.
11) *Triangle on the Head line under the mount of Mercury:* Success in scientific pursuits.
12) *Triangle touching the line of Fate and in between the Fate and Life lines, with a strongly marked mount of Mars :* Success in fight or military.
13) *Triangle on the Fate line :* Monotonous life.
14) *Triangle attached to Heart line in the Quadrangle :* Period of income and improvement in financial position.
15) *Triangle attached to the line of Sun and also to the line of Heart :* Unusual enjoyment of wealth and reputation.
16) *Triangle on the line of Mercury :* Illness with quick recovery.
17) *Triangle with a cross within it on the first bracelet :* Large fortune by inheritance.

Sign of a square

1) *Square on the mount of Venus :* a) Convent career, b) Prison life.
2) *Square is a favourable sign. It is a sign of protection against any possible harm*
3) *Square found near a star :* Escape from danger.

Appendix I

4) *Broken square :* Neutralisation of ill-effects.

5) *Square on a broken line :* Escape from danger.

6) *A square on a vertical influence line :* a) Self imposed restrictions, b), Unsocial behaviour or bed-ridden sickness, c) Seclusion in a hospital or asylum.

7) *An influence line penetrating through a square:* Imprisonment of the influencing person.

8) *Influence line ending in a square :* Death of the influencing person in a hospital due to an accident.

9) *Vertical influence line starting from a square and going to the mount of negative Mars :* Death in battle of the influencing person.

10) *A square on the line of Life:* a) usually a mark of preservation from danger. b) healing power

11) *A square enclosing a cross on the line of Life :* Protection from sickness.

12) *Square on the Head line :* Protection from sickness or accident.

13) *A square on the Fate line :* Protection from loss of business or money.

14) *A square touching the Fate line in the plain of Mars :* Danger from accidents in relation to home life.

15) *A square on the Fate line on the side of Life line :* Danger in travel.

16) *A squre on or close to the Heart line :* Escape from love sorrows.

Island or Yova

According to Western palmistry, an island is a defect in the line whereas according to Indian palmistry, a yova is an auspicious sign on the hand.

1) *A yova on the second joint of Saturn finger :* Wealth through adoption, lottery or heredity.

2) *Island under the mount of Saturn :* Deafness.

3) *Island in the Head line under the mount of Saturn :* Deafness.

4) *Island on the influence line on the mount of Venus*: Sickness.

5) *Long island at the beginning of the influence line*: Change in the attitude or relationship.

6) *If the island is cut by a bar*: Separation by death.

7) *Island at the beginning of the Fate line*: Mystery of birth.

8) *Yova on the Fate line with many short voyage lines*: Interest in two countries.

9) *Island at the termination of the line of influence*: Prolonged illness to the influence ending in fatality.

10) *Two yovas forming a figure of eight at the beginning of the Fate line*: Gift of second sight.

11) *Island on the Fate line on the mount of Uranus with a cross on the mount of Saturn*: Rigorous imprisonment.

12) *Island on the higher side of the Fate line and towards the centre*: a) Unlicenced passion, b) Loss of money, c) Guilty intrigue, d) Marriage troubles.

13) *Island on the Marriage line*: Quarrels and troubles as long as the island lasts.

14) *Many islands on the Marriage line*: Unhappiness.

15) *Island attached to the Marriage line*: Criticism and unhealthy comments about the marriage.

16) *Large island on the Marriage line*: Intimacy with a close relative.

17) *Island on the mount of Jupiter*: Loss through a friend or relative.

18) *Island at the start of the line of Mercury or line of Intuition*: Somnabulism.

19) An island at the beginning of the Life line shows mystery of birth

Mole

1) *Mole on the Life line*: Serious diseases or operation.

2) *Mole at the starting of the Head line*: Luxurious life.

3) *Mole at the beginning, at the centre or at the end of Head line*: All happiness and executive position.

4) *Mole at the end of the Head line*: Acquisition of conveyance.

5) *Mole on the Heart line :* Failure and disillusion.

6) *Mole on the line of Heart with a fresh line from the mole :* Faith surviving the disappointment.

7) *Small indentation on Heart line :* Auto stimulation.

Bars

1) *Bars on the Head line :* Head aches.

2) *Number of bars on the mount of Saturn and crossing Fate line :* Obstacles constantly arising in life.

3) *Bars with ladder-like formation on the Fate line :* a) Succession of misfortune, b) Imprisonment.

4) *Number of bars on the Fate line enclosed by a square :* Evil results minimised.

5) *Number of bars cutting the Heart line :* Repeated disappointments in love and troubles of Heart and liver.

6) *A straight line cutting the Heart line :* Danger or injury from weapon.

7) *An oblique bar across the line of Heart on the mount of Jupiter :* Danger through horse riding.

1) **Sign of Jupiter**

On the mount of Mars of a bad Martian : a) Murderer, b) Lady killer.

2) **Sign of Saturn**

a) *On Jupiter mount :* Occultism.
b) *On Saturn mount :* Hypnotism.
c) *On the mount of Mars :* Murderous tendency with revengeful attitude.
d) *On Venus mount :* Unnatural kind of love.

3) **Sign of Apollo**

a) *On Jupiter finger :* Eloquence.
b) *On mount of Venus :* Platonic love.

4) **Sign of Mars**

   On Moon mount :   Dangerous madness.

5) **Sign of Mercury**

   On Jupiter mount :   Administrative capacity.

6) **Sign of Moon**

   a) *On Saturn mount :*   Insanity.
   b) *On Moon mount :*   Insanity.
   c) *On Mars mount :*   Dangerous madness.

7) **Sign of Uranus**

   On Mercury mount :   a) Scientific knowledge, b) Author of scientific subjects.

8) **Sign of Neptune**

   On Mercury mount :   Author of childrens' stories.

Shankh or the Loop

On one finger only :	The person is happy.
On two fingers :	It is an unfavourable sign.
On three fingers :	It is a bad sign.
On four fingers :	It is not a good sign.
On five fingers :	It is not an auspicious sign.
On six fingers :	The person has prowess.
On seven fingers :	The person gets the comforts of a king.
On eight fingers :	The person is as good as a king.
On nine fingers :	The person enjoys like a king.
On Jupiter finger :	The person is a spend-thrift.
On Saturn finger :	The person is wise and has scientific outlook.
On Apollo finger :	The person loses his wealth in business.
On Mercury finger :	The person loses his money in manufacturing concern.

Appendix I

Chakra or the Whorl

On the thumb :	The person inherits property.
On one finger :	The person is a knight and enjoys life.
On two fingers :	The person is honoured by a king.
On three fingers :	The person becomes wealthy.
On four fingers :	The person becomes a pauper.
On five fingers :	The person enjoys pleasure.
On six fingers :	The person satisfies his passions.
On seven fingers :	The person is virtuous.
On eight fingers :	The person suffers from diseases.
On nine fingers :	The person becomes a king.
On ten fingers :	The person realises the "Self".
On Jupiter finger :	The person benefits through friends.
On Saturn finger :	The person is an authority on religion.
On Apollo finger :	The person benefits through trade.
On Mercury finger :	The person is an author.

Appendix II

A

Abdominal troubles: Deformed second finger.

Ability to impart mental peace and solace: Line of Life ending on the mount of Neptune and the Mercury line touching the Life line.

Abortion: A cross above the line of Marriage.

Accident (see Danger also): a) *From Fire:* 1) A line below the nail of Mercury finger on the left hand. 2) A star on the outer edge of the mount of Jupiter.

b) *to the head:* A break in the line of Head.

c) *accident crippling the person, generally on the legs:* 1) Straight branch from the Heart line ending on a hook on the finger of Mercury. 2) Black spot on the mount of Mercury.

d) *of a motar car:* Rising line from the Life line going upto the mount of Saturn.

Accident in general: e) Short Head line connected to the Life line at its beginning.

f) Break in the Life line.

g) Cross on the line of Head.

h) Absence of the Fate line in the beginning.

i) Influence line from the mount of Moon cutting the Fate line and ending abrutly.

j) Star in the Quadrangle.

Achievement in scientific pursuits: a) Rising branch of the Head line going between the third and the fourth fingers.

b) Head line terminating between the line of Sun and the Mercury finger.

Appendix II 677

Achievement—successful : a) Upward going branch from the Fate line.
   b) Vertical line on the top phalange of the thumb.
   c) A line at the base of the Mercury finger.
Acidity : Smooth fingers.
Acquisition : a) *Acquisition of others' money :* A crose line on the third joint of the Jupiter finger.
   b) *Acquisition of conveyance :* Mole at the end of the Heart line.
   c) *Acquisition of property, land or agriculture :* i) Small triangle on the line of Life. ii) Lines of Life and Head joining at the beginning. iii) Line from positive Mars touching Mercury line under the mount of Sun
Active development : a) Deep and well-cut Head line with pink colour.
   b) Sprouts either rising or falling from the Life line.
Active development periodically : Line of Sun alternately deep and thin on an artistic hand.
Activity : a) Elastic consistency
   b) Broad hands
   c) A martian.
Actor : a) Long and forked line of Head.
   b) Long and conical fingers.
Administrator : a) Jupiter-Apollo combination.
   b) Jupiter-Mercury combination.
   c) Sign of Mercury on the Jupiter mount.
   d) Sign of a fish on the Jupiter mount.
Successful administrator with good control over others : Head line starting from the mount of Jupiter but touching the line of Life.
Adoption : Fate line starting with a fork.
Adventure : a) Star on the lower mount of Moon connected to the voyage line from the Life line.
   b) Powerful mount of Moon.
   c) Apollo finger equal to Saturn finger.
   d) Cross on the Fate line.

Affections: a) *Affections everlasting*: A long, clear and well-traced Heart line.

b) *Affections deprived*: Lines of Head and Heart without branches and lying far apart.

c) *Failure in affections*: A branch from the Heart line to the Mercury mount.

d) *Intense affections and love*: Deep and red Heart line.

e) *Morbid affections*: Deep and yellow Heart line.

f) *Worries in affections*: Cross bars cutting the Heart line.

g) *Impetuous interuptions in affections, violent too*: A wide break in the Heart line.

h) *Deep affections*: Double line of Heart.

i) *Affections suffering adversely due to influencing person*: A break in the line of Fate after touching the line of influence.

j) *Affections influenced by a person in travel*: The line of Voyage turns up and joins the Heart line.

k) *Affections of married partner once lost cannot be regained*: Marriage line ending in a hook.

Aggression: a) A Martian.
    b) A Saturnian.
    c) Sign of sword.

Aggression due to fame and fortune: a) Head line with red colour.
    b) Sun line starting from the upper mount of Mars.
    c) Sun line stating from the mount of Uranus.

Agriculture: a) Yava on the joint of the thumb.
    b) Vertical line on the first phalange of the Saturn finger.
    c) Strong Saturn finger and Saturn mount.
    d) Broad hands.
    e) Hard and stiff hands.

Alcoholism: a) Line of Mars ending in a fork.
    b) Red colour of Mars line.
    c) Black spot on the line of Head under the mount of Saturn.
    d) Star on the mount of Moon.

e) Line from the line of Mars to the mount of Moon.
f) Prominent line across the lower mount of Moon.

Distress for alcoholism : A vertical line on the top phalange of the thumb.

Alergy to allopathic drugs : A prominent line across the lower mount of Moon separating this lower mount trom rest of the mount of Moon.

Ambassador : All the three phalanges of the Mercury finger equal in length and the Head line having branches.

Ambition : Third phalange of the Jupiter finger longer than the third phalange of the Mercury finger.

Worldly ambition : Bracelet on the lower side of the hand.

Ambition not ealised : a) Breaks in the Sun line.
b) A line with a curve from the negative mount of Mars and cutting the line of Sun.

Ancestral qualities : Strong and straight line of Life.

Anxieties : a) Too many cross lines in the Hollow.
b) A line descending from the Head line.
c) A very deep line of Fate.

Apoplexy : a) Sign like a spring on the mount of Jupiter.
b) A Jupiterian.
c) Life line joining a red dot on the mount of Jupiter and an island in the Life line.
d) A Jupiterian with third phalange of the Jupiter finger developed.
e) Head line terminating on the mount of Sun.
f) Island on the Head or the Heart line and downward branch of the Fate line.
g) Deep and well-cut Head line with red colour.

Apoplexy-danger of : a) A very deep and red Heart line runing stiff and clear across the hand with a similar line of Head and a strong mount of Mars.
b) Elongated dot on the Heart line.
c) Uneven line of Mercury.

Appendicitis : Cross lines on the upper mount of Moon.

Appreciation : Square hand.

Aptitude in industry : Fate line ending on the mount of Mercury.

Architect : a) A sloping line of Head with spatulate fingers.
   b) Good line of Head.
   c) Long nails.
   d) Strong mounts of Apollo and Venus.

Ardent disposition : Hair on all phalanges of fingers.

Ardour : Deep and well-cut line of Life.

Arrogance : a) Excess development of the Jupiter mount.
   b) Wide gap between Head and Life lines.

Art of mimicry : Line of Head reaching upto the line of Heart but not touching it.

Artistic temperament : a) Conic hand.
   b) Conic fingers with square hand.
   c) Medium sized hand.
   d) Palm slightly tapering.
   e) Line of Fate terminating on the mount of Sun.
   f) Strong mounts of Venus and Moon.

Aristocrat : A Jupiterian.

Asceticism : Narrow Quadrangle with excess development of the mount of Jupiter.

Aspirations with noble and elevated ideas : Bracelet placed higher on the hand and closer to the palm.

Assasination : a) Star on the mount of Saturn at the end of the Fate line.
   b) Cross or star on the upper mount of Mars.
   c) Large cross in the centre of the Big Triangle.
   d) Black spot at the end of the broken line of Life.
   e) Cross on the mount of Saturn.

Asthma : a) Narrow Quadrangle with poor line of Mercury.
   b) Abnormal development of the Jupiter finger.
   c) Spot in the Quadrangle.
   d) Hedge like formation on the line of Life.
   e) Head line running close to the Heart line and thus narrowing the Quadrangle.
   f) Cross line from the mount of Venus ending on the mount of Jupiter in an island.
   g) Line from the Jupiter mount touching the Life line.
   h) Trident on the third phalange of saturn finger.

i) Whorl-like formation between the mounts of Saturn and Sun.

Atheism : Vertical line on the back side of the Jupiter finger and on the third phalange.

Attitude : a) *Loveable, healthy and happy attitude* : The Heart line ending its course has even breadth, depth and pink colour.

b) *Business-like attitude* : Fate line ending on the mount of Mercury.

c) *Carefree attitude to one's capability and brilliance* : Sun line starting from the mount of Neptune.

d) *Analytic attitude* : Knotty fingers.

Audacity : a) Martian.

b) Fine line of Heart.

c) Jupiter mount prominent.

d) Life and Head lines separated at the start.

Author of scientific subjects : Sign of Uranus on the mount of Mercury.

Author with power of language and imagination : a) Sun line starting from the top of the mount of Moon but nearer the percussion with mental world developed.

b) Rising branch of the Sun line going to the mount of Moon with a star at the end of the Sun line.

c) Sign of a chakra or a whorl on the tip of the Mercury finger.

d) Long second phalange of the Mercury finger.

Authority on religion : Sign of a whorl or chakra on the first phalange of the Saturn finger.

Avarice : a) An extremely long and straight Head line going directly to the other side of the hand and turning upward at the end.

b) Deep and well-cut Head line with white colour.

c) Square fingers bent inward.

d) Absence of the Heart line.

B

Baldness : A line starting from the first phalange of the thumb and going to the backside of the thumb.

Banker : A rising branch from the Mercury line to the mount of Saturn.

Bankruptcy : a) Whenever an island is seen on the Mercury line and if the line of Saturn or Sun is broken or cut by a deep bar.
    b) A wide break on the Fate line.
    c) Poor mount and line of Apollo.

Benefits of characteristics of art and literature : Head line terminating on the mount of Sun.

Benevolence : a) Broad Big Triangle.
    b) Good mount of Jupiter.
    c) Excellent mount of Venus.
    d) Soft hands.
    e) Long nails.
    f) Fate line starting from the line of Life and with Jupiter and Venus mounts well-developed.

Bigotry : A narrow Quadrangle.

Bilious trouble : a) A falling line from the mount of Mercury touching the line of Life.
    b) A wavy line of Mercury with an island on the Life line.
    c) Presence of Mercury line.

Blackmailer : a) Developed and crossed mount of Mercury.
    b) Crooked fingers.
    c) Thin long hands.

Bladder trouble : a) A Martian.
    b) Cross lines or cross on the lower third of the mount of Moon.
    c) Exaggerated mount of Moon.
    d) Any defect in the Mercury line.

Blindness (also see Eye trouble) *:* a) Star in the Big Triangle touching the line of Mercury.
    b) Star on the Heart line.

Blindness of one eye : One circle on the line of Life.

Total Blindness : a) Two circles on the Life line.
b) Circle on the Head line and a cross on the line of Mercury on the upper side.
c) A star on the Heart line.
Blind passion : Head line joined to the line of Life at its beginning and then rising towards the line of Heart then coming down resuming its normal course.
Blood disorder : a) Cross lines on the upper Mars.
b) Black bluish spots on the nails.
c) Deep and red colour cross-bars cutting the line of Head.
d) Head line with a dot.
Blood disease : a) A bad Jupiterian.
b) Mercury line ending on the Head line and Life line cut by many bars.
Blood poisoning : a) Double or triple or broken Girdle of Venus.
b) Black or bluish spots on nails.
Blood pressure : a) A Jupiterian.
b) Head line connected at the start to the Life line but short
c) Cross on the influence line cutting the line of Life.
d) Ray like lines from the Heart line going to the mount of Saturn.
e) Exaggerated or much lined mount of Saturn.
Bluntness : A Martian with short fingers.
Brain disorder : a) Deep and red coloured cross-bars cutting the line of Head.
b) Dot in the Head line.
Brain disease : Ending of Mercury line on the Head line and the Life line cut by many bars.
Brain fever : a) An island in the line of Life accompanied by dots on the Head line.
b) Head line running close to the Life line for a while.
c) Islands on the line of Head.
d) Line of Mercury ending on the Head line.

Brain haemorage : Absence of the Heart line with negative mount of Mars prominent.

Brain-Healthy brain : The line of Via Lasciva starts either from the line of Saturn or the line of Mercury and goes to the mount of Moon, unbroken and uniformity.

Brain troubles due to relatives and friends : a) Black spots in the Head line with a fork at the start in the Life line.
b) Line from the mount of Venus which ends in a star on the Head line.
c) Whenever thinness is found in the Head line during its course.
d) Head line crossed by deep bars.
e) Defects in the Head line.

Brain weakness : Late start of the Fate line with a defective Head line at the start.

Bravery : a) Bulging of the Big Triangle on the hand.
b) A Martian.

Bronchitis : a) Cross lines on the upper mount of Mars.
b) Short and narrow island on the Mercury line.
c) A Jupiterian.
d) Line from the Jupiter mount joining the line of Life.

Brothers : a) Vertical lines on the second joint of the thumb.
b) Vertical lines on the mount of Venus and parallel to the line of Mars.
c) Line rising from the Life line and going to the mount of Jupiter and with branches.

Brothers-troubles from : The mount of Saturn leaning towards the mount of Jupiter.

Brutality : a) Clubbed thumb.
b) Exaggerated mount of Jupiter.
c) Cross in the Big Triangle.
d) Very thick and hard hands.

Burglar : a) Cross in the Big Triangle.
b) Star or Grill on the mount of Mercury or on the upper mount of Mars.

c) Short and red lines of Life, Head and Heart.

d) Star on a badly developed mount of Mars.

Businessman :   Long second phalange of Mercury.

Business–excellent :   Mercury line starting from the rascette.

Business–success in :   a) Thin and narrow line of Mercury.

b) Line of Head forked with one prong going to the mount of Mercury.

Business-failure in :   a) The line of Heart cut under the mount of Mercury by a branch on that mount.

b) A semi-circle in the line of Heart resembling an island.

C

Calamity :   A branch from the Heart line going to the positive mount of Mars.

Calculative nature :   A Mercurian.

Cancer :   a) A break on the Mercury line if encircled by a square and a star in the square.

b) An island on the line of Mercury.

Capacity organizing :   Trident-like formation at the start of the Heart line on the mount of Jupiter.

Career :   a) *Dazzling :* Sun line ending in two stars.

b) *Two distinct careers :* i) Fate line ending in two powerful branches, one to the mount of Jupiter and the other to the mount of Sun. ii) Double line of Fate.

c) *Checkered career :* Wavy line of Fate.

d) *Continuous obstruction in the career :* i) Ladder-like formation of the Fate line. ii) Presence of the ring of Saturn. iii) Star in the Big Triangle on both the hands.

e) *Hard career :* i) Chained line of Fate. ii) Star in the Big Triangle on both the hands.

f) *Career-abroad :* i) Strong line of Voyage on the mount of Moon with a break in the Fate line. ii) Life line ending on the mount of Moon.

g) *Change in career :* Break in the Fate line.

h) *Career-diplomatic :* Triangle on the mount of Jupiter.

i) *Career-loss of :* i) One prong of the Head line going to the mount of Moon and another touching the line of Heart. ii) Grill on the mount of Jupiter.

j) *Career-obstruction due to animal passion :* Wavy line of Sun.

k) *Career-trouble due to disastrous attachment :* Branch from the Heart line reaching the mount of Saturn and then turning back abruptly.

l) *Career-success in :* Good line of Mercury.

m) *Career-success due to shrewdness, brilliance and good manner :* Rising branch from the line of Mercury going to the mount of Sun.

n) *Career-literary or scientific :* Branch from the line of Mercury merging into a strong line of Head.

o) *Career-impaired :* Rising branch from the Mercury line going to the mount of Saturn and cut by the line of Saturn.

p) *Career-disturbed :* The line of Mercury ending on a star.

q) *Career-adversely affected :* Break in the line of Fate after touching an influence line on the mount of Moon.

Catalepsy : Low position of the Big Triangle with the mount of Moon developed with one Bracelet.

Catarrh : Angle of the Big Triangle formed on the mount of Moon.

Catastrophe : Star touching the line of Fate near the point where the influence line joins the Fate line.

Catastrophe due to a relative : Star touching the line of Life on the mount of Venus.

Cautious : a) Carriage of the thumb close to the hand.
b) Life line closely connected to the Head line.

Celebrity : a) *In fine art and literature :* Fate line ending on the mount of Sun.

b) *Celebrity as an artist :* Sun line strong on the mount of Sun.

c) *Celebrity and wealth from mental efforts :* A well marked

Trident at the end of the Sun line or a star at the end of the Sun line.

Celibacy : a) Cross on the first phalange of the Apollo finger.
b) The line of Marriage turning up at the end.

Charity : Mercury line starting from the mount of Neptune.

Chastity : A cross on the first phalange of the Apollo finger.

Chest and lung delicacy : a) A Jupiterian.
b) An island above and below the Head line near the line of Mercury.

Children : a) Number of yova on the second joint of the thumb.
b) *Only one son :* Saturn mount prominent and Sun mount secondary.
c) *Son :* Two clear vertical lines on either side of the mount of Saturn.
d) *Clever and strong children :* Deep and long lines of children.
e) *Delicate and sick child :* Breaks and islands in the lines of children.
f) *Long lived and healthy children :* Well-developed lines of children on both the hands.
g) *Boys :* Strong lines of children.
h) *Girls :* Faint or fine lines of children.
i) *Delicacy of childrens' health :* A black spot or a star on the line of children.
j) *Not more than one child :* Star on the Mercury line.
k) *Twins :* Two lines of children rising from the same point.
l) *Many children :* Many lines of children.
m) *Death of the child :* i) line of children terminating on a black spot or a star. ii) A line on the back side of the Jupiter finger.
n) *Child–illegitimate :* Star on the edge of the Jupiter mount but not touching the Life line.
o) *Presence of children :* i) The line of Heart forked at the end and on the mount of Mercury. ii) A sign of a fish

clearly marked on the hand of a woman. iii) Red colour of the palm and all the principal lines clearly marked and traced. iv) Sign like a yova on the joint of the thumb. v) Small lines on the mount of upper Mars. vi) Vertical lines on the first phalange of the thumb. vii) Lines at the base of the thumb ; thicker lines show boys and thinner lines show girls. viii) Presence of the lines of children

p) *Possibility of childred :* i) Red lines on the hand of a woman. ii) Single sign like a trident, a pot, or a lotus or a fish.

q) *Children and grandchildren :* i) Falling branches from the first Bracelet and from the other side of the hand. ii) A line on the second phalange of the Mercury finger and on the second phalange of the Saturn finger. iii) On the hand of ladies, a clear vertical line on the first phalange of the Jupiter finger or the Sun finger.

r) *Childlessness :* i) A cross or a star on the mount of Saturn. ii) A star at the intersection of the Head and the Mercury lines. iii) Line of influence from the upper Mars going deep into the root of the Saturn finger. iv) The Heart line ending on the mount of Mercury but branchless.

s) *Child-bearing difficulties :* i) On the hand of a woman, Life line running normal for sometime and then taking a turn towards the mount of Moon and going upto the Bracelet. ii) Life line close to the second phalange of the thumb and a star at the intersection of the Head and Mercury lines. iii) The first Bracelet curving too much inside the palm on the hand of a woman. iv) Horizontal cross line on the mount of Moon going upto the line of Life with a cross in the line of Mercury. v) The mount of Venus leaning towards the Bracelet.

Chronic colitis : Longitudinal ridges on the nails.

Chronic complaints : A branch starting from a black spot on the Life line.

Clairvoyance : a) Mercury line forms a small triangle with the lines of Head Life.

b) Cross in the Quadrangle.

c) Drooping line of Head with a fork on the mount of Moon.

Clairvoyance-humbac : a) A poor line of Mercury with the presence of the line of Intuition.

b) Cross on the line of Intuition with a badly marked mount of Mercury.

Gift of Clairvoyance : a) The line of Intuition starting from an island.

b) Two islands forming a figure of eight at the beginning of the Fate line c) Mercury line starting from near the percussion

Clarity of mind : Small distance between the lines of Head and Life.

Clash : a) *Between reason, logic on one side and emotion and sentiment on the other :* Collusion of the lines of Head and Heart.

b) *Between idealism and materialism :* A straight line of Head on a psychic hand.

Cleverness : Abnormal Head line with one prong of the fork going a little away down to the mount of Moon.

Cold, merciless and avaricious : Absence of the Heart line.

Cold-blooded : Absence of the Heart line.

Unscrupulous : A Martian with absence of the Heart line.

Growing cold : Heart line fading slowly.

Combativeness : a) Red lines.

b) Prominent Mars.

c) A large cross in the Big Triangle.

Commonsense : a) Broad hands.

b) Sharp upper angle of the Life and Head lines.

Concentration-power of concentration : a) The mount of Moon developed by way of a strip along the percussion.

b) Long knotty fingers.

c) Strong long thumb.

d) All mounts well-developed.

Confidence : a) A Jupiterian.

b) Head line starting from the mount of Jupiter but slightly separated from the line of Life.

Confident, self-reliant and never discouraged : A branch of the Sun line going to the negative mount of Mars.

Conflict-Mental : A branch from the Heart line falling towards the line of Head.

Constipation : Long line of Fate terminating on the mount of Saturn.

Constitution : a) *Weak :* i) Chained line of Life. ii) Capillary lines. iii) Broad, shallow and chained Bracelet.

b) *Consumes strength and vigour :* i) Falling lines from a deep line of Life. ii) Life line ending in a fork iii) Life line ending in a tassel.

c) *Healthy and robust :* Absence of Mercury line.

Consumption : Long, thin, curved and fluted nails.

Contempt for the opposite sex : Chained line of Heart, and pale in colour.

Conveyance : Mole at the end of the Heart line.

Corporal punishment : Absence of the mount of Saturn.

Corrupt : a) Crooked finger.
    b) Girdle of Venus.
    c) Wavy line of Heart.

Courage : a) Upper Martian.
    b) Firm palm.
    c) Fingers unusually long.
    d) Fine mounts of Jupiter and Venus.

Cowardice : a) Narrow Triangle.
    b) Upper Mars lacking.
    c) Long, narrow and thin nails.
    d) Fingers bending inward.

Criminal : a) Double thumb.
    b) Clubbed thumb.
    c) Black spots on nail of the thumb (crime out of passion).

Criminal jealousy : a) Excessive development of the mount of Jupiter.
    b) A Saturnian with yellow colour of the hand.
    c) Bad Mercurian.

Criminalities : a) Venusian with red colour of the hand who will kill his wife or relatives for the sake of selfish passions.

b) Combination of a bad Lunarian with a bad Saturnian.

Criminal tendencies : a) Absence of the Heart line on a bad hand.

b) Yellow colour of the Heart line of strong Saturnian.

c) Head line terminating on the Heart line between the Sun and the Mercury mounts,d) Head line on the upper side of the

Brutal murder or rape : well-marked line of Via Lasciva with strong line of Mars, deep and red ; strong mount of Venus and a thick or clubbed thumb.

Cruelty : a) Conic hand.

b) Narrow Quadrangle with Mars or Mercury mount developed.

c) Absence of the Heart line with the negative mount of Mars very prominent.

d) Exaggerated mount of Jupiter.

e) Hair on the hands of women.

f) Very low Heart line on a bad hand.

Culprit : Grill on the mount of Saturn.

Cunning : a) Large, firm and conic hand.

b) Under-developed mount of Moon.

D

Danger : (also see 'Accident')

1) *Danger and difficulty :* Cross or star anywhere on the hand.
2) *Danger from animals :* a) Island on the mount of Saturn.
   b) Line from the mount of Venus going upto the mount of Saturn.
3) *Danger from drowning or shipwreck :* a) Star on the Voyage line on the mount of Moon.
   b) Circle on the mount of Moon.
   c) Spot on the mount of Moon.
   d) Heart line broken at three places and with sphere-like formation at the termination of the line under the mount of Mercury.

    e) Heart line broken on the left side of the left hand.
    f) Cross on the mount of Moon.
    g) Wavy cross lines on the first phalange of all fingers.
    h) Island on the line of Voyage.
    i) Circle on the mount of Mercury.

4) *Danger from electricity :* Star between the mount of Saturn and the mount of Apollo.

5) *Danger from elephant :* The Heart line ending in a hook on the mount of Mercury.

6) *Danger from fire :* a) Heart line broken at the right side on the right hand.
    b) Wavy line cutting the Heart line from below.
    c) Star on the outer edge of Jupiter finger.

7) *Danger of Hallucination :* Head line sweeping down the wrist.

8) *Danger to health :* a) Life line with several breaks.
    b) Star on the Fate line.

9) *Danger through high fall :* Two vertical lines in the middle of the Heart line. ii) Heart line broken at several places.

10) *Danger through horse riding :* Oblique bar across the Heart line on the Jupiter mount.

11) *Danger from hydro-phobia :* Break in the Head line under the mount of Sun.

12) *Danger of insanity :* Cross touching the Sun line but with mounts of Moon and Saturn badly developed.

13) *Danger from kingdom :* Saturn mount leaning towards the Jupiter mount.

14) *Danger to longevity :* a) Break both in the Life line and the Fate line.
    b) Any defect seen on the double line of Life.

15) *Danger from poisoning :* a) Circle on the mount of Mercury.
    b) Line of Heart broken on the right side of the right hand.
    c) Black spot on the Heart line.

16) *Danger from snake bite :* Star between the mounts of Saturn and Apollo.

17) *Danger from sun-stroke :*   Break in the Head line under the mount of Apollo.
18) *Danger from weapon :*   Straight bar cutting the Heart line.
Dashing :   A Martian.
Day dreaming of the future events :   Line of Intuition on a square hand.
Deafness :   a) Island on the centre of the mount of Saturn.
   b) Black spot on the line of Head with a fork at the start in the Life line.
   c) Black spot on the Head line and a line from the upper mount of Mars to the mount of Jupiter.
   d) Island on the line of Head under the mount of Saturn.
   e) Black spot on the Head line with the mount of Venus developed.
Deaf and dumb :   Island at the beginning of the Life line and at the end of the Head line and Life line cut by many bars.
Death :   a) *Death–violent :* i) Star in the Big Triangle on both hands. ii) Grill on the upper mount of Mars. iii) Cross on the middle of the Head line. iv) Cross at the end of the Fate line with a grill on the mount of Mercury.
   b) *Death possibility of :* The line of Mercury joined to the line of Life.
   c) *Early–Death (short life) :* The line of Via Lasciva starting from the mount of Venus and joining the Life line.
   d) *Death of the influencing person :* Line of influence cut by a strong cross line and the influence line having an island after the cut and then ending in a star.
   e) *Death of the influencing person in a hospital :* Line of influence ending in a square.
   f) *Death of the influencing person in battle :* A line from the influence line going to the negative Mars.
   g) *Death–accidental :* Life line ending in a cross bar or a dot or a mole.
   h) *Death of a close relative :* Horizontal influence line starting from a star and cutting the line of Life.

i) *Death of a partner :* i) Cross on the Marriage line at the place where it droops down towards the line of Heart. ii) Break in the Head line under the mount of Saturn and it is distinct and sharp without over-lapping. iii) The Fate line cutting through a break in the Head line. iv) Black dot on the Marriage line. v) Yellow dot on the nail of Saturn finger

j) *Death of the partner in happy circumstances :* Two Marriage lines running parallel and equal in length.

k) *Death of the partner in severe illness or accident :* The line of Marriage strongly drooping towards the line of Heart with an island on it.

l) *Death before the death of the married partner :* i) The line of Marriage nearer to the Heart line longer than the upper Marriage line. ii) The line of Marriage ending on the Heart line.

m) *Death-premature :* i) Head line stopping abruptly before it reaches the Fate line and the line of Heart which also stops abruptly. ii) Heart, Head and Life lines closely connected. iii) Short Head line ending under the mount of Saturn. iv) Heart line crossing from side to side with a developed mount of Moon and joining the Head line in a wavy termination under the mount of Mercury.

n) *Death of the parent prevented :* Fate line starting from inside the Big Triangle in both the hands with influence line on the mount of Venus ending in a star.

o) *Sudden death :* i) Heart line starting from the Head and Life lines with a cross on the Head line. ii) Star on the Heart line. iii) Short Head line ending in a star

p) *Death-dishonourable :* Deep line of Fate with red colour cutting the third phalange of the Saturn finger with a star on the line.

q) *Death of one of the parents :* Fate line starting from a star with another star on the mount of Venus.

r) *Death far from birth place :* i) Life line ending in a wide fork. ii) Double line of Life quite parallel to the later portion of the Life line.

Death of mother : Star at the edge of Jupiter mount and touching the life line

s) *Death in a voyage :* i) A line from the rascette crossing the mount of Moon and terminating on the Life line. ii) Cross at the end of the voyage.

t) *Death by drowning :* Cross on the Ring of Saturn with a cross on the mount of Moon.

u) *Death from metalic weapon (sword, dagger) :* i) Star on the third phalange of the Saturn finger. ii) Line from the first phalange of the thumb to the line of Life.

v) *Death on the scaffold :* i) Sharp and distinct break in the Head line under the mount of Saturn without overlapping. ii) Line encircling the thumb on the first joint. iii) Star on both the hands on the mount of Saturn. iv) Cross in the plain of Mars.

w) *Death by accusation :* Line from the Jupiter finger upto the first joint of the thumb.

x) *Death in war :* i) Wavy line from the root of the Saturn finger going to the first phalange of the Saturn finger. ii) Star on the upper mount of Mars.

Death at a holy place: Sign of yara on the Heart line under the mount of Jupiter.

Debauchery : Bad Jupiterian.

Delays : Saturnian.

Deceipt : a) Absence of the Heart line.
b) Widely forked line of Head.
c) Mercury finger long and crooked.
d) Short and pale nails,

Deceipt from enemies : Branch from the Mercury line reaching the mount of Venus after cutting the Life line.

Desire for death : Much larger first phalange of the Saturn finger.

Desire to become great : Line from the mount of Jupiter joining the Head line.

Desires fulfilled according to one's will and satisfaction : a) Mercury line throwing a branch towards the mount of Moon.
b) Thick line at the base of the Jupiter finger going on the back side of the hand.

Desire for power : Jupiter finger equal to Saturn finger.

Despondency : Broken Girdle of Venus.
Determination : a) Stiff and large thumb.
  b) Strong thumb.
  c) Straight line of Head.
Devotion to friends : A Martian.
Dexterity : A Mercurian.
Diabetis : Confused vertical lines with a cross on lower mount of Luna.
Dictatorship and cruelty : a) Life line starting high on the mount of Jupiter.
  b) Excess development of the mount of Jupiter.
Difficulties : a) *Pecuniary due to family responsibilities :* i) Lines from the mount of Venus cutting the lines of Head and Life. ii) Fate line rising low on the left hand and high on the right hand.
  b) *Just difficulties :* Rising line from the Bracelet to the negative mount of Mars.
  c) *From family or marriage partner :* Line from the second Bracelet going to the mount of Moon.
Digestion : a) *Digestive system defective :* Loop formation on the tips of the fingers.
  b) *Impaired digestive system in old age :* Thick and short line of Mercury not reaching the negative mount of Mars.
  c) *Powerful digestive system :* Mercury line starting from the Rascette.
  d) *Good digestive system :* Thin, narrow and good line of Mercury.
Diphtheria : a) A Jupiterian.
  b) Spot in the Head line under the mount of Jupiter.
Diplomat or politician with success and honour : a) Rising branch from the Life line going to the mount of Jupiter and rising branch from the Fate line going to the mount of Sun.
  b) Triangle on the mount of Jupiter or Mercury.
Disaster (serious) : a) Bad Fate line starting with a wide fork of which one prong goes to the mount of Venus.

b) Fate line cut by a line from the influence line on the mount of Venus and the Fate line broken for the rest of its course.

Disciples : The lines of children on the hand of a yogi or a sanyasi.

Dishonesty : a) Over-developed mount of Mercury.
  b) Cross line on the second joint of Jupiter finger.
  c) Absence of the Heart line.
  d) Absence of the Heart line on a bad Mercurian.
  e) Grill on the mount of Mercury.

Dishonesty–cold blooded : Mercury finger twisted and narrow with short nails.

Disposition : a) *Alert and quick disposition :* Absence of Mercury line.
  b) *Amorous disposition :* Minute splits from the Heart line.
  c) *Avaricious disposition :* Break in the Heart line under the mount of Mercury.
  d) *Changing disposition :* Broken Head line with bars or branches.
  e) *Distrust for social environment :* Head line going deep into the mount of Moon.
  f) *Double dealing and hypocrisy :* Head line forked at the end with one prong going to the mount of Moon.
  g) *Flirtatious disposition :* Chained line of Heart.
  h) *Lying disposition and duplicity :* Heart line sinking towards the line of Head and forming narrow Quadrangle with the mount of Moon powerful.
  i) *Murderous disposition :* Wavy branch from the Heart line going to the mount of Moon.
  j) *Disposition–quarrelsome :* i) Line of Mars on a square or broad hand. ii) Wide space between the Life and Head lines.
  k) *Disposition–romantic :* i) Fate line after crossing the Heart line ends in a trident and the Heart line forked, one branch going to the mount of Jupiter. ii) Well-developed Heart line with exaggerated mounts of Venus and Moon.

l) *Disposition–sympathetic and affectionate:* i) Branch from the Sun line merging into the Heart line. ii) Double line of Life covering both the mounts of Mars and Venus.

m) *Disposition–ultra-nervous:* i) Line of Mercury starting from the percussion. ii) Wavy line of Intuition with exaggerated mount of Mars.

n) *Disposition–uncontrollable:* Breaks on the Head line on a bad hand.

Divorce : a) Island across the line of Fate between the lines of Head and Heart and the island ending in a fork.

b) Rising branch from the Life line crossed by a line from the mount of Mars or Venus.

c) Cross line from the mount of Mars or Venus ending in a fork on the Heart line.

d) Cross line from the mount of Mars or Venus cutting the line of Marriage.

e) Cross line starting from a spot on the mount of Venus and cutting a rising branch from the line of Life with a cross on the mount of Jupiter.

f) Marriage line ending on the mount of Venus.

g) Marriage line ending in a fork.

h) Breaks in the Marriage line.

Divorce due to guilty intrigue : Heart line ending in a fork at the termination with one prong deep into the mount of Mercury and an island in the Fate line.

Doctor : a) Jupiter–Mercury combination.

b) Medical stigma.

Domestic troubles : Hollow inclining towards the Life line.

Dreamer : a) Long and narrow hand.

b) A Lunarian.

c) Drooping line of Head.

d) Pointed finger.

Dropsy : a) Cross lines on the lower third of the mount of Moon.

b) Star on the mount of Moon.

Drowning : (see danger from drowning).

Drunkard: a) Curved line starting on the mount of Jupiter and going to the base of the Jupiter finger.

b) Line starting from the line of Mars and going to the mount of Moon.

c) Thick cross line dividing the middle mount of Moon.

Dutiful: a) A Saturnian.

b) Heart line with even breadth depth and pink colour throughout its course.

Dyspepsia: a) Mercury line having ladder-like formation.

b) Broad and shallow line of Mercury.

E

Early retirement: Fate line ending on Heart line

Ear trouble: A Saturnian.

Eczema: Jupiterian.

Effeminacy: a) Flat mounts.

b) Pale and soft hands.

c) Hands without hair.

Efforts: Falling lines from the line of Sun.

Egotism: a) Excess development of the Jupiter mount.

b) Grill on the mount of Jupiter.

c) Straight line of Head.

d) Wide distance at the start between the Head and Life lines.

Eloquence: a) An Apollonian.

b) A Mercurian.

c) Sign of Jupiter on the mount of Apollo.

d) Sloping line of Head with a fork at the end.

Embezzler: a) Longer finger of Apollo.

b) Grill on the mount of Mercury.

c) Crooked finger of Mercury.

d) Star on the mount of Mercury.

Emotional tendencies: a) Conic hand.

b) Psychic hand.

c) Fate line starting with a fork one prong going to the mount of Neptune and another to the mount of Moon,

Extreme emotionalism, sensitivity and timidity: a) Head and

Life lines joined at the start and run together for sometime.

b) Heart line starting high on the mount of Jupiter.

Endurance: a) Mount of Mars inclining towards the mount of Jupiter.

b) A Saturnian.

Enemies: a) Grill in the Big Trangle.

b) Lines from the Bracelet just reaching the mount of Moon. c) A Branch from a star on the mount of Jupiter cutting the line of sun. d) Five vertical lines between Jupiter and saturn mounts.

Energetic: a) Deep and well-cut Head line with pink colour.

b) Hard and firm spatulate hand.

c) Supple conic hand with small thumb.

d) Elastic consistency.

e) Head line starting from the mount of Jupiter and touching the Life line.

f) Small space between the Head and Life lines at the start.

g) Single Girdle of Venus partially traced under the mount of Sun.

h) Presence of the Girdle of Venus.

Engineer: a) Spatulate tip to the Mercury finger.

b) Flat mounts.

c) Broad palms.

d) Medical stigma on the mount of Mercury.

e) Straight line of Head.

Engrossed in family affairs: Conic tips to the Saturn finger.

Enthusiasm: a) Spatulate hand.

b) A Martian.

c) Head line starting from the mount of Jupiter but touching the Life line.

Envy: a) Poor line of Sun.

b) Cross lines on the the third phalange of the Apollo finger.

c) Many lines on the mount of Sun.

Epilepsy: a) Three circles touching each other in the Quadrangle.

b) Middle angle of the Big Triangle formed on the mount of Moon.

c) Short nails with much broken line of Head.

d) Life line suddenly going at right angles to the mount of Moon.

e) Broken Head line with number of branches.

f) Long island on the Mercury line with breaks on the Fate line.

Evil influence : Spot on the mount of Saturn.

Evil temper : Head line not touching the Life line but is connected by small lines or branches.

Execution : a) Life line with badly formed tassel.

b) Cross in the plain of Mars.

c) Star on the Saturn finger.

Experience–painful : Fate line from the line of Mars penetrating into the third phalange of the Saturn finger.

Extravagant : a) Three Bracelets poorly formed.

b) Flexible thumb.

c) Chinks between the fingers.

Eye trouble : a) An Apollonian.

b) Circle in the Quadrangle.

c) Break or circle in the Head line under the mount of Sun.

d) Break or circle in the Heart line under the mount of Sun.

See also blindness.

F

Failure at the eleventh moment : Crooked finger of Sun.

Failure in realisation of ambition : A rising branch of the Head line ending in a bar or cut by a bar.

Failures : Hole In the Heart line.

Failure in life due to ill-health or dishonesty : Line of Mercury ending on a grill.

Failure in intellectual pursuit due to lack of concentration : Two or three branches rising on the line of Sun but irregular uneven or broken or crossed by many bars.

Failure miserable : Good line of Sun in a hollow hand but with twisted fingers.

Fainting fits : Narrow Quadrangle and the line of Mercury joining the Life line.

Faithlessness : Poor line of Heart with a poor line of Head.

Falsehood : Triangle at the end of the Life line.

Fame : a) Star on the middle mount of Moon and connected to the line of Head.
b) Star on the mount of Jupiter.

Fame and fortune but poor success achieved : a) Starting of the Sun line from the Rascette.
b) Sun line starting from the mount of Neptune.
c) Chained line of Sun.

Fame and riches : Sun line starting from the negative mount of Mars ending in a trident.

Universal fame : Good line of Sun ending in three equal furros.

Fame, fortune and unexpected success : Line of Sun stronger than the Girdle of Venus.

Family troubles : The gap between the Head line and the Life line joined by a cross.

Fatal accidents : Break in the Life line and the upper end or the lower end of the line turns inward into the mount of Venus.

Fatality : a) line starting from the first rascette and penetrating into the third phalange of the Saturn finger.
b) Red dot under the mount of Saturn on the line of Heart.

Fatal events : Head line joining the Heart line under the mount of Saturn.

Fatal termination of life : Dot on the Head line followed by a cross or a star.

Fault finding nature : a) Too wide a gap between the Life and Head line.
b) Two stars near the nail of the thumb.
c) Knotty fingers.
d) Mount of Mars developed.

Faulty blood circulation : Arch type formation of the capillary ridges on the tips of the fingers.

Favour for woman : Line of the Via Lasciva starting either from the Saturn line or the line of Mercury and going to the mount of Moon unbroken and uniformly constituted alongwith a good amount of Venus.

Fear of sex : Vertical line on the second phalange of the Saturn finger on the left hand of a woman.

Feeble mindedness : a) Pointed tip of the thumb.
   b) Narrow lower angle of the Triangle.
   c) Lunarian with upper mount of Moon more developed.

Female troubles-exemption from : Double line of Heart on the woman's hand.

Fever-forever : Red or bluish dots on the Heart line.

Fever-malerian : Spot on the first phalange of the Saturn finger.

Fidelity : a) Jupiter finger with square tips.
   b) Life line starting with a fork.

Financial difficulties :
1) a) Cross on the mount of Apollo or Mercury.
   b) Life line ending in a fork.
   c) Island in the Mercury line.
2) *In old age :* Entire space between the Head line and the Heart line filled with an island.
3) *Due to law-suits :* Deep lines from the line of Head cutting the Fate line.
4) *Due to love affair :* Cross on the Heart line at the intersection of the Fate line.
5) *Financial losses :* a) Mercury line connected to the line of Apollo by a line that cuts the Apollo line.
   b) Via Lasciva connected to the line of Apollo by a line that cuts the Apollo line.
   c) Ring of Saturn throwing out a branch to the line of Sun.
   d) Downward branches on the line of Fate.
   e) Cross on the mount of Mercury.

f) Star at the beginning of the Fate line.
g) Fate line ending abruptly on the Head line.

6) *Loss of money due to sickness or death of a relative or a friend :* a) Falling lines from the Life line.
b) Life line ending in a badly formed tassel.
c) Line from a star on the mount of Venus crossing the line of Apollo.
d) Influence line ending in a star within the Big Triangle but after crossing the line of Fate.

7) *Loss of money after marriage :* Line of Marriage terminating on the mount of Sun and cutting the Sun line.

Financial position improved : a) Line from the mount of Mercury touching the line of Heart.
b) Triangle attached to the line of Heart in the Quadrangle.

Flirtation : Chained line of Heart.

Fondness : a) *For leisure, novelty and liberty :* Supple conic hand of moderate development with small thumb.
b) *Fondness for external appearance :* Conic hand.
c) *Fondness for pleasure and romance :* Large and firm conic hand.

Food analyst : Jupiter-Saturn combination.

Fool's hardiness and over confidence : Wide distance between the lines of Head and Life.

Force of character : a) Square hand.
b) Very deep line of Sun on an artistic hand.
c) Very deep line of Sun.

Foresight : Square hand.

Foretelling power : Mount of Moon developed towards the wrist.

Foreign travels : See 'travels'.

Forger : a) Crooked fingers.
b) Flat mount of Jupiter.
c) Excess development of the mounts of Mercury and Moon.
d) Star on the mount of Mercury.

Appendix II

Forgetfullness : a) Jupiter finger with spatulate tip.
  b) Island on the mount of Saturn.
  c) Series of breaks in the Head line.
Fortunate and lucky life : Cross in the Quadrangle under the mount of Saturn.
Fortune : a) Square or triangle attached to the Fate line in the zone of action (between Heart and Head lines).
  b) Mercury line making a good triangle with the lines of Head and Life.
  c) Two parallel lines on either side of a straight and deep line of Sun.
  d) Line from a star on the mount of Venus merging into a good line of Apollo.
Fortune by large inheritance (also see inheritance) : Triangle with a cross in it on the first Bracelet.
Good fortune in old age : a) Chained first Bracelet.
  b) Straight and good Fate line starting from the Heart line and going upwards.
  c) Fate line after crossing the line of Heart ends in a trident and if the Heart line is forked with one branch going to the mount of Jupiter and with the presence of the line of Sun.
Free life in early age : Rising branch from the Life line to the mount of Jupiter.
Friends–devotion to them : a) Martian.
  b) Double Heart line.
Friends–rich friends : a) Cross on the second phalange of the Jupiter finger.
  b) Line from the Quadrangle to the mount of Mercury.
  c) Fate line ending on the mount of Sun.
  d) Line of Mercury ending on the mount of Mercury.
Friends–undependable : Chained line of Heart fretted by many small lines crossing it.
Frivolity : a) Poor line of Sun.
  b) Weak first phalange of the thumb.

G

Gains beneficial :   A parallel line to the line of Heart.
Gall duct inflammation :   Chained line of Mercury.
Gambler :   a) Apollo finger longer than the Saturn finger.
   b) Large mount of Moon.
   c) Soft hands.
   d) Sign of an angle on II phalange of saturn finger.
   e) Cross on the over developed mount of Mercury.
Generative organ-trouble of :   a) A woman's hand with a rayed mount of Venus and vertical lines on the mount of Saturn and Life line ending on the mount of Venus.
   b) Star at the connection of the line of Mercury with the line of Head and with a deep dot at the bottom of the mount of Moon.
   c) Presence of the Girdle of Venus.
   d) Bracelet rising in the centre of the hand.
Generosity :   Low det and large thumb.
Genius misdirected :   Two parallel wavy lines on either side of the straight and deep Sun line.
Gloomy outlook :   a) Powerful Saturn finger.
   b) Quadrangle in the centre of the palm.
   c) Broad and shallow formation of Life line.
Glory, wealth and success :   Rising branch of the Life line to the mount of Apollo.
Glory-immortal and celebrity :   Prominent line of Sun on both the hands and a star on the mount of Sun.
Glory and untold fortune :   Two parallel and straight lines on either side of the straight and deep line of Sun.
Glutton :   Third phalange of the Jupiter finger developed.
Gonadic troubles :   a) Abnormal development of the Mercury finger, especially the third phalange more affected.
   b) Life line ending deep on the mount of Moon on the hand of a women.
   c) Whorl-like formation between the Sun and Mercury mounts.
Gossip :   Poor line of Heart and poor line of Head and a triangle at the end of the Life line.
Gout :   a) Cross lines on the middle mount of Moon.

b) Line from the mount of Saturn touching the Life line.
   c) A Jupiterian.

Gout and rheumatism : An islanded line from the Saturn mount joining an island on the Life line and another line from the middle mount of Moon joining the island on the Life line.

Grief and sorrow : Black spots on nails.

Grief-intense : Line of Fate starting from the third Bracelet.

H

Happy and virtuous life : a) Vertical lines on the second and third phalanges of the Jupiter finger.
   b) Long and unbroken line of the Via Lasciva ending on the mount of Mercury and running parallel to the line.

Hardships due to ill-health : Line from the mount of Jupiter touching the line of Head which starts from inside the line of Life.

Hasty nature : Short fingers.

Hatred for traditions and customs : Spatulate hands.

Hatred for mankind : a) Saturnian with coarse texture.
   b) Saturnian with square or spatulate tips.
   c) Absence of the Heart line.

Head-aches : a) *Mild headaches :* i) Small lines crossing the line of Mercury. ii) Several branches of the Via Lasciva running across the line of Head.
   b) *Severe headaches :* i) Island in the line of Life with small bars in the Head line. ii) Bars on the Head line. iii) Series of breaks in the Head line. iv) Ladder-like formation of the Head line. v) Branch starting from the beginning of the Life line and ending on the Rascette.
   c) *Violent headaches :* Broad and shallow line of Mercury.

Health : a) *Delicate health :* i) Cross lines on the entire percussion of the mount of Moon. ii) Sun line ending in a deep bar. iii) Mercury line touching the line of Life. iv) Short and thin line of Mars.
   b) *Good and robust health :* i) Absence of the Mercury

line. ii) Upward branches of the line of Fate. iii) Life line with rising branches. iv) Closeness of Head and Life lines at the start. v) Strong line of Life with the line of Mars.

c) *Health troubles :* i) Life line covered with dots. ii) Mercury line touching the Life line. iii) Breaks in the course of the Heart line. iv) Downward splits in the line of Heart. v) Strong vertical lines on the first phalange of the Mercury finger. vi) Circle on the mount of Venus. vii) Crosses at the end of the Life line.

d) *Deterioration of health due to old age :* Forked line of Mercury ending on the mount of Mercury.

e) *Health, wealth and tranquility of mind :* Presence of three good coloured Bracelets.

Heart : a) *Heart burn :* Broad and shallow line of Mercury.

b) *Heart disease :* Islanded Life line with dots on the Heart line.

c) *Heart-noble and charitable :* Sun line starting from the Heart line.

d) *Heart physically defective :* i) Absence of the Heart line on a Venusian or an Apollonian. ii) Break in the Heart line under the mount of Sun. iii) Good line of Head disturbed by a poor line of Mercury. iv) Splits from the Heart line drooping towards the Head line.

e) *Heart trouble :* i) Broad nails. ii) Circle on the mount of Saturn towards the line of Heart. iii) An Apollonian. iv) Influence line from the mount of Venus cutting an upward branch from the line of Life terminating in a star. v) Fate line starting from the mount of Moon and ending on the Heart line. vi) Break on the Heart line. vii) Heart line with a break and a star. viii) Dot at the end of the break of the Heart line.

f) *Heart-warm and delicate :* Small hands.

g) *Heart-weak :* Poor line of Heart and a wavy Mercury line.

Appendix II

   h) *Palpitation of the heart :* i) Dark dots on the Heart line.
   ii*)* Poor and wavy line of Mercury with deep dots.

Hemorroids :   A Saturnian.

High ideals :   Long fingers.

High-way robber :   Star on the mount of Mercury.

Honour :   a) *To the parents :* Two or more forks at the start of the Life line below the mount of Jupiter.
   b) *Through the influence of powerful friends :* Rising line from the Bracelet upto the plain of Mars.
   c) *Love of honour and power :* Mercury line ending on the Head line and forked at the termination so as to form a triangle.
   d) *Public honour :* i) Star on the mount of Jupiter. ii) Star on the middle mount of Moon and connected to the Head line.
   e) *Military honour :* i) Star on the upper mount of Mars. ii) Triangle on the mount of Mars.

House property :   Lines of Head and Life joining at the start.

Hydrophobia :   a) Break in the Head line under the mount of Sun.
   b) Star on the mount of Moon in both the hands.

Hypnotic power :   a) Upper mount of Mars leaning towards the mount of Moon.
   b) Mount of Mercury leaning towards the upper mount of Mars.
   c) Sign of Saturn on the mount of Saturn.
   d) Upper mount of Moon more developed and a clear line of Mercury.
   e) Line of Intuition ending on the negative mount of Mars.
   f) Head line forked at the end; one fork going to the mount of Mercury, other to the mount of Moon.

Hypocricy :   a) Crooked finger of Mercury.
   b) Star on the mount of Moon.

Hysteria :   a) Excess development of the mount of Moon.
   b) Combination of the mounts of bad Saturn and bad Mercury.
   c) Crooked Saturn finger.

d) First phalanges of all the fingers abnormally long.
   e) Short vertical lines on the lower mount of Moon.
   f) Star on the mount of Moon.
   g) Girdle of Venus cut by many bars.
   h) Double or triple Girdle of Venus.
   i) Life line ending in an island.
   j) Heart line ending on the mount of Saturn.
   k) Broken Girdle of Venus.

I

Idealism : a) Square and smooth fingers.
   b) Pointed finger tips.
   c) Sloping line of Head.
   d) Long finger of Apollo.
Idiot : a) Powerless and atrophied high-set thumb.
   b) Fingers abnormally developed.
   c) One of the main lines missing.
   d) Very ill-shaped hand.
Idleness : Conic hand.
Ill-luck : Grill on the mount of Saturn.
Illness : a) *Normal illness :* i) Horizontal line rising from the line of Life and going to either of the mounts of Mars (positive or negative). ii) Cross at the end of the Life line.
   b) *Due to sorrow or disappointment in love :* Connecting lines between the line of Heart and the line of Life.
Illegitimate birth : a) Fate line or Life line starting from an island.
   b) Star at the edge of the Jupiter mount but not touching the Life line.
Illegitimate child having brilliant future : Sun line starting with an island.
Imagination : a) *Healthy :* Sloping line of Head with square fingers.
   b) *Diseased or excited imagination :* Mercury line forming a cross with the Head line on the mount of Moon.

c) *Wild and aggravated imagination :* **Head line ending deep on the mount of Moon.**

Imbecile : a) Powerless or atrophied thumb.
b) High set thumb.
c) Elementary thumb.

Immodesty : Two crosses at the beginning of the Life line on the hand of a woman.

Immoral character : a) Triangle on the third phalange of the Saturn finger.
b) Star on the first phalange of the thumb.
c) Wavy line of Mercury starting from the mount of Venus and ending on the mount of Mercury.
d) Wavy line of Via Lasciva.

Impotence (due to slow washing away of the energy) *:* Line of Via Lasciva forked at the end.

Impractical : Conic tip to the Apollo finger.

Imprisonment : a) Square touching the Life line from inside.
b) Fate line starting from inside the Quadrangle.
c) Fate line turning backward into the hollow of the hand and towards the mount of Moon in a semi-circular way.
d) Crooked line of Fate starting from the mount of Mars and terminating on the mount of Saturn.
e) Island on the Fate line on the mount of Uranus with a star on the mount of Saturn.
f) Deep Fate line cutting the third phalange of the Saturn finger with a star on the first phalange of the Saturn finger.
g) Influence line from the positive Mars touching the Sun line with a cross on the mount of Saturn.
h) Grill on the mount of Saturn or Venus.

Imprudence : a) Broad Quadrangle.
b) Mount of Saturn very small.
c) Saturn finger conical.
d) Short phalange of the thumb.

Inability to execute plans and ideas to the full extent : Dropping Head line on a square hand.

Inclination towards sex : Single Girdle of Venus.
Income-period of income : Triangle attached to Heart line.
Incoming danger : Overlapping of the Life line on both the hands.
Inconsistency in thought and action : a) Wavy line of Head.
   b) Thinness in the Head line.
Increase of fortune : Line from a star on the mount of Venus merging into a good line of Apollo.
Independent nature : a) Small space between Head and Life lines at the start.
   b) Branch from Life line going to the mount of Jupiter.
Indifferent educational career : Line from the mount of Jupiter touching the line of Head which starts from within the Life line.
Indigestion : Island under the line of Heart.
Individuality–self centred : a) Fate line starting from the wrist or the mount of Neptune and proceeding straight to the mount of Saturn.
   b) Large space between the lines of Life and Head.
   c) Spatulate hand.
Indulgence in wine and women : a) Branch from the line Mars going to the mount of Moon.
   b) Line of Via Lasciva ending on the mount of Moon.
Industrial life (Interest in machinery) *:* Head line terminating on the mount of Uranus.
Industrious : a) A Saturnian.
   b) Triangle with a cross within it on the first Bracelet.
Infidelity : a) Very long finger of Mercury.
   b) Star on the second phalange of the second finger.
   c) Sign of Moon on the mount of Moon.
   d) Narrow Quadrangle on both the hands with a grill on the mount of Mercury.
Influence of the opposite sex (good) : a) Influence line beginning from the line of Life at a later date on the hand.
   b) *Bad influence of opposite sex :* Influence line across the

hand stopping after crossing the lines of Saturn and Apollo.

c) *Influence of opposite sex or a marriage :* i) Line of influence rising on the mount of Moon and touching the Fate line. ii) Star on the mount of Venus near the thumb.

d) *Influence of a foreigner :* Influence line joining the Voyage line.

e) *Influence of parents or governess :* i) Vertical line starting on the mount of Venus and from the commencement of the Life line. ii) Head line closely connected with the Life line and running together for sometime.

Inheritance : a) Cross in the Big Triangle.
   b) Life line connected by other lines at the start.
   c) Star on the first Bracelet.
   d) Small vertical lines near the nail of the thumb.
   e) Sign of yova or lotus on the thumb.
   f) Influence line running parallel to Sun line.
   g) Branch from Mercury line merging in the Head line.
   h) Sign of angle on the Bracelet.
   i) Triangle with a cross in it on the first Bracelet.

Insanity : a) Drooping line of Head with many lines in the Triangle.
   b) Excess development of mount of Moon.
   c) Sign of Moon on the mount of Saturn.
   d) Abnormally long first phalanges.
   e) Psychic type of hand.
   f) Sign of Moon on the mount of Moon.
   g) Life line ending in a tassel and a branch of the tassel going deep into the mount of Moon.
   h) Head line rising towards the line of Heart under the mount of Saturn.
   i) Head line sloping abruptly to the mount of Moon with a star on the second phalange of the Saturn finger.
   j) Head line sloping to the mount of Moon and with a break in it under the mount of Saturn (sure sign if fond on both hands).

k) Head line ending under the mount of Mercury.
l) Wide fork of the Head line, one fork on the mount of Moon ending in a star or a dot.
m) Uneven Head line with a star or a cross or a dot on it.
n) Star on the second phalange of the Saturn finger.
o) Wavy Head line slanting in an abnormal upward curve towards the line of Heart under the mount of Sun or Mercury.

Insanity-alcoholic : Star on the lower mount of Moon.

Insanity-danger of : Cross touching the Sun line with mounts of Moon and Saturn badly developed.

Insanity-hereditary : Star at the end of the branch from the Heart line going to the mount of Moon.

Insanity-eroti : Presence of double of triple or broken Girdle of Venus.

Insanity due to excess sexual activities even self abuse : Several branches of the Via Lasciva running across the Head line and a star or a cross or a bar or a break in the Head line.

Insignificant life : Flat Triangle with low mount of Saturn.

Insomia : Vertical and confused lines on the mount of Moon.

Intellect : a) A Martian.
b) Developed first phalange of the Apollo finger.

Intellectual-dull : Fate line starting from the line of Head with low mounts of Apollo and Jupiter.

Intellectual conquest of inventive type : White dots on the Heart line.

Intellectual gift with refinement and grace : Presence of the Ring of Saturn on a woman's hand.

Intellectual pursuits : Life and Head lines closely connected at the start.

Intellectual type : Sun line starting from the rascette.

Intelligence impaired : Very deep and often red Girdle of Venus cutting through the line of Fate and Sun.

Interest in two countries : Island on the Fate line with many short lines of Voyages.

Interest organs delicate : Third Bracelet formed like a series of small islands.

Intestinal inflammation : a) Cross lines on the upper mount of Mars.
b) Cross on the upper mount of Moon.

Intestinal weakness : Strong red line between the first and second finger.

Intuition :
1) a) Development of the first phalange of the Jupiter finger.
   b) A Mercurian.
   c) Triangle on the mount of Moon.
   d) Line of Intuition.
   e) Fate line starting from the base of the mount of Moon with long fingers of Jupiter and Apollo.
   f) Fate line starting from two islands forming a figure of 8 (eight).

2) *Intuition strongly developed and significant dreams :* a) Presence of double line of Life.
   b) Intuition line ending in a star.
   c) Rising branch from the line of Intuition going to the mount of Jupiter or Sun.
   d) Mercury line forming a small triangle with the lines of Head and Life.

3) *Assistance of intuition in the career :* Rising branch of Intuition line merging into the line of Fate.

4) *Limited power of intuition :* Broken line of Intuition or its branch.

5) *Poor success in intuition :* Islands in the line of Intuition.

Inventor : a) Spatulate hand.
b) Saturn finger with spatulate tip.

Inventive genius : Hair on the thumb.

Invincibility : A thick vertical line on the first phalange of the Mercury finger.

Irresponsive nature, cold and lack of human warmth : Disgraceful curve of the Life line and somewhat straight descending of the Life line.

Irritable nature and ill-luck in profession : a) Girdle of Venus on a hand with wide gap between the lines of Head and Life.

b) Heart line ending on the mount of Venus.

Irritation :   A Saturnian.

J

Jack of all trades :   a) Square hand with mixed fingers.

b) Low set thumb.

Jaundice :   a) Star on the Mercury line.

b) Mount of Mercury with many lines.

c) Star or spot on the mount of Moon.

Jealousy :   a) Conic hand.

b) Girdle of Venus.

c) Vertical lines on the first phalange of the Saturn finger.

d) Cross lines on the third phalange of the Apollo finger.

Journey :   a) *Both by land and sea :* i) Rising branch from the Bracelet. ii) Via Lasciva starting either from the line of Fate or the line of Mercury and going to the mount of Moon unbroken and uniformly constituted.

b) *Fortunate journey :* The line of Via Lasciva extending upto the mount of Moon and going downward into it.

c) *Successful earning of wealth by journey :* Rising branch from the Bracelet which goes to the mount of Jupiter and having a cross or an angle or a star on it.

d) *Journey profitable :* i) Two lines from the Bracelet going across the mount of Moon. ii) Star on the first phalange of the Jupiter finger.

e) *Disappointment in journey :* Cross on the Voyage line.

Judge :   a) Jupiter finger straight.

b) First phalange of the Mercury finger long.

c) Good Head line.

Judgement lacking :   Drooping line from the Heart line.

K

Kidney troubles :   a) Weak, long and thin finger Apollo.

b) Cross on the mount of Moon.

c) Defect in the third finger.
d) A Martian.
e) Cross on the lower third of the mount of Moon.
f) Any defect in the line of Mercury.
g) Whorl on the middle mount of Moon.
h) Prominent cross line on the mount of Moon.

L

Lack of artistic touch in writing : Square hand.
Lack of clear ideas and thinking : Head line with a bunch like formation at the start.
Lack of concentration and self control : Break in the line of Head.
Lack of confidence : Head line like a bunch at the start.
Lack of courage : a) Head line terminating on the mount of Uranus and a badly developed mount of Mars.
b) Broad and shallow line of Head.
Lack of decision and weak mental power : a) Chained line of Head.
b) Wide gap between the lines of Head and Life.
Lack of discretion : Short Mercury finger.
Lack of energy and vitality : Fork at the end of the Life line or the Fate line.
Lack of intelligence : a) Head line starting from within the line of Life with a branch going to the mount of Venus.
b) Short Head line with a poor line of Heart and a triangle on the Life line.
Lack of mental efforts : Wavy line of Head.
Lack of mental power : Obscuring of lines.
Lack of morals : Conic hands (see morality-lack of).
Lack of natural human warmth : Disgraceful curve of the line of Life.
Lack of originailty : Square hand.
Lack of perception creating danger and difficulties : Joining of the lines of Heart, Head and Life.

Lack of sense of responsibility and lack of patriotism : Drooping Head line with a fork on the mount of Moon.
Lack of Sympathy : Absence of the line of Heart.
Lack of social adaptability : a) Absence of the Fate line.
b) A Saturnian.
Lack of tubercular resistance : Deformed second phalanges of fingers. *Laryngitis* Abnormal development of Jupiter finger
Lascivious tendencies : a) The Via Lasciva starting from the mount of Venus and joining the Life line.
b) The Via Lasciva starting from the mount of Venus and going to the mount of Moon in a loop style with soft and flabby hands.
c) *Lascivious tendency ruling success in life* : Branch of Via Lasciva cutting the line of Sun.
Law suits : a) i) Cross on the Life line. ii) Cross inside the upper angle of the Triangle. iii) Two or more forks at the start of the Life line. iv) See litigation
b) *Law suits due to death of someone :* Influence line from a star cutting a short upward branch of the line of Life.
c) *Loss of law suit :* Influence line from a star cutting a branch of the Life line and also cutting the line of Sun.
d) *Success in the suit :* Influence line from an island crossing the upward branch of the Life line and merging into the line of Sun.
Lawyer : a) Jupiter-Mercury combination.
b) Development of the first phalange of the Mercury finger.
c) A Mercurian.
Laziness : a) Drooping line of Head.
b) Short and conical fingers.
c) Weak line of Heart.
Learned person : Straight line from the root of the Saturn finger going upto the first phalange of the finger.
Leadership : a) Head line starting from the mount of Jupiter.
b) Branch of the Head line rising to the mount of Jupiter.
c) Sun line ending on the mount of Jupiter.

Legacy and inheritance :   a) Small vertical lines near the nail of the thumb.
b) Sign of yova or lotus on the thumb.
c) Star or cross on the first Bracelet.
d) Cross in the Big Triangle.
e) Influence line running parallel to the Sun line.
f) Branch from the Mercury line merging in the Head line.
g) Sign of an angle on the Bracelet.
h) Triangle with a cross in it on the Bracelet.
i) Life line connected by other lines at the start.

Leg-troubles with legs :   a) A Saturnian.
b) Life line connected to the Head line at the start and poor and short Head line.
c) Small lines on the mount of Saturn.
d) Cross lines on the mount of Mercury.
e) Straight branch from the Heart line ending on a hook on the Mercury finger.
f) Black spot on the mount of Mercury.

Leprosy :   A bad Jupiterian.

Liar :   a) Crooked finger of Mercury.
b) Under developed mount of Jupiter.
c) Head line drooping and forked.
d) Cross on the mount of Mercury.
e) The line of Heart sinking towards the line of Head and forming a narrow Quadrangle and the mount of Moon prominent.
f) Grill on the mount of Mercury.

Life :   a) *Good ending of Life :* i) Vertical lines on the mount of Saturn. ii) Faint line of Fate at the beginning becoming clearer later on.
b) *Effect of short life nullified :* Split or a branch from the Life line joining the Fate line.
c) *Life-bright and lively :* Good development of the mounts and fair lay out of the Life line.
d) *Change in life :* Cross near the Mercury line but not touching it.

e) *Disastrous change in life :* Cross on the Fate line.

f) *Laborious life :* Fate line starting from the Head line, taking a turn and then going to the mount of Saturn.

g) *Luxurious life :* Mole at the beginning of the Head line. ii) Straight Head line upto middle of the hand and then sloping to the mount Moon.

h) *Short span of life :* Heart line ending on the mount of Saturn.

i) *Monotonous life :* Triangle on the Fate line.

j) *Good and comfortable life :* i) Double line of Life running full length to the line of Life. ii) Thick vertical line on the first phalange of the Jupiter finger. iii) Four vertical lines on the second and third phalanges of the Jupiter finger.

k) *Life spoiled on account of passionate attachment :* Finely marked Girdle of Venus cut by a bar line under the mount of Sun.

l) *Hard life but ending in tranquility :* Cross in the centre of the Bracelet.

m) *Inclination to spiritual life :* i) Life line ending on the mount of Neptune. ii) Presence of the Ring of Solomon with or without a star on it.

n) *Life in seclusion, philosophic or of a monk :* Presence of the Ring of Saturn with a star.

o) *Mysterious life :* Star on the lower mount of Moon.

p) *Life in prison :* See imprisonment.

Literary qualities : a) Good Girdle of Venus.
  b) Long finger of Mercury.
  c) Cross on the finger of Jupiter.
  d) Star or white spot on the mount of Sun.

Literary success : White spots on the line of Head under the mount of Sun with cross bars on the line of Heart.

Literary talent of the imaginative order : Head line ending in a fork.

Literature—love for it and wit : Strong and good line of Fate or line of Sun cutting a thin Girdle of Venus.

Appendix II 721

Litigation-love for litigation : Double line of running too close to the line of Life. b) Two squares close together on the upper mount of Mars.
Liver trouble : a) Deformed Saturn finger.
   b) A Saturnian. (also see Law suits)
   c) Dark spots on the mount of Moon.
   d) Island on the Mercury line.
   e) Line from the mount of Saturn touching the Life line.
   f) Mercury line but by the line of Via Lasciva.
Longevity: a) Three Bracelets on the wrist.
   b) Natural development of the line of Life.
   c) Life line ending on the mount of Neptune.
   d) Good line of Mercury.
   e) 100 years if the Mercury finger is longer than the first joint of the Apollo finger.
   90 years if the Mercury finger reaches the first joint of the Apollo finger.
   70 years if the Mercury finger just reaches the first joint of the Apollo finger.
   60 years if the Mercury finger is shorter than the first joint of the Apollo finger. f) see seperate chapter at the beginning of the book.
Loss : a) *Loss in general :* Grill on the mount of Jupiter.
   b) *Loss of career :* Fate line ending on the Head line.
   c) *Loss of commercial enterprise* : Heart line starting from the line of Head.
   d) *Loss through a friend or a relative :* Island on the mount of Jupiter.
   e) *Loss of fortune :* i) Star at the beginning of the Fate line. ii) Fate line ending abruptly on the Head line.
   f) *Loss of Memory* : i) Island on the centre of the mount of Saturn. ii) Series of breaks in the Head line. iii) Jupiter finger with spatulate tip.
   g) *Loss of money due to sickness or due to the death of a relative or friend :* i) Falling line from the Life line. ii) Life line with badly formed tassel. iii) Line from a star on the mount of Venus crossing the line of Apollo. iv) Influence line ending in a star within the Triangle but

after crossing the line of Fate. v) Star at the beginning of the Fate line.

h) *Loss of money through women* : Spot on the third phalange of the Saturn finger.

i) *Loss of mother* : Star at the edge of the Jupiter mount and touching Life line.

j) *Loss of partner (married)* : Fate line starting with a fork, one prong going to the mount of Neptune and the other to the mount of Venus (more true in the hands of men).

k) *Loss of prospects due to guilty intrigue* : Line starting from an island on the mount of Venus and ending under the mount of Mercury.

l) *Loss of reputation and money in later life* : i) Sun line ending in an island or a dot. ii) Spot on the mount of Jupiter. *Lottery* - see luck - unexpected through lottery.

Love : a) *Conquest on love* : Fate line ending on the mount of upper Mars.

b) *Fortune in love* : Mercury line starting from the mount of Venus.

c) *Frustration in love* : i) Head, Heart and Life lines joined at the start. ii) Spot on the mount of Venus.

d) *Guilty love* : Island on the Fate line or on the Heart line. ii) Chained line of Heart.

e) *Ideal love* : i) Heart line starting from the base of the Jupiter finger. ii) Heart line encircling the mount of Jupiter. iii) Heart line ending under the mount of Sun.

f) *Idealistic love* : Fate line ending in a fork and a trident with one branch going to the mount of Jupiter.

g) *Ideality and jealousy in love* : Heart line starting from the base of the Jupiter mount.

h) *Intense love though outwardly cool, jealous and selfish* : Heart line starting from the mount of Sun.

i) *Lack of demonstration in love* : Deep cut, well coloured and even line of Heart.

j) *Pure, steady and deep love :* i) Heart line starting from the middle mount of Jupiter. ii) Double line of Heart.
k) *Strength of love unusual for the married partner :* Marriage line starting with a fork.
l) *Strong and sensible about love, not having foolish ideas :* i) Island on the Fate line. ii) Island in a cross line which ends on the Heart line. iii) Heart line starting between the mounts of Jupiter and Saturn.
m) *Sorrow and disappointment in love :* i) Dark dots on the Heart line under the mount of Mercury. ii) Falling splits from the Heart line.
n) *Love for small details :* i) Large hands. ii) Square hand with knotty fingers.
o) *Love for large things :* Small hands.
p) *Unreliable in passion and love :* The line of Heart and the line of Head forming a single line and joining to the Life line.
q) *Love of beauty :* Supple conic hand with moderate development and small thumb.
r) *Brutal love :* Hair like lines on the mount of Mars.
s) *Unnatural kind of love :* Sign of Saturn on the mount of Venus.
t) *Platonic love :* Sign of Sun on the mount of Venus.
u) *Love for revolution :* Mount of Uranus developed.
v) *Love of solitude :* i) A Saturnian. ii) Life line ending on the mount of Neptune.
w) *Love of public life :* An Apollonian with the Apollo mount leaning towards the Apollo finger.
x) *Love for study and scientific investigation :* i) A Mercurian. ii) Mercury finger equal to the first phalange of the Saturn finger.
y) *Love for amphitheatres and libraries :* Square hand.
z) *Love of children :* A Mercurian.
1) *Love for domestic animals :* Smooth fingers with spatulate tips.
2) *Love for recitation :* Jupiter finger with conic tips.

3) *Love for mother :* Mercury finger longer than the first phalange of the Saturn finger.

4) *Unfortunate in mother's love :* A Lunarian with bad Saturn.

5) *Love for mathematics :* Saturn finger with square tip.

6) *Love for punishment :* Third phalange of the Jupiter finger longer than the third phalange of the Mercury finger.

7) *Love with a person of distinction :* Star on the mount of Venus near the thumb.

Love affairs : a) *Broken love affair due to capricious conduct :* Break in the Heart line under the mount of Sun.

b) *Love affair at an early age :* Presence of the double line of Life.

c) *Strong love affair :* i) Starting point of the line of Mars significant. ii) Sun line starting from the line of Heart.

d) *Two love affairs :* Small line from the line of Fate joining the Heart line on the side of the Jupiter mount and presence of two parallel lines of Marriage.

e) *Sustained love affairs :* i) Many longer and deeper lines of Marriage. ii) Two parallel lines from the mount of Venus to the mount of Mars. iii) Small branches at the end of the Heart line.

f) *Success in love affair :* Star at the centre or at the base of the mount of Venus.

g) *Love with a person of distinction :* Star on the mount of Venus near the thumb.

Lower part of the body trouble : a) A Saturnian.

b) Line from the mount of Saturn touching the line of Life.

Luck-good luck : a) Line from the mount of Mercury touching the line of Fate on the mount of Moon.

b) Large Big Triangle.

Luck-unexpected through lottery : a) Star on the line of Mercury.

b) Sudden appearance of the double line of Sun.

Appendix II

    c) Line from the mount of Moon touching the line of Mercury.

    d) Yova on the second joint of the Saturn finger.

Ill-luck : Vertical lines on the third phalange very near to the root of the Saturn finger.

Lucid expression required for a teacher : A clear square on the mount of Jupiter.

Lunacy : Obscuring of the lines on the hand. See also 'insanity'.

Lung trouble : a) Wide and long island on the line of Mercury.

    b) Line from the mount of Jupiter touching the line of Life.

    c) Abnormal development of the Jupiter finger.

    d) Pale lines.

    e) Thin palm.

Lust and intemperance : Double Girdle of Venus.

M

Madness : a) Grill in the Quadrangle.

    b) Sign of Mars on the mount of Moon.

    c) Sign of Moon on the mount of Mars.

    d) Line of Heart formed by islands or small lines.

    e) Lines running across the hand from positive mounts of Mars to negative mount of Mars.

Madness-romantic : Star on the mount of Moon.

Malaria : Bars cutting the line of Mercury.

Manner-stiffness in manner : Straight and thin line of Mercury. *Mahatma :* Signs like garland, mountain, swastic on th hand

Marrriage : a) *Happy marriage :* i) Cross or star on the mount of Jupiter. ii) Double line of influence on the mount of Venus. iii) Sister line to the Fate line. iv) Influence line from the mount of Moon merging into the the Fate line. v) Girdle of Venus present only in one hand. vi) Cross on the mount of Jupiter and a line from the Bracelet going to a vertical line on the mount of

Venus. vii) Single line of Marriage running straight and parallel to the line of Heart. viii) Long and clear line of Marriage with a cross on the mount of Mercury. ix) Deep and well-cut line of Marriage with good colour. x) Line starting from a star on the mount of Venus and going to the line of Heart and ending in a fork.

b) *Marriage–brilliant :* i) Fate line starting from the mount of Moon and merging in the Heart line. ii) Good and parallel distance between the lines of Heart and Head. iii) Rising branch from the line of Marriage going to the mount of Sun. iv) Rising branch from the line of Marriage going to the mount of Sun and a star at the end of the Sun line. v) Line of influence from the mount of Moon joining a small line running parallel to the Head line.

c) *Unhappiness in marriage :* i) A Saturnian. ii) Presence of the Girdle of Venus and a wide gap between the lines of Head and Life. iii) Head line separate from the Life line and running to the mount of Moon, poor line of Heart and the first phalange of the thumb broad and short. iv) Line of influence on the mount of Venus joined at the start to the Life line. v) Line of influence from the mount of Venus cutting the line of Fate. vi) Rising line from the line of Life crossed by a line from the mount of Mars or Venus. vii) Horizontal cross line from the Venus mount touching the line of Marriage. viii) Grill on the mount of Jupiter.

d) *Occasional unhappiness in marriage :* Appearance of an island on the line of Marriage.

e) *Late marriage :* i) A Saturnian. ii) Marriage line starting with fork or an island.

f) *No marriage :* i) Cross on the first phalange of the Mercury finger. ii) Influence line on the mount of Venus turning away from the Life line. iii) Line of Marriage curved upward.

g) *Obstructions and objections to marriage :* i) Line from

the mount of Mercury cutting the line of Marriage. ii) Marriage line starting with an island.

h) *Clash in marriage :* i) Line from the second phalange of the thumb touching the line of Life. ii) Spot touching the Marriage line. iii) Life line ending in a fork on the mount of Venus. iv) Influence line cutting a forked Life line. v) Falling lines from the Heart line. vi) Marriage line pointing towards the Heart line.

i) *Marriage between near relatives :* Island at the termination of the Marriage line with another island at the base of the reason phalange of the thumb.

j) *Physical disparity between husband and wife :* Grill on the mount of Venus and horizontal lines on the mount of Venus.

k) *Loss of riches and position after marriage :* Marriage line terminating on the mount of Sun and cutting the Sun line.

l) *Prosperity and riches after marriage :* i) Marriage line terminating on the mount of Sun and not cutting the line of Sun. ii) Rising branch from the Marriage line. iii) Sun line starting from the Heart line. iv) Bulging Bracelet. v) Rising branch from the Life line to the mount of Saturn.

m) *Married love ending in separation :* i) Line starting from a spot on the mount of Venus and cutting the rising branch of the Life line and a cross on the mount of Jupiter. ii) Island on the Marriage line. iii) Other line of Fate running close to a wavy and chained line of Fate.

n) *Periodical separation :* Fork in the Marriage line at both the ends.

o) *Co-wife :* Branches rising from the Heart line under the mount of Mercury.

p) *Triumph over all obstacles in marriage :* The lines of Head and Heart forked at the start and the line of Head going to the mount of positive Mars.

q) *Broken engagement :* i) Break on the Heart line.

ii) Influence line on the mount of Moon crossing the Fate line.

r) *Misfortune in marriage*: Island on the line of influence on the mount of Moon. ii) *Loss of partner:* a) Cross at the place where the Marriage line droops down to the line of Heart. b) Fate line starting from a fork and one branch of the fork going to the mount of Neptune and the other to the mount of Venus.

s) *Marrying a widow:* First phalange of the Jupiter finger as short as the nail.

t) *Marrying more than once:* Thicker finger of Saturn.

u) *Marrying an old person:* Line from the Bracelet to the mount of Neptune and thence to the mount of Venus

v) *Marrying a trader:* A line from the Bracelet to the mount of Venus and thence to the mount of Mercury.

w) *Second marriage:* i) Two marriage lines and a small line from the Fate line joining the Heart line on the side of the Jupiter mount. ii) Break in the Fate line and the overlapping line ending on the mount of Jupiter.

x) *Married partner:* See partner-Marriage Partner.

Masterbation: Small indentation on the Heart line.

Maternity happy: Two vertical lines on the mount of Saturn, one on the side of the Jupiter mount and the other on the side of the Apollo mount.

Maternity-danger in: Line from the upper part of the mount of Venus to the mount of Saturn.

Maternity-abortion: Cross above the line of Marriage.

Mechanic: a) Spatulate tip to the Mercury finger.
b) Longer second phalange of the Saturn finger.

Medical study: Medical stigma on the mount of Mercury.

Meditation: a) Development of the mount of Moon by way of a narrow strip along the percussion. b) Mount of Moon leaning towards rascc
c) Life line ending on the mount of Neptune.

Melancholia: a) A Saturnian.
b) Wavy and drooping line on the third phalange of the Saturn finger.

c) Grill on the mount of Moon.

d) Wavy line of Head inclining towards the mount of Mercury.

Memory: a) *Memory-good:* i) Jupiter-Apollo combination. ii) Good Head line extending across the hand with a good line of Mercury. iii) Long, narrow, clear and straight line of Mercury with a long line of Head across the hand.

b) *Memory-loss of:* i) Yova or island on the mount of Saturn. ii) Series of breaks in the Head line. iii) Jupiter finger with spatulate tip. iv) An island at the end of Head line.

c) *Memory-remembering previous birth:* Circle on the mount of Jupiter.

Mentally defective: Concave and spoon-like nail.

Mentally retarded: Many breaks and splits in the Head line.

Mental power lacking: Broken line of Head.

Mental degradation: Chained line of Heart rising towards the mount of Saturn.

Mental troubles: Downward branches of the Fate line.

Mental defect arising out of hereditary syphilis: a) Hollow towards the line of Head.

b) Lack of Fate line.

c) Middle angle of the Big Triangle on the mount of Moon.

Mental depression: Chained line of Mercury.

Mentality-changing: Life line ending on the mount of Moon.

Mental power-unusual: Formation of a triangle at a point where a branch of the Sun line reaches the Head line.

Mental strength accentuated: Rising line from the line of Mars merging on the line of Head.

Military renown: a) Triangle attached to the Fate line between the Life and the Fate lines.

b) Star on the upper mount of Mars.

Mimicry: Line of Head reaching upto the line of Heart but not touching it.

Mind: a) *Quick mind:* Short fingers.

b) *Analytical mind:* Philosophic type of hand with a Head line which is straight and high-set.

c) *Powerful mind:* Head line starting from the mount of Jupiter but touching the Life line.

d) *Unsteady mind:* Uneven curve or course of the Life line.

e) *Balanced mind:* Broad hand.

Minerology: Jupiter-Saturn combination.

Minister: A Jupiterian.

Misanthrope: a) Short line of Heart.
    b) Depressed mount of Venus.
    c) A Saturnian.

Miser: a) Narrow Quadrangle and fingers bending inside.
    b) The third phalange of the Saturn finger most developed.

Misfortune: a) Deep hollow on the hand.
    b) Black or red spot on the Jupiter mount.
    c) Hollow towards the Fate line.
    d) Fate line ending in a star.
    e) Abrupt ending of the Fate line on the Head line.
    f) Chained line of Fate.
    g) Island on a line of influence from the mount of Moon to the line of Fate.
    h) Head line starting with a bent downward.
    i) Circles on the line of Mercury.
    j) Grill on the mount of Saturn.

Misfit in the community: Short line of Fate.

Misuse of extra-ordinary intelligence for selfish purpose: Head line extremely long and straight and going directly to the other side of the hand.

Monetary gains: a) Triangles attached to the line of Heart.
    b) A Saturnian with good Fate line.
    c) An independent star in the Big Triangle.

Money: a) *Money making tendency through art:* Straight line of Head on conic hand.
    b) *Money obtained through land, property or agriculture:*

Rising branch of the Sun line going to the mount of Sun and a star on the branch of the Fate line.

c) *Money obtained through commercial and business enterprise:* Rising branch from the Sun line to the mount of Mercury.

Morality: a) Spatulate hands.

b) A Jupiterian.

Morality–lack of: a) Third type of conic hand.

b) Small thumb with high setting.

c) Cross or star at the upper side of the first phalange of the thumb.

d) Narrow Quadrangle on both the hands. Also see 'Immoral character'

Mother–loss of mother: Star at the edge of the mount of Jupiter and touching the Life line.

Murder: a) Star on the mount of Saturn at the end of the Fate line.

b) Crooked Saturn finger.

c) Red dots in the Quadrangle.

d) Cross in the Big Triangle on both the hands.

e) Cross on the mount of Saturn.

f) Star on badly developed mount of Mars.

Murderer (lady killer): a) Sign of Jupiter on the mount of Mars on a bad Martian.

b) *Murderer of wife:* Marriage line ending in a cross on the mount of Saturn.

c) *Murderer:* i) Clubbed thumb. ii) Large cross in the Triangle. iii) Star on the second finger.

d) *Murderous tendency:* i) Knotted Head line. ii) Blue spot on the Head line which is one side of the Triangle with the Life and Mercury lines and a powerful mount of Mars. iii) Line of Mars only at the final portion of the hand and a deep red colour of the line. iv) Strong mount of Mars with deep and straight line of Head and Heart. v) Grill or star on badly developed mount of Mars. vi) Wavy branch from Heart line going to the mount of Moon.

e) *Murder out of Jealousy :* i) Martian with deep red colour of the hand. ii) Grill on the mount of Mars of a Martian.

f) *Murderous tendency with revengeful attitude :* Sign of Saturn on the Mount of Moon.

Musician of great distinction : Rising branch from the Sun line to a strong amount of Venus.

Musician passionately fond of melodious music : Branch from Sun line to a strong mount of Venus.

Mystery of birth : Island either at the beginning of the Life line or the Fate line.

Mysterious life : Star on the lower mount of Moon.

Mysticism and imagination : a) Rising branch of the Head line going to the mount of Moon.
b) Head line deflecting downwards.

N

Nature : a) *Ambitious nature :* i) Life line starting on the mount of Jupiter. ii) Influence line going to the mount of Jupiter. iii) Rising branch from the Head line reaching the root of the first finger.

b) *Emotional and sensitive nature :* i) Long line of Heart. ii) Girdle of Venus found only at the start and at the end.

c) *Fault finding nature :* Too wide a gap between the Head and Life lines.

d) *Obstinate and extrovert nature :* i) Heart line rising high towards the mount and far apart from the line of Head. ii) A Martian.

e) *Quarrelsome nature :* i) Cross in the Big Triangle. ii) Wide space between the lines of Head and Life.

f) *Restless and excitable nature :* Hard, firm, spatulate hand.

g) *Stubborn, hysterical, puzzling, determined, inflexible type of nature :* The line of Heart and the line of Head forming a single line and joining to the Life line.

Nervous constitution : a) Short, shaky, interrupted line of Life.

b) Life line starting with island and filled with small cross bars

c) Head line with open formation at the beginning and sharply bending down from its commencement.

d) Chained line of Mercury.

e) Deep and irregular line of Fate in much rayed hand.

Nervous energy, nervous break-down : a) Absence of Life line (Very rare thing).

b) Head line having ladder-like formation.

c) Girdle of Venus terminating on the mount of Mercury.

Nervousness : a) Nervous thumb.

b) Spots on nails.

c) Narrow nail.

d) Ridges on nails.

e) Blue colour of the nails.

f) A Saturnian.

g) Loop formation of capillary ridges on the tips of the fingers.

h) Tented arch on the finger tips.

i) Two perpendicular lines from a poor line of Heart drooping straight into the mount of Moon.

j) Darkly coloured and deeply cut line of Mercury.

Nervous trouble and morbidity : a) Head line sweeping down to the wrist.

b) Deep cross bars with red colour cutting the Head line.

c) Fluted nails.

d) Small and meaningless lines in the Quadrangle.

e) Obtuse upper angle of the Big Triangle formed by the Head line and the Mercury line.

f) Upper mount of Moon most developed.

g) Grill on the mount of Moon.

Neuralgia : Dots on the Heart line.

Notoriety : Rising branch from the Head line going to the mount of Sun.

Nurse : a) Two clear cut lines on the Mercury finger.

b) Long knotty fingers.

c) Medical stigma on the mount of Mercury.

O

Obstacles : a) Cross lines on the first phalange of the thumb.
b) *Obstacles from relatives :* A Martian with a sign of an island on the lower mount of Mars.
c) *Obstacles from friends :* A Martian with a sign of an island on the upper mount of Mars.

Obstinacy and quarrelsome disposition : a) Head line starting from the mount of Jupiter and not touching the Life line and sloping down to the mount of Moon with broad and short first phalange of the thumb.
b) A Martian.

Occultism : Love and faculty for occult science :
1) Rising branch from the Head line going to the mount of Moon.
2) Heart line encircling the mount of Jupiter.
3) Rising branch from the Sun line to the mount of Saturn and a star on the branch of Fate line.
4) Mercury line ending on the Head line in a fork so as to form a triangle with the Head line.
5) A Mercurian with the line of Intuition.
6) Mystic cross.
7) Single Girdle of Venus.
8) Line connecting the Jupiter and Mercury mounts.
9) Heart line completely encircling the mount of Mercury at its termination.
10) Two or three vertical lines on the middle phalange of the Mercury finger.
11) Pointed tip to the Mercury finger.
12) Sign of Saturn on the Jupiter mount.
13) First phalange of the Saturn finger developed.
14) Lines on the second phalange of the Saturn finger and the Head line sloping upto the wrist.
15) Rising branch from the Mercury line to the Jupiter mount and a star on the Jupiter mount.
16) Triangle on the mount of Saturn.

Occult power-misuse of : Cross on the mount of Saturn.

Appendix II

Old age-happy : Vertical lines on the mount of Saturn.
Opera singer : a) Fingers with conical tips.
    b) Head line forked at the end.
Operation-surgical : a) Island on the Mercury line between the lines of Heart and Head.
    b) Clear break on the Mercury line in the middle, having bar lines at the two ends of the break.
Opportunity : a) *Creative :* Fate line starting from inside the Triangle in both the hands.
    b) *Favourable opportunity :* Fate line starting from the line of Mars.
    c) *Opportunities marred by circumstances :* Fate line ending on the Heart line.
    d) *Less opportunities in life :* i) Life line starting from the positive mount of Mars. ii) Thin Life line upto the end.
Oratory : a) An Apollonian.
    b) A Mercurian.
    c) Line from the bottom of the Mercury finger to the second phalange.
    d) Forked line on the first phalange of the Mercury finger.
Orderliness : Square hand.
Originality : a) Spatulate hand.
    b) Spatulate fingers with straight Head line.
Out look-affectionate and sympathetic : Heart line longer than the Head line.
Over self-confidence and egoism resulting in serious troubles : Head line turning back at its end on the mount of Mars.

P

Painter : a) Conical hand.
    b) Strong mount of Venus.
    c) Head line going to the mount of Moon.
Palpitation of the heart : a) Dark dots on the Heart line.
    b) Poor and wavy line of Mercury with deep dots.
Paralysis : a) Fluted nails.

b) A Saturnian.
c) Star on the mount of Saturn.
d) Flat nail which is narrow at the bottom.
e) All lines obscuring.
f) Abnormal depth of the line of Life.
g) Head line terminating under the mount of Saturn with dots or islands in the line.
h) Star or a cross on an uneven Head line.
i) Line from a grill on the mount of Saturn joining an island on the Life line with dots or island in the Head line.
j) Fate line and Life line both ending in a star.
k) Very deep line of Sun on an artistic hand.
l) Star on the mount of Moon.
m) Grill on the mount of Moon.
n) Dark spot on the mount of Mercury.

Partner–Marriage partner : a) *Married partner–affectionate and faithful :* Girdle of Venus present only on one hand.
b) *Of affluent circumstances :* Double line of Life running full length to Life line.
c) *Dominating :* Influence line from the mount of Moon clear and stronger than the Fate line.
d) *Deformed through accident or sickness :* Dot on the Marriage line.
e) *Governed by Martian qualities :* Double line of Life starting from Life line.
f) *Of hypersensitive nature :* Marriage line ending on the Heart line.
g) *Having long life :* Long and clear line of Marriage.
h) *Married partner's illness causing anxiety :* Falling lines from the Marriage line towards the Heart line.
i) *Of indifferent and cold nature :* i) Very thin line of Marriage. ii) Broad and shallow or chained line of Marriage. iii) White colour of the Marriage line.
j) *Married partner very selfish causing injury to the extent of being fatal :* i) Marriage line ending in a distinct cross

on the mount of Saturn. ii) Marriage line ending in a cross.

k) *Of strong affection :* Pink or red colour of the line of Marriage.

l) *Of stronger individuality :* Line of Mars stronger than the Fate line.

m) *Impediment in partner's love :* i) Dot on the Marriage line. ii) Star on the Marriage line that turns upward.

n) *Conjugal misery :* Black spot not on the Marriage line but on the mount of Mercury.

o) *Partner's death giving shock :* i) Cross at the place where the line of Marriage droops down towards the Heart line. ii) Star on the line of Marriage.

p) *Partner dying before the individual :* Upper Marriage line longer than the lower marriage line.

q) See 'Death'

Passions : a) *Exaggerated sensuality and selfishness :* Heart line starting from the finger of Saturn.

b) *Refinement of passion :* Girdle of Venus connecting the mounts of Jupiter and Mercury.

c) *Passionate nature :* Development of the mount of Venus.

Patriot : Martian with conic fingers.

Pecuniary troubles due to love sorrows : Cross on the line of Heart at the intersection of the Fate line.

Pecuniary success due to person's intellegence : Line from the Head line touching the Sun line.

Perseverance : a) Square hand.
 b) Upper Martian.
 c) A Saturnian.
 d) Strong Head line.
 e) Fingers knotty and square.
 f) Will phalange of the thumb developed.

Perseverance with decision taking abiliy : Mars line deeper and more pink in colour than the colour of the skin.

Personality-magnetic : Fate line after crossing the Heart line ending in a trident and the Heart line forked with one branch going to the mount of Jupiter.

Pessimistic : a) Chained line of Mercury.
    b) A Saturnian.
    c) Mount of Saturn leaning towards the mount of Sun.

Philosophic attitude: a) Mercury finger as long as the Jupiter finger.
    b) Long fingers with well developed knots.
    c) Thin hard palm.
    d) Spatulate fingers.
    e) Finger tips conical.

Physical handicap : A line joined to the first joint of the Mercury finger.

Pick pocketer : a) Long and thin fingers.
    b) Mount of Moon exaggerated.
    c) Mount of Mercury much lined.
    d) Thin and narrow palm.

Piles : A Martian.

Planning–intellectual : Fate line starting from the line of Mars.

Pleader : Jupiter–Mercury combination.

Pleurisy : a) A Jupiterian.
    b) Line rising from the line of Life and ending on an island on the mount of Saturn.
    c) A line with an island from the mount of Jupiter touching the Life line.
    d) Small lines crossing the Mercury line and also the Head line.

Pneumonia : Abnormal development of the Jupiter finger.

Poet : Psychic hand.

Poetry of imagination : Conic hand.

Poisoning : a) *Danger from poisoning :* Circle on the mount of Mercury.
    b) *Blood poisoning :* Black or bluish spots on nails.
    c) *Poisoning by enemy :* Blue dot by the side of the line of Life.

Appendix II

    d) *Self-administered poison:* Blue dot on the Life line.

Politician: clever and wity: a) The line of Via Lasciva ending on the mount of Mercury.
    b) Drooping line of Head.
    c) Powerful mount of Jupiter.

Popularity and reputation: Line from the mount of Venus joining the line of Apollo on the Life line.

Position-high and of power: a) Descending line from the mount of Sun and touching the Heart line.
    b) Long and uncrossed line of Apollo.

Poverty: Star on the mount of Saturn.

Poverty in old age: Cross at the end of the Life line.

Power: a) *Power of concentration:* Broad line of Sun.
    b) *Power neutralised by distraction of concentration:* Forked line of Sun ending on a sign like the letter 'V' on the mount of Sun.
    c) *Power-yogic:* All the lines on the hand form a tree like formation. d) Power of healing ; Square on the Life line.

Precision in manner: Square hand.

Pregnancy: Red dots in the Big Triangle.

Prevention from danger: a) Square on the fault in the line.
    b) Sister line joining the break on the line.

Prevention and protection from all evil: a) Sun line ending in a Square.
    b) Long and narrow hands with a neat line of Life and the line of Mars.

Pride: a) A Jupiterian.
    b) Exaggerated mounts of Sun and Jupiter.
    c) Grill on the mount of Jupiter.

Pride-stupid: Red dots under the mount of Sun.

Pride-too much: Break in the Head line under the mount of Sun.

Priesthood. a) Good balance of Head and Heart lines.
    b) Cross in the Quadrangle under the mount of Saturn.
    c) Straight and developed finger of Jupiter.

Prophet: Mount of Neptune developed.

Prophetic vision : Ring of Solomon.
Prosperity : a) Upward branches of the Fate line.
  b) Fate line about to stop and at the same time another Fate line starts.
  c) Fate line ending on the mount of Mercury.
Prosperity-intermittent periods of : Uneven Fate line alternately deep and thin in character.
Prudence : a) Life and Head lines form a sharp angle.
  b) Mercury line making a clear and good triangle with the lines of Head and Life.
Punctuality : Square hand.
Pursuit : a) *Worthless :* Fate line running close to the line of Life for sometime and taking a turn towards the mount of Saturn.
  b) *of sensual pleasures :* Girdle of Venus crossing both the lines of Fate and Apollo.
  c) *of effective arts :* Girdle of Venus broken under the mount of Apollo.

Q

Quarrelsome : a) Cross in the centre of the Triangle.
  b) A Martian with stiff hands.
  c) Short but broad nails.
  d) Wide gap between the lines of Head and Life.

R

Rash attitude : a) Wide gap between the Head and Life lines at the start.
  b) A Martian.
  c) Wide distance between Apollo and Saturn fingers.
Realisation of ambition : a) Long fork of the Life line going deep into the mount of Jupiter.
  b) Branches from the line of Head going to the mount of Jupiter.
Restlessness and conceit : Wide distance between the lines of Head and Life at the beginning.

Appendix II

Recovery : a) *From grave illness :* Bar across the two broken but overlapping ends of the line of Life.
b) *Quick recovery :* Triangle on the Mercury line.

Religion : Change of religion : a) Grills on the mount of Venus and also on the Head line and both the grills touching the Life line.
b) Sloping line of Head and chained line of Heart spatulate and knotty fingers and a cross on the top phalange of Saturn finger. c) Island in the Head line

Religious : Developed mount of Jupiter.

Religious faith giving consolation : A cross attached to the line of Fate inside the Quadrangle with smooth fingers and first phalange of the first finger well developed.

Religion-respect for : First phalange of the Jupiter finger developed.

Remembrance of previous birth : Circle on the mount of Jupiter.

Renunciation : Horizontal line or a cross at the base of the Jupiter finger.

Respiratory system trouble : a) Head line islanded at the start.
b) Narrow Quadrangle.
c) Line from the Jupiter mount touching the Life line.
d) Abnormal development of the Jupiter finger.
e) Spot in the Quadrangle.
f) Hedge formation on the line of Life.
g) Cross line from the mount of Venus ending on the mount of Jupiter in an island. h) Sign of trident on the Third phalange of Saturn finger

Rheumatism and gout trouble : a) Islanded line from the mount of Saturn joining the island in the line of Life and another line from the middle of the mount of Moon joining the same island.
b) Heart, Head and Life lines joining each other.
c) Bluish dot on the line of Heart.
d) Island on the Head or Heart line and downward branch of the Fate line.

e) Line descending from the mount of Saturn and touching the Life line.
   f) Ridges on the nails.
   g) A Saturnian.
   h) Cross lines or a cross on the middle mount of Moon.

Riches and wealth : see also luck unexpected through lottery. p. 724
1) *Acquisition of others' money :* A cross line on the third joint of the Jupiter finger.
2) *Acquision of conveyance :* A mole at the end of the Heart line.
3) *Acquision of property, land or agriculture :* a) Small triangle on the line of Life.
   b) Lines of Head and Life joining at the start.
4) *Fame and riches :* Sun line starting from the negative mount of Mars and ending in a trident.
5) *Financial position improved :* a) Line from the mount of Mercury touching the line of Heart.
   b) Triangle attached to the line of Heart in the Quadrangle.
6) *Fortune :* a) Square or triangle attached to the Fate line in the zone of action.
   b) Mercury line making a good triangle with the lines of Head and Life.
   c) Two parallel lines on either side of a straight and deep line of Sun.
   d) A line from a star on the mount of Venus merging into a good line of Apollo.
7) *Fortune by large inheritance :* a) Triangle with a cross in it on the first Bracelet.
   b) Cross in the Big Triangle.
   c) Life line connected by other lines at the start.
   d) Star on the first Bracelet.
   e) Small lines near the nail of the thumb.
   f) Sign of yova on the thumb.
   g) Influence line running parallel to the Sun line.
   h) Branch from the Mercury line merging in the Head line.

Appendix II

i) Sign of angle on the Bracelet.

8) *Good fortune in old age* : a) Chained first Bracelet.
b) Straight and good Fate line starting from the Heart line and going upwards.
c) Fate line after crossing the line of Heart ends in a trident and if the Heart line is forked at the start with one branch going to the mount of Jupiter and with the presence of the line of Sun. d) Branch from Head line going to plain of Mars and then to the mount of Apollo.

9) *Riches* : a) Two lines from the first phalange of the thumb to the line of Life.
b) Sign of rainbow on the first phalange of the thumb.
c) Prominent and slanting line on the first joint of the thumb.
d) Line from the second joint of the thumb to the line of Life.
e) Sign of a trident on the mount of Saturn.
f) Many lines on the Apollo finger from the root going to the first phalange.
g) Independent star in the Big Triangle.
h) Star on the mount of Apollo.
i) Long and uncrossed line of Sun.
j) Presence of Double line of Life.
k) Mole at the starting of the Head line.
l) Branches from Heart line pointing straight in the direction of the thumb

10) *Wealth* : a) *Wealth in general* : i) Line from the positive mount of Mars going to the mount of Saturn and acting like a sister line to the Fate line. ii) Rising branch from the Head line ending in a cross and touching the root of the first finger.
b) *Wealth spent on charity purpose* : Mercury line starting from the mount of Neptune and ending on the mount of Mercury.
c) *Unusual enjoyment of wealth and reputation* : Triangle attached to the line of Sun and the line of Heart.
d) *Wealth earned but equally spent* : Line of Mercury pointing towards the mount of Apollo and then taking its course towards the mount of Mercury from near the Head line.

e) *Great wealth :* i) Rising branch of Mercury going to the mount of Apollo and a branch from the Sun line joining the line of Mercury. ii) Mercury line terminating on the mount of Sun with well marked three Bracelets. iii) Star on the mount of Apollo iv) Branches from Heart line pointing towards the thumb

Robber : a) Star or a grill on the mount of Mercury.
   b) Red colour of the lines on the hand.

Romance : a) Line on the back of the thumb and starting from the base of the nail.
   b) Line of Heart starting from the mount of Saturn.
   c) Developed mount of Venus.

S

Sage or a saint : a) Mystic cross.
   b) Line of Intuition.
   c) Pointed and smooth fingers.

Sailing easy life : Fate line starting at a higher level on the hand.

Scandal : a) *Scandal monger :* Jupiter and bad Mars combination.
   b) *Scandal due to guilty intrigue :* Line from the mount of Venus cutting the line of Apollo and terminating in an island.
   c) *Scandal due to foolish talkativeness :* Short Head line with a poor line of Heart and a triangle on the line of Life.

Scar on the skull : Line encircling the first joint of the Jupiter finger.

Scientific approach : a) Low set and large thumb.
   b) Line on the Mercury finger from the bottom upto the first phalange.

Sculptor : a) Mounts of Venus and Moon developed.
   b) Soft hands.
   c) Square finger tips.

Sea trouble : Defective fourth finger.

Second sight gift : Two islands forming a figure of '8' at the starting of the Fate line.

Appendix II

Self administered poisoning : Blue dot in the Life line.
Selfish and cold : a) Deep and well-cut Head line with yellow colour.
b) Absence of the Heart line.
c) Heart line placed low on the hand with unhealthy closeness to the Head line.
Selfish and materialistic : Breaks in the Girdle of Venus.
Sense of romantic idealism and unconventionality in manners and habits : Head line ending in a fork where both the prongs are sloping down.
Sensitive nature : Many lines in the Big Triangle.
Sensual nature : Conic hand.
Sensuality : a) High-set thumb but small thumb.
b) Bad Jupiterian.
c) Mount of Venus leaning towards the mount of Moon.
d) Heart line rising from the mount of Saturn.
Sex :
1) *Early sexual development :* Long line of Heart.
2) *Hatred for sexual act :* Much broken Heart line.
3) *Sexual cravings with coarser instinct :* Line of Via Lasciva starting from the mount of Venus in a Loop type formation and going to the mount of Moon.
4) *Sexual passions :* a) Developed mount of Venus.
b) A Martian.
c) Conic hand.
d) Development of the lower world on the hand.
5) *Sexual relations with the idea of pleasure :* Heart line rising from the mount of Saturn and the mount of Venus large and of pink or red colour.
6) *Selfish sexual tendency of brutal and mental type :* Short Heart line.
7) *Sex trouble :* Deformed Mercury finger.
8) *Conjugal misery :* Black spot not on the line of Marriage but on the mount of Mercury.
9) *Weakness of sexsual activity :* Black spots on the Heart line.

Shrewdness : a) Twisted thumb.
   b) A Mercurian.
   c) Large, thick and short conic hand.
   d) Rising branch from the Sun line going to the mount of Mercury.
Sickness : Life line broad anywhere during its course.
Skin disease : A Jupiterian with grill on the mount of Jupiter. Sisters - Faint Vertical lines between bracelets and Life line
Small pox : A Martian.
Snake bite : Star between the mounts of Saturn and Sun.
Soil analyst : Jupiter-Saturn combination.
Somnambulism : The line of Mercury or the line of Intuition starting from an island.
Sorrow : a) *Sorrow in young age, middle age and in old age :* Large space respectively between first and second fingers between second and third fingers and between third and fourth fingers.
   b) Black spots on nails.
   c) Horizontal line rising from the line of Life and going to either positive or negative mount of Mars.
Speculator : a) Spatulate hand.
   b) Soft hands
   c) Strong mounts of Moon and Venus.
Spending lavishly for fiancee : Many lines on the Apollo finger going from the root upto the first phalange.
Spendthrift : a) Flexible thumb.
   b) Space between Head and Life lines.
   c) Smooth fingers.
   d) Chinks between the fingers.
Spinal cord weakness : a) Narrow, short and curved nails.
   b) Star on the mount of Saturn.
   c) Many lines on the mount of Moon.
Spirit of independence : a) Soft and flabby spatulate hands.
   b) Presence of double line of Life.
   c) A line joining the line of Head and Heart and a high mount of Mercury.

Spirit medium : A Lunarian with medium texture.
Spiritualist : a) Neptune mount developed.
  b) Fine mount of Jupiter.
  c) Slender and soft hands.
  d) Smooth pointed figure. e) also see occultism and mysticism.
Sportsman : a) Only three main lines.
  b) Large hands.
  c) Spatulate finger tips.
Statesman : a) Head line starting high on the mount of Jupiter and forked at the end.
  b) Jupiter and Mercury mounts developed.
Stealing : a) Star on the mount of Mercury.
  b) Cross on the upper mount of Mars.
Sterility of the wife : a) Star or cross at the root of the Saturn finger.
  b) Star on the line of Mercury.
Stock broker : a) Spatulate hands.
  b) Saturn and Apollo fingers of equal lengths.
  c) Straight line of Head.
Stomach : a) *Delicate :* Broad and shallow line of Mercury.
  b) *Acute attach of stomach or bilious trouble :* Dots on the Mercury line.
Strange and unexpected favourable happenings : Two parallel lines from the Uranus cutting the line of Life.
Stubborn : a) Thick vertical line on the first phalange of the Mercury finger.
  b) Square hand.
  c) Hair on the lower phalanges of finger.
Studious : Development of the first phalange of the Saturn finger.
Success : a) *Through difficulties :* i) Line crossing the third knot of the Sun fingers. ii) Sun line starting from inside the Triangle.
  b) *In business due to personal efforts and shrewdness :* Branch from the Fate line rising to the mount of Mercury.
  c) *In military :* i) Triangle touching the Fate line on the side of the Life line. ii) Mars line with red colour.

d) *In scientific pursuit or business :* i) Rising branch from the line of Life going to the mount of Mercury. ii) Rising branch from the Head line going between the third and fourth fingers. iii) Head line curving upward and close to the mount of Mercury. iv) Good line of Mercury. v) Sign of triangle on the mount of Sun.

e) *In art, music and literature :* i) Line of Apollo starting from the line of Life. ii) Sun line starting from the mount of Moon and a sloping line of Head. iii) Branch of the Fate line rising to the mount of Sun.

f) *In getting finance and riches :* i) Three branches rising from the Head line and going to the mount of Jupiter. ii) Fate line ending on the mount of Mercury.

g) *In law and high position :* Line from the Bracelet going to the mount of Jupiter.

h) *Success due to ambition :* i) Fate line with usual course ending on the mount of Jupiter. ii) Rising branch from the Sun line to the mount of Saturn and a star on the branch of the Fate line. iii) Sun line ending in a star. iv) Line of Mercury rising near the line of Life and forming a Triangle on the hand.

i) *Success in life :* i) *Connected with foreign country :* a) Presence of the Sun line. b) Sun line starting from the top of the mount of Moon. ii) *Due to guilty love* : Sun line starting with an island. iii) *Due to talents and powers of high order :* Sun line starting from the mount of Uranus. iv) *Through hard labour :* Falling lines from the line of Mercury. v) *Success in second half of life :* Sun line starting from the Heart line. vi) *Success through soberness, frugality and wisdom :* Rising branch from the Mercury line to the mount of Saturn.

j) *Success ruined by excessive love of opposite sex :* Line joining the lines of Sun and Mercury cuts the line of Sun.

k) *Late success :* Cross inside the lower part of the Big Triangle.

Suffocation : See Respiratory system troubles. P. 741

Suicide : a) *Suicide in water :* i) Star on the lower developed mount of Moon with sloping line of Head. ii) Two stars on the third phalange of the Saturn finger and Head line broken under the mount of Saturn.
b) *Suicide by poisoning :* i) Star on the Girdle of Venus under the mount of Saturn. ii) Presence of the Ring of Saturn.
c) *Suicidal tendency :* i) Lack of upper mount of Mars. ii) Star right on the line of Life. iii) Star at the terminatian of the Fate line with another star on the mount of Moon. iv) Cross on the lower mount of Mars. v) Star on the mount of Saturn or on the mount of Moon.

Sustained life : Life line untouched by the Mercury line.

Sun stroke : a) An Apollonian.
b) Island or break in the line of Head under the mount of Sun.

Support to family, relatives and friends : Triangle on the Life line.

Surgeon : a) Clear and deep Head line.
b) Second knots of the fingers developed.
c) Medical stigma.

Swindler : a) Yellow colour of the Heart line and a Mercurian.
b) Crooked fingers.

Syphilis : a) Concave spoonlike nail.
b) Star in the middle of the double or triple Girdle of Venus.
c) Cross or star on the mount of Mercury.

T

Tact : a) Low set and large thumb.
b) Fine plain of Mars.
c) Long fingers.
d) Triangle near the end of the Life line.
e) Good lines of Head and Heart.

Talent : a) Fork at the end of the Head line.

    b) Rising branch from the Head line going to the mount of Sun.

    c) Drooping line of Head with a fork in it on the mount of Moon.

Talent diversified : Sun line ending in a tassel.

Talent in science and eloquence : The line of Via Lasciva starting from inside the Life line and extending towards the mount of Mercury.

Teacher :   a) A Jupiterian.

    b) Fine lines of Head and Heart.

    c) Fine mount of Sun.

    d) Long and well-shaped thumb.

    e) Branch from Head line going to the mount of Jupiter.

Teeth trouble :   a) A Saturnian.

    b) Black spots on the Head line with powerful mount of Saturn.

Teeth–bad and calcium deficiency :   a) Line from the mount of Saturn touching the Life line.

    b) Wavy and long Heart line.

    c) Wavy line of Mercury.

Telepathy :   Line of Intuition.

Temper :   a) *Violent temper :* Elementary hand.

    b) *Sour temperament due to extremely irritable and passionate nature :* Presence of double line of Life.

    c) *Irritable temper prone to quarrels and disputes :* Double line of Life running too close to the line of Life.

Theatrical success :   Head line ending in a fork.

Theft :   a) *By a person who has been appointed for religious duty :* Broken line at the root of the Jupiter finger.

    b) *By one in the family :* Spot on the Saturn finger.

    c) Star on the mount of Mercury.

Thief :   a) Crooked finger of Mercury.

    b) Flat mount of Jupiter.

    c) Mount of Moon bulging.

    d) Head line wavy with a narrow Quadrangle and exaggerated mount of Mercury.

Appendix II

Throat trouble : a) Upper mount of Moon with cross lines.
  b) Large and round nails.
  c) A Jupiterian.
Thyroid gland trouble : a) Under developed small, broad and fat hand which is flabby with sausage-shaped fingers.
  b) Over-developed long bony hand with long bony fingers.
Timidity : a) Narrow Triangle.
  b) Mounts of Mars, Mercury and Jupiter very low.
  c) Thin and soft palm.
  d) Long knotted fingers bent inward.
  e) Head line starting from within the Life line.
Tonsils : a) A Jupiterian.
  b) See Throat trouble.
Tranquility : Presence of three good coloured Bracelets.
Travels : a) Star on the first phalange of the Jupiter finger.
  b) Mercury line starting from the Rascette without touching the Life line.
  c) Rising branch from the Rascette going to the mount of Mercury.
  d) Line from the Life line going to the mount of Moon.
  e) Horizontal line on the mount of Moon.
  f) *Long travel or voyage :* i) Horizontal line on the middle mount of Moon from the side of the percussion. ii) Line from the Bracelet going from near the percussion and to the mount of Jupiter. g) White spot on the nail of Saturn finger
  g) *Travel or voyage of business nature :* Line of voyage turning up and joining the line of Head
  h) *Advantage from voyage :* Voyage line turning up towards the mount which would indicate the nature of advantage.
  i) *Protection from danger in the travel or voyage :* Square on the voyage line.
  j) *Fatal accident during voyage :* i) Star on the voyage line. ii) Voyage line turning down and joining the Life line.

k) *No return from voyage :* Rising line from the Bracelet from near the percussion to the mount of Jupiter changes its course at the end and goes towards the mount of Saturn but does not reach the mount.

l) *Stay in foreign country :* i) Life line ending deep into the mount of Moon. ii) Line from the mount of Moon crossing the line of Fate and proceeding towards the line of Life and at the same time two parallel lines starting from the line of Fate and pointing towards the mount of Mercury. iii) Influence line from the mount of Moon touching the Life line

Treachery : Star on the mount of Mercury.

Trouble from relatives : a) Cross on the mount of Venus touching the Life line.
   b) Star touching the Life line on the mount of Venus.

Trouble from the opposite sex : Circle in the Big Triangle.

Trouble to parents : Star at the beginning of the Fate line.

Tuberculosis : a) Filbert nail and an island on the Mercury line.
   b) Long, thin, curved nails with ridges.
   c) A Jupiterian.
   d) Second phalanges of the fingers narrow.

Tuberculosis of the intestines : A Martian with a grill on the upper side of the mount of Moon.

Tyranny : a) Jupiter finger longer than the Saturn finger.
   b) Long hard nails.
   c) A Jupiterian.

Typhoid : a) Black spot in the Head line.
   b) Crimson or purple dot on the Life line.
   c) Mercury line broken and a square covers the break.

U

Unhappiness : Star on the first phalange of the Saturn finger.

Unhappy with brothers : Jupiter finger shorter than the first knot of the Saturn finger.

Unscrupulous : A Martian with absence of the Head line.

Untrustworthy : Head line terminating in a small fork, a thick soft palm, short thumb and the third phalange of the fingers bulging inside the hand.

V

Vanity : a) Excess development of the Sun mount.
  b) Long third phalange of the Sun finger.
  c) Third finger leaning towards the second finger.
  d) Mount of Jupiter displaced towards the mount of Saturn.

Vanity and religious fanaticism : Rising branch from the Life line going to the mount of Jupiter finally turning to the mount of Saturn.

Vanity-insane : Break in the Heart line under the mount of Sun. Vehicle : Mole at the end of Heart line.

Vericose veins : A Saturnian.

Venereal disease : a) Affected thumb.
  b) Star in the middle of the double or triple Girdle of Venus.
  c) Black spot on the mount of Venus.

Versatility : a) Moderate length of Mercury finger.
  b) Broad hand.
  c) Line of Sun enexpectedly and exceptionally good.
  d) Fine and long third and fourth fingers.
  e) Palm shorter than fingers.
  f) Double line of Head.
  g) Mixed type of hand.

Vigour : a) Elastic consistancy.
  b) A Martian.
  c) Double line of Life.

Vindictiveness : a) Excess development of the Jupiter mount
  b) Flat and thin Saturn finger.
  c) Very narrow Quadrangle.
  d) A Martian with wide gap between the lines of Life and Head.

Vitality : a) *Excessive vitality and greater sex urge :* Life line encircling a developed mount of Venus.
b) *Animal vitality :* Abnormally deep line of Mercury.
c) *Tremendous vitality and aggression :* Deep line of Mars as powerful as the Life line.

Vivacity : Absence of Mercury line but developed mount of Mercury.

Violent passions : Unusually higher placing of the Heart line.

Violent resolutions but equally changing : Line of Head starting from within the line of Life.

Violent temper : a) Excess development of the upper Mars.
b) Lines on the hand with red colour.
c) Nails long, thick and curved clawlike.
d) Very deep line of Life.
e) Deep Head line with red colour.

Vicious thinking : Excess development of the mount of Venus.

Vision prophetic : Ring of Solomon

Voyage : See travel.

W

Wealth : See 'Riches' also. a) *Wealth in general :* i) Line from the positive mount of Mars going to the mount of Saturn and acting like a sister line to the Fate line.
ii) Rising branch from the Head line ending in a cross and touching the root of the first finger.
b) *Wealth spent on charity purpose :* Mercury line starting from the mount of Neptune and ending on the mount of Mercury.
c) *Unusual enjoyment of wealth and reputation :* Triangle attached to the line of Sun and the line of Heart.
d) *Wealth earned but equally spent :* Line of Mercury pointing towards the mount of Apollo and then taking its course towards the mount of Mercury from the Head line.

e) *Great wealth :* i) Rising branch of Mercury going to the mount of Apollo and a branch from the Sun line joining the line of Mercury. ii) Mercury line terminating on the mount of Sun with well marked three Bracelets. iii) Star on the mount of Apollo. iv) Single line from the second joint of the thumb to the Life line.

Weird music : Conic hands.

Widowhood : a) Mount of Mercury leaning towards the mount of Sun.
   b) Broken line of Fate.
   c) Black spot on the line of Marriage.
   d) Deep lines from the line of Heart cutting the line of Fate at the date at which the line of Fate is cut.
   e) The line of Marriage drooping on the line of Heart.
   f) Line of Marriage drooping down and a cross at the point of drooping.
   g) Line of influence on the Venus mount associated with a star.
   h) Small bar cutting the above line.
   i) Line from the Heart line cutting the Fate line and ending on the Head line.
   j) Fingers with more than three phalanges.
   k) Break in the Head line and a branch from the Heart line cutting the Fate line.

Will power : a) Lack of nervous thumb.
   b) Stiff thumb.
   c) Large thumb.
   d) First phalange of the thumb developed.

Will and great determination : Double line of Head or double line of Mercury.

Wisdom : a) Fork at the end of the Sun line, one branch going to the mount of Mercury and another to the mount of Saturn.
   b) Rising branch from the line of Mercury going to the mount of Sun.
   c) Vertical line on the first phalange of Apollo finger.

Womb trouble-causing sterility : Star at the intersection of the line of Mercury and the line of Head and a deep dot at the bottom of the mount of Moon.

Wound : a) Line from the negative mount of Mars joining the Life line.

b) *Wound in the chest :* i) Capillary cross line on the mount of Saturn. ii) Small lines on the mount of Mercury.

c) *Wound in the fight :* i) Spot on the mount of Mars. ii) Line on the upper mount of Mars.

d) *Wound in the eye :* Circle on the mount of Mars.

e) *Wound on the Head :* i) Capillary cross lines on the mount of Jupiter. ii) Head line ending on the mount of Saturn.

f) *Wound to the leg :* i) Cross on the mount of Mercury. ii) Black spot on the mount of Mercury. iii) Straight branch from the line of Heart ending in a hook on the finger of Mercury.

Writer : a) Line from the negative mount of Mars meeting the line of Head below the mount of Sun.

b) Sun line starting from the top of the mount of Moon and nearer the percussion with the mental world of the hand developed.

c) Rising branch of the Sun line going to the mount of Moon and a star at the end of the Sun line.

d) Long second phalange of the Mercury.

Writer of scientific subjects : Sign of Uranus on the mount of Mercury.

Writer of children's stories : Sign of Neptune on the mount of Mercury.

Y

Yogi : a) Mount of Jupiter developed.

b) Horizontal line or a cross at the base of the Jupiter finger.

c) Narrow Quadrangle.

d) Line of Life ending on the mount of Neptune.

Bibliography

Samudrik Probodh	Nawathe
Samudrik Kuchhika	Kalikaprasad
Hasta sanjivanam	Ganeshdutta
Samudrik Dipika	Laxminarayan Tripathi
Sariraka Shastra	V. A. K. Ayer
Hast Samudrika Shastra	K. C. Sen
Advanced Palmistry	S. Banajri
Palmistry for Everybody	Dhundiraj M. Naik
Modern Cheirosophy	G. V. Dass
The Science of Palmistry	Devachrya
Treatise on Indian School of Palmistry	B. R. Bhat
Read Your own Palm	A. L. Bhagwat
The Book of the Hand	Catherine Hill
The Hand Speaks	Noel Jacquin
Secret of Hand Reading	Noel Jacquin
The Hand of Man	Noel Jacquin
The Science of Hand	D' Arpentigni
The Mystery of your Palm	Psychos
A Doctor's Guide to better Health Through Palmistry	Eugene Scheimann M. D.
Hands Up	Capini Vequin
Hand Reading	An Adept
The Modern Palmist	Dennis Barry Jackson
A Hand Book on Hands	Beryl B. Hutchinson
Palmistry for Everyone	Vera Compton
The Human Hand	Dr. Charlotte Wolff
Palmistry for pleasure and Profit	V. A. K. Ayer
Palmistry at a Glance	Martini
Ilm-ul-kaff	Gaffar

Palmastra	Gaffar
How to Read Hands	Mir Bashir
Laws of Scientific Hand Reading	William G. Benham
How to choose Vocations from Hand	William G. Benham
Language of the Hand	Cheiro
You and your Hand	Cheiro
Study of Palmistry	The Compte C. De Saint Germain